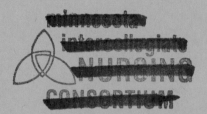

HANDBOOK
on STRESS
and ANXIETY

❖ ❖ ❖ ❖ ❖ ❖ ❖ ❖ ❖ ❖ ❖ ❖

Contemporary Knowledge,
Theory, and Treatment

Irwin L. Kutash
Louis B. Schlesinger
and Associates

❖ ❖ ❖ ❖ ❖ ❖ ❖ ❖ ❖ ❖ ❖ ❖ ❖

HANDBOOK
on STRESS
and ANXIETY

✤ ✤ ✤ ✤ ✤ ✤ ✤ ✤ ✤ ✤ ✤ ✤ ✤

Jossey-Bass Publishers
San Francisco • Washington • London • 1980

HANDBOOK ON STRESS AND ANXIETY
Contemporary Knowledge, Theory, and Treatment
by Irwin L. Kutash, Louis B. Schlesinger, and Associates

Copyright © 1980 by: Jossey-Bass Inc., Publishers
433 California Street
San Francisco, California 94104

&

Jossey-Bass Limited
28 Banner Street
London EC1Y 8QE

Library of Congress Cataloging in Publication Data

Main entry under title:
Handbook on stress and anxiety.

   Bibliography: p. 474
   Includes index.
   1. Stress (Psychology) 2. Anxiety. I. Kutash,
Irwin L. II. Schlesinger, Louis B. [DNLM:
1. Anxiety. 2. Stress, Psychological. WM172 H236]
BF575.S75H36   152.4   80-8014
ISBN 0-87589-478-X

Manufactured in the United States of America

JACKET DESIGN BY WILLI BAUM

FIRST EDITION

Code 8038

The Jossey-Bass
Social and Behavioral Science Series

❖ ❖ ❖ ❖ ❖ ❖ ❖ ❖ ❖ ❖ ❖ ❖ ❖

Foreword

The editors of the *Handbook on Stress and Anxiety* have assembled a galaxy of authorities. The contributions vary from literate recapitulation of established information, through fascinating accounts of new findings, to creative speculation on possible new ways of looking at these ancient human problems—stress and anxiety. Like all galaxies, some stars loom brighter than others, but all contribute their bit to the illumination of the subject.

The volume presents theory, research, and treatment from a broad spectrum including social, behavioral, psychoanalytic, and psychophysiological perspectives. Psychoanalytic theory is presented in a historical perspective, and some of Freud's original views are questioned in light of the evolution of theory and practice. Learning and behavior theories of stress and anxiety are included, as are sociological theories; and a holistic blend is found in the ethological and neurobiological material in Chapters Five and Six. A mixture, with some seasoning, of the theories also appears in the chapters on feminism, childhood and adolescence, and later life. The same applies to the role of anxiety and stress in such areas as crime, violence, and substance abuse. Some contributors used this opportunity to further expound and expand their previous work on the subject in both theory and treatment; an excellent review of seminal work in stress and anxiety results. Hans Selye restates his major contributions on stress and adaptation and introduces an ethical concept on coping with stress. Work on cognition and on the role of individual reactions to potentially stressful situations is elaborated in Chapter Eight. In the final chapter, Irwin L. Kutash provides an important conclusion: We cannot and should not attempt to prevent the development of anxiety or to avoid stress; instead, effort should be directed toward development of increased capacities to cope with the vicissitudes of life.

In considering the varied approaches to the subjects of this book—from pharmaceutical preparations, to society, to psychoanalysis, to neurobiology, to ethology—I had a free association to a glass of beer being described in turn by an artist, a chemist, and an alcoholic. Each would approach the task from his own perspective, background, and training. Each would use language and terminology appropriate to his task. The descriptions would be very different yet accurate, and the combined perspectives would vastly enrich our conception of that glass of beer. Similarly, a book such as this one will broaden our conceptions of stress and anxiety and of their relationship.

Washington, D.C.   JACK EWALT
June 1980   *Director, Mental Health*
                                                    and Behavioral Sciences Service,
                                                    Veterans Administration

Preface

By 1947 Albert Camus had labeled the twentieth century "the century of fear," and W. H. Auden had proclaimed the "age of anxiety." At midcentury Rollo May (1950) pointed to the many anxiety-creating situations facing humans, highlighting "the threats of war, of the uncontrolled atom bomb, and of radical political and economic upheaval" as the obvious and "the inner confusion, psychological disorientation, and uncertainty with respect to values and acceptable standards of conduct" as the less obvious. These threats have not diminished. In fact, mankind is now under such stress— as a result of dramatic changes in the industrial, economic, and social spheres— that many look back to those years as a simpler, calmer age and even try to recapture the values of the era. Some of the pressing problems in contemporary society include the population explosion, environmental pollution, the energy crisis, poverty, and the threat of nuclear destruction. Each individual not only is beset by the pressures of his or her own daily life but is privy to every disaster in the country and the world through modern news media and communication methods. Perhaps the gains of modern civilization will be outweighed by the stress-created side effects if we do not come to understand, control, prevent, or adapt to stress and anxiety.

Out of this concern, we have assembled this state-of-the-art handbook. We asked leading authorities from representative theoretical viewpoints to present the latest theories, research findings, or treatment approaches. Every effort has been made to include all major basic concepts and theories from a psychodynamic, behavioral, developmental, sociological, ethological, and biological standpoint.

Part One presents theories of stress and anxiety, encompassing all prevailing schools of thought. Perspectives on stress are discussed in Part Two and on anxiety in Part Three. Part Four focuses on assessment, treatment, and prevention of stress- and anxiety-related disorders.

As in an earlier volume, *Violence: Perspectives on Murder and Aggression,* the editors have refrained from making final statements or conclusions, since that would be at variance with our purpose for these "perspectives" handbooks. Further, the authors' contributions do not represent a consensus of opinion. That is, we have invited contributions that can compete with each other, so that readers can form their own opinions and follow up on the line of research they feel would be most profitable to pursue.

We cannot ignore the warning signs of today, and we hope this handbook will be a positive contribution toward consolidating our contemporary knowledge and precipitating concerted future efforts.

Maplewood, New Jersey   IRWIN L. KUTASH
September 1980   LOUIS B. SCHLESINGER

Contents

The Authors

✻ ✻ ✻ ✻ ✻ ✻ ✻ ✻ ✻ ✻ ✻ ✻ ✻

IRWIN L. KUTASH, Ph.D., faculty member, New York Center for Psychoanalytic Training, New York City; clinical assistant professor of psychiatry and mental health sciences, New Jersey College of Medicine and Dentistry; chairman, Mental Health, Alcohol and Drug Review and Goals Committee, Regional Health Planning Council, Newark, New Jersey; and psychological consultant, Alcohol Rehabilitation Program, Veterans Administration Medical Center, East Orange, New Jersey, and Cedar Grove Residential Treatment Center, Department of Human Resources, Trenton, New Jersey.

LOUIS B. SCHLESINGER, Ph.D., coordinator, Violence Treatment and Prevention Program, Veterans Administration Medical Center, East Orange, New Jersey; clinical assistant professor of psychiatry and mental health sciences, New Jersey College of Medicine and Dentistry; and consultant, Department of Psychology, Fair Oaks Hospital, Summit, New Jersey.

RICHARD R. BOOTZIN, Ph.D., professor of psychology, Northwestern University.

JOSEPH V. BRADY, Ph.D., professor of behavioral biology, Johns Hopkins University.

THOMAS H. BUDZYNSKI, Ph.D., director, Biofeedback Institute of Denver, University of Colorado Medical Center.

SANDRA BUECHLER, Ph.D., assistant professor of psychology, University of Delaware.

JESSE O. CAVENAR, JR., M.D., chief, Psychiatry Service, Veterans Administration Medical Center, Durham, North Carolina, and professor of psychiatry, Duke University Medical Center.

ALAN COMPTON, M.D., faculty, Los Angeles Psychoanalytic Institute.

JAMES C. COYNE, Ph.D., assistant professor of psychology, University of California at Berkeley.

ROBERT K. DAVIES, M.D., medical director, Fair Oaks Hospital, Summit, New Jersey, and lecturer, Yale University School of Medicine.

JOHN M. DAVIS, M.D., director of research, Illinois State Psychiatric Institute and University of Chicago School of Medicine.

JERRY L. DEFFENBACHER, Ph.D., associate professor of psychology, Colorado State University.

JOHN DORIS, Ph.D., professor of psychology and director, Department of Human Development and Family Studies, Cornell University.

DANIEL L. ELY, Ph.D., assistant professor of biology, University of Akron.

NORMAN S. ENDLER, Ph.D., professor of psychology, York University.

MARK S. GOLD, M.D., director of research and training, Fair Oaks Hospital, Summit, New Jersey, and lecturer, Yale University School of Medicine.

JAMES P. HENRY, M.D., Ph.D., professor, Department of Physiology, School of Medicine, University of Southern California.

ROBERT HICKS, M.D., research associate, Illinois State Psychiatric Institute, and assistant professor, University of Chicago School of Medicine.

MARDI J. HOROWITZ, M.D., professor of psychiatry, University of California at San Francisco and Langley Porter Institute.

CARROLL IZARD, Ph.D., professor of psychology, University of Delaware.

HOWARD B. KAPLAN, Ph.D., professor and director of Sociological Research Lab, Baylor College of Medicine.

CHASE PATTERSON KIMBALL, M.D., professor of psychiatry, medicine, and behavioral science, University of Chicago.

THOMAS S. LANGNER, Ph.D., professor of clinical psychiatric epidemiology, Columbia University.

RICHARD S. LAZARUS, Ph.D., professor of psychology, University of California at Berkeley.

MICHAEL LEWIS, Ph.D., professor and director, Institute for the Study of Exceptional Children, Educational Testing Service, Princeton, New Jersey.

ANNE MCINTYRE, Ph.D., associate professor, Department of Psychology, University of Tennesee at Knoxville.

DAVID MAX, Department of Psychology, Northwestern University.

ROLLO MAY, Ph.D., supervising and training analyst, William Alanson White Institute, New York City.

RICHARD E. MINTER, M.D., instructor in psychiatry, University of Michigan.

RUTH MOULTON, M.D., training and supervising analyst, William Alanson White Institute, New York City.

ANNA OKONEK, A.B., research assistant, University of Chicago.

KIRK E. PEFFER, Ph.D., assistant clinical director, Biofeedback Institute of Denver.

A. L. C. POTTASH, M.D., associate medical director, Fair Oaks Hospital, Summit, New Jersey, and lecturer, Yale University School of Medicine.

ROBERT J. POWERS, Ph.D., chief, Alcohol Rehabilitation Program, Veterans Administration Medical Center, East Orange, New Jersey.

EUGENE REVITCH, M.D., clinical associate professor of psychiatry, Rutgers University Medical School.

HANS SELYE, M.D., Ph.D., D.Sc., president, International Institute for Stress.

MILES E. SIMPSON, Ph.D., associate professor and chairman, Department of Sociology and Anthropology, Murray State University.

EMILIE F. SOBEL, Psy.D., clinical psychologist, Brooklyn Community Counseling Center.

RICHARD M. SUINN, Ph.D., professor, Department of Psychology, Colorado State University.

DONALD R. SWEENEY, M.D., Ph.D., clinical director, Fair Oaks Hospital, Summit, New Jersey, and lecturer, Yale University School of Medicine.

MICHAEL TAMAROFF, Ph.D., clinical assistant psychologist, Department of Pediatrics, Sloan-Kettering Cancer Center, New York City, and clinical assistant instructor of psychology in psychiatry, Cornell Medical College.

THOMAS ASHBY WILLS, Ph.D., research associate, Columbia University.

WILLIAM W. K. ZUNG, M.D., professor of psychiatry, Duke University Medical Center and Veterans Administration Medical Center, Durham, North Carolina.

HANDBOOK
on STRESS
and ANXIETY

❖ ❖ ❖ ❖ ❖ ❖ ❖ ❖ ❖ ❖ ❖ ❖

Contemporary Knowledge,
Theory, and Treatment

To Samuel B. Kutash

who died while preparing a chapter on psychodynamic theories of anxiety. Samuel B. Kutash coauthored the Encyclopedia of Criminology, The Graphomotor Projection Technique, Perceptual Changes in Psychopathology, *and* Violence: Perspectives on Murder and Aggression. *His influence lives through the works he left behind and the people he inspired, including the editors.*

Part I

* * * * * * * * * * * * * *

Stress and anxiety are clearly a pervasive part of the human condition—perhaps more so in today's crowded and complex world than ever before. In this section, the editors have assembled theories from six significant points of view that perhaps come closest to doing justice to such a complex phenomenon. If not individually, perhaps collectively, these points of view might explain the totality.

Alan Compton, in the opening chapter, traces developments in the psychoanalytic theory of anxiety, from Freud's reformulations of his theory in 1926 through the most recent psychoanalytic contributions. He focuses on areas that Freud left unclear but that have since been clarified, on new observations that have resulted in changes in theory, and also on additions to the theory that have been proposed on theoretical grounds. From the most exhaustive review of such literature undertaken to date, Compton draws

Theoretical Perspectives on Stress and Anxiety

✻ ✻ ✻ ✻ ✻ ✻ ✻ ✻ ✻ ✻ ✻ ✻ ✻

many critical conclusions—for example, that *Aktual* neurosis is not a viable clinical entity; that the anxiety that occurs in traumatic neurosis is not essentially different from other anxiety; that infants do not manifest fear or anxiety before the age of 3 to 6 months; and that the energic explanation of traumatic moments in adult life is less tenable than an explanation involving total impact and global response.

Richard R. Bootzin and David Max, in Chapter Two, cover the learning and behavioral theories of anxiety and stress. The important consideration, according to learning and behavioral theory, is that anxiety and avoidance behavior are responses elicited and maintained by specifiable proximal stimuli. In considering anxiety acquisition, the authors cover Pavlovian or classical conditioning explanations and discuss their shortcomings—for example, the finding that some stimuli have more potential than others to become conditioned to an unconditioned stimulus. They then discuss newer additions to the theory, such as preparedness or the biological predisposition to learn certain CS-UCS pairs, which have explained some of these flaws. They also review (1) the information models, which emphasize information processing and expectancy rather than learning through association or contiguity alone; (2) avoidance learning, highlighting the dual-process theory and its failings and then covering the newer theories, which emphasize the information component of the conditioned stimulus; (3) operant conditioning and anxiety acquisition; and (4) the two important variables of predictability and controllability. They believe that Bandura's (1977a) theory represents an effective and useful synthesis of behavioral procedures and cognitive theory. They do not believe, however, that any one theory fully explains all the data concerning anxiety acquisition.

In Chapter Three, Michael Lewis discusses fear and anxiety from a developmental point of view and emphasizes the following general principles: (1) Fear is a feeling state. (2) Neither situations nor responses alone can be used to reference fear. (3) A wide variety of situations and events can produce fearful states and experiences. (4) Early development involves the change from affective states to affective experiences. (5) Situations that elicit fear and responses that reference it are open to such forces as maturation, cognitive development, and cultural norms. (6) Affect development is best viewed as embedded in the child's total social, psychological, and physical development. Lewis believes that these principles can help guide future inquiry.

Chapter Four, by Howard B. Kaplan, provides coverage of the sociological theories of stress and anxiety—emphasizing the relationship between sociocultural characteristics and patterns of individual experiences of stress and anxiety. He considers three sets of mutually interacting variables that are part of the sociological systems or patterns of subjective distress: (1) those relating to the personal need-value system, (2) personal systems of adaptive coping/defensive patterns, and (3) life events. Finally, he presents a strategy for further developing a general sociological theory of stress by systematically focusing on the sociocultural systems and processes that influence patterns of subjective distress. He concludes that sociological theories of stress should develop models of the mutually interacting sociocultural and personal circumstances which induce stress.

In Chapter Five, James P. Henry and Daniel L. Ely demonstrate that ethology and physiology can provide information about behavior patterns, coping processes, and the patterning of neuroendocrine responses. They found from their ethological studies that an individual's social rank and, therefore, predominant behavior pattern influences the central nervous system's (CNS) perception of psychosocial stimuli and so in turn the specificity of the efferent limb of the physiological response. They further found that the subsequent biochemical patterning is determined by the individual's social role, personality factors, life style, and CNS perceptual mechanisms. Relating the findings from animal studies to humans, they compare Type A people to the dominant mice within the closed social environment of their complex population cage. They suggest, moreover, that we should include in stress theory the idea that environmental stimuli may be perceived and processed differently depending on conditions of threat, uncertainty, social role, personality factors, motivational conditions, and coping strategies; consequently, different neuroendocrine response patterns may emerge.

In Chapter Six, Donald R. Sweeney, Mark S. Gold, A. L. C. Pottash, and Robert K. Davies deal with neurobiological theories of stress and anxiety. They focus most intensively on evidence that supports relationships between brain norepinephrine systems and stress, since the information on noradrenergic systems is more completely developed than information supporting other mechanisms. The authors present compelling evidence of the important role of the CNS noradrenergic system in forming the neurobiological substrate of stress or anxiety response. Specifically, they report the following findings: (1) Measurement of MHPG (the primary CNS metabolite of norepinephrine) is related to affective disorder and stress. (2) Alteration of locus coeruleus function (the major brain center controlling noradrenergic activity) is related to modification of fearful behavior in animals. (3) The drug clonidine, which inhibits the locus coeruleus and decreases brain levels of norepinephrine and MHPG, is effective in alleviating the symptoms of opiate withdrawal. (4) Opiate withdrawal and panic have a common neurobiological mediation. (5) Measurement of noradrenergic function in clinical samples may help in designing new and more effective psychopharmacological treatments for anxiety or stress syndromes.

1

Psychoanalytic Theories

Alan Compton

❀ ❀ ❀ ❀ ❀ ❀ ❀ ❀ ❀ ❀ ❀ ❀ ❀

In a recent study, we traced the development of Freud's theory of anxiety, with special emphasis on the role of the discharge theory of affect in determining his early, immediate, and final formulations on anxiety (Compton, 1972a). Two questions served as general guidelines for the inquiry: What is anxiety? What accounts for its particular quality? These questions will now be applied to the formulations of other psychoanalysts who have addressed themselves to the problem since Freud published *Inhibitions, Symptoms and Anxiety* in 1926.

We shall be interested in determining to what degree the areas Freud left unclear have been clarified. What additional pertinent observations have been made? What changes in the theory of anxiety follow from these observations? What changes or additions have been proposed on theoretical grounds, and what is their value?

Note: This chapter is a revised version of a paper published in the *Journal of the American Psychoanalytic Association*, 1972.

From the beginning of Freud's work, affect and excitation were conceptually indistinguishable. The theory of affects was necessarily a discharge theory. Of central concern in a discharge theory is the source of the energy to be discharged. For anxiety, the excitation might originate somatically or mentally, but in either case it was sexual in nature. Unpleasure affects, of which class anxiety is a member, presented a special problem, since discharge in general was thought to be associated with pleasurable feelings. Without a specific unpleasure energy, such affects had to be indirectly derived. The particular content of an anxiety experience was viewed by Freud as a "grafting" to the underlying disturbance. Once the libido theory was developed, the source of anxiety was seen as warded-off, transformed libido.

By 1919, anxiety in a situation of real danger had been brought into the theory by Freud as a manifestation of the self-preservative or ego drives. In order to unify the theory, Freud tentatively proposed that in such danger situations narcissistic or ego libido might be transformed into anxiety. The particular quality of the affect was explained as a result of the phylogenetic experience of birth.

In 1920, Freud loosened the relationship between pleasure/unpleasure and quantities of excitation, thus making possible the description of non-discharge affect states as well as other theoretical clarifications (Freud, 1920a). Once the ego was defined as a system, affect, as an aspect of conscious, perceptual experience, fell within the province of that system. It had also become clear from clinical observation that anxiety motivates defense, rather than being a product of defense. Freud now gave considerably more weight to the concept of anxiety as a signal, and he relatively deemphasized the libido transformation theory. In the revised theory of 1926, however, he described two kinds of anxiety, *signal* and *traumatic* (or *economic*), and the latter variety remains as a discharge of libido. Instinctual or traumatic or generated (energic) anxiety is the type that occurs in *Aktual* neurosis, traumatic neurosis, certain traumatic moments of adult life, at birth and in early infancy, and in the neuroses of childhood. For all other conditions, the concept of signal anxiety applies. Signal anxiety involves the idea of a danger situation, always including an "outside referent"; that is, something in the environment that is at least believed to be real.

For reasons established in the study of the development of Freud's work on anxiety, the subsequent literature will be reviewed in the following areas:

1. Early alterations, revisions, and additions
2. Alterations of anxiety theory based on changes in drive or instinct theory
3. *Aktual* neurosis
4. Trauma and traumatic neurosis

5.   Psychoanalytic "physiological" approaches
6.   Studies of early infancy
7.   Attempts at further articulation or refinement of Freud's anxiety
      theory
8.   Experimental and extra-analytic developments

Early Alterations, Revisions, and Additions

In 1927, Jones introduced the term *aphinisis*, defined as total, permanent extinction of the capacity and opportunity for sexual enjoyment as a whole. Aphinisis, he proposed, is what is "fundamentally feared" in every neurosis, and castration anxiety is a derivative of this fear (p. 440). In 1929, in order to explain the mechanism of anxiety in hypochondria and "war shock," he put this concept together with Freud's (1917) suggestion that in situations of real danger anxiety is derived from narcissistic libido (Jones, 1929b). Part of the response to danger is an increase in ego libido; this amounts to strong excitation without relief, which is tantamount to loss of capacity for erotic gratification. Anxiety results from this danger; that is, the danger of aphinisis (pp. 300-301). Jones goes on to say, without explanation, that in the situation described "it is plain" that the source of the danger is "in the sadistic or aggressive component" (p. 302).

While Jones's invocation of aggression is somewhat mystifying, other early contributors to anxiety theory also emphasized "the sadistic or aggressive component," with some (often fragmentary) clinical material to support their contentions.

Federn had been working with psychotic patients for some years, when, in 1929 (pp. 335-337, 348-349), he proposed that anxiety flows directly from inhibition of flight from a feared object; the inhibition of flight is caused by a masochistic tie to the object; thus, the assumption of aggression is necessary for understanding anxiety. (Also see Glauber, 1963.)

Laforgue (1930) proposed in similar terms a somewhat different idea: anxiety may be libidinized. He also suggested that sexual excitation in early infancy may be indistinguishable from anxiety.

Klein (1932, 1948), on the basis of analysis of young children, attributed anxiety directly to the danger of the death instinct. Anxiety thus has its origin in the fear of death. She saw two fundamental forms of anxiety: (1) persecutory, related to "annihilation of the ego"; and (2) depressive, related to "the harm done to the internal and external loved objects by the subject's destructive impulses" (1948, p. 282).

Rado (1933) attributed far-reaching significance to the idea of libidinized anxiety. Castration fear in women is the signal of instinctual danger emanating from "genital masochism" (p. 454). Paralysis is the nucleus of anxiety and can be brought about only by masochism (p. 455). An anxiety attack is "an explosive discharge of masochism in the field of the ego's psychosomatic functioning" (p. 456). In *Aktual* neurosis, suppressed genital excitement is transformed into genital masochism, which is discharged as anxiety (p. 457).

    Comment. It seems reasonable to view these contributions in part as responses to Freud's introduction of the ego-id-superego model and his 1926 reformulation of anxiety in terms of that model. From that view, all five remain at the level of drive psychology; that is, they do not—as Freud did—attempt to conceptualize responses to instinctual and environmental events as functions of an ego organization. While exclusive adherence to drive psychology imposes extensive limitation, it does not necessarily render the propositions false. In fact, Freud had little or no direct experience in the analysis of young children and did not specifically study anxiety in the psychoses. Narcissistic and masochistic manifestations are more prominent in these clinical conditions, and in recent decades analysts have generally emphasized the role of aggression in psychoses. At least for Federn and Klein, the clinical material was somewhat different from that on which Freud based his hypotheses. What does seem especially questionable in these hypotheses is the attribution of universality to the mechanisms. Such attribution is linked with an error in logic, resulting in a more serious problem, particularly in the work of Klein, though the same error is apparent in Jones's hypotheses. The error is an example of what Hartmann (1955, pp. 221-222) has called the "genetic fallacy"; that is, the confusion of a function with its history, so that the function is reduced to its genetic precursors. This reduction is embodied in the notions of "fundamental fear" or "basic anxiety." The result is a generalization which is both existentially and conceptually inappropriate for the earliest developmental phases and inapplicable for later phases, because it does not recognize development in any meaningful sense.

    Laforgue's idea of the sexualization of anxiety has been rather widely accepted. We might rephrase his concept in this way: The anxiety response may occur in the service of a masochistic drive, and the evocation of anxiety can be a sadistic drive aim.

    Evaluation of the role of aggression in anxiety is a more complex problem, one with which we shall continue to be concerned. Freud limited his considerations of the relation of aggression and anxiety to guilt, conceptualized as a "topographical variety of anxiety," "moral" or "social anxiety," and as an expression of aggression via superego function (Freud, 1930, p. 135). This limitation had to do with Freud's recognizing aggression as not an independent drive, not subject to the pleasure principle, and not playing a role in mental conflict parallel to that of the sexual drives. (For discussion, see Brenner, 1971; Compton, in press.) Subsequently, an opposite view was proposed (Hartmann and Loewenstein, 1949), according to which aggression is taken as an independent instinctual drive, regulated by the pleasure principle. From the latter viewpoint, the relation of aggression to anxiety would be, in large part, the same as or parallel to the relation of libido to anxiety.

Alterations of Anxiety Theory Based on Changes in Instinct Theory

From the beginning, Freud's conceptualization of unpleasure was a problem, as we have mentioned above, especially in regard to sudden augmentations of unpleasure affect, whether or not in response to external stimuli. If drives are given the basic attribute of seeking gratification (whether or not gratification is thought of as energy discharge), unpleasure affects necessarily have to be indirectly derived. The libido transformation theory of anxiety is the prime example. This theory, as we have shown in the Freud study, became cumbersome as the variety of phenomenological data increased. It would be expedient to provide the theory with a more direct source of unpleasure—for example, an "unpleasure energy" or a drive or instinct that could directly account for the unpleasure manifestation. Both the nature and particular quality of the affect might be accounted for in this way.

In work directly related to anxiety theory, three proposals have been made for reclassifying drives. The first of these was by Brunswick (1954), who suggested the addition of defensive drives to Freud's libidinal and aggressive drives, and a revised dual classification of vital-libidinal instincts and defensive-aggressive instincts.

In 1958, Schur revised his hypotheses on anxiety (which will be taken up later) by postulating an instinct (not drive) to avoid danger, present in animals and man. In man, with the development of psychic structure, the "internal drive element of the instinct to avoid danger grows into a 'wish' " (p. 205). In 1966, Schur extended this idea by postulating different bases for the unpleasure and the pleasure regulatory principles: unpleasure is rooted in the basic biological response pattern of withdrawal; pleasure, in the basic approach pattern.

> There is no motivational force to *seek* an object in order to withdraw from it. *We therefore cannot speak of an instinctual drive to withdraw from pain and danger.* There is only a propensity to respond to certain stimuli with withdrawal and certain species-specific discharge patterns. This response is the model both for the anxiety response and for defense . . . and it is regulated by the unpleasure principle. . . . The development of many ego structures is required before the *need* to withdraw from danger (pain) develops into a *wish* to avoid danger [pp. 151-152].

Rangell (1955) proposed a similar idea without attempting to develop a biological basis for it. Estimation of danger, he said, involves a sampling of it, which releases an instinctive reaction of tension and discharge. This instinctive reaction is a historical precipitate of the alertness or vigilance of lower forms and is "supplied by a pool of defensive, *instinctive* energy" (pp. 413-414). Later (1968, pp. 398-399) Rangell said, "Anxiety is a psychobiological organismic event." There is transmission from "nonspecific instinctual pressure" (unpleasure) via the soma to anxiety.

> *Comment.* Schur's conclusion regarding the relation of anxiety to drive is the opposite of Brunswick's. Both Schur and Rangell are proposing to add not another instinctual drive, and not a regrouping of instinctual drives, but rather an instinct in the ethological sense, with a mental component.
>
> The alteration in the theory of aggression made by Hartmann, Kris, and Loewenstein (discussed above) has been so widely accepted that it is usually taken simply as the psychoanalytic theory of aggression. It does, however, represent a view of aggression different from Freud's view, and it vastly extends the frequency and variety of instances in which aggression is involved in mental conflict and therefore in the anxiety response. Unlike the propositions of Schur and Rangell, which are advanced on purely theoretical and biological grounds, the Hartmann, Kris, and Loewenstein modification is a purely clinical theory, lacking in biological referents.

Aktual Neurosis

Because there have been questions concerning both the theory of economic anxiety and its observational bases, we shall look initially at developments in those areas where Freud utilized energic explanations, one of which is *Aktual* neurosis.

The *Aktual* neuroses have received relatively little attention since Freud, although Fenichel (1945) and Nunberg (1955) accept the existence of this condition. Nunberg, in fact, states that every neurosis has an *Aktual*-neurotic core. Blau (1952) and Rangell (1968) see anxiety neurosis as a common condition. Fink (1970) attempts to correlate Freud's description of the symptoms of anxiety neurosis with Masters and Johnson's "pelvic congestion syndrome."

For the most part, however, ever since the early days of the Vienna Psychoanalytic Society (see, for example, Nunberg and Federn, 1962, pp. 175-182), analysts have found Freud's nosological entity hard to accept. Brenner (1953) reviews the idea of anxiety neurosis and concludes that there is neither compelling evidence for the concept nor evidence which necessitates its abandonment. Stewart (1967) also reviews Freud's ideas in this area at length. He suggests that certain specific criteria would have to be met to fulfill Freud's early definition of *Aktual* neurosis: (1) There must be a chemical basis for the sexual urge. (2) In anxiety neurosis, "the major portion of the chemical substance must not achieve psychic representation as conscious or unconscious sexual affect." (3) The accumulation of the chemical substance must lead to discharge through the vegetative nervous system with the production of symptoms of anxiety. Stewart concludes, "There is no evidence that such a condition exists" (pp. 70-71).

> *Comment.* There is no currently known reason to eliminate the supposition that physiological changes, including sexual changes, may trigger neurophysiological responses related to "anxiety" patterns in the central nervous system. This is, however, very far from the specificity of hypotheses involved in the concept of *Aktual* neurosis, as Stewart suggests. With these facts in mind, and the additional conclusion, drawn from the study of Freud's early work, that the basis of the concept of *Aktual* neurosis was spurious to begin with (Compton, 1972a), it seems unwise to base any far-reaching conclusions on the entity *Aktual* neurosis. Specifically, it is not an acceptable basis for establishing a class of anxiety responses as energically and somatically determined, with mental content only secondarily "grafted on."

Trauma and Traumatic Neurosis

The anxiety that occurs in traumatic neurosis and in association with trauma is generally explained by Freud in directly energic terms.

Brenner (1953), reviewing the literature on traumatic neuroses of war (see especially Grinker and Spiegel, 1945; Kardiner and Spiegel, 1947; Simmel, 1944; Sperling, 1950), found no conclusions that the condition is the result of an influx of unmasterable stimuli. Brenner concluded that "an external stimulus creates neurotic anxiety rather because of its relationship to unconscious conflicts of the individual it affects, than because of its physiological intensity" (p. 21).

The psychoanalytic concept of trauma was assessed by a number of analysts independently (Furst, 1967) and by a section of the Kris Study Group (1967). Generally, these studies do not directly question the energic definition of trauma; only Sandler (1967, pp. 160, 163) appears to specifically suggest another direction. Most indicate that they find the energic concept useful. Most of the discussion about what trauma is or is not, however, has little to do with energic factors.

> *Comment.* What is of interest for the study of anxiety is this: If trauma is an energic concept, then the anxiety associated with trauma is also, almost necessarily, seen in energic terms; if trauma

can be adequately characterized in some other way, then there is no *necessary* implication about related anxiety.

For reasons fully developed elsewhere (Compton, in press), the energic *definition* of trauma seems both unnecessary and untenable. The following definition appears to encompass the relevant phenomena: A *psychic trauma* is a disruption of the current function of the mental apparatus, produced by the reaction of the apparatus itself to the meaning of a perceived event. No developmental stage is excluded, and no quantitative factors outside the apparatus are of direct importance. Psychic trauma differs from physical trauma especially if there is a loss of psychic differentiation between past and present. The past trauma can feel as if it is taking place in the present.

If trauma can be adequately conceptualized in some such way as this (see A. Freud, 1967, p. 242, for a similar characterization, not, however, offered as a definition), then there is no necessity to view the anxiety in trauma and traumatic neurosis as a raw energic product, or, in fact, as different in any fundamental way from anxiety in other contexts.

Psychoanalytic "Physiological" Approaches

In 1941, Kubie developed an anxiety theory in Pavlovian terms and then showed the correspondence of this theory to Freud's 1926 anxiety theory. Nunberg (1955) simply says that anxiety has two sources, psychic and somatic; it may originate in the one, the other, or both (p. 190).

Other psychoanalytic "physiological" approaches are concerned with the sensation of pain and its relation to unpleasure affects (Szasz, 1955, 1957; Ramzy and Wallerstein, 1958). Ramzy and Wallerstein carefully distinguish between sensations and affects and, on that basis, between bodily pain, mental pain or painful affect, fear, and anxiety. They conclude that anxiety is always a derivative phenomenon, based on memory traces of fear or pain, while pain is always a primary experience; fear may be either primary or derivative (pp. 184-187). They also muster evidence from the data of neurophysiology (Conel, 1947, p. 147), academic psychology (Hebb, 1955), and ethology (Lorenz, 1935) to establish that any psychic experience of pain or fear before the age of 3 months is extremely unlikely. The experience of anxiety, because it is a derivative phenomenon, is even more unlikely.

The part of the formulation of Ramzy and Wallerstein with which we are concerned here is similar to the learning theorists' conception of anxiety as a conditioned fear response. According to Eysenck (1969, p. 7), pain is a "primary drive" analogous to hunger and thirst. Natural stimuli associated with pain give rise to fear responses, which are very similar to pain responses;

the "proprioceptive consequences" of these learned responses produce the "drive stimulus" that serves the "secondary drive," anxiety.

> *Comment.* A methodological objection occurs at this point: It is unacceptable to characterize a psychic state by description in purely physiological terms. Such characterization results in terminology that blurs the problem of anxiety while giving the appearance of elucidating it. Two questions, although loosely phrased, can help to highlight the issue. Do somatic response patterns "invade the mind," leading to secondary "grafting on" of content appropriate to anxiety? Or may somatic response patterns, as a quasi-independent part of the anxiety response, be perceived by some ego apparatus with possible secondary augmentation of the anxiety affect in response to the perception?
>
> There are, however, several approaches that decrease the ambiguity of the psychobiological concepts. We shall return later to this point and to the question raised by Ramzy and Wallerstein regarding the developmental precedence of anxiety and, further, whether it is possible to make this distinction. The cross-sectional dynamic problem is different from the longitudinal or genetic problem (Hartmann and Kris, 1945).

Studies of Early Infancy

Besides anxiety neurosis and trauma, the major bases of Freud's view of anxiety as an energic discharge process are birth and early infancy.

Greenacre (1941, 1945) reviewed the literature reporting observational and experimental data on the fetus and the neonate. In both there is demonstrable responsivity, readily discernible as separate or loosely constellated reflexes. The responses occur if "untoward conditions" develop during intrauterine life or if painful stimuli are applied neonatally. Greenacre proposes that these reflex responses to untoward conditions or painful stimuli may be regarded as components of a "preanxiety response" and that they form the basis of the organic (physiological) components of the anxiety reaction. She further proposes that the birth experience is important *ontogenetically* in patterning these loosely constellated reflexes into the physiological preanxiety response. Events *in utero*, during birth, or during the first few weeks of life may produce a special sensitivity of these physiological preanxiety responses, with lifelong consequences: a "predisposition to anxiety." Her studies are based on analytic work with severely neurotic or borderline adults who had an unanalyzable "basic anxiety."

> *Comment.* Greenacre alters Freud's hypotheses concerning anxiety and birth, from phylogenetic to ontogenetic; she specifies

a mechanism at a neurophysiological level. Besides making the theory of early anxiety relatable to the ethological concept of imprinting (see below), Greenacre shows that the study of anxiety in very early life is concerned with the transition from neurophysiological states to subjectively experienced and observed or communicated behavior; that is, psychic states. This approach decreases the area of ambiguity in Freud's anxiety theory and deemphasizes the phylogenetic proposition, which has generally been found unacceptable. We have already objected to the term *basic anxiety*, but Greenacre uses it in a somewhat different way.

Spitz (1950, 1965) extensively and intensively studied infant development by observation. He also speaks of the "anxiety response" and postulates three stages in its development. From birth through the first month, the perceptive threshold is high. Reaction to stimuli is brief, inconsistent, diffuse, and nonspecific. Neither anxiety nor pleasure can be observed; the only psychological correlates that can reasonably be inferred are unpleasure and quiescence. During months 2 through 6, pleasure responses can be distinguished: smiling at 2 months, social smiling at 3 months. Unpleasure responses become more specific—"in the nature of fear" (1950, p. 139)—and sustained. Both pleasure and unpleasure responses occur in relation to the infant's partner (mother). Unpleasure responses are occasioned by percepts associated with previous unpleasure experiences—for example, with repeated preventive inoculations—or by the mother's leaving. In months 7 through 10, there appear "drastic fright reactions" at the approach of a stranger. Spitz regards these reactions as the first unequivocal manifestation of anxiety proper. Spitz appears to agree with Ramzy and Wallerstein that fear, or something like fear, occurs before anxiety does.

Szekely (1954), reinterpreting Spitz's findings, suggests that the percept "two eyes and a forehead" (sufficient to evoke a smiling response in the 3-month-old child) is a key stimulus, in the ethological sense, that releases the "animal fear instinct." Smiling, then, when the child learns to recognize the mother, is a manifestation of the relief of anxiety. The later "stranger anxiety" is simply a manifest continuation of what was there before. In 1965, Spitz paid a good deal of attention to this "ingenious reinterpretation," but was unable to detect in the infants he observed any evidence of a fear response to the mother's face.

Benjamin (1961, 1963) also reported on careful longitudinal studies of infants by direct observation, with some special interest in the anxiety response. According to Benjamin, at about 4 weeks most infants have outbursts of "undifferentiated negative affect expression" (1961, p. 660). This is concomitant with a period of rapid neurophysiological maturation at 3 to 4 weeks (1963), which entails increased perceptual capacity for external stimulation—a "lowering of the stimulus barrier" (1961, pp. 659-660). At 3 to 5 months, there are "clear-cut manifestations of fear," as judged by facial expression, gross motor behavior, and attempts at visual avoidance (1961, pp. 660-661). Benjamin does not find that previous unpleasure percepts are necessary for this response and considers these responses as an early stage of anxiety. In his description of responses in the second half of the first year, he distinguishes separation anxiety and stranger anxiety, which, he finds, show independent variations in intensity, peak time, and persistence (1961).

Both Spitz and Benjamin draw one identical important conclusion directly from their observations: "What is the evidence to justify the statement that no differentiated object exists at the age of 6 to 10 weeks? It is very simple, consisting of the fact that, as Spitz (1950) put it, the preobjects are interchangeable" (Benjamin, 1963, p. 132).

For present purposes, the differences in the observations of Spitz and Benjamin are not marked. Their studies are not entirely parallel: Benjamin follows the reaction to being left alone ("separation anxiety"); Spitz does not. In 1950, Spitz designated the unpleasure responses observable as early as 3 months "in the nature of fear"; in 1965 he said, less cautiously, "fear." Spitz and Benjamin agree that such responses occur in reaction to being left by the "adult partner." They also occur, Spitz says, in association with percepts related to previous unpleasure experiences. Benjamin says that the fear responses appear as a result of maturation and are not dependent on previous unpleasure experiences, but that "differential previous experiences significantly codetermine the frequency and nature of these early responses" (1961, p. 661). (I have not been able to discover an example in Benjamin's publications.) They agree that anxiety cannot be experienced until there is a sufficiently mature ego to experience it. The question is when that begins. It also follows from Benjamin's view that fear does not necessarily precede anxiety developmentally.

Benjamin says that the response at 3 months is an early stage of anxiety, not just a precursor; in contrast, Spitz says that the "8 months" response is the first unequivocal manifestation of anxiety. Benjamin agrees with Spitz's differentiation of the 3-month and 8-month responses, but he proposes that what is new at 8 months includes (1) more definitive organization of the libidinal investment in the mother; (2) further development of the distinction between the mother and others, and between the I and non-I; (3) increased capacity of the ego to anticipate and predict; (4) the maturational organization of aggression as such into object-directed hostility and anger, with the resultant marked increase in fear of object loss (1961, pp. 661-662).

Spitz does not discuss aggression in relation to anxiety. In his 1950 paper, narcissism is the unifying concept in his theoretical discussion of anxiety: anxiety is a response to threatened integrity of the ego, an impending narcissistic trauma. In 1965, he no longer mentions this idea.

Brody and Axelrad (1966, 1970) also focus on early infancy as a period of transition from somatic to psychic response. They report extensive data of their own, as well as reviewing infant observation studies by non-analysts (see especially Ambrose, 1961, 1963) and the ethological concept of imprinting (Hess, 1959). Imprinting, they hypothesize, is a phylogenetic process and is responsible for a number of events in human development. Imprinting occurs during certain physiologically critical periods in early life. In human infancy, there are two such periods. The first, imprinting to the human species in general, occurs during the first three months of life; the second, imprinting to the mother or her surrogate, occurs in months 3 through 7 (1966, pp. 222, 227). These are the "two phases of socialization." Preparedness for anxiety exists in physiological paths; the development of the affect anxiety occurs in conjunction with the two imprinting processes, combined with development of the ability to perceive psychologically the physiological reactions.

Emde, Gaensbauer, and Harmon (1976) pursued the study of separation reactions and stranger reactions, using Spitz's (1959) ideas that rates of development in infancy are uneven and that affect behaviors can serve as useful indicators of times of rapid change. They confirmed Benjamin's findings that separation distress and stranger distress follow different developmental curves (pp. 107-121) and clearly are separable phenomena (p. 117). They also found that stranger distress occurs even when the mother is present and in infants who have never shown separation distress (p. 117). They conclude that stranger distress cannot be directly derived from separation distress. Nor can it be explained cognitively, since the infant is capable of discriminating adequately between the mother and unfamiliar people some months earlier (p. 121). Stranger distress, they conclude, requires a new explanation.

The method of differentiating affective states in infancy is of interest: the evaluation of the facial expressions and other motoric behavior of infants by adult observers. It is only at the time of "stranger distress" that adults consistently describe the baby as looking "fearful" or "afraid" or "frightened" (p. 128). The investigators postulate that a new level of organization has occurred or is occurring at that time which justifies the descriptive shift from "distress" to "fearfulness" (p. 127)—a "differentiation of emotionality" (p. 122). They suggest that a maturational factor is involved, one that controls further differentiation of emotionality (p. 128). The new level of organization is apparent in physiological and social sectors as well (p. 123).

Comment. In relation to anxiety in early infancy, Freud presented two fundamental hypotheses: (1) The form and quality of the anxiety response is determined by the phylogenetic experience of birth as an inherited precipitate in the mental apparatus. (2) Prior to lasting object cathexis, there is little or no psychic content, and only raw energic events can be postulated; after lasting object cathexis occurs, affective experience, including anticipation, may be described. Most of the studies in this area that we have reviewed—Greenacre, Spitz, Szekely, Benjamin, and Brody and Axelrad—take a somewhat different orientation: the transition from physical to psychic response. Greenacre accomplishes an advance from Freud's hypotheses by placing the patterning affect of birth in an ontogenetic and neurophysiological context, with the subsequent psychic experience in some way influenced by the prepsychic patterning. Brody and Axelrad attempt to formulate the process of object cathexis in terms that interdigitate with ethology, with emphasis on *how* this process occurs. They also call attention to the necessity to consider neurophysiological maturation. Spitz and Benjamin are perhaps primarily interested in *when* this process occurs; that is, when there are manifestations of fear (differentiable from unpleasure) and when the fear response is dissociated from stimuli learned to be unpleasant. For both, the criterion for an anxiety response is apparently that there are manifestations of fear not directly produced by a previously unpleasure percept, not realistic, learned fear but something stemming from within the infant, and not explicable without inferring a psychic process more complex than a reflex-like response to stimulus. It is of interest that neither Spitz nor Benjamin nor Emde nor anyone else describes a state of fear or anything more closely resembling fear than "unpleasure" in early responses to appetitive needs or other disequilibria or discomfort. Benjamin, in addition, notes that neurophysiological maturation, instinctive behavioral responses, and learning processes are all considerations in the early months of life. From the standpoint of theory, Benjamin—like Jones, Federn, Klein, and Brunswick—suggests that aggression is involved in the anxiety response and offers a specific hypothesis about object-directed aggression (above). Greenacre and Spitz attempt to extend hypotheses relating narcissism to object relations, ego development, and anxiety.

This work, then, offers confirmation and specification of some of Freud's hypotheses and, in a few instances, alternatives that seem preferable. We are left with the idea of some concordance of object cathexis and affective states as the earliest *possible* evidence of ego organization. There are also the notions of the psychic experience of affect, the probability of prior influence on the organization, and the experience by neurophysiological patterning, instinctive behavioral patterns, and primitive learning.

Besides these papers derived directly or indirectly from infant observation, other studies which deal with the transition from somatic to psychic anxiety responses include Ramzy and Wallerstein (1958),

Schur (1953, 1955, 1958), DiCara (1970), Hess (1959), Eibl-Eibesfeldt (1970), and Andrew (1971).

Perhaps it is worthwhile to state the problem again, utilizing the background of this discussion. What is anxiety? What accounts for its particular quality? Before birth and in the neonatal period, motoric and physiological responses to physiological disequilibria and painful stimuli occur. At least some of these responses occur in later life in association with mental states of fear and anxiety. One problem is to determine the onset of psychic states as opposed to purely physiological responses. The second problem, given the existence of psychic states, is to determine the differentiation of affects. When we are dealing with preverbal periods, the only method available is direct infant observation. Decisions about affects that the infant may be experiencing must be made by adult observers, judging from the facial expressions and other behaviors of the infant. By this method, diffuse "unpleasure" or distress responses may be held as the prototype of an affect class, out of which a later form, fear or anxiety, becomes differentiated. The cause, content, and timing of this earliest possible experience of fear/anxiety are to some extent decidable on the basis of the phenomena—separation versus stranger distress, for example—and to some extent dependent on the investigator's concepts of fear and anxiety.

In any event, it seems clear that appropriate research methodologies obviate the necessity for bald energic hypotheses concerning this period of life. One complication—or, perhaps, benefit—that results from these direct observational methods is the recognition of marked individual differences among the observed infants, in intensity, timing, form, and quality of the several anxiety-related responses (Benjamin, 1963; Emde, Gaensbauer, and Harmon, 1976; Mahler, Pine, and Bergman, 1975, p. 56).

Attempts at Further Articulation or Refinement
of Freud's Anxiety Theory

Nunberg, Fenichel, Brenner, Zetzel, Flescher, Schur, Waelder, Stewart, and Rangell have all dealt at length with Freud's anxiety theory, mainly in terms of theoretical considerations. Differences among these contributors are largely, but not entirely, differences in relative emphasis on signal anxiety or on economic anxiety. Aside from the observational studies of infants, these papers represent the major contributions from psychoanalysts directly concerned with anxiety and its understanding. There are, in addition, pertinent contributions by other authors, not made in the context of a general discussion of anxiety; some of these are also included here.

Where the author has fully detailed his theory of anxiety, his own work is certainly the best presentation of his theory as a working model. The study of the development of psychoanalytic theory is better served by breaking down the various contributions into their elements and grouping related elements for critical consideration. Accordingly, we shall follow the organizational scheme used for Freud's later work—summarizing for each author under each of the usual five metapsychological points of view. The selection of material for the categories is somewhat arbitrary, and there is a great deal of overlapping. The discussions are, however, so complex—at times abstruse—that the redundancy is unavoidable and will perhaps even be welcome. We shall begin by indicating the central concept from which each writer seems to take his orientation and end with comments on his clarification or emendation of Freud's anxiety theory.

The primary guiding questions remain: What is anxiety? What accounts for its particular quality? Some rephrasing of our secondary questions will be helpful in following these discussions. Is there *always* some content in a fear response, at the "root" of the fear, or is it sometimes only a contentless energic state or discharge? What is the relationship between sensory perceptions associated with painful stimuli and the sensations of internal disequilibria or "need"? Why and how or under what conditions do these perceptions and sensations coalesce into a common affective state? Can we explain motoric responses to danger which occur without accompanying anxiety? Can the "ego" register losses of "its powers"? If so, how?

It is sometimes implied that psychoanalysis has a well-worked-out theory of anxiety. To emphasize that this is perhaps not the case, we shall repeat the questions about the conceptualization of anxiety as phrased by Zetzel (1955, p. 370): "(1) To what extent is anxiety a response to a danger situation, internal or external? (2) To what extent is anxiety produced by the frustration of an instinct (drive), again whether internal or external? (3) Should anxiety be regarded as a subjective awareness of instinctual tension, or, and to what extent, does anxiety represent a mode of instinctual discharge?" She also adds that a comprehensive theory of anxiety must take into account the important role of aggression (p. 379).

Orientation of Contributors. The central concept of Fenichel's theory of anxiety (1937), of affects generally (1941), and of neurosis (1945) is the "dammed-up state"—a relative insufficiency of the discharge apparatus with quantities of dammed-up excitation resulting either from excessive influx of stimuli (of external or internal origin) or inhibition of discharge. Such states are associated with subjective feelings of tension. Trauma is energically defined in accord with Freud. Danger is the possibility of a traumatic excess of excitation. Anxiety is a mode of experiencing tension "arising from urgent needs" (1937, p. 49). All anxiety is "at base" a fear of experiencing a traumatic state (1945, p. 133).

Comment: Given only this much, it may already be asked why the perception of an actual situation recognized as dangerous immediately produces essentially the same affective reaction.

Rangell's central concepts are very similar to Fenichel's. Mounting psychic tension is a common condition in the genesis of symptom formation (1968, p. 381). When there is psychic intersystemic conflict, discharge is blocked and a tension state exists (1963, p. 89). The tension state in psychic conflict, the dammed-up state, and the actual-neurotic state are equivalent terms (1955, p. 396). In such a state, relative "discharge" insufficiency of the ego produces a trend toward a traumatic situation or traumatic state (economically defined), differing from other tension states in degree (1968, pp. 380-381). Thus, external and internal dangers converge in the traumatic situation: the relative insufficiency of the ego may be in relation to heightened influx of stimuli or blockage of discharge (1955, pp. 398-399). Anxiety is always a response to danger and always economically justified (1968, p. 395).

Flescher (1955) has a purer excitation/discharge orientation and a simpler theory: anxiety is a substitution of autoplastic discharge for aim-directed aggression.

Nunberg (1955) makes explicit the mind-body dichotomy, and his discussion follows these lines: anxiety has two sources, psychic and somatic; it may originate in either or both. All neuroses have a component of actual anxiety; that is, discharge of drive tension in the form of anxiety (p. 190).

Brenner (1953) is oriented to the ego experience. Anxiety is an affect which the anticipation of danger evokes in the ego (p. 23).

Arlow (1963, p. 13), in a discussion of symptom formation, addresses only anxiety in the limited sense (excluding "real fear"); anxiety is the signal that alerts the ego to the imminence of some internal danger. The danger is the emergence of derivatives of a previously repressed drive.

Stewart (1967) carries this approach further to demonstrate the adequacy of formulations for anxiety without invoking discharge hypotheses.

Schur's formulation carefully balances the ego experience and energic aspects of anxiety theory. Anxiety is always a response and always economically justified, a response of the ego or its matrix to a traumatic situation or to a danger, present or anticipated (1953, p. 93). In this reaction, the affect anxiety, which is an ego reaction, and the discharge phenomena, which are also id manifestations, must be distinguished (1958, pp. 217-218).

Comment. Although Schur's formulation sounds identical to Rangell's, it is not. Schur approaches the problem of economic versus danger responses on a structural basis—ego contribution, id contribution. Rangell's approach is fundamentally energic, as is Fenichel's, with structural considerations secondary.

Genetic Propositions. Fenichel's starting point in developmental time is not clearly specified: "In infancy," biological helplessness leads to painful states of high tension—traumatic states. The "pain" of these states is undifferentiated, but they may be designated as states of "primary anxiety." They are the root of other affects as well as anxiety (1945, p. 42). The first fear is the wordless fear of further traumatic states (1945, p. 44).

Comment. Some questions should be raised. How does the "first fear" arise? What is its mechanism? How does the "capacity to fear" arise? Is the physiological need state reflected psychically in proportion to its intensity? Moreover, it seems misleading to call such states primary *anxiety* if they are the root of other (unpleasure) affects as well, including affects that are fundamentally different from anxiety. The more general term *unpleasure* (or displeasure or distress) would be preferable, and more consistent with the limitations of the infant observation, as we have indicated above. (Hartmann preferred the designation *anxiety* as an emphasis of genetic continuity. See Brenner, 1953, p. 23, for discussion of this point.)

Brenner's position (1953, pp. 23-24) concurs with our objection, as well as with the observations of Spitz, Benjamin, Emde, Ramzy and Wallerstein, and Freud. Anxiety as such is not present from birth; only pleasure and unpleasure can be inferred from observation as very early psychic experience. Even the physiological "anxiety syndrome," which is present from birth, is better described from the psychic viewpoint as a nonspecific unpleasure response.

Most investigators in this area agree that the psychic experience of anxiety can occur only after some degree of ego-id differentiation has taken place. Nunberg, for instance, says that the anxiety of the infant is initially biological; the transition to psychic anxiety is via the repeated perception and cathexis of the mother as object, which gradually transforms the reaction to anticipation of danger. The "psychic contents" then make use of the original somatic mechanisms of anxiety as a means of expression (1955, pp. 196-199). From a genetic viewpoint, anxiety is a reaction to trauma (p. 193).

Comment. Again, it seems misleading to designate a physiological response by its eventual psychic correlate. If this phrasing is taken as an expression of the organismic response view, it still blurs the problem when we are attempting to consider the genesis of anxiety. It also leads to a blurring of the psychoanalytic concept of psychic energy with physical or physiological energy. If, however, the transition from somatic response to somatic plus mental response is emphasized, the formulation resembles the viewpoints of Greenacre and Schur.

Schur describes this earliest stage in terms of motoric responses to physiological disequilibria. He also offers by far the most carefully detailed genetic theory of the anxiety response. In his view, biological response mechanisms related to anxiety are present in animals, fetuses, and newborns, as well as older human beings. They are part of homeostatic mechanisms for adjusting physiological disequilibria. As ego functions develop maturationally and through "realization" of the need-gratifying "function" of the object, psychological response is added to the physiological patterns, with a resulting tendency to "desomatization" of these responses. With further development of the ego, danger can be anticipated (1953, pp. 67-74). There then gradually develops a spectrum of normal ego responses, from panic in a traumatic situation to thoughtlike awareness of danger (Freud's signal anxiety) (1953, p. 90). A hierarchy of situations and responses can be consistently described (1958, pp. 190-193).

Because his initial genetic theory left gaps in accounting for traumatic states in adults and omitted discussion of the role of the id in anxiety, Schur later expanded his theory in the following way. The simplest psychic element is the wish; with the appearance of the wish, psychic structure, in contrast to physiological need satisfaction, begins. Thus, the concept of instinctual drive (related to wish) can be differentiated from the drive element of (ethological) instinct (related to need). In the instinctual sense, there is an "internal drive to avoid danger." Before the differentiation of psychic structure, the releasing excitations (of the internal drive) are physiological disequilibria and perceptual stimulation; the reactions consist of "diffuse discharge." The (psychic) energy involved is undifferentiated. With the development of psychic structure, the internal drive element of the instinct gives rise to a wish (to avoid danger), and the physiological prototypes of the anxiety response become subject to the (psychological) pleasure principle. Libidinous and aggressive energy are now involved (1958, pp. 203-205). The anxiety response thus includes instinctual patterns (in the ethological sense) and psychic structure (p. 205). In 1966, as we have mentioned, Schur further modified this postulate.

Comment. The effect of this ethological interpolation is to link anxiety with the id, which solves certain energic problems of traumatic experience in adults at the cost of placing the wish to avoid danger on a footing with other unconscious wishes. In 1966, Schur presented some biological background to justify the assumption

of such an instinct. One difficulty, however, is that, given such an
instinct, most of the problems of anxiety could probably be resolved
without recourse to Freud's anxiety theory.

We should also note here, from the work of Spitz and
Benjamin, that perhaps, from a genetic viewpoint, fear and anxiety
should be distinguished from each other. Later we shall consider the
value of this distinction from other viewpoints. A. Freud (1977,
p. 86) takes a strong position in favor of distinguishing the terms
fear and *anxiety* generally.

Dynamic Propositions. Fenichel (1937, pp. 59-61) explains his dynamic formulations with his view of the necessary energic state: what is
feared in excessive excitation is collapse of the ego or loss of voluntary control—loss of control of anal and urethral sphincters or fear of bursting, fear
of being washed away, fear of death, or fear of falling down. At this point
it is not clear whether Fenichel is using "ego" in the system sense or the self-
representation sense, or both. In 1945 (p. 133) he says, "The organization
of the ego may be overwhelmed by excitation," which seems to imply the
system sense.

Lewin (1952), remaining more clearly at the level of mental content,
points out that anxiety is not only a signal but a sort of memory; that is,
the anxiety experience has a content. Anxiety attacks reproduce earlier
life events. Given the phase sequence of anxiety situations postulated by
Freud, the existence of one phase does not exclude the simultaneous presence
of earlier forms (Lewin, 1952, p. 311). Nunberg (1955, p. 209) adds that
there are secondary fantasies (for example, womb fantasies) attached to the
phasically determined content of anxiety experiences.

Brenner (1955, p. 84) suggests that the perception of danger gives
rise to a fantasy of the traumatic situation and that this fantasy causes
signal anxiety. Arlow (1963) does not mention trauma in his formulation
of anxiety in conflict and symptom formation. In his view, the danger is
given a concrete expression in fantasy, revealing the level of drive and ego
functioning at the time of the original conflict, just as the regressively re-
activated id impulse is expressed in fantasy derivatives (p. 22).

Waelder (1960) notes some other suggested content of anxiety besides
Freud's phasic sequence of danger situations. Fear of one's own masochism,
casually mentioned by Freud (1926), Waelder feels, is a derivative of castration fear rather than an additional special category. Anna Freud's idea of fear
of the strength of one's own drives (1936, chap. 12), however, is a "content" of a different kind, which amounts to a fear of "ego disintegration"
(pp. 158-162). The dangers "can be reduced to . . . loss of object, desertion,
emasculation, and ego disintegration" (p. 162); that is, they are all "narcissistic castastrophes" (p. 164). Freud's ([1917] 1963, p. 165) thought

that the response to danger may be relatable to ego-libido should not be dismissed.

Rangell (1955, 1963, 1968) accepts the sequence of danger situations, as modified by Anna Freud. His own additional discussions are not, however, formulated primarily at the level of content and mechanism but, rather, at the level of structure-energy and mechanism. In Rangell's formulations, the dynamic content of anxiety states in general is helplessness.

Comment. The paucity of contributions in the dynamic framework that we have cited is partly the result of convenience in allocating material and partly an artifact of the method. A review which pursued contributions concerning particular developmental phases and clinical conditions would yield more dynamic propositions about anxiety. We have chosen to focus on the areas that were obscure in Freud's work, and the subsequent observational and theoretical developments in these areas, rather than to review points where there has generally been confirmation.

Structural Propositions. Investigators generally agree that Freud's formulation of signal anxiety (anxiety produced by the ego) is anthropomorphic and therefore should not be maintained (Fenichel, 1945, p. 43; Schur, 1953, p. 92; Brenner, 1955, p. 84; Flescher, 1955; Rangell, 1955, p. 398; Stewart, 1967, p. 174). They also agree that at least some of the differences in anxiety reactions are attributable to ego development or regression (Fenichel, 1945, p. 133; Brenner, 1953, pp. 23-24; Schur, 1953, p. 74; Rangell, 1955, pp. 401-402).

Other structural hypotheses require more detailed discussion. For Fenichel (1945, p. 43), the "primary anxiety" of early infancy—that is, states of pain due to excessive excitation—is experienced passively by the "ego," as is anxiety resulting from traumatic events later in life. In his view, signal anxiety results from the ego function of judging danger; that is, the possibility of a traumatic excess of excitation. Such judgment "sets up conditions in the id similar to those of a traumatic situation itself, though in lesser degree. And this too must necessarily be experienced by the ego as anxiety" (1937, p. 50). This anxiety is purposefully used by the ego; the affect is thus "tamed" (1941, p. 217). Fenichel also includes the idea that there may be regression of "anxiety," from the signal form to the traumatic form. Apparently, this regression has again to do with the interaction of structure and energy: "All anxiety is a fear of experiencing a traumatic state, of the possibility that the organization of the ego may be overwhelmed by excitation" (1945, p. 133).

Comment. Fenichel was one of the first to offer structural hypotheses in an attempt to refine Freud's theory. His first approximations have regularly led us to questions. In this instance, it is not clear why or how the judgment of danger sets up conditions in the id similar to those of a traumatic situation, or even what those conditions might be. (Freud's formulations of trauma, which Fenichel accepts, are, in the theory development sense, prestructural.) How can the exercise of an ego function instantaneously result in excess excitation? If something other than that is involved, it is not clear why "the ego" should experience anxiety, since the experience depends on excess excitation, according to Fenichel. The pervasive effect of the discharge theory of affects is evident in these formulations.

Rangell's position again appears similar to Fenichel's. He attempts to fill in some of the gaps in this type of proposition. The ego passively experiences both traumatic and signal anxiety (1955, pp. 398-399). Anxiety is always automatic and direct, and always a signal of danger (1968, p. 386). In an *existing traumatic situation*, the danger is external pain or instinct cumulation that will not stop or cannot be discharged or will get worse or never stop (1955, pp. 392, 399). In a *potential traumatic* (danger) *situation*, the ego arrives at an estimate of the danger, and signal anxiety occurs (1955, p. 399). Evaluation (estimation) of the danger involves a sampling of it. "An instinctive reaction of tension and discharge" follows (1955, p. 404). On closer inspection, the evaluation involves permitting a small amount of discharge and sampling the gratification and superego reaction. A series of preliminary signals thus occurs, which may lead to signal anxiety of variable intensity (1963, pp. 75-102). The degree of control of the anxiety response reflects ego development or regression (1955, pp. 401-402).

How does Rangell visualize the mechanism of the anxiety response itself? He seems to offer two slightly different though related formulations, both of which are primarily energic. One is that in signal anxiety the "instinctive reaction of tension and discharge is a historical precipitate of the alertness or vigilance of lower forms, supplied by a pool of defensive, *instinctive* energy" (1955, pp. 403-404). The other formulation is as follows. Anxiety is always preceded by a "small traumatic state," which elicits the memory of a previous trauma (1968, pp. 386-388). (Compare Fenichel's idea that the judgment of danger creates conditions in the id similar to those of a traumatic state.) In both cases—that is, in signal and traumatic anxiety—how does the traumatic state lead to the experience of anxiety by the ego? There is transmission from nonspecific instinctual pressure via the soma to the experience of anxiety (1968, pp. 398-399).

    Comment. Rangell's careful and closely reasoned exposition of the theory of anxiety still leaves some major questions at the most central points. In order to keep the energic orientation for signal anxiety (the usual form), he has to postulate the "small traumatic state" and supply it with instinctive, somatic energy. I cannot conceive of the idea of an excess of excitation relative to the sufficiency of the apparatus as anything other than an "is" or "is-not" phenomenon. It seems inherent in the definition that some set of conditions must be *exceeded* for the concept to apply. "Will be" or "will not be" is a different order of decision, requiring a different deciding apparatus. In that case, as Waelder (1967, p. 17) says, the whole secret is in how the ego does the anticipating. We shall return to Rangell's ideas in the more purely economic framework.

Brenner emphasizes the role of the ego. The experience of anxiety requires the anticipation or prediction of a state of unpleasure. This requires some significant degree of development of ego functions, such as memory and sensory perception (1953, pp. 23-24). Certain ego functions are involved in the recognition of danger; others, in the reaction to recognition (1955, p. 84).

Loewenstein (1964, pp. 156-157) suggests that *intra*systemic conflict may also result in anxiety, including severe anxiety attacks, based on threatening loss of control of the ego's own functions. He suggests that such states represent a regression to traumatic anxiety.

In Schur's formulation, genetic and structural elements are inextricable, and, as we have said, he carefully balances the ego-experience and energic aspects. The ego utilizes awareness of danger as a signal. Two separate groups of ego functions should be distinguished: evaluation of danger and the response to this evaluation (1953, pp. 93-94). The ego regulates or taxes or structuralizes the anxiety response (1958, pp. 207-208). Ego functions of delay, inhibition, and anticipation are involved (1958, pp. 208-209). What the ego regulates is the "affect charge" emanating from the id, along with the internal drive to avoid danger. Regulation means, in this instance, neutralization of the energy involved (1958, p. 208). Either or both of the ego functions involved in the response to danger are subject to regression, including regression to resomatization (1953, p. 74). Neurotic anxiety is a regressive response involving loss of time distinction between past and present (1953, pp. 88-89). Ego regression is disruptive of the ego and assumes increasingly the aspect of danger, becoming a source of anxiety (1966, p. 147). Perception of the "discharge" resulting from resomatization also augments the anxiety response (1966, p. 150). Regression of ego responses can restore archaic situations and thus recreate the old economic conditions (1953, p. 91). The process is explained by the assumption that the capacities to utilize secondary process, to neutralize energy, and to desomatize responses are interdependent (1955, p. 124).

Comment. We gratefully accept the two points on which there seems to be general agreement. (1) For us, Freud stands corrected: the ego never produces anxiety in any form. (2) At least some of the differences in anxiety reactions are attributable to ego development or ego regression, or, more specifically, following Bohur, to development or regression of certain ego functions. Brenner and Bohur suggest essentially the same distinction of functions involved in the anxiety response: (1) evaluation or recognition of danger and (2) response.

Economic Propositions. In this area, the concepts of trauma and types of psychic energy are, of course, prominent. Freud left major unresolved problems in both cases. On the one hand, there is his distinction between economic and signal (nonenergic) anxiety; on the other, his omission of any specific discussion of the role of aggression in anxiety. In order to follow the development of these ideas in the work of subsequent analysts, we shall have to set aside our objection to Freud's concept of trauma and our proposed redefinition.

Most of the authors who discuss energies—Fenichel, Nunberg, Flescher, Schur, and Rangell—explicitly accept the energy discharge theory of affect. Only Flescher is entirely specific about the type of energy involved: aggression. Flescher (1955) says that a danger situation always mobilizes aggressive drives. Anxiety appears as a substitute for aggressive action—specifically, a substitution of autoplastic discharge for aim-directed aggression. The intensity of the anxiety is a measure of the intensity of undischarged aggression.

> *Comment.* Flescher's formulation is open to the following objections: (1) There is no way clearly to distinguish libido and aggression, and all psychoanalytic hypotheses concerning drive energies postulate their invariable fusion in some proportion. (2) There is no explanation of how or why the aggression is transformed into anxiety. (3) The theory is overly mechanistic in that it is baldly energic and tends to be unpsychological. It also sounds like a variation of Freud's libido transformation theory, and it is open to the same kinds of objections. (4) As Hartmann (1948, pp. 83-87) has indicated, once the ego-id-superego model was introduced, the ego or self-preservative drives lost their theoretical status. Self-preservation is seen largely, in man, as the task of ego functions, to which both sexual and aggressive drives contribute. Aggression, as an instinctual drive, is not synonymous with aggressive actions.

For Fenichel, energy buildup and discharge are, as we have indicated, central. An excessive influx of stimuli (trauma) or an excessive accumulation of drive due to inhibition of discharge may result in a dammed-up state, in which the discharge apparatus is relatively inadequate. Anxiety is a mode of experiencing such "tension due to urgent needs" (1937, p. 49) and is an "archaic discharge syndrome" (1945, p. 43) composed of emotional feelings and physiological discharge phenomena (1941, pp. 215-216). Anxiety is approximately the same as, or a type of, "traumatically determined vegetative unpleasure" (1937, p. 52).

According to Nunberg, anxiety is a specific painful affective eruption of discharge in response to excessive augmentation of stimulus or damming up of instincts (1955, p. 194). What is discharged is the stimulus (p. 194), drive tension, and psychic energy (p. 204). Anxiety has two sources, somatic and psychic (p. 190), and is itself of instinctual origin, and not only a reaction of the ego (p. 204). The psychic energy involved is "displaceable" between libido and aggression (pp. 203-204). In neurotic anxiety, there is always a component of *Aktual* anxiety; that is, instinctual tensions discharged as anxiety (pp. 204-206).

> *Comment.* If anxiety, like other affects, is a "discharge phenomenon," something must be discharged. Freud, as we have seen, believed this to be libido. Flescher says that aggression is discharged. For Fenichel, "tension due to urgent needs," or "traumatically determined vegetative unpleasure," is discharged. In Nunberg's view, "stimulus," "drive tension," and "displaceable or free psychic energy " are discharged. Nunberg's drive tension includes somatic drive tension as well as psychic. "Discharge phenomena" for all three is a term indicating, at least in some respects, physiological processes.

Schur (1953, p. 74) concurs with the standard formulation that the anxiety response is determined by the relation of the quantity of excitation to the reactive organization. In the earliest stages of development, the psychic energy is undifferentiated. With the formation of psychic structure, libidinous and aggressive energy appear and subsequently occur in various states of fusion and neutralization (1958, p. 205). We can also speak at this point of an affect charge, emanating from the id, along with the hypothetical wish stemming from the drive to avoid danger, and of an affect anxiety which is the ego reaction. The ego neutralizes the id energy and regulates the anxiety response (1958, pp. 207-208). The ego's ability to use secondary process and to neutralize energy is interdependent with the desomatization of responses (1955, p. 124).

> *Comment.* If I follow Schur correctly and the following interpolations are permissible, what is discharged is, at one end of the spectrum, nothing: in the "thoughtlike awareness of danger" (1953, p. 90), the ego has successfully neutralized whatever emanated from the id and continues secondary process operations. (Alternatively, this discharge could be regarded as de facto, in that energy is removed from the system by neutralization or binding. But that hypothesis refers to displacement of energy within a system, not to removal from the system.) At the other extreme, when there

is regression of evaluation of danger and of response, primary process prevails; that is, free drive energies are operating, unneutralized. Perhaps there is dedifferentiation of the psychic energy which reopens the path to physiological response patterns—resomatization, or physiological discharge of the (codifferentiated) energy. Between the two extremes—panic and thoughtlike awareness of danger—are all the variations of experience of the affect anxiety, dependent on the quantity of excitation to be dealt with and the state of the reacting apparatus (ego). Presumably, there would be variations in the proportion of neutralization and discharge. Most of the phenomena that are the basis of these discussions fall "between the two extremes." As long as there is affect, and not only thoughtlike awareness of danger, there is discharge. Here, still, affect charge and discharge are indispensable concepts. To put this in the terms of our discussion of Freud's work, affect and energy are now distinguishable in the ego—but not in the id.

Rangell also begins with the idea that whenever there is relative insufficiency of the ego, a state of psychic helplessness exists. An "unpleasure affect" occurs, and danger exists (1955, pp. 398-399). If the response is *signal* anxiety, the question of the energy source raises the question of the energy sources of defense mechanisms in general. Perhaps there is "an innate, phylogenetically determined pool of such defensive, affective energy, instinctive in contrast to instinctual, a historical precipitate of the alertness or vigilance of lower forms" (p. 403). In a traumatic state, there is direct conversion of "instinctual tension" into affect by massive internal discharge. In a more differentiated state, the discharge is accompanied by the ego's perception and judgment of the uncontrolled affect; that is, by anxiety (p. 404). In his 1968 paper, Rangell reformulates the "microdynamic sequence" involved in the signal response: the ego, confronted with instinctual tension pressing for discharge, permits a small sample or trial discharge. A "small traumatic state" may ensue, evoking a memory of previous trauma and leading to judgment of the potential effect if further discharge is permitted (pp. 387-388). The "small traumatic state" is equivalent to the "unpleasure affect" of the earlier paper (p. 391). Undischarged instinctual pressures produce the (potential) traumatic state (p. 393). But how does the traumatic state lead to anxiety? Or how does the instinctual flooding from the id lead to the experience of anxiety by the ego (p. 395)? The answer is psychosomatic: "Anxiety is a psychobiological organismic event." There is transmission from "nonspecific instinctual pressure" (unpleasure) via the soma to anxiety (pp. 398-399). (Compare Freud, [1895] 1966, pp. 320-321.)

Comment. I have already raised objection to the idea of a "small traumatic state." Even if this state is called an "unpleasure affect," a more acceptable term, the problem of explanation has merely been shifted from "anxiety" to "unpleasure affect." The terms are at the same level and therefore not explanatory of one another except possibly in a genetic sense; we must now begin all over to explain the dynamic mechanism of the unpleasure affect. I think recognition of this is inherent in the final statements quoted above, which postulate an eventual psychosomatic explanation. This and earlier comments are in no way intended as an objection to Rangell's (1968) assertion that a theory of anxiety should include both physiological and psychological phenomena. Rangell's idea that danger is an intrinsic part of a state of helplessness also seems valuable.

Brenner's approach differs significantly from that of Fenichel, Flescher, Nunberg, Schur, and Rangell. He does not invoke discharge hypotheses and in fact minimizes energic hypotheses in general. Brenner reviews the lines of evidence on which Freud based his hypotheses of economic anxiety—anxiety neurosis, traumatic neurosis, and psychic states of early infancy. He concludes that there is no good evidence that actual neurosis exists and that the literature on traumatic neurosis generally reflects the idea that neurotic anxiety arises because of the relationship of external events to unconscious conflict. This leaves only the experience of early infancy as a situation providing evidence for economic anxiety. (This is not, in fact, quite accurate: Freud included childhood, up to age 5 or 6.) But what can be observed at that time can best be characterized as unpleasure (1953, pp. 18-21). In 1955, Brenner pointed out that Freud's last statements on the pleasure principle are that the relation between the phenomena of accumulation and discharge of mobile drive energy, on the one hand, and affects of pleasure and unpleasure, on the other hand, are neither simple nor determinable. "We cannot satisfactorily formulate the pleasure principle in terms of later concepts which deal principally with psychic energy. We must therefore hold to the earlier version of it, which is formulated in terms of subjective experiences of pleasure and unpleasure" (pp. 75-76).

Brenner is, in effect, saying that we can arrive at satisfactory explanations, proceeding on firmer ground, by not utilizing energic hypotheses about anxiety except in a derivative way, at least for the time being. Stewart (1967) carries this approach further. He traces the derivatives of Freud's early work and points out that the application of an energy concept in psychoanalysis is meaningful only when it is coordinated with genetic, dynamic, and structural views (p. 118). Psychic energy is a concept only analogous to physical energy, and energy hypotheses are not provable or disprovable at a clinical level (p. 119). He goes on to suggest four sets of distinctions: (1) two types of energy formulations in Freud's writing, a mechanical model and a field theory, whereby structures are organizations of energy (pp. 114-120); (2) the distinction of cathexis hypotheses and discharge hypotheses (mentioned earlier); (3) two meanings of the constancy principle: (a) a form of the principle of conservation of energy and (b) the assumption that justifies the discharge hypotheses, an input-output concept (pp. 127-128); (4) the distinction of the *pleasure principle,* a general trend in psychic life where behavior is governed by wish, not by need, and the *pleasure-unpleasure series,* the means or signals by which the principle operates (pp. 136-137). He mentions the toxicological theory of anxiety and the chaining of affect theory to simple economic formulas. The latter he sees as the disadvantage of overemphasizing the discharge hypotheses (pp. 150-152).

The description of automatic anxiety in Freud's work, Stewart says, was based on an economic view, with little or no necessary psychic content. Signal anxiety, in contrast, was described from a genetic and dynamic view related to the *aim* of the libidinal impulse (p. 167). Except for the problem of accounting for "primary repression," "the early traumatic states are no different from signal anxiety except that the signal and the response are crude and global" (p. 171). Stewart then reformulates the importance of the feeling of helplessness (traumatic moment) that results from a change in the *mode* of the energy involved, toward primary process, and in the binding capacity of the ego, rather than a "simple quantitative" change (p. 173).

> The most parsimonious view of anxiety would then be that at first it manifests itself in the diffuse state of unpleasure and is the early ego's passive response to danger. External danger is responded to because key stimuli produce automatic patterned responses, including secretory changes. Internal danger is at first not distinguishable from physical pain. Pain or appetitive need has a total impact, and response is global. Later this total response is tamed via maturation and object ties. When the total response is combined with the anticipatory function of the ego, the signal function can occur [p. 174].

The role of affects in general is to allow signals of drive-related processes to achieve consciousness, making more discriminating regulation possible (p. 179). "We do not speak of anxiety in response to external danger as having a tension reduction function. It does not therefore seem correct to assume that affects reduce tension" (p. 181).

> *Comment.* Stewart's discussion seems to lead toward two conclusions, both of which he stops short of making. (1) The most straightforward discharge hypothesis in relation to anxiety is that there is an "unpleasure energy," which is secreted or freshly generated, and that the discharge of this energy is manifest as anxiety (compare Schur, Fenichel, Brunswick, Rangell, and also Freud, [1895] 1966, p. 320). (2) Discharge hypotheses, at least in the

extrapsychic sense, are generally simplistic or concretistic and should probably be abandoned. Stewart's alternative formulations raise many questions, of which the following are the most obvious: Is there evidence for automatic patterned "danger responses" to key stimuli in the human infant? In establishing "internal danger," what has a "total impact" on what, and what "responds globally"? One of the problems of anxiety theory emerges perhaps particularly clearly in Stewart's formulations. How is it that endogenous (drive) stimuli and external (danger) stimuli can "converge" in precisely the same response? Freud's theory does account for this, by deriving the danger concept from the preexisting unpleasure (traumatic) state plus experience. Rangell has also proposed an answer to this question, one which rests, however, on premises we have questioned.

Experimental and Extra-Analytic Developments

Perception Studies. On the basis of his experimental studies of preconscious perception of tachistoscopic images, Fisher (1956, pp. 45-46) concludes: "Instead of thinking in terms of an organism as a being that is stimulated, then perceives or recognizes, and then reacts, the evidence suggests that it would be preferable to think in terms of an organism that is stimulated, then reacts, and finally part of the reaction appears as conscious perception. Consciousness and response are not identical, and not all response involves consciousness. Adaptive response can involve preconscious and unconscious processes also."

The implication for anxiety theory is that the experience of anxiety —even signal anxiety—is not necessarily a part of the perception of and response to danger. This does not, however, alter any propositions concerning the role of the ego in the anxiety response, since ego is not synonymous with consciousness. Fisher's observations lend further credence to the idea of affects as indicators of alterations within the organism that occur outside of consciousness. Perhaps we might distinguish between a danger-situation response and an anxiety experience.

Biology of Sleep and Dreaming. Of particular interest here is the rather well-established fact that dreaming as a psychological process emerges from an underlying matrix of physiological processes. As Fisher puts it, "Dreaming is thus associated with a primitive form of sleep which is ontogenetically early and phylogenetically old" (1965, p. 273). Rapid eye movement (REM) sleep is present at birth in man, in newborn kittens, and in decorticate animals and man (pp. 272-273). Fisher points out that the physiological changes accompanying REM periods have been assumed to be correlated with dream effects in the adult, but there is little evidence on this, and all the changes are present in the neonate, when dreaming is not occurring in any psychological sense (p. 275).

If we say that dreaming as a psychological process emerges from the previously existing and underlying neurophysiological processes, that, of course, says nothing about how the transition occurs. It does offer a parallel to the propositions concerning the transition of the somatic to the psychic anxiety response—or danger response, with or without anxiety effect.

Visceral Learning. Learning theorists distinguish two types of learning. In classical or Pavlovian conditioning, a conditioned stimulus (signal) is presented along with an innate unconditioned stimulus (such as food) that normally elicits a certain innate, unconditioned response (salivation); after repetitions, the conditioned stimulus elicits the same response. This type of learning is thought to be involuntary. In instrumental learning or operant conditioning, a reinforcement or reward is given whenever the desired conditioned response is elicited by the unconditioned stimulus; a given response can be reinforced by a variety of rewards, and a given reward can reinforce a variety of responses. This type of learning is thought to be voluntary (DiCara, 1970).

Neal Miller has demonstrated in a long series of careful experiments that rats are capable of learning visceral responses by instrumental training procedures. For example, rats can be taught to modify their heart rate by rewards, as well as to alter their intestinal motility. In recent experiments, electrical activity of the brain has been shown to be modifiable by reward. "This finding forces us to think of the internal behavior of visceral organs in the same way we think of the external, observable behavior of the skeletal muscles, and therefore to consider its adaptive value to homeostasis" (DiCara, 1970, pp. 36-37). It also appears that human subjects are capable of visceral learning: medical students were taught to raise or lower their blood pressure to obtain a reward, without knowing what response was being measured (pp. 37-38).

This finding suggests that "psychosomatic symptoms" may in some way be learned. It also may have some bearing on the problems of anxiety. Learning is thought to occur before 3 months (see, for example, Benjamin, 1961). Physiological patterns may be especially susceptible to instrumental conditioning (at the hand of the mother) during this time, thus altering the matrix out of which the anxiety response develops. In addition, either physiological or psychic response could be encouraged during this time, the one at the expense of the other. Greenacre's "predisposition to anxiety" is susceptible to explanation in this way. Her concept says nothing about the nature of very early unpleasure experiences. It does say that modification or augmentation of such experiences can be dependent on type, quality, and timing of maternal responses, independent of any quantitative factor such as amount of physiological disequilibrium or amount of external stimulus.

Ethological Studies. Lorenz (1935) introduced the term *imprinting* to describe interspecies sexual fixations in adult birds, resulting from specific kinds of interspecies exposure during a "critical period" early in the life of the animal. He postulated that the first object to elicit a social response later released not only that response but also related responses, such as sexual behavior. According to Hess's (1959) review, the phenomenon has been shown to occur in insects, fish, sheep, deer, and buffalo, as well as several kinds of fowl (p. 133). Hess found that the critical period for imprinting fowl is limited at the one end by locomotor ability and at the other by the onset of fear. He feels that at least the end of susceptibility to imprinting with the onset of fear is true for all animals, perhaps including man (p. 137).

Besides imprinting, a number of ethological concepts—such as instinctive reaction, key stimuli, and innate releaser mechanism—appear in the psychoanalytic literature of anxiety. The implication of all this is, once again, that that general area of phenomena designated in psychoanalysis as "primary"—primary anxiety, primary repression, primary narcissism—is subject to explanation in terms other than energic. Energic hypotheses tend to be used when data are lacking. Prior to the developmental time when we can receive reports of, infer, or reasonably postulate psychic content, neurophysiological events occur which are perhaps parallel to and perhaps genetic precursors of the neurophysiological events homologous with later psychic content. Whatever energic theory we may find necessary for explanation of this early developmental time is meaningful only when articulated with, and subordinate to, the "neurophysiological dynamics" or their observable correlates, just as energic hypotheses concerning later psychic function are meaningful only when coordinated with genetic, dynamic, and structural views related to clinically observable phenomena.

It is of interest that the ethological theories most generally criticized by other biologists are those concerned with discharge hypotheses. Andrew (1971), for example, points out that while rises and falls in threshold are associated with the performance of a response, a variety of mechanisms are known to be involved. He mentions that the discharge model obscures the complexities and also fails to distinguish three separate factors: (1) appetitive behavior directed toward opportunity for performance, (2) progressive changes caused by the lack of performance, (3) the recovery from performance.

Nonpsychoanalytic psychological theories of anxiety (theories employing neither psychoanalytic drive psychology nor psychoanalytic ego psychology) have been reviewed by May (1950a), Guntrip (1961), and Fisher (1970).

2

Learning and Behavioral Theories

Richard R. Bootzin
David Max

Theorists generally agree about the various responses that constitute anxiety: *verbal reports* of apprehension, impending danger, inability to concentrate, feelings of tension, and expectations of being unable to cope; *behavioral responses,* including attempts to avoid the situation, impaired speech and motor coordination, inhibition of ongoing behavior, and performance deficits on complex cognitive tasks; and *physiological responses,* such as muscle tension, increased heart rate and blood pressure, rapid respiration, dryness of the mouth, drop in resistance in galvanic skin response, coldness in the extremities, nausea, diarrhea, and frequent urination. There is, however, considerable disagreement about the stimuli that elicit anxiety. As Martin (1971) points out, anxiety about being castrated differs from anxiety about being rejected—not because the anxiety response itself is different but because different stimuli are thought to have elicited the anxiety. Similar distinctions are made between anxiety and fear; that is, fear is regarded as reality based and anxiety as irrational. With respect to the response itself—instead of the eliciting stimuli—there is little distinction between fear and anxiety; therefore, we will use the terms interchangeably.

Learning and behavioral theories differ from psychodynamic theories of anxiety in that they focus on proximal rather than distal causes or stimuli (Kaplan, 1974). In psychodynamic theory, anxiety or avoidance behavior is interpreted as a sign of underlying intrapsychic conflict (a distal stimulus); in learning and behavioral theories, anxiety is taken as a response to some immediately preceding stimulus and is maintained by reinforcing consequences (proximal stimuli). Proximal stimuli can be external (such as an upcoming examination or expressions of rejection or approval by an important other) or internal (such as self-statements about worthlessness or imagined stimuli and consequences). The important consideration, according to learning and behavioral theories, is that anxiety and avoidance behavior are responses elicited and maintained by specifiable proximal stimuli.

While it might be expected that anxiety is a unitary response, with all components working in harmony, just the opposite seems to be true. Frequently, there are low intercorrelations between verbal, behavioral, and physiological measures of anxiety (Lang, 1968, 1970; Lang, Melamed, and Hard, 1970; Paul, 1966). Different measures produce different estimates of the severity of the anxiety response, and these measures vary somewhat independently of one another.

The desynchrony between different measures of anxiety is frequently seen in treatment outcome studies, where improvement is observed at a faster rate on some measures than on others. Thus, with the repeated presentation of a phobic stimulus, physiological measures habituate much faster than the subject's verbal report (Meyers-Abell, 1976). Further, subjects may report that they no longer feel anxious but at the same time engage in considerable avoidance behavior, or vice versa (Rachman, 1978; Rachman and Hodgson, 1974). Marked desynchrony occurs even between different physiological measures—to some extent because individuals may have unique patterns of responses, so that, for example, some people are primarily heart rate responders and others are GSR responders (Lacey and Lacey, 1958). Biofeedback experiments have indicated that people can learn to be desynchronous; that is, given the appropriate feedback, people can learn to increase one physiological measure at the same time they decrease another (Schwartz, 1978).

Rachman (1978, p. 20) provides the following summary of the relationship between different measures of fear or anxiety: "Self-reports of fear correlate well with each other; they correlate moderately well with the ratings of fear made by external judges and also with the avoidance behavior observed in a fear test; self-reports correlate modestly with physiological indices of fear; physiological indices of fear correlate modestly with each other and hardly at all with muscle tension."

Synchrony between measures is likely to be increased during conditions of extreme fear or anxiety (Rachman, 1978). An interesting illustration of both synchrony and desynchrony is present in a comparison of veteran and novice parachute jumpers (Fenz and Epstein, 1967). Among ten veteran jumpers, desynchrony was observed. Physiological measures increased moderately but steadily throughout the day of the jump and then leveled off and stayed near their peak aboard the plane and during the jump. Subjective reports of fear showed a different pattern. There was an increase in the morning of the jump, a decrease beginning with arrival at the airport and continuing aboard the plane, and then another increase during the jump before the chute opened. Novice jumpers, in contrast, showed a synchronous reaction. Both subjective and physiological measures built to a very high peak shortly before the jump occurred (for example, the mean heart rate was 145 beats per minute) and then subsided after landing. The veteran jumpers showed only moderate changes in all measures, while the novice jumpers showed very marked reactions.

Anxiety Acquisition

Pavlovian Conditioning

In Pavlovian or classical conditioning, the investigator attempts to change the stimulus value of a neutral stimulus (the conditioned stimulus, CS) by pairing it with a stimulus that reflexively elicits a response (the unconditioned stimulus, UCS). Through repeated pairing, the neutral stimulus becomes conditioned to elicit a response similar to the one elicited by the UCS. A conditioned response (CR) can be unlearned through extinction procedures, in which the CS is presented repeatedly without the UCS.

The first demonstration that fear or anxiety could be conditioned in humans was the classic study conducted by Watson and Rayner (1920) with an 11-month-old infant, Albert. The UCS, a loud noise that elicited a startle and fear reaction in Albert, accompanied each presentation of the CS, a rat. After seven conditioning trials, Albert cried and crawled away during presentations of the rat. In addition, he cried and whimpered at the sight of certain other animals and objects (a rabbit, a dog, a sealskin coat, and a Santa Claus mask), although he showed no negative reaction to the experimental room and its furniture.

In later experiments with human subjects, the typical UCS is a mildly painful electric shock applied to a hand or leg. In such experiments, the acquisition of conditioning effects requires many trials, and the conditioned response does not persist. In fact, instructing subjects that they will no longer be shocked is usually sufficient to extinguish the CR (Grings, 1976).

Long-lasting effects, in contrast, have resulted from naturally occurring disasters. For example, Leopold and Dillon (1963) reported the effects on survivors of a collision between a gasoline tanker and a freighter in the Delaware River in 1957. The tanker's captain, deck officers, pilot, and five crewmen were killed instantly in an explosion. All twenty-three of the freighter's crew survived. Most of the thirty-five survivors from the tanker were given a psychiatric examination at the time and again about four years later.

During the first examination, 78 percent of the survivors reported symptoms, including nervousness, tension, general upset, sleep disturbances, and gastrointestinal disturbances. Four years later, the number of disturbances had increased, and all but one survivor reported symptoms. There was a marked increase in complaints of restlessness, depression, and phobic reactions. New complaints also appeared: feelings of isolation, of being watched, of hostility and distrust toward other workers. The number of survivors who had sleep disturbances increased, and the number who had gastrointestinal disturbances stayed about the same.

Although all the survivors were veterans of long service at sea (over half had served more than ten years, and none had been at sea less than a year), most of them could not continue working at sea. At the time of the follow-up, only 35 percent were working regularly at sea. A few never returned, another 35 percent returned but were forced to give it up because of the severity of their symptoms, and the rest were able to work only sporadically.

The personalities and adjustment of the seamen before the collision were unrelated to the severity of the symptoms afterward. The similarity of reactions from seaman to seaman leaves inescapable the conclusion that the symptoms resulted from the collision. An important question, however, is why the symptoms intensified rather than extinguished with time. All the men who continued to work at sea, out of economic necessity, were "tense, anxious, nervous, and fearful aboard ship" (p. 917). Thus, despite repeated experiences without a recurrence of an unconditioned stimulus, anxiety continued to be elicited by their being aboard ship. This is directly opposite to what would be expected according to a Pavlovian conditioning model.

Preparedness Model

Other evidence indicates that Pavlovian conditioning may not be a complete explanation of the acquisition of anxiety. Early models of Pavlovian conditioning assumed that all stimuli have an equal potential for becoming conditioned to an unconditioned stimulus. However, only some stimuli do become associated. For example, the rat became a conditioned fear stimulus for Albert, but the experimental room and its furniture did not. The Hull-

Spence version of Pavlovian conditioning deals with this stimulus selection problem by proposing that, with repeated trials, conditioning of irrelevant cues extinguishes because these cues occur just as often when the unconditioned stimulus is absent as when it is present (Reiss, 1979). However, this explanation seems to be incomplete, since some stimuli are easy to condition while others are quite difficult. Watson and Rayner (1920) were able to condition Albert to fear a rat in only seven trials; however, attempts to condition children to fear wooden shapes and colored cloths (Bregman, 1934) or opera glasses (Valentine, 1946) failed after as many as fifty trials.

Seligman (1971) has proposed that people have a biological predisposition—a *preparedness*—to learn certain CS-UCS pairs. *Prepared* phobias have natural importance to the survival of the species and are therefore easily acquired and resistant to extinction. The anxiety among survivors of the marine collision seems to fit with the idea of preparedness. Fears associated with being on water and off the safety of land could have evolutionary significance, and the anxiety was acquired as the result of only one traumatic event and did not extinguish. However, other prepared phobias, such as snake phobia, although easy to acquire, are very amenable to treatment. Still others, such as agoraphobia, have a gradual onset but are resistant to treatment.

In a systematic attempt to evaluate the clinical implications of preparedness, de Silva, Rachman, and Seligman (1977) examined the records of sixty-nine phobic and eighty-two obsessional patients treated at the Maudsley Hospital in London. The patients' fears were rated for their preparedness on the basis of their evolutionary significance. The results were that degree of preparedness was not correlated with either rapidity of acquisition or resistance to treatment. Thus, although some fears undoubtedly are more likely to be acquired than others, it does not follow that such fears will be rapidly acquired or resistant to extinction.

Information Models

The traditional American interpretation of Pavlovian conditioning is that the organism has been conditioned to respond reflexively in a particular way. Bolles (1972) attributes this misinterpretation to a faulty English translation of Pavlov's work. In that translation, "conditional response" became "conditioned response"; thus, Pavlov's original emphasis on the stimulus side of the problem was lost. A "conditional" response implies that the organism interprets the stimuli according to previous experience, whereas a "conditioned" response implies that the organism has learned to respond in a particular way.

Recent modifications of Pavlovian conditioning theory emphasize information processing and expectancy rather than association through contiguity. For example, Wagner and Rescorla (1972) have proposed that

Pavlovian conditioning of a CS depends on the new information that the CS provides about the magnitude or occurrence of the UCS. A number of unique predictions from this model have been confirmed in animal experiments. For example, if an animal is given a series of conditioning trials in which a particular CS (B) is always followed by a UCS, and then another series of conditioning trials with a compound CS (A and B) followed by the UCS, a conditioned response is not elicited by A alone. According to Wagner and Rescorla, A does not acquire associative strength because it provides no new information about the occurrence of the UCS.

Except for a few theoretical discussions (Rizley and Reppucci, 1974; Reiss, 1979), there has been little attempt to apply recent information models of Pavlovian conditioning to clinical research. However, these discussions suggest that cognitive variables may be a vital part of anxiety acquisition.

Avoidance Learning

In animal research, avoidance learning is typically investigated in a shuttle box with two compartments. When the animal is in one of the compartments, a light or a tone is presented; then, a few seconds later, electric shock is delivered through the floor of the compartment. The animal can avoid the shock by leaving the compartment in the interval between the signal (CS) and the shock (UCS). Once the animal has learned this avoidance response, it can be given hundreds of trials with the shock equipment unplugged, and it will continue to shuttle back and forth between compartments in response to the CS.

An ingenious solution to the problem of the persistence of avoidance behavior was proposed by Mowrer (1947) and is known as the dual-process theory. The first process is the Pavlovian conditioning of fear to the conditioned stimulus (the tone or the light) that signals the occurrence of the electric shock. Fear is an aversive state and motivates the animal to engage in escape behavior. The animal is escaping from the CS and the fear it elicits, thus avoiding the shock. The avoidance behavior is reinforced by fear induction (the second process). Since the avoidance behavior is motivated by fear arousal, elicited by the CS, and is reinforced by fear reduction, the presence of the UCS becomes irrelevant to maintaining the response.

Paradoxically, the animal engaging in avoidance behavior exhibits very little emotional behavior. It is only when the avoidance response is prevented that emotional behavior is observed. Nevertheless, fear arousal and reinforcement from fear reduction are seen as central to understanding the persistence of avoidance behavior in the dual-process theory. Almost all the research on avoidance behavior has been animal experimentation. However, the dual-process theory has been the traditional learning model used to explain symptomatic behavior (such as compulsive rituals) in human anxiety disorders.

Although there is considerable intuitive appeal to the dual-process theory, numerous objections have been raised in recent years. First, autonomic reactions take much longer to activate than avoidance responses (Bandura, 1977a). Thus, although they may occur concurrently during acquisition, it is unlikely that the autonomic response causes the avoidance response. Second, autonomic feedback is apparently not necessary for either the acquisition or the maintenance of avoidance behavior. Surgical removal of autonomic feedback does not eliminate either acquisition or maintenance (Rescorla and Solomon, 1967). And third, fear reduction does not seem to be necessary, since escape responses will be acquired even if they do not lead to the immediate termination of the UCS (Bolles, 1972).

If anxiety is not central to understanding avoidance behavior, what alternatives are available? As is true in recent Pavlovian conditioning theories, recent theories of avoidance behavior emphasize the information component of the conditioned stimulus. Thus, Herrnstein (1969) concludes that the CS in avoidance-learning experiments is a discriminative stimulus and not a conditioned stimulus. That is, it signals the occasion for reinforcement or punishment but is not, in its own right, reinforcing or aversive. Similarly, Bandura (1977a) stresses the predictive value of formerly neutral stimuli associated with aversive experiences: "It is not that the stimuli have become aversive but that the individuals have learned to anticipate aversive consequences" (p. 209). Once established, defensive behavior is difficult to eliminate because consistent avoidance prevents the animal or person from learning that the real-life conditions have changed. According to Bandura, anxiety and defensive behavior are coeffects of centrally processed expectations and are not themselves causally linked. We will discuss Bandura's theory in more detail in the section on cognitive processes.

Operant Conditioning

Operant conditioning refers to the process of changing the frequency of a response by controlling the consequences of the response. In Pavlovian conditioning, the CS and the UCS are presented independently of the organism's response. In operant or instrumental conditioning, the presentation of a reinforcing or a punishing stimulus is contingent on an appropriate response by the organism.

In discussing anxiety and stress reactions, operant theorists focus not on autonomic arousal or cognitive processes but, instead, on avoidance behavior and its consequences. A major contribution from this perspective is the recognition that reinforcing consequences—such as attention from others, reduction in work requirements, and monetary compensation (for example, disability pay)—can be primary determinants in the acquisition and maintenance of "symptomatic" behavior.

Operant treatments of avoidance behavior typically involve positive reinforcement of successive approximations of the desired approach behavior

(Leitenberg, 1976). In this respect, operant treatments are not very different from treatments generated from a Pavlovian conditioning analysis. Both involve repeated exposure to the stimuli that have been avoided. From the Pavlovian conditioning perspective, repeated exposure would result in extinction of the anxiety conditioned to those stimuli. From the operant perspective, the anxiety is irrelevant, but repeated exposure is necessary in order to reinforce approach behavior.

In the operant conditioning perspective, stimuli that signal the occurrence of reinforcement are discriminative stimuli, not conditioned stimuli. Individuals learn to respond to the discriminative stimuli in order to receive reinforcement. Responses in the presence of discriminative stimuli can become persistent because they have been reinforced frequently in the past. "Symptomatic" behavior can also come under the control of discriminative stimuli. Such behavior occurs in some situations more frequently than in others. For example, chronic insomniacs, who have considerable difficulty falling asleep in bed at bedtime, often have no difficulty falling asleep on a couch or when away from home. Insomnia is an apt illustration because it is usually interpreted as a reaction to stress or some emotional problem. There is considerable intuitive appeal to this assumption, since people who ordinarily have no trouble sleeping often develop insomnia during periods of stress (Grinker and Spiegel, 1945). However, the sleeping problems of chronic insomniacs have persisted for so long that the insomnia is likely to be independent of situational stresses. The chronic insomniac has learned to associate bed and bedtime with worrying or with other behavior that is incompatible with sleeping. A treatment designed to strengthen the stimulus control properties of bed for falling asleep quickly and to eliminate cues for incompatible behavior has been successfully used with insomniacs (Bootzin and Nicassio, 1978).

Cognitive Processes

In animal research on the acquisition of anxiety, both the CS and the UCS are observable, physical stimuli. That would be a major limitation, however, for theories about human anxiety acquisition. In case histories of many phobics, for example, no traumatic incident can be reconstructed (Marks, 1969). Similarly, the high prevalence of snake phobics in epidemiological studies (Agras, Sylvester, and Oliveau, 1969) is unlikely to be due to a high incidence of actual traumatic events with snakes. Human research, however, indicates that anxiety can be conditioned to symbolic and imaginal events, as well as to physical stimuli. In one of the first studies on cognitive mediation, Miller (1935) shocked subjects to the letter T but not to the number 4 read out loud. Subjects were then instructed to think T and 4, alternately, in a series of trials. Subjects had galvanic skin response (GSR) reactions when they thought T, but not when they thought 4.

Additional evidence that cognitive processes are crucial comes from the extensive research on modeling and observational learning (see Rosenthal and Bandura, 1978). Subjects can acquire emotional responses vicariously, by observing others react with pain (Berger, 1962), and there is anecdotal evidence of fears transmitted from mother to child (Rachman, 1978).

The modeling research indicates that subjects can acquire emotional responses when both the CS and UCS are symbolic. The capacity of images and verbal self-statements to elicit marked emotional changes has been well documented by research on hypnosis, autogenic training (Schultz and Luthe, 1959), verbally induced anxiety (Lang, 1977; Sipprelle, 1967), verbally induced depression and elation (Velten, 1968), and aversive conditioning procedures, such as covert sensitization, which employ imagined CS-UCS pairs (Cautela, 1967).

Symbolic processes are also involved in the transmission of information about feared objects or events. Although there is little formal evidence, experience from everyday life clearly indicates that anxiety can be induced by information alone (Rachman, 1978). Information and instruction are constantly used—by parents, for example—to teach distinctions between situations that are not dangerous and situations that *are* dangerous and therefore to be feared. A person walking alone at night in parts of a city that he has been told are dangerous may become anxious even if he has never previously been mugged or observed a mugging. The anticipation of feared consequences is likely to lead to cognitive rehearsal of the feared event, thereby inducing emotional arousal.

Because of the important role that modeling, information, imagery, and language have in emotional arousal, it seems plausible that emotional reactions are centrally controlled rather than purely the result of prior Pavlovian conditioning. From a traditional Pavlovian conditioning view, images and language are covert stimuli that have acquired their capacity to elicit emotional responses through prior conditioning (Wolpe, 1978). This proposition seemed more tenable before the advances in biofeedback, when it was thought that emotional responses could only be elicited reflexively and could not be brought under voluntary control. However, biofeedback research undermined the distinction between voluntary and involuntary responses (see, for example, Miller, 1969). When the appropriate feedback is provided, all the physiological indices of anxiety can be brought under some degree of voluntary control (see Blanchard and Young, 1974). Most important, with practice individuals can improve their ability to regulate their own physiological responses. This practice effect is also observed with the verbally induced emotional arousal procedures mentioned earlier. However, if symbolic stimuli are covert CSs, then repeated practice (without the presentation of a UCS) should lead to extinction of the emotional reaction. That this does not happen indicates that emotional reactions are at least partially centrally controlled rather than purely the result of prior Pavlovian conditioning.

Predictability and Controllability. Two variables that have important implications for cognitive processes are the extent to which aversive events are predictable and controllable.

Predictable aversive events are less stressful than unpredictable aversive events. For example, in experiments on the development of ulcers in rats, shocks preceded by a signal were much less ulcerogenic than shocks that occurred unpredictably (Weiss, 1977). A related phenomenon may have been observed in the London blitz during World War II. Londoners, who were bombed with considerable regularity, showed remarkably few anxiety reactions. In contrast, there was considerable anxiety and apprehension in the surrounding country villages, where bombing was much less frequent but more unpredictable (Vernon, 1941). Such predictable events may be less stressful because individuals, being forewarned, can prepare for the stressor or because individuals thereby know when the aversive event will *not* occur and thus when it is safe to resume normal activities. In research with animals, the safety function of predictability seems to be most important (Weiss, 1977). With unpredictable aversive events, anticipatory stress and anxiety are relatively constant, whereas there are longer periods of relief from stress with predictable stressors.

Like predictable stressors, stressors that are controllable usually are experienced as less aversive than stressors that are not controllable. In avoidance-learning experiments, for example, rats who can escape or avoid shock develop fewer ulcers than rats who receive the same number of shocks but whose behavior has no effect on the shock (Weiss, 1977). Controllability also seems to have been a factor in the development of anxiety among air crews during World War II. Pilots of heavy bombers reported less fear than their gun crews. Fighter pilots experienced the least fear, even though casualties were much higher for fighters than for bombers (Rachman, 1978). Although these differences may be due to differential selection, the pattern of results is consistent with a relationship between controllability and stress reactions. Pilots clearly have more control than their crew members to avoid disastrous consequences, and fighter pilots have more flexibility and, thus, more control than bomber pilots. Bomber pilots, for example, must fly in formation and have less ability to engage in evasive action. As this example indicates, the perceived control, not the actual control, determines anxiety reactions. Fighter pilots have a higher degree of perceived control, even though casualty rates are higher for fighters than for bombers.

Perceived control is also central to Seligman's (1975) theory of learned helplessness and its applications to depression (Miller, Rosellini, and Seligman, 1977). It is not clear when a perceived lack of control will lead to anxiety and when it will lead to helplessness and depression. Both anxiety reactions and depression are usually reported as observed reactions to natural and war-inflicted disasters. However, individual differences may play an important role in determining the person's response to the stressing condition.

Averill (1973) reports that for some subjects (between 10 percent and 20 percent in various studies) the availability of control over the stressor is stress inducing rather than stress reducing.

Efficacy Expectations. A theory related to expectations of control is Bandura's (1977a) theory regarding efficacy expectations and their relationship to avoidance behavior. Bandura distinguishes between two types of expectations: outcome expectations, the belief that a given behavior will lead to particular outcomes; and efficacy expectations, the belief that "one can successfully execute the behavior required to produce the outcomes" (p. 193). Thus, a pilot might believe that he will return to the base safely if the plane is flown skillfully (an outcome expectation). The pilot might further believe that he *can* fly the plane as skillfully as is needed (an efficacy expectation).

In Bandura's view, efficacy expectations—and not anxiety—are the primary determinants of coping and defensive behavior, since people who are anxious sometimes do continue to engage in coping behavior despite emotional arousal. Efficacy expectations are derived from four types of information. The major determinant is performance feedback from prior experiences. Thus, experiences of mastery enhance self-efficacy. Vicarious experience, verbal persuasion, and autonomic arousal also affect efficacy expectations, but not as strongly as performance feedback.

Bandura has proposed a comprehensive theory of behavior change. He suggests that the mechanisms by which behavior is regulated are primarily cognitive. Thus, Bandura's theory represents a synthesis of behavioral procedures with cognitive theory and has been influential in moving learning and behavioral theories to a more cognitive position.

Conclusion and Treatment Implications

The three components of anxiety (subjective discomfort, autonomic arousal, and defensive behavior) are not always synchronous and at times seem to be under the control of different variables. At this point, no one theory fully explains all the data concerning anxiety acquisition. Thus, it is likely that anxiety can be acquired in many different ways—from Pavlovian conditioning to the cognitive rehearsal of aversive consequences.

Just as there has been increased recent interest in cognitive theories of anxiety acquisition, so there has been a parallel movement toward cognitive behavior therapy techniques. A more explicit cognitive orientation has encouraged therapists to help patients identify their self-defeating, anxiety-inducing self-statements. Treatment procedures to teach patients more functional anxiety-reducing self-statements (Meichenbaum, 1972) are a promising addition to the armamentarium of the behavior therapist.

In many ways, the behavioral perspective is primarily a treatment perspective. The major contribution of learning and behavioral theories to clinical practice has been the implementation of successful treatment procedures for a wide range of clinical problems (see Chapter Twenty-Two for a review of behavioral treatment procedures). Advances in theories about anxiety acquisition may result in the development of even more effective treatment procedures.

3

Developmental Theories

Michael Lewis

❋ ❋ ❋ ❋ ❋ ❋ ❋ ❋ ❋ ❋ ❋ ❋ ❋

Since fearful states occur under a wide set of events, any theory of the development of fear must be prepared to deal with these complex events as well as the relationship between fear and cognition and between fear and other affective states.

Although examples of fear-eliciting situations are widely available, the research literature has surprisingly focused on only a narrow segment of them. Here, we shall look first at various examples of the phenomenon called fear. We shall argue that the feeling state in each example may be the same (fear) but that the conditions and therefore the processes that elicit the feeling are different. Although this argument, in fact, may not be accurate, it has heuristic value in the study of affective development and will be used as a starting point.

Example 1. A 2-year-old child and his mother sit in the pedia-
trician's office. When it is their turn to see the doctor, they enter
the room. The child stares at the doctor and his white coat, screams,
turns away, and clutches at his mother's leg.

This example appears to be a case of *conditioned* or *learned fear.* The
infant has previously experienced some unpleasant action (such as an injection), the agent of which was the doctor. Now, two months later, the child
associates the previous noxious event with the current situation. Specifically,
he associates the doctor and the white coat (which is a salient stimulus dimension) with the injection, and the feelings of pain, and now responds with fear
to the situation. This fearful behavior may generalize to other situations that
have similar and salient dimensions. For example, the child may react fearfully to any new office or to any strange male or to anyone wearing a white
coat. Learned fear has not been given its due place in the literature on the
development of fearful states. This is rather surprising, since learned fear
and its generalization must surely account for a large portion of children's
fearful states. The reasons for its neglect have to do, at least in part, with
the interest in fears associated with attachment behavior, another affectual
response, and with the interest in fear as a measure of cognitive-motivational
processes. Any theory, however, must be prepared to consider learned fear
and its relationship to the child's growing cognitive abilities; for example,
the ability to store information and retrieve it as well as to represent events
and outcomes in some available and useful fashion.

Example 2. A month-old infant is lying in its crib, looking at
the mobile above it. Suddenly a loud bang sounds behind the crib;
someone has dropped a pile of dishes. The infant startles, its blood
pressure and heart rate increase, it throws out its limbs, and it starts
to cry.

In this example, the young organism experiences an intense, sudden,
and unexpected change in the level of energy reaching its sensory systems.
Stimulus events having these three elements can elicit a fearful state—not
only in the young immature organism but in children and adults as well.
Thus, it is reasonable to consider the class of events that produce *unlearned
fearful* states, since the nervous systems of humans of any age are designed to
respond to such stimuli as noxious. Fear may be part of that response to the
noxious event; that is, fear may protect the organism by enabling it to avoid
(or try to avoid) such situations in the future. For example, the rushing of
the express train as it passes the local station may be painful and, therefore, fearful, thus providing the conditions necessary for people to learn to
avoid it by staying in the station building while the train passes. In general,

however, events such as the crash of dishes or the noise of a passing train probably account for a relatively small percentage of fearful states—especially since, with increasing age, such events become increasingly associated with other events.

> *Example 3.* A 3–year-old child is riding her tricycle with her mother as she walks through the park. A stranger walks over to the little girl, says "Hello" to the mother, and asks the child if she likes to ride her tricycle. The mother smiles and returns the greeting. The child freezes, stops peddling, turns toward the mother, frowns, and starts to whine.

In this situation, commonly called "stranger fear or anxiety," the child becomes frightened of new people and, at the same time, shows positive behavior toward her caregiver and to other people who are familiar. The development of this fearful state (sometimes called a "wary state") usually occurs after the first eight months of life. Before that time, the child usually exhibits positive behavior toward all social experiences. Thus, at an earlier age, this stranger, who now elicits a fearful state, may have evoked both smiling and approach behavior—although Bronson (1972) has demonstrated fearful behavior at ages as early as 3 months. Once elicited, stranger-induced fearful behavior reaches its highest intensity around 18 to 24 months. Whether the response disappears or is transformed into more socially accepted forms is unknown. There is no reason to imagine, however, that adults are not wary of impinging strangers.

This phenomenon has been likened to imprinting. As such, some researchers consider it a maturationally determined, biologically derived response that serves to limit the number of people to whom the infant can become attached (Scott, 1963; Schaffer and Emerson, 1964). Others consider it a manifestation of the child's cognitive ability to compare the various social events (strange people) to an internal representation of its caregivers. It is also considered an index of the infant's primary relationship with significant others (that is, the infant's attachment to its primary caregiver), since it represents a discriminably different response toward various adults in its world.

Why these discriminably different reactions to various adults should take the form of fearful response is not easily explained. It is tempting to postulate some conditioned or learned fear state. For example, the appearance of a stranger—say, the arrival of a babysitter—may be associated with the loss of the mother. Another possibility is that the infant has a schema for each of its familiar adults and that the violation of this schema by the appearance of a stranger elicits fear. But, again, why should the violation of an existing schema cause fear rather than, say, *arousal* or *interest*? Moreover, studies have shown that the nature of the stranger plays an important role in the nature of the child's response. For example, adult strangers are more likely to elicit a fearful state than are child strangers (Lewis and Brooks, 1975). The introduction of a new schema, therefore, cannot explain stranger fear. Finally, most children who manifest stranger fear are able to make friends within a relatively short period of time. The 3-year-old girl in our example made friends with the stranger, a business associate of her father's, within five minutes of the original fear episode. How this friend-making pattern fits into stranger fear is poorly understood and rarely addressed.

Example 4. An 8-month-old infant is sitting in his mother's bedroom. In the bathroom, his mother is dressing for the evening and has put on her new long-haired wig. As she steps into the bed-room, the infant stares at her intensely for a moment and suddenly begins to cry.

In this example, we see a clear case of the violation of expectancy. The child has formed a complex schema of its mother, including not only the visual, auditory, and olfactory modes but also intersensory integration. This sudden and unexpected change results in interest and arousal. The child orients and tries to make sense of this change in a familiar stimulus array. This transformation cannot be easily assimilated, nor can the child accommodate its old schema to this new event. The result is a fear state. Most theorists, following Hebb (1949), have opted for this view; there is, however, some difficulty in understanding why the failure to assimilate an event would be fearful. Alternatively, one could argue that the infant, failing to perceive in this "new" mother its "old" mother, is confronted with the loss of its "old" mother. The loss itself, whether through a conditioning or innate mechanism, becomes fear-inducing. Another view is related to loss of control and the consequent eliciting of fear (Gunnar-Vongnechten, 1978). In this view, fearful states are elicited by the child's inability to control the new situation or make sense of it. Fear, then, is a function of both arousal (caused by the inability to assimilate the new information) and the inability to control the event.

Example 5. A 2-year-old child is playing in a sandbox in the park. Her mother is standing close by. As the child glances up from the sandbox, she sees her mother walking away. She begins to call "Mommy, Mommy" and starts running toward her with her arms outstretched.

This final example involves the child's fear of the loss of its mother. It is clear that, among the primates at least, the loss of the primary caregiver increases the probability of the death of the child. The distancing (or loss) of the mother is associated with painful events or with the disruption of ongoing patterns of behavior (Cairns, 1966). The disruption, which cannot be controlled by the infant, then becomes the cause of the fearful state. Therefore, the infant must help to regulate and control the interaction—in particular, the physical distance—between itself and its mother (Lewis and Rosenblum, 1975). Initially, due to the infant's helplessness, the mother is the most active regulator within the dyad; however, through crying, eye contact, and smiling, the infant also helps regulate this distance. As the infant matures and is able to both leave and follow, it becomes increasingly capable of assuming a major role in the regulation of the distance between them. Thus, in this example the child moves toward the mother and signals for her return as she leaves her daughter. Mere distance is not the only or indeed the most salient elicitor of fear. Just as important appears to be who leaves whom or who controls the distance. Thus, the child has relatively little difficulty in leaving the mother; however, when the mother attempts to leave the infant, considerable upset and fear result (Rheingold and Eckerman, 1973). Apparently, it is the loss of control or fear of loss, rather than just distance as such, that motivates the child's responses.

Another interesting issue involves the definition of leaving. In a series of studies, we found that children manifest fearful states not only when they are left alone but also when their mothers cease interactions with them or are separated from them by a barrier, even though the mothers remain visible (Goldberg and Lewis, 1969; Young and Lewis, 1979). We concluded that leaving should be considered in its broadest sense; that is, to imply not being in interaction with. It is the inability to control the interaction that can elicit fearful behavior patterns.

As we can see, these five examples of fear are quite different. Nevertheless, they all can be characterized by an affective response in the infant which most of us would readily label fear. Whether the child itself experiences fear or whether it is our attribution of the child's internal state will be held in abeyance until later. We recognize that the study of affective behavior must take both behavior of the child and attribution of the observer into account. We will now turn to these factors, especially the meaning of behavior, specific stimuli, and the context of behavior.

The Meaning of Behavior

The issue of the meaning of a response is not new to our inquiry (Lewis, 1967; Lewis and Starr, 1979). A review of the literature on affect in general and fear in particular indicates that, for subjects of all ages, no single behavior constitutes a necessary and sufficient reference for fear. Crying, perhaps the most likely candidate, fails to meet this requirement, since crying may signal feelings of anger, unhappiness, or even joy. Even inhibition of action can be in the service of such different states as thoughtfulness, interest, or fear. A given stimulus may initially evoke smiling and laughter; with repeated presentations, however, it may evoke crying. Indeed, some stimuli may at different moments produce a number of patterns in a given infant. In this regard, neither approaching nor withdrawing, looking toward or away, reaching for or holding back, among various possibilities, offers us the single operationally defined distinctions we seek. In a word, there is no one-to-one correspondence between a response and a particular affect. Consequently, a study of the pattern of interrelated responses, not a particular response itself, offers us the best hope of finding a relationship between behavior and the internal experience we term fear. Toward such an effort, Campos and associates (1975) suggest the possibility of a relationship between such behavioral responses as facial expression and autonomic nervous system response of heart rate acceleration. These measures in combination may reflect fearful behavior. Such attempts to understand fearful behavior must be applauded, although relatively little headway in looking at behavior relationships has been made (Lewis, Brooks, and Haviland, 1978). Moreover, the patterns of behavior we observe may differ between classes of individuals, between members of the same group, and even within the same individual at different times. Genetic and ontogenetic factors, cognitive and motor abilities, and prior life experiences, as well as immediate antecedent events, will all alter the structure of these response patterns in any given individual.

The ontogenetic differences are particularly salient, since the capacities that are critical for the expression of fear themselves vary with age. For example, how can physical withdrawal serve as a measure of fear in a child who is too young to move about? Is eye aversion an index of fear in the child who is too young to walk but only an index of distraction or lack of interest in the toddler-aged child? In short, does a given behavior or even a set of behaviors maintain its relationship to the underlying feeling state, or is a more fluid combination of behaviors (those open to transformation with age) required for us to infer the state of fear?

Since single behavioral responses may not reflect the affective state we call fear, some have postulated a fear system in the infant; that is, a uniquely organized set of responses integrated within the nervous system and functionally independent of other such systems. However, most of the relevant data suggest that no one single system, independent of other systems, is elicited by a class of events (Bretherton and Ainsworth, 1974; Sroufe, Waters, and Matas, 1974). Haviland and Lewis (1976) found, for example, that the approach of strangers evokes both smiling and prolonged gaze as well as aversion, lip quivering, and even crying.

Another problem with the meaning of responses has to do with the difficulty of trying to capture intensity of response. Thus, some children can be said to be less fearful than others. How are we to capture differences in degree of affective behavior? In such an attempt, the terms *wariness* and *sobering* have come into use (Rheingold and Eckerman, 1973). Thus, fear could be reserved for intense negative responses, while wariness could be used to indicate moderate levels. *Sobering* might reflect even less intensity, more like children paying attention to the events around them. The problem of what to call the behavioral pattern presents us with an example of the type of difficulty that needs to be overcome. It has been widely recognized that the appearance and approach of the new, or the loss of the familiar, results in an inhibition of ongoing activity and in attentive behavior. If one chooses to call this set of behaviors "wariness" or "sobering," one takes the risk of biasing the response as a negative affective behavior.

Of considerable interest is the potential biasing effect when we look at large numbers of subjects and attempt to find some central tendency by which to characterize their responses. Consider a situation where children sitting next to their mothers watch a stranger slowly move toward them. Let us assume that half of the children are rated on a five-point scale as most fearful (that is, are rated 5) and that half the children are rated as not fearful at all (that is, are rated 1). If we average their scores, we obtain a rating of 3, which on the scale indicates sobering or wary behavior. Of course, none of the children exhibited wariness. In fact, half of them showed no fearful behavior at all. The fact that only half are fearful should have important consequences for a theory of affect development, so that data presentation—the use of data on percentage of subjects showing particular affects and the use of specific behavior rather than scales—becomes an important consideration.

Specific behaviors or sets of behaviors used to reference fear include facial, physiological, and postural or gestural. Facial expressions revealing fear have been well articulated by Darwin (1895), Tomkins (1962), Ekman (1961), and Izard (1971).

Campos and associates (Campos and others, 1973; Schwartz, Campos, and Baisel, 1973) have shown that heart rate acceleration, a response associated with stress, accompanies children's responses to fearful events. Many explanations for this heart rate change are possible; for example, the crying or flight associated with fear may cause general motor arousal, which in turn naturally leads to heart rate increases. We found, however, that attentive faces are highly associated with heart rate deceleration but that neither fearful nor happy faces appear related to heart rate (Lewis, Brooks, and Haviland, 1978). In general, the relationship between physiological indices and facial expression remains relatively unexplored. That a covarying set of facial and physiological responses exists is still widely held, although the search for such sets has yet to prove useful. Besides heart rate, other autonomic nervous system (ANS) responses—including respiration, GSR, and vasodilation—have been used; none in itself has proved any more useful than heart rate.

Postural responses in humans probably have received the least attention, which is surprising since bodily movements probably carry considerable information. Fear responses have been associated with bodily tension and flight and are often used by others to reference fear. Consider the child who rapidly moves away from the stranger and hides behind its mother. Both facial and physiological responses are unavailable for use by the observer; however, the postural/movement cues are quite sufficient to reference the behavior as fearful. In conditions where mobility is restricted, either because the child is motorically immature or is unable to get away (as in a high chair), postural cues are still available (although limited). In such instances, children will push themselves backward, moving as far as possible from the strange object or person. Proxemics also are used as references for fear. Consider children who grab their caregivers and hold tightly to them. These behaviors, at least in everyday encounters, are used as indicators of fearful behavior. Unfortunately, they have been underused in research.

One further point needs to be made in this regard; specifically, the relationship between facial and postural activity. Facial-postural activities can be used on some occasions in an additive or a substitutive fashion. For example, under intense fear, the child may show both facial and bodily cues which we can reference as fear. Or the child may use one set rather than another. In fact, facial expressions of fear may be intensified if the child is prevented from fleeing.

At this point in the research activity on emotional expression, both in adults and children, many of the issues of measurement remain unanswered. We do not know whether one set of responses better references the internal state of fear than another. We do not know the relationship between sets of responses, nor do we have any idea of their change as a function of ontogeny. Clearly, as the child develops, new responses appear; thus, as the child becomes more mature, the bodily expressions change. Around 1 year of age, children are sufficiently mobile so that they can move toward their caregivers in times of fear rather than call. Thus, activity should increase and crying decrease. While new responses are added, old ones become increasingly inappropriate. While crying is acceptable in the opening year or two of life, it is discouraged in the preschool child. Thus, crying as a referent changes. Finally, we recognize the possibility of vast individual differences in responses which individual children use to reference fear. The source of these differences is unclear, and many have their origins in such general response tendencies as temperament differences.

Within any discussion of individual differences in response tendencies, we are naturally forced to consider individual differences in degree of fearfulness. This issue, rather than addressing the topic of transient affective states, raises the more general topic of enduring states or characteristics of the child. The difference between fleeing and enduring affects is of central importance to any theory of affective development and needs to be considered.

Specific Stimuli

Certain social characteristics related to fear—specifically, familiarity (prior experience), sex, size, and age of the people—have been explored in some detail. For the specific stimulus event, it must be known whether the stimulus is a stranger, a familiar, or an attachment figure. Furthermore, the child's experience with the class to which the individual belongs may have an important impact on the child's response, even on first exposure to that specific person. Thus, for example, a stranger or even a known person wearing a white laboratory coat may provoke fear independent of the person but dependent on the child's negative past experience with doctors' white coats. More generally, on repeated exposure, through processes ranging from simple stimulus habituation, complex assimilations, to changes in overall levels of arousal, the child shows changed responses to the same stimulus. For example, two equally novel toys may evoke very different responses, depending on the state of the child, the state itself being dependent on the history of past events. In one case, the first novel toy (or person) presented to the child may evoke arousal, interest, exploration, and pleasure. However, the second presentation to an already aroused child may provoke upset and fear as the threshold of arousal is raised beyond the pleasurable level and the child is unable to control the arousal. From a more cognitively oriented point of view, a consideration of this temporal sequence of stimuli, in terms of both immediate and more remote antecedent events, invokes some hypothetical memory capacity which allows children to recognize previously experienced figures and to alter their response configuration accordingly. The development of such cognitive structures, especially in early childhood, is essential in considering the effect of past experiences—familiarity—on the child's fear behavior. Even here, there is no single one-to-one relationship between familiarity and fearfulness. Many children are not frightened of unfamiliarity per se. Therefore, the simple notion of a fear release evoked in some automatic sense in the presence of novelty, either person or object, seems questionable. Indeed, without the positive response to some novelty, the intellectual development of the child would be in serious jeopardy. Strangers at a distance are interesting, not fearful.

In a series of studies in our laboratory, we have been able to show that children appear to show less frowning and more smiling to strange children than they do to strange adults (Lewis and Brooks, 1974). It was not clear what cues young infants and children (8 to 24 months) use to differentiate children and adults. In an attempt to explicate whether facial configuration, height, or both play a role in this differentiation, a second study of children this age was undertaken. Not only were adults and children used as social objects, but we were able to find an adult female midget who was willing to help us. Since the midget had the facial configuration of an adult and the height of a child, we sought to determine which, if either, of these two cues was invoked in the differentiation. Our results indicated that young children reliably elicit less fearful behavior than adults. As to the midget, the children showed neither the pleasure in seeing a child nor the frowning as in seeing the adult. The response to the midget was one of surprise (Brooks-Gunn and Lewis, 1978). Thus, even by 7 months of age, children have knowledge of the facial configuration-height relationship; and when this is violated, as in the case of the midget, they show surprise. That this violation of the familiar did not cause fearful behavior indicates again the complexity of fearful behavior and the fact that violation of expectancy is not in itself fear-producing.

Male strangers evidently elicit more fear than females (Benjamin, 1961; Greenberg, Hillman, and Grice, 1973; Morgan and Ricciuti, 1969; Shaffran and Gouin-Décarie, 1973; Skarin, 1977). Again, the question of which cues are the particularly salient ones in sex differences has been considered. Because height might again be a factor, and male strangers in the studies reported were taller than female strangers, it is difficult to determine whether sex differences or height were responsible for the reported findings. In two studies from our laboratory, no sex differences were found when height was controlled; and, as Weinraub and Putney (1978) and Feinman (in press) have now shown, height appears to be an important factor in children's fearful responses. The nature of the stimulus itself is important in affecting whether children will be likely to respond with fearful behavior; nevertheless, fearful behavior has no single one-to-one connection between a class of events (elicitors) and response. Sroufe and Wunsch (1972), for example, have shown that a particular type of stimulus is capable of eliciting *both* laughter and fear behavior.

Context or Situation

Contextual factors include (1) the size and complexity of the environment, (2) its familiarity, (3) the presence or absence of the mother, (4) the mother's own response to the stimulus, and (5) the state of the child prior to the stimulation. For example, context familiarity and the presence of a familiar person have been shown to affect children's fear behavior. Thus, children are less fearful of strangers in their own homes than in the unfamiliar laboratory setting, and children's fear behavior is markedly affected by the presence or absence of the mother. For example, Campos and associates (1973) have shown that children show considerable fear when they are left alone with a stranger but relatively little fear when the mother is also there.

Weinraub and Lewis (1977) have shown that children are upset on being left alone when their mothers fail to mediate their behavior by reducing the disruption of their loss. When mothers instruct the children in what to do once they are gone, the children are less disrupted and fearful than the children of mothers who just simply leave. We found that 15-month-old children were considerably less fearful and made friends with a stranger in a shorter time if the mothers demonstrated a positive rather than a neutral attitude toward the stranger upon the stranger's entrance into the room (Lewis and Feiring, 1980). These data confirm our view that fearful responses to people (and perhaps objects) for children can be mediated by their observation of their caregivers' responses to these same events.

Relationship of Fear to Cognition and Other Affective States

Fear and Cognition. In the various examples of fear-eliciting situations presented at the beginning of this chapter, all but one required some form of cognitive activity. If we hold that fear or, for that matter, any affect has a simple one-to-one correspondence with a set of elicitors, then the elicitation of fear needs no cognitive support. In the simplest case, some classes of events—those that are intense, sudden, and unexpected—have the capacity to elicit fear independent of any cognitive activity. Even here, we have argued, there may be a need to consider some form of cognitive activity. A distinction is drawn between "fearful state" and "feeling fearful" or a fearful experience (Lewis and Rosenblum, 1978). Select events, such as a noise, can produce "fearful states," with accompanying physiological responses. Nonetheless, in order to "feel fearful," one must reflect on or attend to the "fearful state," these actions being cognitive in nature.

Implicit in the literature on fear are several important cognitive processes and capacities, the development of which is critical for the elicitation of fear states and experiences. Moreover, their developmental course appears to parallel that of fear, especially fear elicited by strangers and fear elicited by the loss of mother. We shall consider several of these cognitive factors, recognizing that more could be added. These factors are certainly considered to be central and serve as a good example of the relationship between fear and cognition. Memory, both recall and recognition, must play an important role in fear-producing events. For example, the child must be able to *recognize* and *associate* past events which were noxious. The white coats of doctors or their offices, associated with pain, now have the capacity to elicit fear. While *recall* is a more difficult skill, taking longer to appear, it too is needed in order to utilize past experience. How can the child be upset if the mother is gone and the child cannot recall her? Schaffer (1974) has commented on several cognitive factors necessary to support an infant's fear of the strange—among them, the ability to recall and to make simultaneous comparison. In terms of expectancy, we have seen that violation of expectancy per se is not fear inducing. The child's response depends on how he assimilates the event (Kagan, 1974; Lewis and Goldberg, 1969). Thus, fear results from arousal, the failure to assimilate, and the loss of control. The importance of the child's perception of control was highlighted in a study by Gunnar-Vongnechten (1978).

One final cognitive event appears necessary for understanding feeling experiences rather than states. Notice that the child or adult, when making reference to internal states, says "I am fearful." The use of the self-referent is particularly important, for, as we have stated, feeling states require that the agent of the statement and the object of the feeling both be the self (Lewis and Rosenblum, 1978). We have recently considered the development of self and have argued for the necessity of such a concept as self or consciousness when considering feeling experiences. Moreover, we see the development of self, object, and person permanence as arising together in a complex process in which each is dependent on the others (Lewis and Brooks-Gunn, 1979). Lewis and Brooks-Gunn (1978) have shown a direct relationship between self-recognition in mirrors and fear of strangers, those children showing self-recognition being those who are more fearful of the stranger.

Fear and Other Affects. While the relationship between cognitive development and emotional experience has received some attention, especially in terms of fear and cognition, there is almost no work on the relationship between affective states. One of the distinctions that have been made between different affective states is that of primary and secondary or derived affects. Primary affective states are those which are present at birth or develop within the first year of life, at least in terms of facial expression, and which require relatively little cognitive capacity in order to be expressed. The need for cognitive development appears to be the chief difference between these primary and derived affects. Fear would be a primary affect while shame would be a secondary one. Shame is secondary since in order to feel shame one must have learned a standard. It is the deviation from that standard which produces shame. This being the case, shame cannot occur until the standard is learned, something which will take several years to occur. However, as our examples on fear have shown, even within a primary affective state, some events require past experience in order to elicit fear. Thus, the doctor's coat is only fear eliciting after the child has learned the association between the coat and pain. Nevertheless, although different causes can produce fear, fear states occur after the first half year of the child's life.

This differentiation between primary and secondary affects may be useful, but it still does not allow us to explore the relationship between different affective states or experiences. One way in which different affective states may be related is through models of general arousal. Schachter and Singer (1962) have postulated that general arousal, in addition to the context in which the arousal takes place, forms the particular affect experienced. If this is the case, those children who are more readily aroused would be more likely to show a variety of affective states or experiences; children who are easily fearful may also be easily angry or even happy. Unfortunately, there are almost no data on this topic, although we found that infants and young children who show high fear states are not necessarily those who show more angry or happy states (Lewis and Michalson, in press).

As we have shown earlier, it is possible for the same event to elicit different affects. Consider again the example of the mother putting on the wig (Example 4). While the first time she places the wig on her head elicits upset and fear in her child, the next time she puts the wig on, the child may show considerable interest; by the third time, the appearance of the wig may elicit laughter. Other examples come readily into view: the tickle which usually elicits laughter now elicits a cry or upset when the child is tired. While not all affects can be elicited by the same event, there appears to be more than a casual relationship between some. The nature of the affect expressed appears to depend on (1) the ambient arousal level of the child and (2) the ability to assimilate the event into its meaning system and to control the event. While these two principles certainly cannot account for all the affects experienced by children, they are useful in looking at the relationship between affects. Even so, unless we know of the immediate history of the child in addition to the ability of the child to control the event, we are not able to predict in advance what particular affect experience the particular event may elicit. The example of the tickle makes clear that laughter, upset, or fear may result, depending on the arousal level of the child. Unless we know that level in advance, we will not be able to predict the child's particular response.

There are several affects whose relationships have been based upon a more theoretical basis; in particular, the relationship between attachment and fear. The original explanations of stranger fear were based on the belief that fear of the strange, which was thought to occur around 8 months, operates within an imprinting-like model. Initially, children could be imprinted on any social object; but, because of their limited physical mobility, they were for the most part imprinted on their own parents. However, as they became physically mobile at around the last quarter of the first year, it was necessary to ensure that they would not become imprinted on anyone besides the parents. Stranger fear was thought to be that mechanism whereby children become frightened of strange others and therefore do not become imprinted on them. While such a theory may not be true, it does provide a theoretical framework in which to place fear and attachment affects. Alternative versions of the relationship between attachment and fear have been offered by others. The child's trusting, loving, and secure relationship with its mother (or caregiver) is related to fear such that children who have more trust and security are expected to be less fearful. Unfortunately, the relationship between fear (for example, fear when the mother leaves) and attachment has never been resolved. For example, should children who are more securely attached be more or less upset when their mother departs? It could be argued that secure children will be less fearful, since they know that their mother will come back. On the other hand, securely attached children may miss their mothers more and therefore be more upset by their loss.

In order to look at the relationship of fear to other affects and to examine other problems, Lewis and Michalson (in press) examined over seventy children, ranging in age from 3 months to 3 years. Each child was rated on five affective states (fear, anger, happiness, attachment/dependency, and competence) by observing its behavior across a large number of situations. In the case of fear, children were observed in over thirteen different situations in which fear is often the expected experience; for example, the approach of a stranger, the threat of a peer, the breaking of a toy, the scolding of an adult, etc. After children were rated on these five affects, the correlation between them was observed. Of interest for our discussion here is the relationship between fear and the other four affects. Fear was found to be significantly related to both attachment/dependency and competence. Children rated high on fearfulness were also rated high on attachment/ dependency and low on competence. Thus, children who were fearful also showed attachment/dependency and showed relatively little competence —competence defined as being able to meet the task demands of the day care environment. In addition to the relationship with attachment/dependency, there was an interesting developmental trend between fear and anger. For infants under 12 months of age, fear and anger were unrelated; however, children over 18 months showed a strong relationship between fear and anger such that the more fearful children were also the more angry.

In this particular study, the relationship between affects was explored by relating individual differences in affective expression. Whether these results on individual differences can be related to the relationship between affects within an individual still remains to be explored. Nevertheless, these data point up the interrelated nature of the different affects. Both inter- and intraindividual differences in affective expression/experience need more consideration.

There is one final issue in the relationship between affects which receives far too little attention. We tend to think that a particular situation or event elicits one particular affect at a time. Thus, while a wig may elicit several different affects over multiple presentations, we tend to describe events as elicitors of particular singular states or experiences. The question of mixed or multiple affects is rarely considered but it is probably a more common event for a mixture of affects to be produced. In general, events probably elicit a mixture of affects; sometimes these various affects are congruent, other times opposites. The relationship of different affects cannot be fully understood until we are prepared to recognize that the elicitation of pure affect states or experiences, that is, those of only one affect, is probably rare. It is more likely the case that a mixture involving perhaps many different affects is usually elicited. We should be prepared to see if there are any highly occurring groups of affects, in this way determining the relationship between simultaneously occurring affects.

Conclusion

The study of the development of affect has just begun; we have only the barest outline to guide us in our understanding of the development of fear. We have, however, learned certain facts that will aid us in our inquiry.

1. Fear is a feeling state, having the same properties and standing as a thought. While the stimuli which contribute to its experiences or responses which reference it may change with age, the feeling state remains; infant and adult both feel fear.

2. Neither situations nor responses alone can be used to reference fear. Indeed, the complex interactions between both situations and responses, guided by the cultural norms and developmental level, are necessary to infer fearfulness.

3. There is a wide number of situations and events which have the capacity to produce fearful states and experiences. The most important of these are learned elicitors (those associated with past events which are noxious) and the loss of control. Unlearned elicitors include sudden and intense stimulation, violation of expectancy coupled with the inability to assimilate the change, and presentation of the unfamiliar, including objects, events, and people.

4. Early development involves the change from affective states to affective experiences as self-development occurs and young children are now able to identify the state as belonging to them: "*I am* fearful."

5. Situations which elicit fear and responses which reference it are open to a variety of forces, including maturation, cognitive development, and cultural norms.

6. Affect development may be best viewed as embedded in the child's total social, psychological, and physical development.

4

Sociological
Theories

Howard B. Kaplan

❖ ❖ ❖ ❖ ❖ ❖ ❖ ❖ ❖ ❖ ❖ ❖ ❖

In the history of sociological theory, neither subjective distress (the global concept used here to refer to anxiety and stress) nor the more inclusive concepts of emotion or affect have normally been central concerns. Dodge and Martin (1970, p. 58) have noted correctly that "the literature on stress does not specify the social determinants of stress except in a vague sense."

Kemper (1978, p. 21), considering sociological theories of *emotions,* concludes that emotions are rarely the subject of main interest but goes on to note: "Although there is no systematic sociological theory of emotions, sociologists from Marx to Homans have dealt with emotions and kinds of coping response that particular emotions produce." Thus, Marx interpreted alienation as a psychological condition resulting from particular patterns of ownership and control of the means of production. For Durkheim (1897), stable differences in suicide rates among various social categories are the result of variable degrees of social integration and social regulation. More recently, Homans (1961) has proposed that to the extent that one does not understand that one's profits should be in proportion to one's investments, the more one is likely to display anger. The view is sociological in two respects. First of all, individuals exchange rewarding activities with each other in the context of social interaction. Further, the interacting parties "perceive and appraise their rewards, costs, and investments in relation to the rewards, costs, and investments of other men" (Homans, 1961, p. 75). Thus, the emotions arise in the course of social interaction against the background of what is perceived as normative.

Sociocultural theories of subjective distress may be distributed between two broad classes: those asserting direct relationships between mutually influential characteristics of the sociocultural system and those asserting relationships between such characteristics, on the one hand, and other *personally* relevant characteristics, on the other.

Within the first class are theories of status integration. One of the more systematic statements of this approach is that of Dodge and Martin (1970), who argue that since almost all of man's goals are achieved through participation with other men in their structure of social relationships, participation in this structure with his fellows comes to be highly valued, and threats of disruption of this participation are sources of stress. Thus, it is postulated that *the extent of socially induced stress in a population varies inversely with the stability or durability of social relationships in that population.* Since society in its nature is "a complex arrangement of social statuses or 'positions' interrelated in lesser social structures through socially defined and sanctioned demands and expectations that incumbents of given statuses are permitted and expected to make upon incumbents of other specified statuses, the maintenance of stable and durable social relationships with others depends upon the conformity of members of the population to the demands and expectations made upon them in the context of the social relationships" (Dodge and Martin, 1970, p. 63). Thus, it is postulated that *the stability and durability of social relationships within a population vary directly with the extent to which individuals conform to the pattern and socially sanctioned demands placed upon them by others.*

Insofar as individuals occupy numerous statuses simultaneously, conformity to the expectations defining one status may interfere with those related to another. Thus, it is postulated that *the extent to which members of a population conform to the patterned and socially sanctioned demands placed upon them by others varies inversely with the degree to which members of that population are subjected to role conflicts.*

Whether or not an individual will experience role conflict depends directly on the extent to which he occupies incompatible statuses and indirectly on the conditions influencing the likelihood of occupying incompatible statuses. Incompatible statuses are those statuses which, when occupied simultaneously by the same person, demand conformity to role expectations that interfere with one's ability to conform to role expectations associated with other statuses. Such situations threaten the stability and durability of the individual's social relationship. Thus, it is postulated that *the extent to which members of a population are confronted with role conflict varies directly with the extent to which members of that population occupy incompatible statuses.*

If incompatible statuses are related to the subjectively threatening disruption of social relationships, it seems reasonable to assume that social rules would preclude the occupation of incompatible statuses or, if they should be occupied, would sanction the resolution of the incompatibility by having the individual leave one or the other of the incompatible statuses. Further, in view of the subjectively distressful nature of the incompatibility, the person should be motivated to resolve the conflict himself, even if he were not aware of the relevant social sanctions. Therefore, incompatible statuses should be simultaneously occupied infrequently, and the degree of compatibility between multiple statuses (that is, the degree of *status integration*) should be reflected in the extent to which they are actually occupied simultaneously. "Theoretically, maximum status integration would be the situation in which knowledge of only one of an individual's statuses would make it possible for the remaining undisclosed statuses to be predicted with certainty" (Dodge and Martin, 1970, p. 66). Illustrative of a situation of maximum status integration would be communities where it can be predicted with reasonable certainty that a woman aged 30 is a wife, a mother, and a housewife and that a male aged 40 is a husband, a father, a farmer, and a member of a particular religious group. In short, status integration is indicated by an observed pattern of status occupancy. In contrast, in certain areas in large cities, the knowledge that a person is a 40-year-old male does not provide a basis for predicting marital, parental, occupational, or religious status.

The above leads to the final postulate, that *the extent to which members of a population occupy incompatible statuses varies inversely with the degree of status integration in that population* (Dodge and Martin, 1970, p. 66).

Unlike the theoretical statements considered above, which detailed stress-inducing characteristics of the more inclusive social systems, Kemper's (1978) approach treats subjectively distressful (as well as the other) emotions as deriving from the characteristics of the less inclusive social relationship. Kemper presents a model of social interaction located in the empirically derived dimensions of power and status: "History, ethnicity, and local conditions may particularize the manifest shape of cultural items that indicate power and status magnitudes, and there may be differential normative and structural patterning of who has how much power and status. The important ground fact for knowledge is that social relations are comprised of two fundamental dimensions that transcend local and temporal distinctions" (Kemper, 1978, p. 346). Power is a mode of social relationships in which compliance is obtained from others who do not give it willingly. Status is reflected in the voluntary compliance received from those with whom one interacts. The "distressful emotions" of guilt, shame, anxiety, and depression are derived from patterns of excess or insufficient power and status. For example, when one perceives that he has lower status than he deserves, the emotion of shame is evoked. The experience of insufficient status evokes the emotion of depression. When the other person has insufficient status, the emotion evoked is guilt or shame.

Kemper (1978) is essentially dealing with a microcosmic approach to social relationships. He does not address in any detailed way the question of what macrosociocultural factors influence the differential likelihood of experiencing an excess or a deficiency in power or status; therefore, he does not consider the macrosociocultural factors which influence the probability of experiencing distressful emotions. The approach, however, is useful in focusing our efforts toward the goal of isolating the macrosociocultural factors which indirectly influence subjective distress. This may occur by influencing the likelihood of experiencing excesses or deficiencies in power and status on the part of the interacting parties in a relationship.

More recent theoretical statements, in addition to considering the distress-inducing influences of sociocultural systems, have incorporated a number of other elements, including need-value systems, life events, and coping mechanisms. Much of the failure to develop more systematic and detailed sociological theories of stress/anxiety than those considered above is likely accounted for by the failure to specify these more proximate circumstances associated with the genesis of stress/anxiety. The initial specification of these circumstances would facilitate further delineation of the mutually influencing sociocultural variables that influence such conditions and, through their influence on these circumstances, in part determine the probability of individual experience of stress.

The following statements are offered as illustrative of those emphasizing one or the other of such sets of more proximate influences on stress. However, these statements frequently implicate more than one set of such influences.

The role played by *internal goals and values* in the induction of stress is apparent in B. P. Dohrenwend's (1967) formulation of sociocultural factors in coronary heart disease. Dohrenwend posits that societies characterized by a relatively high degree of industrialization, a relatively open class system, and achievement and autonomy as dominant values of the elite tend to recruit relatively large numbers of individuals (for example, neophytes or the upwardly or downwardly mobile) into social positions that predispose individuals to experience conflict between important internal goals and values and external social environmental demands. Intense, prolonged experience of such conflict is said to predispose the individual to heart disease.

In one theoretical model centering on *coping resources,* life events are viewed as arising from the person's psychological and biological constitution, the culture, and the social environment (Warheit, 1979, p. 503). These events pass through adaptive-nonadaptive screens representing the coping resources available to individuals as they attempt to meet the demands imposed on them by the life events. In addition to genetic predisposition, biological constitutions, and personality, these screens include culturally transmitted systems of belief that give persons explanations for events and symbolic definitions that attach meaning to events. The screens also include social-environmentally given personal resources (socioeconomic statuses, families, interpersonal networks, and secondary organizations). Stress, an altered state of the organism occurring when demands on the person exceed his response capabilities, is "a function of the number, frequency, intensity, duration, and priority of the demands viewed in apposition to coping resources."

Moss (1973) conceives of social relations as *information-communicating networks,* consisting of groupings of communicating and interacting people who transmit a particular configuration of information. People "resonate" with the information in the networks through interaction and communication media. The networks resonate with each other through communication channels that link them. The type of involvement the person has with communication networks is based on the degree to which the information he utilizes is taken from a communication network and the extent to which the information is observed to be accurate and effective by the person in his milieu. If the person finds his information taken from the network to be accurate and effective, he feels involvement in the communication network—that is, he identifies with the network. If he perceives incongruities between the information he has learned and what he determines to be accurate and effective in the environment, he feels negative involvement with that network—that is, he is alienated from the network. If he does not take his information as a whole from the network but, rather, finds his own configuration of information and values accurate and effective in his environment and in that network, he is detached in his involvement with that network—that is, he experiences autonomy. Finally, if the person does not take his information as a whole from the given communication network and observes that what information he does have is neither accurate nor effective in that milieu or network, the person is uninvolved with that communication network—a noninvolvement characterized as anomie. Information incongruities may produce changes in physiological processes and in social involvement.

The probability of encountering incongruities in a communication network's information involves at least four factors. The first is heterogeneity of information and norms in a given milieu—that is, quantity of incongruous information, values, and norms found in the communication networks associating in a particular milieu (including incongruities within a particular network's information). "In modern societies communication networks contain, are contained within, overlap, and communicate with other networks. The variety of networks resonating together and the rapid rate of change increase heterogeneity, which enhances the probability of incongruities being encountered" (Moss, 1973, p. 150). The second factor is the degree to which direct contact with natural environmental conditions incongruous with the communication network's information is unavoidable. A third factor is the extent to which the communication network's norms encourage or require activities that may entail contact between participants of incongruous communication networks, as when requirements of military service brought together in close contact participants of many incongruous networks operating within the nation. The fourth factor is isolation—that is, the use of norms to prevent awareness of and contact with incongruous information in other networks and to prevent access to information within the network that may be incongruous with the network's more widely shared information.

Illustrative of sociologically relevant theoretical perspectives incorporating *life events* are the expectations that persons in low social status are disproportionately exposed to stressful life events and that the differential exposure would provide an explanatory link between the low social status and individual psychological distress (B. S. Dohrenwend, 1973).

Intervening Variables

From the overview just considered, it is apparent that the following three *mutually interacting* elements must be considered as variables intervening between sociocultural determinants and the experience of subjective distress: the personal need-value system, the personal system of adaptive/coping/defensive patterns, and life events.

Need-Value System. The extent to which particular life circumstances are distress inducing is a function of the subjectively perceived relevance (value) of life events for a subject's congenital and acquired (psychosocially developed) needs. Each individual has internalized a hierarchy of valued and disvalued end states such that the achievement of certain goals and/or the avoidance of others has a higher priority than the achievement or avoidance of alternate goals. Depending on the order of the goals in the value system and the individual's perception of his proximity to or distance from the goals, and depending on the person's sense of approaching or distancing himself from the end state in question, the person will experience more or less intense and lasting subjective distress. The person who anticipates, recalls, or experiences life events that evoke perceptions of distance from positively valued end states, or of approaching disvalued end states, will experience an increasingly greater sense of need to achieve the positively valued goal and to avoid the disvalued goal. The intensification of felt need will be experienced as subjective distress.

The implication of the personal need-value system in the genesis of subjective distress is apparent in a large body of research, including that which takes psychophysiological indicators to be reflections of subjective distress. Thus, Kaplan (1972) observed that subjects interacting with liked or disliked others were significantly more likely to manifest physiological (galvanic skin) responses, as well as other (particularly socioemotional) responses, than were subjects interacting with neither liked nor disliked social objects. Congruent with these findings are observations of higher subject diastolic blood pressure when the interviewer showed a warm and interactive as opposed to a neutral and noninteractive style (Williams, Kimball, and Williard, 1972), and of significantly greater rises in plasma free fatty acid level where the experimental induction suggested that the task was important rather than unimportant (Back and Bogdonoff, 1964).

Adaptive/Coping/Defensive Responses. Whether or not the person experiences subjective distress will in large measure be a function of the individual's ability to adapt to, cope with, or defend against adverse life experiences. These terms, frequently employed in various, overlapping ways (Coelho, Hamburg, and Adams, 1974), are used here to refer to the capability of (1) meeting situational requirements (subjectively perceived as legitimate), thereby forestalling the experience of subjective distress, or (2), in the face of failure to forestall the stressful experience, mitigating the intensity and/or duration of the subjectively distressful experience.

When we consider the adaptive/coping/defensive capacity of the individual, we include those resources cited by others as social resources, psychological resources, and specific coping responses. "Social resources are represented in the interpersonal networks of which people are a part and which are a potential source of crucial supports: family, friends, fellow workers, neighbors, and voluntary associations" (Pearlin and Schooler, 1978, p. 5). Psychological resources "are the personality characteristics which people draw upon to help them withstand threats posed by events and objects in their environment. These resources, residing within the self, can be formidable barriers to the stressful consequences of social strain." These include self-esteem, self-denigration, and mastery (the extent to which a person perceives his life chances as being under his own control rather than being fatalistically ruled). Coping responses "represent some of the things that people *do,* their concrete efforts to deal with the life strains they encounter in their different roles."

The association between inadequate adaptive/coping/defensive resources, on the one hand, and subjective distress, on the other, is suggested
by numerous studies employing psychophysiological indicators of stress, in
which physiological activation was observed to be more likely if appropriate
adaptive patterns were not available (whether because the situation was
novel or because such patterns were precluded) or if the individual lacked
coping ability or demonstrated failing ego defenses. In the context of U.S.
Navy underwater demolition team training, Rubin and Rahe (1974) noted
that elevated mean serum cortisol coincided with novel experiences about
which the men had some anticipatory anxiety, but declined with practice
and familiarity. Using data from self-reported anxiety, pulse rate, and skin
resistance measures, Holmes and Houston (1974) reported that the threat of
painful shocks increased stress but that subjects using redefinition (thinking
of shocks as interesting new physiological sensations) and isolation (remaining
detached and uninvolved) showed smaller increases in stress than subjects
who were not told to use these coping strategies.

Using other indicators of distress, Vaillant (1976) reported that long-
term psychological health could be predicted from knowledge of the maturity
of ego-defensive coping styles that subjects characteristically used in the face
of environmental crises. Andrews and his associates (1978) noted that both
maturity of coping style and a measure of crisis support (having relatives,
friends, or neighbors, as well as others available for help in an emergency)
were related to psychological health. These variables appear to be related
to psychological impairment independently of the relationship between
life event stress and impairment.

Life Events. Life events may reflect either change or continuity in
personal experiences. Where the events reflect changing circumstances, life
events are manifested as an individual's loss, addition, or redefinition of
social positions. Any one event may imply one or more of these changes.
Death of a wife, for example, implies the loss of the status of husband, the
redefinition of the role expectations of the status of father (insofar as functions normally performed by the mother must now be performed by the
remaining members of the family), and the addition of the status of widower,
with its new set of rights and obligations. The events have a clearly demarcated
beginning against which the change may be noted. This class of events, after
Pearlin and Leiberman (1979), may be divided into two classes of events:
normative and nonnormative. *Normative events* are expected and regular
in their occurrence. Illustrative events in a number of different role areas
include first job, retirement, getting married, death of spouse, becoming a
parent. *Nonnormative events* are frequently crises which, while of common
occurrence, are not easily predictable by people, since they are built into the
movement of these people across the life span. These events include being
fired from a job or divorced.

Other life "events" reflect continuity in the social positions a person occupies and the roles he performs in those positions. "Problems of this order are often chronic, low-keyed frustrations and hardships that people have to contend with in their occupations, their economic life, and their family relations" (Pearlin and Leiberman, 1979, p. 220): job pressures or overload, lack of marital reciprocity, children's failure to be attentive and considerate of parents.

Whether reflecting change or continuity in life circumstances, life events (as they interact with the person's need-value system and adaptive/coping/defensive resources) more or less directly influence the experience of subjective distress. More directly, some events induce stress by virtue of being judged intrinsically undesirable. The event reflects the anticipation or experience of the person's inability to fulfill felt obligations or otherwise satisfy felt needs (including both the attainment of valued goals and the avoidance of noxious circumstances). Less directly, events may induce stress insofar as the *consequences,* rather than (or as well as) the event itself, are undesirable. The indirect stress-inducing influence of life events may occur through either of two routes. First, events (whether negative, positive, or neutral in evaluative significance) may impose new requirements on the individual, the fulfillment of which is problematic. These requirements take the form of self-imposed obligations to others or expectations of personal achievements, perhaps occasioned by the adoption of new social positions or sanctioned role redefinition in old social positions. Problems in fulfilling various obligations or expectations increase the likelihood of actual failure, which is a stress-inducing experience. The second indirect route through which life events influence the experience of subjective distress is through their disruption of the person's normal and characteristic ways of forestalling the experience of adverse life events or, if the adverse events were not forestalled, mitigating the intensity and duration of concomitant subjective distress.

In the context of the life events literature, a debate has been occurring as to whether the change per se or the negative valuation of the change accounts for the various adverse outcomes. It is becoming increasingly clear, however, that the relationship is accounted for by the subjective undesirability of the event. This conclusion has been forestalled because of the lack of recognition that even positive events may increase the likelihood of *subsequent* undesirable events or may render the person increasingly vulnerable to the experience of the events and correlated subjective distress (by disrupting the personal resources available for forestalling the intrinsically undesirable events or containing the intensity and duration of the associated subjective distress). In short, where the event is stress-inducing, it is so because it is intrinsically undesirable or has undesirable consequences. Consistent with this conclusion is the observation that life events (specifically, the effects of desirable and ambiguous events, change, and number of events) cease to be related to subjective distress *after undesirability is controlled* (Ross and Mirowsky, 1979). Perhaps what makes events subjectively undesirable involves all three effects: judgments of intrinsic undesirability; perceptions of new obligations or needs, the fulfillment of which is problematic; and the disruption of normal response patterns ordinarily employed to forestall the experience of (and contain the subjective distress associated with) undesirable life events, thus rendering the person vulnerable to the future experience and effects of such adverse life circumstances. Relevant to this speculation are data indicating that persons rate undesirable events as requiring more readjustment than other events (Ross and Mirowsky, 1979).

The relationship between life events and subjective distress has been noted in a number of studies. Andrews and his associates (1978) noted a relationship between life events scaled for emotional stress and psychological impairment.

Mutual Influences Among Intervening Variables. The intervening variables considered immediately above may have a relatively direct influence on the experience of stress, as we have seen above, or may generate subjective distress through their mutual and interactive influence. The mutual influence may take any number of forms. Thus, the need-value system determines the personal acceptability of particular adaptive/coping/defensive patterns and (due to their variable compatibility with the person's need-value system) influences the motivation toward pursuing certain life events and avoiding others. The adaptive/coping/defensive structure may influence the need-value system, for example, by leading to a defensive reordering of priorities and may influence the number and kind of life events through defensive avoidance of life change. Life events may have a profound influence on both personal systems, as when the accession to a new social position leads to a reordering of values, or when social mobility disrupts established adaptive/coping/defensive patterns.

The mutual influence of life events and coping mechanisms has been noted by Pearlin and Schooler (1978, p. 6), who observed that "some of the most persistent strains originate in conditions impervious to coping interventions, thus discouraging individual ameliorative coping efforts." Not all modes of coping mechanisms are equally effective in different role areas: "With relatively impersonal strains, such as those stemming from economic or occupational experiences, the most effective forms of coping involve the manipulation of goals and values in a way which psychologically increases the distance of the individual from the problem. On the other hand, problems arising from the relatively close interpersonal relations of parental and marital roles are best handled by coping mechanisms in which the individual remains committed to and engaged with the relevant others" (Pearlin and Schooler, 1978, p. 18).

Toward a General Sociological Theory of
Subjective Distress

Neither general sociocultural theories of stress nor overviews of the empirical literature permit specification of the mechanisms through which sociocultural factors influence subjective distress. Any given sociocultural factor may influence the experience of subjective distress through any or all of several routes. Since there appears to be good reason to accept assertions that the mutually interacting variables of personal need-value systems, personal adaptive/coping/defensive resources, and life events are implicated in the genesis of stress, perhaps the most effective strategy at this point would be to systematically consider the mutually influential sociocultural factors that affect each of these mediating variables.

Need-Value System. Since characteristics of the personal need-value system are known to be implicated in the genesis of subjective distress, a general sociological theory of subjective distress should assert relationships between macrosociocultural factors and such characteristics. What are the need-value complexes which, if frustrated, induce distress in all societies or in particular societies? What sociocultural characteristics influence the internalization of needs that the individual cannot satisfy? What features of the social system increase the likelihood that the personal need-value system will include equally valued but incompatible goals, thereby ensuring the subsequent frustration of one or the other need? Such features as patterns of socialization and the consistency of these experiences in the person's various membership groups as well as the various positions the person occupies in the social system will be implicated.

Which social experiences will be intrinsically disvalued by the person and therefore induce subjective experience of distress will be a function of the value systems of the society. Certain of the valued goals will be universal by virtue of the person's initial dependency on a sociocultural network for satisfaction of his needs. Elsewhere (Kaplan, 1975), it has been argued that the need for self-esteem is universally a characteristically human motive. The genesis of this motive stems from the individual's initial dependence on other human agencies for the satisfaction of constitutionally given needs. Stemming from a similar source is the earlier developed need for the company of other humans. As Dodge and Martin (1970, p. 59) have pointed out, man as a species survives through collective organization to meet his biologically given or acquired psychological and social needs by exploiting his environments. Since almost all of man's goals are achieved through participating with other human beings in a structure of social relationships, participation in this network comes to be highly valued in itself. Thus, banishment or enforced silence would be interpreted as a highly disvalued circumstance.

By association, any event that disrupts or threatens to disrupt social participation would similarly be interpreted as subjectively disvalued and cause for the experience of subjective distress.

The *particular* values internalized by the subject will be influenced by the particular sociocultural matrix in which he is socialized. People do not universally value money, courage, or academic achievement. In certain cultures and for certain positions within the social structure, the frustration of these values would be highly stressful.

Just as these values and their structure are determined by the stable sociocultural matrix, so will sociocultural change influence these factors by creating new values and a reordering of old consensually defined values. In the process of change, new expectations are imposed on individuals, depending on their various positions in the social position. However, social mobility *within* stable sociocultural structures (particularly in sociocultural systems that define the mobility as normative) will also lead to the adoption of new values associated with the new positions adopted in the course of the mobility experience.

A growing empirically based literature illustrates the influence of the social systems in which individuals participate. Among Navy enlisted men, for example, recent disciplinary problems were the only life change which predicted illness (Rahe, 1974, p. 68). In view of the requirements for discipline in the military, it is not unexpected that such events should be of great emotional significance. In the more inclusive sociocultural system, observations by Scotch (1963) among the Zulus are consistent with the interpretation that the same characteristics and behaviors are differently evaluated in rural tribal as opposed to urban settings, and thus differentially related to the development of hypertension in the two settings.

Different social positions within the same system appear to influence the nature of personal need-value systems. For example, a growing number of studies suggest that individuals who occupy positions of leadership and responsibility are significantly more likely to manifest higher levels of *psychophysiological activation in response to life events* that are specifically associated with requirements to accept responsibility for others—presumably a value-relevant role requirement of the position. Thus, student aviators making their first aircraft carrier landings had higher mean serum cortisol levels and higher levels of urinary excretion of cortisol and 17-OH-CS metabolites than the radar intercept officers in the rear cockpit, who had no flight control and had to rely completely on the pilot's skill (Rubin, 1974). In an earlier study, the only men in a special combat unit in Vietnam anticipating enemy attack that showed elevated 17-OH-CS levels were the two officers and the radio operator (Bourne, Rose, and Mason, 1968). Kiritz and Moos (1974) cite reports of higher heart rates in pilots than in copilots, a difference that reversed itself when individuals changed positions; a positive association between responsibility for other individuals and diastolic blood pressure; greater amplitude of gastric contractions in subjects who were able to press a button to avoid the strong auditory stimulus to both members of the pair than in the passive members of the pair; highest levels of 17-OH-CS secretion in aircraft *commanders;* and sharp increases in heart rate by key NASA personnel when they were suddenly given additional responsibility.

What remains to be accomplished, however, is the systematization of the current empirically based propositions and future specifications about the sociocultural factors influencing the genesis, structure, and content of personal need-value systems.

Adaptive/Coping/Defensive Resources. The experience of subjective distress has been shown to be a function of personal adaptive/coping/defensive resources. Therefore, any general sociological theory of subjective distress will have to consider the sociocultural factors that influence such resources.

Sociocultural systems are highly variable in the extent to which they permit, for example, an ideology of self-justification for the failure to achieve valued goal states and/or for the experience of disvalued states. More inclusive social systems are highly variable in their capacity to respond to distress experiences in ways which forestall or contain the distress associated with adverse events. Where societies do not provide patterned mechanisms for reducing the intensity and duration of subjective distress, the individual is more likely to experience intense and lasting distress.

Whether or not the individual has the capacity to adapt to value-relevant environmental requirements (thereby forestalling the experience of subjective distress) will depend on such factors as the range of early life experience he had, the degree of responsibility he was awarded in various life roles, the adequacy of his socialization experiences with regard to the transmission of specific adaptive patterns for current and anticipated roles, and general capacities such as flexibility and autonomy. These variables in turn will be influenced by a person's position in the social structure. Birth order will influence training in autonomy and flexibility, social-class position will influence the predisposition to anticipate subsequent life roles, different social classes will provide specific adaptive patterns in various areas of life experience and a general tendency to regard life experience within or beyond one's own control.

To the extent that the environment is characterized by rapid social change, individuals will have less opportunity to learn stable response patterns to known stimuli. They will be, in these circumstances, more exposed to novel stimuli for which stable adaptations are not available. Nor will individuals be willing to teach younger generations specific adaptations if they anticipate that these adaptations will be outdated by the time occasions for their use arises. Even in relatively stable societies, where large portions of the population migrate into the society or from one part of the society to the other (where the society is multicultural in essence), the probability of not possessing effective adaptive patterns is increased. Since adaptation to the requirements of the system is affectively relevant in the context of the person's need-value system, the failure to successfully adapt to the felt obligations of the situation will evoke more or less severe and lasting subjective distress.

Numerous reports have implicated these and other features of sociocultural systems and their component social statuses in the processes influencing the nature and effectiveness of adaptive/coping/defensive resources.

In their study of children's psychological reactions to artillery shelling of their surroundings in Israel, Ziv and associates (1974) suggest that particular modes of coping are in part influenced by prevailing social norms. Examining some of the effects of job loss, Kasl, Gore, and Cobb (1975) noted that in a rural setting, where the community and social support system was less severely disrupted by the closing of a plant than in an urban setting, adverse effects of anticipating an actual job loss were softened. Matsumoto (1970) hypothesized that Japan's low rate of heart disease, as compared with that in the United States, is due not the the presence of lesser occupational or social stress but to the nature of the Japanese work and other institutional structures, which provide greater social support.

Scotch (1963), considering hypertension among rural and urban Zulus, concluded that in the urban community the individuals most likely to be hypertensive appeared to be those who maintained traditional cultural practices and therefore were unable to adapt successfully to the demands of urban life. It is unclear, however, whether the maintenance of traditional cultural practices was a reflection of the inability to adapt and/or an above normal identification with the traditional cultural practices, which precluded the adoption of the more adaptive patterns suitable to urban life.

With regard to the general capacity of the individual to adapt to or cope with new requirements of life events, Gutman (1963) attributed the presumed lack of difficulty experienced by middle-class American migrants to the internalization of typical American character traits, including the ability to initiate conversations with strangers and the recognition of the legitimacy of a wide range of behaviors in others. Kelly (1968) used residential mobility as an index of diversity of experience, presumed to be directly associated with future coping capacity. P. Mann (1972) found that students from families who had made many moves reported less anxiety and placed more value on autonomy and independence than students from nonmobile families.

As in the case of more inclusive social systems, less inclusive systems are variable in the extent to which they facilitate adaptive/coping/defensive functions. Thus, intact families are likely to increase the probability of containment of subjective distress associated with life events. While unattached persons are likely to be isolated and required to face problems on their own, intact marriages permit the sharing of crises and the giving of mutual support (Myers, Lindenthal, and Pepper, 1975, p. 126). In this connection, Medalie and associates (1973) observed a lower incidence of coronary heart disease among subjects who receive love and support from their wives. In the course of his study of stress response among graduate students involved in Ph.D. preliminary examinations, Mechanic (1962b) concluded that successful adaptation depends on developing the skills, techniques, and solutions which permit a person to meet the pressures of the situation.

The person's positions in the social systems in which he participates, as well as the characteristics of the system itself, influence both the pattern and effectiveness of adaptive/coping/defensive responses. With regard to pattern, males tended more than females to be repressors in coping style (Brown and Rawlinson, 1976). Findings reported by Speisman and associates (1964) suggested a relationship between occupational category and coping style. Executives who were high in a disposition to employ denial as a coping device manifested the greatest reduction of stress response upon listening to a denial message emphasizing that the stimulus film was staged and the actors suffered no injury. In contrast, a student group that was relatively low in disposition to employ denial showed very little stress reduction in response to the denial message but did show marked reduction to an "intellectualization" message encouraging a detached, analytic attitude toward the events and persons in the stress-inducing film.

With regard to effectiveness of patterns, mechanisms that have been found to be effective for adapting to, coping with, or defending against the distressful implications of life circumstances are not equally available to all in the society; rather, the availability depends on the person's positions in society. Thus, Pearlin and Schooler (1978) found that the effective coping modes were disproportionately available to men, the educated, and the affluent.

Much of the task of systematizing our knowledge of how sociocultural factors influence adaptive/coping/defensive resources, however, remains to be accomplished.

Life Events. Both the normal range of life events and major catastrophes such as flood, famine, and war may be stressful not only because they involve approximation of intrinsically disvalued states (frustration of organic needs, death of loved ones, loss of valued possessions, disruption of career and family aspirations) but also because they subsequently require new response patterns. The life events also have consequences for disrupting the individual's normal ways of adapting to a situation. The old rules may no longer apply. The organized social patterns through which one fulfilled one's needs in the past may no longer obtain. Since such life events are known to induce stress, a systematic sociological theory of subjective distress would necessarily consider the *mutually influencing* sociocultural patterns which determine the prevalence of various stress-inducing life events.

What sociocultural factors (as reflected in the theoretical statements and research reports considered above) appear to influence the experience of intrinsically disvalued life events? In the course of his socialization experiences, a person normally becomes emotionally invested in a set of values and a system of normative expectations which regulates social relations and facilitates the approximation of such values. At a relatively abstract level, any life event is intrinsically disvalued to the extent that the event either calls into question the set of values or system of normative expectations or frustrates the person's attempts to approximate the values and conform to the set of normative expectations.

As in the case of intrinsically undesirable life events, numerous sociocultural factors may be specified (although not in any systematic way at this point) which influence the likelihood of life events that have future implications for frustration of values and violation of personally internalized normative expectations. For example, social expectations regarding upward mobility will increase the likelihood of failure to achieve values and conform to personal and social expectations. Positions of responsibility require conformity to expectations, and the fulfillment of high expectations can be difficult to meet. The ability to fulfill the expectations becomes even more problematic as the person's control over system outcomes is diminished and as his responsibilities become more diffuse.

What mutually influencing sociocultural factors are likely to influence the occurrence of events that imply disruption of normal and characteristic modes of forestalling or reducing the experience of subjective distress? The characteristics of the social system influencing the potential for experiencing life events that disrupt normal defensive/adaptive/coping patterns are numerous and varied. Cultural patterns requiring geographical and social mobility are likely to disrupt the normal range of interpersonal patterns and familiar modes of response that individuals employ. Most generally, the individual's repertoire of effective adaptive/coping patterns may become ineffective and maladaptive as social changes create new conditions which render existing patterned responses ineffective.

Empirical support for these and other tentative conclusions regarding sociocultural factors influencing life events is provided by an ever-growing body of literature. For example, the thesis that "disvalued" social positions increase the likelihood of experiencing stress-inducing life events is consistent with a number of empirical findings. Thus, members of the lower class and women were observed to be disproportionately exposed to stressful life events (B. S. Dohrenwend, 1973). Lower-class individuals were said to experience more unpleasant events characterized by a high readjustment impact than higher-class individuals (Myers, Lindenthal, and Pepper, 1974). Generally, women, the young, and those of lower socioeconomic position were observed to be most vulnerable to those life strains which are most clearly associated with psychological distress (Pearlin and Leiberman, 1979).

The extent to which leadership roles and the accompanying felt requirements to adapt to life events (along with the increased probability of such life events) are stressful appears to be a function in part of the interpersonal affective relationships among the group members. Back and Bogdonoff (1964) compared plasma free fatty acids (FFA) between natural groups of existing friends brought into the laboratory and groups of strangers. The task required one group member to assume a leadership role and make a judgmental decision, with the rest of the group indicating whether or not they agreed. In the group of strangers, being the leader as well as being agreed with and being the best performer all produced increased FFA.

Consistent with the status integration hypothesis, Mettlin and Woelfel (1974) reported that among rural high school students stress was positively related to a discrepancy in the expectations of subjects' significant others and to the number of significant others (which presumably would be related to the probability of conflicting expectations). The authors concluded that stress is proportional to the heterogeneity and extensiveness of the communicative network within which the individual is embedded.

Reviewing a large number of studies, Graham and Reeder (1979, pp. 87-88) concluded as follows: "This rather diverse body of literature supports the position that culture change—that is, a change in social world and in the structure of social relationships—tends to predispose individuals to CHD [coronary heart disease]. Breakdown in expectations and cues, and the person's being ill equipped culturally and psychologically to cope with new situations, may be among the processes at work."

Clearly, this literature requires further systematization. What has been proposed in this section is that such systematization might most easily proceed by considering the relationship between mutually influencing macrosociocultural factors and, in turn, each of the sets of variables said to exercise more proximate influence upon the experience of subjective distress.

Conclusion

Sociological theories of stress and anxiety contribute to the understanding of stress induction not only by pointing to the sociocultural factors correlated with indices of stress but also, to the extent that the relationship between sociocultural factors and stress is mediated by other personal factors, by tracing the chain of influence leading to the experience of distress. It is not enough to demonstrate that socioculturally defined mobility is related to stress. One must explain why mobility should be related to stress. Is it the result of deprivation of intrinsically valued goals, disruption of normal modes of forestalling or reducing the impact of stress associated with life crises, and/or some other circumstances? In short, sociological theories of stress should be expected to develop models of the mutually interacting sociocultural and personal circumstances which induce stress and/or stress-facilitating circumstances. It is fortunate that the attempts to fulfill this expectation will facilitate along the way the systematization of current knowledge and the assimilation of new research findings and tentative theoretical formulations regarding the genesis of subjective distress.

5

Ethological and Physiological Theories

James P. Henry
Daniel L. Ely

Lorenz, Tinbergen, and the classical ethologists of the 1940s and 1950s have shown what can be gained by observing natural behavior and then searching for the laws that control it. Later investigators questioned whether endocrine responses are affected by such behavorial and psychological components. Today, as a result of great advances in neuroendocrinology, there is concern about the possible relationship among environmental stimuli, behavior patterns, the ensuing physiological responses, and the disease processes that may result from them. It is our intent here to illustrate with quantitative data how ethology and physiology can provide information about behavior patterns, coping processes, and the patterning of neuroendocrine responses.

Note: The authors acknowledge the technical assistance of Linda Ely, Mary Manderbach, Virginia Allanson, and Dan Hart in the preparation of this chapter.

81

Historical Perspective

At the outset, the pioneering work of two individuals must be mentioned. In 1929, Cannon described the flight-or-fight response—notably, the activation of the sympathetic adrenal-medullary system in emergency situations. In the 1930s, Selye began his work in stress research. He described an alarm reaction involving the adrenocortical system in emergency situations (Selye, 1950). If either system is driven too hard or too long, the arousal can become a health hazard. The early behaviorists, using conditioned reflexes, showed that humans and animals respond to the same behavioral stimuli. The subsequent behaviorist theory of human behavior, associated with the theoretical contribution of Hull (1934) and the experimental results of Skinner (1938), was based on satisfaction of instinctual needs. Since these studies did not observe the animal in a natural habitat, ethologists filled this gap by studying the adaptive evolutionary significance of behavior (Eibl-Eibesfeldt, 1971). Specifically, they focused on (1) the significance of a specific behavior for the survival of man, (2) the reasons for a specific behavior set at a specific time, (3) the psychophysiological mechanisms involved, and (4) the phylogenesis and ontogenesis of any behavior pattern. (For a valuable discussion of the significance of ethology for psychiatric research, see Serban, 1976.)

Hamburg and associates (Hamburg, Hamburg, and Barchas, 1975) propose that emotions evolved as expressions of motivation that an animal must experience in order to accomplish the adaptive tasks necessary for survival. He must regularly seek food and water, avoid predators, mate, successfully care for the young, and train them to cope effectively with the demands of the environment. The normal animal finds these activities intrinsically pleasant. Indeed, they result in activation of the rewarding areas of the brain studied by the neurophysiologist Olds (1976). Rolls (1975) has described the prime function of the amygdalar nuclear complex as that of attaching value to acts; thus, it drives attachment and agonistic behavior patterns by use of the mechanism described by Olds (1976). The effect of this neurophysiologically based arousal of these reward and punishment systems is to make the animal try harder to accomplish the particular task he perceives as connected with the reward or to avoid what he finds punishing.

MacLean (1976) has presented evidence that the limbic and striatal regions are the locus for the neuronal complexes mediating the emotions and the behavior that are critical for self-preservation and species preservation. These complexes are wired by genetic determination in such a way that the individual will engage in territorial and attachment behavior appropriate for the occasion, as long as he has had certain socializing experience while maturing.

Tiger and Fox (1972) speak of a biogrammar. That is, in just the same way that baboons growing up in captivity spontaneously produce a baboon social system, we have language and a complex culture because we are wired to produce them when given the right inputs at the right times.

So, in addition to their subjective aspect, emotions have both behavioral and physiological or neuroendocrine components. When considering the evolutionary necessity that a mother mammal must be motivated to care for her baby, we meet a genetically determined attachment behavior pattern, whose profound importance has been detailed by Bowlby (1970), and we find that there are neuroendocrine changes associated with her care of the young. Indeed, shifts abruptly occur in these patterns when the attachment bond is disrupted by removing the mother from her infant. In the primates this attachment behavior persists and, with modifications in man by symbolism, motivates a lifetime of socialized behavior (Bowlby, 1970). The social ethological concept of the secure base is central to Ainsworth's empirical studies of children and mothers (Ainsworth, Bell, and Stayton, 1974) and also to Bowlby's (1976) theory of personality development. Their evidence shows that individuals with stable, affectionate, encouraging parental figures become self-reliant and capable of cooperation. Conversely, those with parental figures who have the opposite traits show a lack of self-reliance and difficulty in cooperation and are more prone to neurotic symptoms, especially anxiety and depression.

Studies of Stress in Dominant and Subordinate Animals

Social ethology is concerned with the interactions between various members of a group of animals as they seek food, nests, and mates (Crook, 1970). Attachment and territorial behavior, as well as the role of the male and female and of the young and aged within the social hierarchy of a normal animal community, are critically dependent on emotional stability. Recently a concerted effort has been made to observe the alteration in behavioral patterns and the nervous and hormonal consequences that result from a disturbance of equilibrium in such a hierarchy.

Ethologists, following in the tradition of naturalists, laid the foundation. The work of Van Lawick-Goodall (1971, 1973) with chimpanzees and of Kummer (1968) and Eimerl and associates (1965) with baboons in their natural habitat has beautifully illustrated the mechanisms of attachment behavior that binds the primate social group. Bernstein and Gordon (1974) have shown that aggression also can serve to hold a baboon troop together. Crowcroft (1966) made similar observations in his studies of mice socially interacting in the habitat of a large room.

Following Crowcroft's approach, in our laboratories we have used population cages that provide a seminatural environment for social interaction (see Figure 1). When mice are provided with an adequate social environment, they develop specific social roles and can be ranked from dominance to subordinance by their characteristic behavioral profile. A typical

**Figure 1. Typical Population Cage Used for Most of the
Rodent Experiments**

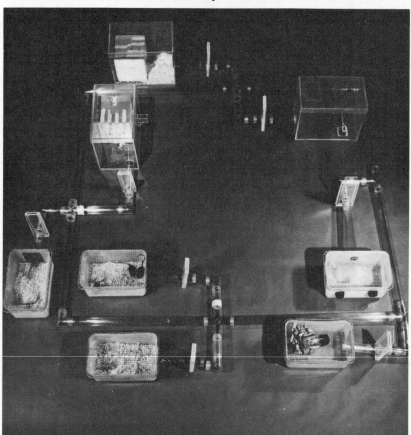

colony consists of five nonsibling males and ten females from several litters. At about 3 to 4 months of age, the animals are placed in the population cage on a large shelf. In due course, they establish territories and socially interact as they seek for the food and water provided ad libitum. A simple technique is to record behavior by dropping gates that routinely trap the mice in their various cages. The males are then scored for physical appearance, amount of territory occupied, and the number of females trapped with them per unit of time (Ely and Henry, 1974). This system of determining social rank provided us with a good indication of the dominant male, but a more sophisticated behavioral recording system was needed to further differentiate the males of descending social rank. Our needs in taking a social ethological approach were to record aggressive behaviors, feeding behaviors, territorial conflict, withdrawal behavior, and other patterns.

Therefore, John Henry of the biomedical engineering group in our laboratory at the University of Southern California developed a computer-based behavioral monitoring system that utilized magnetic tagging (Ely, Greene, and Henry, 1976). Small Alnico VIII magnets (2 x 9 mm) were dorsally or ventrally implanted in invaginations of muscle tissue (Ely and others, 1972), and the direction of polarity and the location of the magnet were used to produce a binary code for individual mouse identification. Each box runway had Hall effect detectors, which generated a signal in response to a magnetic pulse. One was placed in an upper and one in a lower groove in the portal to each box, so that an electric signal was generated as a mouse traversed it. Interfacing circuitry converted the signals into binary code, which fed into a minicomputer to be stored or printed out on a teletype.

Typical Dominant-Subordinate Behavior Patterns. During the first two weeks of social interaction in a population cage, aggressive encounters are high as the males compete for social position. The aggressive activity typically decreases after about forty days, and social gestures tend to substitute for overt aggression. A characteristic behavior pattern of the dominant (D) male is a "patrol," which has been ethologically described by Crowcroft (1966) as rapid locomotor activity whereby an individual moves about an area checking on other individuals. During the early development of the social hierarchy, the dominant male actively "patrols" the colony; as the social positions become established, however, the patrol behavior of the D male decreases, as does his overt aggression. Because of the high activity of the D males, the subordinate (S) males are confined to small areas of the colony and exhibit a behavioral restraint. When the D male is active, the S male is inactive and confined to a single colony area.

Behavioral patterns over fixed time intervals were then processed by the computer and diagrammed with an X-Y plotter in order to obtain a print-out showing every transaction made by specific individuals and the amount of time spent in specific areas in the colony. The D male not only is more active than S males but also spends more time in the female nest areas and feeding area, and his general locomotor patterns appear relatively constant with time (Figure 2). Specific analysis of feeding behavior shows that the D males spend more total time in the feeding area than S males do.

Role of Early Social Learning in the Development of Social Rank. A technique used in our laboratory was that of early social deprivation followed by placement in a colony. Four months of social deprivation after weaning followed by a placement into a social enrichment environment

Figure 2. Representative Behavior Patterns of a Dominant and a
Subordinate Male

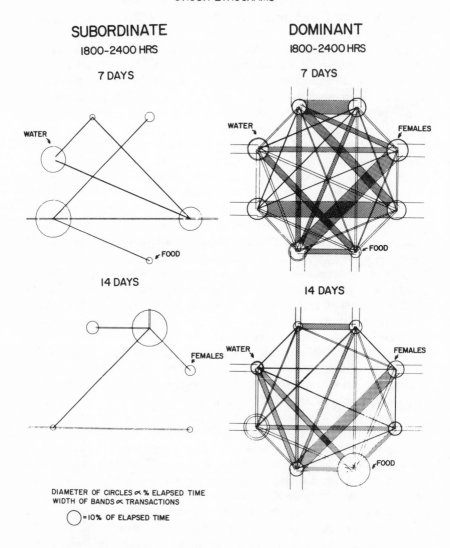

CONTRASTING
BEHAVIOR PATTERNS
6 HOUR ETHOGRAMS

produced a high level of psychosocial stimulation and resulted in hypertension that was mediated cognitively (Henry, Meehan, and Stephens, 1967; Henry and others, 1971b) with associated cardiovascular and renal pathophysiology (Henry and others, 1971a; Henry, Stephens, and Santisteban, 1975). These mice were extremely aggressive and maintained a high level of overt aggression for the duration of the experiment (up to six months). Mice placed in a colony after six months of social deprivation lived in chronic social disorder (Ely and Henry, 1974). These psychosocially stimulated animals also had higher adrenal weights and higher systolic blood pressures as compared to the socialized colony animals. Six months of social deprivation had produced permanent deficiencies in the appropriate stimulus-response relationships which form the basis for social communication and recognition.

Supporting these findings, Watson, Henry, and Haltmeyer (1974) have shown that mice raised in isolation from the time they could feed alone (from about 14 days until adulthood) develop deficiencies similar to those in socially deprived monkeys. All males were equally badly bitten, showing that there was no stable hierarchy and that territory was not respected. As in Calhoun's (1962) disturbed rodent colonies, no young were successfully raised by socially disordered female mice. In repeated observations, we found that colonies of socially deprived mice remain disordered for months. As a consequence, they show repeated arousal of the sympathetic nervous system and of the adrenal medulla (Henry and others, 1971a) and cortex (Henry and Stephens, 1977a). Thus, the conditions needed to induce chronic disease had been fulfilled (Henry, Stephens, and Santisteban, 1975).

Limbic System Involvement. To determine the extent of limbic system involvement in perception and modulation of the psychosocial stimuli to which the mice were exposed, we reexamined the question of the role of the hippocampus in the control of emotional responses and social behavior (Papez, 1937; MacLean, 1949). Specifically, we monitored patterns of social behavior (territorial defense, eating and drinking behavior, aggression, and dominant-subordinate relationships) by using the previously mentioned computer-based behavioral-monitoring system in the following groups of mice: hippocampus removed, cortically lesioned controls, sham controls, and unoperated controls.

Using the standard criteria for evaluating social rank (Ely and Henry, 1974), we found that normal social organization developed in the three control colonies, but there was a lack of social differentiation in the animals with hippocampus lesions. These animals showed no overt signs of aggression but manifested extremely high levels of general activity. Hippocampal-lesioned animals were more like D animals in their activity, showing significantly more transactions in most of the colony areas and far more patrols and larger territories than S animals. However, they were unlike D animals in that they did not inflict injuries. Furthermore, there was a synchrony of feeding behavior in the lesioned colony, whereas in a normal colony the subordinate males rarely feed in the presence of the dominant animal. In general, the group did not exhibit much behavioral individuality; all appeared similar to D animals in hyperactivity and patrols but were completely unlike the D in aggression. This is consistent with several reports of abnormal aggression and defense in animals with hippocampus lesions; for example, less biting of objects (Glickman, Higgins, and Isaacson, 1970), a decrease in shock-induced aggression (Eichelman, 1971), and impairment of defensive behavior (Kim and others, 1970; Blanchard and Blanchard, 1972).

These behavioral results prompted the question concerning the physiological correlates of hippocampal lesions in socially interacting animals. Numerous investigators have failed to find any effect of hippocampal stimulation on respiration or blood pressure in the cat, dog, monkey, and rabbit (Kaada, 1951; Kaada, Feldman, and Langerfeldt, 1971; Koikegami and others, 1957; Pampiglione and Falconer, 1956). However, several studies have suggested hippocampal involvement in adrenocortical function (Moberg and others, 1971; Nakadate and deGroot, 1963; Pfaff, Silva, and Weiss, 1971). Moberg and associates (1971) found a reduced corticosterone circadian rhythm in fornix lesioned rats. Kawakami and associates (1968) showed that, in rabbits, stimulation of the hippocampus inhibits corticosterone levels under stressful conditions but increases corticosterone levels under nonstressful conditions. Pfaff, Silva, and Weiss (1971) showed that corticosterone decreases hippocampal unit activity in the rat, and ACTH increases it.

The evidence suggests that the hippocampus is involved in cardiovascular and endocrine responses when the organism is aroused. Therefore, we evaluated autonomic nervous system function and adrenocortical function in hippocampal animals under various social situations. Using CBA mice again in the same type of population cage, we measured blood pressure, plasma corticosterone, and behavioral indices of aggression. Again, we found the absence of aggressive activity and the lack of development of a social hierarchy. The hippocampal-lesioned males were hyperactive and their blood pressure was significantly elevated, as compared to the control groups (Figure 3). However, the hippocampal-lesioned males grouped in the standard laboratory cage (which did not permit territorial behavior or maximal social interaction) did not exhibit elevated blood pressure as compared to the controls. The same was true for plasma corticosterone (Figure 4). It appeared that the colony conditions enhanced the rise in blood pressure and plasma corticosterone in the hippocampal-lesioned animals. However, the data did not suggest direct hippocampal involvement in blood pressure control, since the hippocampal animals in the noncolony conditions were not affected.

Nauta (1956) has suggested that some of the fibers of the ventral fimbria continue as the medial cortico-hypothalamic tract to the paraventricular zone of the anterior hypothalamus. Here, then, is a possible pathway for hippocampal influence on blood pressure. When the hippocampus was removed, the balance of autonomic nervous system reactivity may have

Figure 3. Systolic Blood Pressure of Three Groups of Animals
Socially Interacting in the Territorial Situation (A), and of
Three Groups Living in a Nonterritorial Situation
(Standard Laboratory Cages—B)

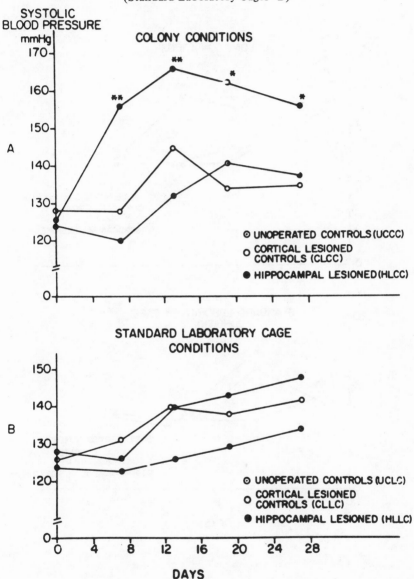

Note: Day 0 represents the day before animal placement into the territorial colony conditions and the day before placement into the laboratory caging for the nonterritorial
cage condition. The asterisks indicate levels of significance as compared to the controls:
$* = p < .05$, $** = p < .001$.

Figure 4. Plasma Corticosterone of Three Groups of Animals in the
Territorial Colony Condition (A), and of Three Groups in a Nonterritorial
Condition (Standard Laboratory Cages—B)

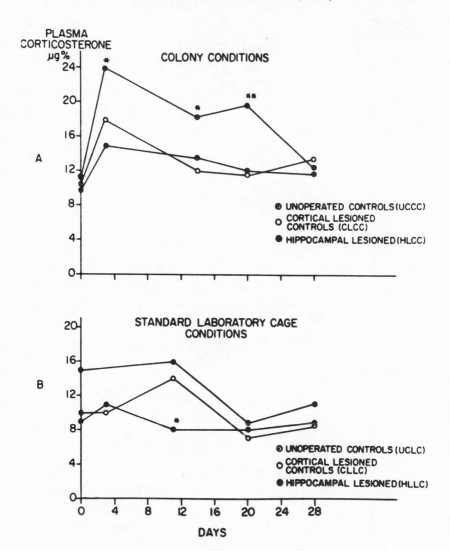

Note: Day 0 represents the day before animal placement into the territorial colony conditions and the day before placement into the laboratory caging for the nonterritorial
cage condition. The asterisks indicate levels of significance as compared to the controls:
$* = p < .05$, $** = p < .01$.

been altered, and with the removal of septal influence on the hippocampus there was an increase in activity in the sympathetic nervous system. Holdstock's (1970) data support this concept, since lesions of the hippocampus-related septal region produced less general autonomic reactivity with decreased sympathetic tone.

Kawakami and associates (1968) showed that stimulation of the hippocampus increases ACTH in nonstressful conditions but decreases ACTH in stressful conditions. This evidence suggests that under stressful conditions (such as those in a colony) the hippocampus may normally inhibit the hypothalamic corticotropin-releasing factor, and thereby pituitary ACTH. However, without hippocampal control and in the presence of stressful conditions, an increase in plasma corticosterone could be expected, as was found in this study.

The Hippocampus and Territorial Activity. The hippocampus, with inputs from other areas of the frontal cortex, appears to regulate the activities of the corticotropin-producing hypothalamic cells when control of territory has been lost or when old patterns of responding fail to produce rewards. Several investigators have proposed that the hippocampus is involved in cognitive spatial mapping (Kimble and Greene, 1968; Samuels, 1972; Greene and Stauff, 1974; Nadel and O'Keefe, 1974; Olton and Werz, 1978). This mapping function may apply not only to location in physical space but also to the concepts of territory and home range in their broadest sense. Social organizations require their members to have an acute sense of location; they must "know their place," not only in the physical but in the hierarchical space. This premise holds true for all mammalian societies, but for civilized man the relations between various aspects of social roles become enormously complex and refined.

The idea that the hippocampal formation has primary involvement in control of the pituitary ACTH adrenocortical mechanism is in keeping with Mason's convincing detailing of the evidence that psychological influences are potent releasers of cortical hormones (Mason, 1968; Mason and others, 1976). The summary paper by Mason and associates (1976), outlining the selectivity of corticosteroid and catecholamine responses to various natural stimuli, presents contrasting data for animals and humans that throws further light on this problem. Monkeys frustrated by being forced into hard physical work for food or depressed by unexpectedly being passed by and left hungry by their attendant responded to their loss of control with sharply elevated urinary 17-hydroxycorticosterone (17-OH-CS) excretion. In contrast, human volunteers carefully primed to understand and cooperate in an experiment showed no change in 17-OH-CS excretion during three hours of exhausting exercise, despite a near doubling of urinary catecholamine excretion. The sense of control these men retained protected them from feelings of helplessness and depression (Seligman, 1975).

In a recent survey of neuroendocrine abnormalities in depressive illness, Sachar (1976) found that the mean hourly cortisol concentration of depressed patients is significantly higher in the afternoon, evening, and early morning hours—the hours when secretion normally ceases—rather than during the interval from 5 A.M. to 11 A.M., when the bulk of the day's cortisol is normally excreted. He concludes that an excessive driving (or removal of inhibition) of the hypothalamic cells secreting the corticotropin-releasing factor (CRF) plays a significant part in severe depressive illness in man.

Carroll (1976) has established that a dysfunction in a depressed man's limbic system affects the pituitary control of the adrenal cortex and leads to an elevated plasma cortisol. This condition occurs in primary depression found after bereavement, but not when the individual behaves similarly but suffers from a schizophrenic disturbance of the cognitive (reasoning) process. Carroll also showed that an impaired response to dexamethasone, which normally suppresses the release of cortisone by competing, eliminates the feedback to the ACTH mechanism. In primary depression the limbic drive overrides the normal feedback.

Physiological Correlates of Social Rank. Many studies have shown differentiation of responses between D and S males in the gonadal axis. Dominants have heavier sex accessory glands than subordinates (Brain, 1972; Brain and Nowell, 1970; Bronson, Stesson, and Stiff, 1973; Evans and MacKintosh, 1976). Since the weight of these glands is dependent on circulating androgens, it is suspected that the subordinates have lower blood levels of androgens (McKinney and Desjardins, 1973).

When hierarchies develop in rats and mice, the subordinate animals exhibit greater adrenocortical activity (measured by weight or histological changes) than dominant animals (Barnett, 1955; Davis and Christian, 1957; Southwick and Bland, 1959). More recently, several investigators have measured plasma corticosterone in mice (Louch and Higginbotham, 1966) and rats (Chapman, Desjardins, and Bronson, 1969; Popova and Naumenko, 1972) and found that the S males have higher adrenocortical activity than D males, as indicated by higher corticosterone levels.

Sympathetic adrenal-medullary activity has been studied in environmental stress situations, with increases found in the catecholamine enzymes (dopamine B-hydroxylase, tyrosine hydroxylase, and phenylethanolamine-N-methyltransferase) in mice and rats due to repeated immobilization, stress, isolation, induced aggression, and spontaneous fighting (Henry, Ely, and Stephens, 1972; Henry and others, 1971a; Hucklebridge, Nowell, and Dilks, 1973; Kvetnansky and others, 1971; Kvetnansky, Weise, and Kopin, 1970; Lamprecht and others, 1973; Maengwyn-Davies and others, 1973; Weinshilboum and others, 1971). Therefore, we performed experiments to explore the relationship between the following dominant-subordinate parameters:

long-term behavior patterns and pituitary adrenocortical and sympathetic adrenal-medullary response patterns. Again the same basic population cage was used, as well as the same population type, age, and size. After about forty days of colony interaction, the social hierarchy was firmly established, and aggressive activity subsided. At this time there was a maximum differentiation between the adrenal-medullary catecholamine biosynthetic enzymes of the dominant and the subordinate animals (Ely and Henry, 1978). The data indicated that neuroendocrine response to social interaction is correlated with the behavior profile of the individual (Figure 5). Figure 5-A shows that tyrosine hydroxylase (rate-limiting enzyme for catecholamine synthesis) increased in all animals after fourteen days of social interaction; however, the D males exhibited a greater increase than did the S males (200 versus 50 percent, $p < .001$, respectively). Tyrosine hydroxylase (TH) continued to increase in the D males, peaking at Day 42. After this time until the termination of the experiment, TH declined toward control values in all animals. Figure 5-B shows the same general early trend of phenylethanolamine-N-methyltransferase (PNMT) increasing in all animals on Day 14 and declining toward control levels after 105 days. However, on Day 42 the S males exhibited a return toward control values, whereas the D males showed a peak PNMT response which was significantly greater than that of the S males ($p < .01$). Adrenal gland weights did not differ significantly between animals (Figure 6); however, the S males did exhibit higher plasma corticosterone values on Day 14 as compared to D males ($p < .01$).

As observed with TH and partially with PNMT, the plasma corticosterone returned toward contol values after Day 42, even though it remained elevated above control on Day 105. This increased pituitary adrenocortical response in subordinates has recently been verified in another set of experiments on animals from a different biological class, Japanese quail. In collaboration with Scott Orcutt (University of Akron), we have recently shown (unpublished observations) that in social groupings of Japanese quail the S males have significantly elevated levels of plasma corticosterone as compared to D males during the early period of social hierarchy establishment. The S males exhibited significant increases in plasma corticosterone after seven days and fourteen days of social interaction in a colony. As in the studies with mice, these differences decreased with time.

Candland and Leshner (1974), using squirrel monkeys, found that after several weeks or even years in a colony situation, dominants had higher 17-hydroxycorticosteroid levels than did subordinates, with little difference occurring in catecholamine levels. In previously isolated animals, however, immediately after a social order was established, the subordinates did have higher levels of 17-hydroxycorticosteroids than did the dominants. At the same time, the urinary catecholamines increased in those mid-ranking monkeys who successfully fought to maintain status but decreased in those who

Figure 5. Percentage Increases in (A) Tyrosine Hydroxylase (TH)
and (B) Phenylethanolamine-N-Methyltransferase (PNMT)
in Dominant, Subordinate, and Control Males.

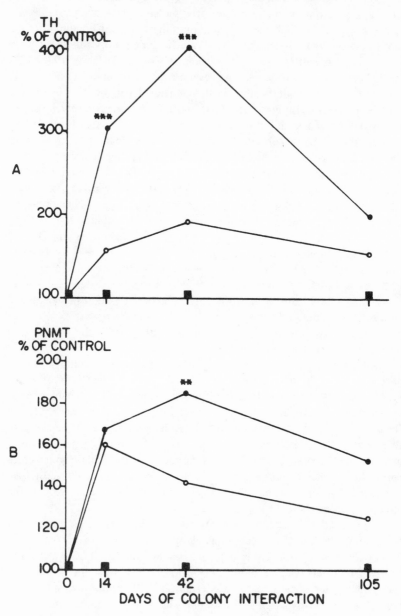

Note: Solid circles = dominant males; open circles = subordinate males; squares = controls.
**$p < .01$, ***$p < .001$.

Figure 6 (A) Paired Absolute Adrenal Weight (Wet) and
(B) Plasma Corticosterone of Dominant, Subordinate, and Control Males

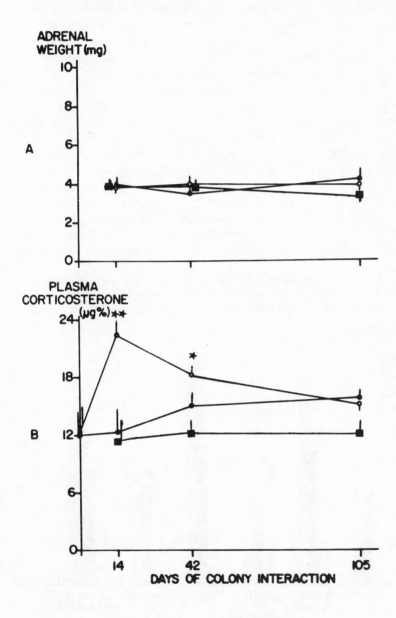

Note: Solid circles = dominant males; open circles = subordinate males; squares = controls.
*p <.05, **p <.01.

were unsuccessful and became further subordinated. Since the species and the methodology used in this study differ from ours (urine rather than plasma, measurements, and different time scale), it is difficult to make direct comparisons. In both studies, however, dominant animals responded to the environment with neuroendocrine patterns different from those of the subordinates. These patterns are dependent on behavior profile, physical condition, and length of time spent as a dominant or subordinate.

In further tests of the responsiveness of the pituitary-adrenocortical axis (PAC) and sympathetic adrenal-medullary axis (SAM) in D and S animals, we found that the elevated SAM activity in D males decreased when they were removed from social interaction and showed further increases if the level of psychosocial stress was increased; however, the S males did not show such responsiveness in the SAM axis under similar manipulations but, instead, showed more responsiveness in the PAC axis to restraint stress, ACTH injection, and role reversal (Ely and Henry, 1978) than D males did. Figure 7 shows that the S males had a greater response of plasma corticosterone to restraint stress (two hours' immobilization) and ACTH injection than D males did. Figure 8 shows that D males had a greater response of tyrosine

Figure 7. Plasma Corticosterone Levels of Control, Dominant, Subordinate, Dominant Made Subordinate, and Subordinate Made Dominant Males During Immobilization, ACTH Administration (10 units sc), and Role Reversal

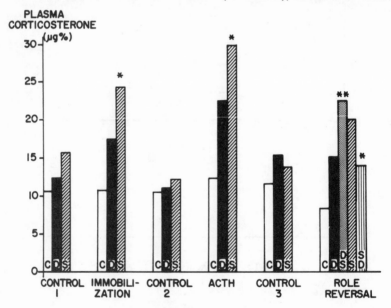

Note: C = controls; D = dominant; S = subordinate; DS = dominant made subordinate; SD = subordinate made dominant.
*$p < .05$, **$p < .01$, comparing dominant to subordinate levels.

Figure 8. Percentage Tyrosine Hydroxylase (TH) Increase over Controls
in Dominant Controls, Dominants Removed, Dominants as Intruders,
Subordinate Controls, Subordinates Made Dominant, and
Subordinates as Intruders

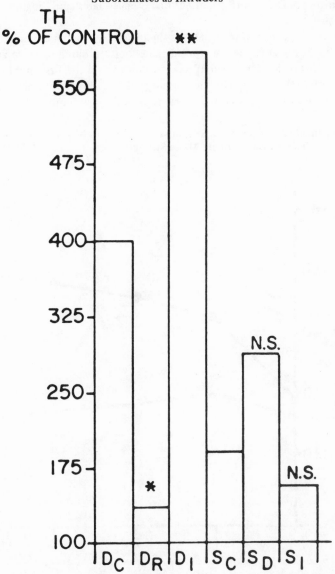

Note: D_C = dominant controls; D_R = dominants removed; D_I = dominants as intruders;
S_C = subordinate controls; S_D = subordinates made dominant; S_I = subordinates as
intruders.
Student's *t* tests were performed between D_C vs. D_I and S_C vs. S_I.
*$p < .05$, **$p < .01$; N.S., not significant.

hydroxylase to intruder stress and that the tyrosine hydroxylase began to
increase when an S male assumed the dominant position (SD). Benton and
associates (1978) recently found that the adrenal content of noradrenaline
was higher in D than in S males but that S males had slightly higher adrenaline
content.

To further investigate the increased sympathetic nervous system
activity in the D males, we studied the effects on blood pressure and found
that the D males developed a hypertension around the first month of social
interaction (Figure 9) (Ely and Henry, 1971; Ely, Henry, and Ciaranello,
1974), and maintained this hypertension for four months; in contrast, the

**Figure 9. Blood Pressure Response of Dominant Males as Compared to
That of Subordinate Males Socially Interacting in a Colony**

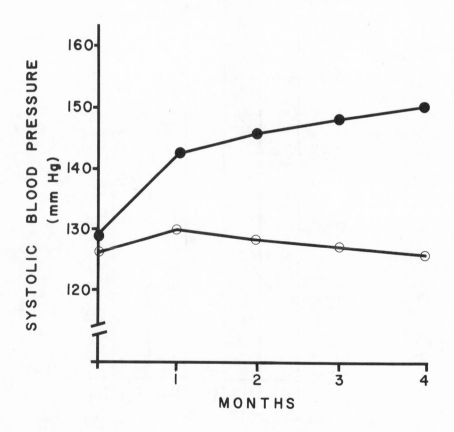

Note: Solid circles = dominant males; open circles = subordinate males.

S males had normal systolic blood pressures. The blood pressure response was reversible, however, if the D was removed from social interaction after forty days. If an S male achieved dominant status, then he developed an increased blood pressure. We also found that the D males had greater blood pressure responsiveness to acute psychosocial stress than S males did (Figure 10).

Figure 10. Blood Pressure Responses of Dominant and Subordinate Males
in Different Social Conditions

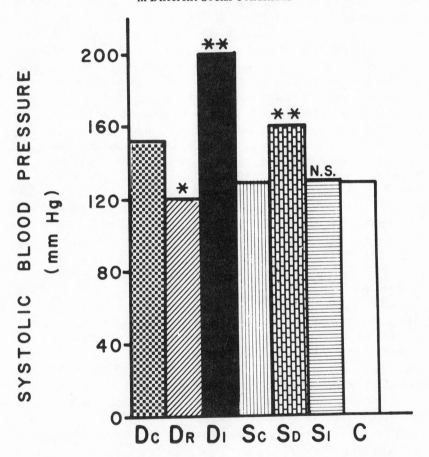

Note: Each pressure represents four pressures averaged over a month, with N = 4-10 for each group.

D_C = dominant control; D_R = dominant removed from social interaction; D_I = dominant intruder into another colony; S_C = subordinate control; S_D = subordinate made dominant; S_I = subordinate as an intruder into another colony; C = control males in standard lab cages.

D_R and D_I groups are compared to D_C; S_D and S_I groups are compared to S_C.

* = $p < .05$, ** = $p < .01$; N.S. = not significant.

Somewhat similarly, Folkow and Rubinstein (1966) found that months of repeated episodes of stimulation of the "defense area" in the hypothalamus (frontal-lateral area) produced an arousal of the sympathetic nervous system, with increases in blood pressure and heart rate.

Adrenal Gland Morphology. Ultrastructural differences within the adrenal gland may explain the difference in responsiveness of the pituitary-adrenocortical axis in D and S males (Ayers and Ely, 1979). There is a significant correlation between social rank (as measured behaviorally and by preputial gland weight) and the type of cristae within the mitochondria of the zona fasciculata of the adrenal cortex. Ultrastructural examination of the zona fasciculata of subordinates with high corticosterone levels (40-50 $\mu g\%$) showed round mitochondria with tubulo-vesicular cristae, large-diameter profiles of agranular endoplasmic reticulum, and large accumulations of cell products in subendothelial and intercellular spaces (Figure 11). Animals in the middle of the hierarchy had lower corticosterone levels (17-18 $\mu g\%$) than the subordinates and oval mitochondria with tubulo-vesicular or lamellar cristae, and smaller-diameter profiles of agranular endoplasmic reticulum. Dominants showed the lowest corticosterone levels (11-15 $\mu g\%$), with the majority of mitochondria exhibiting lamellar cristae (Figure 12). In control animals, the mitochondria in zona fasciculata cells were found to be generally ovoid or spherical. Cristae of the control mitochondria most often appeared to take the form of vesicles or tubules which may contain angles of 90° or less. Occasionally, mitochondria with cristae in lamellar arrangement were seen (Figure 13).

There have been reports that the zona fasciculata mitochondria are responsive to ACTH injections (Kahri, 1970; Sekiyama and Yago, 1972) and those in the zona glomerulosa to aldosterone changes (Fisher and Horvat, 1971). In general, adrenocortical mitochondria are responsive to prostaglandin administration (Penney, Olson, and Averill, 1973). These changes can be reversed by injections of ACTH. Our preliminary results support these data, since the S animals with high plasma corticosterone levels have a tubular vesicular mitochondria suggestive of those animals in previous studies with ACTH treatment. Further work is needed to clarify the relationship and temporal sequence of events occurring in the mitochondria between D and S animals, but indications currently suggest a morphological and physiological differentiation.

Summary and Theoretical Implications

Dominant and subordinate animals can be uniquely characterized by physiological, morphological, and behavioral indices. Note that we are using the terms *dominant* and *subordinate* in the ethological sense, which reflects the idea that these are social roles developed over a long period in a "home"

Figure 11. A Representative Electron Micrograph of the Adrenal Cortex Zona Fasciculata in a Subordinate Male

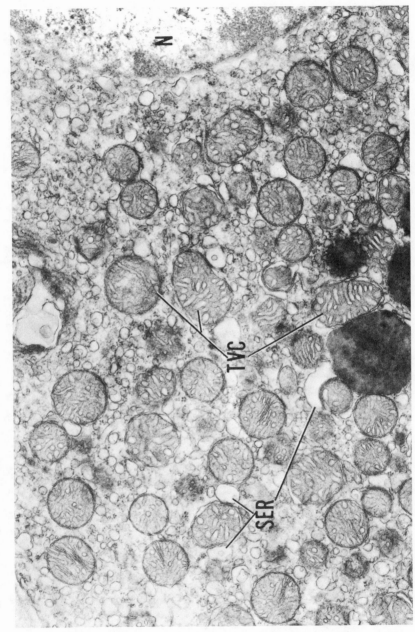

Note: Mag. 22,500; SER = smooth endoplasmic reticulum; TVC = tubulo-vesicular cristae in the mitochondria; N = nucleus.

Figure 12. A Representative Electron Micrograph of the Adrenal Cortex Zona Fasciculata in a Dominant Male

Note: Mag. = 22,500; LC = lamellar cristae in mitochondria.

Figure 13. Control Animals with Plasma Corticosterone Levels of 5-10μg%, and Ovoid or Spherical Mitochondria in Zona Fasciculata Cells

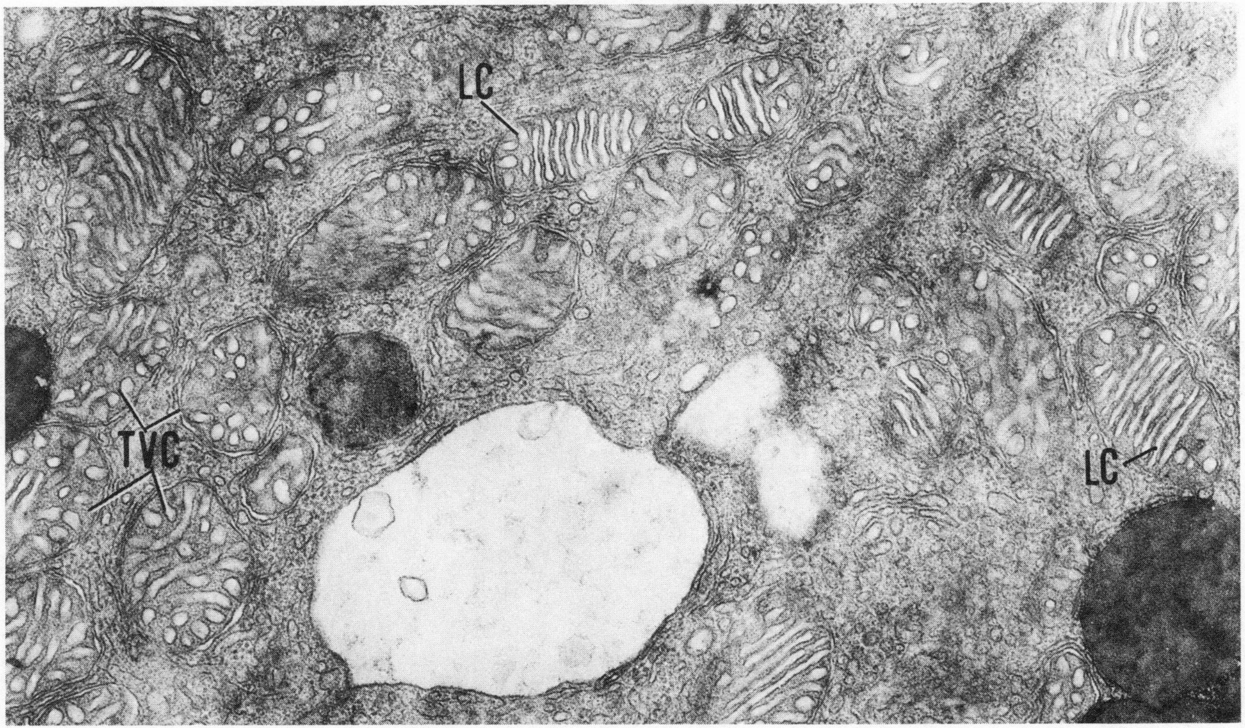

Note: Mag. = 22,500; SC = spherical cristae; LC = lamellar cristae.

environment and not acute roles seen in types of paired conditions of one animal dominating another in a test environment. Table 1 summarizes the characteristics of the D animal, as compared to the S, in long-term ethological types of studies using mice. In summary, the D male is characterized by increased activity in the following systems: gonadal axis, sympathetic adrenal-medullary axis with elevated blood pressure, and locomotor activity accompanied by vigilant patrolling behavior. The S male is characterized by increased activity in the pituitary adrenocortical axis, decreased locomotor activity, suppression of the gonadal axis, and normal blood pressure.

In mice, rats, and men, uncertainty can elicit activation of the limbic system, resulting in exploratory activity that may provide new information about the environment and thereby reduce the uncertainty and fear (Levine, Goldman, and Coover, 1972; Russel, 1973; Halliday, 1968). Complex coping processes, which reduce the activation process, also can occur at this stage. Coping refers to the process elicited when a certain stimulus is appraised as a threat (Lazarus and Averill, 1972) and threat is the anticipation of harm. Effective coping processes can prevent or minimize further activation of specific efferent outflows from the diencephalon (Ursin, 1978). Activation of the diencephalon can be either phasic (short-lasting) or tonic (long-lasting), as suggested by Ursin (1978). In conditions of intense phasic activation or, in some cases, intense tonic activation, the activation would be nonspecific. In other words, a majority of the body's effectors are stimulated to meet the metabolic demands of the situation. This is the basic Selyean concept of non-specific arousal. However, in situations of more mild and tonic activation, specific response patterns would selectively stimulate effectors, such as the somatomotor axis or the pituitary adrenocortical axis. These responses consequently stimulate their respective target organs with appropriate secretions and adaptive responses. Further, if the activation is prolonged and coping is not adequately established, structural change may occur in the target organs and result in pathology and disease (Henry, Stephens, and Santisteban, 1975; Folkow, 1975). (For more specific details, see Henry and Stephens, 1977b.)

In our studies we have differentiated the animals into a dominant type with a strong SAM response and a subordinate type with a strong PAC response pattern. We suggest that the two responses reflect different reactions to social environment stimulation. Other investigators (Levine, Goldman, and Coover, 1972; Weiss, 1972), in studies of operant conditioning with rats, have shown that the corticosterone level of the animal rises when the realities of the situation fail to meet the animal's expectations based on prior experience. This broad concept would include the general theme that when the organism, be it a rodent or a higher primate, perceives that his expectations are not being met, his behavior will be either fight or flight, with the consequent possibility that he may improve his situation. If the

Table 1. Physiological and Behavioral Characteristics of a Typical Dominant Male as Compared to a Subordinate Male Mouse.

Physiological and Behavioral Parameters	Direction of Change in Dominant Animal (as Compared to Subordinate)	Reference
Gonadal axis		
Plasma testosterone and FSH	Increased	Bronson, Stesson, and Stiff, 1973
Preputial gland weight	Increased	Bronson, Stesson, and Stiff, 1973; Brain, 1972; Evans and MacKintosh, 1976
Pituitary-adrenocortical axis		
Adrenal weight	Decreased	Barnett, 1955; Davis and Christian, 1957; Southwick and Bland, 1959
Plasma corticosterone	Decreased	Louch and Higginbotham, 1966; Ely and Henry, 1978; Bronson, Stesson, and Stiff, 1973
Zona fasciculata (percentage tubulo-vesicular mitochondrial cristae)	Decreased	Ayers and Ely, 1979
Sympathetic adrenal-medullary axis		
Adrenal catecholamines	Increased	Benton and others, 1978
Adrenal catecholamine enzymes	Increased	Ely and Henry, 1978; Ely, Henry, and Ciaranello, 1974
Physical condition (signs of body scars and wounds)	Decreased	Ely and Henry, 1971, 1978
Blood pressure, systolic	Increased	Ely and Henry, 1971; Ely, Henry, and Ciaranello, 1974
Behavioral axis		
General activity	Increased	Ely and Henry, 1974, 1978
Patrol behavior	Increased	Ely and Henry, 1974, 1978
Amount of territory	Increased	Ely and Henry, 1974, 1978

behavior that follows results in a successful reestablishment of the security of the organism's expectations, then the sympathetic adrenal-medullary responses decrease. If this response is not effective and the expectations are simply not being met, then the organism experiences helplessness (Seligman, 1975). In this case, the physiological changes will tend to follow the classical Selyean alarm-response pattern. Behaviorally there will be withdrawal and decreased motor activity, and the stage is set for endogenous depression (Sassenrath, 1970; Sachar, 1976). This withdrawal is accomplished by increased corticosterone output and by the classical depressive emotional response. According to Price (1969), this depressive or yielding reaction has evolutionary value because it decreases social conflict and tends to stabilize the control of the hierarchy.

The animal model with which we are working provides us with the opportunity to test these theoretical ideas. During initial periods of social interaction, the response patterns of both D and S mice were typical of general nonspecific arousal, with activation of both the PAC and SAM systems preparing the organism to meet the demands of the new environment. Mason (1975b) refers to this type of response as a "Pattern II" response, in which there is a high degree of unpredictability, uncertainty, or ambiguity associated with the situation. Several experimental studies with monkeys have shown that this Pattern II response is associated with elevated plasma norepinephrine and 17-hydroxycorticosteroids (Mason and others, 1961a; Mason, Brady, and Tolson, 1966).

However, once the social hierarchy had become established and the environment was no longer novel and uncertain, the response patterns of the D and S animals differentiated. The S males maintained a typical Selyean alarm pattern with elevated pituitary-adrenocortical activity, and the D males assumed a Cannon type of defense pattern with elevated adrenal-medullary activity. The S animals were being threatened and behaviorally inhibited by the D males, but social gestures and territorial defense substituted for overt aggression and the arousal was mediated cognitively. The S animals then withdrew behaviorally in a helpless type of conservation-of-energy pattern, similar to that described by Engel and Schmale (1972). We interpret this pattern as an appropriate adaptive response, which functions to minimize confrontations with the D male and enhance the survival of the S male. This adrenocortical pattern has been reported in withdrawn, depressed humans (Stokes, 1972) and may be related to a specific type of depression (Sachar and others, 1972). Bronson, Stesson, and Stiff (1973) have also shown that S male mice maintained higher plasma corticosterone levels due to grouping effects longer than did D animals. In contrast to this response pattern, the D males in our study assumed an aggressive energy-consuming response, with activation of the catecholamines which stimulate cyclic AMP and the enzymes responsible for lipolysis and glycogenolysis for energy mobilization. This pattern appears to permit the D male to maintain his vigilant patrolling behavior and consequently the social stability of the colony. The studies of Corley, Mauck, and Shiel (1975), using squirrel monkeys, support the concept of response-pattern differentiation. The monkeys who actively avoided a shock showed increased sympathetic nervous system activity and high blood pressure, whereas the monkeys yoked to the same shock stimulus but helpless to control the situation collapsed of bradycardia.

Potential mechanisms for the increased responsiveness of the neuro-endocrine system range from neural feedback differences in hormone regulation to differences in target organ sensitivity. Sassenrath (1970) found that subordinate *M. mulatta* monkeys in a chronically stressful social environment showed higher plasma corticosterone levels in response to ACTH than dominant animals did. She concluded that the fear-evoking component of chronic social stress may be the predominant stimulus for endogenous ACTH release.

Human Applications

We have demonstrated that drugged (Δ 9-THC) animals or animals that are socially displaced downward fail to perform expected social organizational tasks (Ely, Henry, and Jarosz, 1975). Such conduct is compatible with endogenous depression in man (Sachar, 1976), and the raised corticosterone levels support this idea (Ely, Henry, and Ciaranello, 1974). Paralleling our animal studies is the work of Friedman and Rosenman (1974), who behaviorally characterize humans as Type A and Type B personalities. Type A persons are those whose behavior evidences the urgency of time pressure, excessive competitive drive, or undue hostility when thwarted. Men with Type A behavior patterns carry an approximately twofold risk of coronary heart disease (Rosenman and others, 1976).

Do Type A and Type B individuals differ in neuroendocrine response patterns? The observations of Jones, Bridges, and Leak (1970), who examined the differences in urinary noradrenaline excretion and changes of plasma 17-hydroxycorticosteroids when different types of persons are stimulated, suggest that this distinction may be feasible. They studied male students during a critical oral examination in anatomy, measuring their biochemical changes while they were under the influence of this challenging psychosocial stimulus. They typed the students into two groups: one had high muscularity and a low component of fat; the other, a long thin body and limbs and low muscularity. Those with high muscularity had the most marked noradrenaline response to stress but showed a significantly lower response of plasma cortisol than the linear men. Jones suggests that in the muscular individual the challenging social stimulus may have primarily evoked anger, activating adrenal-medullary activity with the release of noradrenaline, which has been associated with active aggressive behavior (Frankenhaeuser and Gardell, 1976). In contrast, the pituitary-adrenocortical mechanism may have been more readily activated in the predominantly linear individuals, whose personality exposed them to a withdrawal response (Jones, Bridges, and Leak, 1970).

The biochemical studies of Friedman, Rosenman, and St. George (1969) suggest a difference between the responses of the pituitary-adreno-cortical system in the two contrasting types of subjects whose behavior they have been observing since the late 1950s. They found the same average levels of cortisol in both Type A and Type B. However, when persons show-ing the fully developed Type A response pattern were challenged with large doses of the adrenocorticotrophic hormone (ACTH), they excreted sig-nificantly less cortisol than Type B subjects.

The group then used a mental contest to contrast the plasma cate-cholamine response of Type A coronary-prone subjects to a specific challenge with that of Type B subjects. At the end of the experiment, the Type A subjects (due to the experimental design) were angry, whereas Type B subjects remained unperturbed. The mean plasma noradrenaline value for Type A subjects (0.54 mg/ml) during the contest was significantly different from the resting value (0.41 mg/ml). There was no significant difference be-tween the corresponding values of Type B subjects (0.41 mg/ml) (Friedman and others, 1975).

They also contrasted the urinary excretion of noradrenaline in the two groups. Both noradrenaline and its metabolic end products increased significantly more in Type A persons during a tense working day than in the Type B. Yet, during bed rest at night, neither type had an increase (Byers and others, 1962). Thus, the Friedman group found contrasting responses: the pituitary-adrenocortical system of Type B individuals responded more to the ACTH stimulus, and the sympathetic catecholamine system of Type A responded more to the stimulus of competition.

The behavior of Type A persons appears related to that of a dom-inant animal being challenged, whereas that of the Type B has more of the relaxed, noncompetitive aspects of subordinates who have accepted their position. The excessive production of noradrenaline by the Type A person being stimulated is compatible with that in dominant male mice. The bio-chemical work of Friedman, Rosenman, and St. George (1969), showing that the adrenal response to excess ACTH is less in Type A individuals, is compatible with the results of our animal studies and suggests that dominant versus subordinate role differentiation may be at the basis of A and B typol-ogy, at least to the extent that Type A is competitive and readily slips into a sympathetic adrenal-medullary mode, whereas Type B is more inclined toward an adrenocortical mode.

In his review of stress behavior patterns and coronary heart disease, Glass (1977) found Type A college students to be more ambitious; they earn more honors, and more go on to graduate school. Treadmill tests showed that Type A men push themselves harder and suppress feelings of fatigue. They work closer to the limits of endurance; and when they are defeated in spite of their efforts, they experience the loss of control as more threatening. Indeed, when the loss is severe, they become more vulnerable to a helpless response than Type B individuals. Glass speculates that when Type A perceives a threat to his control of the environment, he struggles to reestablish control. During this period, the active coping efforts will be associated with increased plasma noradrenaline, but adrenaline is unchanged. Upon perceiving that control has been lost, Type A will become passive and give up, and his noradrenaline levels are likely to decline. The more frequent and the more intense the cycling between the sympathetic nervous system arousal of the effort to control and the onset of helplessness with parasympathetic activity, the more vulnerable the individual may be to the acceleration of pathophysiological precursors of coronary heart disease (Glass, 1977). Several related studies indicate that hypertension may be associated with anxiety (Vlachakis and others, 1974), anxiety and anger (Whitehead and others, 1977), and anxiety and depression (Friedman and Bennet, 1977). Grings and Dawson (1978), after examining numerous personality factors and associated physiological response patterns, conclude that individuals do not just respond autonomically with sympathetic or parasympathetic activation; instead, there are mixed patterns, and the pattern remains consistent in the individual across a variety of situations. Their results support the concept that individuals with high ego strength (somewhat like the dominant animals in our colony situations) are physiologically more responsive to their environment than are those with low ego strength.

An important human study that has recently examined psychological variables, coping processes, and neuroendocrine responses is the elegant and unique investigation by a team of twenty-one scientists examining parachutist trainees in a Norwegian Army Parachute School (Ursin, Baade, and Levine, 1978). Blood and urine samples (collected before training started and on jump days 1, 2, 5, and 11) were analyzed for seven different biochemical factors. The central thesis of the study was that adequate coping behavior would be characterized by a significant reduction in internal physiological activation. In general, the results support the work of Roessler (1973), who found more psychophysiological reactivity in the sympathetic nervous system during the process of coping development but decreased activity after coping was established. In the study of parachutist trainees, the investigators found that general ability level, defense mechanisms, motivation, and role identification factors explained "considerable portions" of the variance. After coping was developed, the variance depended on the relationship between resultant achievement motivation and performance. Increased activation in the pituitary adrenocortical axis was positively correlated with high defense mechanisms and low performance. With the development of coping processes, however, the cortisol levels returned toward baseline on the second jump day and remained at that level. The sympathetic adrenal-medullary axis, as indicated by urinary levels of catecholamines, showed activation on the first jump day and slowly declined toward baseline levels by Day 11, but there was a difference between prejump and postjump responses of epinephrine and norepinephrine. Prejump conditions apparently activated more fear responses and epinephrine secretion, whereas the norepinephrine response was influenced by a less well-defined challenge to the coping potential of the individual (Hansen and others, 1978). The work of Frankenhaeuser and co-workers (1971) supports the idea that epinephrine is involved in the active coping behavior of healthy individuals, not only in fight-or-flight situations but also in coping with everyday stressors. The results of the parachutist data, however, are somewhat difficult to interpret with regard to the norepinephrine responses, since tasks involving muscular use increase norepinephrine levels (Folkow, Häggendahl, and Lisander, 1967). However, there is a similarity between these men (their neuroendocrine responses and their coping processes) and the dominant mice in our experiments. The cortisol response rapidly returned to normal after the first jump, and the postjump catecholamine levels remained elevated throughout all jumps. Although the general ability and technical comprehension of the parachutists were similar to those of the ordinary Norwegian soldier, they differed in their preference for skiing, diving, flying, and mountain climbing. Thus, the parachutists had a stronger identification with the masculine role and a higher preference for thrill and adventure (Baade and others, 1978). In general, this new study (Ursin, Baade, and Levine, 1978) supports the idea that an individual's perception of a threatening situation, rather the situation as such, is the primary determinant of coping level and of the ensuing neuroendocrine response pattern.

Conclusion

Both human and animal data suggest to us that there are subtle specific responses to stressful stimuli in the environment. Fundamental to Selye's nonspecific arousal response was the finding that the changes elicited by various stressor agents are basically the same, irrespective of the specific nature or perception of the eliciting stimulus. This holds for strong arousing stimuli. However, from our studies it appears that an individual's social rank and, therefore, predominant behavior pattern influences the CNS perception of psychosocial stimuli and so in turn the specificity of the efferent limb of the physiological response.

The subsequent biochemical patterning is determined by the individual's social role, personality factors, life style, and CNS perceptual mechanisms. The two discrete pathways that we have examined are the fight-or-flight response pattern typical of the dominant animal, first described by Cannon, and the Selyean depressive alarm response typical of the subordinate animal. An analogy can be made between the Type A individual and his work and the dominant mouse within the closed social environment of a complex population cage. Granted, man has different coping and perceptual abilities; however, both are responding to the subtle patterns of activation of instinctual mechanisms at limbic hypothalamic levels; both are engaged in an activity that is species-preservative, not just self-preservative; both are active, intense, and competitive, with a sense of time urgency.

Perhaps we should include in stress theory the idea that environmental stimuli may be perceived and processed differently in the CNS, depending on conditions of threat, uncertainty, social role, personality factors, motivational conditions, and coping strategies. Consequently, different neuroendocrine response patterns may emerge.

6

Neurobiological Theories

Donald R. Sweeney
Mark S. Gold
A. L. C. Pottash
Robert K. Davies

❊ ❊ ❊ ❊ ❊ ❊ ❊ ❊ ❊ ❊ ❊ ❊ ❊

During the last several years, there have been increased efforts to clarify the psychobiological mechanisms that underlie stress and anxiety. The progress of this work has depended, in part, on parallel efforts to develop a meaningful phenomenology of the complex, multidimensional system of signs and symptoms associated with these states. Although the terminological boundaries between "stress," "anxiety," and "arousal" remain unclear (Spielberger, 1972b), considerable progress has been made in the direction of more reliable clinical subcategorization (Spitzer, Endicott, and Robins, 1977). For the sake of simplicity, we will here use the word *stress* to represent the broader category typically described by terms such as "stress syndrome," "anxiety reaction," and "arousal state."

Knowledge of the neurobiology of stress has benefited most substantially from advances in the fields of neurochemistry and psychopharmacology.

In neurochemistry, efforts of basic researchers to identify and describe the function of central nervous system (CNS) neuroregulators have been followed closely by attempts of clinical researchers to relate such neuroregulator function to normal and abnormal behavior. The thrust of this clinical research has involved the development of assays that, when performed on specimens of peripheral fluids (urine, cerebrospinal fluid, and blood), reflect the functional CNS activity of the neuroregulator system under investigation. The neuroregulators that have received the most attention are the catecholamines (specifically, norepinephrine and dopamine) and the indoleamines (specifically, serotonin). These particular neurotransmitter systems have been studied extensively because the pharmacological agents shown to be beneficial in the treatment of the major psychiatric disorders also have major effects on these same neuroregulator systems. Thus, we hear of the "dopamine" hypothesis of schizophrenia (Kety, 1978) and the "amine" hypotheses of the affective disorders (Schildkraut, 1965; Asberg and others, 1976). However, the catecholamine and indoleamine systems, critical as they may be in mediating behavior, represent only a partial picture of the complex neurochemistry of the central nervous system. The roles of amino acid neurotransmitters, such as glycine and gamma-amino-butyric acid (GABA), are under current active investigation (Aprison, 1977). Furthermore, potentially important interactions between neurotransmitters and neuroendocrine systems have received much recent attention (Kizer and Youngblood, 1978). Finally, the recent discovery of endogenous opiate-like substances in the brain has generated much speculation and some initial data supporting their role in the regulation of behavior (Goldstein, 1978).

Results of investigations in clinical psychopharmacology have also contributed to progress in elucidating neurobiological mechanisms of stress. For example, the efficacy of antidepressants in treating some patients with panic anxiety disorder has aided in creating newer classifications of anxiety disorder in general, and in constructing new theories of anxiety (D. F. Klein, 1967; Tyrer, Candy, and Kelly, 1973). Another example is the successful use of the drug clonidine in the treatment of opiate withdrawal (Gold, Redmond, and Kleber, 1978a, 1978b). The heuristic implications of the similarities between the syndromes of opiate withdrawal and panic anxiety have stimulated hypotheses that are currently being tested (Gold and others, 1979). Both of these examples will be discussed below in further detail.

As noted, one of the ways in which neurochemical theories of behavioral dysfunction are developed is by establishing the efficacy of a certain class of psychopharmacological compounds and then examining the effect of these compounds on neuroregulator systems. However, since most drugs exert their effects on multiple brain systems, it is unlikely that a single specific neurochemical mechanism will account fully for the efficacy of any given drug or for the etiology of any given syndrome. For example, the benzodiazepine group is among the most widely used classes of drugs for the treatment of anxiety states (Greenblatt and Shader, 1974). The benzodiazepines have effects on several neuroregulator systems, including GABA, glycine, norepinephrine, and serotonin, and we do not know which of these systems are most important in defining the mechanism of action of these drugs. Linear, univariate models of neurochemical mechanisms, including many of those currently being entertained, clearly are only crude approximations.

In the present discussion, we will focus most intensively on evidence that supports relationships between brain norepinephrine systems and stress. In doing so, we do not suggest that the noradrenergic system is the most critical variable in forming the biological substrate of stress. However, the information on noradrenergic systems—from basic laboratory studies and from clinical psychopharmacological studies in humans—is more completely developed than information supporting other mechanisms. Other major theories of anxiety, such as the lactate theory (Pitts and McClure, 1967) and the beta-adrenergic receptor theory (Jefferson, 1976), are reviewed in Chapter Twenty-Four of this volume.

Measurement of Noradrenergic Function

There is extensive literature on relationships between human emotional states and peripheral changes in epinephrine and norepinephrine (Frankenhaeuser, 1971, 1975). Heightened states of arousal, whether generated by psychological or physical stimuli, are associated with increased peripheral levels of epinephrine produced by the adrenal medulla and norepinephrine produced by the peripheral sympathetic nervous system (Levi, 1972). Only during the last several years, however, have measures of noradrenergic systems that appear to reflect the activity of *central* norepinephrine systems become available. Evidence from basic laboratory studies indicates that norepinephrine is metabolized within the central nervous system to yield either 3-methoxy-4-hydroxyphenethylene glycol (MHPG) or di-hydroxyphenethylene glycol (DHPG). These glycols leave the brain in free or conjugated form, and they are then excreted into urine (Meek and Neff, 1972; Maas, Landis, and Dekirmenjian, 1976).

Further evidence for the central nervous system origin of MHPG as the primary metabolite of norepinephrine stems from animal studies of the nucleus locus coeruleus. This pontine center contains the highest density of norepinephrine-containing neurons in the central nervous system (Dahlstrom and Fuxe, 1964). The cell bodies located in the nucleus locus coeruleus give rise to axons that diffusely innervate the entire cerebral cortex as well as subcortical limbic structures such as the hypothalamus and cingulate cortex. Thus, experimental alteration of locus coeruleus activity may provide a major avenue to knowledge regarding the function of the noradrenergic system.

In both rats and primates, lesioning of the locus coeruleus results in decreased concentration of brain norepinephrine and brain MHPG (Korf, Aghajanian, and Roth, 1973; Huang and others, 1975). Electrical stimulation of the locus coeruleus produces increased concentration of brain MHPG (Korf, Aghajanian, and Roth, 1973). These results suggest that there is a direct relationship between brain MHPG concentrations and the functional activity of the locus coeruleus. A second major question, however, is whether the amounts of MHPG recovered in peripheral fluids are sufficient to reflect central nervous system events. Several earlier studies in animals and in humans resulted in estimates that between 30 and 80 percent of urinary MHPG originates in the central nervous system (Maas and Landis, 1971; Kopin, 1978). More recently, a human study of brain arteriovenous differences in plasma MHPG has resulted in an estimate that more than 60 percent of urinary MHPG is derived from the brain (Maas and others, 1979). To summarize, MHPG is the major CNS metabolite of norepinephrine, and its measurement in urine appears to reflect brain noradrenergic activity.

Affective Disorder and Noradrenergic Function

In order to discuss relationships between stress and noradrenergic function, we must first describe recent work relating norepinephrine to affective disorders, since there seems to be a significant overlap between the role of norepinephrine in stress and in affective disorder. In the first place, many individuals exhibit "mixed" depression-anxiety syndromes. In addition, it is commonly held that the affective disorders themselves are "stress" syndromes. Finally, there is significant diagnostic overlap between anxiety syndromes, such as agoraphobia, and affective disorder (Bowen and Kohout, 1979).

The "catecholamine hypothesis" of depression, proposed several years ago (Jacobsen, 1964; Schildkraut, 1965; Bunney and Davis, 1965), holds that there may be a functional deficiency of norepinephrine at central nervous system synapses in certain types of affective disorder. The hypothesis stemmed from psychopharmacological evidence showing that drugs that deplete CNS norepinephrine produce depression in some individuals, while drugs that increase the functional availability of CNS norepinephrine may alleviate depressive symptoms.

One pathway for the investigation of the "catecholamine hypothesis" of affective disorder has been to measure urinary MHPG in depressed patients. The results of these studies are based on urinary MHPG excretion in the "baseline" state; that is, in patients who have not been taking medications for at least several days and who have not been treated pharmacologically for their depressive disorders. Initially, it was reported that clinically heterogeneous depressed patients for whom no further diagnostic subcategorizations had been made excreted significantly less urinary MHPG than healthy comparison subjects (Maas, Fawcett, and Dekirmenjian, 1968). Subsequently, studies employing the research diagnostic criteria of Feighner and associates (1972) have indicated that the strongest evidence for decreased urinary MHPG in depressives exists in groups diagnosed either as bipolar depressives (patients studied when depressed, but with histories of mania or hypomania) or as having primary affective disorders, whether unipolar or bipolar (Schildkraut and others, 1973; Goodwin and Post, 1975; Jones and others, 1975).

Another possible basis for subcategorizing depressed patients has emerged from investigations of relationships between baseline urinary MHPG excretion and response to treatment with tricyclic antidepressants. Three separate studies have indicated that patients with low baseline urinary MHPG tend to have a favorable treatment response to imipramine, whereas patients with normal or high baseline MHPG have favorable treatment responses to amitriptyline (Maas, Fawcett, and Dekirmenjian, 1972; Schildkraut, 1973; Beckmann and Goodwin, 1975). While the clinical implications of these findings have been somewhat controversial, a more recent study has reported that the use of baseline urinary MHPG levels to select tricyclic antidepressants produced significantly more favorable clinical results than selection of a tricyclic on more typical clinical grounds (Cobbin and others, 1979).

Stress and Noradrenergic Function

Animal studies have shown that brain norepinephrine turnover increases under conditions that are likely to produce increased arousal, such as foot shock, treadmill running, or cold-water swimming. These studies have been reviewed in detail elsewhere (Stone, 1975). Such animal studies, in postulating relationships between brain events and "stress," must define stress exclusive of its experiential component. Since terms such as *anxiety* are usually defined by both objective signs and subjective symptoms, animal studies are limited. However, recent studies on primates have proved valuable in extending information on the role of the brain noradrenergic system in mediating the behavioral components of fearful states.

These studies have focused on observation of primate behavior both prior and subsequent to the above-described techniques of lesioning or electrically stimulating the nucleus locus coeruleus. Animals with lesions of the locus coeruleus displayed marked decreases in fearful behavior elicited in response to threat (Huang and others, 1975). In contrast, animals exposed to electrical or pharmacological stimulation of the locus coeruleus showed increments in behaviors such as yawning or scratching, thought to be associated with fearful states (Gold and Redmond, 1977; Redmond, Huang, and Gold, 1977). It should not be assumed, however, that these results demonstrate noradrenergic specificity in mediating fearful behavior. Beyond its noradrenergic function, the locus coeruleus has been shown to interact with GABA (Cedarbaum and Aghajanian, 1977) and with opiate receptors (Bird and Kuhar, 1977; Korf, Bunney, and Aghajanian, 1974).

As in depression, urinary MHPG has been investigated in studies of stress responses. Several studies have reported that urinary MHPG varies with mood in bipolar patients studied longitudinally. More specifically, urinary MHPG excretion was higher when such patients were manic or hypomanic and lower when they were depressed (Bond, Jenner, and Sampson, 1972; Post and others, 1977). Since manic states appear to involve increased arousal, these results are consistent with the animal studies described above. Other investigations have postulated short-term urinary MHPG increases as possibly related to stress. In many cases, however, this interpretation has taken stress as a "nonspecific" factor, and no attempt has been made at direct measurement of responses on the stress-anxiety continuum. In one study, stress was postulated as a possible factor in explaining urinary MHPG elevations in patients undergoing increased physical activity (Ebert, Post, and Goodwin, 1972). In a study involving intravenous infusion of labeled norepinephrine, the investigators concluded that the observed increases in urinary MHPG were possibly related to the stress of the infusion procedure itself (Maas, Dekirmenjian, and Fawcett, 1971). In a study that attempted to control for stress, patients who had recovered from depressive illnesses underwent a six-hour protocol that included both control and stress periods. During control periods, subjects were allowed to relax and read magazines. The stress period was composed of a fifteen-minute performance test followed by the viewing of a film showing scenes of traffic accidents and surgical operations. Although both patient and comparison groups showed increases in self-rated anxiety during the stress periods, urinary MHPG changes did not appear to reflect these differences (Takahashi, Nakahara, and Sakurai, 1974).

In another investigation of urinary MHPG and stress, naval aviators were studied during training involving both simulated and actual landings of aircraft on aircraft carriers (Rubin and others, 1970). Urinary MHPG was significantly elevated for the periods preceding and during the actual landings, but not for the simulated landing. Increases in MHPG ranged from 25 to 58 percent higher than the control periods. This study did not report between- and within-individual relationships between stress and urinary MHPG, so that individual differences in urinary MHPG could not be examined as they covaried with intensity of arousal or stress.

A more recent study was designed to evaluate the effects of both stress and physical activity on urinary MHPG (Sweeney, Maas, and Heninger, 1978). Depressed patients were exposed, during a baseline hospitalization period, to eight-hour periods of either increased or decreased physical activity. Throughout the study, patients used the State-Trait Anxiety Inventory (Spielberger, Gorsuch, and Lushene, 1970) to carry out self-ratings of anxiety.

Although increased or decreased physical activity did not affect urinary MHPG, analysis of within-individual changes in state anxiety showed highly significant positive relationships between urinary MHPG and state anxiety. Those patients who showed significant increases in state anxiety also showed significant increases in urinary MHPG, while those with a decrease in state anxiety showed decreases in urinary MHPG. Thus, the data supported the statement that urinary MHPG covaries significantly with state anxiety in a diagnostically heterogeneous sample of acutely depressed inpatients. Further-more, the data suggested that patients with increased anxiety and increased MHPG had lower baseline urinary MHPG than those with decreased anxiety and decreased MHPG. It is noteworthy that the group showing increased MHPG and the group showing decreased MHPG could not be distinguished on clinical grounds. These two groups may have represented two distinct modes of norepinephrine metabolism, perhaps associated with differing modulation of norepinephrine by other neuroregulators. The results also suggest that urinary MHPG may be a measure of noradrenergic reactivity. The baseline MHPG differences between the two groups may be associated with differences in vulnerability to anxiety. It is commonly held that some individuals are more vulnerable to stress than others and that such vulner-ability may be related to the development of psychopathological syndromes (Sweeney, Maas, and Pickar, 1979; Sweeney and Maas, 1979b).

The data described above on urinary MHPG are partially supported by some more recent investigations of plasma MHPG. The development of assays for plasma MHPG is important primarily because plasma mea-surements are more likely to reflect short-term or transient changes in nor-adrenergic function and are therefore more appropriate for the study of noradrenergic reactivity (Sweeney and Maas, 1979a). Furthermore, plasma measurements, when compared to the laborious and time-consuming process of collecting twenty-four-hour urine specimens, are more easily obtained in nonresearch settings. Thus far, only a few studies have been carried out on plasma MHPG. Plasma MHPG has been reported to vary directly with mood in bipolar patients studied longitudinally and to increase in patients who have been treated successfully with antidepressant medications. Other data, collected on relatively small numbers of individuals, suggest that plasma MHPG may be significantly related to urinary MHPG (Sweeney and others, 1979). However, further data will have to be obtained in order to strengthen this finding.

In a study of a small number of psychiatric inpatients undergoing a lumbar puncture (usually an anxiety-provoking procedure), there was some evidence to suggest a within-individual relationship between plasma MHPG and state anxiety. Patients showing the most marked increases in anxiety prior to the lumbar puncture also tended to show the largest in-creases in plasma MHPG (Sweeney and others, 1979). Finally, patients undergoing a short-term, two-day trial on d-amphetamine, a drug that increases the central nervous system availability of norepinephrine and dopamine, showed a significant decrease in plasma MHPG during this pharmacological challenge (Sweeney and others, 1979). The data suggested that patients responding with a brightening of mood to d-amphetamine had lower baseline plasma MHPG than patients with no response or a dysphoric response to d-amphetamine, a result that is consistent with previous studies of urinary MHPG (Sweeney and Maas, 1978). Measures of baseline noradrenergic function may predict the direction in which mood will respond under either environmental or pharmacological provocation. Specification of both baseline noradrenergic function and change in that function after provocation may, in the future, help to predict, on the basis of "noradrenergic reactivity," which individuals are vulnerable to anxiety or depression.

Panic Anxiety and Opiate Withdrawal: Possible Common Neurobiological Mediation

Studies within the last two years have provided major new information on the possible role of the noradrenergic system, in interaction with brain endorphin systems, in mediating anxiety states. As we have noted, lesioning of the nucleus locus coeruleus inhibits brain norepinephrine activity, while electrical stimulation increases brain norepinephrine activity. Pharmacological studies of the nucleus locus coeruleus have also added important information. Drugs such as piperoxane and yohimbine, which are known to activate the locus coeruleus, also produce marked increases in anxiety and fear (Goldenberg, Snyder, and Aranow, 1947; Holmberg and Gershon, 1961).

In contrast, the drug clonidine, which inhibits locus coeruleus function, blocks and reverses the electrophysiological (Cedarbaum and Aghajanian, 1976, 1977) and behavioral (Redmond, Huang, and Gold, 1977; Gold and Redmond, 1977) effects of piperoxane.

Other evidence supports important interactions between the locus coeruleus and brain opiate receptors (Extein and others, 1979). Anatomical studies have described a widespread distribution of opiate receptors throughout the locus coeruleus (Atweh and Kuhar, 1977; Young, Bird, and Kuhar, 1977). In single-unit electrophysiological studies, locus coeruleus inhibition has been produced by intravenous or microiontophoretic administration of opiates such as morphine, further demonstrating this interaction by pharmacological means (Bird and Kuhar, 1977; Korf, Bunney, and Aghajanian, 1974).

These basic findings led to the hypothesis that the noradrenergic system, interacting with opiate receptor systems, may mediate the physiological and affective changes associated with the administration of opiates as well as the syndrome of opiate withdrawal (Gold, Redmond, and Kleber,

1978b; Gold and Kleber, 1979). In a study designed to test the effects of clonidine on the symptoms of opiate withdrawal (Gold, Redmond, and Kleber, 1978b), addicted patients who were being maintained on methadone were abruptly withdrawn from methadone and allowed to develop significant withdrawal symptoms. Clonidine was then administered to these patients. In all cases, cessation of withdrawal symptoms took place within several hours. Subsequently, other studies have extended these findings to larger numbers of addicted patients with equally impressive results, demonstrating the efficacy of clonidine in opiate withdrawal (Gold and others, in press).

There is a striking similarity between the signs and symptoms of opiate withdrawal and those of naturally occurring panic anxiety (Gold and others, in press). Table 1 lists these common signs and symptoms. Despite

**Table 1. Common Signs and Symptoms of
Panic Anxiety and Opiate Withdrawal**

Signs	Increased heart rate
	Increased blood pressure
	Increased respiratory rate
	Pupillary dilation
	Increased perspiration
Symptoms	Anorexia
	Nausea
	Diarrhea
	Insomnia
	Irritability
	Restlessness
	Fear of death or impending danger

this similarity, the previous literature contains no reports of direct and quantitative comparison of these syndromes. In a recent investigation, ten opiate addicts and ten patients with panic disorder were studied (Gold, Sweeney, and Pottash, 1979). Observer and self-rating scales were administered to the opiate addicts during a baseline methadone maintenance period and then during acute withdrawal after discontinuation of methadone; and to patients with panic disorder during a baseline period and immediately upon the onset of at least two spontaneous panic attacks. The two groups did not differ during the baseline period. During withdrawal or panic, both groups showed significant increases in heart rate, blood pressure, temperature, tremulousness, anorexia, insomnia, restlessness, and gastrointestinal discomfort. The opiate withdrawal patients demonstrated a significantly greater elevation of anger and irritability than the patients with panic disorder, who, in turn, demonstrated greater elevation in fear ratings. Despite these differences, the data demonstrated quite clearly that the two syndromes overlap, suggesting that they may have a common neurobiological mediation and supporting the laboratory studies cited above on the role of the locus coeruleus in mediating fearful behavior.

We have also reviewed the clinical evidence supporting the importance of the noradrenergic system in stress. Further possible clinical support emerges from psychopharmacological studies of panic anxiety. Several studies have noted the efficacy of antidepressants, such as imipramine and phenelzine, in the treatment of panic disorder (Klein, Zitrin, and Woerner, 1977; Kelly and others, 1970; Sheehan, 1979). In general, antidepressants seem to be effective in reducing or eliminating spontaneous panic attacks but not in modifying the phobic anxiety that is frequently part of the syndrome in patients with panic disorder. The antidepressants that have been successful in this syndrome have, as one of their neurochemical effects, the release and/or reuptake blockade of norepinephrine (that is, they increase the functional availability of norepinephrine in the CNS). Like clonidine, norepinephrine inhibits the activity of the locus coeruleus (Cedarbaum and Aghajanian, 1977). Therefore, this locus coeruleus inhibitory mechanism may be partially responsible for the efficacy of antidepressants in panic anxiety. Clonidine also should alleviate panic symptoms. We have administered clonidine to two patients with panic disorder who had previously failed to respond to imipramine, a tricyclic antidepressant. Both patients showed significant decreases in frequency of panic attacks while on clonidine. These preliminary results are currently being pursued with larger numbers of subjects.

Summary

We have presented evidence to support the important role of the CNS noradrenergic system in forming the neurobiological substrate of stress or anxiety responses. This material may be summarized as follows:

1. Measurement of urinary MHPG (and, more recently, plasma MHPG), the primary CNS metabolite of norepinephrine, has been shown to be related to affective disorder and to stress.

2. Pharmacological, surgical, or electrical alteration of the function of the locus coeruleus, the major brain center controlling noradrenergic activity, is related to modification of fearful behavior in animals.

3. The drug clonidine, which inhibits the locus coeruleus and decreases brain levels of norepinephrine and MHPG, is effective in alleviating the symptoms of opiate withdrawal.

4. Opiate withdrawal and panic anxiety are strikingly similar in their symptoms, giving rise to the hypothesis that they have a common neurobiological mediation. Some antidepressants that inhibit the locus coeruleus

also reduce or eliminate both intensity and frequency of panic attacks in patients with this syndrome. There is some evidence that clonidine has at least an equally potent effect in this syndrome.

5. Measurement of noradrenergic function in clinical samples may help not only in categorizing individuals on the basis of their noradrenergic reactivity but also in designing new and more effective psychopharmacological treatments for anxiety in particular and the stress syndromes in general.

Part II

✻ ✻ ✻ ✻ ✻ ✻ ✻ ✻ ✻ ✻ ✻ ✻ ✻

Part Two of this volume contains chapters representing some of the most current research and theory in the stress field. The section begins with an elaboration of "the stress concept" by Hans Selye, the distinguished scientist and researcher who first expounded the consequences of stress on the human body over forty years ago. Selye first classifies and defines "stress," because it is, as he states, a term "too well known and too little understood." In his view, there are two general types of stress: "distress," which is unpleasant; and "eustress," which is pleasant. He then outlines the three stages of the general adaptation syndrome, detailing how the body reacts to stress on a physiological and hormonal level, and discusses the diseases of adaptation—how stress causes disease and how disease causes stress. Dr. Selye states that his concepts are merely a means of organizing a consistently observed set of phenomena; their use enables us to learn more about stress

Stress Research
and Findings

❋ ❋ ❋ ❋ ❋ ❋ ❋ ❋ ❋ ❋ ❋ ❋ ❋

and its consequences. Finally, he presents a "code of ethics" drawn from a wealth of experience—his own and that of his patients—on how best to cope with the stress of life.

In Chapter Eight, James C. Coyne and Richard S. Lazarus present their research and thinking in the areas of cognition and individual variation as they mediate the perception of external stress. Here, the individual's method of appraising his experience and using this information to cope is highlighted. Each individual's reaction to stress is unique, based on numerous psychological factors. Coyne and Lazarus argue that the relevant psychological and social processes must be directly examined in stress research.

In Chapter Nine, Thomas A. Wills and Thomas S. Langner discuss psychosocial stress from an epidemiological perspective. They review the research relating psychological disorder and socioeconomic status and conclude that individuals of lower socioeconomic status have a higher incidence of psychological disorder. Several factors make up the psychosocial stress of the lower classes: lack of control, insecurity and unpredictability of the future, lowered self-esteem, generalized demoralization, and fragmented social support systems. The authors elaborate each of these psychosocial stressors and present research that bears on it. Concluding the chapter, Wills and Langner discuss some implications for prevention and therapy.

Louis B. Schlesinger and Eugene Revitch elaborate, in Chapter Ten, the relationship of stress, violence, and some forms of criminal behavior. Stress is divided into two chief types: mainly external (social and situational) and mainly internal (psychogenic). A common consequence of external stress, such as poverty and other poor social conditions, is child abuse and domestic violence. Situational stress is also discussed as a determinant of about 70 percent of homicides and other violent crimes. Unresolved psychological conflicts that break into consciousness often place the individual in a state of great inner tension, resulting in explosive violent crime, often murder. The concept of catathymic crisis is discussed as an explanation of the psychodynamic process of these acts. Individuals with compulsive urges to act out fantasies of a violent or nonviolent, but still antisocial, nature experience extreme stress if they do not relieve the tension by the deed. Schlesinger and Revitch cite their own case material to illustrate all these points. The authors add a note about prevention and intervention, highlighting the role of internal and external stress.

Chapter Eleven pertains to the very current topic of life events, personality traits, and the onset of illness. Richard E. Minter and Chase P. Kimble present a comprehensive and systematic review of the available research. Throughout, we are cautioned to be particularly cognizant of the methodology of the various studies. The psychological variables discussed are life events, life stress, personality traits, and their interrelationship. Sick-role tendency, the effect of stress on others' behavior and on personality variables, and factors affecting visits to a physician are also considered. For the most part, the authors conclude that attempts to show a correlation between life stress or personality characteristics and illness are inconclusive because most studies have significant methodological flaws.

In the last chapter of this section, Joseph V. Brady, a pioneer in the research on the effects of stress and anxiety, reviews the experimental evidence in this field. He divides the chapter into classical and instrumental conditioning paradigms and comprehensively organizes the findings, illustrating many of the interesting relationships graphically. A variety of responses are dealt with, including the behavioral and the biochemical. The chapter provides mention of Brady's classic, early-1950 studies with his "executive monkeys," along with his most up-to-date neurochemical interests.

7

The Stress Concept Today

Hans Selye

❖ ❖ ❖ ❖ ❖ ❖ ❖ ❖ ❖ ❖ ❖ ❖ ❖

Stress, like relativity, is a scientific concept which has suffered from the mixed blessing of being too well known and too little understood. We are exposed to stress every moment of our lives, and our response to it often determines the quality of our life and health. Perhaps the first step is to learn exactly what stress is, because the more we know about its causes and effects, the better we are able to control them to our advantage.

Stress is the nonspecific response of the body to any demand. In some respects, every demand made on the body is unique; that is, *specific.* Heat, cold, joy, sorrow, muscular exertion, drugs, and hormones elicit highly specific responses. For example, heat produces sweating; cold produces shivering; exertion, such as cycling up a hill at top speed, predominantly affects the muscles and the cardiovascular system. All these agents, however, have one thing in common: they increase the demand for readjustment, for performance of adaptive functions which reestablish normalcy. This rise in requirements is independent of the specific activity that caused the increase. In that sense, the response is *nonspecific*.

The nonspecific adaptive response of the body to any agent or situation is always the same, regardless of the particular stimulus; what varies is the degree of response, which in turn depends only on the intensity of the demand for adjustment. Thus, it is immaterial whether the stress-producing factor—or *stressor,* as it is properly called—is pleasant or unpleasant. A game of chess, a kiss, pneumonia, and a broken finger all produce the same systemic reaction, though their specific results may be quite different or even completely opposite. While it is difficult to see how such essentially differing conditions can produce an identical reaction in the body, the truth of this has been experimentally verified beyond doubt.

Stress is not something to be avoided. Indeed, by definition, it cannot be avoided, since during every moment of our lives some demand for life-maintaining energy exists. Even while we are asleep, the heart, the respiratory apparatus, and many other organs continue to function. *Complete freedom from stress is death.*

Since nonspecific reactions to demands occur in lower animals, and even in plants, which have no nervous system, stress is not to be confused with nervous tension. Nor, as we have seen, is it always the nonspecific result of damage, since any kind of normal activity can produce considerable stress without causing harmful effects. However, we commonly distinguish between two types of stress: *eustress,* pleasant or curative stress; and *distress,* unpleasant or disease-producing stress.

The origins of the stress concept predate antiquity. Even prehistoric man must have recognized a common element in the loss of vigor and sense of exhaustion that overcame him after hard labor, intense fear, lengthy exposure to cold or heat, starvation, loss of blood, or any kind of strenuous exertion. First, the task was experienced as a hardship; then he grew used to it; finally, he could endure it no longer. In this way a few men, through subjective observation, may have learned to modify their behavior intuitively in order to exploit stress to their best advantage. However, objective research could not begin until measurable indexes of the body's reaction to stress were found.

The General Adaptation Syndrome (G.A.S.)

About forty years ago, in the course of experiments with rats, I learned that a variety of impure and toxic gland preparations produce a stereotyped syndrome, characterized by enlargement and hyperactivity of the adrenal cortex, atrophy of the thymus gland and lymph nodes, and the appearance of gastrointestinal ulcers. Further research showed that this triad and other simultaneously occurring organ changes can also be induced by heat, cold, infection, trauma, hemorrhage, nervous irritation, and many other stimuli. Some of these changes are merely signs of damage; others are manifestations of the body's mechanism of defense against these diverse agents. The entire syndrome, including its pattern of development in time, was called the *general adaptation syndrome*. The G.A.S. is made up of three stages:

1. *Alarm Reaction.* The organism's reaction when it is suddenly exposed to diverse stimuli to which it is not adapted. The reaction has two phases:
   a. *Shock phase.* The initial and immediate reaction to the noxious agent. Various signs of injury—such as tachycardia, loss of muscle tone, decreased temperature, and decreased blood pressure—are typical symptoms.
   b. *Countershock phase.* A rebound reaction marked by the mobilization of defensive phase, during which the adrenal cortex is enlarged and secretion of corticoid hormones is increased. (Most of the acute stress diseases correspond to these two phases of the alarm reaction.)
2. *Stage of Resistance.* The organism's full adaptation to the stressor and the consequent improvement or disappearance of symptoms. At this stage, however, there is a concurrent decrease in resistance to most other stimuli.
3. *Stage of Exhaustion.* Since adaptability is finite, exhaustion inexorably follows if the stressor is sufficiently severe and prolonged. Symptoms reappear, and, if stress continues unabated, death ensues.

With this formulation, the vague outlines of primitive man's intuitive perception of stress were brought into sharper focus and translated into precise scientific terms that could be appraised by intellect and tested by reason.

Adaptation Energy. The triphasic nature of the G.A.S. gave the first biological indication that the body's adaptability, or *adaptation energy,* is finite. Experiments on animals have shown that exposure to stressors can be tolerated only so long. We still do not know precisely what is lost, but something must be, or else, given enough food, the body would be able to resist indefinitely. After exhaustion from excessively stressful activity, sleep and rest can restore resistance and adaptability almost to previous levels, but the emphasis here is on the word *almost.* Just as any machine eventually wears out even if it has enough fuel, so the human body sooner or later becomes the victim of constant wear and tear.

The stages of the G.A.S. are analogous to the three stages of a man's life: childhood (with its characteristic low resistance and excessive responses to any kind of stimulation), adulthood (during which adaptation to most commonly encountered agents has occurred, and resistance is increased), and senility (characterized by irreversible loss of adaptability and eventual exhaustion, ending with death).

It is still too early to say whether this connection between age and the G.A.S. is real or only apparent. All we know is that every biological activity causes wear and tear; it leaves permanent "chemical scars," which accumulate to constitute the signs of aging. In this way, aging may be regarded as the sum of all the stresses to which the body has been exposed during a lifetime. A newborn baby, while crying and struggling, is under considerable stress but shows no trace of aging, whereas a man of 90 sleeping quietly in his bed is unmistakably old.

Adaptation energy has not been shown to exist in the same way that, for example, caloric energy has. Rather, it is a convenient symbol that sheds some light on a process about which we are still much in the dark. If we picture extraterrestrials looking down and trying to understand how a car runs and why it may break down although it has all the gasoline it needs, we get an inkling of the problem that scientists face with the human body. These beings might speak about a car's "drivability," or driving energy, which, once exhausted, causes the car to break down permanently. They see that with a reckless driver the car breaks down much more quickly, and they may recognize the value of good driving in allowing the car the longest possible life. They know that if something goes wrong a car may be repaired, even as a living body may be helped to cure itself. However, with their limited information, they cannot wholly understand the causes of the many breakdowns a car is subject to, and so they introduce the idea of drivability.

Like all metaphors, this one has its limitations. We know the mechanics of a car well enough to make the concept of drivability unnecessary. But while a car does not have "drivability," in man adaptation energy may indeed exist. In any case, until we find evidence to the contrary, it is useful to speak as if it did.

There seem to be two types of adaptation energy: the superficial kind, which is ready to use; and the deeper kind, which acts as a sort of frozen reserve. When superficial adaptation energy is exhausted during exertion, it can slowly be restored from a deeper store during rest. Thus, acute fatigue automatically stops us from wasting adaptation energy too lavishly in certain foolish moments. The restoration of the superficial adaptation energy from the deep reserves tricks us into believing that the loss has been made good, when actually all we have done is transfer adaptation energy from a less accessible to a more accessible form.

Mechanisms of the G.A.S. The identity of the alarm signals that first relay the stress message has yet to be determined. These signals may be metabolic by-products released during activity or damage, or they may be the lack of some vital substance consumed whenever any demand is made on an organ. Since the only two coordinating systems that connect all parts of the body with one another are the nervous and the vascular systems, we can assume that the alarm signals use one or both of these pathways. While nervous stimulation may cause a general stress response, denervated rats still show the classic syndrome when put under stress; so the nervous system cannot be the only route. It is probable that often, if not always, the signals travel in the blood. Alternatively, perhaps no one substance or deficiency has a monopoly on acting as an alarm signal; instead, perhaps a number of messengers carry the same signal. The various cells could send out different messengers, as long as their messages would somehow be tallied by the organs of adaptation, such as the pituitary.

Whatever the nature of the *first mediator,* however, its existence is assured by its effects, which have been observed and even measured. The discharge of ACTH, the involution of the lymphatic organs, the enlargement of the adrenals, the corticoid hormone content of the blood, the feeling of fatigue, and many other signs of stress can all be produced by injury or activity in any part of the body. Some way must exist to send messengers from any cell to the organs which are so uniformly affected by all stressors.

Through this first mediator, the stressor eventually excites the hypothalamus, a complex bundle of nerve cells and fibers that acts as a bridge between the brain and the endocrine system (see Figure 1). The resulting nervous signals reach certain neuroendocrine cells in the median eminence (ME) of the hypothalamus, where they are transformed into CRF (corticotrophic hormone-releasing factor), a chemical messenger. In this way, a message is relayed to the pituitary, causing a discharge of ACTH (adrenocorticotrophic hormone) into the general circulation.

Upon reaching the adrenal cortex, ACTH triggers the secretion of corticoids, mainly glucocorticoids, such as cortisol or corticosterone. These compounds supply a readily available source of energy for the adaptive reactions necessary to meet the demands made by the stressor agent. The corticoids also facilitate various other enzyme responses and suppress immune reactions as well as inflammation, thereby helping the body to coexist with pathogens.

Normally secreted in lesser amounts are the proinflammatory corticoids, which stimulate the proliferative ability and reactivity of the connective tissue, enhancing the "inflammatory potential." Thus, they help to put up a strong barricade of connective tissue, which protects the body from further invasion by the pathogenic stressor agent. Because of their prominent effect on salt and water metabolism, these hormones (for example, desoxycorticosterone and aldosterone) are also referred to as "mineralocorticoids." The somatotrophic hormone (STH) of the pituitary likewise stimulates defense reactions.

Figure 1. Principal Pathways Mediating the Response to a Stressor Agent
and the Conditioning Factors that Modify Its Effect.

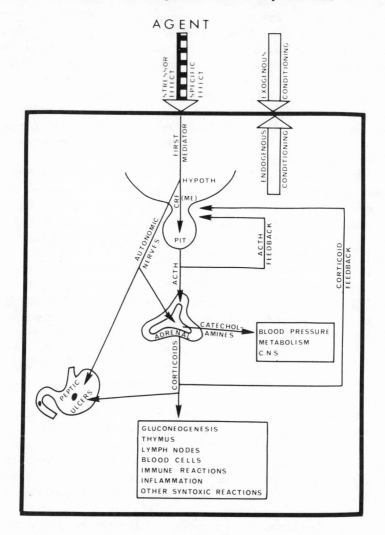

As soon as any agent acts on the body (thick outer frame of the diagram), the resulting effect will depend on three factors (broad vertical arrows pointing to the upper horizontal border of the frame). All agents possess both nonspecific stressor effects (solid part of arrow) and specific properties (interrupted part of arrow). The other two heavy vertical arrows, pointing toward the upper border of the frame, represent exogenous and endogenous conditioning factors, which largely determine the reactivity of the body. Since all stressors have some specific effects, they cannot elicit exactly the same response in all organs. Furthermore, even the same agent will act differently in different individuals, depending on the internal and external conditioning factors that determine their reactivity. (Reprinted by courtesy of Butterworths, Reading, Mass., from H. Selye, *Stress in Health and Disease,* 1976.)

This chain of events is cybernetically controlled by several biofeedback mechanisms. For instance, if there is a surplus of ACTH, a short-loop feedback returns some of it to the hypothalamus-pituitary axis, and this axis shuts off further ACTH production. In addition, through a long-loop feedback, a high blood level of corticoids similarly inhibits too much ACTH secretion.

At the same time as these events are taking place, another important pathway is utilized to mediate the stress response. Other stress hormones, such as catecholamines, are liberated to activate mechanisms of general adaptation. Adrenaline in particular is secreted to make available energy, to accelerate the pulse rate, to elevate blood pressure and the rate of blood circulation in the muscles, and to stimulate the central nervous system (CNS). The blood coagulation mechanism is also enhanced as a protection against excessive bleeding if injuries are sustained in the encounter with the stressor.

Innumerable other hormonal and chemical changes check and balance the body's functioning and stability, constituting a virtual arsenal of weapons by which the organism defends itself for survival.

Undoubtedly, in man, with his highly developed central nervous system, emotional arousal is one of the most frequent activators of the G.A.S. Yet it cannot be regarded as the only factor, since typical stress reactions can occur in patients exposed to trauma or hemorrhage while under deep anesthesia. Since stress is not necessarily the result of nervous arousal, many experts in this field speak more precisely of "neurogenic stress" or "psychogenic stress" when this particular form is meant.

According to Mason (1975a), when psychological influences are minimized, stressors such as heat and fasting do not provoke certain hormonal responses characteristic of stress, while other stressors, such as cold and hypoxia, continue to evoke these reactions. I agree with him, but, in my opinion, all this is explained by the effects of different conditioning factors and by the well-documented fact that not all stressors reach the headquarters of the "hypophysiotrophic area" in the hypothalamus through the same pathways. There is no doubt that humoral stimuli can initiate the stress response, even when emotional arousal or any other cortical stimuli are no longer able to reach centers producing the corticotrophic hormone-releasing factor (CRF).

In addition to the general adaptation syndrome, there develops in tissues more directly affected by stress a *local adaptation syndrome* (L.A.S.). Inflammation is undoubtedly one of the most important features of this response. Chemical alarm signals are sent out by the directly affected tissues, from the L.A.S. area to the coordinating regions in the nervous system and hence to the endocrine glands, especially the pituitary and the adrenals. The endocrine regulators participate in the control of localized inflammation and also produce hormones to combat wear and tear on the body. Hence, there are close interactions between the L.A.S. and the G.A.S. A primarily local stress, if sufficiently severe, can produce a G.A.S., and general stress influences the L.A.S.

The Stress Response. The stress response has a tripartite mechanism, consisting of (1) the direct effect of the stressor on the body; (2) internal responses that stimulate tissue defense or help to destroy damaging substances; and (3) internal responses that cause tissue surrender by inhibiting unnecessary or excessive defense.

Every agent that acts on the human body, from outside or from within, does certain things more than others. Those that it does more are relatively specific or characteristic for the agent, as compared to those that it does less. The latter, the nonspecific actions, may therefore be viewed as incidental side effects. But they are incidental only from the standpoint of classical medicine, which is always interested in the specific causes of disease and the specific cures with which to combat them. Stress research is primarily concerned with nonspecific actions. Whatever our point of view, we must keep in mind that, in actual practice, it is impossible to separate the specific from the nonspecific effects. For example, the end result of exposure to any of the agents represented by the double arrows in Figure 2 could not be the same, even though their stressor effects are identical. The two

**Figure 2. The Stressor (Solid Arrows) and the Specific (Broken Arrows)
Actions of Three Agents.**

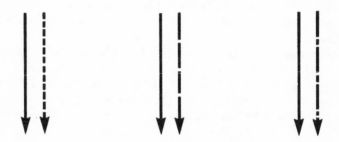

types of actions of the same agent can influence one another. Here the nonspecific effects are conditioned (modified) by the specific effects of each agent. Indeed, the specific actions of agents can, even totally, block certain nonspecific effects whenever the two happen to be diametrical opposites. The inevitable modifying and masking by specific actions was one of the main reasons why it took so long to draw a clear picture of stress as such.

This state of affairs is encountered whenever we try to make any generalization. For instance, one of the typical features of the G.A.S. is its characteristic blood sugar curve. However, if stress is produced by the injection of insulin (the antidiabetic hormone of the pancreas), the typical blood sugar response will be obscured, because the specific action of insulin is to lower the blood sugar at all times. It would be false to conclude that the blood sugar is not an indicator of stress or that insulin cannot produce a G.A.S. The stressor effect of insulin can still be recognized because, like all other stressors, at excessive dose levels, the hormone causes adrenocortical stimulation, thymus involution, and so forth. We have learned this lesson by examining many effects of many agents.

Syntoxic and Catatoxic Agents. Adaptive hormones are collectively called *syntoxic* when they facilitate coexistence with a pathogen, either by diminishing sensitivity to it or by encapsulating it within a barricade of inflammatory tissue. In contrast, catatoxic hormones enhance the destruction of potential pathogens, mostly through the induction of poison-metabolizing enzymes in the liver.

Syntoxic and catatoxic reactions are the body's only defense against internal stressors. When the stressor comes from outside, however, a third possibility exists: instead of putting up with the enemy or trying to destroy him, one may attempt to escape from the enemy. Walter Cannon spoke of the "fight-or-flight response" of an organism to its environment: an emergency discharge of adrenaline quickens the pulse rate, raises the blood pressure to improve blood circulation to the muscles, and stimulates the central nervous system; digestion by the stomach and intestine is temporarily suspended; blood clots more quickly to protect against excessive bleeding if injuries are sustained during its encounter with the stressor; and the blood sugar is raised to supply additional energy to the muscles. These changes represent different phases of the alarm reaction to stressors.

Cross-Resistance and Cross-Sensitization. Even the earliest studies on the G.A.S. showed that several stressors applied simultaneously can have a cumulative effect. For example, cold and hunger decrease resistance to almost any stressor, and concurrent application of various drugs and/or physical agents may result in an increase of their stressor potency. In such instances, it became customary to speak of "cross-sensitization." On the other hand, during or immediately following an alarm reaction produced by one stressor, there may develop a "cross-resistance" against the damaging effect of another. In all these instances, it is important to distinguish between specific and truly nonspecific or stressor effects. Certain agents (for example, specific antidotes, blocking agents, and remedies, as well as factors that cause specific hypersensitivity) may augment or diminish the toxicity of another agent merely because they increase or decrease the specific effect of the other.

Cross-resistance and cross-sensitization depend on a large number of factors, such as intensity and duration of the stressor action, associated specific effects of the stressors, genetic background, and species susceptibility. It is unlikely that all forms of cross-resistance or cross-sensitization rely on a single mechanism: a pituitary or adrenal hormone discharge could hardly be implicated in the types of cross-resistance that have been demonstrated after those organs have been removed.

According to one theory, schizophrenics are less responsive to stressors because they are already under stress, and virtually all forms of so-called nonspecific prophylaxis and therapy (for example, muscular exercise, hot or cold baths, and shock treatments) are actually instances of cross-resistance.

Since there are no two identical individuals, it is not surprising that the same stressor may affect different people in different ways and to different degrees. We all know that in the same room some people can feel too hot, others too cold, and others just right. There exist many endogenous and exogenous factors that can selectively enhance or inhibit a stress response. "Endogenous" refers to such internal factors as genetic predisposition, sex, age, early training, and previous damage to specific organs, while "exogenous" applies to the many external conditions operating at the time of the stress, such as treatment with drugs or hormones, dietary deficiencies, and the physical surroundings. Most exogenous conditioning agents may be regarded as acting through cross-resistance or cross-sensitization, as long as their effect is nonspecific.

Diseases of Adaptation. Stressors can disrupt homeostasis in two ways: by being beyond our power of adaptability or by causing disease because there is a particular weakness in the structure of our organism. Think of a chain placed under tension—that is, physical stress. No matter what pulls on the chain and no matter in which direction, the result is the same—in other words, *nonspecific.* The chain is faced with a demand for resistance. Just as in the chain the weakest link (or in a machine the least resistant part) is most likely to break down, so in the human body there is always one organ or system which, owing to heredity or external influences, is the weakest and most likely to break down under general biological stress. In some people the heart, in others the nervous system or the gastrointestinal tract, may represent this weakest link. That is why people develop different types of diseases under the influence of the same kind of stressor. That is also why, strictly speaking, the pure stage of exhaustion is never reached. Before all adaptation energy is depleted, the weakest link breaks down, causing an immediate general collapse. Although I have performed over one thousand autopsies, I have not come across one case of death from old age, where all parts of the body, wearing at equal rates, give in at the same time.

Every disease, of course, causes stress, since it imposes demands for adaptation upon the organism. In turn, stress plays some role in the development of every disease; its effects are added to the specific changes caused by the disease, and may be curative or damaging, depending on whether the stress reactions combat or accentuate the trouble.

Unremitting stress can break down the body's protective mechanisms. This is true both of adaptation that depends on chemical immunity and of that due to inflammatory barricades. Therefore, when we are run down, we are far more likely to "catch" a malady that, in peak condition, we could usually resist. Potentially pathogenic microbes are in or around us all the time; yet they cause no disease until we are exposed to stress. In this case, the illness is due neither to the microbe nor to stress but to the combined effect of both. In most instances, *disease is due neither to the germ as such nor to our adaptive reactions as such but to the inadequacy of our reactions against the germ.*

Diseases in whose development the nonspecific stressor effects of the eliciting pathogen play a major role are called *diseases of adaptation,* or stress diseases. But just as there is no pure stressor—that is, an agent that causes only the nonspecific response and has no specific action—so there are no pure diseases of adaptation. Some nonspecific components participate in the pathogenesis of every malady, but no disease is due to stress alone, since the cause of nonspecific responses will always be modified by various "conditioning factors" that enhance, diminish, or otherwise alter disease proneness.

In stress research, the term *conditioning* is not used in the Pavlovian sense but in the sense of setting the conditions for something to take place (for example, susceptibility or resistance). In relation to psychological and psychiatric problems, conditioning factors are undoubtedly of great importance. Overdosage with corticoids and similar steroid compounds can cause a state of excitation, followed by deep anesthesia; mineralocorticoids may produce damage to brain vessels conducive to epileptoid convulsions or serious disturbances of neuromuscular functions, which resemble those seen in familial periodic paralysis. The production of convulsions by metrazol or electroshock can be greatly influenced by steroid hormones; androgenic and estrogenic hormones (which are produced by the gonads and also by the adrenals) exert an important effect on the sexual and fighting instincts. Most important among these conditioning factors are the specific effects of the primary pathogen and the factors influencing the body's reactivity by endogenous or exogenous conditioners. Hence, the diseases of adaptation cannot be ascribed to any one pathogen but only to "pathogenic constellations"; they are pluricausal or multifactorial diseases, which depend on the simultaneous effect of several potentially pathogenic factors that alone would not always produce disease.

The justification for calling any malady a disease of adaptation is directly proportional to the role that maladjustment to stress plays in its development. In some instances (for example, in surgical shock), stress may be by far the most important pathogenic factor. In other cases (instantly lethal intoxications, traumatic injuries to the spinal cord, most congenital malformations), it is of little or no significance, either because the damage is inflicted so rapidly that there is no time for any adaptive process or because the pathogen is highly specific. In the latter event, whatever develops represents a secondary result and is not the primary component. Typical diseases of adaptation are due to insufficient, excessive, or faulty reactions to stressors, as in inappropriate hormonal or nervous responses. Thus, the term should be used only when the maladaptation factor appears to be more important than the eliciting pathogen itself.

Some diseases in which stress is particularly important are kidney disorders, high blood pressure, hardening of the arteries, heart accidents, gastric or duodenal ulcers (the "stress ulcers"), and various types of mental disturbances.

The pathogenicity of many systemic and local stressors depends largely on the function of the hypothalamus-pituitary-adrenal axis, which may either enhance or mitigate the body's defense reactions against stressors. We think that derailments of this adaptive mechanism are the principal factors in the production of certain maladies, which we therefore consider to be essentially "diseases of adaptation."

Among the derailments of the G.A.S. that may cause disease, the following are particularly important:

1. An absolute excess or deficiency in the amount of adaptive hormones —for example, corticoids, ACTH, and STH (the somatotrophic hormone, also known as the growth hormone)—produced during stress.
2. An absolute excess or deficiency in the amount of adaptive hormones retained (or "fixed") by their peripheral target organs during stress.
3. A disproportion in the relative secretion (or "fixation") during stress of various antagonistic adaptive hormones; for example, ACTH and antiphlogistic (antiinflammatory) corticoids, on the one hand, and STH and prophlogistic (proinflammatory) corticoids, on the other.
4. The production by stress of metabolic derangements which abnormally alter the target organ's response to adaptive hormones through the phenomenon of "conditioning."
5. The abnormal response to the G.A.S. of participating organs, other than those involved in the hypothalamus-pituitary-adrenal mechanism (for example, the nervous system, liver, and kidney).

Direct and Indirect Pathogens. Direct pathogens are those that act directly against the body irrespective of any vital tissue reaction. Thus, mechanical trauma, intense heat, and strong acids or alkalies will cause tissue damage irrespective of the body's response and, more particularly, of the defensive reactions characteristic of stress. That these pathogens are really direct and independent of any vital activity is best demonstrated by the fact that they will affect even a cadaver, which obviously could not develop morbid lesions as a consequence of its own vital reactions. Other examples of direct pathogens are endotoxins, spinal cord transection, and x-radiation. Their effects (fever, paralysis, the radiation syndrome) are not evident after death, yet they do act directly, to a large extent. It is true that the body's defensive reactions (particularly the stress response) can be elicited by direct pathogens in the living organisms as a secondary consequence of their specific effects. However, these specific actions are not, or only very slightly, influenced by the stress they produce.

Indirect pathogens act only, or predominantly, through the excessive or inappropriate defensive reactions that they elicit. For example, the main purpose of inflammation is to localize irritants by enclosing them within a barricade of inflammatory tissue. This prevents their spread into the blood, which could lead to blood poisoning and death. However, there are times when, as in the case of allergy, the foreign agent itself is harmless and causes trouble only by inciting inflammation. Here, inflammation is what we experience as the disease, and so the invader is an indirect pathogen. Again, the rejection of grafts and transplants represents an immunological reaction that evolved to protect organisms against potentially dangerous foreign materials, but in these cases the mechanisms are inappropriate and man can improve on nature by suppressing them.

In a sense, inflammation is intermediate between syntoxic and catatoxic responses. The encapsulation of a potential pathogen, or its enmeshment in a restraining tissue mass, is syntoxic, since it merely permits coexistence with an aggressor by separating it from the rest of the body. However, when this separtion is followed by aggression, through inflammatory cells and enzymes, a true catatoxic element is added, since these latter responses are designed to destroy the enemy, not merely to ignore it.

Homeostasis and Heterostasis. One of the most characteristic features of all living beings is their ability to maintain the constancy of their internal milieu, despite changes in the surroundings. The physical properties and chemical composition of our body fluids and tissues tend to remain remarkably constant despite all the changes around us. For instance, if we are exposed to extreme cold or heat, our bodies will try to maintain a constant temperature. If this self-regulatory power fails, disease or even death will ensue. Homeostasis, the staying power of the body in an ever-changing environment, is therefore the all-important criterion of health.

The aim of the body's stress response is to restore its internal equilibrium, which the stressor has upset. Natural mechanisms usually are enough to maintain the fixity of the internal milieu; however, during exceptionally heavy demands, ordinary homeostasis is not enough. The "thermostat of defense" must be raised to a higher level. For this process, I proposed the term *heterostasis:* the establishment of a new steady state by treatment with agents that stimulate the physiological adaptive mechanisms through the development of normally dormant defensive tissue reactions. In both homeostasis and heterostasis, the internal milieu participates actively.

In homeostatic defense, the potential pathogen automatically activates usually adequate catatoxic or syntoxic mechanisms; when these do not suffice, natural catatoxic or syntoxic agents in additional quantities can be administered by the physician. These agents are not the same as, for example, antibiotics, which combat disease without the body's active participation. Heterostasis depends on treatment with artificial remedies that have no direct curative effect but can stimulate the production of unusually high amounts of the body's own natural chemical defenses despite abnormally high demands, which could not be met without outside help.

The most salient difference between homeostasis and heterostasis is that the former maintains a normal steady state by physiological means, whereas the latter "resets the thermostat" of resistance to a heightened defensive capacity by artificial interventions from the outside.

Implications

Now that the main features of stress have been introduced, a final word of caution is needed. The stress concept is a tentative explanation of proven facts and should not be taken too literally. In science in general, and in biology particularly, the measure of a theory is in its usefulness; it does not attempt to be right in the same sense as a mathematical problem. I said some fifty years ago, "Our facts must be correct; our theories need not be as long as they are useful in inventing new facts." So it is with the stress concept. I have coined the phrase *general adaptation syndrome* to describe a set of symptoms consistently observed in a variety of situations. A common denominator must exist; I have called it *biological stress.*

Similarly, the alarm reaction, the stage of resistance, and the stage of exhaustion are not as distinct as they may look on paper. How much simpler things would be if they were! However, they are artificial divisions of what in nature is a continuous process. The transition from one to another is gradual, like a spectrum. As in our division of visible light, we distinguish between red, yellow, blue, when actually there are no sharp lines of division between them.

I have tried to make the same thing clear concerning the first mediator. There must be a first link in the chain of effects, regardless of whether that first link be a substance, a chemical deficiency, several distinct things, or a combination. *There must be a first link.* Until we know more about it, let us simply call it the "first mediator."

I have also pointed out that no diseases are caused only by maladaptation to stress. However, when stress plays a critical role, the term *disease of adaptation* is appropriate, just as it is appropriate to call certain other sicknesses pneumonia, leukemia, and colds, though they are not exclusively related to pneumococci, leukocytes, or cold.

The purpose of this digression has been to explain what is usually tacitly assumed but which not everyone realizes: while in the study of nature, as in nature itself, pure black or pure white does not exist, it is often necessary to assume otherwise. Once this is understood, no confusion will arise when we speak of stress, adaptation energy, the stage of exhaustion, or diseases of adaptation, as if not only their effects but they themselves were concrete, rather than merely useful abstractions.

Undoubtedly, many psychosomatic derangements are due to stress and particularly to derailments of the G.A.S. The most common stress-induced minor nervous derangements are headaches, chronic fatigue, and bruxism (gnashing of teeth). These and many types of neurotic behavior are often viewed as manifestations of maladjustment to the stress of life.

Stress is also important in the pathogenesis of various types of war neuroses, stuttering, motor disturbances, autism, and anorexia nervosa. Floating anxiety, with its characteristic vague fears and uneasiness, may be regarded as a mildly pathological way of reacting to stress. As with schizophrenia, there seems to be a predisposition to anxiety in some people, which may be aroused by stressful life situations.

Diseases, particularly diseases of adaptation, often depend not so much on the apparent pathogen as on the way we react to it. The same may be said of stress itself. We have already seen the importance of conditioning in this respect. Some of these factors we have little control over. Often, however, deliberate effort, guided by an understanding of stress and of ourselves, can accomplish a lot.

Some general ways of dealing with stress include (1) removing unnecessary stressors from our lives, (2) not allowing certain neutral events to become stressors, (3) developing a proficiency in dealing with conditions that we do not want to or cannot avoid, and (4) seeking relaxation or diversion from the demand. In addition, we must learn to recognize "overstress" (hyperstress), when we have exceeded the limits of our adaptability; or "understress" (hypostress), when we suffer from lack of self-realization (physical immobility, boredom, sensory deprivation).

The stress of life has four basic variations (shown in Figure 3), although in their most characteristic nonspecific manifestations they all depend on the same central phenomenon. Our goal should be to strike a balance between the equally destructive forces of hypo- and hyperstress, to find as much eustress as possible, and to minimize distress. Clearly, we cannot run away timidly from every unpleasant experience; in order to achieve our purposes, we must often put up with unhappiness, at least for a time. Here faintheartedness would in the long run prove even more distressing, by depriving us of the joy of ultimate success. Unnecessary or too much distress—all distress, in general, that does not hold promise of eustress—is what is to be avoided.

From what the laboratory and the clinical study of somatic diseases have taught me concerning stress, I have tried to arrive at a code of ethics

Figure 3. The Four Basic Variations of Stress.

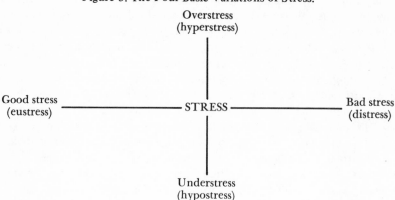

based on the scientifically verifiable laws that govern the body's reactions in maintaining homeostasis and living in satisfying equilibrium with its surroundings.

It is a biological law that man—like the lower animals—must fight and work for some goal that he considers worthwhile. We must use our innate capacities to enjoy the eustress of fulfillment. Only through effort, often aggressive egoistic effort, can we maintain our fitness and assure our homeostatic equilibrium with the surrounding society and the inanimate world. If we are to achieve this state, our activities must earn lasting results; the fruits of work must be cumulative and must provide a capital to meet future needs. To succeed, we have to accept the scientifically established fact that man has an inescapable urge to work egoistically for things that can be stored to strengthen his homeostasis in the unpredictable situations with which life may confront him. These are not instincts we should combat or be ashamed of. We can do nothing about having been built to work, and it is primarily for our own good. Organs that are not used (muscles, bones, even the brain) undergo inactivity atrophy, and every living being looks out first of all for itself.

How, then, can we develop a code of ethics that accepts egoism and working to hoard personal capital as morally correct? I shall summarize my main conclusions in the form of three basic guidelines:

1. *Find your own natural predilections and stress level.* People differ with regard to the amount and kind of work they consider worth doing to meet the exigencies of daily life and to assure their future security and happiness. In this respect, all of us are influenced by hereditary predispositions and the expectations of our society. Only through planned self-analysis can we establish what we really want; too many people suffer all their lives because they are too conservative to risk a radical change and break with traditions.

2. *Practice altruistic egoism.* The selfish hoarding of the good will, respect, esteem, support, and love of our neighbors is the most efficient way to give vent to our pent-up energy and create enjoyable, beautiful, or useful things.

3. *Earn thy neighbor's love.* This motto, unlike "Love thy neighbor as thyself," is compatible with man's biological structure, and although it is based on altruistic egoism, it can hardly be attacked as unethical. Who would blame him who wants to assure his own homeostasis and happiness by accumulating the treasure of other people's benevolence toward him? Yet this makes him virtually unassailable, for nobody wants to attack and destroy those upon whom he depends.

These are the main principles derived from observations of the basic mechanisms that maintain homeostasis in cells, people, and entire societies, and that help them face the stressors encountered in their constant fight for survival, security, and well-being. Once they are understood and clearly formulated, we can use them best by conscious control.

It must, however, be clearly understood that there is no universal prescription for success. I think the best that a professional investigator of stress can do is to explain the mechanisms involved as far as he understands them; to outline the way he thinks this knowledge could be applied to daily life; and, finally, to describe how he himself applied it, leaving the reader to judge how successful these efforts can be to him.

This last I have attempted elsewhere, particularly in *The Stress of My Life* (Selye, 1977). Here I may best finish by recounting the story of the alcoholic's two sons: one a teetotaler and the other a drunk. When asked to explain their drinking habits, both replied, "With a father like that, what do you expect?" This illustrates perhaps the most important moral that we can draw from stress research: that it is not what we face but how we face it that matters. Though internal and external factors influence or even determine some responses, we do have limited control over ourselves. It is the exercise of this control, or the lack of it, that can decide whether we are made or broken by the stress of life.

8

Cognitive Style, Stress Perception, and Coping

James C. Coyne
Richard S. Lazarus

❖ ❖ ❖ ❖ ❖ ❖ ❖ ❖ ❖ ❖ ❖ ❖ ❖

Thirty years ago, psychological stress researchers were primarily interested in the answers to two questions: "Under what conditions of stress does human performance deteriorate?" and "Who are the people most vulnerable to such deterioration?" (see Lazarus, Deese, and Osler, 1952). Interest in these questions continues, and many issues remain unresolved, but the scope of stress theory and research has greatly expanded to include the determinants of morale, social functioning, and physical health. Consider the striking increase in research examining stress and coping processes thought to influence not only the etiology and onset of disease but also the experience, course, and outcome of illness, as well as the utilization of medical care and compliance

Note: Writing of this chapter was supported in part by a research grant from the National Institute on Aging (AG 00799).

with and response to treatment (Moos, 1977). Within medicine, there is a growing recognition than an exclusion of psychosocial considerations distorts perspectives and interferes with patient care, and there is a demand that the dominant biomedical model of disease be expanded to a broader biopsychosocial model (Engel, 1977), in which psychological stress has a key role.

The past thirty years have also witnessed some fundamental changes in the way in which stress is conceptualized. The limitations of simple drive and tension reduction and linear stimulus-response (S-R) concepts have become apparent. Psychological stress is now viewed as a general rubric for somewhat different though related processes of person-environment transaction, in which demands tax or exceed the resources of the person. Such stress is neither simply an environmental stimulus, a characteristic of the person, nor a response, but a balance between demands and the power to deal with them without unreasonable or destructive costs. Our model of stress is explicitly cognitive-phenomenological, emphasizing how the person appraises what is being experienced and uses this information in coping to shape the course of events. This appraisal of the significance of an ongoing relationship with the environment for one's well-being leads to coping processes consistent with personal agendas. The effects of the coping are in turn appraised and reacted to as part of the continuous flow of psychological, social, and physiological processes and events. Stressful commerce with the environment thus involves extensive psychological mediation and reciprocal feedback loops, which cannot be reduced to stimulus and response terms. The nature of stress phenomena therefore requires that any comprehensive model of it be developed within a transactional, process-oriented perspective.

What are the implications of adopting such a perspective, and how does it differ from more traditional approaches? Dewey and Bentley (1949, p. 108) propose three levels of organization of inquiry through which the development of knowledge and the history of science progress: *self-action,* where things are viewed as acting under their own power; *interaction,* where thing is balanced against thing in causal interaction; and *transaction,* where systems of description and naming are employed to deal with aspects and phases of action, without final attribution to "elements" or other presumptively detachable or independent "entities." Nineteenth-century instinct theory can be classified as an inquiry at the self-action level. Current structural models of stress, which emphasize environmental stressors, dispositional properties of persons, and stress responses, are at an interactional level. Conventional studies of stress thus assume that person and environment exist as substantially separate entities and that key person and environment variables can be described prior to their connection to each other. With these variables as static or "given," attention can be focused on their action and reaction rather than on any reorganization or redefinition of the variables themselves. The search is for linear sequential causation. As an alternative, the transactional level of inquiry assumes that prior knowledge of person or environment alone is inadequate and that key person and environment variables must be designated relationally. No constituents of the ongoing flow of stress and coping can be specified completely apart from the specification of other constituents. Furthermore, the designation of variables as independent and dependent, antecedent and consequential, is merely provisional and can be revised as needed. Variables can thus be redesignated, redetermined, and renamed as the observer's interest in phases of ongoing events shifts.

When one thinks in process-oriented, transactional terms and acknowledges the existence of feedback loops, he is forced to abandon firm notions of linear causality. The designation of variable a as coming first and variable b as determined by it is recognized as dependent on where one chooses to break continuity of process. One might just as well start with variable b as a determinant of subsequent changes in variable a. The fact that a transactional description is inherently circular is not to be deplored but exploited in observation, description, and theory building (Dewey and Bentley, 1949; Riegel and Meacham, 1978; Watzlawick, Beavin, and Jackson, 1967). However, it remains legitimate to dissect a transactional description of stress in order to make our analysis of it provisionally deterministic and therefore researchable. Indeed, a failure to propose ways of defining stress has thus far limited the impact of proponents of transaction in psychology, such as the communications theorists and the dialectical movement. We can partition our relational categories of description into person and environment antecedent variables and employ an analytic model following the logic of analysis of variance. Problems arise only when we accept our partitioning of variables as necessary, fixed, or the sole distinctions that can be made, or when we interpret statistical interaction of static or structural variables as if it represented direct observation of actual transactional processes (Lazarus and Launier, 1978).

Unfortunately, confusion arising from such problems dominates the study of stress. We have distinct bodies of literature focusing on antecedent environmental conditions of stress, on intervening states and traits, and on responses to stress. With apologies and compromises, these conflicting definitions side-slip across each other, with little coherence and minimal integrative efforts. Fractions of variance accounted for by arbitrary partitioning and sampling of person and environment variables are interpreted as if they represented proportions of causal responsibility. Linear causal relationships, dictated by the constraints of experimental design, are taken as adequate representations of what occur naturalistically as mutually causative, reciprocal relationships.

Many researchers in this area make one or at best a few assessments of persons and situations and assume that they have identified relatively stable traits or properties. The relevant psychological and social processes—

how the subjects construe or appraise their ongoing transactions with the environment, how they cope, the social contexts of adaptation, and the kinds of patterns involved—are inferred rather than directly examined. Yet it is these very processes that enable any personal or environmental characteristics to be expressed in somatic disturbance or adaptational failure and that allow some individuals to handle a given stressful event better than other individuals do. Moreover, the assumed correspondence between stable characteristics of persons or environments and actual process often does not hold. For example, trait measures of coping have been related to the strength of stress responses before and after surgery, and it has been assumed that the inferred coping processes account for differences in reaction. However, in some instances no relationship has been found between trait measures of coping and the actual process of coping that has been observed (Cohen and Lazarus, 1973).

From a transactional perspective, many of the current problems in the study of stress result from the employment of rigid structural concepts; that is, from the reification of the particular variables and the sequence chosen for study. The solution lies in giving up the comfortable myth that a single order of phenomena dominates the psychological world, and the related myth that a study of certain basic elements and their relations can enable one to arrive at a final analysis of a psychological event. Instead, a transactional explanation consists of explicating *for some purpose* the quality of a psychological process that we find important or interesting. That entails a description of its spread in time, the strands or textures supporting the quality of the process, and its relationship to its context (Jenkins, 1974, p. 794).

Thus, in examining the role of a person's cognitive appraisal in a coping episode, we might look to the particular combination of personal and situational variables fused in the appraisal, whether it be threat, harm-loss, or challenge; the resultant patterns of emotion and coping efforts; and how these, along with environmental response, feed back to subsequent appraisals. Therefore, we recognize a two-way street between cognition and emotion. Rather than mechanisms or well-delineated structures, psychological processes and their contexts are the units of analysis within a transactional perspective. The boundaries of the process and its relevant context are determined by the purposes of the analysis and can be expected to vary in accordance with our interests.

Traditional research methodologies retain a legitimate place within such a perspective, but they are subject to a more intense critical scrutiny than before. An experimental paradigm does not always make a significant contribution to knowledge because its situation is often unrepresentative and artificial (Jenkins, 1974). For instance, traditional interest in the effects of stress on task performance has been revived in the learned helplessness paradigm, and it has been asserted that learned helplessness is a suitable model for a variety of naturalistic phenomena, including depression (Seligman, 1975). A large body of laboratory research has been focused on the role of cognition in learned helplessness and subsequent impaired performance (Abramson, Seligman, and Teasdale, 1978; Buchwald, Coyne, and Cole, 1978; Wortman and Dintzer, 1978). The transactional perspective, however, requires a critical examination of the experimental context of such studies. In the typical learned helplessness study, subjects are asked to solve a cognitive task after having been first deceived as to the controllability of noise in a first task. Yet the elaborate explanations that have been offered for learned helplessness effects have generally ignored the key role of such deception and have simply assumed that subjects respond to the manipulation as intended by the experimenter. Questions such as exactly what features of naturalistic phenomena are being modeled by the deception are rejected.

A transactional perspective requires that ecological validity be demonstrated, not simply assumed. It calls for alternative methodologies appropriate to describing the continuous flow of person-environment relationships as they occur in stress and coping in the natural setting. Such flow needs to be examined in purely descriptive terms before one asks the more analytic, deterministic questions in controlled experimental studies.

Given the relative paucity of naturalistic descriptive data, much of the current laboratory study of stress is premature. Laboratory studies provide an important way of isolating specific components of stressful transactions and testing hypotheses about their determinants. They are not, however, a substitute for naturalistic data, and there are recognizable limitations to the information they can provide—namely:

1. Laboratory studies do not provide descriptive ecological information concerning the sources of stress, resources, and constraints faced by ordinary people in their daily lives, or their patterns of emotional reaction and coping responses. Neither can such studies indicate how these vary as a function of age, sex, type of community, socioeconomic status, or personality type.

2. Such studies provide no information about the relationships that emerge and change over an extended period of time between stress and coping and adaptational outcomes such as health, social functioning, and morale.

3. In duration, severity, and complexity, experimental stressors must fall short of the stressors of everyday life. There are ethical restrictions on what human subjects can be exposed to, and there are practical limitations in our ability to simulate the configuration of stressors faced in daily life.

4. The precise control of key variables afforded by laboratory studies

is often illusory. Experimenter-defined parameters of stimulus dimensions only narrowly sample the dimensions of the experimental context to which subjects respond. Precision in the specification of dependent measures is often accomplished by constraining the resources the subject can mobilize and the responses that can be made, so that an unrepresentative response sample is obtained.

5.   The lack of robustness of many laboratory phenomena is in stark contrast to the broad generalizations about naturalistic phenomena that are typically made from laboratory studies. Experimental procedures have been refined and elaborated with little reference to precisely the features of naturalistic stress and coping that are being simulated. A lack of attention to external validity leaves many experimental studies as ventures in triviality.

In the 1960s, Lazarus and his associates sought to develop a means of creating and studying stress processes in the laboratory that more closely approximated naturalistic conditions. Motion picture films were chosen because they did not depend on deception but relied on the natural tendency of people to react emotionally while watching others have a damaging experience (Lazarus and others, 1962). The studies repeatedly showed that normally stressful events can be made considerably more benign through cognitive means of achieving emotional control. When situational manipulations facilitated denial and intellectualization, subjects showed lower levels of stress response, including autonomic levels of arousal, but the effectiveness of these experimental inputs depended on the subjects' natural defensive dispositions (see Lazarus, Averill, and Opton, 1970, for a review). This research provided the substantive data for the proposition that how a person appraises and copes with an environmental stressor has an important bearing on the emotional and adaptational outcome. At the same time, the theoretical issues that emerged proved to be somewhat refractory to laboratory-derived data and highlighted the limitations of a strictly laboratory approach. Our call for a transactional level of inquiry in the study of stress and the current direction to our research are direct results of these insights.

Currently we are engaged in a research project in which the adaptation of normal adults in various environmental contexts is repeatedly assessed throughout a one-year period. Using a variety of instruments and in-depth interviews, we examine fluctuations in person-environment relationships by measuring major life changes, daily hassles, uplifts, coping processes, patterns of emotion, and adaptational outcomes such as health, morale, and social functioning.

In summary, a transactional perspective for the study of stress requires a relational conception of variables and a greater emphasis on process, fluctuation, and change. It has important implications for how we interpret phenomena and what counts as an explanation, and it emphasizes the need for naturalistic study and realistic methodologies (Jenkins, 1974). In the next section, we present our cognitive-phenomenological approach to stress conceptualized within this transactional perspective.

A Cognitive-Phenomenological Approach to Stress

The studies of film-induced stress reactions conducted by Lazarus and his associates are part of a larger body of literature clearly demonstrating that cognitive-mediational accounts of human stress and coping are preferable to strictly personal or environmental ones (see Lazarus, 1966, 1968; Lazarus, Averill, and Opton, 1970; Lazarus and Launier, 1978). Indeed, the cognitive orientation has shown such a general resurgence in psychology in recent years that it has been described as a "cognitive revolution" (Dember, 1974).

When operating within a transactional perspective, one must be alert to the dangers of leaving the organism "lost in thought," as Guthrie once accused Tolman of doing. The key role we give to cognitive processes must be understood as one aspect of ongoing person-environment transactions. Cognitive processes do not simply terminate in a static cognition, but rather are viewed as phases of activity relating the person to the environment. Bateson (1971, p. 1) has provided a metaphor that captures a sense of this: "Consider a man felling a tree with an axe. Each stroke of the axe is modified or corrected, according to the shape of the cut face of the tree left by the previous stroke. This self-corrective . . . process is brought about by a total system, tree-eyes-brain-muscle-axe-stroke-tree; and it is this total system that has the characteristics of . . . mind."

Although we argue that stressful emotions and coping are products of cognition—that is, the way a person appraises or constructs his relationship with the environment—we do not mean that the relationship goes only one way. In an adaptational encounter, environmental demands, cognitive appraisal processes, coping, and emotional response interpenetrate, each affecting the other. Depending on how the observer punctuates the unfolding sequence, antecedent status can be assigned to any of a number of configurations of these variables. Our predominant emphasis on cognition, however, stems in part from a sense that its role has been understated in the past and in part from a belief that it often represents a critical juncture in the person-environment transaction, such that small differences can have an amplified effect on the course of subsequent stress, coping, and outcome.

Cognitive Appraisal. Since the 1960s, the Lazarus group has applied the concept of *cognitive appraisal* to the person's continually reevaluated judgments about demands and constraints in ongoing transactions with the environment and his or her resources and options for managing them. These evaluative processes determine the person's stress reactions, the various emotions experienced, and adaptational outcomes.

Primary appraisal refers to the cognitive process of evaluating the significance of an encounter for one's well-being, answering the question "Am I okay or in trouble?" It comes in three forms: judgments that the transaction is (1) irrelevant, (2) benign-positive, or (3) stressful. An encounter evaluated as *irrelevant* is one that is considered to have no personal significance and therefore one that can be ignored. A *benign-positive* encounter involves a judgment that a state of affairs is beneficial or desirable. *Stressful* appraisals involve judgments of harm-loss, threat, or challenge; all three involve some negative evaluation of one's present or future state of well-being, but challenge provides the least negative or most positive one.

The person's current time perspective is important in distinguishing between *harm-loss* and *threat*. Harm-loss refers to damage already sustained, such as loss of significant relationships or social roles, blows to self-esteem, or incapacitating injury or illness. Threat refers to the same type of damage but involves an anticipation of what has not yet happened. Field studies of the stress of a complex event, such as serious illness or injury, suggest that harm-loss and threat can occur as alternating or concurrent themes as the person appraises and reappraises harm that has occurred and threats to well-being that may result from the harm (Hamburg, Hamburg, and deGoza, 1953; Visotsky and others, 1961). Thus, a stroke victim might focus on the resulting paralysis and speech and thought disturbance, or the threat of a recurrence, or both, as he or she attempts to come to terms with the condition (Moss, 1972).

Appraisals of threat and harm-loss are sometimes difficult to separate empirically, yet the distinction is theoretically important. Since a harm-loss appraisal involves an evaluation of damage already done, current concerns and coping efforts will center on overcoming, tolerating, making restitution for, or reinterpreting the harm in the context of the present. Yet with threat, the focus will be on the future, on attempts at maintaining the status quo or preventing the harm by heading it off or neutralizing it. Shifts in these observable coping patterns would, we believe, reflect changes in the person's appraisal—either because he has had access to new information or because he has reevaluated existing information. In adopting a transactional, process-oriented perspective, one becomes sensitized not only to the need to describe the flow of events but also to the fact that in such a description theoretically distinct concepts may at times fuse.

The distinction between *challenge* and *threat* may be one of the more crucial ones in the study of stress, although it involves a number of unsettled issues. It rests on positive versus negative emotional tone, whether the person focuses on the potential for mastery and gain or on the potential for harm. Challenge involves a judgment that the demands of a transaction can be met and overcome. Because challenged persons have better morale and are more cheerful in the face of adversity, we would expect them to have a better outcome in the wide range of stressful transactions in which such an outlook can make a difference. The advantage may be simply attitudinal and behavioral, but there may also be implications for somatic health. Elsewhere, Lazarus (1978a; Lazarus and others, in press) has speculated that the distinction between threat and challenge might overlap with Selye's (1974) distinction between harmful and constructive stress and that such appraisals might produce distinguishable hormonal and tissue response patterns.

Many stressful transactions are sufficiently rich in ambiguity that an appraisal of challenge versus one of threat could be attributed to selective attention, without the need for motivational inferences. In other instances, a challenge appraisal might represent gross self-deception or distortion of reality. The traditional view has been that such self-deception is tantamount to mental disorder, whereas accurate reality testing is the hallmark of mental health and successful adaptation. Yet an examination of the stress and coping literature suggests that the matter is not so simple (Lazarus, 1978b).

Lazarus's (1966) research review indicates that defensive functioning is successful in a variety of contexts. For instance, in the high-tension atmosphere of a coronary care unit, the patient who ignores or denies the diagnosis and who shuts out the possibility of sudden death may fare the best, both physically and psychologically (Gentry, Foster, and Harvey, 1972). Even Carl Rogers has acknowledged that the closed, well-defended person is likely to cope with stress better than his ideal of the open, sensitive person (see Bergin and Strupp, 1972, p. 316). Traditional considerations of defensive functioning have typically assumed that what is being evaluated is a stable style, a disposition, or even a rigid character armor that deforms the personality. However, a study of men judged to be healthy and successful revealed that they selectively and adaptively employed immature defense mechanisms and that those men who had least access to such strategies were least adjusted overall (Vaillant, 1977).

Clearly, an evaluation of a person's cognitive appraisal processes must distinguish between their *adaptiveness*—their success or failure in terms of morale, social functioning, somatic health, and preservation of options for future coping—and clinical judgments narrowly emphasizing veracity of perception or sensitivity. A transactional perspective, with its emphasis on fluctuation and change, suggests further that evaluative questions must involve a sense of timing, sequence, and context. Thus, the denial processes that allow a victim of myocardial infarction to cope with the coronary care unit can also have disastrous consequences if they delay or prevent the seeking of indicated treatment. In still other instances of sudden illness or injury, temporary self-deception, in order to make the recognition of threatening elements manageably gradual, may enable the victims to buy time for later rehabilitative efforts. After they are past the worst and most debilitating period and feel stronger, they can constructively turn to more reality-based appraisals and actions aimed at rehabilitation (Hamburg and Adams, 1967).

If primary appraisal answers the question "Am I okay or in trouble?" then *secondary appraisal* can be seen as an answer to the question "What can I do about it?" Secondary appraisal refers to the person's ongoing judgments concerning coping resources, options, and constraints. The essential difference between primary and secondary appraisal is in the content of what is being evaluated. Actually, the evaluative processes are highly interrelated and even fuse. A firm sense of self-efficacy (secondary appraisal) can lead one to appraise transactions as benign or irrelevant that would otherwise be threatening; in contrast, if one believes that his coping resources are depleted, then he may perceive a transaction as threatening where it otherwise would not be.

As the work of the Lazarus group has progressed, secondary appraisal processes have acquired a greater emphasis. Primary appraisal remains important, but there is now greater attention to the shaping of coping activities by secondary appraisal (Lazarus and Launier, 1978). Yet we know relatively little about secondary appraisal processes. Essentially, secondary appraisal involves the evaluation of coping strategies with respect to their cost and probability of success. The determinants of secondary appraisal in a given stressful transaction are likely to include the person's previous experiences with such situations; generalized beliefs about self and environment; and the availability of resources, such as the person's morale and assessments of health/energy, problem-solving skills, social support, and material resources (Folkman, Schaefer, and Lazarus, in press).

Secondary appraisal processes in naturalistic stress transactions are likely to prove quite complex. Secondary appraisal must involve balancing competing concerns as the person simultaneously or sequentially evaluates personal and social resources that can be mobilized, the adequacy of alternative coping strategies, and feedback from coping efforts. The choices are seldom clear-cut, and as the person's perspective shifts from one encounter to another, priorities determining coping may be radically altered. Information processing under such circumstances is highly selective and influenced by the individual's primary appraisals, emotional state, and personal agendas. Experimental simulations of secondary appraisal processes, using subjects' probability estimates to construct utility functions, are likely to provide only inadequate representations.

Methodological Considerations. Although cognitive appraisal is often a matter of conscious deliberation, unconscious or impulsive appraisals are not excluded. Furthermore, although various forms of self-report can prove useful in assessing ongoing appraisals, subjects may not always report accurately on the determinants of their behavior. Nisbet and Wilson (1978, p. 233) suggest that "when reporting on the effect of stimuli, people may not interrogate a memory of the cognitive processes that operated on the stimuli; instead, they may base their reports on implicit, a priori theories about the causal connection between stimulus and response." Cognitions remain an inferential variable, and there are limits to the certainty with which we can determine the particular cognitions a person is experiencing. Klinger (1978) notes that one cannot verify a person's report of a cognition, and it is even questionable whether one can record the event accurately. In the study of cognition, the "validating process resides in ruling out artifacts, in replications, and, ultimately, in the usefulness of data or theory for making other forms of prediction and perhaps control" (p. 227).

What, then, are appropriate methodologies for the study of appraisal processes? In experimental studies, it is important to avoid the tautology inherent in using the same measure to define the presence of a cognition as one used to evaluate its effects. In a study of the cognitive control of emotional response, such as the Lazarus film studies, one can define the presence of the cognitive activity (as opposed to its effects) with joint reference to (1) the instructions facilitating denial or intellectualization; (2) individual difference variables; (3) a comprehension check involving some signal that the subject understood the instructions; (4) self-report of cognitive strategies; and (5) a debriefing in which the subject is encouraged to disclose any unreliable self-reporting (Mahoney, 1977).

When one is attempting to reconstruct appraisal processes in descriptive studies of stress and coping in naturalistic settings, converging evidence from a variety of sources can be employed: the person's self-report; knowledge of the characteristics of the person and environment; observed patterning of emotion, physiological response, and coping; and, most important, the congruence or fit among these variables.

Reappraisal. Cognitive appraisals are not static, but rather shift in response to changing internal and external conditions. *Reappraisal* refers to the changes in a person's evaluative judgments; it is evident in changes in the patterning of emotional response and coping or in the person's depiction of the situation. Reappraisal is a feedback process and takes two forms. The first involves new information or new insights about the changing person-environment relationship and its significance for well-being. The other, *defensive reappraisal* (Lazarus, 1966, 1978b), represents cognitive maneuvering to reduce distress rather than to assess accurately the troubled person-environment relationship with a view to changing it. What was originally appraised as harm-loss or threat is reappraised and nonthreatening or desirable. The appropriateness of such reappraisals must be judged relative to the observer's vantage point and the transactional context of the appraisal.

Coping. Defensive reappraisal represents the interpenetration of cognitive appraisal processes and coping; depending on the observer's purposes, either aspect of it can be emphasized. Lazarus and Launier (1978, p. 311) define coping as "efforts, both action oriented and intrapsychic, to manage (that is, to master, tolerate, reduce, minimize) environmental and internal demands and conflicts among them which tax or exceed a person's resources." Among the important features of such a definition is that reference to taxing demands limits the concept of coping to stressful transactions rather than to adaptation in general. Even so, the concept may prove to be excessively broad and in need of restriction. Second, the definition is process oriented, as opposed to more structural definitions that are keyed to generalized dispositions or styles or to hierarchies of coping and defensive mecha-·nisms. Third, it is broader than many traditional delineations of the function of coping in that it admits to an action or problem-solving function as well as that of regulating the emotional response.

In our model, coping thus serves two main functions: the alteration of the ongoing person-environment relationship *(instrumental* or *problem oriented)* and the control of stressful emotions *(emotion regulation).* Problem-oriented coping refers to efforts to deal with the sources of stress, whether by changing one's own problem-maintaining behavior or by changing environmental conditions. Emotion regulation refers to coping efforts aimed at reducing emotional distress and maintaining a satisfactory internal (for example, hormonal) state for processing both information and action.

The two coping functions frequently occur simultaneously (Folkman, 1979). The coping process is a dynamic constellation of many acts, and both the demands and the strategies of the person change as the transaction unfolds. As we noted earlier, coping with extreme stress often involves an acute phase, in which efforts are most appropriately directed toward minimizing or defensively distorting the impact of the event (emotion regulation); and a reorganization phase, in which the harm, loss, or threat is recognized and coping efforts are focused on altering the troubled person-environment relationship. However, it is also possible for the two functions to be in conflict, as when palliative (emotion-focused) coping obstructs or delays actions required to protect people against illness (Hackett and Cassem, 1975; Pranulis, 1975; Von Kugelgen, 1975).

Coping strategies can be distinguished along a number of dimensions in addition to function. Noting that the lack of an adequate taxonomy has hampered the study of coping processes, Lazarus and Launier (1978) have proposed a working classificatory scheme. Full discussion of it is beyond the scope of this chapter, but it may be noted that coping strategies can additionally be distinguished according to mode employed (direct action, action inhibition, information search, or cognitive). The scheme proposed by Lazarus and Launier will most likely undergo further refinement as it is tested in actual research, but it provides provisional means of ordering data concerning intraindividual and interindividual differences in the constellation of coping over the period of one or more stressful transactions.

The importance of coping as a mediating variable in the outcome of stress is now being appreciated even in those areas of research where it was once ignored. Thus, one review of the life events literature concludes: "In practical terms . . . life event scores have not been shown to be predictors of the probability of future illness" (Rabkin and Struening, 1976a, p. 1015). Another suggests: "As our research develops, we need to give greater attention to such variables as coping skills and supportive relationships that may intervene between the occurrence of life events and the initiation of illness" (Mechanic, 1974, p. 92). Yet relations between environmental sources of stress and coping have been narrowly construed, with coping simply a response to environmental conditions.

In our model, coping actively shapes the course of the ongoing person-environment relationship. Rather than a fixed entity that inevitably impinges on the person, much of the environment remains only a potential until it is actualized by coping efforts. Environmental influences may shape the constellation of coping efforts that come into play in a stressful transaction, but coping also partially determines which environmental influences are activated and what form they will take. As a number of writers have noted, much of the observed consistency in human behavior may be the result of people's selecting and generating environmental conditions that are typical for them and to which they react in a characteristic way (Bandura, 1977b; Bowers, 1973; Mischel, 1973; Runyan, 1978; Wachtel, 1973).

If one fails to take into account the intricacies of such person-environment relationships, one is likely to attribute to the person characteristics not possessed or to leave significant aspects of that person's experience unexplained (Watzlawick, Beavin, and Jackson, 1967). From a cognitive-phenomenological viewpoint, it is important to reconstruct the psychological situation in which the person's cognitions and behavior make sense. Current stress and coping research has generally ignored this. For instance, laboratory research has demonstrated the achievement striving, time urgency, and interpersonal aggressiveness with which the coronary-prone or Type A individual approaches a variety of tasks (Carver and Glass, 1978). In the context of the laboratory experiment, such behavior may seem pointless and irrational, and we get little sense of the naturalistic contexts in which it is sufficiently adaptive to persist. As well as the reactive characteristics of Type A persons, we need to know the pressures they typically face and the structure of opportunities and responsibilities that maintain Type A behavior. Type A persons may indeed shape their typical environments, but the resulting demands may constrain them from adopting alternative behavioral strategies.

The existence of bidirectional influences between person and environment complicates attempts to describe cognitive processes. When one assumes the existence of feedback processes, it becomes important to integrate assumptions about cognitive processes with considerations of the person's ongoing commerce with the environment. Coyne (1976a, 1976c) has argued that assumptions about rigid cognitive structures and distortions in depression have distracted investigators from considering the feedback from the depressed person's transactions with the environment. The depressed person is inept in meeting role responsibilities (Weissman and Paykel, 1974), induces hostility and depression in others, and gets rejected (Coyne, 1976a). The depressed person's ineffectual coping produces an idiosyncratic environment that gives ample validation to a negative self-concept, which in turn leads to more ineffectual coping. One can get little indication of all this when one attempts to conceptualize cognitive processes outside of a transactional context.

Recognition that coping may determine subsequent environmental conditions adds a new dimension to the evaluations of coping effectiveness. If one looks at the individual in isolation, the cost of coping can be divided into several components: pain of stressful emotions, psychic cost of violation of value integrity, and physiological cost of harmful disturbance in bodily function (Folkman, Schaefer, and Lazarus, in press). However, in examining the individual in an environmental context, one must introduce considerations of the ecological impact of coping efforts—that is, their effect on the individual's larger social or environmental network and the ramifications for subsequent coping efforts. This of necessity vastly increases the potential for incongruence among competing considerations (Boszormenyi-Nagy and Sparks, 1973; Coyne, 1976b). How do we evaluate the coping efforts of the executive who is able to master the demands of a competitive work situation but whose wife becomes dependent on prescription drugs and whose children develop psychological problems in the face of his neglect? Ortega y Gasset (1961, p. 104) has conveyed a poetic sense of this issue in relationship to a transactional perspective: "I am myself plus my circumstances, and if I do not save it, I cannot save myself. This sector of circumstantial reality forms the other half of my person; only through it can I integrate myself and be fully myself. The most recent biological science studies the living organism as a unit composed of the [adaptation of the] body to its environment, but also of the adaptation of the environment to its body. The hand tries to adjust itself to the material object to grasp it firmly; but at the same time, each material object conceals a previous affinity with a particular hand."

Concluding Remarks

Many writers remain optimistic about the potential of traditional approaches to the study of stress, and they can find little necessity for the metatheoretical shift we describe here. For some, the problems facing the field require only conceptual refinement and technical innovation. The expectation is that, for example, new scaling techniques will substantially increase the predictability of subsequent adaptation from recent life events, or that improvements in laboratory studies of failure-induced stress will lead to major new insights into naturalistically occurring stress and coping.

While the issue may not yet be entirely settled, we ourselves are impressed with the need for some radical redirection in our conceptualization of stress and coping.

Adoption of a transactionally oriented, cognitive-phenomenological model of stress brings with it a host of new conceptual and methodological challenges, and the model is clearly in its infancy. Nonetheless, we believe it will grow increasingly attractive as traditional investigators are required by their data to invoke notions of cognitive mediation and bidirectional influences between person and environment.

How people appraise their ongoing commerce with the environment and how their coping selects and transforms the environment must be recognized as important to the understanding of stress and coping. Such recognition leads to an interesting problem. It suggests that we can describe, predict, and even control stress and coping better than in the absence of these considerations, but also that there are limits to what our efforts can accomplish. Cognitive appraisal processes are of necessity selective and sometimes idiosyncratic, and fantasy, attentional deployment, and recall processes are among the important determinants. Stressful transactions in naturalistic settings are also usually sufficiently rich in ambiguity to support multiple appraisals. Furthermore, couplings between the individual's coping and the environment, and between environmental response and the individual's cognitive-perceptual processes, are less than perfect. At each phase of the stress and coping process, there is a role for chance and uncertainty (see Meehl, 1978; Neisser, 1976). We are, however, far from reaching the limits of our model, and at the present time the main implication of this line of reasoning is that we should look for just so much precision and determinancy as the nature of stress phenomena permits.

9

Socioeconomic Status and Stress

Thomas Ashby Wills
Thomas S. Langner

❖ ❖ ❖ ❖ ❖ ❖ ❖ ❖ ❖ ❖ ❖ ❖ ❖

What is stress? What is psychological disorder, and how is it distributed in the community? These two issues are of central importance for research in psychiatric epidemiology. The formulation of "stress" as a theoretical construct—a construct that enables investigators to deal with evidence on psychological disorder—is essential to the theoretical basis for epidemiological research. In addition, empirical studies in psychiatric epidemiology almost invariably show a greater prevalence of psychological disorder among persons of lower socioeconomic status (SES). These two issues are related. If we are to have an effective theoretical explanation for the variation in prevalence rates

Note: Preparation of this chapter was supported by grant MH-18260 from the National Institute of Mental Health. Thanks to Daniel Katz and Marjorie McMeniman for their comments on a draft.

with SES, we must have a clear definition of stress. Moreover, if a stress formulation of psychological disorder is correct, then it should provide the most plausible explanation for observed correlates of prevalence.

Conceptual Status of Stress

The notion that psychological problems are caused by stress is intuitively appealing. One can vividly imagine examples of stressful experiences, and it is easy to recall instances where there were problems in reaction to stress. Stress concepts have been applied with some plausibility to evidence on the relationship between life events and both physical and psychological disorder (for reviews see B. P. Dohrenwend and B. S. Dohrenwend, 1974; Rabkin and Struening, 1976b). Nevertheless, there are a number of conceptual and methodological problems with current stress formulations. With regard to research on life stress and illness, the absolute magnitude of the relationship is rather low (see Rabkin and Struening, 1976a); and, despite the volume of research in this area, there is still considerable uncertainty whether life events are causes or consequences of symptomatology. Another problem concerns the definition of "stress" itself. With regard to this issue, perhaps the most than can be said is that it is many things to many people (for excellent critiques see Cassel, 1975; Dohrenwend and Dohrenwend, in press). The prevailing tendency among investigators has been to simply define stress as whatever seems stressful to them or, alternatively, to define stress in terms of some vague category such as "aversive stimuli," without bothering to specify the inclusion or exclusion criteria for this category. The observation of individual differences in reaction to life events has led to postulation of mediating constructs such as "vulnerability" or "resistance" to the stressor, and these constructs can be invoked on a post hoc basis to account for almost any conceivable finding. (Of course, there is nothing wrong with using these concepts to formulate hypotheses that are then tested, but this has not always occurred.) With a collection of vague definitions and mediating constructs, it is possible to account for any finding after the fact, but one really has a weak and flabby theory that does not permit one to make predictions. An additional problem has been the occasional practice of defining a "stressor" as anything that turns out to be correlated with symptomatology. This leaves aside the problem of accounting for events that turn out not to be stressors, and use of this practice on a post hoc basis produces an airtight system that is immune to disproof (since the "stressors" are always correlated with symptoms) but is incapable of generating a prediction.

Lest the reader be too ready to shrug off the theoretical issues as idle nitpicking, consider the example of frustration-aggression theory. It was intuitively appealing, one could readily think of instances where there had been frustration and aggression, and the theory seemed to be applicable to real-world problems. Observational studies soon showed, however, that the frequency of frustrating events in everyday life was sufficiently high that aggression should be a daily or hourly occurrence, an implication that did not seem credible to most people (for a review see Bandura, 1973, chap. 1). Moreover, laboratory studies indicated that events meeting any reasonable definition of frustration showed only a weak and erratic relationship to aggression, whereas other events showed a strong and consistent aggression-evoking effect (see Tedeschi, Smith, and Brown, 1974). This led to steadily loosening definitions (to the extent that frustration was defined as anything that evoked aggression), with invocation of numerous hypothetical mediators and multiple ad hoc explanations, and finally the whole thing just collapsed of its own weight and was abandoned even by most of its original adherents, to be replaced by more specific formulations.

Without an operational definition of stress, then, one is left in a weak theoretical position. One approach that has been taken toward an empirical definition is to obtain ratings of perceived stressfulness for various events by lay or professional judges (Dohrenwend and Dohrenwend, in press), but there are some problems with this approach because of the substantial inter-rater variability in rated stressfulness of given events (see Redfield and Stone, 1979). An alternative approach is to identify the basic social-psychological processes that produce stress, and then index stress by determining the extent to which these processes are involved for a particular individual. In the following sections, the latter approach is taken, and stress is considered with respect to (1) lack of perceived control over events and (2) threat to self-esteem.

Predictability, Lack of Control, and Stress. From a psychological standpoint, it is very important to have (or to believe that one has) control over events, particularly aversive events. When people are placed in situations where aversive events occur unpredictably and outside their personal control, the result is feelings of helplessness, incompetence, frustration, depression, anxiety, and fatigue (see Miller and Norman, 1979), all of which are typical items on psychiatric symptom checklists. The relation between unpredictable events and stress reactions has been demonstrated repeatedly in the laboratory (see Pennebaker and others, 1977; Schulz, 1976; Weidner and Matthews, 1978).

The construct of *learned helplessness* has been particularly successful for encompassing the extensive literature on the effects of lack of control. Recent reviews (Abramson, Seligman, and Teasdale, 1978; Miller and Norman, 1979) have noted the finding of performance deficits and emotional reactions among persons exposed to noncontingent aversive events, and have concluded that the phenomenon arises when failure is attributed to stable causes internal to the self. It is the latter that results in self-deprecation and negative affect, together with low motivation and generalized expectancies for failure.

Although life events researchers typically have not classified events in terms of perceived control, several studies have indicated the importance of this variable. Myers, Lindenthal, and Pepper (1971) noted that negative events outside the control of the individual were particularly important for discriminating persons with high versus low scores on psychiatric impairment. Similarly, B. S. Dohrenwend (1973) found that correlations between life events and impairment scores were greatest for events classified as outside the control of the individual.

Perceived Control and Problem-Solving Resources. In naturalistic settings, the essential conditions for learned helplessness probably are produced by continued failure over a period of time; this would seem necessary to produce attributions to stable, internal causes. Now, it is stating the obvious to note that people do not ordinarily set out to fail. If they do fail, it is not because they did not try to succeed but because (among other things) their efforts were ill timed or unsuccessful, or they had bad luck, or they had fewer problem-solving skills, advantages, and resources to begin with. When one's best efforts have not been wholly successful, resultant discouragement and feelings of helplessness, incompetence, and depression set in. This process, however, is not usually something that occurs overnight, but is the gradual summation of learning and experience that span many years.

In some situations, such as unemployment (see Gore, 1978), the onset of stress is sudden. Yet again, stress-related symptomatology is produced not only by the unpleasant nature of the experience but by the fact that some persons do not have resources and skills that enable them to solve the problems with which they are confronted. In any event, for persons in lower SES levels (those with the least resources and fewest marketable skills), unemployment is not a one-time thing but a chronic aspect of their experience.

Thus, in trying to sharpen stress theory and improve prediction of what events will be stressful for a given individual, we must consider the problem-solving skills and resources that a person has available to cope with particular problems. It is this variable that probably accounts for considerable variation in what has been termed "vulnerability to" or "perception of" the stressor. Viewing stress in terms of predictability and problem-solving resources also clarifies the finding that psychiatric impairment is particularly prevalent among migrant and immigrant groups (see Rabkin and Struening, 1976b); these are exactly the persons who have the most problems to solve (including language deficiency) and the fewest resources to deal with them.

Self-Esteem. Another crucial aspect of many stressful situations is that they present a threat to self-esteem. Surprisingly, this aspect of stress has received little attention in the epidemiological literature, and there seems to be a widespread tendency among social scientists to regard self-esteem as if it were merely a point on an attitude scale. But self-esteem is not an abstract concept; it is a central theme in a person's life, and the particular point marked on a self-esteem scale represents an individual's evaluation of his or her own worth as a person. Moreover, judgments of self-esteem are not made lightly, but are formed from years of experience with other persons. In particular, judgments of low self-esteem reflect the consequences of an individual's daily interactions with people in the larger society. The effect of low self-esteem as a stressor in itself should be seriously considered, because it represents an everyday experience of devaluation and rejection in interactions with other persons.

Another point worth emphasizing is that personal acceptance or personal rejection does not just come out of the air, but comes from other people. There is no clearer demonstration of this fact than the literature on measurement of subjective well-being. The most consistent finding in this literature is that overall happiness is strongly related to interpersonal relationships, whether this variable is indexed as successful involvement with people (Wilson, 1967), involvement in formal social activities (Beiser, Feldman, and Egelhoff, 1972), social-emotional support relationships (Campbell, 1976), leisure activity with family or friends (London, Crandall, and Sears, 1977), or sociability and social activity (Lewinsohn and Amenson, 1978). The converse of this finding is that subjective unhappiness is most strongly determined by interpersonal discord: conflict and rejection in interactions with others. This was shown quite clearly in the study by Lewinsohn and Amenson (1978), where empirical procedures were used to obtain sets of pleasant events and unpleasant events. (These sets were correlated with mood self-ratings for both psychiatric patients and normal controls.) The set of pleasant events was composed almost exclusively of items concerning acceptance from and interaction with other persons (for example, "Having friends come to visit"). Analogously, the set of unpleasant events contained items primarily reflecting interpersonal discord and rejection from others (for example, "Having my spouse dissatisfied with me," "Being insulted"), as well as some items reflecting time constraint ("Working under pressure"), physical discomfort ("Being physically uncomfortable"), or failure ("Failing at something").

The epidemiological literature again is consistent with this formulation. There is no self-esteem threat more powerful than rejection by an intimate partner, and the literature on marital disruption (Bloom, Asher, and White, 1978) indicates that separation and divorce represent profoundly stressful events, associated with a wide range of physical and emotional disorders; separated persons in particular are markedly overrepresented in impaired and institutionalized groups. Of course, divorce presents a number of instrumental problems as well, but studies of divorced persons have consistently focused on the feelings of failure and shame, loss of self-esteem, rejection, and incompetence as a person (see Bloom, Asher, and White, 1978, pp. 876 ff.).

A study by Kobasa (1979) of life stress and illness among public utility executives showed that a variable termed "alienation from self" (that is, low self-esteem) was the strongest single discriminator of the group who showed high illness rates under stress. With regard to the stressful effects of unemployment, several reviews have noted that loss of self-esteem is the most consistently reported observation among unemployed persons (see, for example, Kasl, 1974). (An additional effect of unemployment is the financial insecurity created by job loss.) Finally, perhaps the most consistent finding in the literature on child psychopathology is the association between parental rejection of the child and various types of child behavior problems (see, for example, Langner, Gersten, and Eisenberg, 1977).

Stress and Social Supports. A focus on threat to self-esteem as a crucial element in stress clarifies at least two issues. One is the literature showing that, among persons exposed to high stress, those with social supports of various kinds (friends, marriage partners, or community relationships) have much lower levels of symptomatology, compared with those lacking social support (for reviews see Cobb, 1976; Rabkin and Struening, 1976b). Investigators have sometimes expressed puzzlement about why social support systems should have such marked effects. The present analysis suggests that part of the reason is that the supporting persons offer reassurance and acceptance of the stressed person and convey, as Cobb (1976, p. 300) puts it, "information leading the subject to believe that he is esteemed and valued."

Another issue concerns a tendency in the literature to discuss results from social support studies as if the subjects had been randomly assigned to groups. In fact, persons who fall in the "divorced" or "living alone" categories did not randomly assign themselves to that condition, but in a great number of cases were there because they had been rejected (for good or bad reasons) by someone else. With this fact recognized, it follows almost necessarily that persons in the "low social support" category will show high rates of impairment, and, in fact, many studies show that subjects in this category are markedly elevated in symptomatology relative to everyone else, stressed or unstressed (see Cobb, 1976). Moreover, in some studies there is a main effect for social support (see Myers, Lindenthal, and Pepper, 1975). Note carefully the implications of this finding. Even under low stress, which presumably should not be conducive to impairment, persons without social support show elevated rates of symptomatology, suggesting that the condition of low social support is itself a source of stress. Eaton's (1978) reanalysis of the New Haven longitudinal data also showed that, although there was a relationship between life events and psychiatric symptoms for all subject groups, the strength of this relationship was particularly great for persons in the "low social support" category (those living alone or not married).

Undoubtedly, social support provides predictability, security, and

additional assistance to help solve instrumental problems. We suggest, therefore, that the *combination* of predictability and reassurance makes social
support a potent insulator against stressful conditions. In this context, note
Beiser's (1976) finding that a group of persons who showed spontaneous
remission of neurotic disorder had originally scored higher on indices of self-
esteem and obtaining emotional support from other people. Conversely, the
lack of predictability, and lack of reassurance against threats to self-esteem,
by itself is almost the definition of stressfulness.

    Demoralization and Psychological Disorder. Integrating the concepts
of lack of control and low self-esteem, which have previously been noted as
essential aspects of stressful conditions, we arrive at the construct of *demoralization.* The best definition is that by Frank (1973, p. 316): "A person
becomes demoralized when he finds that he cannot meet the demands placed
on him by the environment and cannot extricate himself from his predica-
ment." The consequences of this situation are the feelings of helplessness,
hopelessness, and depression that are commonly represented in measures
used by psychiatric epidemiology researchers. The symptoms themselves are
not the items of central interest; rather, they are best viewed as consequences
of a situation where an individual has not been successful in solving the
problems that he or she faces.

    The construct of demoralization has a solid empirical basis in the
epidemiology literature; in fact, recent research by Dohrenwend and associates
(1978a, 1978b) has indicated that this construct is tapped by all the commonly used psychiatric epidemiology screening instruments. This conclusion
originally emerged from a study in which a number of measures of symptomatology and role functioning were administered to a total sample
comprising 227 adult respondents, of whom 124 represented a community
sample from the Washington Heights area of New York City and 103 represented a sample of psychiatric patients (both inpatient and outpatient). The
symptomatology items used in this study were originally classified by three
judges (board-certified psychiatrists) into five groups that were thought to
represent independent and nonoverlapping areas of psychological disorder.

    The five scales proved successful for differentiating between the
community sample and the patient sample. For all five, the psychiatric
patients on the average had higher scores than the nonpatients, when sex,
ethnicity, and education were controlled for. In addition, high symptomatology was correlated with impairment in role functioning, especially in the
area of marital relationship. These results replicated the usual findings for
psychiatric screening instruments, and a composite measure based on the five
subscales was essentially identical to other psychiatric epidemiology instruments—for example, correlating .91 with the Langner (1962) screening
inventory. There were, however, two unexpected results. One was that the
five symptom scales, although thought to be independent, in fact were all

intercorrelated to the limit of their reliabilities; the five scales all measured exactly the same dimension. This was true both for the community sample and for the patient sample. The other unexpected finding was that, although the composite score was related to psychiatrists' ratings of overall psychological impairment in the community sample, there was no such relationship in the patient sample; and in both samples, the composite measure showed no relationship to diagnostic category, being equally elevated for persons in different categories. Thus, the composite measure successfully discriminated between patient and nonpatient groups and, at least in the community sample, was successful in discriminating between more impaired and less impaired persons, but it did not differentiate between diagnosed types of psychological disorders. The authors summarized their initial results by likening the composite measure to an elevated body temperature measurement for physical disorder: "It tells you that there has been a departure from normality, but it does not tell you what type of disorder or disturbance is involved" (Dohrenwend and others, 1978a, p. 28).

If screening inventories measure a phenomenon that is present in psychological disorder, but do not measure any particular disorder, what do they measure? A second study, based on a sample of 200 adult respondents (Dohrenwend and others, 1978b), indicated that the construct of demoralization best fit the evidence. Here, a group of eleven scales emerged that were highly intercorrelated. These included scales termed Poor Self-Esteem, Hopelessness-Helplessness, Dread, Confused Thinking (not delusions or hallucinations), Sadness, Anxiety, Psychophysiological Symptoms, and Perceived Physical Health, as well as scales concerned with guilt, enervation, and somatic problems. These various aspects are exactly the properties that Frank (1973) proposed as the common characteristics of persons who seek psychological help, and the composite measure was termed Demoralization. In contrast, scales measuring symptoms for which people usually do not seek help, such as antisocial behavior, were not strongly related to the Demoralization composite. Perhaps the most compelling evidence for the construct was the fact that a single item correlated .66 with the composite score based on eight scales. This item was: "How often since last year have you felt difficulties were piling up so high that you could not overcome them?"

Construing epidemiology screening inventories as measures of demoralization leads to a number of important and useful corollaries. It should be noted immediately that the various symptoms encompassed by the demoralization composite measures (for example, helplessness, low self-esteem, sadness, and depression) are exactly the reactions that were previously identified in relation to the definition of stressful situations. Also, construing psychological disorder as demoralization helps to clarify stress formulations; that is, although difficult situations are common in everyday life, only the lack of control over situations produces stress, and psychiatric symptomatology is present among those persons who for one reason or another are overcome by the demands on them and are unable to cope with the problems they face. This formulation also accounts for the fact that there is a substantial level of untreated psychological disorder in the population (see Dohrenwend and Dohrenwend, 1969). Persons who confront the possibility of being overwhelmed by their problems can seek help and reassurance from a number of people, including friends, family members, ministers, and medical doctors, and hence will not show up in rates based on treated cases known to psychotherapists. This is just as true for child behavior problems as for adult problems. The Family Research Project study showed that, even at the highest levels of children's impairment, only about half of the children were referred for professional treatment (Langner and others, 1974). Moreover, persons who become demoralized may simply endure their problems and carry on until things change for the better with the passage of time. This probably accounts for the substantial "spontaneous remission" rate commonly noted in studies of neurotic disorder (see, for example, Lambert, 1976). The formulation also suggests an explanation for the generally low magnitude of the correlation between life event measures and symptomatology. These measures were not conceptually derived and include many events that may cause considerable distress but are generally within the coping ability of most persons and can be resolved in good time. In contrast, events that have long-term consequences, that are outside the individual's control, and eventually wear people down are likely to produce demoralization (with attendant physical and psychological symptomatology); an example is the death of a spouse, which is generally observed to be the most stressful of all life events.

The demoralization formulation also accounts for the stress-strain relationship (in epidemiological terminology, a dose-response relationship) that has been observed in epidemiology studies. The finding by Langner and Michael (1963) from the Midtown Manhattan study, that an increasing level of stress is associated with increasing levels of symptomatology (the more stress, the more symptoms), has since been replicated in several different contexts (Berkman, 1971; Ilfeld, 1977a; Langner, 1975). The stress-strain finding is predicted by the stress-demoralization formulation; since psychiatric symptomatology presumably arises when one is overcome by numerous problems, then the more problems, the more likely it is that a person will be overwhelmed. Note that there is also a dose-response relationship in life events research: On the average, the more life events (hence the more problems to deal with), the higher the level of symptomatology (see Rabkin and Struening, 1976a). This finding also is consistent with the demoralization formulation.

One fact that is not immediately accounted for by the construct of demoralization is the association between stress and physical illness. There is certainly no doubt about the existence of the relationship (see, for example, Cobb, 1976; Lipowski, 1977; Rabkin and Struening, 1976a), and the commonly used screening inventories represent a combination of psychological symptoms and physical ailments. A complete discussion of this issue is beyond the scope of this chapter. We shall simply note that, above and beyond the physical effects of chronic anxiety, several investigators have suggested that a breakdown in motivation (sometimes termed the "giving-up syndrome") is a crucial element in the development of psychosomatic disorders and may represent the common pathway for several types of illness (see Schmale, 1972). This syndrome, as it has been described by some investigators, seems essentially equivalent with the construct of demoralization.

An interesting corollary of the demoralization formulation is that it accounts for some perplexing findings on psychotherapy outcome. If a common element in psychological disorder is a motivational problem, then what people seek from psychotherapists is reassurance, sympathy, ego support, and encouragement, which would enable them to deal with the failure to cope with their problems. This may account for the fact that psychotherapy outcome is unrelated to length of treatment (Smith and Glass, 1977); the empirical evidence indicates that the demonstrated benefit from one session of psychotherapy is equivalent to that noted for extended treatment. Similar findings have been noted in studies of the effect of psychotherapy on medical ailments. For example, Rosen and Wiens (1979) examined subsequent use of medical facilities by persons who had received psychotherapy (an average of seven treatment sessions), persons who had received a single-session diagnostic evaluation, and a control group of persons who received neither evaluation nor therapy. They found that, across a number of measures, the psychotherapy group showed a significant reduction in clinic, hospital, and drug usage, compared with the controls. The surprising finding in this study was that the group who received only a single evaluation session showed as much reduction as the psychotherapy group and, in fact, showed more reduction on most measures. In the Rosen and Wiens study, there was a possible confound because there were diagnostic differences between the groups, with an overrepresentation of organic and retardation diagnoses in the evaluation-only group. Note, however, that the Rosen and Wiens findings replicated the results of another investigation (Goldberg, Krantz, and Locke, 1970).

Apparently, then, a single session with an attentive and sympathetic person has a powerful effect. All the evidence suggests, therefore, that the essential element of psychotherapy that produces improvement is sympathetic attention from an accepting and encouraging person, a proposition that has been advanced by a number of reviewers (for example, Gomes-Schwartz, Hadley, and Strupp, 1978; Luborsky, Singer, and Luborsky, 1975). This suggestion is consistent with evidence indicating generally equivalent effectiveness of many psychotherapies—of widely differing theoretical bases—

for treatment of emotional problems (Luborsky, Singer, and Luborsky, 1975; Smith and Glass, 1977) and evidence indicating generally equivalent effectiveness of psychotherapists with or without professional training (Durlak, 1979).

Social Class and Psychological Disorder

A basic finding in psychiatric epidemiology is the greater prevalence of psychiatric impairment among persons of lower SES. This finding was noted in a community sample of New York City residents (Langner and Michael, 1963) and has been replicated across a number of different methods and geographical locations (for reviews see B. S. Dohrenwend and B. P. Dohrenwend, 1974; King, 1978). It is sometimes noted that the relationship derives not so much from an overall linear effect as from a markedly disproportionate rate of disorder among persons of lowest status (see Ilfeld, 1978; Warheit, Holzer, and Arey, 1975). With respect to diagnostic categories, higher rates for lower-status persons are usually noted for the schizophrenias and personality disorders. Some studies have found no correlation between social class and neurotic symptoms, but when a distinction is made between *prevalence* of neurotic symptoms (presence of the symptom at any time) and *persistence* of the symptoms (presence of the symptom for five to seven days), a higher rate of persistent depression is found among persons of lower SES (Craig and Van Natta, 1979). Also noteworthy is the fact that lower SES is associated with failure to show remission of neurotic disorder (Beiser, 1976).

Several different processes probably are involved in the overall finding of a correlation between social class and psychological disorders, and we shall not treat them all here. It is likely that there is some downward mobility of disturbed persons, especially for schizophrenic disorder (associated with poor role functioning and interpersonal relations) and antisocial behavior (associated with aggressiveness and unstable employment). Even so, prospective research has shown that the beginnings of these disorders are related to social class in community samples of children (see Langner and others, 1979). The modified stress formulation implies a higher rate of psychiatric disorder, given the conditions that low-status persons face daily, such as insecurity, lack of social support, and lack of problem-solving resources.

Insecurity and Unpredictability. "There is nothing so degrading as the constant anxiety about one's means of livelihood. . . . Money is like a sixth sense without which you cannot make a complete use of the other five." The author of this passage was not a marginally employed low-status person but a member of the English intelligentsia (Somerset Maugham, writing in *Of Human Bondage*), who nevertheless lacked the snug security of an academic position and clearly appreciated the pervasive effects of not being sure how one is going to pay the rent next month. On the face of it, this is exactly the situation of any person whose occupational skills are minimal, whose job may be eliminated at any time, and whose paycheck is swallowed up immediately by expenses, leaving nothing for a cushion. Conversely, there may be no better form of security than having a lot of money in the bank. With regard to problem-solving resources, we will just assert flatly that a great many problems are very easily solved by money and are most difficult to solve without money. The less money one has, the more problems pile up, the more difficult they are, and (since money buys time) the less time one has to deal with them.

A clear demonstration of the direct effect of money on symptomatology was noted in the Chicago-area study (Ilfeld, 1977b). In this study, the percentage of respondents with high symptomatology increased more than twofold between the lowest income level (33 percent with high symptomatology) and all other income levels (approximately 15 percent with high symptomatology). Numerous control analyses indicated that this correlation was not accounted for by any of twenty-five control variables. The only variable that modified the relationship was an index of current financial stressors, such as difficulty in paying monthly bills and in having enough money for adequate living quarters, transportation, food, medical care, and leisure activities; this was evidence for a direct effect of income on symptomatology. Variables such as low self-esteem and low social support also were correlated with symptomatology, but neither of these variables was uniquely responsible for the observed association between low income and psychiatric symptoms.

Social Supports and Marital Stability. An unfortunate fact about low social status is marital instability. A large number of studies have found divorce, separation, and self-reported marital dissatisfaction to be related to SES variables (for review and discussion see Galligan and Bahr, 1978). The evidence suggests that the correlation between low status and marital instability is mediated primarily by economic dissatisfaction and arguments about economic matters (Galligan and Bahr, 1978; Scanzoni, 1975). Null results were obtained in a recent study by Glenn and Weaver (1978), but there are questions about whether the methodology of this study was adequate. For one thing, the criterion variable was a single item in a questionnaire survey. Another remarkable aspect of this study was that nonwhites were excluded from the analysis.

Evidence of this process was noted in the Chicago-area study (Ilfeld, 1978), which examined a representative community sample of 2,299 respondents. In that sample, at the lowest income level there were four times as many unmarried respondents as married respondents, and in fact hardly any of the latter at all (the ratio was 180 to 39). This study also noted (as have other studies of social supports) a strong association between low social support and psychiatric symptoms, with divorced and separated respondents overall exhibiting a two- to threefold increase in prevalence of high symptomatology, compared with married respondents.

A study by Brown, Ni Bhrolchain, and Harris (1975) of middle- and working-class women in London also is particularly informative. These investigators found a higher prevalence of psychiatric disturbance in the lower-status group, but also noted four variables that when controlled for eliminated the class differential. These variables were (1) absence of a close, intimate relationship with a husband or boyfriend; (2) lack of full- or part-time employment; (3) loss of mother by death or separation before age 11; and (4) having three or more children at home. Item 1 is obviously a social support variable, reflecting the relationship between psychiatric impairment and lack of social support and also the association between low SES and marital instability. The third item (loss of mother) might also be interpreted as a social support variable, inasmuch as the mother was not present to provide support. Item 2 reflects the correlation between low income and symptomatology, as was noted in the Ilfeld (1977b) study.

Self-Esteem. The Chicago study (Ilfeld, 1978) is one of the few that have specifically measured self-esteem in a community sample. These investigators used the Rosenberg ten-item scale, an instrument that has been well validated in other contexts. The results can be briefly summarized: From high SES levels to low SES levels, there was a steady decline in self-esteem. This was true whether status was indexed by income, education, or occupation. At the lowest income level, 61 percent of the respondents reported low self-esteem, compared with 40 percent for the next income level and 19 percent for the highest income level. Low self-esteem also was substantially correlated with high symptomatology.

Social Class, Demoralization, and Symptomatology. It has been suggested that the conditions of lower-status living present exactly the factors that conduce toward demoralization, exerting a constant pressure that is likely to wear people down. The results of the Chicago study (Ilfeld, 1978) seem particularly consistent with this formulation. In this study, the primary measure was the Psychiatric Symptoms Index (PSI), a self-report symptom checklist that was highly correlated with the Langner (1962) screening inventory. It was found not only that low SES was related to high symptomatology but also that a number of different stress factors (including low social support and low self-esteem) tended to occur in combination at the lowest SES level. These investigators also developed a seven-item scale termed the "Self-Efficacy" index; this scale was substantially intercorrelated with the Self-Esteem scale ($r = .56$), and low self-efficacy was related to high symptomatology. The content of the Self-Efficacy scale is most interesting, for the three highest-loading items read as follows: "I have little control over the things that happen to me," "I often feel helpless in dealing with the problems of my life," and "There is really no way I can solve some of the problems I have." Clearly, this is a demoralization scale, measuring exactly the same construct as the Demoralization composite found by Dohrenwend and associates (1978b). In the Chicago study, there was a dramatic association between SES and self-efficacy scores, and in absolute terms this was the strongest relationship reported in the Ilfeld (1978) article: $\chi^2(8) = 157.9$, $p < .001$. In the Chicago study, self-esteem, self-efficacy, symptomatology, and SES were all substantially interrelated, and the results of this study provide a clear picture of the relation between social class, demoralization, and psychological disorder.

The generality of the demoralization process has perhaps been insufficiently appreciated because studies of psychological assessment have concentrated on obtaining discrete diagnostic clusters. This procedure is of course justified, because the purpose of diagnosis is to guide treatment decisions for different types of persons. Also, if one takes items concerning depressed mood and social withdrawal, disordered thinking and bizarre thoughts, and manipulativeness and antisocial behavior, then a factor analysis is surely going to produce a Depression cluster, a Psychoticism cluster, and a Sociopathy cluster—especially if one uses a clinic sample. At the same time, such a procedure may underemphasize attributes that are characteristic of distressed persons in general, particularly persons in the community. Consider the results of a study by Borgatta, Fanshel, and Meyer (1960), where clients representing the general caseload of a social agency were rated on a broad-based item pool by social workers. For this sample, factor analysis of the ratings indicated a single predominant factor, which was replicated across client groups of adult females, adult males, and young unmarried mothers. The factor was loaded by items reflecting lack of optimism, not being energetic, not liking people, being wrapped up in the self, and lacking a sense of humor. This seems to be almost exactly the general character of the demoralization construct. The investigators summarized the content of the factor as representing a client who was "overwhelmed and discouraged" (Borgatta, Fanshel, and Meyer, 1960, p. 28). There were several other noteworthy aspects to the factor. For adult males, the factor was correlated with low-status occupation. (Most of the females were not in the labor market.) In addition, for all client groups, the factor was correlated with judgments by the social workers that casework help would be unproductive. Like their colleagues in other helping professions, the social workers preferred clients who were optimistic, energetic, and healthy to those who were discouraged, apathetic, and impaired; yet it is the latter who need help the most (see Wills, 1978).

Two Unanswered Questions. There are two issues that are not immediately resolved by the stress-demoralization formulation but at least are not incompatible with it. One is that the learned helplessness process (Miller and Norman, 1979) requires that failure be attributed to internal, stable causes. This is consistent with the finding that psychiatric symptomatology is related to low self-esteem. The difficulty is that persons low in SES, who score low on self-esteem, also tend to view events as outside their control (Lefcourt, 1976). One might ask why, if events are outside personal control, there would be internal attributions for failure. We might resolve this matter if we recognize that low-status persons have less control over events mainly because they have fewer skills and resources to control events; these are internal, relatively stable qualities. Thus, what kind of answer one gets depends on how the question is asked. The fact that low-status persons rate themselves as having less control over events is not incompatible with the possibility that they attribute the lack of control to their own lack of resources; this is in fact what the evidence suggests.

Another unresolved issue is the fact that, in addition to the correlation between SES and adult psychopathology, epidemiological studies also show a greater prevalence of child psychopathology at lower SES levels (see, for example, Achenbach, 1978; Lapouse and Monk, 1964; Tuddenham, Brooks, and Milkovich, 1974). Since children are not exposed to the same stressors as adults, what processes may account for this finding? A complete discussion is beyond the scope of this chapter (for a discussion of organic factors to which children in lower-income families may be more often exposed, see Abel, in press; Hutchings and others, 1978; Landesman-Dwyer and Emanuel, 1979; Needleman and others, 1979). There is considerable evidence that people under stress do tend to derogate other persons and wish to see others unhappy. The most plausible interpretation of this process may be a social comparison theory (see Wills, 1979), not the frustration-aggression theory. The probable mediating process between parents' unhappiness and children's disorder is the association between parental rejection and child psychopathology.

Implications for Prevention and Treatment

One is repeatedly struck by the association between financial stress and psychological disorder, and there is good reason to expect that the way to have a healthy populace is to have a healthy economy (see Brenner, 1973). In addition, there is a disproportionate prevalence of psychological disorder among persons at the lowest socioeconomic level, and it is clear that prevention and treatment efforts should be focused on providing services to these persons, as has in fact been done in a recent program designed specifically for that purpose (Edwards and others, 1979). With regard to psychological assessment and psychotherapeutic treatment, the importance of the demoralization construct should be seriously considered, and psychotherapy practice might place more emphasis on the basic therapeutic relationship rather than on the tenets of some particular school of therapy. Finally, the importance of social support for psychological health should be emphasized. In particular, stable marriage and family relationships seem to be of great value, and we suggest that government policy, therapeutic practice, and social values should be directed toward this goal.

10

Stress, Violence, and Crime

Louis B. Schlesinger
Eugene Revitch

❈ ❈ ❈ ❈ ❈ ❈ ❈ ❈ ❈ ❈ ❈ ❈ ❈

There is no generally agreed-upon definition of the concept of stress. Researchers in the field of physiology (for example, Mason, 1971; Selye, 1946) regard stress as a response, a reaction, or an adaptation, usually somatic in nature, to environmental stimulation or change. However, in common parlance and generally in the fields of psychiatry, psychology, and sociology, stress is considered not a response but a stimulus. The Random House dictionary, for example, defines stress as "any stimulus, such as fear or pain, that disturbs or interferes with the normal physiological mechanisms of the organism." Engle (1953, p. 22) provides a more complete definition of stress, including both internal and external sources of stimulation: "Stress refers to all processes, whether originating in the external environment or within the person, which impose a demand or requirement upon the organism." In this chapter, we conceive psychological stress to be a stimulus that creates a disturbance in intrapsychic homeostasis. The stress may be external (socio-logical and situational) or internal (intrapsychic) noxious stimuli. Stress is often experienced as suffering or displeasure.

Most research and theory in the stress field emphasize physiological effects, such as changes in the viscera, rather than psychological or behavioral reactions. Violent and criminal behavior, as a consequence of stress, is virtually ignored. One of the few to recognize the relationship of stress and crime is Halleck (1971), who regards crime as a kind of adaptation to life's stresses. He writes: "Sometimes these stresses are realistic and direct, sometimes they are realistic and indirect, and sometimes they do not have an objectively measurable source" (p. 84). According to Halleck, criminal adaptation to realistic and direct stress (such as poverty or crowded living conditions) can be thought of as "rational" crime and is studied by sociologists. Stress that is realistic and indirect or objectively unmeasurable (such as psycho-logical conflict) mediates criminal adaptation through the individual's own personality or psychopathology and can be considered "irrational" crime.

In prior publications (Revitch, 1975, 1977; Revitch and Schlesinger, 1978), we have attempted to classify criminal or antisocial behavior along a spectrum of motivational stimulation. On one end of the spectrum are offenses that are the result of external factors, such as social environment and situational circumstances. On the opposite end of the scale are offenses committed because of internal sources of a psychogenic, rather than a socio-genic, origin. There are also categories falling between the extremes, with borderline cases having characteristics of adjacent areas. This system of classification is, in many respects, similar to Halleck's in that both external and internal factors are brought together in the same universe of discourse. Since any criminal act is an interaction between the individual and the environment, it is necessary to deal with both. In our analysis of the role of stress, violence, and crime, we divide stress into two chief types—external and internal—and discuss each one's effects on the individual.

External Stress

There is no doubt that the recent crime rise in the United States (see F.B.I. *Uniform Crime Reports,* published annually by the U.S. Government Printing Office) is due, in large part, to external, environmental, and social factors. Our society is currently experiencing a weakening of social controls and a breakdown of established values. Rapid social change, the effects of the computer and atomic age, strained economic conditions for the lower and, more recently, the middle class—all provide for extreme environmental stress. Such conditions of stress have been well elaborated by sociological theorists. For example, Merton (1957), elaborating on the seminal work of Durkheim (1897) and his concept of anomie, believes that the breakdown of social order—as a result of economic depression, prosperity, or rapid tech-nological change—contributes directly to crime. According to Faris (1955), the breakdown or disruption of interpersonal bonds and the deterioration of morale create social disorganization, stress, and crime. Other sociologists, such as Teeters (1959), take an eclectic position, stating that there are nu-merous causes of crime, but environmental stress still plays a prominent role. There are many historical examples of increased antisocial behavior, including wanton murder, during times of social upheaval (see Wedgewood, 1957). The atrocities of Nazi Germany provide a classic example of the rela-tionship between violence and rapid social change in values, social unrest, and tremendous social stress—conditions that not only foster violence but also condone it.

Among the most common of the socially stimulated antisocial acts are child abuse and family violence, which are almost always due, in large part, to external stress. In child abuse, those under the age of 5 are the most common victims, and the mother or primary caretaker is the most common offender. Beating is the most common form of abuse, although burning of hands, immersion in boiling water, starvation, and murder have been fre-quently reported. One case of abuse seen by one of us (E.R.) involved a sadistic father who would squeeze his son's genitals when the child wet him-self. Ironically, many child abusers have themselves been abused as children, and they frequently state that they love their children (Kempe, 1962). Psy-chological factors are certainly involved in child abuse (as was clearly seen in the case above); without stress, however, abuse is not likely to occur, despite the psychopathology.

Major theorists and researchers in the field of family violence recog-nize the important role of external stress. Gil (1969, 1970), a leading ex-ponent of the environmental stress theory of child abuse, finds such abuse concentrated mainly in the poor. Psychological factors that predispose to abuse are present in all classes, but the poor are subject to the special environ-mental distress and strains associated with socioeconomic deprivation. Middle-class families do experience violence, but it is less publicly visible, less fre-quent, more restrained, and less lethal. Gelles (1973) views family violence as an adaptational maneuver in response to social stress. He cites cases where pregnant wives have been assaulted and concludes that such acts indicate the family's use of physical aggression as a response to stress (Gelles, 1975). Steele (1978) argues that psychodynamics are extremely important in understanding child abuse but that social stress and life crisis are also major ingredients.

Recent empirical evidence supports the social stress concept. Justice and Duncan (1976) found a significant correlation between life crisis (as measured by a rating scale) and child abuse; other conditions, such as family isolation (Garbarino, 1977), have also been cited. One experimental study (Passman and Mulhern, 1977) tested and confirmed the hypothesis that heightened stress results in increased punishment of children by their mother. The following cases of family violence are illustrative:

Case 1. A recent immigrant from a South American country, a 27-year-old female, was first examined by one of us (E.R.) when signs of injuries were found on her 3-month-old baby. The child was placed in a foster home. Six months later, the mother was reexamined by order of the court, since she had requested termination of the foster home placement and return of the child. She was an attractive, well-groomed woman of bright intelligence and with a college education. In the second interview, she revealed the following history with an outburst of emotion: Her birth was some kind of family scandal, since she was born out of wedlock and adopted by her aunt. Her adoptive parents belonged to the country's high society, and she was taken care of and raised by servants. Early in life, she developed a feeling of being discriminated against by her uncles, aunts, and cousins, who openly discussed her origins. She recollected a feeling of intense shame when, in her childhood, an older girl mentioned her illegitimacy in the hearing of others. She married an immigrant to her homeland, a man of a much lower social station than her adoptive parents.

Upon arrival in the United States, she felt displaced in a strange land, and she believed that the neighbors rejected her. When she became pregnant a few months later, her unhappiness increased, and she had nausea and vomiting throughout the nine months of pregnancy. She said: "I was afraid because I did not know the doctor. I was afraid of the hospital. I did not speak English well, and I had no friends." The newborn child was placed in an incubator and was brought home three days after the mother's discharge from the hospital.

In the first interview, she denied her guilt, rationalizing her child's injuries as follows: "He fell from my arms. I jumped and I think my foot hit a rock and I fell on top of the baby." She seemed to have more confidence in the examiner at the second interview, and she admitted neglecting the baby. She said: "I was afraid of the hospital. I did not know English well. I know American hospitals are good, but I didn't know anyone. I had no friends." Furthermore, she stated that she had no help, that she didn't like her doctor, and "I felt it was too much for me. I was so thin, I never had time for anything. I also worried about my appearance. I had no time for myself. I was conscious about my looks. I was not a very good picture." She claimed that her husband wanted her to be the same woman he married and that he always told her that a woman should look like a woman even if she were a mother.

Comment. The patient as much as admitted to willful neglect of the child. Throughout her life, she felt isolated, rejected, and inferior. These feelings were accentuated in marriage to a person of foreign birth and culture and of inferior social status. Nevertheless, she was now more isolated in the United States than she had ever been previously and therefore was completely dependent on her husband for love and support. Because she believed that her attractiveness was her only positive quality, the assumed loss of good looks through pregnancy and child care seemed threatening. Taking care of an unwelcome child in the situation described was overwhelmingly stressful. The stress was external, impinging on her fragile and insecure personality make-up.

Case 2. A 23-year-old woman smothered her 2-year-old son while he was sick in bed. Finding him lifeless sometime later, she called police for assistance. Three to four weeks prior to this incident, the child had been brought to the local hospital emergency room because of lacerations on the body and forehead. Healed scars were found on the chin, both cheeks and tongue. On the day of the incident, she tied the child to the bed because he was restless. In the interview, she was unable or unwilling to tell exactly what took place. She denied her offense. She claimed that the child did not eat and seemed sick, so she gave him aspirin. She added: "I just don't know how this could happen." She had two other children, aged 4 years and 8 months. The description given to me (E.R.) of the boy (specifically, his hyperactivity and clumsiness) suggested that he suffered from minimal brain dysfunction.

The mother of the dead boy had had a difficult childhood. Her parents divorced when she was 2 or 3 years old, and immediately after finishing high school she married. She had met her husband at a diner, where both were employed at the time. The marriage was stressful, dull, and without outlets. The husband had a volatile temper and on occasion struck her. Bills at times were not paid, which was upsetting to her. She complained that she never had a honeymoon or vacations and that her only recreation was shopping and TV. The three times she went with her husband to Puerto Rico she had to stay with his family, unable to participate in family discussions, since she did not know Spanish. She said: "I never had fun; I never had a good time in my life." She complained of headaches, blurred vision, chest pains, fainting spells, and depression. Her husband frequently left her alone, and she complained that she had to spend evenings all by herself. The husband preferred the dead child to the other children, although, according to her, he was the most troublesome of the three.

Comment. The environmental stress is obvious in this case. Her husband was unsupportive and indifferent. She had absolutely no outlets and rest. Her whole existence consisted in chores and the care of the children. She may have singled out the 2-year-old boy because of his identification with her husband and because his illnesses demanded greater attention and effort.

Adolescents (particularly around 15-17 years of age) are much more crime prone than adults. The recent rise in crime in general is, in large part, caused by the disproportionate rise in juvenile crimes and delinquency. Approximately fifteen years ago, juvenile delinquency centered mainly on school and behavioral problems, family incorrigibility, and minor acts of vandalism and stealing. In recent years, however, there has been an increase in violent criminal acts committed by adolescents, including mugging of the elderly, rape, and murder. Even youth gangs of the late 1950s had some purpose to their antisocial behavior. Today we see more purposeless acts of violence perpetrated by teenagers, including middle-class youths.

The adolescent period has always been considered a time of instability and turmoil (A. Freud, 1958). But why has juvenile crime increased in recent years? Explanations center on increased loosening of family ties, quickly changing values, more leisure time, and boredom, as well as on the by-products of increased affluence: a nation "crammed with an incredible variety of attractive goods," where youths find "their inhibitions overridden by the cumulative temptations of a materialistic wonderland" (Christenson, 1970, p. 213). Bandura (1973) and others also argue that the media, particularly television, have glorified violence and crime. The common denominator in many of these explanations is an increase in stress resulting from external factors. The developing adolescent is more sensitive to stress than the adult and reacts behaviorally, whereas many adults react to stress somatically.

The stress of poverty in the lower classes, as well as the stress of boredom and meaninglessness in the upper classes (see Grinker, 1978), provides conditions of tension, anger, and a readiness to act out against almost anything. Recent acts of terrorism throughout the world furnish further examples of this phenomenon. Perpetrators of such acts are often middle-class young adults with good educations who lack direction and purpose in life and are confused by the stress of conflicting social principles. This social stress leads to psychological disequilibrium, which the individual attempts to reduce in some fashion—for example, by joining a left-wing radical group or a religious cult to gain some type of meaning in life. Cult leaders such as Jim Jones, Reverend Moon, and Charles Manson have an unusual charismatic influence over others; however, the social climate of disillusionment and anomie clearly plays a large part in their ability to control the followers. We have examined and treated many adolescent offenders whose crimes were perpetrated mainly because of external stress. The following case is illustrative:

Case 3. A 17-year-old youth was admitted, by order of the juvenile court, to the now defunct New Jersey State Diagnostic Center because of violation of probation, running away from home, and car theft. His father's whereabouts were unknown. His mother was a colorless, apathetic woman with only a grammar school education. One of the boy's sisters was diagnosed as borderline defective, and was in a state hospital while he was a patient at the Diagnostic Center. A half sister was in a sanitarium for tuberculosis. His stepfather, over 6 feet tall and weighing 235 pounds, was described as a brutal man employed in loading trucks.

The patient himself measured only 4 feet 10 inches and weighed 85 pounds. He looked undernourished and emaciated. There was no evidence of beard growth or of pubic or axillary hair. His intelligence was within borderline range. Neurological examination did not reveal distinct abnormalities, but his EEG was characterized by fluctuating rhythm with runs of 5- to 6-per-second frequencies. The stepfather inflicted physical punishment and at times injured the boy without any attempt by the mother to interfere. The patient weighed only 5 pounds at birth. He had had severe temper tantrums since early life, as well as breath-holding attacks until the age of 3 years. Tantrums and mere excitement were frequently followed by soiling his pants, even at the age of 17 years. When he left school at 16, he could read only at the third or fourth grade level. Psychiatric examination and projective tests elicited a marked feeling of inadequacy, a painful perception of his short stature and immature bodily development. He felt that people took advantage of him. He also developed claustrophobia, headaches, and dizzy spells. While at the Diagnostic Center, he had severe temper tantrums, which suggested the diagnosis of psychomotor epilepsy. However, the tantrums were always reactive in nature and without amnesia. One of these attacks occurred when he was placed in a small room. There he developed dizziness and anxiety due to his claustrophobia. He screamed. When the attendants did not pay attention to him, he became highly aggressive, causing extensive damage to his room.

Comment. Poor body development and short stature in themselves are stressful to a 17-year-old boy. The stress was increased, however, as his immature development set him apart from his peers, and his abusive stepfather and indifferent mother offered a family environment that was not only unsupportive but also threatening. His weak and immature body build was contrasted by the stepfather's size and weight. The theft of cars gave him some feeling of power and control and thus released the stressful feelings of inadequacy and inferiority. His unstable existence, with poor school and work adjustment and impulsive behavior, placed him in the impulsive category of offenders in our scale of the motivational spectrum. In spite of an abnormal EEG, we felt that he did not suffer from epilepsy but of what is described in French literature as "crises catathymiques" (Gayral and others, 1956; Revitch, 1964).

External stress can also be more immediate, stemming from a situation, rather than from society, the environment, or a stage of development.

Many crimes are purely a reaction to a stressful situation. Approximately 70 percent of all homicides, for example (see F.B.I. *Uniform Crime Reports*), occur under stressful circumstances, such as family arguments and barroom brawls. Much white-collar crime is due to stress of circumstances such as threatened financial strain, loss of self-esteem, or loss of job. Gas line violence, a fairly recent phenomenon, is a classic example of situational stress. Many armed robberies are basically reactions to stressful situations (see MacDonald, 1975) or a combination of psychopathology and situational stress (Johnson, 1978). Yukio Mishima, a Japanese novelist who deals with the psycho-dynamics of violence in his 1971 novel *Thirst for Love,* graphically describes a murder which is the result of tremendous situational stress created by anger, humiliation, and jealousy. Etsuko, the principal character, has been recently widowed by a man who was unfaithful to her. She subsequently falls in love with a peasant boy, who also rebuffs her affection, so that, once again, she feels betrayed. She describes the tremendous stress she has been under as "unbearable agony. . . . You can't imagine how much I suffered." Carrying a knife, Etsuko's aged father-in-law appears in the garden in time to witness the peasant boy's attempts to have sex with Etsuko. Etsuko seizes the knife and slays the young man.

Immature and impulsive people and adolescents are particularly sensitive to stress and may respond to various stressful situations in an anti-social manner. Such offenses may be aggressive, nonaggressive (such as stealing), or a combination of both. Bagley (1969) cites one type of incest that is accidental and impulsive; it stems from the stress of disorganized living. Prison life is another example of an extremely stressful situation. Stress factors such as close, overcrowded living conditions, lack of free-dom, lack of privacy, and a monotonous routine dictated by rigid regula-tions often rise to such a crescendo that violent activity is precipitated. The following case is illustrative:

> *Case 4.* A 48-year-old bank robber (C.C.) impulsively stabbed another inmate when the victim borrowed a pack of matches and did not immediately return it. C.C. stated that this action implied that he was a "weak spot." During the week prior to the attack, C.C. was in constant pain from an infected foot and a toothache. He was also worried about an impending parole hearing. Criminal history included many impulsive crimes, such as robbery of banks and stores; however, his history of violence was minimal, and he was well respected in the prison, serving on several committees and the like.
>
> *Comment.* Obvious background stress is discernible here. C.C. was incarcerated and subject to all the difficulties that this state suggests; furthermore, he was in real physical discomfort while await-ing a parole hearing. To these factors is added the immediate stress of a blow to self-esteem; thus, all these factors contributed to trig-gering the violent attack. In the interview, C.C. spoke of the constant

tension he was under and he said: "It probably wouldn't have happened if I hadn't been in so much pain. When he didn't give back the matches, I would probably have just let it go." If not for the stress, this offense probably would not have occurred.

Internal Stress

The relationship of internal stress to violence and crime has never been fully elaborated, probably because internal stress is hard to measure objectively. The closest attempt has come from the psychological theories of crime, based on the Freudian hypothesis that "the conflict in the unconscious mind gives rise to feelings of guilt and anxiety, with a consequent desire for punishment to remove guilt feelings and restore proper balance of good against evil. The criminal then commits the criminal act in order to be caught and punished" (Vold, 1958, p. 119). This psychodynamic theory, however, as well as other elaborations based on it (see, for example, Abrahamsen, 1960; Glover, 1960), does not fully describe the role of internal stress; its focus is primarily on conflict.

Menninger, Mayman, and Pruyser (1963) view psychopathology in general, and violence in particular, as an adaptation to external *and* internal stress. Episodic dyscontrol (outbursts, attacks, assaults, social offenses) is the result of the ego's failure to adapt to strain; at the same time, it is an avoidance of lower-level adaptation, such as psychosis. According to Menninger (1966, p. 32), "The strain resulting from attempted adaptation with inadequate powers may reach the point where it is a choice of breaking or being broken. . . . Sometimes something must yield, and a 'crime' is committed to prevent a crack. . . . Internal balance is thus and thereby reestablished." Menninger's concept, then, refers to crimes that are the result of both external and internal stress. The following case, seen by one of us (L.B.S.), is graphically illustrative of both external and internal stress:

> *Case 5.* A 46-year-old man (D.P.) fatally shot his wife and three children, aged 6, 9, and 12 years. He then called police and waited for his arrest. D.P. had been unemployed for two years prior to the murders and had also served time in prison for several impulsive assaults while intoxicated. His wife was employed part time as a Tupperware saleswoman and often belittled D.P. for not working, calling him a "bum" in front of the children. They lived in overcrowded conditions in an inner-city neighborhood and had frequent, violent arguments.
>
> On the day of the homicides, the couple had another argument, and D.P. was asked to leave the house. He accused his wife, in the course of the argument, of infidelity, and she, in turn, accused him of listening in on her telephone conversations. Apparently be-

coming hysterical, Mrs. P. threw food at him and swore at his dead parents, screaming "They should burn in hell!" She also told the children that D.P. was "worthless and no good." He started to leave the apartment, but "something snapped. I went into the bedroom and got my gun." D.P. returned and killed his wife and the children. After the murders, he felt relief.

Comment. The external stress, in this case, is clear. D.P. was unemployed and constantly belittled by his wife. The stress, in the way of continual harassment, finally brought him to the breaking point. His internal controls began to break, and tremendous inner stress was relieved by the explosion, which possibly averted further psychotic decompensation.

In previous publications (Revitch, 1975, 1977; Revitch and Schlesinger, 1978), we have elaborated on a psychodynamic process described as catathymic crisis (Wertham, 1937). We divided this process into the acute and chronic types. In the acute type (which Menninger considers a subtype of episodic dyscontrol), psychic equilibrium is suddenly upset by an external event or irritant of symbolic significance that touches off a deeply rooted conflict. The release of affect overwhelms the ego and disrupts the psychic homeostasis. The inner stress of the tension caused by this disruption results in an act of violence, which usually is followed by relief. The following case is illustrative:

Case 6. An 18-year-old youth strangled a 22-year-old female nightclub entertainer with a rubber hose after she had entered the gas station where he worked. She apparently asked to use the telephone, after which she returned to the front office and turned on the radio. Shortly afterward, C.S. found her with most of her clothes off, telling him not to be afraid. He stated: "She grabbed me by the wrist and pulled me toward her. I pulled my hand away. She started kissing my neck, and she unbuttoned my pants. I turned around and looked at her. I started having sex standing up." However, C.S. could not effect an erection. The woman then pushed him away and said: "You're a little boy—go back to your mother." C.S. then grabbed a piece of rubber tubing and put it around her neck and strangled her. He placed the body in the trunk of his car and took it to a nearby vacant lot, where he left it. That evening he slept well and functioned adequately the next day at school. Fragments of the event began to intrude consciousness, and C.S. became anxious. He believed at this point that the event was a dream; however, when he found the woman's eyeglasses in his trunk, he realized that he probably had killed her. Several days later, he confessed.

Comment. In this case, the stress is very indirect, sudden, internal, and psychogenic. The irritant was the injury to his pride, when the victim told him to go to his mother. This touched upon a "complex of ideas" (Wertham, 1967) and created a state of sudden inner stress, which was relieved by his destroying the noxious stimulus (the victim).

The chronic catathymic process was originally described by Wertham (1937) as an attempt to explain unusual cases of violence. In these cases, the violence was not sudden, the motive was not apparent, and the act was preceded by obsessional preoccupation with violence. Wertham (1967) described this prodromal period as a buildup of tension, which is released through the violent deed. Revitch and Schlesinger (1978) further elaborated this concept and highlighted this incubation phase as the essence of the chronic catathymic process. This period of inner stress and tension may be manifested by depressed mood and loose, schizophrenic-like thinking. The individual is obsessively preoccupied with suicidal and homicidal ideas. Most often the act is interpersonally directed toward a spouse or lover. At other times, the violence may be diverted toward an inanimate object. Relief follows the violent act. In *The Temple of the Golden Pavilion,* another novel (1971a) by Yukio Mishima, a beautiful description of the chronic catathymic process culminating in an act of arson is presented. The central figure of the work is Mizoguchi, an ugly, stuttering, scrawny boy. He is taunted by his peers and feels unattractive and unloved. He becomes preoccupied with the beauty of the temple, and this preoccupation then shifts to an urge to destroy it by arson. During the incubation period, he is unable to perform sexually because visions of the temple intrude consciousness and he loses his erection. Once Mizoguchi makes definite plans to set fire to the temple, he feels relief, and this same relief is experienced after he carries out the act and watches the temple burn. Arlow (1978) believes that the underlying conflict was Mizoguchi's witnessing the primal scene. The temple, symbolizing the mother, had to be destroyed in order to restore psychic equilibrium. We believe that the conflict, whatever it might be, created a tremendous state of tension and inner stress in Mizoguchi, which was relieved through the destruction of the temple.

The following case was seen by one of us (L.B.S.) and is classic of the chronic catathymic process. Here, the internal stress of the incubation period is clearly illustrated:

Case 7. A 29-year-old male (W.G.) was seen in the county jail to help in the determination of sanity; he stood charged with murdering his wife. W.G. was steadily employed as a salesman and had a good work record and no prior involvement with the law. He had previously been married to his childhood sweetheart and had one child from this union, which ended after one year. He stated that when he met his second wife (the victim), he felt uncomfortable because she was "overly protected as a child; she was weak-minded;

her parents were very dominant." He further stated: "She always went back to her parents when we had an argument or a problem."

The events leading up to the murder are as follows: Approximately nine months before the event (the incubation phase), W.G. and his wife began having serious marital difficulties. The wife threatened to divorce him, and she frequently left home to live with her parents for brief periods. Finally, the wife chose to separate permanently, and this apparently depressed W.G. who had accompanying suicidal ideas. He sought treatment at a local clinic, but the depression did not abate, and the ideas of violence were not taken seriously by the psychiatrist. W.G. bought a gun and went to his wife's place of employment and showed it to her. He stated: "I purchased the gun; I thought of suicide. I talked to her for a final time with the gun in my car, and then I put the gun to my head and told her 'I'm going to kill myself.' She then promised she'd come back to me." The wife brought charges against him for this incident, and W.G. served thirty days in jail and was released on bail. When released, he bought another gun and thought again of suicide. Yet he maintained hope that he and his wife would reunite. The Christmas season was nearing, and this apparently made W.G. feel worse. He stated: "I tried to contact my wife. I felt bad. People were happy, but I wasn't happy. I went to see the social worker at the clinic. I cried and I could feel that something was happening."

"On Christmas Eve, I decided to go to midnight mass and see my wife. I saw encouragement in her eyes. I tried to talk to my wife, but her mother intervened. I followed them home; I had the gun in my car. I followed them into the garage. They pulled in the garage, and I went in behind them. I asked to talk to my wife. It was Christmas Eve, around 1 A.M. The father hit me with a broom handle, and the mother went in the house, apparently to call the police. I pulled out the gun. I put numerous shots into my wife. I wanted them to know I meant business. The parents were all scattered. I stepped into the driver's seat and shot her in the head again and again. She fell out the passenger side; I saw no blood on her. I said to her that I loved her, and I kissed her on the lips. Then I shot her again from close range directly in the head. I think I fired two more shots. I walked away and felt I would throw up. I pulled the hammer back and pointed it to my head. My hands shook so bad I couldn't pull the trigger. I looked at her eyes. I really felt ill. I saw the police coming, so I dropped the gun. I was afraid my father-in-law would go for it and start shooting me. I yelled at the cops to pick up the gun that I dropped. I was glad it was all over."

Comment. In this case, the state of inner tension and stress began nine months prior to the murder, when marital problems started. At points, the stress state was manifested clinically as depression. Both suicide and violence were seen by the subject as possible solutions to his crisis. He knew that "something was happening" to him, but neither he nor the professionals he consulted knew exactly what the active process going on within W.G. was. After the murder, he experienced a sense of relief as the act released the stress state and restored homeostasis. (Crime, including murder, in states of depression has been described by Woddis, 1957.)

On the extreme endogenous end of the spectrum are the compulsive offenses. These are crimes that are repeated over and over in the same, often ritualistic, manner, despite any attempt to stop the offender. These crimes are the result of purely psychological sources, with little influence of the environment. The depth of the inner conflict is profound and places the offender in a state of tremendous psychic stress. The future offender is often plagued by primitive fantasies that have broken into consciousness, and he has an intense urge to act out these fantasies. If he resists, and he often may resist such urges for years, he experiences extreme discomfort. William Heirens, famous for his saying "Catch me before I kill again—I can't help myself," reported headaches when trying to resist the compulsion of burglarizing homes and killing women (Freeman, 1955). He is quoted as saying: "I resisted for about two hours. I tore sheets out of place and I went into a sweat. When I got these urges I would take out plans and draw how to get in certain places. I would burn up the plans. Sometimes they helped" (Kennedy, Hoffman, and Haines, 1947, p. 118).

A case, previously reported in full (Revitch and Schlesinger, 1978), was of a 16-year-old boy who killed two women and brutally tortured a third. He told one of us (L.B.S.) that at bedtime he prayed not to wake up, so that he would not have to commit his crimes again. In another case seen by us, a young man who had been tormented for years with fantasies and urges to rape and kill women stated that he would kill himself before doing anything to someone else. Three years later, this individual was found dead one morning, an apparent suicide. Here, the stress was expressed only in fantasy, and attacks on women never occurred, although he brutally killed small animals.

Not all compulsive crimes are violent. Exhibitionism, the urge to expose genitals to passersby, is almost always compulsive; yet the offenders are passive, inadequate, and nonaggressive. One of our cases, for example, was a 53-year-old married man who was reactively depressed due to unemployment. He exposed himself several times to his teenage daughter's girl friends. He stated he could not control himself, and, although he was "ashamed of himself," he felt relieved following the act. Another of our cases described tremendous inner stress when he did not expose himself. He always had the urge but only "got the guts" to do it when drinking. The man would stand naked in the front window of his home, hoping that "young girls in the neighborhood would ring the bell and talk to me." It is rare that females are arrested for indecent exposure, since those who have such compulsions can release them easily through socially sanctioned means and thus relieve the inner stress. There have been some cases reported, however, of bona fide female exhibitionists (see Hollender, Brown, and Roback, 1977) who were apprehended.

The following case of compulsive fetishism, resulting in murder, illustrates the strength of the compulsion that this type of offender is unable to conquer:

> *Case 8.* A 46-year-old man (W.Y.) who had a fetish for leather was sentenced to life in prison for the murder of a woman. While driving his car, he noticed a woman who was wearing leather gloves, and he followed her for approximately 40 miles to her home. He entered the house after her and asked to fondle her gloves. The woman apparently became terrified, and W.Y. killed her. This man was under psychiatric outpatient treatment at the time for assaults on women and for breaking into houses, all apparently stemming from a need to touch leather objects. While in prison, W.Y. was a model inmate, earning a master's degree and gaining recognition within the institution and local community as a classic case of what proper rehabilitation can accomplish. After fourteen years, he was released on parole. Four days after his release, he was arrested for assaulting seven women "to get their leather pocketbooks." When interviewed by one of us (L.B.S.) shortly after this incident, he stated that for years he had fantasized about "holding women who wore leather." He described headaches and tremendous frustration to the point of explosive angry episodes to relieve tension when the act could not be accomplished. While he was in the structured world of prison, he was able to control the compulsive urge to deal with the accompanying psychic tension. After he was released, however, his own controls were too fragile, and he acted out even though he stated that he absolutely did not want to do it. "It was too much for me, I couldn't control it."
>
> *Comment.* The internal stress, in this case, is highlighted by W.Y.'s description of his psychosomatic reactions in prison when the compulsion could not be carried out. It is not the need to touch leather itself that makes this man dangerous but, rather, the tremendous state of inner stress that he must reduce. The tension becomes unbearable, and it is at this point that he is likely to act out.

Discussion

We have attempted to explain the relationship of stress to violence and to some forms of criminal behavior. External stress, stemming from the environment or from a particular situation, is obvious, direct, and easily measurable. Sociologists have studied such external stress and theorized on its etiology and means of control. Internal stress is less obvious because its effects are indirect and not easily measured. Very little attention has been paid to the manifestations or results of this inner process. By using our previously reported system for classifying antisocial behavior, we have tried to bring together both external and internal stress factors into the same universe of discourse and to explain these forces as they interface with the individual's own personality makeup.

When the problems of violence and crime are approached from the perspective that we have outlined, several implications for prevention become clear. If the external stresses may be minimized by social change or intervention, crime is likely to be reduced. It is doubtful that sociologists or politicians can readily accomplish this task for society as a whole. However, using the degree of external stress as a red flag device for specific families in immediate crisis can help to deter, for example, child abuse or domestic violence. The level of internal stress also needs to be assessed by mental health professionals when a patient presents ideas or fantasies of violence. As in Case 7, inner stress sometimes is evaluated only as reactive depression. Parole boards also need to be cognizant of the degree of inner tension and stress that the compulsive offender harbors, since we believe it is not the compulsion or fantasy itself, but rather the amount of distress it causes the patient, that determines whether the patient will act out the fantasy. Many individuals have sadistic fantasies their entire lives and never act on them, because the fantasy does not create inner distress and disturb the individual. By continued study of both external and internal stress and their vicissitudes, the complex and multidetermined etiologies of violence and criminal behavior will further unfold.

11

Life Events, Personality Traits, and Illness

Richard E. Minter
Chase Patterson Kimball

❖ ❖ ❖ ❖ ❖ ❖ ❖ ❖ ❖ ❖ ❖ ❖ ❖

A number of investigators have attempted to show a correlation between life stress and the onset of illness or between personality traits and illness. While some have worked with specific disease entities—such as coronary heart disease, hypertension, peptic ulcers, cancer, ulcerative colitis, asthma, and rheumatoid arthritis—others have studied the general susceptibility to any illness. Some believe that life stresses are always undesirable events. Others regard stress as any event that requires an adjustment of some sort. Some workers have dealt with life stresses as a whole; others have studied specific life stresses. Some investigators feel that psychological factors, in association with environmental factors, have an etiological role in illness, since they lower host resistance and allow predispositions to specific disease processes to manifest themselves. Others feel that the psychological factors are involved in the development of a predisposition.

This chapter provides a comprehensive and critical review of the work done on illness as a whole. Reviews by Lehmann (1967) and Thurlow (1967) sometimes omit discussion of methodological shortcomings, which we emphasize here. Birley (1972) discusses a number of studies relating stress and illness, but his overview is not a critical review of the literature. Coleman (1973) recently reported the findings of some of the leading investigators in this area, but his review is neither critical nor complete. Studies dealing with biochemical correlates or with animal studies are not reviewed here, although much promising work is being done in these areas.

In this review, illness refers to organic processes; it does not refer to symptoms without demonstrable organic signs identified through clinical and laboratory procedures. Self-reports and medical records often fail to identify a precise explanation for symptoms and to document illness. Many of the studies reviewed here do not provide a clear definition of illness. Others have selected inadequate study samples. For example, some may study only individuals who visit a physician, ignoring individuals who have similar complaints but do not seek physician assistance. The implication is that there may be differences (such as a high sick-role tendency) between these two populations and that these differences, rather than the correlation between illness and selected psychological parameters, are being measured. In order to minimize these problems, more precise documentation of illness and the selection of appropriate control groups for comparison are required. A satisfactory control group may be obtained by examining all persons in a sample rather than just those with symptoms and by carefully matching the groups to be compared. Such measures would assist in determining whether the illness group under study is actually different from a control population in regard to various psychological characteristics.

Life Events and Illness Onset

Early Work. Hinkle and his co-workers (Hinkle, 1961; Hinkle and others, 1956, 1957, 1958, 1960; Hinkle and Wolff, 1957a, 1957b, 1958) were the first to attempt a large study of the relationship between life events and illness. In studies on telephone company employees covering up to twenty years, they reported the following findings: (1) A small number of people (25 percent) have most of the illness episodes (50 percent). (2) As the number of illness episodes increases, the number of organ systems involved also increases (thus, chronic diseases did not bias the results). (3) As the number of episodes of illness increases, the individual exhibits an increased number of etiologies of illness. (4) As the number of episodes of illness increases, the number of disturbances in mood, thought, and behavior also increases. (5) Clusters of illness, which were composed of several "different and ostensibly unrelated syndromes," were observed to occur and were not related to activity, diet, rest, or exposure to infections. (6) Such clusters of illness occurred most often when a person had a life situation described as unsatisfactory or when he experienced difficulty in adapting to his environment. Hinkle and Plummer (1952) reported that most absences from work for illness were restricted to a small number of people and that, compared to the low-absence group, the high-absence group had more major and minor illnesses, operations, injuries, and disturbances of feeling state, thought, and behavior. Those with high absence rates were described as discontented, unhappy, and difficult to supervise; they had more conflict and anxiety (Hinkle and others, 1958); they had been exposed to more stressful situations and experiences. These investigators felt that "something happened . . . in the ill group to render them subject to many bodily disturbances" and that "this had not happened to the well group" (p. 373). They hypothesized that there are inherent differences in constitutional adaptive capacities and that there is a causative relationship between life events and the appearance of illness at a particular time. However, they conceded that some of the differences were secondary to differences in illness reporting (Hinkle and Plummer, 1952). Measurement of the amount of life dissatisfaction was made by three judges who had no access to medical records. All illness data were obtained retrospectively from medical records and reports made by the person. The pioneering efforts of these workers stimulated others to investigate the nature of this life dissatisfaction and its relationship to illness onset. What was needed was a quantitative measure of life events.

The Social Readjustment Rating Scale. Rahe, Holmes, and their co-workers developed the first quantitative measure of life events. As a measurement of life stress, they chose to measure life changes that caused the individual to make an adjustment of some sort. To measure such life changes, they developed the Schedule of Recent Experience (SRE), a list of forty-three life events which had empirically been found to be important for most people, ranging from minor violations of the law to death of a spouse (Holmes and Rahe, 1967). Since different life events require a different amount of adjustment, these workers developed the Social Readjustment Rating Scale (SRRS) (Holmes and Rahe, 1967). This scale gave different weights to each life event; the weights were derived from rankings of the events by samples from the general population, according to the amount of adjustment required for the event (Masuda and Holmes, 1967). The amount of life change was then obtained by multiplying the weight for each event by the frequency that it occurred in the time period under study, the result being expressed as Life Change Units (LCU).

The investigators then utilized the SRE and SRRS to study life events and illness onset (Gunderson and Rahe, 1974). The results of their numerous studies can be summarized as follows: (1) Clusters of life changes preceded the onset of reported illness; increased LCU scores for the several years preceding the study period repeatedly showed a positive, significant correlation with incidence of illness during the study period. (2) A small proportion of men had most of the illness episodes. (3) Most (80 percent) of the illness episodes were minor. (4) More illness episodes occurred during stressful periods (combat on a navy ship). (5) A higher incidence of illness was observed in men performing physically demanding or hazardous tasks. (6) Demographic variables affected the reported incidence of illness: higher incidence in younger men, blacks, unmarried men, men with lesser education, and men with more job dissatisfaction. These studies have the major shortcoming of lack of documentation of illness. All illness data were obtained from self-reporting and from medical records; no protocols of criteria needed for diagnosis of illness were used. Rahe and associates (1972) admitted that visits to the dispensary are not adequate indices of the prevalence of illness.

Rahe, Holmes, and their co-workers did document illness in other studies on tuberculosis (Hawkins, Davies, and Holmes, 1957; Rahe and others, 1964). They studied employees of a tuberculosis sanitarium who had developed tuberculosis within the previous three months, the diagnosis being based on a noted change in routine chest X rays. They compared this group to a matched control group of sanitarium employees who were free of tuberculosis, based on chest X rays and tuberculin skin tests. There was a significant difference between the tuberculous and control groups in that the tuberculous group had higher LCU scores. This was a well-controlled study with well-documented illnesses. Other studies on tuberculosis by these workers did not have good control groups (Holmes and others, 1957).

Other Studies of Life Stress. Other workers have now used the SRRS to study the relationship between life change and illness. Cline and Chosey (1972) administered the SRE to military cadets. Health data were obtained retrospectively from a self-administered health checklist. The number of health changes had a small but significant correlation with LCU scores. Health changes were mostly very minor: runny nose, indigestion, eye strain, pimples, bruises, and nausea; these are the types of symptoms that may be differentially reported according to the individual's threshold for complaint.

Casey, Thoresen, and Smith (1970) administered the SRE to Army personnel in basic training. They recognized that many medical records do not list a diagnosis and do not distinguish the "disease-free health care seeker" from the truly sick person. Since they felt that retrospective diagnosis is a risky procedure, they did not attempt to make "illness" ratings or "seriousness-of-illness" ratings. Rather, they reported a significant correlation between LCU scores and the "level of health care attained" (in the Army medical system, each higher level of health care attainment consists of more extensive and sophisticated diagnostic and treatment measures). However, most of the statistical significance is accounted for by the very large number of low LCU scores in the lower level of the health care system (the dispensary).

Thurlow (1971) studied the medical records of industrial employees. He reported that the perception of the life situation, as measured by the SRE and by the Standard Deviation Score, a measure of the amount of variability which the environment is viewed to have, bears a stronger relationship to illness experience than does the more objective and less judgmental items of social change. With sick-role tendency (as measured by a questionnaire) held constant, the Standard Deviation Score was still found to correlate significantly with subsequent frequency of minor illness episodes. Controlling for sick-role tendency is a useful technique which other researchers should use.

Stewart and associates (1969) studied single platoons in a Marine training camp. They reasoned that if a specific etiology, such as microbial infection or accidents, was the cause of all illnesses, then there would be a clustering of the same illnesses in each platoon, since the platoons were relatively isolated from each other for the eight weeks of training. Using a three-way analysis of variance, they found numerous different causes of illness in each platoon, rather than clusters of a few etiologies. They concluded that the cause of illness was nonspecific and was related to the social environment of each platoon. The data on illness were obtained from sick-call records. Those platoons with the largest number of sick calls had significantly more mild complaints (the men were sent back to full duty), and half of all complaints were of unknown etiology; this suggests a large number of functional complaints.

Mutter and Schleifer (1966) used a semistructured interview to obtain data on family patterns of ill children. To ensure that somatic illness actually existed in the study sample, they included only children who were hospitalized for an acute disease process. The illnesses were those commonly seen in a pediatric setting, and the diagnoses were straightforward. A well-matched control group of healthy children was selected. The social and psychological parameters were well described and were sought in the families of the children of both groups. The families of the ill children were more disorganized and, during the six-month period under study, exposed these children to a greater number of changes in the psychological and social aspects of their lives, compared to the families of the control group. These changes were inherently more threatening and tended to have greater disruptive impact than those experienced by the control group. These workers felt that their findings support a multifactorial concept of disease, one that implicates social, psychological, and biological factors.

Noting that only a small number of persons who become colonized or infected by an infectious agent actually acquire the disease, Friedman and Glasgow (1966) reviewed animal and human studies of psychological and social factors that affect the host-parasite relationship. The animal studies showed that relatively subtle psychological and environmental factors appear to influence susceptibility to a wide range of infectious agents, but the human studies did not warrant such a conclusion. Most human studies had experimental problems. The only study without such problems was one reported by Meyer and Haggerty (1962). In a well-controlled prospective study of streptococcal throat infections, they obtained throat cultures on all subjects at least every three weeks for one year. Studying all persons in the sample was important because other studies (Goslings and others, 1963; Valkenburg and others, 1963) have estimated that 90 percent of the cases of group A streptococcal pharyngitis are never seen by a physician. Meyer and Haggerty defined streptococcal illness as the occurrence of a positive throat culture plus the presence of one or more clinical signs listed on a protocol. Families were interviewed periodically for accounts of stress and other variables. One fourth of streptococcal acquisitions (detection of a new type of Group A betahemolytic streptococcus for that person) and illnesses followed an acute family crisis (the list of crises did not contain trivial events); streptococcal respiratory infection, as well as nonstreptococcal respiratory infection, was four times as likely to be preceded as to be followed by acute family stress, the difference being statistically quite significant. The amount of chronic stress in a family (as independently judged by two observers) correlated significantly with streptococcal acquisition rates, illness rates, and anti-streptolysin-O response. Meyer and Haggerty concluded that the causal role and precise mechanisms were far from clear. However, they accomplished what other researchers did not: they documented the presence of illness by using strict criteria for diagnosis rather than relying on self-reports or medical records.

Aaksten (1974) developed his own questionnarie, similar to the SRE, and administered it to a population in Holland. He found correlations between psychosocial stresses and health disturbances and interpreted the stresses as failures to realize existential goals.

Marx, Garrity, and Bowers (1975) used a College Schedule of Recent Experience and a health questionnaire to report an association between high levels of life change and reported illness.

Coddington (1972a) developed a questionnaire for life change in children, with different questions for different age groups. He then determined the LCU scores for a population of normal children (Coddington, 1972b); no significant differences were found in race and social class, but LCU scores increased with age. He and his co-workers then studied hospitalized patients (Heisel and others, 1973). Two to three times as many of these children had experienced more frequent and/or more severe life events prior to the onset of their illness than did their healthy peers, the difference being statistically significant. Unfortunately, these investigators make no mention of criteria needed for diagnosis of illness.

Not everyone has reported positive correlations between life changes and illness. Wershow and Reinhart (1974) failed to find such a correlation.

They criticize the SRE research and suggest a moratorium on such work. Caplan (1975) disagrees with Wershow and Reinhart and suggests refinements in methodology. Neither paper refers to the documentation of illness.

Specific Life Changes. Other workers have concentrated on specific types of life change. Sheldon and Hooper (1969) studied the health of newly married couples. Compared to the five best-adjusted couples, the five worst-adjusted couples had more symptoms, more days in bed for illness, more current organic disease, and poorer health. Hooper and associates (1972) measured the effect of house change on illness, mental health, and satisfaction. They reported more illness in housing areas containing more mobile families. In both studies, the health data were obtained from self-reports.

Berkman (1969) studied spouseless motherhood and its possible effect on illness. Compared to married mothers, spouseless mothers reported significantly more illness and had lower morale, more psychological predisposition to stress, and lower ego strength. The illness data were obtained by a postal questionnaire.

Hall-Smith and Ryle (1969) postulated that an unstable marriage would be a stress that would correlate with illness. As measures of stability, they used reports of affection and domination discrepancy scores (difference between spouses on level of domination). They found a positive association between the domination discrepancy scores and illness and a negative association between affection and illness. They did not indicate how illness was documented.

Bruhn, Philips, and Wolf (1972) used the SRE and the SRRS to study first-, second-, and third-generation Italian-Americans living in the same community. They reported that LCU scores correlated with illness and were highest in the third-generation subjects and lowest in first-generation subjects. Differences were found in types of life changes: family change occurred more often in first-generation subjects; personal life change, in second-generation subjects; and work and finance changes, in third-generation subjects. The study was retrospective, and illness data were obtained from reports by the individuals.

As their index of stress, Roghmann and Haggerty (1973) used objective evaluation of the amount of coping required by a specific reported event. They reported that onset of illness correlated with a stressful event and that the presence of stress increased utilization of medical services, whether or not illness was present. Illness data came from self-reports.

Concentration camps impose severe physical and psychological stress on people. Arthur (1974) and Eitinger (1973) found increased mortality and morbidity in survivors of concentration camps, compared with the rest of the population.

Eylon (1967) studied the relationship between birth events (a pregnancy, a delivery, or a wedding) and appendicitis. Eylon studied only those cases with both preoperative and postoperative diagnosis of appendicitis and compared them with other surgical patients. Significantly more birth complications had occurred in appendicitis patients (or in a friend or relative). Half of these patients had birth events, compared to one seventh of the other surgical patients. To explain his findings, Eylon cites the Papez-MacLean theory, that emotions affect the viscera via the autonomic nervous system (MacLean, 1949). The few previous studies on appendicitis (Ingram, Evans, and Oppenheim, 1965; Meyer, Unger, and Slaughter, 1964) were concerned with the difference between patients who, on operation, were found to have or not to have actual appendicitis; briefly, those patients with a false positive diagnosis had more emotional problems than did those with actual appendicitis.

The studies we have discussed so far have tried to show that life events cause a decrease in general host resistance to *all* illness and make a person more vulnerable to pathophysiological processes. While numerous studies have reported the same results, conclusive evidence for such a hypothesis is still lacking.

Psychological Vulnerability and Illness

Workers in psychosomatic medicine have described various personality types in psychosomatic disorders. The hypothesis is that certain personality traits make a person more vulnerable to certain diseases; that is, the person has "psychological vulnerability" to those diseases. In addition, some researchers argue that certain personality characteristics make a person more vulnerable to all illness.

Personality Traits. Luborsky, Docherty, and Penick (1973) selectively reviewed fifty-three studies (including retrospective studies and studies utilizing immediate observation) of onset conditions for psychosomatic symptoms. The same main types of psychological antecedents were reported in both types of studies, except that frustration was found more often in immediate observation studies and separation in retrospective studies. The psychological antecedents reported, in order of frequency, were resentment (hostility), frustration (rejection), depression (hopelessness), anxiety, and helplessness. They noted that most studies were retrospective. Unfortunately, in such studies the effect of the disease on the personality and the course of life events cannot be determined. In addition, many studies have been uncontrolled.

In recent years investigators have sought ways to avoid these biases. Canter, Cluff, and Imboden (1972) used the Hypochondriasis, Morale Loss, and Ego Strength scales of the Minnesota Multiphasic Personality Inventory (MMPI) and the total score of the Cornell Medical Index (CMI). An individual who scored above the median on any three of these four scales was considered psychologically vulnerable; nonvulnerability was equated with scores below the median on any three of the scales. All subjects were given a number of skin tests and were checked for hypersensitive reactions. A protocol for diagnosis of hypersensitive reactions was used, and all subjects were required to report for evaluation regardless of presence or absence of symptoms. Twenty-three percent of the psychologically vulnerable persons, compared to 7 percent of the nonvulnerable persons, had a hypersensitive reaction, the difference being highly significant. Canter (1972), again using the MMPI and the CMI to define psychological vulnerability, reported on changes in mood during a febrile illness. Body temperature was taken at least every six hours on volunteers infected with *Pasteurella tularemia.* A list of adjectives describing a person's positive and negative moods was filled out twice each day. The psychologically vulnerable group had more total number of fever hours. The onset of mood change (decreased positive mood and increased negative mood) occurred at least six hours before the onset of fever in twenty-four of thirty-four cases ($p < .01$). The maximum temperature was higher for the vulnerable group, but not at statistically significant levels. In Canter's view, the study suggests that mood changes are sensitive barometers to changes in the biological state and that a psychologically vulnerable person is also biologically vulnerable. Both of these studies documented illness well and had good control groups.

Voors and associates (1968, 1969) administered the MMPI to Marine recruits and then, utilizing a protocol for recording signs and symptoms, examined all recruits daily for objective signs and symptoms of respiratory illness. They also used a weighted score, with different weights for each sign and symptom, depending on severity. Neither the weighted nor the unweighted score correlated significantly with any of the scales of the MMPI. The investigators concluded that the MMPI does not help predict illness.

Dependent Personality. The dependent personality has often been considered a personality type susceptible to diseases. Jacobs and associates (1966, 1967) developed indices to measure exaggerated dependency in allergy subjects. Their battery of tests yielded information concerning maternal domination, paternal rejection, exaggerated dependency, and neurotic emotional lability. Combining these tests, they obtained a total "psychological index" score, higher scores indicating greater dependency. They divided volunteer college students into a group allergic to asthma or hay fever, a normal group, and a vasomotor group having relatively chronic respiratory or dermatological complaints of a nonatopic nature. Independent diagnoses were made on these subjects by allergists on the basis of history and physical examination prior to the experimental procedures. The measure for biological predisposition consisted of eosinophil count on histamine challenge and skin test procedures. Ninety-three percent of the allergy subjects, compared to 33 percent of the nonallergy subjects in the other two groups, reacted to skin tests or to histamine challenge.

Patterns of maternal domination or paternal weakness were present in 78 percent of the allergy subjects, compared to 50 percent of the nonallergy subjects ($p < .05$). Further, 75 percent of the allergy cases had both biological and psychological factors present, while 75 percent of the nonallergy subjects did not have both factors concurrently present. This study is well controlled, and illness is well documented.

These authors believe that the summation hypothesis best explains allergic disorders; that is, both psychological and biological factors together cause more allergy than either by itself. They base this conclusion on the finding that adding the biological index scores and the psychological index scores gave scores that differentiated the allergic group from both other groups.

Maladaptive Coping. Jacobs and associates (Jacobs and others, 1970, 1971; Jacobs, Spilken, and Norman, 1969; Spilken and Jacobs, 1971) used these techniques to study respiratory illness in college students. Students who were treated at the college dispensary for upper respiratory illness and asthma had more disappointments, failures, unresolved role crises, social isolation, manifest distress, and life crises than did matched controls. These workers initially felt that development of an upper respiratory illness is associated with "unresolved distressing life change, maladaptive coping mechanisms, and unpleasant affect." They later felt that the maladaptive coping mechanisms would make a person more likely to go to a physician for symptoms that another person might ignore. In early studies, they studied only those who went to the dispensary; in later studies, they found people with respiratory illness who had not gone to the dispensary. They realized that people who did not seek medical care for such symptoms would be different from those people studied at the dispensary. They also found that subjects presenting at the dispensary with upper respiratory illness and asthma had angry-defiant coping styles and that habitual and excessive defiance was associated with an increased incidence of failure and disappointment. They concluded that people with maladaptive coping mechansims will experience more life crises and failures and will respond to life crises with symptoms more overtly neurotic than the symptoms they manifest at times of lesser life stress.

Psychiatric Disorder and Somatic Illness. Other workers have attempted to show a relationship between psychiatric disorders and somatic disorders. Sainsbury (1960) retrospectively found that patients with psychosomatic disorders scored high on "neuroticism," as measured by the Maudsley Personality Inventory. Weiss (1969) reported a correlation ($r = .63, p < .01$) between somatic symptoms and psychiatric symptoms, as measured by the Cornell Medical Index. Hinkle and associates (Hinkle and Wolff, 1957b; Hinkle and others, 1958) and Roessler and Greenfield (1961) examined individual health records and found that somatic illness was significantly more common in psychiatric patients. Stimulated by Hinkle's work, Kreitman, Pearce, and Ryle (1966) studied this relationship and reported that a positive relationship between psychiatric and somatic illness had not been confirmed. Although they found significant positive relationships between psychosomatic, minor organic, and symptomatic complaints, they felt that the findings were due to lower thresholds of complaint. They found a negative relationship between psychiatric and major organic illness. All these studies were based on patient self-reports or medical records.

Eastwood and Trevelyan (1972b) felt that such results are difficult to evaluate, so they approached the problem another way. They obtained a random selection of patients from a medical practice in England; in this way, they could examine persons in the general population for psychiatric illness, rather than examining only those who visited a psychiatrist. Presence or absence of psychiatric illness was detected by questionnaire and confirmed by interview; objective methods and strict criteria for diagnosis were used; and a well-matched control group was obtained from the same random sample. Health questionnaire and screening tests were used, but the final diagnosis of somatic disorder was based on the physical examination and the use of a protocol for diagnosis of illnesses. These workers found a statistically significant difference in the two groups: 49 percent of the psychiatric group had one or more major somatic disorders, compared to 21 percent in the control group; in minor illnesses, significance was achieved only for men, 73 percent of the psychiatric group having one or more minor illnesses, compared to 46 percent of the male controls. Most of the major somatic illnesses (65 percent in the psychiatric group and 85 percent in the control group) were unknown to the doctor—and probably to the person himself—prior to the screening. In general, these illnesses produced few symptoms or caused little concern to the patient. Thus, it cannot be said that the psychiatric group was reacting to a conscious knowledge of somatic illness, thereby contributing to psychological indices. Eastwood and Trevelyan recognized that a positive correlation does not show a cause-and-effect relationship.

Eastwood and Trevelyan (1972a) used the same methods to study the relationship between psychiatric disorder and a large number of psychosomatic disorders. More such disorders were found in the psychiatric group than in the control group; coronary heart disease and hypertension were particularly more frequent in the psychiatric group. These workers also compared a psychiatric group with a control group for the presence of ischemic heart disease, again using a protocol for diagnosis (Eastwood and Trevelyan, 1971). They found a statistically significant excess of ischemic heart disease among the psychiatric group compared to the control group: 30 percent versus 11 percent for males and 23 percent versus 12 percent for females. The methodology used here was excellent and should serve as a model for other researchers.

Thus, in some studies that have attempted to correlate personality characteristics with physical illness, poor methodology provided inconclusive data. In other studies, the methods were good, and such studies indicate that psychological factors may be important in certain diseases. These diseases need to be considered by themselves, and good studies on these diseases do not demonstrate the importance of personality factors for any and all disease. Of course, the demonstration of significant, positive correlations is not a demonstration of etiology. More work is needed to help us understand the nature of these correlations.

Psychological Vulnerability and Life Events

Some investigators have studied psychological vulnerability to illness in the context of life events. They believe that particular life events will precipitate illness in persons who are susceptible to those events because of past experiences. Rahe and Arthur (1978) have incorporated this susceptibility into their model of illness onset.

Separation. Engel, Schmale, Greene, and their associates have focused on the relationship between illness and separation from significant others (see Schmale, 1972, and Greene, 1965, for reviews of this work). Schmale (1958) interviewed patients on medical floors, asking them about recent losses or threats of loss. Twenty-nine of forty-two patients (69 percent) reported such losses, and he felt that forty-one of the forty-two patients showed feelings of helplessness or hopelessness. In his view, separation was important in precipitating illness in these patients because of past unresolved separation experiences. He had no control group, and his findings of hopelessness and helplessness could have been the patients' reactions to illness, since his study was retrospective. Moreover, only 33 percent of these patients reported "actual" losses or threats of loss (rather than merely "symbolic" losses, such as a friend's forgetting a dinner engagement), whereas Imboden, Canter, and Cluff (1963) studied ostensibly normal, healthy subjects and found that 25 percent reported recent deaths and presently existing illness in their families.

Engel and Schmale (Engel, 1968; Engel and Schmale, 1972) developed the concept of a "life setting conducive to illness: the giving-up-given-up complex." The salient features of this complex are feelings of helplessness and hopelessness. However, Engel and Schmale do not present firm data to support this theory; rather, they rely on anecdotal case histories and studies cited here as having methological flaws.

Parens, McConville, and Kaplan (1966) prospectively studied object loss in student nurses. They used questionnaires to assess depression, adjustment to the new situation of leaving home, past object loss, and other factors that might intensify separation reactions. The findings suggested that prediction of future illness could be made based on the amount of adjustment accomplished and on the depression scores. Students who experienced feelings of helplessness-hopelessness (giving up) in response to separation seemed to become ill more frequently. Also, those with more past object losses had significantly more illness episodes. Data on health were obtained from medical records and self-reports.

Bennett (1970) reported the incidence of illness in people following the flooding in Bristol, England. He found a significant correlation between illness and vulnerable personalities—described as dependent personalities and those with feelings of hopelessness and helplessness. His index for illness was visits to a physician. One finding stands out: The incidence of death (there is no doubt that this indeed was illness) significantly correlated with the vulnerable personality and was not related to the flood itself or to diseases like plague, which may have resulted from poor sanitation secondary to the flood. The increase in death occurred only in the six months following the flood and seemed related to the stress of having the flood disturb the comfortable living styles of the people in Bristol.

Illness During Bereavement. The study of bereavement is the study of severe loss (Klerman and Izen, 1974). Schmale (1971) studied fourteen women whose husbands had died of cancer. Ten of these women experienced "psychic trauma" within thirteen months of the loss, and eight of those ten developed somatic disease as diagnosed by their private physicians. Schmale concluded that the psychic trauma decreased the somatic resistance and allowed a disease predisposition to manifest itself. He used no control group.

Parkes (1964) studied London widows and found an increase in visits to a physician in the first year of bereavement, compared to the previous two years, for the widows. He recognized the problems of using medical records and of having no control group. Parkes and Brown (1972) used structured interviews to obtain data on bereaved American widows and widowers and matched married controls. The bereaved group had more hospital admissions than the control group, and they had significantly more "autonomic" symptoms: dizziness, fainting, trembling, twitching, nervousness, chest pain, sweating without cause, lump in throat, and palpitations. All symptoms were more common in the bereaved group only in the first year of bereavement. Maddison and Viola (1968) reported an increase in deterioration of health in widows in the first year of bereavement, but health data were obtained from a mailed questionnaire.

Death During Bereavement. One area of investigation in which illness is easy to document is that of death following psychological stress. Such reports appear in the press, and Engel (1971) collected newspaper reports of sudden death following disrupting life events. Rees and Lutkins (1967) studied a semirural population of 5,184, in which 488 residents died during the six-year study period. Of these, 371 had close relatives (spouse, child, parent or sibling) within the study area, a total of 903 bereaved relatives. A control group was used, consisting of 878 close relatives of 371 living people who were similar in age, sex, and marital status to those who had died. Of the bereaved relatives, 4.76 percent died within one year of bereavement, compared to .68 percent of the control group ($p < .001$). The death for bereaved males was higher than for bereaved females: 6.4 percent compared to 3.5 percent ($p < .05$). The incidence of close relatives' dying during the first year of bereavement was doubled when the primary death causing bereavement had occurred in a hospital rather than at home ($p < .05$).

These findings confirmed an earlier study by Young, Benjamin, and Wallis (1963). These investigators examined the records of the General Register Office for England and Wales and obtained a sample of 4,486 widowers of age 55 and older whose wives had died during 1957. They studied deaths in these men for up to five years. The deaths among widowers in the first six months following the death of the wife was higher than the expected rate for all married men of the same age in England and Wales, the difference obtaining statistical significance (actual deaths were 214; expected deaths were 148 ± 12). Among the eight different age groups, all showed higher incidence of death among the widowers, and four age groups obtained statistical significance. After the first six months of bereavement, the mortality rate fell back to the expected death rate. Neither of these two studies investigated the causes of death.

Parkes, Benjamin, and Fitzgerald (1969) followed up this sample of 4,486 widowers for nine years, investigating the cause of death, as stated on death certificates. There was increase in mortality in the first six months for several diseases, but only with heart disease was the difference large enough to obtain statistical significance (heart disease consisted of coronary thrombosis and arteriosclerotic and degenerative heart diseases). In addition, 22.5 percent of the deaths were from the same diagnostic group as the wife's death. Of these, over half were in the heart disease groups while less than 20 percent were in the groups of influenza, pneumonia, bronchitis, or "other" causes. These authors believe that the increased mortality was not caused by homogamy (the tendency of the fit to marry the fit and the unfit to marry the unfit), common environment, or common infectious disease.

The studies on death during bereavement were free of several methodological problems commonly found in stress and personality research. The severity of the psychological stress was unquestionable. The occurrence of death was the ultimate documentation of physical illness. Several of these studies used matched control groups or internal controlled comparisons. This is a compelling group of studies. It is significant that, when etiologies of death were examined, only cardiac disease stood out as having a higher incidence of death during bereavement. Psychological stress may cause more deaths from heart disease, but this does not necessarily mean that stress causes more deaths or more illness from other causes.

Illness Behavior

When illness was not documented and when only sick people were studied, the findings cited above could have been the result of a tendency for some people to be more sensitive to bodily complaints than other people and thus more likely to seek medical care. Perhaps what has been found by these investigations is not a general susceptibility to illness in time of life stress or in people with certain personality characteristics but a hypersensitivity to bodily complaints during such times or in such people.

Bursten (1965) discussed several possible ways in which life stress may correlate with a visit to a physician: recognition of an already existing problem for the first time, engagement in disease-provoking activities, assumption of the sick role, and reaction to the illness itself. Kasl and Cobb (1966a, 1966b) believe that health behavior, illness behavior, and sick-role behavior are sociological roles that a person chooses to maintain at a given time, depending on his psychological state and current life situation.

Sick-Role Tendency. Mechanic and Volkart (Mechanic, 1959, 1962a; Mechanic and Volkart, 1960, 1961) developed a questionnaire to measure sick-role tendency; that is, the tendency for a person to seek medical care with a given symptom. They found that a high tendency to adopt the sick role was associated with significantly more visits to a college health center. Mechanic (1963) believes that illness behavior can cause bias in medical sampling for studies of illness. Mechanic and Newton (1965) studied self-reporting of illness and found that the degree of underreporting of illness was greater in the "low-inclination group" (those who are less inclined to use medical facilities when sick).

Zola (1966), in a study of Irish, Italian, and Anglo-Saxon patients, reported that the variable which consistently correlated most highly with illness behavior was ethnic group membership. Persons of Italian descent tended to seek medical aid when their symptoms interfered with social or personal relations; those with Irish ancestry tended to go only after such a visit was sanctioned by others; persons of Anglo-Saxon descent went when they perceived an interference with some specific vocation or physical activity.

Kasl and Cobb (1964) found that subjects with high scores on aggressiveness, jitteriness, and depression made more visits to the medical dispensary than did those without these characteristics. Summerskill and Darling (1957) found group differences in seeking medical care for upper respiratory complaints. Women, students from minority religious groups, urban students, and younger students were most likely to visit the college health center for treatment of such disorders. Jacobs and associates noted that persons who went to the medical dispensary had more maladaptive coping styles (angry-defiant styles) than did persons who never went to the dispensary.

Roessler and Greenfield (1958) reported that college students who made frequent visits to the health center scored lower on self-acceptance scales than did matched controls. Robbins, Tanck, and Meyersburg (1972) found that people who scored high on "psychic tension" and low on ego strength had more somatic complaints than did others. Cluff, Canter, and

Imboden (1966) identified a group of "psychologically vulnerable" people—those with low ego strength and hypochondriacal tendencies. This group showed an increase in reporting of influenza but was no different in viral serologic titers than the control group. The frequency of reported influenzal illness for both groups together was one sixth that of influenzal infection as determined by serologic titer. The psychologically vulnerable persons also had longer symptomatic recovery from influenza (Imboden, Canter, and Cluff, 1961). These findings are similar to those found by the same workers for chronic brucellosis (Imboden and others, 1959).

Thus, a person's threshold of complaint and inclination to adopt the sick role may account for some of the findings reported in the studies on life events and illness onset.

Stress and Illness Behavior. Other studies suggest that stress itself may cause or, at least, have some effect on illness behavior. Stoeckle and associates (Stoeckle and Davidson, 1962, 1963; Stoeckle, Zola, and Davidson, 1963, 1964) studied people who presented to general medical clinics with functional complaints and in whom no bodily illness could be detected. Eighty-four percent reported experiencing psychological distress at the time they were bothered by symptoms. Of all new patients, only 43 percent were judged to have somatic illness. Most patients presenting with only functional complaints were judged to be depressed. Patients reported that their symptoms began after a specific experience which the patients felt had started their illness. Vaillant, Shapiro, and Schmitt (1970) reported that 44 percent of patients admitted to a hospital were motivated at least in part by emotional distress. Both the psychiatrist and the ward physician agreed that physical distress alone was not enough to account for hospitalization in 31 percent of all cases admitted. Most of these patients appeared to use coexisting but usually long-standing physical illness to justify a hospital admission. Satin (1972) found that 86 percent of the people presenting to an emergency unit with health complaints had had a recent life stress. He felt that many people with recent stress used physical complaints as a "ticket of admission" to the hospital. Thus, rather than causing illness, stress may cause a person to use illness behavior as a means of coping with the stress.

Illness and Personality. Finally, illness may have an effect on personality and on the tests used to study personality. Meyer, Golle, and Weitemeyer (1968) divided patients with one of three diseases (asthma, tuberculosis, and cardiac valve lesions) into groups of illness lasting less than one year, those lasting three to six years, and those lasting more than six years for each disease. In patients with asthma and cardiac valve lesions, duration of illness correlated significantly with "neuroticism" scores on the Maudsley Personality Inventory. The authors point out that the "diseases we call psychosomatic might differ from 'pure' organic afflictions in precisely their tendency to develop a disease-dependent neuroticism" (p. 347).

Bendien (1963) also studied "neuroticism" in illness. Patients with "psychosomatic" diseases and those with nonpsychosomatic diseases gave equally high neuroticism scores, both being much higher than for healthy subjects. Bendien rejects the conclusion of other investigators that questionnaire researches of this kind demonstrate the presence of a neurotic personality in so-called psychosomatic patients. Instead, he believes that the high neuroticism scores are secondary to being ill.

Summary of Current Literature

Numerous investigators have studied life events and illness onset and have reported that illness onset occurs after stressful life events more often than can be accounted for by chance. However, their work has methodological shortcomings. We are not the first to point out such shortcomings (see Rabkin and Struening, 1976a; Andrews and Tennant, 1978). Illness has rarely been documented in these studies. Few protocols were used for diagnostic criteria. Most investigators relied on restrospective medical reports or self-reporting. Without documentation of illness, the effect of sick-role tendency and of stress in producing illness behavior without actual illness cannot be controlled for. Therefore, this literature as a whole remains inconclusive and needs to be viewed skeptically at this time. The few good studies utilized strict criteria for diagnosis of illness. For example, tuberculosis was diagnosed by skin tests and chest X rays, sore throats were diagnosed by throat cultures and clinical signs, and appendicitis was diagnosed operatively. We suggest that these methods be used for studies in the future in place of medical records and self-reporting of illness.

The literature on psychological vulnerability to illness tended to have better methodology. Protocols of diagnostic criteria were more often used. Researchers often used control groups and random sampling or studied all persons in a natural group, rather than only those persons who visited a physician. Even so, this literature remains inconclusive because illness has been show to affect personality traits. Further, the studies with better methodology focused on specific diseases such as asthma, allergy, and cardiac disease while studies with poorer methodology examined any and all disease. Perhaps only certain illnesses are influenced by psychological variables.

If good control groups and strict criteria for diagnosis were used, and if all persons in a given population—rather than only those who complain of illness—were studied, sick-role tendency and illness behavior could be controlled for. Such an undertaking would require much manpower, time, and expense. However, the issue of how life stress and personality traits affect illness is so pervasive to all of medicine that we need to discover the nature of these relationships. We now need definitive studies, not studies that are more easily accomplished but inconclusive. If we find that stress and personality influence illness, we can then proceed to investigate what mechanisms are involved and how we may alter these relationships to provide more relief from illness.

Little work has been done on mechanisms involved in stress-induced illness. Some people believe that stress lowers host resistance to illness but do not suggest how this happens. Studies on the effect of stress in precipitating or worsening cardiac, gastrointestinal, or respiratory illness implicate the autonomic nervous system. Is the autonomic nervous system involved in all stress-induced illness, or are there other mechanisms?

Other dimensions of life stress still unexplored are duration of life events, rates of occurrence, and cycles of illness and stress. Intervening behavioral variables between life events and illness need exploring—for example, drinking, accident proneness during times of preoccupation with personal problems, and personal caretaking (eating and sleeping properly). Subjective response to life events has received little attention. Specific life events have been studied, but innumerable ones remain.

Physicians frequently observe that many persons who have physical complaints are instead depressed. Some present with continued, but stable, symptoms which have always been present, while others give new but vague complaints. Have past investigations simply dealt with depression disguised as and mistaken for illness, or is depression somehow etiologically significant in illness onset?

Little work has been done on psychological defense mechanisms. For example, many people use denial to minimize symptoms of true organic disease. Perhaps life stress helps to decrease denial, so that the same symptoms are then recognized as requiring medical attention. Perhaps life stresses produce an increased need for reinforcement, which one then obtains by visiting a physician or by manipulating an admission to a hospital. Perhaps those people who overuse admissions to a hospital and visits to a physician do so because they have no other source of emotional support; such people would also have difficulty in coping with life stress. These possibilities all need exploring in future investigations.

12

Experimental Studies of Stress and Anxiety

Joseph V. Brady

✳ ✳ ✳ ✳ ✳ ✳ ✳ ✳ ✳ ✳ ✳ ✳ ✳

Laboratory studies over the past several decades have provided a productive point of departure for an experimental analysis of the environmental and psychophysiological interactions which define stress and anxiety. Investigative attention has focused on two general models for characterizing the phenomena of interest. The more traditional *concurrent model* emphasizes the effects of previous or accompanying environmental-behavioral interactions as determinants of psychophysiological stress and anxiety responses. The early work of Pavlov (1879) and Cannon (1915), relating autonomic changes to environmental antecedents, provides classical examples of such laboratory studies. Current applications of this approach extend the analysis of both respondent and operant conditioning effects on a broad range of biochemical, physiological, and behavioral processes (Brady and Harris, 1976). The more contemporary *contingent model,* in contrast, calls attention to environmental-behavioral interactions that follow psychophysiological stress and anxiety responses (Miller, 1978).

Experimental approaches within the framework of both concurrent and contingent models continue to provide a vigorous and productive research base for laboratory studies of both the psychophysiology and the psychopathology of stress and anxiety. Such investigative activities emphasize the effects of aversive learning and conditioning procedures on visceral and autonomic processes, and the broad range of laboratory experiments involved can be differentiated on the basis of the temporal ordering of behavioral and physiological events. In the more traditional classical conditioning studies of the concurrent model approach, physiological events (such as heart rate) are initially recorded as unconditioned responses to an unconditional stimulus (UCS), such as an electric shock. These physiological responses then subsequently occur (though not necessarily in identical form) during presentation of a conditional stimulus (CS), such as a clicking sound, which has been paired repeatedly with the UCS. Experimental variations of this concurrent-model approach have also involved operant learning procedures for establishing and maintaining ongoing performances (for example, lever pressing to avoid shock) while measuring associated changes in physiological response systems (for example, corticosteroid levels). The contingent-model approach, in contrast, emphasizes contingency relationships between *antecedent* physiological changes (such as blood pressure elevation) and experimentally programmed environmental *consequences* (such as shock escape and/or avoidance).

Over the past two decades, experimental studies of stress and anxiety within the framework of such aversive learning and conditioning paradigms have clearly focused more on some response systems (for example, cardiovascular psychophysiology) than others. To a considerable extent, this uneven distribution of stress and anxiety response measures is a function of the technological and methodological developments which have paced the emergence of scientifically operational laboratory approaches to the problem (for example, Obrist and others, 1974). As such advances increase the ease and accessibility of psychophysiological measurement techniques, an ever-expanding range of biological and behavioral events and their relationship to stress and anxiety can be studied.

Concurrent-Model Studies

The pioneering work of Pavlov and Cannon has been extended over the past half-century or more and elaborated in numerous volumes that document the effects of *classical conditioning* procedures on physiological processes in general (Beecroft, 1966; Prokasy, 1965; Razran, 1961) and autonomic responses in particular (Adam, 1967; Dykman, 1967; Harris and Brady, 1974). In the past decade alone, for example, there has been a tidal wave of classical cardiac conditioning studies. The basic issue posed by the rhetorical question "Can the heart learn?" has, of course, been addressed extensively, with the answers providing convincing evidence of the wide-ranging variability in the *form* (that is, the acceleration or deceleration) of the classically conditioned cardiac response (Shearn, 1961). Several reports indicate that a characteristically biphasic cardiac response pattern emerges after repeated CS-UCS pairings in a range of different laboratory species (Dykman and Gantt, 1958; Ramsey, 1970; Schoenfeld, Matos, and Snapper, 1967). The form in which this pattern has been observed (for example, an early heart rate acceleration followed by a cardiac deceleration) suggests that separable response components (for example, "orienting") may participate differentially in the temporal course of such classical cardiovascular conditioning (Kakigi, 1971). Ongoing behavioral interactions (for example, "effect of person") may significantly influence the physiological consequences of classical conditioning (Anderson and Gantt, 1966).

Several reports over the past decade have also provided support for the Law of Initial Values (LIV) as a determinant of the physiological effects associated with classical conditioning procedures (Black, Carlson, and Solomon, 1962; Ramsey, 1970; Snapper, Pomerleau, and Schoenfeld, 1969). In all these studies, an inverse relationship was observed between the magnitude of the conditioned heart rate response and the cardiac rate recorded during the time interval immediately preceding the CS presentation. Controlling the pre-CS heart rate with a cardiac pacemaker, however, did not reveal systematic relationships between the classically conditioned heart rate response and the paced pre-CS heart rate level (Snapper, Pomerleau, and Schoenfeld, 1969). This suggests that the interactions that define the LIV effects, so well documented in human cardiovascular conditioning studies (for example, Lacey and Lacey, 1962), probably reflect more the participation of central than peripheral factors.

Of particular significance from the perspective of stress etiology and the origins of anxiety is the observation that single-trial classical conditioning can occur. In an experiment with dogs, Newton and Gantt (1966) found that one CS-UCS (tone-shock) pairing produced a classically conditioned heart rate response which persisted over extended time intervals during repeated extinction trials involving tone presentations in the absence of shock. Partial reinforcement effects in increasing resistance to extinction of classically conditioned autonomic responses have also been repeatedly confirmed (see, for example, Fitzgerald, 1966; Wagner, Seigel, and Fein, 1967). Discrimination effects also have been well documented. Investigators such as Pare' (1970) and Tighe, Graves, and Riley (1968) found that the magnitude of the conditioned cardiac response is significantly greater to a CS presentation followed by the UCS than to a CS presentation that has not been followed by the UCS.

Other circulatory responses—including blood pressure, blood flow, peripheral vasomotor activity, and catecholamine levels—have also been shown to change systematically in relationship to classical conditioning procedures. The correlations (or lack thereof) between these effects and the differentiation of "orienting" or "startle" components from "true" conditioned autonomic response patterns continue to provide areas of controversy and disagreement (Kakigi, 1971). Nonetheless, studies involving determinations made with dogs under both curarized and noncurarized conditions suggest at least some degree of independence between such classically conditioned cardiovascular responses, on the one hand, and respiratory and skeletal muscle changes, on the other (see Newton, 1967).

Clearly, however, the role of central regulatory and homeostatic mechanisms for the control of classically conditioned stress and anxiety responses requires that a broader biological perspective be maintained with regard to the range of interacting visceral and somatic systems which in concert provide for the adjustments and adaptations of the internal environment. Within this context, for example, the relationship between heart rate and other visceral and motor components of a "total" classically conditioned response has provided the focus for a range of investigations. These studies emphasize both the independent variations of multiple interacting systems (Black, 1965; Yehle, 1968) and the complex interrelationships between such response measures (Hein, 1969; Obrist and Webb, 1967). Probably the most parsimonious view of the complexities involved would recognize that all possible combinations and permutations can and do occur under some circumstances. It remains a continuing research challenge to delineate and define the range of independent circumstances under which classically conditioned stress and anxiety effects are established and maintained.

A productive integration of this classical approach with the analysis of performance-related stress and anxiety effects has more recently encompassed a broader range of biochemical and physiological response systems. A basic laboratory technique that has contributed significantly to these advances involves the superimposition of a classical aversive conditioning procedure upon an ongoing instrumental learning performance for food reward (Estes and Skinner, 1941). A modification of this procedure with laboratory primates trained to operate a telegraph key for banana pellets provided for recurrent five-minute presentations of an auditory signal (clicking sound) terminated contiguously with a brief electric shock to the feet (Brady, 1965). Within a few trials, virtually complete suppression of the lever-pressing behavior occurs in response to the clicker (as illustrated in Figure 1), accompanied by piloerection, locomotor agitation, and, frequently, urination and/or defecation.

The development of this conditioned "anxiety" response has been studied in relationship to changes in plasma 17-hydroxycorticosteroid (17-OH-CS) during a series of acquisition trials consisting of thirty-minute

Figure 1. The Conditioned Emotional Behavior as It Appears Typically in the
Cumulative Response Curve

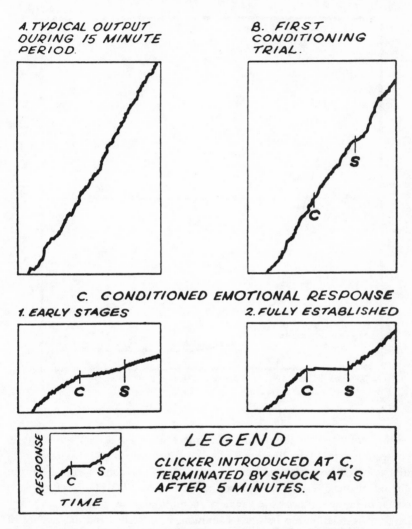

A. TYPICAL OUTPUT
DURING 15 MINUTE
PERIOD.

B. FIRST
CONDITIONING
TRIAL.

S

C

C. CONDITIONED EMOTIONAL RESPONSE

1. EARLY STAGES

2. FULLY ESTABLISHED

C   S

C   S

RESPONSE

C   S

TIME

LEGEND
CLICKER INTRODUCED AT C,
TERMINATED BY SHOCK AT S
AFTER 5 MINUTES.

lever-pressing sessions, with auditory stimulus and shock pairing occurring
once during each session, approximately fifteen minutes after the start
(Mason, Brady, and Tolson, 1966). Seven such conditioning trials were
accompanied by the withdrawal of blood samples immediately before and
immediately after each thirty-minute session; 17-OH-CS levels associated with
successive stages in the acquisition of the conditioned "anxiety" behavior
were also determined. Figure 2 shows the corresponding changes in lever
pressing and 17-OH-CS throughout the series of seven conditioning sessions.
The progressive *suppression* of lever pressing in response to presentation

Figure 2. Changes in Plasma 17-OH-CS Levels Related to
Emotional Conditioning

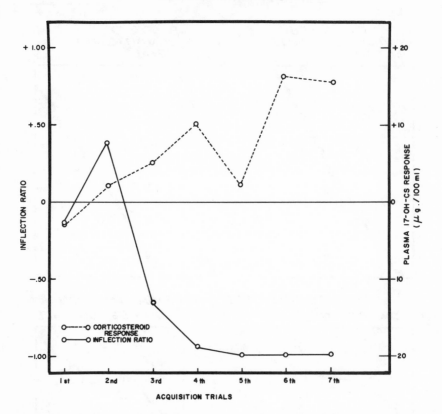

of the auditory stimulus during each successive trial is represented by an "inflection ratio" (the lower solid line on Figure 2) which provides a quantitative measure of the conditioned behavioral suppression. The upper broken line on Figure 2 reflects the progressive *increase* in 17-OH-CS levels over the course of the seven successive "anxiety" conditioning sessions.

The relationship between conditioned "anxiety" and the activity of the pituitary-adrenal system has been further confirmed in a series of experiments with monkeys in which the conditioned suppression of lever pressing had been previously established. Five such animals were studied during one-hour lever-pressing sessions for food reward; in these sessions, five-minute periods of auditory stimulus presentation were alternated with five-minute periods of no auditory stimulus. Blood samples taken before and after several such experiments with each animal, during which no shock followed any of the auditory stimulus presentations, revealed substantial corticosteroid elevations related to the conditioned "anxiety" behavior alone. When measurements of plasma epinephrine and norepinephrine levels were added to the corticosteroid determinations in experiments with this conditioned "anxiety" model, the potential contributions of a "hormone pattern" approach to such a psychophysiological analysis became evident. Preliminary observations, in the course of a rather rudimentary conditioning experiment involving a loud truck horn and electric foot shock with monkeys, suggested the differential participation of adrenal-medullary systems in conditioned and unconditioned aspects of such "anxiety" behavior patterns. Exposure to the horn or the shock alone *prior* to the conditioned pairing of the two produced only mild elevations in catecholamine levels. Following a series of conditioning trials, however, during which horn sounding for three minutes was terminated contiguously with shock, presentation of the horn alone markedly increased norepinephrine levels without eliciting any epinephrine response. This hormone pattern approach has been extended in a series of experiments in which concurrent plasma epinephrine, norepinephrine, and 17-OH-CS levels were determined during monkey performance on the alternating five minutes "on," 5 minutes "off" conditioned "anxiety" response procedure described above. The results obtained during thirty-minute control and experimental sessions involving recurrent "anxiety" behavior segments (see Figure 3) confirmed the differential hormone response pattern characterized by marked elevations in both 17-OH-CS and norepinephrine but little or no change in epinephrine levels.

Observations of autonomic changes related to this same conditioned "anxiety" stress model have been reported with a series of monkeys catheterized for cardiovascular measurements (Brady, Kelly, and Plumlee, 1969). Heart rate and systolic and diastolic blood pressure were recorded continuously during experimental sessions involving both lever pressing alone and exposure to the conditioned "anxiety" procedure. Figure 4 shows the lever-pressing performance, heart rate, and blood pressure values obtained during approximately nine minutes of a one-hour control session prior to "anxiety" behavior conditioning. The stable lever-pressing performance was accompanied by equally stable heart rate and blood pressure values throughout the session. By contrast, Figure 5 shows the results obtained during an early experimental session following a series of only five conditioning trials, which involved three-minute presentations of a clicking noise terminated contiguously with foot shock superimposed on the lever-pressing performance. The complete suppression of lever pressing during clicker presentations was accompanied by a dramatic drop in heart rate and a somewhat less vigorous blood pressure decrease.

Significantly, however, continued pairings of clicker and shock superimposed on the lever-pressing performance produced abrupt reversals in the direction of these autonomic changes, with cardiac acceleration and blood pressure elevation appearing and persisting in response to the clicker during the later stages of anxiety conditioning. Figure 6 shows the sequence of

Figure 3. Mean Plasma 17-OH-CS, Norepinephrine, and Epinephrine Levels
During Conditioned "Anxiety" Sessions

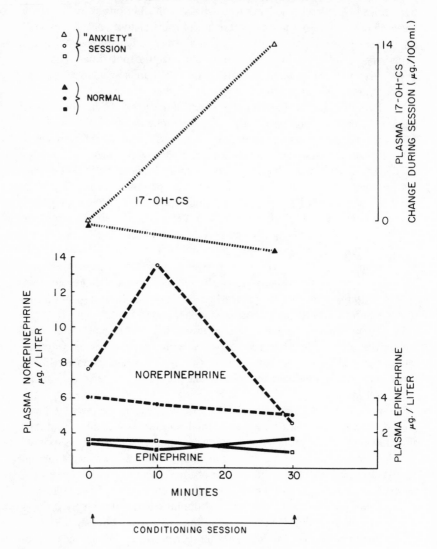

Figure 4. Lever-Pressing Performance, Heart Rate, and Blood Pressure Values
During Control Session Prior to Emotional Conditioning

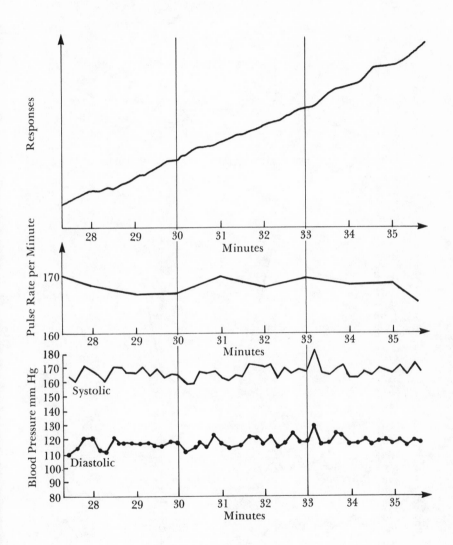

Figure 5. Changes in Lever Pressing, Heart Rate, and Blood Pressure
During Conditioned "Anxiety" Session After Emotional Conditioning

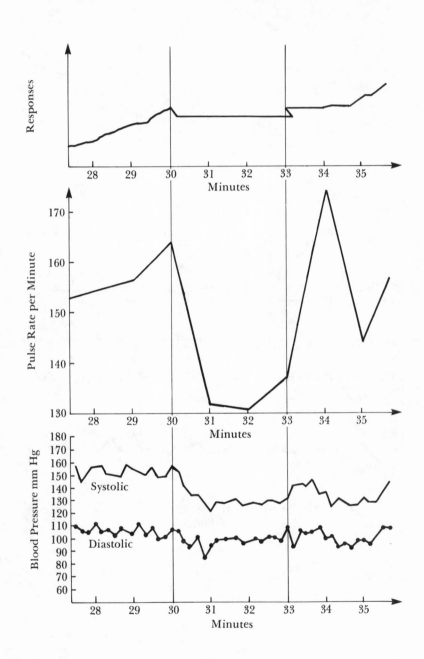

Figure 6. Minute-by-Minute Changes in Blood Pressure, Heart Rate,
and Lever-Pressing Response Rate for Monkey A on
Successive 3-Minute Clicker-Shock Trials During Acquisition of the
Conditioned Emotional Response

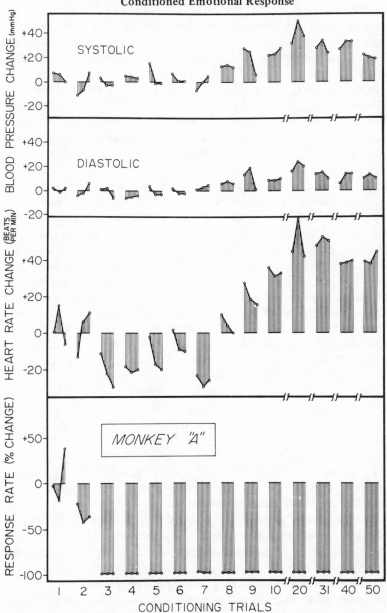

Note: The zero points represent control values calculated from the three-minute interval
immediately preceding the clicker.

changes in the form of the autonomic responses in the course of fifty such anxiety conditioning trials. Blood pressure, heart rate, and lever-pressing rate for successive conditioning trials are shown as changes during the three-minute clicker period as compared to baseline values (the "0" point on each graph), which represent averages for each measure of the three-minute interval immediately preceding the clicker. The blood pressure and heart rate values are shown as absolute changes in millimeters of mercury and beats per minute, respectively. The lever-pressing values are shown as percent changes in response rate during the clicker, as compared to the baseline. Figure 6 shows that lever pressing during the clicker completely ceased by the third conditioning trial for Monkey A, and this behavioral suppression response was maintained throughout the entire course of fifty clicker-shock pairings. The autonomic changes followed a more varied, but nonetheless systematic, course during this acquisition phase. A marked deceleration in heart rate first appeared during presentation of the clicker on the third conditioning trial, which corresponds to the initial development of complete behavioral suppression. During the next four trials, a similar decelerative change in heart rate accompanied the behavioral response, with little or no change apparent in either diastolic or systolic blood pressure. During the eighth conditioning trial, however, an abrupt change in the direction of the cardiac response to the clicker was reflected in both heart rate and blood pressure measures. Increases in heart rate, which approximated forty beats per minute, developed in response to the clicker by the tenth conditioning trial and persisted throughout the remainder of the fifty acquisition trials. Both systolic and diastolic blood pressure showed correspondingly consistent and dramatic elevations in response to the clicker; these elevations first appeared between the eighth and tenth conditioning trials and persisted through trial 50.

When the conditioned "anxiety" response was extinguished, a further divergence between autonomic and behavioral response to stress was observed. Figure 7 illustrates this characteristic difference in extinction rates for the cardiovascular and instrumental components of the conditioned emotional response with Monkey B. Although virtually complete recovery of the lever-pressing rate in the presence of the clicker occurred within ten such extinction trials, both heart rate and blood pressure elevations in response to the clicker alone persisted well beyond the fortieth extinction trial. Finally, reconditioning of the "anxiety" response with this same animal rapidly produced behavioral suppression, accompanied immediately by the tachycardiac and pressor responses. Significantly, the initial cardiac decelerative response, characteristic of the early trials during the original emotional conditioning, failed to appear during reconditioning with any of the animals.

The experimental approaches to the analysis of psychophysiological stress and anxiety responses thus far described have emphasized the *suppressive* effects on behavior of exposure to such conditioning situations. Under

Figure 7. Minute-by-Minute Changes in Blood Pressure, Heart Rate, and
Lever-Pressing Rate for Monkey B on Successive Three-Minute Presentations
of the Clicker Without Shock During Extinction of the Conditioned
Emotional Response

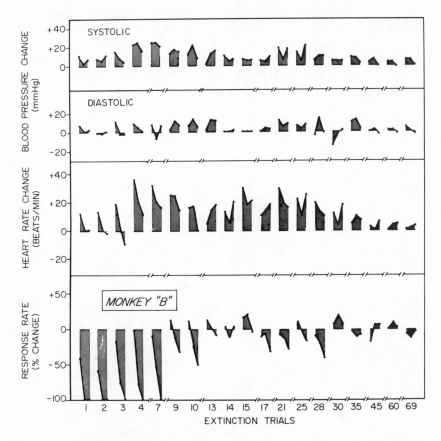

Note: The zero points represent control values calculated from the three-minute interval
immediately preceding the clicker.

certain conditions, however, the arrangement of environmental contingencies
involving avoidance of such aversive events generates marked increases in the
frequency of specific behaviors in response to stress and anxiety. The conditioned avoidance model, which has provided the basis for extensive experimental analysis in this area of stress measurement, has been described in
previous reports on the psychophysiology of emotional behavior (Brady,
1965, 1967; Mason, Brady, and Sidman, 1957; Sidman, 1953; Sidman and
others, 1962). Briefly, the basic procedure involves programming shocks to
the feet of the monkey in the primate chair every twenty seconds, unless the

animal presses the lever within that interval; each lever press postpones the shock for another twenty seconds. This avoidance requirement generates a stable and durable lever-pressing performance (illustrated in Figure 8), which is consistently associated with twofold to fourfold rises in corticosteroid levels for virtually all animals during two-hour experimental sessions (as shown in Figure 9), even in the absence of any shock (Brady, 1966; Mason,

Figure 8. Cumulative Record of Avoidance Lever Pressing, Showing High, Stable Rate of Approximately 1,500 Responses per Hour

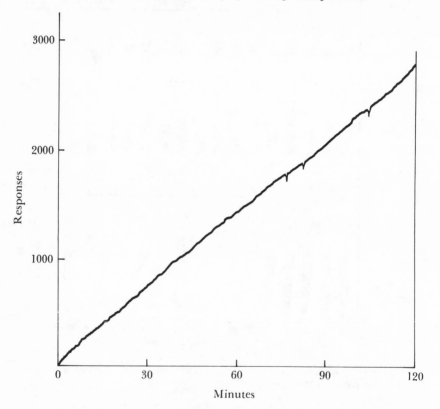

Note: The three small vertical marks on the cumulative record indicate the occurrence of shocks when twenty seconds elapsed between lever responses.

Brady, and Sidman, 1957). It has also been possible to demonstrate quantitative relations between the rate of avoidance responding in the monkey and the level of pituitary-adrenal activity independently of the shock frequency (Sidman and others, 1962). Marked differences in the hormone response have been observed, however, when the avoidance procedure includes a discriminable exteroceptive warning signal presented five seconds prior to administration of the shock whenever fifteen seconds have elapsed since the previous

Figure 9. Changes in Plasma 17-OH-CS During
Two-Hour Avoidance Performance

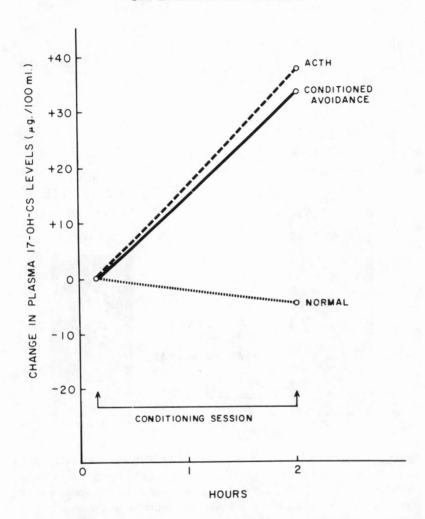

Note: The heavy dotted line labeled "ACTH" shows the rate of steroid rise over a two-hour period following only one intravenous injection of 16 mg/kg ACTH. The heavy solid line labeled "conditioned avoidance" affords a comparison of the rate of steroid elevation during a two-hour exposure to the shock avoidance contingency with the ACTH response and with the "normal" levels for a similar two-hour control period (represented by the smaller dotted line in the lower portion of the figure).

response. Figure 10 compares the 17-OH-CS levels measured during "regular" and "discriminated" avoidance sessions with the monkey and shows the consistently reduced corticosteroid response associated with programming such a warning signal. Conversely, superimposing so-called "free" or unavoidable

Figure 10. Plasma 17-OH-CS Responses During Nondiscriminated ("Regular")
and Discriminated ("Warning Signal") Avoidance Session

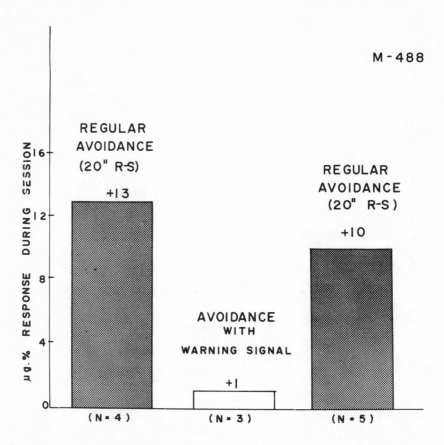

shocks on a well-established avoidance baseline without a warning signal produces marked elevations in 17-OH-CS. Figure 11, for example, shows that presentation of such "free shocks" during two-hour avoidance sessions more than doubles the corticosteroid response as compared to the regular non-discriminated avoidance procedure.

Concurrent biochemical measurements of plasma corticosteroid and catecholamine levels have also been made in the course of several avoidance experiments with the monkey. The results illustrated in Figure 12 confirm the previously described emotional stress pattern of 17-OH-CS and norepinephrine elevations with no significant alteration in epinephrine levels. Two experimental manipulations involving the avoidance procedure, however, produced significant variations in this hormone pattern. At least a modest epinephrine elevation with no change in norepinephrine accompanied presentation

Figure 11. Plasma 17-OH-CS Responses During "Regular"
Nondiscriminated Avoidance and During Avoidance with "Free Shocks"

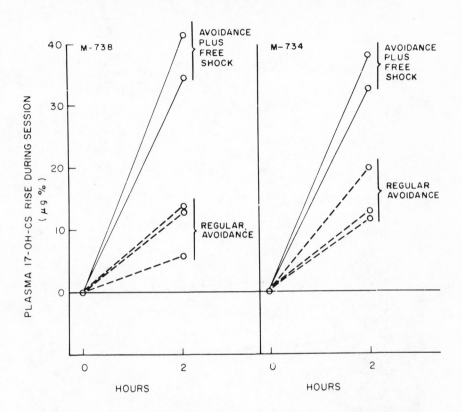

of the avoidance signal to a well-trained avoidance monkey following removal
of the response lever from the restraining chair. Significantly, the effect
occurred within one minute of the signal presentation and could not be
observed following ten minutes of continued exposure. The results obtained
with the second series of experiments involving such variations in catecholamine
levels showed the effects of "free shock" administration to a monkey at
different stages in the course of avoidance training. Mild norepinephrine and
epinephrine elevations were obtained during early conditioning sessions
involving more than 100 "free shocks" before the monkey had acquired
the avoidance behavior. A modest rise in norepinephrine levels with no
change in epinephrine accompanied later experimental sessions involving
performance of the well-learned avoidance response. Finally a series of experiments in which "free" or unavoidable shocks were programmed at the rate of
one per minute showed that the elevation occurred even though the animal
received no more shock than during previous regular avoidance sesssions.

Figure 12. Mean Plasma 17-OH-CS, Norepinephrine, and Epinephrine Levels
During Conditioned Avoidance Sessions

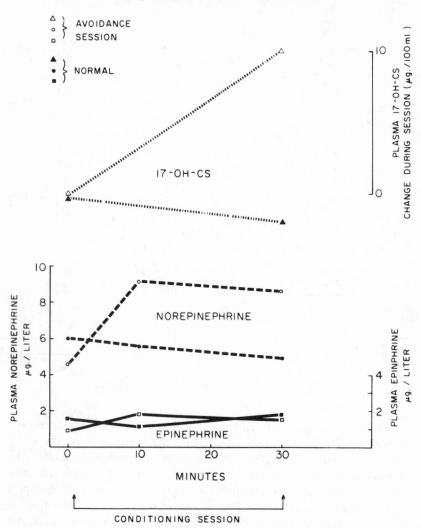

Extended exposure to continuous 72-hour avoidance sessions has
provided the setting for experimental analysis of a broader spectrum of
hormonal changes in relationship to stress and anxiety responses in the
rhesus monkey (Mason and others, 1961b, 1961c). The pattern of corticosteroid and pepsinogen changes observed before, during, and after such a
continuous 72-hour avoidance experiment, for example, is shown in Figure
13. Although plasma 17-OH-CS levels showed the expected substantial

Figure 13. Mean Blood Levels of 17-OH-CS and Pepsinogen During 72-Hour
Continuous Avoidance Sessions

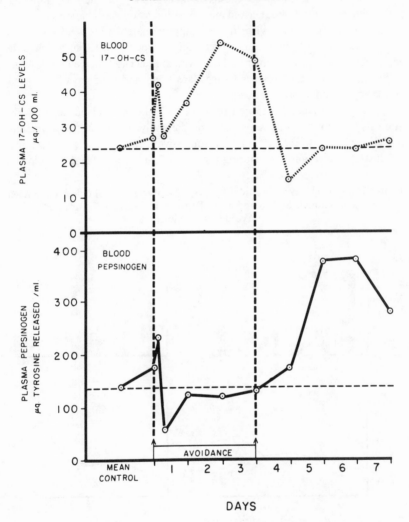

elevation throughout the 72-hour avoidance session, plasma pepsinogen levels were consistently depressed below baseline values during this same period. The postavoidance recovery period, however, was characterized by a marked and prolonged elevation of pepsinogen levels, which endured for several days beyond the 48-hour postavoidance interval required for recovery of the preavoidance corticosteroid baseline. The consequences of repeated exposure to such continuous 72-hour avoidance stress over extended periods (up to—and, in some cases, exceeding—one year) on patterns of thyroid, gonadal, and adrenal hormone secretion have also been described in studies with a series of five chair-restrained rhesus monkeys. Two of the five monkeys participated in the 72-hour avoidance experiment on six separate occasions over a six-month period, with intervals approximately four weeks between the exposures. The remaining three animals performed on a schedule which repeatedly programmed 72-hour avoidance cycles followed by 96-hour nonavoidance or "rest" cycles (three days "on" and four days "off") for periods up to and exceeding one year.

The two animals exposed to repeated 72-hour avoidance at monthly intervals for six months showed a progressively increasing lever-pressing response rate with each of the six successive 72-hour avoidance sessions, as illustrated in Figure 14. During the initial 72-hour avoidance experiment

Figure 14. Steroid Levels, Avoidance Response Rates, and Shock Frequencies for Animals M-736 and M-77 During Six Monthly 72-Hour Avoidance Sessions

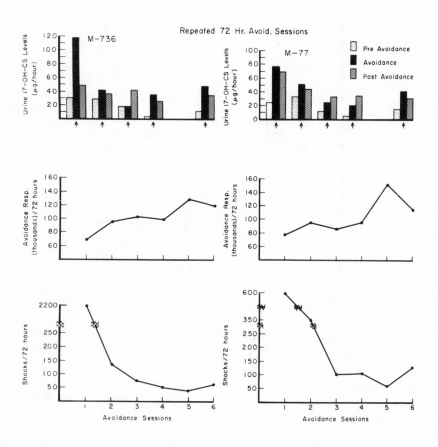

with these two animals, response rates averaged 16 resp/min and 18 resp/min, respectively. Response rate values for these same monkeys during the sixth 72-hour avoidance experiment averaged 28 resp/min and 27 resp/min. In contrast, shock frequencies over this same period showed a sharp decline within the first two 72-hour avoidance sessions and remained at a stable low level (not exceeding two shocks per hour for either animal) for the remaining four 72-hour avoidance cycles. Hormone changes related to the repeated 72-hour avoidance cycles showed consistent and replicable patterns over the six-month experimental period for both animals. During the initial experimental sessions, as shown in Figure 14, both monkeys showed approximately threefold elevations in 17-OH-CS levels during the 72-hour avoidance and returned to near baseline levels after approximately six days. The remaining four monthly experiments were characterized by substantial, though diminished, steroid responses (approximately twofold elevations in 17-OH-CS levels) during avoidance, with essentially the same six-day period required for recovery of basal levels. Significant changes related to the extended avoidance performance were also observed in catecholamine, gonadal, and thyroid hormone levels, with recovery cycles extending in some instances (thyroid) for three weeks following the 72-hour avoidance period.

The three remaining monkeys required to perform on the three days "on," four days "off" avoidance schedule showed an initial increase in lever-pressing response rates for approximately the first ten avoidance sessions. This was similar to that seen with the two animals described above. By approximately the twenty-ninth weekly session with these animals, however, lever-pressing response rates during the 72-hour avoidance period had decreased to a value well below that observed during the initial avoidance sessions, and the performance tended to stabilize at this new low level for the ensuing weeks of the experiment. In contrast, shock frequencies for all animals quickly approximated a stable low level within the first two or three exposures to the avoidance schedule, and seldom exceeded a rate of two shocks per hour for the remainder of the experiment. Typically, for example, Monkey M-157, which had been exposed to this program for some sixty-five weekly sessions (as illustrated in Figure 15), showed an average response rate of 23 resp/min during the initial 72-hour avoidance session, 32 resp/min during the tenth avoidance session, 19 resp/min during the twentieth avoidance session, and 16 resp/min, 20 resp/min, and 19 resp/min during the thirtieth, fortieth, and fiftieth weekly avoidance sessions, respectively. The initial 72-hour avoidance sessions, characterized by progressive increases in lever-pressing rate, were accompanied invariably by elevations in the 17-OH-CS levels. By the twentieth weekly avoidance-rest cycle, however, steroid levels had dropped below initial basal values, and no elevation in response to the 72-hour avoidance performance could be observed. By the thirtieth weekly session, 17-OH-CS levels had returned to their preexperimental basal values,

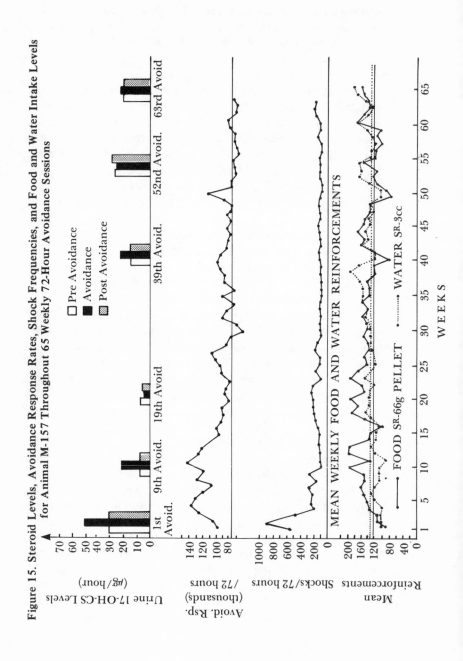

Figure 15. Steroid Levels, Avoidance Response Rates, Shock Frequencies, and Food and Water Intake Levels for Animal M-157 Throughout 65 Weekly 72-Hour Avoidance Sessions

but continued exposure to the three days "on," four days "off" schedule failed to produce any further steroid elevation in response to the 72-hour avoidance requirement up through the sixty-fifth experimental session. Figure 15 also reflects the fact that, following initial adjustments during the early sessions of the program, shock frequencies remained at a stable low level and normal food and water intake was maintained essentially unchanged throughout the extended course of the experiment.

The general pattern obtained with M-157 has been replicated with only minor variations in the two additional animals completing fifty-six and forty-six weeks, respectively, on this same experimental program. The change in responsivity of the pituitary-adrenocortical system to the avoidance stress is the most consistent and striking observation in all three monkeys. These most recent findings, however, indicate that continued exposure to this repeated performance requirement on the time schedule programmed in this experiment produces an apparent dissociation between the stressful avoidance performance and the 17-OH-CS response. Although a definitive analysis of such a relationship is not possible on the basis of these data alone, the critical role of temporal parameters (work-rest cycles) is clearly indicated. Certainly, related findings on the course of recovery for a broad range of hormone measures provide additional support for this focus on temporal factors in the measurement of psychophysiological responses to stressful situations.

A trend toward more extended periods of experimental observation and measurement has been apparent also in concurrent avoidance studies focusing on cardiovascular changes, particularly in primates. Both rhesus (Forsyth, 1969) and squirrel monkeys (Herd and others, 1969) developed hypertensive blood pressure levels with recurrent exposure to free-operant avoidance paradigms for periods up to and exceeding twelve months. Chair-restrained baboons (Findley, Robinson, and Gilliam, 1971) that were performing on a discrete-trial fixed-ratio instrumental escape-avoidance procedure, however, did not maintain elevated blood pressure levels over the year or more during which they participated in the study (Findley and others, 1971). Indeed, the baboons in this extended study did show substantial pressure increases during the actual escape-avoidance performance intervals within the daily experimental sessions, and there were some periods during the first several months on the program which were characterized by general elevations in both blood pressure and heart rate. But the chronically high cardiac output levels (for example, heart rate) suggest a potentially important "physical exercise" factor. This may partly account for the long-term return to normotensive pressure levels not recovered in previous studies (Forsyth, 1969; Herd and others, 1969) with exposures of comparable duration to less demanding free-operant avoidance requirements.

A recent series of studies on cardiovascular changes associated with avoidance stress procedures (Anderson and Brady, 1971; Anderson and

Tosheff, 1973) provide further evidence that is at least consistent with the hypothesized relationship among muscle activity, cardiac output, and peripheral resistance in the behavioral pathogenesis of hypertensive conditions. The focus of these studies with dogs has been on continuous monitoring of blood pressure and heart rate during free-operant (panel press) shock avoidance stress and, significantly, during a fixed-interval preavoidance anxiety period systematically programmed to precede the required avoidance performance. Under these conditions, a unique divergence between heart rate and blood pressure changes was observed during preavoidance anxiety intervals up to fifteen hours in length, with virtually all animals showing a characteristic systolic and diastolic increase accompanied by either a decrease or no change in heart rate. Comparisons involving similar performance requirements on a variable-interval *food* reinforcement schedule revealed a markedly different preperformance cardiovascular pattern characterized by systematic increases in both heart rate and blood pressure. And this differential "preparatory" pattern was confirmed both between individual animals maintained separately on each of the procedures and "within" the same animal alternately performing on the avoidance and food reinforcement schedules. Moreover, direct measurements of cardiac output in dogs prepared with aortic flow probes during exposure to the avoidance program confirmed that the preavoidance pressure changes were attributable to increased peripheral resistance, while the pressure increases during the avoidance performance per se occurred as the peripheral resistance was actually observed to decrease and the cardiac output increased markedly. Additional studies involving beta-adrenergic blockade with the drug propranolol during the same experimental procedure, however, clearly showed that peripheral resistance levels do increase to maintain elevated pressure levels during avoidance when drug-induced heart rate reductions produce decreases in cardiac output (Anderson and Brady, 1973).

The results of these experiments establish firm relationships between a broad range of autonomic-endocrine system activity and behavioral interactions which involve various aspects of stress and anxiety. The initial findings, which emphasized changes in absolute levels of selected hormones, can be viewed as reflecting relatively undifferentiated consequences of arousal states associated with such stress-inducing situations. The definite temporal course of visceral and steroid changes under such conditions and the quantitative nature of the relationship between degree of behavioral involvement and level of physiological response have been well documented. In addition, the critical role of an organism's behavioral history in determining the nature and extent of autonomic-endocrine response to stress and anxiety has been demonstrated in a convincing fashion. Clearly, however, the most meaningful dimension for hormone and visceral analysis in relationship to more chronic stress and anxiety responses is the broader patterning or balance of secretory and visceral change in many interdependent autonomic and endocrine systems. The extensive and prolonged participation of these fundamental systems in behavioral interactions suggests a relationship between such physiological activity and the more durable consequences of stress and anxiety. Indeed, the differentiation of such autonomic-endocrine response patterns in relationship to the historical and situational aspects of behavioral events may well provide a first approximate step in the direction of identifying distinguishable intraorganismic consequences associated with both episodic and persistent stress and anxiety interactions.

The experimental research literature concerned with stress and anxiety also reflects an abiding interest in the effects of such processes on the gastrointestinal system (see, for example, Ader, 1971). Of particular interest is the controversy over the factors that influence the incidence of peptic ulcers in rodents and primates under aversive behavioral control. Some further support for the efficacy of "conflict" and related conditioning procedures in the production of gastric lesions in laboratory rats has been provided by studies focusing on a variety of social-psychological and physiology parameters (for example, Sawrey and Sawrey, 1966), but replication and confirmation of the reported relationships continue to present problems (Ader, Beels, and Tatum, 1960). Similarly, recurrent descriptions of avoidance conditioning effects on the gastrointestinal system have characteristically presented something less than a consistent picture with regard specifically to the conditions under which erosions of the gastric mucosa are most likely to occur. The reported incidence of peptic ulcers in rhesus monkeys intermittently exposed to a free-operant shock avoidance procedure (Brady and others, 1958) has proved difficult to repeat under some laboratory conditions (Folz and Miller, 1964), including those under which the study originated (Brady, 1964). Additionally, several investigations with laboratory rats on escape-avoidance procedures have failed to find an incidence of gastric lesions in experimental animals which exceeded that of controls; in some instances, yoked control animals receiving unavoidable shocks alone showed a greater degree of ulceration than their avoiding partners (Moot, Cebulla, and Crabtree, 1970; Weiss, 1971a).

A clarification and at least partial reconciliation of these apparently conflicting developments in the effect of stress and anxiety on the gastrointestinal system has been suggested by Weiss (1970, 1971c). Laboratory rats that received shocks in a predictable fashion developed significantly less gastric ulceration than rats that received the same shock intensity without the "predictability" of a "warning" stimulus. Weiss then examined the effects of adding an operant escape-avoidance ("coping") panel-press to the procedure. Under these conditions, markedly fewer gastric lesions were found in the experimental animals when compared with "helpless" controls similarly exposed to warning signals and shocks (one per minute for twenty-one hours) but without escape-avoidance responses. When the interactions between warning signals and the escape-avoidance responses were tested in a subsequent experiment involving groups differentiating between two types of preaversive stimuli ("beeping" tone and an "added clock"), presence or absence of escape-avoidance wheel turning, and appropriate "yoked" controls, the results provided a basis for reconciling the apparent contradictions between the rat and monkey studies. While the outcome of this rather mammoth 180-rat experiment confirmed the prepotence of the operant escape-avoidance conditioning in reducing the incidence of ulcers, the addition of a warning signal to the procedure was found to attenuate the development of gastric pathology even further. A similar warning stimulus procedure has been found to reduce the steroid response to operant avoidance performance requirements in the monkey (Mason, Brady, and Tolson, 1966).

In Weiss's view, these findings indicate that the incidence of peptic ulcers may be a function of the interaction between strength of the escape-avoidance performance (that is, the frequency of "coping" responses) and the probability of discriminable response-contingent signals associated with the absence of aversive stimuli (that is, "feedback" about shock-free conditions). Within the framework of this interpretive analysis, the incidence of peptic ulcers in free-operant avoidance monkeys would be accounted for in terms of a high response frequency in the absence of warning stimuli and the relatively low "feedback" discriminability of "safe" signals produced by those responses. The yoked-control monkeys, in contrast, characteristically emitted "avoidance" responses only infrequently, received only a few shocks well distributed in time (due to the high performance rates of the experimental animals), and were found to be free of gastrointestinal pathology. Weiss (1971b, 1971c) has provided some further confirmation of this formulation in a subsequent series of experimental manipulations which increased the frequency of ulcers in avoidance rats punished with shock for responding, and decreased the incidence of ulcers in animals producing a brief tone with each shock-postponing panel-press.

Contingent-Model Studies

Experimental studies within the framework of instrumental psychophysiological learning effects represent a relatively recent development in the basic science foundations of stress and anxiety processes (Harris and Brady, 1974). The systematic series of investigations undertaken at Yale in the mid 1960s by Miller and his colleagues (Miller and Carmona, 1967; Miller and DiCara, 1967), for example, activated a productive decade of "operant" learning research involving visceral and autonomic processes. There were, of course, notable precedents established in the earlier human experimental literature (Kimmel, 1967), and many reports had previously appeared on the "voluntary" control of physiological responses by Yoga and related meditative techniques (see, for example, Wenger and Bagchi, 1961). But the significant recent advances of laboratory animal research in this area seem to be attributable, at least in part, to the prominent experimental focus on explicit contingency relationships between specific antecedent physiological events, on the one hand, and programmed environmental consequences, on the other.

The initial instrumental learning experiments by Miller and Carmona (1967) showed that marked increases in salivation could be produced in fluid-deprived dogs given access to water contingent on such salivatory processes. The magnitude of this effect was emphasized by the fourteenfold difference in salivation rate between these animals and similarly deprived dogs given water only when no salivation occurred. This dramatic learning effect has been confirmed more recently in an experiment using food to operantly reinforce *decreases* in salivation (Shapiro and Herendeen, 1975), the results contrasting sharply with well-documented classical conditioning effects in the opposite direction. Equally convincing demonstrations of instrumental heart rate learning have emphasized the bidirectional control over both increases and decreases in cardiac rate which can be established in laboratory rats (DiCara and Miller, 1969) and rhesus monkeys (Engel and Gottlieb, 1970), while large-magnitude, enduring heart rate elevations have been operantly conditioned in dog-faced baboons (Harris, Gilliam, and Brady, 1976).

The specificity of physiological response effects suggested by such instrumental learning studies has in fact been documented in operant conditioning experiments showing independent control of heart rate and intestinal contractions (Miller and Banuazizi, 1968). Instrumentally learned increases or decreases in the P-R interval of the EKG have also been shown to be independent of changes in the P-P interval (Fields, 1970). Perhaps the most dramatic demonstration of such specificity, however, is the reported selective instrumental learning of vasomotor tone increases in one ear of the laboratory rat and vasomotor tone decreases in the other ear of the same animal (DiCara and Miller, 1968). Significantly, these instrumentally learned blood flow changes were not correlated with heart rate, rectal temperature, or vasomotor tone in the tail, suggesting a remarkable and previously unrecognized localization of sympathetic action. Subsequent replications and confirmations of these findings with respect to the specificity of instrumentally learned physiological responses have included the observation that operantly conditioned blood pressure effects can occur independently of changes in heart rate and skeletal muscle activity (Pappas, DiCara, and Miller, 1970).

Instrumental learning experiments have also focused on the analysis of bidirectional changes in blood pressure with both rats (Pappas, DiCara, and Miller, 1970) and monkeys (Benson and others, 1969), and impressive large-magnitude operantly conditioned blood pressure elevations have been reported with the dog-faced baboon (Harris, Findley, and Brady, 1971). Significantly, these latter studies involved the application of operant "shaping" techniques, with both the amplitude and duration of blood pressure elevations required to avoid shock and obtain food. More chronic stress studies of instrumentally learned blood pressure changes with the baboon have emphasized the analysis of such procedures under conditions which provide for enduring elevations of 25 to 30 mm Hg above baseline during daily twelve-hour "conditioning" sessions alternating with twelve-hour "rest" periods (Harris and others, 1973). Figure 16, for example, shows the stable response pattern (right-hand panel) developed after exposure to such daily

Figure 16. Comparison of Average Blood Pressure and Heart Rate Values for
Four Baboons over Consecutive 40-Minute Intervals During
Sixteen Preexperimental Baseline Determinations and Sixteen 12-Hour
"Conditioning On," 12-Hour "Conditioning Off" Sessions

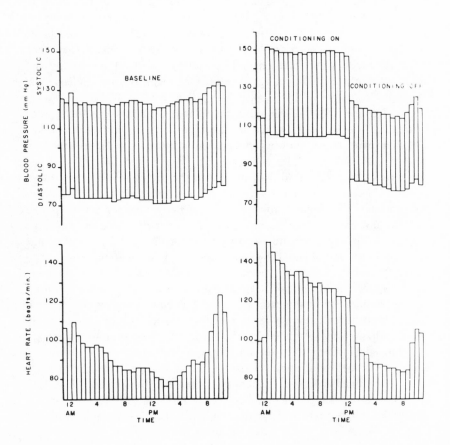

instrumental blood pressure learning sessions for two to three months. Characteristically, sustained elevations of 30 mm Hg or more in both systolic and diastolic blood pressure were maintained throughout the twelve-hour "conditioning on" periods, accompanied by elevated but progressively decreasing heart rate over the course of the twelve-hour interval. During the ensuing twelve-hour "conditioning off" recovery period, heart rate continued to fall somewhat precipitously, and blood pressure returned to approximately basal levels (or slightly above) within six to eight hours. That these large-magnitude sustained elevations in blood pressure were related directly and specifically to the programmed contingency requirements of the instrumental learning procedure was further confirmed by the results obtained with an additional group of baboons. In the same experiment, this group was exposed to virtually identical conditions except that food reward and shock avoidance were made contingent on *decreases* in blood pressure. Extended exposure (six months or more) to this instrumental blood pressure-lowering procedure (including exposure to all the same surgery and chronic catheterization, confinement and chair restraint, food deprivation and reward, and of course electric shocks) produced only small (nonsignificant) *decreases* in blood pressure under the same general laboratory conditions prevailing for the animals that showed instrumentally learned blood pressure elevations.

The role of autonomic mediation in these stress-related instrumental circulatory changes has also been evaluated by assessing the effects of specific pharmacological alpha- and beta-adrenergic blockers on the operantly conditioned blood pressure increases in baboons (Goldstein, Harris, and Brady, 1977b). Beta-adrenergic blockade, for example, completely eliminated the heart rate increases accompanying instrumentally learned blood pressure elevations without attenuating the pressure increase. Similarly, alpha blockade of adrenergically mediated peripheral vasoconstriction did not significantly alter the instrumentally learned blood pressure elevation response. Although combined alpha- and beta-adrenergic blockade did substantially reduce the magnitude of the operant blood pressure increase, the continued appearance of a significant instrumentally learned elevation in both systolic and diastolic blood pressure suggests nonadrenergic participation in such instrumental autonomic learning effects.

Continued exposure to such recurrent experimental stress procedures involving sustained large-magnitude increases in blood pressure may be associated with emergent effects on the "resting" circulation (Harris and Brady, 1977). In the course of repeated daily twelve-hour "on," twelve-hour "off" sessions under these conditions, gradual but progressive pressure increases have been observed during the daily twelve-hour "conditioning off" or "rest" periods (for example, no cardiovascular "feedback" and no food or shock contingencies in effect) over successive months of the program in virtually all animals. Though these "rest period" elevations are of lesser magnitude

(15-20 mm Hg) than the blood pressure increases observed during the twelve-hour "conditioning on" sessions, they have been reported to persist for extended intervals. And selected animals followed for two years or more, with prolonged "vacations" (for example, no instrumental cardiovascular learning sessions programmed, no feedback stimuli or shock, and food freely available) interspersed between the otherwise continuous exposure to daily twelve-hour "on," twelve-hour "off" instrumental blood pressure learning sessions, showed sustained elevations in blood pressure in the absence of contingency control for periods up to five months.

Conclusion

There are, of course, many unresolved procedural, interpretive, and theoretical problems in the analysis of experimental studies which bear importantly on the basic and applied aspects of stress and anxiety. The prominent focus on "mediational" issues, for example, has not only generated physiological controversies about the relationship between autonomic-visceral and somato-motor mechanisms (Black, 1968; DiCara, 1970) but has as well emphasized the need to reexamine some of the conventional distinctions between types of learning and conditioning (see Schoenfeld, 1972). Disagreements regarding mechanism and methodology notwithstanding, the evidence that experimental stress and anxiety learning and conditioning procedures, however mediated, can exert orderly and systematic effects on the functional characteristics of biochemical, anatomical, and physiological systems seems incontrovertible. Clearly the experimental analysis of such interactions involving behavioral and somatic processes seems to hold considerable promise for enriching both laboratory and clinical approaches to the understanding, prevention, and management of stress and anxiety responses. Of at least equal importance to the emerging investigative disciplines in this area is the contribution made by a basic laboratory analysis to a comprehensive psychophysiology of the stress and anxiety domain.

Part III

✳ ✳ ✳ ✳ ✳ ✳ ✳ ✳ ✳ ✳ ✳ ✳ ✳

In this section, the problem of anxiety is dealt with from various perspectives, providing the reader with an overview of the most current thinking on the topic. Rollo May begins the section with an examination of anxiety and values. He develops his central tenet—that anxiety arises when man's value system is threatened—through many clinical and historical examples. He then traces the origin of such values and distinguishes between "normal" and "neurotic" anxiety as a response to a threat to these values. Finally, he outlines some implications for psychotherapy.

In Chapter Fourteen, Norman S. Endler discusses in detail the inter-actional model of anxiety. When trying to understand the complexities of anxiety, one must take into account both the situation and the psychology of the perceiver. The topic of state versus trait anxiety is focused on, and there is a thorough review of the research evidence and varying experimental

Anxiety Research
and Findings

�֎ ✿ ✿ ✿ ✿ ✿ ✿ ✿ ✿ ✿ ✿ ✿ ✿

designs of the interplay between the person and his environment. Throughout the chapter, we are constantly reminded of the complexities of this field and of the need for many perspectives rather than one single viewpoint.

In Chapter Fifteen, Ruth Moulton discusses anxiety and the new feminism. Cultural changes of the 1960s and 1970s have resulted in a new role for women. These changes have caused a great deal of anxiety in both males and females. Women now have new freedoms which are anxiety provoking, and men have to deal with lowered self-esteem as the traditional concept of masculinity is challenged. Moulton discusses all these issues and presents illustrative case material. Other topics—such as marriage and divorce, dual-career marriages, career versus children, and women and men at work—are analyzed with regard to stress and anxiety. The chapter closes with some ideas on psychotherapy with women.

Anxiety patterns in childhood and adolescence are elaborated in Chapter Sixteen by Sandra Buechler and Carroll Izard. Buechler and Izard employ the differential emotions theory as a framework in which their ideas are developed. Anxiety is considered to be not a unitary concept but "a pattern of emotion and affective-cognitive structures." The emergence, experience, and regulation of anxiety in infancy and later life are detailed. The role of emotion in development is highlighted throughout the chapter, along with a discussion of current research and methodological problems. Other issues dealt with by the authors include the adaptive role of fear and anxiety patterns, the phenomenon of the emotion contagion, and the socialization of fear.

In Chapter Seventeen, John Doris, Anne McIntyre, and Michael Tamaroff present their theory and research on separation anxiety in pre-schoolers and its social and cognitive consequences. The authors have developed two scales to measure separation anxiety. By necessity, these rating scales are filled out by parents and teachers, since the preschooler cannot yet read or accurately report his own experience of anxiety. Evidence for reliability and validity is presented, along with a review of several studies utilizing the instruments. The authors then discuss the complex pattern of social adjustment and aggression in different groups of anxious children differentiated by the scales. Separation anxiety and cognitive performance on a variety of intellectual tasks are also dealt with. Doris, McIntyre, and Tamaroff suggest integration of their findings within the framework of learning and psychoanalytic theory. They conclude with a discussion of the optimal level of anxiety necessary for optimal growth and development of the preschool child.

Emilie F. Sobel discusses, in Chapter Eighteen, anxiety and stress in later life. Research relative to personality and cognitive changes of the elderly is reviewed, with several interesting phenomena highlighted. Much of the "regressive" childlike behavior of the aged patient is observed, and its etiology remains complex and multidetermined. Sobel describes detailed modified therapeutic techniques for use with the elderly patient. She also emphasizes that the elderly have to deal with many anxiety- and stress-producing agents in the environment. Finally, the anxiety of death is discussed, and Sobel presents further therapeutic techniques to help the patient cope with and adjust to this most stressful time in his life.

In Chapter Nineteen, Robert J. Powers and Irwin L. Kutash examine the complex relationship of anxiety and stress to alcohol use and abuse. A process model of stress is described, consisting of three stages: Demand Stage, Threat Stage, and Exhaustion Stage. At each stage, alcohol has been found to have paradoxical effects. At times alcohol may relieve anxiety and stress; at other times it may increase them or bring little change. The role of alcohol use at each stage is examined, and factors are identified that contribute to excessive use and to abuse.

13

Value Conflicts
and Anxiety

Rollo May

� � � � � � � � � � � �

The distinctive quality of human anxiety arises from the fact that man is a valuing animal, who interprets his life and world in terms of symbols and meanings. It is the threat to these values—specifically, to some value that the individual holds essential to his existence as a self—that causes anxiety. A classic and dramatic illustration of this type of threat is seen in the remark of the unsophisticated Tom, whom Wolf and Wolff (1943) studied in their significant work on anxiety and gastric functions at New York Hospital. You may recall that Tom and his wife lay awake all one night worrying whether Tom's job in the hospital laboratory would last or whether he would

Note: This chapter is an updated version of a lecture delivered at the annual convention of the American Psychiatric Association in 1956 and published in *Progress in Psychotherapy* (New York: Grune & Stratton, 1957).

have to go back on government relief. The next morning, the gastric readings for anxiety were the highest of any encountered in all those studies. The significant point is Tom's remark: "If I couldn't support my family, I'd as soon jump off the end of the dock." The threat that underlay this great anxiety in Tom was not that of physical deprivation—he and his family could have got along on relief—but was rather a threat to a status which Tom, like so many men in our culture, held even more important than life: the ability to fulfill one's role as a middle-class provider for one's family. The loss of this status would be tantamount to not existing as a person.

We see similar examples in the area of sex. Sex gratification in itself, of course, is a value. But physical gratification itself is only a small part of the question, since a person will be thrown into conflict and anxiety when rejected sexually by one partner but not by another. Obviously, other elements—prestige, tenderness, personal understanding—give the sexual experience with that partner a special value.

Death is the most obvious threat cueing off anxiety; for, unless one holds views of immortality, which are not common in our culture, death stands for the ultimate blotting out of one's existence as a self. But immediately we note a curious fact: some people prefer to die rather than to surrender some other value. The taking away of psychological and spiritual freedom was not infrequently a greater threat than death itself to persons under the dictatorships of Europe. "Give me liberty or give me death" is not necessarily histrionic or evidence of a neurotic attitude. Indeed, there is reason for believing, as we shall indicate later, that it may represent the most mature form of distinctively human behavior. Nietzsche and existentialists such as Jaspers, in fact, have pointed out that physical life itself is not fully satisfying and meaningful until one can consciously choose another value which he holds more dear than life itself.

What is the origin of these values, the threat to which results in anxiety? The infant's first value is the care, nourishment, and love it receives from its mother or parental substitutes; a threat to these, being indeed a threat to the infant's existence, gives rise to profound anxiety. As maturation proceeds, the values are transformed, becoming a desire for approval by the mother, "success" in the eyes of parents or peers, and, later on, status in cultural terms. In the mature adult, the values become the devotion to freedom, to a religious belief, or to scientific truth. I do not mean this as an exact maturation scale; I mean only to illustrate roughly that maturation involves a continuous transformation of one's original values and that in the normal human being these values take on an increasingly symbolic character.

It is an error to think that these later values are merely extensions of the original value of preserving mother's care and love. On the pattern of emergent evolution, the maturing person continually develops new capacities out of the old, new symbols, values in a new form. To be sure, if an individual's anxiety is neurotic, he may repetitiously and compulsively try to satisfy the same values he held at earlier stages. But the values of the mentally healthy adult cannot be comprehended as a mere sum of his previous needs and instincts.

The most important emergent capacity in the human being is self-relatedness. It begins somewhere after the first few months and probably is fairly well developed in the child by the age of 2. Thereafter, the values of love and care take on a new character. They are not simply something received but are reacted to by the child with some degree of self-awareness. He may accept the mother's care, defy it, use it for various forms of power demands, or what not. A patient at a clinic reported that he had learned at an early age to put his hands against the wall and push his high chair over, so that his parents would catch it. The value involved here was not self-preservation—that is, being saved from hitting the floor (he had his parents so well trained that this contingency never arose); the value gained was rather the satisfaction and security involved in his power to force his parents to sit on pins and needles, ready to jump to his aid.

In the mature person—the adult with a degree of autonomy—some choice, some conscious affirmation, some self-aware participation is necessary in loving and accepting love if the experience of love is to yield full satisfaction. The value then lies as much in being able to give to the other person as in receiving; and such a mature individual may well experience his most severe anxiety if his opportunity to give love to the partner is threatened.

Let us look now at this distinctive capacity for self-relatedness of the human being, a capacity which is crucially significant for understanding human anxiety. It is man's capacity to stand outside himself, to know that he is the subject as well as the object of experience, to see himself as the entity who is acting in the world of objects. This quality, which distinguishes man from the rest of nature, can be described in many ways. Goldstein terms it man's capacity to transcend the immediate, concrete situation and to deal with "the possible." Mowrer (Mowrer and Ullman, 1945, p. 2) calls it the human being's time-binding quality: "The capacity to bring the past into the present as a part of the total causal nexus in which living organisms behave (act and react) is the essence of 'mind' and 'personality' alike." Howard Liddel points out that his sheep can keep time for about ten minutes, his dogs for about half an hour, but the human being can keep time into the distant future—he can plan for decades or centuries. And, we should add, he can worry about this future and suffer anxiety in anticipating his own eventual death. Whatever terms are used, the capacity we are here describing, which emerges somewhere in the first two years of life, underlies our capacity to use symbols as tools, to talk, and to reason. It makes us the historical mammals who are not only pushed by history, as all organisms are, but who can also "look before and after" and, by understanding the past, mold and to some small extent influence the future. As Lawrence Kubie has indicated, neurosis has its source in the distortion of these symbolic functions as a result of a dichotomy between conscious and unconscious processes which starts early in the development of each human infant.

Adolf Meyer, Sullivan suggests, held that the human being operates on a hierarchy of organization and that the physiological functions are subordinate to the integrating functions and particularly to man's capacity to use symbols as tools. Thus, in experimental work with human beings, in anxiety or other areas, one must define the context of the particular person being studied; to ask, that is, what symbolic meaning he gives the situation and what his present values are.

What is important here for understanding anxiety is that man, the symbol maker, interprets his experience in symbolic terms and holds these symbols as values, the threats to which give rise to profound anxiety. The understanding of anxiety can thus never be separated from ethical symbols, which are one aspect of the human being's normal milieu. Through his distinctive social capacity to see himself as others see him, to imagine himself empathetically in his fellow man's position, the person can direct his decisions in the light of long-term values, which are the basis of ethics and therefore the basis of ethical anxiety.

I use the terms *symbols* and *values*, incidentally, in the sense of their being the quintessence of experience. They are a boiling down of the most real relationships and satisfactions; thus, a threat to a symbolic value can have tremendous anxiety-arousing power.

An individual's values and, therefore, his anxiety are conditioned by the fact that he lives in a given culture at a particular moment in the historical development of that culture. It is the essence of man's nature to interpret his values in the context of his relation to other people and their expectations. Tom, who believed that he had to be a self-supporting middle-class male, was validating himself by values that have been dominant in Western society since the Renaissance. As Fromm, Kardiner, and others have pointed out, the dominant value since then has been competitive prestige measured in terms of work and financial success. If one achieved such prestige, he considered himself a person and his anxiety was allayed; if he did not, he was subject to powerful anxiety and lost his sense of being a self, like Willie Loman in *The Death of a Salesman,* who, in the words of the playwright Arthur Miller, "never knew who he was."

In the past decade or so, however, this dominant competitive value has apparently been reversed. David Riesman, in his studies in *The Lonely Crowd*, points out that young people rarely have the goal of competitive success any more; they want not to be first in school but rather to stay somewhere in the middle. The dominant value, then, becomes not getting ahead of the next man but being like everyone else—that is, conformity.

One now validates himself by fitting into the herd; what makes him prey to anxiety is to be different, to stand out. This development obviously is part of our special social problem in these days of antiintellectualism, witch hunts, suspicion of the original and creative person, and the general tendency to avoid anxiety by assuming the protective coloring afforded by looking like everyone else.

These contemporaneous cultural values of conformity, adjustment to the "radar type" of person who reflects his signals from the crowd around him, are related to the prevalence of loneliness in our day, about which Sullivan and others have written. Loneliness is a special form of anxiety. As Freud, Rank, and others have suggested, all anxiety may be, at bottom, separation anxiety; thus, loneliness—the awareness of separation—may be the most painful conscious and immediate form of anxiety. As all of us observe, loneliness is a common experience of those who conform. They are driven to conform because of loneliness; however, validating the self by means of becoming like everyone else reduces their experience of personal identity, making for inner emptiness and thus causing greater loneliness.

Shall we say that, in this shift from competition to conformity, the dominant value—and hence the locus for the genesis of anxiety—has changed? Certainly, one of the clearest reasons for the prevalence of anxiety in our culture is the fact that we live in a time when almost all social values are in radical change; when one world is dying, as social scientists too numerous to mention have demonstrated, and the new one is not yet born. But is there not a more specific explanation which underlies both the value of competitive success, dominant from the Renaissance until recently, and its apparent present opposite, conformity? Do not both arise from the same cause; namely, modern Western man's disruption in his relationship to nature, including human nature? Since the Renaissance, Western man has been infatuated with the goal of gaining power over nature. As Tillich points out, he has gradually transformed the broad concept of reason of the seventeenth and eighteenth centuries into technical reason in the nineteenth and twentieth centuries, and he has dedicated himself to the exploitation of nature. Ever since Descartes's dichotomy in the seventeenth century between subjective experience and the objective world, Western man has progressively sought to see nature as entirely separated from himself. The deep loneliness and isolation that such a view entailed was already sensed by Pascal, who said, "When I consider the brief span of my life, swallowed up in the eternity before and behind it, the small space that I fill or even see, engulfed in the infinite immensity of spaces which I know not, and which know not me, I am afraid and wonder to see myself here rather than there; for there is no reason why I should be here rather than there, now rather than then."

But since modern men were successful in validating themselves by power over nature for several centuries, the loneliness and isolation inherent in this situation became widespread only in the recent twentieth century. Particularly with the advent of the atom bomb, sensitive laymen as well as scientists began to experience the loneliness of being strangers in the universe; and it has made many Western men, like Pascal, afraid. Our contemporaneous loneliness and anxiety thus go deeper than alienation in relation to ourselves and our society; they stem also from our alienation from the natural world.

Several straws in the wind show the movements in our society toward recovering an indigenous relation with nature. Modern physics is one such movement. As Werner Heisenberg says, the essence of modern physics is that the Copernican view that nature is to be studied "out there," entirely separate from man, is no longer tenable; nature cannot be understood apart from man's subjective involvement, and vice versa. The West's new interest in Eastern thought points in the same direction. Oriental thought never suffered our radical split between subject and object, between I-the-person and the world "out there," and therefore escaped the special Western brand of separation from nature and consequent loneliness.

I mention these somewhat speculative points because I wish to emphasize strongly that to understand modern Western man's anxiety we must see him in his historical position as the heir of several centuries of radical splitting of subject and object, and consequent disrupted relation with nature.

In any event, we must differentiate neurotic anxiety from normal anxiety. If, as we have said, anxiety is the reaction to a threat to values that one identifies with his existence, no one can escape anxiety, for no values are unassailable. Furthermore, values are always in process of change and reformation. The only apparent escape—albeit a self-defeating one—from the anxiety that goes along with transformation of values is to crystallize one's values into dogma. And dogma, whether of the religious or the scientific variety, is a temporary security bought at the price of surrendering one's opportunity for fresh learning and new growth.

Normal anxiety is a reaction that is proportionate to the threat, does not involve repression, and can be confronted constructively on the conscious level (or can be relieved if the objective situation is altered). Neurotic anxiety is a reaction that is disproportionate to the threat, involves repression and other forms of intrapsychic conflict, and is managed by various kinds of blocking off of activity and awareness.

Actually, neurotic anxiety develops when a person has been unable to meet normal anxiety at the time of the actual crisis in his growth and threat to his values. Neurotic anxiety, that is to say, is the end result of previously unmet normal anxiety.

Normal anxiety is most obvious in the steps in individuation, which, as Rank pointed out, occur at every stage in one's development. The child learns to walk and leaves the past security of the pen; he goes off to school;

at adolescence he reaches out toward the opposite sex; later, he leaves home to earn his own living, marries, and eventually must separate finally from immediate values on his deathbed. I do not mean that these events are necessarily actual crises, though they are potential ones; I mean rather to indicate that all growth consists of the anxiety-creating surrender of past values as one transforms them into broader ones; it consists of the giving up of immediate security in terms of more extensive goals, death being the final step in this continuum.

This transforming of values, and meeting the anxiety related thereto, is one side of creativity. Nietszche well says, "Valuing is creating; hear it, ye creative ones! Without valuation the nut of existence would be hollow. Hear it, ye creative ones!" In Goldstein's phrase, man as the valuator is, in the very act of valuing, engaged in molding his world, making himself adequate to his environment and his environment adequate to himself. This interrelation of transforming of values and creativity indicates why creativity has always been considered, from the myth of Prometheus on down, as unavoidably connected with anxiety.

I wish to underline three implications for therapy in this discussion. First, the goal of therapy is not to free the patient from anxiety. It is, rather, to help him become free from neurotic anxiety and to meet normal anxiety constructively. Normal anxiety, we have seen, is an inseparable part of growth and creativity; the self becomes more integrated and stronger as experiences of normal anxiety are successfully confronted. Hence the famous saying of Kierkegaard: "I would say that learning to know anxiety is an adventure which every man has to affront if he would not go to perdition either by not having known anxiety or by sinking under it. He therefore who has learned rightly to be anxious has learned the most important thing."

Second, our discussion implies grave questions about the use of drugs to relieve anxiety. (We except the rare cases in which anxiety, if not relieved, itself would lead to more serious breakdown, or needs to be relieved to the point where psychotherapy is possible.) The harmful effect of the general use of drugs for normal anxiety is obvious, for to wipe away the anxiety is in principle to wipe away the opportunity for growth; that is, value transformation, of which anxiety is the obverse side. By the same token, neurotic anxiety is a symptom of the fact that some previous crisis has not been met, and to remove the symptom without helping the person get at his underlying conflict is to rob him of his best direction finder and motivation for self-understanding and new growth.

Third, this discussion implies that there is an inverse relation between the soundness of an individual's value system and his anxiety. That is, the firmer and more flexible one's values, the more one will be able to meet his anxiety constructively. But the more the person is overcome by anxiety, the more his values will diminish in strength. Thus, the patient's arriving at sound values is, in the long run, an integral part of his therapeutic progress. This does not relieve the therapist of his responsibility to help the patient in the technical process of slow, steady uncovering of the roots of his conflict; indeed, this has to be done in most cases before the patient is able to arrive at his own enduring values.

Mature values are those that transcend the immediate situation in time and encompass past and future; transcend also the immediate in-group and extend outward toward the good of the community, ideally embracing humanity as a whole. The more mature one's values are, the less it matters to him whether his values are literally satisfied or not. The satisfaction and security lie in the holding of the values. To the genuine scientist (or religious person, for that matter), security and confidence arise from his awareness of his devotion to the search for truth rather than the finding of it.

14

Person-Situation Interaction and Anxiety

Norman S. Endler

❉ ❉ ❉ ❉ ❉ ❉ ❉ ❉ ❉ ❉ ❉ ❉ ❉

Personality theory has been plagued by theoretical, methodological, and empirical ambiguities and confusions. Two important and interrelated issues for personality, and especially anxiety, are the controversy as to whether *situations* or *traits* are the major source of behavioral variance and the belief in cross-situation consistency versus the belief in situational-specificity of behavior (see Endler and Magnusson, 1976c).

Personologists (Cattell, 1946, 1950; Cattell and Scheier, 1961; Murray, 1938) and clinicians (Rapaport, Gill, and Schafer, 1945) postulate that traits (person factors), exhibited in terms of cross-situational consistencies, are the major determinants of behavior. This position emphasizes

Note: This chapter was written while the author was on sabbatical and was partially supported by an SSHRC Leave Fellowship No. 451-790497.

dispositional or intrapsychic variables. Sociologists and social psychologists (Cooley, 1902; Cottrell, 1942a, 1942b; Dewey and Humber, 1951; Lindesmith and Strauss, 1949; Mead, 1934) contend that situations, and the perceptions or meanings of situations in terms of cultural norms and roles, are the basic determinants of behavior.

Instead of asking whether traits or situations are the major source of behavioral variance, one might more profitably ask "*How* do persons and situations *interact* in determining behavior?" (Endler, 1973). This question has general relevance for personality theorizing and research. It has special relevance for anxiety, especially an interaction model of anxiety, in which the multidimensional nature of the construct is emphasized (see Endler, 1975b).

Types of Investigations

The issues of cross-situational consistency and persons versus situations (see Endler, 1975a; Endler and Magnusson, 1976b) have been investigated in at least three major ways: (1) by the multidimensional variance components strategy; (2) by the correlational research strategy; and (3) by the Personality x Treatment factorial experimental design (see Endler and Magnusson, 1976c, for a more detailed presentation).

Multidimensional Variance Components Strategy. The earliest empirical research on the specificity-consistency and person-versus-situation issues employing a multidimensional variance components technique was conducted by Raush, Dittmann, and Taylor (1959a, 1959b); Raush, Farbman, and Llewellyn (1960); and Endler and Hunt (1966). Raush and his co-workers examined the behavior of delinquent boys in various situations and rated the observed behavior. Using a multivariate information transmission analysis (which is analogous to the variance components technique), they found that the person-by-situation interaction accounted for more behavioral variance than did either situations or persons.

The S-R Inventory of Anxiousness (Endler, Hunt, and Rosenstein, 1962) requires subjects to rate their own responses on a number of scales for each of a number of verbally described situations. This yields a Persons-by-Responses-by-Situations three-dimensional data matrix. Endler and Hunt (1966, 1969) administered various forms of the S-R Inventory of Anxiousness (containing different situations and different modes of responses) to samples of subjects differing in education, age, social class, geographical location, and level of mental health. Using a variance components technique (Endler, 1966b) to estimate the relative importance of persons, situations, responses, and interactions, they found that persons accounted for about 4 percent for males and about 8 percent for females, and person-by-situation interactions accounted for about 10 percent. The two-way interactions (persons by situations, persons by response, and situation by response) accounted for more anxiety variance (about 30 percent) than did the sum of the contributions for situations and persons. Endler and Hunt (1968), using their S-R Inventory of Hostility, found that persons accounted for about 19 percent for males and about 15 percent for females; situations, about 5 percent for males and 7 percent for females; and person-by-situation interactions, about 11 percent. The total of the three simple interactions accounted for about 30 percent of the hostility variance.

Ekehammar, Magnusson, and Ricklander (1974) (studying Swedish adolescents), Endler (1975b), and Endler and Okada (1975) (studying Canadians), using variations of the S-R Inventory of Anxiousness, obtained results supporting the relevance of person-by-situation interactions with respect to anxiety. Nelsen, Grinder, and Mutterer (1969) reported analogous results for the variable of honesty, and Argyle and Little (1972) found similar results for social perception. Bishop and Witt (1970) investigated leisure activities; and Endler (1966a) and Endler and Hoy (1967) studied conforming behavior. The results of these studies provided evidence for the importance of person-by-situation interactions.

Moos (1968, 1969) analyzed observations of subjects' actual overt behavior (smiling, smoking, talking) and self-ratings in the actual presence of situations. Moos studied ward staff and psychiatric patients, used ward settings as situations, and examined a number of different variables. He found that the person-by-situation interaction variance was more important than the variance due to persons. (See Argyle and Little, 1972; Bowers, 1973; Endler, 1977; Endler and Magnusson, 1976b, 1976c; and Magnusson, 1976, for summaries and reviews of many of these studies.)

The studies reviewed are based on various personality traits and behaviors and a variety of samples differing in age, social class, geographical location, and mental health. A good portion of the data base is derived from self-report measures, and it would have been preferable to have more results based on actual behavioral measures. However, the results do represent a phenomenon that generalizes across various personality variables, situations, and samples of subjects. These variance components studies describe interactions; they do *not* explain them. Nevertheless, we can conclude, as Endler and Magnusson (1976c, p. 964) do, "that persons and situations per se are less important sources of behavioral variance than are person-situations interactions."

Correlational Research Strategy. Whereas the variance components strategy provides an indirect test of the assumption of cross-situational consistency, the correlational strategy provides a direct test of cross-situational stability. Hartshorne and May (1928) assessed honesty, in young boys, in various situations. They found correlations of honesty across *various* situations of about +.30. Rushton (1976) has recently reviewed studies of children's altruism and found that the average correlation of altruism scores across various situations was +.30. The results of the various studies on altruism and honesty do *not* support the trait theory assumption of trans-situational consistency. Newcomb (1931) studied introversion-extraversion behavior patterns in adolescent boys across thirty situations. The correlations averaged about .30, which accounts for only 9 percent of the variance.

Magnusson and associates (Magnusson, Gerzén, and Nyman, 1968; Magnusson and Heffler, 1969; Magnusson, Heffler, and Nyman, 1968) examined the cross-situational consistency of ratings with respect to cooperative ability, self-confidence, leadership, and talking time. In their various studies, Magnusson and his colleagues systematically varied the situation constructs of tasks and groups composition. For *similar* situations, the correlations were high (about .70); for *dissimilar* situations, the correlations were low (about zero). There is evidence for consistency for *similar* situations but no evidence for relative consistency across dissimilar situations.

Transsituational consistency can also be examined via factor analysis. The trait hypothesis of cross-situational consistency would postulate that one general factor would account for most of the total variance. Burton (1963) factor-analyzed the Hartshorne and May (1928) honesty data, and Nelsen, Grinder, and Mutterer (1969) reanalyzed their own honesty data. The results of these studies indicate that honesty was only moderately consistent across various tasks. Endler and associates (Endler, Hunt, and Rosenstein, 1962; Endler and Magnusson, 1976a; Endler and Okada, 1975) factor-analyzed S-R Inventory of Anxiousness data and found no evidence for a general anxiety factor. Similarly, Endler and Hunt (1968) found no evidence for transsituational consistency with respect to hostility.

Personality x *Treatment Experimental Design Strategy.* The variance components studies describe interactions; they do not explain them. The correlational studies demonstrate consistency or fail to demonstrate it. Sarason, Smith, and Diener (1975) point out that, although the typical variance components studies are useful because they inform us *what* the state of affairs is (for example, that interactions are important), they do not tell us *why*. We should be concerned with *how* persons and situations interact in eliciting behavior. We should plan studies that simultaneously incorporate situation (treatment) and personality variables in their experimental designs. By doing this, we can obtain information about the role of particular personality variables and particular situations and the way in which they interact in eliciting behavior.

During the 1970s, there have been a number of personality-x-treatment experiment design studies on the issues of interactionism. Endler and Edwards (1978) have provided an extensive review of these studies relating them to the variables of anxiety, conformity, and locus of control. At this point let us briefly summarize some of the personality-x-treatment experimental design studies as they relate to various personality variables.

The studies on anxiety will be deferred until the section on the interaction model of anxiety.

Cronbach and Snow (1977), after reviewing the school achievement literature, point out that there are numerous aptitude-by-treatment interactions which relate to instruction. Domino (1971) investigated the relationship between personality factors and college achievement. He found an interaction between situation (instructor's style of teaching), personality (achievement via independence and achievement via conformance) as manifested in college course outcome (for example, course grades, exam results).

Fiedler's (1977) contingency model provides a theoretical background and empirical support for the relevance of person-by-situation interactions for leadership. Field studies and laboratory data have demonstrated how the situation influences the relationship between leadership style (person variable) and group performance. Situation variables and leadership style interact in influencing group effectiveness.

A discussion of the multidimensionality of anxiety and the evidence for interactionism with respect to anxiety will be deferred until the discussion of the interaction model of anxiety.

Evaluation of the Evidence for Consistency. Argyle and Little (1972), Bowers (1973), Endler (1973, 1975b), Magnusson (1976), Mischel (1968, 1969), Pervin (1968), and Vernon (1964) have all evaluated the trait stability hypothesis and have pointed out that there is little empirical support for cross-situational consistency of behavior. In general, personality validity coefficients range from .20 to .50, with a mean of .30 (Endler, 1973; Mischel, 1968). The empirical results on stability, discussed above, point to the limitations of the trait model as a general basis for the use of personality empirical data for describing and predicting behavior in actual situations. The stability (or consistency) correlations, averaging about .30, are based primarily on empirical studies of noncognitive personality constructs and social behavior, including such variables as altruism, anxiety, conformity, honesty, hostility, leadership, rigidity, and self-confidence. These studies are primarily cross-situational rather than longitudinal. Block (1977), Epstein (1979), and Olweus (1979) have found some empirical evidence for longitudinal consistency in social and personality variables.

In studies of intellectual and cognitive factors, there is some evidence for both longitudinal and cross-situational consistency (see Mischel 1968, 1969; Rushton and Endler, 1977). Endler (1977) and Magnusson and Endler (1977)—in discussing three kinds of mediating variables; namely, structural (cognitive), motivational, and content (personality social)—suggest that one would expect high consistency for structural variables such as cognitive style but low consistency for motivational and content variables. One would expect greater consistency in similar situations than in dissimilar situations (see Magnusson, Gerzén, and Nyman, 1968). Possibly one of the reasons for greater similarity in longitudinal data than in cross-situational data is that there is probably a greater opportunity to select the situations one encounters throughout the course of one's life (longitudinally). We will be discussing the role of situations in the next section.

According to Endler and Magnusson (1976c, p. 966), "The empirical evidence from the variance components studies, from the correlational studies, and from the personality-x-treatment experimental designs seriously questions some of the assumptions of the trait theory of personality and its traditional measurement model." Many inconsistent findings are probably due to higher-order interactions (Cronbach, 1975), failures to distinguish between overt reactions and mediating variables, and treating self-reports and actual behaviors as identical (Magnusson and Endler, 1977). There is also often a failure to distinguish between mechanistic and dynamic interaction (Endler and Edwards, 1978).

Mechanistic Versus Dynamic Interaction. In personality theory, the interaction concept has been discussed in terms of (1) *statistical* interactions of main factors (independent variables), such as persons, situations, and modes of response, as part of a data matrix; and (2) *process models* of behavior, concerned with reciprocal causation or reciprocal action between behavior and situational factors. Endler (1975a) has used the terms *mechanistic* (structural or statistical) and *dynamic* (process or organismic) interaction. The statistical sense of the term focuses on interaction in terms of *structure*, and the other sense of the term is concerned with the *process of interaction.*

The mechanistic model of interaction, using the analysis of variance statistic, makes a precise distinction between independent and dependent variables. This model assumes an additive and linear relation between situational and person (trait) factors in determining behavior. For this model, interaction is concerned with the interdependency of determinants (independent variables) of behavior. It is not concerned with the interaction between independent and dependent variables. In this case the interaction is between causes and not between cause and effect.

Typically, studies on person-by-situation interactions (whether using variance components techniques or person-by-treatment analysis of variance designs) have exemplified the mechanistic model of interaction. Although this model helps us to demonstrate and explain interactions, it is limited in that it is inadequate for studying the dynamic interaction model of personality.

The dynamic or process model of interaction focuses on the reciprocal interaction between behavior and situational events. According to this model, events affect the behavior of organisms; but, in addition, the person is also an active and intentional agent, selecting and influencing environmental events. Dynamic interaction is multidirectional and refers "to the mutual interdependence of persons-situations and behavior, so that persons-situations influence behavior and vice versa" (Endler, 1975a, p. 18). Dynamic interaction focuses on process and attempts to integrate mediating variables, person reaction variables, and situations.

Much of the research on person-by-situation interactions has illustrated the mechanistic model of interaction. Basically "this is probably due to the fact that we have not yet perfected the techniques and measurement models for investigating dynamic interaction" (Endler and Edwards, 1978, p. 149).

The research which we will be discussing relevant to the interaction model of anxiety will focus primarily on the mechanistic model of interaction. However, we will then suggest some directions for future anxiety research, which could enable us to obtain some insights and understanding of the dynamic process of interaction. Prior to discussing the interaction model of anxiety, it is necessary to discuss the role of situations within the context of person-by-situation interactions.

Role of Situations in Interactional Psychology

In addition to person variables, interactional psychology is also concerned with situation variables. There have been few attempts to study situations psychologically, and much of the early research on personality overestimated the role of *person factors* and underestimated the role of *situation factors* (Endler, 1980a). There has been more emphasis on the study of *traits* than on the study of *situations* in personality research. The recent increase in research and theorizing about situations has to some extent been influenced by the interaction model of personality (Endler and Magnusson, 1976c).

We often select the situations with which we interact and the situations we encounter. However, there are circumstances where situations are imposed on us. Life is a mixture of selected and imposed situations. This is a continuous lifelong ongoing process. However, instead of examining situations longitudinally, we are prone to observe and examine a cross-sectional slice of situations, at one specific point in time.

By selecting a specific occupation (for example, machinist) and working for a specific company (for example, an automobile company such as Chrysler or Ford or General Motors), we are more likely to encounter certain people rather than others (for example, mechanics rather than lawyers) and certain environmental situations rather than others (for example, working indoors rather than outdoors). A mechanic or a woodsman is more likely to encounter physical danger than a doctor or a lawyer is. A business executive is more likely to encounter psychological stress in his job than a lumberjack is. (However, the lumberjack may possibly encounter as much stress or more stress in his home environment.) If there is any consistency in behavior, it is probably because, to a certain extent, we encounter and interact with similar situations, both at work and during our leisure hours, from day to day. We are all creatures of habit, and we seek similar situations as we go through similar routines from day to day. If we are plumbers, we are more likely to interact with other plumbers than with physicians. If we are professors, we are more likely to interact with other professors than with painters. Other people form an important part of our environment and influence us. Although we shape our environment, our environment also shapes us.

According to Magnusson (1978, p.1), "The total environment influences development and behavior," but "the influence of environment is always mediated via actual situations." One can examine the life style or life course of a person in terms of the situations he or she encounters. Runyan (1978) proposes that we investigate the life course in terms of sequences of person-by-situation interactions. All of us have certain goals in life and certain projects that we engage in (for example, buying a car or a boat, buying a suit or a dress, studying for an occupation or vocation, taking a trip). These projects differ in degree of involvement, in relevance in degree of planning, and in size. Because of this, it may be necessary to ask persons to scale their projects along various dimensions if we wish to make interindividual comparisons (see Endler, 1980b).

The meaning that a person assigns to a situation or life event, or his perception of the situation or event, appears to be the most influential situational factor affecting the person's behavior. Magnusson (1971, 1974) has proposed an empirical psychophysical method for investigating the *perception* of situations. Magnusson (1971) and Magnusson and Ekehammar (1973) examined situations common to university students in their studies. They found two bipolar situational dimensions—(1) positive versus negative and (2) active versus passive—which are analogous to the semantic differential factors. They also found a unipolar dimension, a social factor. Ekehammar and Magnusson (1973) then extended their research to stressful situations and found essentially the same results as in their previous studies. The *perception* of the situation (or its meaning) appears to be an essential factor that influences behavior.

One can also investigate the person's *reactions* to situations. Frederiksen (1972) and Rotter (1954) have both suggested that situations can be classified according to the similarity of responses that they elicit in persons. Here the aim is to develop taxonomies of situations. Many of the studies that have used the situation reaction approach have employed data from inventories originally developed for research purposes: the S-R Inventory of Anxiousness (Endler, Hunt, and Rosenstein, 1962), the Interactional Reactions Questionnaire (Ekehammar, Magnusson, and Ricklander, 1974), and the Stressful Situations Questionnaire (Hodges and Felling, 1970). A factor analysis of persons' responses to the various situations of the S-R

Inventory of Anxiousness yielded three situational factors: (1) Interpersonal Status Threatened, (2) Inanimate Personal Physical Danger, (3) Ambiguity. With respect to the S-R Inventory of General Trait Anxiousness, Endler and Okada (1975) and Endler and Magnusson (1976a) found the same situational factors. Most of the situation reaction studies have investigated the dimensionality of situations on the basis of individuals' reaction to situations as wholes.

Magnusson and Ekehammar (1975, 1978) and Ekehammar, Schalling, and Magnusson (1975) have investigated the relationship between peoples' perceptions of situations and their reactions to situations. Reactions to a situation are to a large extent dependent on the person's perception of situations or events. The relationships between perceptions of and reactions to situations are important for an interactional psychology of personality. Magnusson and his colleagues, in their research on situations and interactional psychology, compared the situation perception and situation reaction strategies within a single study. Magnusson and Ekehammar (1975) obtained situation *reaction* and situation *perception* data on the same forty subjects. There were four kinds of stressful situations covering a total of twelve different situations. They found that the coefficient of congruence between perceptions and reactions for three of the four a priori groups of situations ranged from .89 to .92; for the fourth group of situations, the coefficient of congruence was .69. In an analogous study, Ekehammar, Schalling, and Magnusson (1975) obtained basically the same results. The above studies used group data. Magnusson and Ekehammar (1978), analyzing individual data, also obtained results that were congruent with an interaction model of personality.

When we investigate the psychological significance of situations, it is important to differentiate between situation *perception* dimensions and situation *reaction* dimensions. Two persons may *perceive* the identical situation, and another one may *react* by withdrawing from the situation. The investigations by Magnusson and his co-workers provide a useful approach for investigating how perceptual factors in situations affect reactions. Another important aspect relating perception to reaction is the temporal one. On one occasion the individual may react to stress by withdrawing from the situation, while at another point in time the same individual may react by attacking. It is important to note that all situations are multidimensional and multifaceted. Various contextual and motivational factors may mediate the relationship between perception and reaction, in addition to the specific situation.

The Person-by-Situation Interaction Model of Anxiety

The interaction model of anxiety (Endler, 1975b) provides a methodological context for research in anxiety with respect to the selection of experimental designs and with respect to anxiety assessment techniques (Shedletsky and Endler, 1974). The multidimensional interaction model of anxiety (Endler, 1975b) originates from the rationale and research in the S-R Inventory of Anxiousness (Endler, Hunt, and Rosenstein, 1962). The extent or the degree to which a trait is expressed is influenced by a number of factors, such as the types and proportions of situations in which specific responses are exhibited; the type, intensity, number, and duration of these responses; and the relative provocativeness of the various situations in arousing specific responses. The assessment of a trait such as anxiousness must necessarily consider both the responses that characterize anxiousness and the appropriate eliciting responses.

Spielberger (1972a) has proposed that research on the state-trait anxiety theory should investigate and specify the stressful stimuli that evoke differential levels of A-State for high and low A-Trait persons. Because high A-Trait persons are self-deprecatory and concerned with "fear of failure," according to Spielberger, they should be more likely to perceive situations that are ego involving as more threatening than would low A-Trait persons. High A-Trait individuals should exhibit more intense levels of A-State arousal in ego-threatening situations than low A-Trait persons. In neutral or non-threatening situations, the level of A-State arousal should not be appreciably higher for high A-Trait persons as compared to low A-Trait persons.

Rappaport and Katkin (1972), O'Neil, Spielberger, and Hansen (1969), Hodges and Spielberger (1969), and Hodges (1968) have all found that high A-Trait persons in *ego-threatening conditions* or *situations* report greater changes in A-State levels than do low A-Trait persons. However, for *physical danger conditions,* high A-Trait persons do *not* show greater increases in A-State arousal than do low A-Trait persons. Katkin (1965) and Hodges and Spielberger (1966) found that the threat of shock (physical danger) produced increases in reported A-State, but that these reported changes were not related to the level of A-Trait, as measured by the Taylor (1953) Manifest Anxiety Scale (MAS). Auerbach (1973) and Spielberger, Gorsuch, and Lushene (1970) found similar results, in that stressor stimuli such as physical dangers, which do not pose a "psychological threat" to self-esteem, did *not* interact with A-Trait in eliciting A-State arousal. That is, high A-Trait persons did not perceive the physical dangers as more threatening than did the low A-Trait persons. In these cases the level of A-Trait did not influence the intensity of A-State arousal. Most of the studies cited above used the Taylor (1953) MAS or the A-Trait Scale of the State-Trait Anxiety Inventory (STAI) (Spielberger, Gorsuch, and Lushene, 1970) as the measure of trait anxiety.

Hodges (1968) separately investigated the effects of both physical threat and ego threat on A-State arousal, for individuals differing in A-Trait. For ego-threat failure instructions, high A-Trait persons reacted with greater increases in A-State arousal, as assessed by the Zuckerman (1960) Affective

Adjective Check List, than did low A-State persons. However, for physical danger threat of shock instructions, there was no relationship between A-State arousal and the level of A-Trait.

Endler and Shedletsky (1973) examined the generalizability of the Spielberger (1972a) state-trait anxiety theory to another personality trait—namely, authoritarianism—and also attempted to replicate Hodges' (1968) study. In regard to anxiety, Endler and Shedletsky (1973) found that the threat of failure (ego-threat) and threat of shock (physical threat) elicited A-State arousal but that increases in A-State for the ego-threat instructions were unrelated to the level of A-Trait. For the physical threat of shock instructions, however, the high A-Trait persons manifested greater A-State increases than did the low A-Trait persons.

Differences between the Endler and Shedletsky (1973) findings and those of Hodges (1968) may be due to a number of factors. The physical threat condition in the Endler and Shedletsky (1973) experiment may have contained an ego-threat component and/or the ego-threatening condition may not have been sufficiently intense to produce differential levels of A-State arousal for low and high A-Trait persons. For example, McAdoo (1969) found that A-State arousal was positively related to the level of A-Trait when the degree of ego threat was forceful (for example, a strong failure feedback) but was not systematically related to the level of A-Trait when ego threat was less intense (for example, a mild failure feedback).

However, the discrepancy between the Endler and Shedletsky (1973) results and those of others may well be due to the fact that Hodges (1968), Spielberger, Gorsuch, and Lushene (1970), and Rappaport and Katkin (1972) measured A-Trait via the Taylor MAS and the STAI, which are both unidimensional, while Endler and Sheldletsky (1973) measured A-Trait via the multidimensional S-R Inventory of Anxiousness. Endler and Shedletsky (1973) and Shedletsky and Endler (1974) point out that both the STAI and the MAS assess primarily ego threat or interpersonal trait anxiety and that interpersonal or ego-threatening conditions on situations interact with congruent interpersonal A-Trait (STAI or MAS) to evoke differential A-State changes for high and low interpersonal A-Trait persons. When a physical danger threat situation occurs in conjunction with the noncongruent interpersonal A-Trait (MAS) or STAI, no differential changes in A-State occur. The multidimensional S-R Inventory of Anxiousness assesses interpersonal (ego threat), physical danger, and ambiguous facets of A-Trait. Therefore, A-Trait measures based on the S-R Inventory of Anxiousness would assess potential interpersonal (ego threat) and physical danger anxiety and may account for A-Trait interacting with physical danger in eliciting differential A-State changes.

The assumption that the STAI A-Trait Scale assesses primarily A-State proneness to ego threat is supported by findings of Hodges and Felling (1970) and Spielberger, Gorsuch, and Lushene (1970). These results indicated that the correlations between the STAI A-Trait and STAI A-State scores were higher in ego-threatening situations than in physical danger situations. In addition, Shedletsky (1972) found that correlations of STAI A-Trait scores were significantly higher with the interpersonal situation scales than with the physical danger or ambiguous threat scales of the S-R Inventory of Anxiousness.

Spielberger's (1972a) state-trait *theory* of anxiety accurately describes the relationship between A-State, type of threat, and A-Traits. However, the STAI A-Trait measure is restricted to interpersonal A-Traits and ignores other facets of the domain of trait anxiety. Endler, Hunt, and Rosenstein (1962), as indicated earlier, have found three situational factors for anxiety. Trait anxiety is multidimensional (Endler and Magnusson, 1976a), and a person-by-situation interaction approach must take cognizance of this.

The Multidimensionality of Anxiety. Individual differences in A-Trait can occur in at least three situational domains: interpersonal, physical danger, and ambiguous types of situations (Endler, Hunt, and Rosenstein, 1962; Endler and Okada, 1975). Endler and Shedletsky (1973) classified persons into high and low A-Trait on the basis of total anxiety scores, using the multidimensional S-R Inventory of Anxiousness. This approach may be misleading because it confounds physical danger trait anxiety, ambiguous trait anxiety, and interpersonal trait anxiety. That is, individual differences in trait anxiety can occur in at least three domains: physical danger, ambiguous, and interpersonal. In most cases it is probably necessary to amplify interpersonal components of A-Trait. Possibly for extremely anxious people interpersonal interaction *per se* may be anxiety provoking. However, for most persons it is the possibility or threat of being evaluated or observed by others (social evaluation) that is anxiety provoking. We are suggesting that there are a number of facets of A-Trait, including, for some people, daily routines. The multidimensionality of A-Trait is presented schematically in Figure 1.

The S-R Inventory of General Trait Anxiousness. Although one can measure multidimensional trait anxiety by summing across specific situations of the S-R Inventory of Anxiousness, this has certain limitations. It assumes that summing across specific situations within a facet of A-Trait (a factor domain) provides some degree of generality. In addition, because the S-R Inventory of Anxiousness has more than 150 items, it may be too long. Therefore, Endler and Okada (1975) developed a general measure of A-Trait for each facet (factor category) and devised scales with fewer items.

The multidimensional S-R Inventory of General Trait Anxiousness (S-R GTA) (Endler and Okada, 1975) was developed with the aim of maximizing the effects of individual differences and minimizing the effects of situations. The original inventory consisted of four general situations and nine modes of response for each situation, thus providing a 36-item scale. The first three general situations, derived from the three situational anxiety

Figure 1. Facets of A-Trait

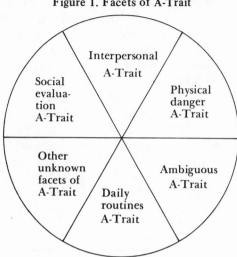

factors (interpersonal, physical danger, and ambiguous) identified by Endler, Hunt, and Rosenstein (1962), were as follows: "You are in situations where you are about to or may encounter physical danger," and "You are in a new or strange situation." The fourth general situation was designed to assess anxiety in innocuous daily routines and stated "You are involved in your daily routines."

Nine modes of response, derived from three mode-of-response factors (distress-avoidance, autonomic-physiological, and exhilaration-approach) found by Endler, Hunt, and Rosenstein (1962), were defined as follows: seek experience like this, perspire, have an "uneasy feeling," feel exhilarated and thrilled, get fluttering feeling in stomach, feel tense, enjoy these situations, heart beats faster, and feel anxious. Each item used a five-point scale, ranging from "not at all" to "very much." Subjects were asked to indicate the felt intensity of their own responses to the situation in question. Endler and Okada (1975) administered the original S-R GTA to samples of normal high school students (182 males, 204 females), college students and adults (150 males, 197 females), and neurotic (34 males, 91 females) and psychotic (35 males, 10 females) adults. Means, standard deviations, standard error of mean scores, and alpha reliability coefficients were computed for the four situations scores and the nine mode-of-response scores for the various samples. These results are reported by Endler (1975b) and by Endler and Okada (1975).

The S-R GTA was subsequently revised. A fifth general situation—namely, "You are in situations where you are being evaluated by other people"—was added. The aim here was to assess social evaluation A-Trait. To improve stability, six new modes of response also were added (feel upset, feel relaxed, feel comfortable, feel secure, feel self-confident, and feel nervous); and "look forward to these situations" was substituted for "feel exhilarated and thrilled." The revised S-R GTA thus has five general situations and fifteen modes of response. Information about the revised inventory appears in Flood and Endler (in press). Table 1 presents the Social Evaluation Scale of the S-R GTA.

Table 1. The Social Evaluation Scale of the S-R Inventory of General Trait Anxiousness

"You Are in Situations Where You Are Being Evaluated by Other People"

(We are primarily interested in your reactions in *general* to those situations where you are being *evaluated or observed* by other people. This includes situations at work, school, in sports, social situations, and so on.)

Circle one of the five alternatives for each of the following 15 items.

Seek experiences like this	1	2	3	4	5	
	Very much				Not at all	

Feel upset	1	2	3	4	5	
	Not at all				Very upset	

Perspire	1	2	3	4	5	
	Not at all				Very much	

Feel relaxed	1	2	3	4	5	
	Very relaxed				Not at all	

Have an "uneasy feeling"	1	2	3	4	5	
	Not at all				Very much	

Look forward to these situations	1	2	3	4	5	
	Very much				Not at all	

Get fluttering feeling in stomach	1	2	3	4	5	
	Not at all				Very much	

Feel comfortable	1	2	3	4	5	
	Very comfortable				Not at all	

Feel tense	1	2	3	4	5	
	Not at all				Very tense	

Enjoy these situations	1	2	3	4	5	
	Very much				Not at all	

Heart beats faster	1	2	3	4	5	
	Not at all				Much faster	

Feel secure	1	2	3	4	5	
	Very secure				Not at all	

Feel anxious	1	2	3	4	5	
	Not at all				Very anxious	

Feel self-confident	1	2	3	4	5	
	Very much				Not at all	

Feel nervous	1	2	3	4	5	
	Not at all				Very nervous	

State Anxiety. There is also evidence for the multidimensionality of A-State (see Endler and Magnusson, 1976a; Endler and others, 1976). These empirical results, plus the theorizing of Sarason (1975a, 1975b) and Wine (1971), lead us to conclude that there are at least two components of A-State: a cognitive-worry component and an emotional arousal component. In addition, Sarason (1975a, 1975b) points out that anxiety is related to self-evaluation (the highly anxious person is self-centered and focuses on self-evaluation and self-worry rather than on the situation task). With these factors in mind, we have developed a new measure of A-State, the Present Affect Reactions Questionnaire (PARQ), which is a revision of the Hoy and Endler (1969) Behavioral Reactions Questionnaire (BRQ). The PARQ consists of ten cognitive-worry items, ten autonomic-emotional items, and in the present version (PARQ III) six buffer items. For each item there is a five-point intensity scale ranging from not at all to very much. Examples of cognitive-worry (C-W) items are "feel calm, unable to focus on task, unable to concentrate, self-preoccupied, and feel worried." Examples of autonomic-emotional (A-E) items are "hands feel moist, breathing is irregular, heart beats faster, perspire, and mouth feels dry."

Person-by-Situation Interaction and State-Trait Anxiety. As indicated earlier, Spielberger's (1972a) conceptualization of the relationship between A-Trait, A-State, and type of situational threat appears to be restricted, since it encompasses only one aspect of A-Trait (primarily interpersonal or ego-threatening) within the context of the person-by-situation interaction anxiety model. As indicated earlier, Endler and associates (Endler and Hunt, 1969; Endler and Magnusson, 1976a; Endler and others, 1976) provide evidence to support their contention that both A-Trait and A-State are multidimensional. A multidimensional A-Trait measure (Endler and Okada, 1974, 1975) enables one to extend the state-trait theory to physical danger A-Trait, to social evaluation A-Trait, and to ambiguous A-Trait personality dimensions.

One of the assumptions of the interaction model of anxiety (Endler, 1975b) is that both A-Trait and A-State are multidimensional. A second basic assumption is that in order for the person-by-situation (trait-by-situational stress) interaction to be effective in inducing A-State, it is necessary for the A-Trait measure to be congruent to the threatening situation. For example, the interaction model of anxiety would predict that interpersonal ego threat A-Trait will interact with an interpersonally ego-threatening situation to elicit A-State changes (see Endler and Magnusson, 1977), but will not interact with physical danger A-Trait or with an ambiguous threat situation. Social evaluation A-Trait will interact with a congruent social evaluation threat situation to elicit A-State changes; but physical danger A-Trait will *not* interact with a noncongruent social evaluation threat situation in eliciting A-State changes (see Flood and Endler, in press). However, physical danger A-Trait will interact with a congruent physical danger threat situation to evoke changes in A-State.

The interaction model of anxiety, which focuses on a *differential* hypothesis (predicting significant interactions when traits and situational threats are congruent and predicting no interactions when traits and situations are not congruent), goes beyond merely proclaiming that interactions are important. This approach enables one to *predict* (rather than postdict) the nature and direction of the interaction between trait (personality) and situational factors and to examine their joint effects on behavior (for example, A-State).

Empirical Investigations of the Interaction Model of Anxiety

The interaction model of anxiety has been empirically investigated both in the laboratory and in real-life situations. One of the laboratory experiments reported by Endler and Okada (1974) examined the joint effects of physical danger A-Trait and a physically threatening situation on A-State. Seventy female and sixty-two male undergraduate students at York University served as subjects in an experiment in which the physical danger situation was the threat of shock. The results for females were that a greater change in A-State, as measured by the Behavioral Reactions Questionnaire (BRQ) (Hoy and Endler, 1969; Endler and Okada, 1975), occurred for women with high physical danger A-Trait scores, as compared to those with low physical danger A-Trait scores. An interaction occurred between the physical threat situation and congruent physical danger A-Trait in eliciting changes in A-State. This pattern did not emerge when the A-Trait classification was based on interpersonal A-Trait because physical danger threat is *not* congruent with interpersonal A-Trait. This predicted pattern of interaction did not occur for male subjects.

Endler and associates (1979), studying twenty-five Canadian high school students, used the S-R GTA and the PARQ to assess the interaction model of anxiety in a classroom situation. The component social evaluation A-Trait by stressful classroom situation interaction was significant in eliciting changes in A-State arousal as assessed by the PARQ. The noncongruent person-by-situation interactions were not statistically significant. Both this study and the Endler and Magnusson (1977) study provide empirical support for the differential predictions of the interaction model of anxiety and attest to the multidimensionality of trait anxiety.

Diveky and Endler (1977) studied middle-management male bankers in both stressful social evaluation "on-the-job" situations and nonstressful "off-the-job" situations (as reported by the bankers themselves). The interaction between social evaluation A-Trait and congruent social evaluation situational stress was significant regarding A-State arousal as assessed by the PARQ.

Endler, Edwards, and McGuire (1979) investigated anxiety in stage actors, both during a rehearsal and prior to an important stage performance. There was a marked trend toward an interaction between social evaluation

A-Trait and the congruent situational stress of a performance in inducing A-State as assessed by the PARQ.

Flood and Endler (in press) investigated the interaction model of anxiety in a real-life track meet. The differential hypothesis predicted that there would be a significant interaction between social evaluation A-Trait and a congruent social evaluation track-and-field meet in inducing A-State changes, but no significant interaction between the other noncongruent facets of A-Trait (for example, physical danger, ambiguous, and innocuous). Forty-one male athletes (aged 15 to 30) competing in short-, middle-, and long-distance track events completed the revised form of the S-R GTA and the BRQ measure of A-State two weeks prior to competition. This was the nonstress condition. The BRQ was completed again just before a major competition that the athletes considered important (the stress condition) and that they perceived as a social evaluation situation. The interaction between social evaluation A-Trait and the stressful track-and-field situation was significant. High social evaluation A-Trait athletes manifested greater increases in A-State between the nonstress and stress situations than did low A-Trait athletes. There were no significant interactions between the track-and-field situation and the noncongruent facets of A-Trait. The Flood and Endler (in press) study supports the differential hypothesis and the interaction model of anxiety.

In the various studies discussed above (except for Endler and Magnusson, 1977, and Endler and Okada, 1974), we assessed the individuals' perception of the stressful situation, via the Perception of Situations Rating Form (PSRF), and in all cases (except for Endler and others, 1979) the situation was perceived as a social evaluation situation. All of the studies support the interaction model of anxiety.

Kendall (1978) compared the Spielberger (1972a) state-trait anxiety model and the Endler (1975b) interaction model of anxiety. Kendall used failure on an intellectual task as a social evaluation stressor situation and a car accident film as a physical danger situation. Kendall's results supported the interaction model of anxiety. The high social evaluation A-Trait group, as assessed by the S-R GTA, manifested a greater increase in A-State following the social evaluation stressor situation than did the low social evaluation A-Trait group. The high physical danger A-Trait group reported a greater increase in A-State after the physical danger threat than did the low physical danger A-Trait group. None of the other differences between high and low A-Trait groups were significant. The Kendall results support the interaction model of anxiety.

Conclusions

We have discussed person-by-situation interactions and have described three sources of evidence regarding the person-versus-situation issue: the variance components strategy, the correlation strategy, and the personality-by-treatment experimental design strategy. The evidence indicates that person-by-situation interactions are more important than either persons or situations, with respect to personality theory. After contrasting mechanistic versus dynamic interaction, we discussed the role of situations in interactional psychology. After discussing the multidimensionality of trait and state anxiety, we presented an interaction model of anxiety and provided empirical support for this model.

Where do we go from here? What direction should our theorizing and research with respect to situations and interactions take? It is essential to investigate ongoing processes and dynamic interactions. It is necessary to focus on persons' perceptions of situations and the meanings that situations have for them. We should isolate the kinds of situations that make individuals anxious and the cues in the situations that they perceive as threatening (Endler, 1978). The message that the environment is sending may not be the message that the individual is receiving.

15

Anxiety and the New Feminism

Ruth Moulton

❋ ❋ ❋ ❋ ❋ ❋ ❋ ❋ ❋ ❋ ❋ ❋ ❋

The recent wave of feminism is best understood as one phase of a vast socioeconomic development which began when the Industrial Revolution precipitated a series of cultural changes that have slowly been escalating, with forward thrusts and backward pulls, during the last two centuries. Thus, the "new feminism" (1960s and 1970s) is the result, not the primary cause, of current events. Women have chafed under the restrictions of a patriarchal society since the beginning of Western civilization; and despite repeated waves of feminism, each more successful than the last, real equality between the sexes has never been attained. Our culture has never accepted drastic changes in traditional sex-role stereotypes. Current socioeconomic conditions, however, have altered concepts and expectations about sexual roles. More than half the American female population is working outside the home, the divorce rate is steadily increasing, and there is new skepticism about the viability of traditional marriage. The changes of the last twenty-five years have been so rapid that massive anxiety has burdened both males and females. Human beings are caught between a need for excitement and change and a need for the stability and familiarity that seem to promise security.

Although women have won new freedoms from overt sexual discrimination and have more choices of careers and life styles, they feel caught between divergent cultural pressures and are more aware than ever before of personal stress (Moulton, 1977b). Moreover, they face a continuing battle to make use of the sexual equality now theoretically available to them if they wish to escape from or drastically modify their traditional domestic role. Many are surprised by the amount of prejudice they encounter as they move out into the world; sex discrimination is now illegal, but prejudice has merely become more buried and covert.

Men, too, have new problems—and new sources of anxiety—as sexual equality increases. Although they have much to gain by the new choices in life styles—they may not have to work so hard if their wives also earn; they need not focus on a narrow area of job activity to the exclusion of all other interests; they can get to know their wives and children better—they may suffer a loss of self-esteem. In addition, to whatever degree men have been in power, they cannot be expected to give it up easily. For most people, power is too gratifying. Laws may legislate equal opportunity, but they cannot enforce equal access to that opportunity. Laws cannot ensure that those who have traditionally been discriminated against can automatically take advantage of new options (Hennig and Jardim, 1976). There are many blocks in the way, both outer prejudice and inner resistance.

Sociohistorical Background

To become aware of the slowness of social change, one can look briefly at the history of feminism in America over the past 150 years. The early feminists, Elizabeth Cady Stanton, Susan B. Anthony, and Lucy Stone, failed to get the results they hoped for because their attack on marriage threatened the entire culture. The next generation of social feminists were more socially acceptable, favoring continence over contraception, supporting prohibition, devoting themselves to social welfare causes, and concentrating on getting the vote (Moulton, 1972). Even with these modifications, it took 72 years—from the first women's rights convention in 1848 at Seneca Falls, New York, to 1920—for American women to get the vote. This victory did little to relieve their plight; many lacked the education, social awareness, and independence from their husbands' attitudes to use the vote constructively (O'Neill, 1969). Fifty years later, it was clear that men had maintained their firm grasp on the commanding positions in American life (Moulton, 1972). Although the number of working women doubled between 1940 and 1967, their participation in prestigious professions was no higher in 1968 than it had been in 1898 (Epstein, 1971).

The current women's movement has a much broader socioeconomic base and thus more chance for continued development. Some mark its beginning with Betty Friedan's exposure of the feminine mystique in 1964, but it also coincided with the renewed battle for civil rights, the movements against racial and sexual discrimination, the so-called sexual revolution, student uprisings against the war in Vietnam, and concern with overpopulation and environmental issues. The threat of atomic annihilation, depletion of natural resources, famine, and birth defects and cancer due to radiation, all have made people more aware of their powers for self-destruction and of man's inhumanity to man. Women's sense of restricted participation in improving social conditions was an important factor in their drive for more equal roles with men, who had usurped the instruments of power for so many centuries.

Stress and Cultural Change

Human beings have always felt stress; it is only the nature of the stress that changes. Since cultural change causes anxiety in proportion to its rapidity, it is no surprise that the sudden emergence of large numbers of women into the outer world will cause conflict and will affect men, women, children, and families in both positive and negative ways until the changes have been integrated (Moulton, 1977a). Stress, however, is both a natural component of living and a major stimulus for growth if it is not too overwhelming. Challenge motivates people to work for change if there is reasonable chance for improvement. Selye (1956) likens stress to the irritating grain of sand that causes an oyster to form a pearl. He enumerates a long list of factors that could cause stress, from excessive cold to bacteriological agents and other noxious stimuli, and adds that psychological stress can produce the same kinds of physical effects. He describes three stages: the first, of shock, such as a sudden anxiety when one is confronted with a new job; the second, of mobilization to master it; and the third, demobilization or breakdown of effective activity because the stress was too great. These stages parallel the challenges that face women to motivate them to work for change. Stress may bring out the best in them, but this will only continue if there are rewards and positive reinforcement. If women run into dead ends when prejudice, regulations, or other blocks make it impossible to advance past a certain point, they may feel defeat and react by losing interest and by becoming hostile, bitter, and discouraged. The generally accepted fact that depression and suicide are more frequent in women, especially those with high educational levels and high social achievement, can be interpreted as a reflection of their not being able to reach their aspirations.

Despite efforts to be different from previous generations, women have inner and usually unconscious obstacles, revealed through psychotherapy, which stand in their way. These inner, hidden inhibitions include restrictions such as (1) hidden dependency needs; fear of disapproval by male authorities and women competitors; (2) fear of being self-assertive, which might be seen as hostile aggression, both unladylike and unlovable; (3) fear of success, which might alienate others and raise expectations that cannot be fulfilled; (4) fear of being unfeminine, spurned by parents, mate, children, peers, whether due to jealousy or inability to understand and accept a new kind of woman (Moulton, 1979b). A woman may be seen as a threat when she is merely trying to establish her autonomy and sense of self.

The most deeply buried, unconscious conflicts that may be stirred up by the need for autonomy are connected with the quality of early relationships to parents and the amount of anxiety connected with separation from them. The parent may have originally encouraged the child to succeed but become increasingly critical and rejecting when the young person's achievements surpassed those of the parent, who now feels threatened and envious. This process may be completely unconscious. The parent is merely subtly undermining, but it plays on the young person's guilt about wishes to surpass and get even with the parent for the omnipotent control of the early years. In the boy's oedipal battle with his father, he may identify with the father and try to be dominant in the same traditional way; or he may see assertion as hostile aggression against the father as a rival who may retaliate. This guilty fear about the father may take on a special quality in young women, who may fear that they will be accused of wanting to *be* men, to possess a penis of their own, of wanting to castrate the father and/or possess the mother. They may certainly envy the man his power in the outside world, if not literally the penis (Moulton, 1970, 1972); but this need not curtail the girl's achievements for the rest of her life unless the father is overtly rejecting, lacks respect for women, and punishes his daughter for daring to be different. She may turn back to her mother for some encouragement but get more disapproval, especially if the mother has lived a life of sacrifice for her family and is envious of the daughter's efforts to have a life of her own. The daughter may fear that her success will be at the expense of her mother and show up her mother's failure (Schecter, 1979). This inner anxiety may be realistically reinforced by the mother's threats: "If you go into medicine, law, a serious career, you will be unmarriageable and an unfit mother, should you try to be one." Some girls submit and renounce success; others refuse and fight to attain it. The outcome depends not only on the girl's ego strength, which is built on early acceptance by her parents, but also on their later ability to let her go, their willingness to encourage her to make her own life without the threat of totally losing them.

One girl, who was programmed into a career by her parents, was obedient to them until she went away to college and discovered freedom. She refused to return home, kept a separate apartment near them, and chose a very successful man to marry. They were opposed to this marriage because she would thereby acquire a more prestigious, sophisticated life style, which made them feel devalued. They fought her openly until it was ineffective; she went ahead with the marriage but developed ulcerative colitis and had to start therapy. At this point, she was desperate because her mother especially had refused to talk to her for months; it was as though the separation were final. Her mother had been nourishing in childhood, laying the basis for her daughter's later obesity, but she could not be a good mother of separation at a later stage, because she felt too much need to keep her daughter close and had expected her to use her education to strengthen the family business and to protect the mother from the father's domination. The battles for control in this family were spectacular. There were reconciliations and new battles. She felt anxiety at work when she had to take independent responsibility or stand up for herself, because her parents had kept her from learning to do either. Job problems alone did not cause exacerbation of her colitis, but renewed threats of abandonment by her parents did, indicating that the latter aroused the deepest fears. When she acquired the strength through treatment to hold her own against her parents, her colitis disappeared; and eventually her parents, now afraid of losing her, began to admire what she had done.

Another young woman came for a consultation due to the return of claustrophobia, which coincided with her boyfriend's pressure for marriage. She had never been close to either parent; they never discussed feelings, but the mother was visibly upset because her daughter was not the prettiest girl in the class, and she showed no interest in the daughter's excellent schoolwork. The girl tried to be a "good girl" to please her mother but felt that "she never heard me." Her premature separation from mother gave her a façade of self-sufficiency, a pseudoindependence (Moulton, 1977c); but she had bouts of claustrophobia in locked bathrooms, closed beach cabanas, and later in buses and elevators; she must have felt locked in by her family's narrowness. She had a tendency to depression, also connected with early maternal deprivation, and had a severe depression when she lost her virginity in college. Shame prevented her from talking about it, so she had no support or consensual validation. Her father was concerned only with her getting married; and when she wanted to go to law school, he said, "Isn't that cute?" In rage and rebellion she applied, but was too discouraged to function well and did not get into law school despite high board scores. She was too depressed to explore further and got a job with limited possibilities. Her recent boyfriend was a lawyer who encouraged her to push ahead, but she seemed unable to believe him and assumed that she would have to stay home with children as her mother had. Her father's putting her on the spot about marriage in front of a room full of relatives precipitated the attack of claustrophobia that sent her to seek psychiatric help.

Both of these cases illustrate how parental attitudes can undermine a girl's belief in her professional future and her chance to combine it successfully with marriage and children. This can happen with boys also; but since they are generally expected to have a career and earn money, they are not as vulnerable to being undermined as are girls, who have so little tradition of career success and are not trained for it. Thus, the sudden pressure to achieve in a new way often leaves them immobilized or in danger of failing or giving up along the way.

Areas Affected by Cultural Change

The effects of cultural change can be seen in many areas of life, and these areas can be separated as follows.

Sexual Attitudes and Behavior. In the past, women could hide their lack of full responsiveness and accept passive receptiveness as a natural role for women. Society's permission for women to enjoy sex has removed many overt inhibitions, so that frigidity is much less frequent (Moulton, 1966) and extramarital affairs more frequent (Moulton, 1977c). Now, women can openly admit and enjoy their natural sexuality. For some, however, new burdens have been imposed. With the new awareness of sexual physiology (Masters and Johnson, 1966), they may feel inadequate without multiple orgasms. If they feel pressure to be orgasmic, more casual, more free about sex, and yet are unable to respond quickly, they block even more and experience a new sense of self-consciousness and failure. They cannot live up to the new expectations, being unable to get their own inner permission. Under the new rules, some men can no longer feel a sense of macho over having been able to perform sexually, but feel, instead, failure if the woman does not experience multiple orgasms. Secretly they blame themselves, although overtly they may blame the woman for being unresponsive. This problem has led to a phenomenon of impotence in young men (Ginsburg, Frosch, and Shapiro, 1972), who feel that women demand too much of them sexually. That which could be joyous and gratifying to both partners becomes heavy. Men do not want to be used as sex objects or studs merely to gratify the woman or to make her feel feminine any more than women have wanted to serve men's needs without affection.

There has been a shift, from the old concept of male sexual dominance and responsibility, with helpless female submission, to emphasis on female responsibility for equal participation in mutual sexual satisfaction (Thompson, 1942). This new equality demands good communication between sexual partners, an equal acceptance of responsibility for each other's satisfaction, an ability to drop old concepts of domination and submission. Equality does not mean sameness; there are differences between the sexes which can be exciting rather than anxiety provoking. Victorian women feared sexual injury from men. Now the male fear of sexual engulfment, castration, and humiliation resurfaces. It was always present in folklore (Bettelheim, 1954; Lederer, 1968; Moulton, 1977a).

Some women can empathize with men's fear of ridicule; other women have tended to use this weapon to get even with men who have controlled, dominated, and made servants of them. In the past, many women accepted the submissive role, either because they really were helpless or because they were fearful of the outside world and felt a need to be taken care of. Women fighting the Equal Rights Amendment, who are largely housewives, are still clinging to their age-old rights for support, joining men who have other reasons for keeping them at home, to make it seem that domestic and childrearing functions are their sole contribution. Many of these men really want to be taken care of like children but never admit it even to themselves and cover their need with male chauvinism (Woods, 1976). To admit dependency in this society is more embarrassing than to admit sexual need, which is now recognized as everyone's prerogative. This new acceptance of equal rights to sexual satisfaction has decreased the tendency of women to withhold sex as a weapon, to feel freer to ask for what they want, and to enjoy it without guilt. They are less resentful of men's sexual pleasure if they feel included and are less apt to feel oppressed and submissive in intercourse. Cooperation between the sexes is an ideal goal, but it has many obstacles in the way of its implementation. I will try to illustrate this in other areas where men and women interact.

Marriage and Divorce. Marriage, or some form of commitment between man and woman, has existed since the beginning of recorded history. Almost every kind of relationship imaginable has been tried at some time in some culture: monogamy, polyandry, polygamy, exogamy, endogamy, self-selection of mates, parental selection of mates, marriages for convenience, and marriages for love. All variations seemed quite natural to those who lived with them, and all seemed to serve a useful purpose at some time. According to sociologists such as Jessie Bernard (1972), there is no evidence that either human nature or any of our instincts demands any special form of marriage. The traditional patriarchal marriage, typical of nineteenth-century America, can be explained in many ways: man's need to protect his wife and children as property; his need to restrain his acquisitive yearnings and competitive drives; his need to curtail his appetite for adventure and variety for the sake of security, his own and that of his children. Sociologists have said that monogamy produces jealousy. Psychoanalysts feel that the adult extensions of infantile jealousy of the mother tend to produce monogamy, whereas oedipal conflict makes it hard to maintain (Horney, 1928). In any event, the deep human need for intimacy seems to make some kind of pairing inevitable. It is the best solution for loneliness. The issue is what kind of pairing is most suitable for a given culture.

It was not until the late 1960s that women finally faced the fact that the typical marriage is too restricting; binds them to household work and child care, for which they do not get paid either in recognition or money; and cripples their personal growth. Later in marriage, when they are freer, they either have no place to go or no basic training to rely on and are too insecure in the outer world to be able to fight their way into it (Epstein, 1974). Marriage is a safe refuge for the husband where the wife supplies emotional support at the expense of her own growth. The wife can remain essentially childlike and dependent while seeming to take care of her family. Only when she tries to move outward does she discover how phobic, narrow, uninformed, and unprepared she really is (Symonds, 1971). The buried resentment or overt hostility to her husband is often the underlying factor in the development of her phobias, depression, alcoholism, the sense of emptiness and boredom when the children are gone, the lack of sexual interest, the alienation from her husband.

Marriage, in the past, was seen as a trap by many men, although they seemed to profit by it, live longer, and remain healthier. Whereas women in the past saw marriage as the only security, it made them literally sicker, and they died sooner than those who kept their freedom (Bernard, 1972). Women are now beginning to see marriage as a trap for them. As a result, they are increasingly seeking divorces; postponing marriage to a later age; or living with men without legal commitment, which gives women an increased sense of autonomy, a voluntary relationship where services can be given, not owed. A division of labor can be achieved based on individual preferences and aptitudes rather than on traditional sex-typed expectations. Of course, there are many problems in working out such new arrangements. There are some chores that no one wants. Men can fall back on the old concept of "women's work," feeling unloved or emasculated when asked for a new kind of participation. Women are more apt to feel guilty and comply, but with resentment. When they rebel totally, a household may fall apart. It takes good communication, good will, and mutual respect to work out the details without resorting to outworn recipes or premature breaking of relations in bitterness and vindictiveness. The presence of children obviously makes such arrangements much more difficult, and many couples postpone parenthood.

Two other solutions to the static marital trap are extramarital affairs and the return to professions or jobs outside the home. These two solutions are often linked (Moulton, 1977c). The working woman is exposed to interesting new men, has valid reasons for being away from home, may go on business trips and conventions without her husband. These may give her many sexual opportunities similar to those that men have become accustomed to. Traditional men, narrow-minded and unsure of their own sexual attractiveness, may feel threatened by their wives' freedom, saying, "Financial freedom will lead to sexual freedom. I want to know where my woman is at all times." This kind of man may refuse to show any interest in the woman's outside activities, although he may expect her to share and help with his. He may demand that she fulfill his creature comforts and undermine her as a woman by complaining that the household is suffering. He may especially point out that the children are feeling deserted, although, in fact, it is *he* who feels deserted. Many men find a working woman more stimulating and less clinging. Those with a negative reaction, as described before, often force their wives into the very thing they fear: extramarital affairs, increased time away from home, and eventually divorce.

The woman's need for a second man is stronger if her husband is uninterested or critical. Men are more accustomed to tolerating or may even prefer an uninterested wife. Women, however, who may be relatively new to professional lives and who have had long training in dependency and self-doubt, generally need approval for their professional work. They may seek such approval from a male mentor or boss and may then become involved in a sexual affair. Such an affair may be handled with discretion by the more self-reliant woman who wants to preserve her marriage and who can take responsibility for her sexual behavior without having to report to her husband as though to her father, to get permission. She may also use her financial independence to get out of an unsatisfying marriage, an option most women have not had, not only because of lack of money but also because of social ostracism and blame. Making a marriage work was considered one of the woman's jobs. A divorce was *her* disgrace, just as not marrying was seen as her failure, and spinsters were treated with pity or contempt.

Many divorced women are delighted with their new freedom and use it well for growth and personal development. Many remarry wisely. Others may remarry without insight into their choice of partner and make the same mistake. One phenomenon that has recently appeared (Moulton, in press) is that of the financially independent professional woman who takes the initiative for a divorce, only to discover that living without a man is very painful to her. She can find sexually exciting men who give her more sexual satisfaction than she had before because they have enough sexual experience to become good lovers. They also have the advantage of novelty. If her husband has been sexually unimaginative, boring, alienated, alcoholic, she may find an exhilarating new sense of self-confidence about her femaleness. She may then experience an unexpected desire to remarry, only to find that the man does not share it. Many of the men she had thought were available for a lasting relationship are, in fact, not available. They have been divorced, may have children to whom they are committed, and are determined never to remarry, never to commit themselves to another woman. They may avoid remarriage by never quite completing their divorces, using their pseudomarriage as an excuse to limit intimacy. They may have several mistresses simultaneously or change from one woman to another in series when relationships become too close. This behavior can be very frustrating to the woman, who may find that she is not as independent as she had thought. Indeed, she may feel lost or panicky without a man in the house—especially if she was lonely as a child, suffered from night-time phobias, or felt unvalued by her parents. These problems may have been completely hidden while she was busy being a home-maker, a young mother, or an active professional woman building her career—only to reappear when she is alone or without a dependable man. Even if she has children at home, she still feels a need for male companionship in the evening and for male approval and support.

In therapy it often becomes clear that she relied heavily on her father and, later, on male teachers for encouragement and backing even when she became in reality a completely self-sufficient professional woman. She is still dependent on male approval and feels empty or helpless without it. She finds that there is prejudice against the single woman, who is often seen as a threat, whereas the single man is seen as a social asset. She is unaccustomed to using female support systems or making new social networks of her own. Although more of these exist now—American Women in Science, women's studies groups, women's caucuses—some women who had weak or under-mining mothers with whom they could not identify do not trust female support. Women can be very competitive, vying for power and putting each other down—a phenomenon seen in many insecure minority groups until they reach a point of recognizing the need to work together and can organize into effective groups directed toward constructive action. The fear of lone-liness and age is seen more often in women in their 50s, who struggled hard to achieve autonomy in the 1920s and 1930s, often in isolation and with little outside help. Young women today have grown up with more ideas of equality and sense of self, expect to get more, and are working together better to help each other achieve. Thus, they may not be as vulnerable as the previous generation.

Dual-Career Marriages. One might expect more understanding and cooperation in couples who both work and can empathize with conflicts between professional and personal needs. The two members of the couple may alternate tasks or may relieve each other at points of maximum stress. When one has to travel or work late, the other takes care of home chores, improvising as needed. This requires a great deal of flexibility and a fairly equal balance of ability and self-respect. The confident male can take over for his wife without feeling emasculated, especially if his mother has had a successful career and was also loved and respected. If the young couple had good role models, such as parents who worked well together in a teamship where neither had undue power over the other, they can more easily avoid the traps inherent in a dual-career marriage, like competition as to whose work matters more. In the past, the needs of the man's career came first. The wife was expected to follow, and usually did if she wanted to preserve her marriage. This fact has been exploited by institutions that not only fail to consider the wife's or family's needs but make the man feel he is too dependent, not dedicated to his work, if he brings up these problems. The old rules against hiring both husband and wife in the same department were designed to guarantee that the husband did not exploit his position to try to get benefits for his wife. Now that women have equal or superior competence, institutions often refuse to consider them on their own merits or seem to punish them by offering promotions or new jobs in distant localities that pit marriage against work.

Caroline Bird (1979) talks about the two-career collision course, the dangers of the wife's earning more, the struggle that ensues when power and money change hands. She also describes the "cool, super-couple" who make it all work. They seldom come to my office. Those who do are not so cool. Two people who worked in the same corporation thought that they were safe because he was several years ahead and she felt secure in following. However, she was unusually competent and, when cultural pressure came to give equal employment opportunities to women, was appointed to the highest rank ever held by a woman. When the organization offered him a job overseas where there would be no place for her to work, marital crisis ensued. He was tempted not only because the job seemed exotic but also because he saw her rising faster than expected. The dilemma was solved when the man turned down the tempting offer because his wife refused to follow. He changed jobs to a similar, but smaller, organization where he had higher pay and a more prestigious title. This settled the issue temporarily, but resulted in much hard feeling and eventually in divorce.

In another example, the wife and husband were in the same department of a small college. Offered a professorship at a prestigious eastern university, she turned it down because he would not go with her. Commuting seemed untenable, although she has since discovered couples working hundreds of miles apart and enjoying weekend marriages. Years later, during treatment, she discovered how resentful she was at the increasing confinement of the small college. Work blocks and psychosomatic symptoms periodically immobilized her. When offered a position as department head at a very exciting, large, West Coast university, she found herself too enraged to talk to her husband. The deadlock was relieved through therapy of both husband and wife. They became less afraid of talking about the problem. He was reassured that she did not want to leave him but desperately wanted a wider field of professional action. He then began to look for a job near where she wanted to go. She was more ambitious and enjoyed change more than he, but she respected his work and was finally able to help him consider new options.

Women must often take the initiative in looking for new solutions to the couple's problems. This may be a leadership role to which the woman is not accustomed and may be reluctant to assume. Her solutions may be fair and feasible, but she may feel a backlash of irrational guilt and even consider taking it all back and returning to what was once the status quo, a self-defeating impulse to be studied and resisted.

Couples differ widely as to who likes to move, who enjoys commuting, who gets more lonely when sleeping alone two or three times a week. I am more apt to see energetic, restless wives in therapy. They are anxious and frightened, often with good reason, when their careers seem to move faster than the husband's. One man told his wife, "Don't ever try to surpass me; I can't take it." When she reminded him later of the remark, he had no memory of it. Another woman steadily advanced, supporting the family while her husband had several career failures. Rather than face her disappointment in him, she filled her life with many children and many interesting jobs, thus delaying depression. When he finally became successful, she was too busy to care, and their sexual relationship had seriously deteriorated. He had become like one of her sons. His buried resentment often made him awkward, forgetful, apologetic. Marital therapy helped to rebalance the relationship. He saw the hostility in his boyish passivity; she saw her escape into hyperactivity and her refusal to talk as precluding any new equilibrium.

Concern is sometimes expressed that changing sex-role stereotypes will confuse children, making them unable to distinguish between male and female behavior. It is true that a clear division of labor may make it easier for the developing ego to order experience into simple bipolar concepts of "masculine" and "feminine." However, one can question whether it is adaptive to use outmoded models in a world of transition, where wide variations in sexually appropriate behavior exist. The old stereotypes may be more adaptive where parents themselves have unstable gender identities and need more rigid patterns to follow (Lerner, 1978). Clear bipolar concepts may be simpler for the child, but they do not prepare him for the complexities of modern life, where flexibility has enormous advantages.

When parents are both nurturing and intellectual, work together at a variety of tasks, share authority, collaborate in a pragmatic way without hostile competition, the growing child may be free to enjoy a wide range of behavior patterns, varied experiences, and open expression of spontaneous and understandable feelings. Cultural transitions are stressful, but flexible parents can prepare the next generation to expect and welcome change with a minimum of anxiety.

Careers Versus Children. With all the vicissitudes of careers for women in a world not quite ready for them, and the complications of dual-career marriages, the most pressing extra burden is the presence of children. Women have been programmed to see motherhood as their unique and most valuable function. Men and society have joined to underline this view, partly as a way to keep women safely at home, under control. With the new power to regulate family size, women have mounting anxiety as they must choose between their traditionally child-oriented role and the new options available. Their response has varied between two extremes. Women now in their 50s often had a third or fourth child at a time when they were about to be free to enter the outside world, thus making it impossible to do so. A writer, frightened by the success of her first novel, became "accidentally" pregnant just in time to obstruct the writing of a second book. Other women have postponed having a first or second child in order to pursue careers without the extra burden. Some younger ones, now in their 40s, were childless by default, having waited until it was unsafe or until their fertility was at a low ebb (Moulton, 1979a). They were often relieved to have the choice taken out of their hands. Others were disappointed, especially if their careers were not proving to be as satis-fying as they had hoped. To be able to relinquish the option of motherhood without deep regret requires that a woman believe in herself, in her value as a useful human being aside from her reproductive capacities.

Parenthood is no longer deemed necessary for maturation and con-tinued personal development (Welds, 1976). According to Erikson (1950), generativity, the style of ego maturity associated with adulthood, can be achieved by those who are not biologically generative. The stigma of non-motherhood must be removed, so that it becomes a viable alternative with its own dignity (Bernard, 1975). There is evidence that the woman who can successfully manage both roles—motherhood and career—may engender and maintain a degree of enthusiasm and creativity into her later years. She is envied by the unfulfilled woman who reluctantly gave up one for the other. Those who choose both must be aware of the likelihood that they will often despair, feeling that they could have been *really* successful in one *or* the other. Trying to do both takes much energy and drive, a minimum of self-doubt, and an ability to relinquish perfectionistic goals in all areas. It is useful to have had a role model—mother, aunt, teacher—who combined various activities and who enjoyed her work free of undue guilt or harassment (Hoffman, 1974). If the career woman is impatient with her children and puts undue or premature importance on independence, the daughter may feel rejected. She may feel unable to live up to expectations and flee into a traditional, protected marriage. The daughter of a social worker said with bitterness at age 5, "When I grow up, I'm going to be the kind of mommy who stays home and bakes cookies for her children."

The difficulty of finding an adequate housekeeper is the single most important complaint of working mothers. Some professional women are trying to elevate the status, prestige, and pay of those women who take their place at home, giving them the appreciation and dignity they deserve. It has been suggested that they be given special training, like that of the metapelet in the kibbutz, who looks after children while their mothers work. In our culture older women who have successfully raised their own children and who need to earn money and feel useful might fill this need. Older girls finishing their education and needing a place to live have also been used for child care and have profited by being in an interesting home.

The need for new kinds of family support systems has come about because of the loss of the extended family and the advent of the isolated, nuclear family. The need for child care facilities has become more pressing. The educated woman often has higher standards for child care and cannot accept inadequate substitutes without experiencing immobilizing quantities of guilt (Rossi, 1977). It is the quality, not the quantity, of parental attention that matters. Academic fathers and fathers who work free-lance at home can spell their working wives. Some men feel that this is a more varied and humane life than that of the overworked businessman who never has time for his family and becomes alienated from them. There is evidence of decreased drive for success in younger men (Knudsin, 1974). Many welcome the opportunity for a dual-paycheck marriage and a more varied distribution of activities (Bird, 1979). Their attitude may mitigate the excessive role strain and overload suffered by working mothers (Johnson and Johnson, 1976).

Although men suffer from role proliferation, they are more able to compartmentalize and insulate their professional work and thus are less guilt ridden and do not agonize as much about childhood illnesses, expecting the mother to handle them. Since she has the same expectations, the mother finds it more difficult to suppress her worries about home and children. Society's emphasis on the full-time mother as the norm, backed up by the popularization of psychoanalytic theory about the basic role of the mother, has resulted in assigning her more than her share of blame for failures in childrearing. Overlooked until recently was the role of fathers, siblings, peers, schools, and cultural activities. As a result, the professional woman must often choose between lowering her career commitment or seeming to neglect her husband and children, even when this "neglect" may merely be a matter of having an outsider cook and clean.

Successful career women often suffer from depression after the birth of the first or second child. Often they had never liked housekeeping and, while childless, had employed part-time cleaning help and eaten meals out with colleagues or husband. Some look back on their student or bohemian life with nostalgia and yearn for the simplicity, the freedom of choice, the many options to use time for relaxation that have been drastically curtailed by having children. Marriage itself may make a dramatic difference in the equilibrium of a couple because unconscious, outdated models of parental roles interfere with the development of a new, unique life style. Successful

rebellion against parents seems much easier without a legal tie that institu-
tionalizes and curtails the relationship. If unconscious, outdated models of
parental roles persist, although hidden, the arrival of a child can tip the former
balance. The mother may be terribly torn between the baby, her husband,
and her job, always guilty about one of the three. She is afraid that she will
ruin the child, lose her husband, or fail at her job. The mother may rush back
to the job before she is ready, thus depriving herself and her baby of a fair
chance to make good contact. Or her guilt may make her resign from the job
to give the baby all it needs, which is only temporarily satisfying. If part-time
jobs were available, this aspect of the problem would improve. With more
flexibility in sex-role stereotypes, there are increasing numbers of men who
enjoy helping with the children, who will give up some working time to enjoy
them, and who are able to share new parenting pleasures with their wives.

   Women and Men at Work. Statistics compiled in 1974 show that although women make up more than half the labor force, less than 5 percent
of those earning more than $10,000 a year are women (Hennig and Jardim,
1976). It is clear that equal opportunity has changed things, but *slowly.* A
few more token women have been allowed into areas that were previously
closed to them, such as law firms, corporations, and banks; but it is still
extremely difficult for women to reach levels of high responsibility, such as
presidency of a firm, senior law partner, or head of a department. They are
usually junior members of the team, assistants rather than heads. Every exception to this, when a woman arrives at a top position, is publicized. Their
numbers are few, however, and many problems remain. Most obvious is the
stubborn persistence of male prejudice against women as subject to raging
hormones, less stable than men, less predictable, in need of more time off,
and not able to maintain rational, objective points of view.

   Another problem: Both men and women have trouble breaking away
from the old sex-role stereotypes of man as the ultimate decision maker and
source of power, and woman as facilitator, keeping a low profile while she
works behind the scenes (Moulton, 1972). Both men and women have great
difficulty in treating each other simply as human beings working together,
focusing on the job to be done, and recognizing merit as it evolves regardless
of the sex of the other. Sex cannot be completely overlooked, but it can be
used as a pleasant, essentially irrelevant, peripheral fact, an occasional harmless diversion, rather than an obstacle to cooperation or a ploy for manipulation. Men and women are so unused to working together as equals that
they are often awkward and anxious and do not know how to react. Some
women may need help in therapy to see the problem clearly and to have
enough belief in their own value to quietly but firmly insist that it be respected. Women are caught in a real double bind here. If they make demands,
however appropriate, or merely assert their rights, they may be called castrat-
ing, unfeminine, or hysterical. If they comply like good girls, they allow

themselves to be used and fail to win the respect and recognition they need and deserve.

The way in which most girls have been raised adds to their handicaps, imposing internal inhibitions and depriving them of certain basic skills necessary for survival and growth in a male, competitive world. They are told that aggression is unfeminine; that men want them to be passive and submissive; that they should not allow their intelligence or ability to show because it is threatening to men, who will then avoid them and not marry them. As a result, women grow to fear success. In the early grades, girls often surpass boys not only in reading and writing skills but also in mathematics and science (Maccoby, 1966). This early superiority steadily declines throughout schooling, so that women who were "A" students in high school often fail or drop out in college and may never dare to go to graduate school.

Although large numbers of women are now entering professions, many psychological problems remain. If women automatically wait to be chosen rather than stepping forward, they probably will be ignored in an organizational environment where there is need for maximum visibility. It is not enough to do a good job, to be a "good girl," and to finish assignments on time. Men will often take credit for what women have done. Women's names have been omitted from research papers even though they may have been equal collaborators, or even originated the idea (Moulton, 1979b). Women must call attention to their contributions; they must put pressure on men at the top to clear the way for an interesting project, to allow access to the necessary equipment, to give them the same helpful suggestions that would automatically be given to young talented male colleagues but are withheld from females either through malice or through oversight. Many women expect to be encouraged and to be treated fairly, as they had been by their fathers, teachers, or mentors. It is hard for them to accept the need for fighting and the fact that they are threatening to men in their jobs and professions, especially under the present economic conditions.

There is also the problem that girls have rarely been taught to fight, to throw themselves violently into team sports, to handle winning and losing, to deal with criticism and demanding authorities (Hennig and Jardim, 1976). Women are said to take criticism too personally and to depend too much on praise as a catalyst or as necessary permission to go ahead. Men grow up knowing that they will have to work all their lives. Women grow up in ambiguity, not knowing whether they can count on a long-term career or whether they will be permitted to go just so far and then be eased out. In academia, they may get postgraduate scholarships but not be put on the tenure ladder or never promoted to full tenure. Jobs are often given to men because they are supposed to need them more and to be more committed to the work (Moulton, 1977b). Even dress can be a problem. The woman who dresses in a way that attracts little attention may find it easier. She is one of the boys, less of a sexual threat. This is another double bind for women. If they dress in a mousy or dowdy old-fashioned way, people will feel that they lack self-respect. If they are too attractive, people may assume that they are out to use sex to get ahead or are not serious about their careers. Often a woman must take the responsibility of retraining the men with whom she works, showing them that they can eat lunch with her or to talk business with her without needing to be chivalrous or to take care of her or fear her seductiveness.

There are many subtle, covert, time-honored patterns that put women at a disadvantage. For example, they are excluded from the informal structure of organizations that consist almost solely of men. The men support each other; they exchange valuable information about important external events that may happen in the future. These off-the-cuff relaxed interchanges have a gossipy nature, occurring over coffee, at bars, and at lunches from which women are excluded (Hennig and Jardim, 1976; Moulton, 1979b). They are similarly excluded from "bull sessions," where many problems are slowly threshed out before being made available to younger or female members of a department or organization. Men learn a certain kind of functional group behavior, or team spirit, which prepares them to adopt corporate manners; most women, however, want more personal and meaningful relationships. They may find it easier to become good teachers or supervisors, showing empathy and understanding. Men will often rank such a woman as a con-scientious supervisor, a reliable worker, but lacking in management potential, because she has not shown the aggressiveness that they have discouraged her from using.

Role of Therapy

Some of my patients were quite successful in their chosen fields, some less so, and some felt a great sense of failure. All were in conflict about their dual roles—professional versus personal. Most were too busy to come often, averaging one to two times weekly. At times the central issues were easily brought into focus and were clarified sufficiently so that therapy could be rationally terminated within weeks or months. In other cases there was profound self-doubt, low self-esteem, and lack of ego strength; and therapy continued for several years.

Wise judgment may be necessary to choose the right orientation and the right therapist. Therapists with a feminist orientation need to be careful not to proselytize women patients into a more liberal role than they can manage. It is nontherapeutic to liberate a patient from sex-role stereotypes if the patient has used them for most of her life to shore up and maintain a shaky sense of gender identity. For a healthier patient, it may be necessary to question their needs for conformity, but the therapist should thought-fully decide whether to analyze or to support defensive traditional tendencies based on an assessment of the patient's ego strength and expressed goals (Lerner, 1978). Therapists must avoid imposing their own personal ideology.

16

Anxiety in Childhood and Adolescence

Sandra Buechler
Carroll Izard

❖ ❖ ❖ ❖ ❖ ❖ ❖ ❖ ❖ ❖ ❖ ❖ ❖

Differential emotions theory presents the developmental psychologist and the child psychotherapist with a framework for study of the unique role of each of the fundamental emotions in promoting personality integration. Its view of emotions as adaptive, motivating, organizing experiences focuses attention on the role of each discrete emotion in the development of adequate coping skills and exploratory, creative abilities. The emotions (in interaction with the homeostatic, drive, perceptual, cognitive, and motor subsystems) shape and color conscious experience and control of the limits of awareness by their effects on the focusing and selectivity of perception. In infancy (and throughout development), the individual's experience of each of the fundamental

Note: This material is based in part on work supported by the National Science Foundation under Grant No. BNS 78-04236.

human emotions makes a distinct contribution to intrapersonal and inter-personal growth. Thus, differential emotions theory directs our attention to study of the essential role of each fundamental emotion in the child's adaptation to its personal and nonpersonal environment.

Central Tenets: The Emotions as Defined by
Differential Emotions Theory

Since extensive formulations of differential emotions theory have been presented elsewhere (Izard, 1977, 1979), only some of its central tenets, and, more particularly, its view of anxiety as an emotion experience in early life will be outlined in this chapter. A more detailed statement of the differential emotions theory conception of anxiety is available in Izard's (1972) work on patterns of emotions. After brief summary of some of the key components of the theory, our attention will focus on the emergence, experience, and regulation of anxiety patterns in infancy and later development.

According to this theory, the emotions constitute the primary motivational system in the human being, alongside the three other major types of motivation (drives, affect-perception and affect-cognition interactions, and affective-cognitive structures and orientations). Affects (emotions and drives) interact with perceptions and cognitions, resulting in the great variety of human motivations. When an affect (or pattern of affects) interacts frequently with an image or cognition, the pattern assumes the stability of an affective-cognitive structure and may combine with other such structures to form complex personality traits, such as passivity, skepticism, or egotism.

Differential emotions theory describes eleven fundamental emotions, each with its own characteristic neurophysiological, expressive, and motivational-experiential components. At the neurophysiological level, a fundamental emotion is a particular, innately programmed pattern of electrochemical activity in the nervous system. At the expressive level, it is primarily a characteristic pattern of facial activity, with bodily responses (postural-gestural, visceral-glandular, and sometimes vocal behaviors) as other components. At the experiential level, a fundamental emotion is a quality of consciousness that organizes and focuses sensation, perception, and cognition. All three levels, the neurophysiological, expressive, and experiential, are essential to the concept of the fundamental emotion, so no single component can suffice as a definition.

The eleven fundamental emotions are interest, joy, surprise, sadness, anger, disgust, contempt, fear, shame, shyness, and guilt. None are inherently positive or negative experiences, since their effect depends on individual-environment interactions. However, for convenience they are categorized according to their most probable social evaluation, with interest and joy as positive emotions, surprise as a transient emotion state preparatory for new input, and sadness, anger, disgust, contempt, fear, shame, shyness, and guilt as negative emotion experiences.

Anxiety as a Pattern of Emotions. When two or more of these funda- mental emotions are experienced simultaneously, or in rapid sequence, they form a pattern of emotions. Anxiety, depression, social affection, and hos- tility are four of the more frequently encountered patterns of emotion. In any pattern of emotions, each discrete or fundamental emotion has some motivational impact on the individual. Its essential, unique qualities are experienced. If a particular emotion pattern is a frequent experience, it may form a stable emotion trait, which may then become a likely response when similar conditions recur.

This theoretical framework has several implications for the study of anxiety. Rather than defining anxiety as a unidimensional experience, differ- ential emotions theory considers anxiety to be a pattern of emotions and affective-cognitive structures. An anxiety pattern always includes fear as the key component, with two or more of the emotions of sadness, anger, shame, shyness, guilt, and interest. The conception of anxiety as a variable pattern (that is, fear interacting with other emotions) suggests the importance of studying the significance of each of the fundamental emotions in the pattern rather than focusing on anxiety as a consistent entity. The consequences, in terms of intrapersonal experience and interpersonal interactions, when one individual's early experience results in a predominant fear/shame/guilt anxiety pattern, while another individual develops a fear/anger/sadness anxiety pattern have yet to be explored. There are many anxiety patterns. Whether specifiable biological differences, early experiences in infancy, vicissitudes in the caregiving relationship, or other factors result in the development of different anxiety patterns is a major question for future inquiry. Whether during childhood (and beyond) certain anxiety patterns interfere in the process of normal development more than others is only one of the many clinically relevant issues to be addressed. A subsequent section of this chapter will explore some further implications of these issues.

Research investigating anxiety patterns as experienced by adults has been summarized by Izard (1972, 1977). The data reported generally support the view proposed by differential emotions theory that anxiety is a pattern of emotions and affective-cognitive structures. One study (Bartlett and Izard, 1972) compared the emotions experienced during real and imagined anxiety conditions. The data suggested that, in both situations, fear was central to the experiences of anxiety, but interest, anger, guilt, shame, and shyness were variable components. Thus, empirical evidence supports the concept of anxiety experience in adults that has been proposed by differential emotions theory. An extensive research project focusing on experiences likely to elicit fear and anxiety patterns in infancy and early childhood is currently in progress.

The Role of Emotions in Development. As background for the discussion of anxiety in early childhood, first it is necessary to present an outline of the role of emotions in development, as proposed by differential emotions theory. A more detailed treatment of this topic has been presented by Izard (1977, 1978b) and by Izard and Buechler (in press).

Differential emotions theory proposes a view of the role of emotions in development that may be briefly summarized by several basic tenets:

1. The fundamental emotions are primarily activators and organizers of experience.

2. The emotions have a functional, adaptive role in development. From infancy onward, emotions serve to organize, direct, and motivate behavior in the other subsystems of the personality. In contrast to conceptions of the emotions as disruptive to ongoing experience, or as merely responses to cognitive processes, discrete emotions theory views each of the fundamental emotions as playing a unique but significant part in furthering sensory, perceptual, cognitive, and motoric growth.

3. Emotions are continually present in consciousness and serve to regulate the processes of awareness. As each emotion emerges during infancy, it increases the individual's conscious awareness, preparing the infant for a particular type of learning and development. Phenomenologically, emotion experiences are invariant from their emergence, providing an essential continuity to conscious experience from infancy onward.

4. Each emotion emerges in conscious experience when it can play an adaptive role in development. The order of emergence of emotion expressions and felt experiences is innately determined. Through its relationship to sensory, perceptual, cognitive, and motoric processes, each newly emerged emotion adds to the complexity of consciousness.

5. The facial expressions of fundamental emotions, which are innate and universal, play a key role in emotion activation and provide the sensory data that are integrated through cortical-limbic interactions as emotion experience. These expressions also play a key role in social-emotional communication and in the establishment of the infant-caregiver bond.

Anxiety Patterns in Infancy: Issues and Research

Before we explore the earliest experiences of anxiety patterns in infancy, some of the general issues in studying the emergence of any emotion and, more particularly, the problems in understanding the emergence of anxiety patterns should be mentioned.

One issue that has been the subject of debate is whether the emergence of an emotion is primarily a function of maturational processes or learning and experience. Differential emotions theory holds that, while the neural substrates for the experience and expression of each of the fundamental emotions are innate, the emergence of five of the emotions awaits age-related maturational processes. Other theorists, such as Bridges (1932) and, more recently, Sroufe (1977), hold that by a process of differentiation the separate emotions derive from a single emotion or arousal state. Sroufe, for example, suggests that "early obligatory attention" later differentiates into "wariness" and, finally, into fear. In contrast, discrete emotions theory holds that the capacity for experiencing and expressing fear results primarily from maturation and that, from the point of its emergence, fear has characteristic, identifiable, unchanging neurological, expressive, and experiential components. The invariance of fear as a quality of consciousness contributes to the development of the sense of continuity and the concept of self. The differential emotions theorist would expect the facial expression of fear in the infant to be essentially the same as its universal (and cross-culturally validated) adult expression (except for certain differences between infant and adult faces, such as degree of roundness and amount of subcutaneous fatty tissue). The theory also posits that the emergence of fear occurs at a point in infant development when its experience and expression can serve adaptive purposes in promoting learning and social (infant-caregiver) attachment. It assumes that the emergence of fear adds to the complexity of the infant's conscious experience. Finally, the theory holds that fear experiences are qualitatively distinct from (not derivative of) other fundamental emotion experiences.

A second broad issue is the relationship between emotion emergence and cognitive attainments. Since differential emotions theory views emotions as organizers of conscious processes, rather than merely as responses to concomitants of cognitive events, and views emotion emergence as more a function of maturation than of learning, the theory suggests that the emergence of an emotion is not necessarily preceded by any particular cognitive attainment. As shall be elaborated below, this issue has particular relevance for the study of the onset of fear-related experiences in infancy, since much empirical effort has been expended in the search for the experiential and cognitive "prerequisites" for the emergence of fear.

A third issue in the study of emotion emergence is the relationship between the earliest behavioral expression of an emotion and its experiential component. The question can be raised as to whether, for example, the 6-week-old smiling infant really feels joy as we feel the emotion. The question of the invariance of emotion expressions and experiences is relevant to study of the emergence of every emotion. The differential emotions theory holds that the process of activation of felt emotion experiences involves proprioceptive and cutaneous feedback from the facial expression and that, therefore, once an infant shows the complete facial pattern indicative of a particular emotion, it is capable of the corresponding discrete emotion experience.

One persistent problem specific to the study of the emergence of fear in infancy is the lack of consistency among investigators and theoreticians in their terminology and criteria for the presence of an emotion or emotion pattern. In the literature on the emergence of negative emotion responses to strangers, for example, some researchers use the term *stranger fear,* while others use *stranger anxiety,* and still others use *stranger distress.* From the differential emotions theory point of view, fear, anxiety, and distress are not interchangeable terms, and the criteria for their presence should be clearly differentiated. If (as is the case in much of this literature) presence of the "stranger response" is indexed by crying and other negative emotion behaviors that could be components of one or more of several discrete emotions, it is difficult to interpret the results as indicative of the age of emergence of any particular discrete emotion. The 7-month-old infant who cries at the approach of the stranger may be expressing sadness, fear, or a pattern of negative emotions. Unless criteria for the presence of a specific discrete emotion (such as a set of specific facial behaviors) are used, these data cannot inform us what particular emotion or pattern of emotions the infant is expressing.

The lack of consistency in the use of terminology and criteria for the presence of fear is also evident in the experimental designs employed to study fear emergence. In the stranger response literature, for example, procedural variations that may contribute to the discrepancies in reported onset of the response include sex, height, and facial behavior of the strangers, manner and speed of approach, type and duration of infant-stranger contact, competing emotion elicitors in the context, physical constraints on the movement of the infant, presence and proximity of the mother, and aspects of the scoring procedure. Close examination of the major investigations of the "stranger response" suggests that this paradigm is a stimulus complex with elements that have different degrees of salience at varying ages in infancy. As a result of these age-related differences, some experimental designs that have been used to investigate "stranger fear" have incorporated elements that were likely to elicit negative emotion expressions at young ages, while other designs were unlikely to elicit negative responses at any of the ages tested; hence, their results are discrepant regarding the age of onset of fear.

The issue becomes especially complex when one considers that most investigators have studied the emergence of "fear" in a particular limited experimental context but have not exposed their subjects to several eliciting situations to explore whether at a particular point in development the infant becomes able to express fear. Thus, we have a literature on stranger responses, separation responses, and visual cliff responses, but less work has been done to study whether the onset of "fear" in one of the three situations corresponds to its emergence in the other two. This gap has significant theoretical implications for the question of whether fear (and the other discrete emotions and emotion patterns) emerges at a particular, maturationally determined point in development.

Despite these difficulties in the literature, a review of the theoretical and empirical research reveals considerable support for the view that fear emergence is largely a maturation-determined phenomenon. One line of investigation consistent with this viewpoint is the series of studies conducted by Emde and his associates (Emde, Gaensbauer, and Harmon, 1976; Emde and Robinson, 1976). Their work has yielded evidence of the onset of "stranger fear" at about 8-9 months of age. These investigators have interpreted their results as supporting the existence of an age-related biobehavioral shift in the infant's functioning at this point in development. The emergence of fear expressions at 8-9 months of age is considered indicative of a more pervasive change in infant experience. These results are consistent with differential emotions theory, which holds that the expression of each discrete emotion emerges at a maturationally determined point.

Some investigators, however, have reported different results. The work of Tennes and Lampl (1964) and Bronson (1972), for example, suggests that the stranger response may occur much earlier than the last quarter of the first year of life. Studies by Rheingold and Eckerman (1973) and Morgan and Ricciuti (1969) challenge the universality of the stranger response, with data suggesting that many infants may never show a negative emotion response to strangers. The lack of comparability in the terminology, experimental paradigm, criteria for the presence of stranger "fear," subject ages, and experimenter behavior across these studies limit the generalizability of their results and leave still unanswered the question of whether there is a maturationally determined stranger response that reliably emerges at 8-9 months of age.

Even if the point of emergence of stranger fear were clear, several issues of importance to differential emotions theory remain largely unexplored. Does fear in general emerge as an emotion response at this maturationally determined point, so that the infant is now capable of expressing fear of other stimuli besides strangers? What is the functional, adaptive value of fear in the infant's experience at this point? Why can fear be activated in conscious experience at 8-9 months, and how does it motivate growth in the social, sensory, perceptual, cognitive, and motor areas? How do fear experiences expand conscious awareness and contribute to progress in mastery of the basic tasks of development? What is the relationship between fear emergence and anxiety pattern emergence? Do the various anxiety patterns emerge in the experience and expressive repertory of the infant at the same maturational point as the key discrete emotion component (fear)? What role do these patterns play in emotion experience, mastery of developmental tasks, and individual personality growth? The remaining sections of this chapter will explore some of these issues, although their study (from a discrete emotions point of view) has only recently begun.

Adaptive Role of Fear and Anxiety Patterns

The emergence of fear and anxiety patterns fosters a new awareness of the vulnerability of the self (Izard, 1978b) and strengthens the infant's social bond to the caregiver. But if the emergence of fear is maturationally determined (as differential emotions theory suggests), what could account for its activation, in the last half of the first year of life, by such previously nonnegative stimuli as the approach of a stranger? One speculation might be that the increasingly mobile infant, newly able to crawl, just about to begin to walk, is "launched" toward motoric and social independence. Awareness of vulnerability (fear) could serve to balance exploratory inclinations (interest), keeping the infant within safe proximity of help, since its ability to cope with environmental hazards is still quite limited. While this suggestion is speculative, several lines of research lend it some support. Several "stranger fear" studies suggest that the infant's behavior in the stranger paradigm is not a simple response to the mere presence of the stranger but, rather, results from the interplay of emotion elicitors present in the situation. Thus, the infant's response to the stranger depends on the presence and proximity of the mother (Gaensbauer, Emde, and Campos, 1976) and the presence of (interest-eliciting) distracting stimuli. For example, in the Rheingold and Eckerman (1973) study, many interest-eliciting toys were present, and stranger fear was not elicited reliably. Presumably, then, fear may be a response to a context in which fear elicitors predominate. Similarly, work by Bowlby (1973), Ainsworth, Bell, and Stayton (1971), and Mahler (1969) indicates that the securely attached infant responds differently from other infants to "fear"-eliciting situations, suggesting that these situations may in fact differ for these infants. A secure attachment bond may make the fear-interest balance in a new situation shift more easily toward interest as the predominant emotion elicited, allowing the securely attached infant to use mother as a base for wider exploration of the novel environment.

The motivating experience of fear is distinctly different from the experience of sadness and from each of the anxiety patterns (Izard and Tomkins, 1966). Specifically, fear motivates urgent defensive strategies geared toward escape and avoidance of reexperiencing of the situation and of the fear itself. Sadness, in contrast, elicits less crisis-oriented strategies, including time-consuming cognitive efforts. The child whose efforts at motoric functioning meet failure should (theoretically) be able to continue to work on improving these skills. But in the face of fear (or, perhaps, in the face of fear unmitigated by major interest components) the urge will be to avoid motorically challenging situations that might result in reexperiencing the fear, thus limiting skill development in that area.

The anticipatory avoidance behaviors motivated by fear also differ from those motivated by a given anxiety pattern. The intense, toxic, constricting quality of fear facilitates immediate efforts to change the situation, such as rapid escape from the "steep" side of the visual cliff. This is, obviously, an adaptive response to heights in early infancy. In contrast, anxiety, which may be elicited by the interesting yet fearful presence of a stranger, might allow (under certain conditions, with slow approach by the stranger and with mother present) for some interaction with the new person. Given the inherently adaptive functions of a social existence for human beings, such tentative, context-related responsiveness is adaptive for the infant. Although the ensuing exploratory interaction would certainly have a different quality from an interaction motivated by interest-joy, for example, the anxiety-motivated examination of the novel-threatening person allows some new learning to occur, with intermittent interruptions for search for contact with a source of security (such as the caregiver). But this could permit social, sensory, perceptual, and cognitive experiences that would not be available to the infant in a state motivated only by fear or by interest.

Furthermore, fear and a given anxiety pattern often differ in the manner and extent to which they recruit memory. It seems plausible that fear (for example, of a painful experience of recently being inoculated) might quickly evoke similar past affective experiences. The increase in stimulation in fear is sharply focused and, perhaps, relatively easy to associate with contextual cues for the infant who is developing long-term memory skills. In contrast, certain anxiety patterns (such as a fear-shame pattern) might be less distinctly associated in memory with specific contextual cues, particularly since shame heightens self-awareness rather than the scanning of the surround. These differences in the functioning of memory in fear and anxiety patterns suggest that it might be quite adaptive for fear to motivate escape from environmental situations with specifiable, memorable features (such as heights or high-temperature surfaces). However, in other contexts (particularly in social situations), the "noxious" qualities are much harder to isolate, store in memory, and retrieve. Hence, patterns of emotions that do not motivate quick retrieval of a salient cue and quick escape, but, rather, that are accompanied by a more "diffuse memory" of similar threatening yet interesting experiences, would allow for some interpersonal exploration.

Emotion Contagion

A basic principle of differential emotions theory, the concept of emotion contagion, has important implications for our understanding of fear and anxiety patterns in infancy. Emotion contagion is the activation of an affect by expression of that affect by another person. This principle suggests, for example, that fear expressions of the caregiver can elicit or enhance the infant's experience of fear. Thus, when one feels fear or is in the presence of a fearful person, the experience tends to be fear evoking for all individuals, but it may also evoke anger, excitement, shame, sadness, interest, or other discrete emotions or anxiety patterns, depending on the context and the individual's history of emotion experiences. What does this suggest about the experience of an infant who is frequently exposed to a highly anxious caregiver? Presumably, such experience evokes some type of anxiety pattern, but whether it will evoke the same pattern as is present in the adult may be questioned. The adult's anxiety pattern could, for example, include discrete emotions (such as guilt) that are not yet within the infant's experience. Hence, by the process of emotion contagion, the infant could experience an anxiety pattern, but the pattern might have a very different quality from that of the caregiver. The process of emotion contagion seems to provide a fascinating future research area of great theoretical as well as clinical importance.

Socialization of Fear

Differential emotions theory postulates an increase in the possible number of different patterns of anxiety as the capacity for experiencing new emotions emerges during infancy. There are several implications of this postulate.

1. Anxiety accrues new interpersonal meanings with the emergence of shame in the latter half of the first year. Shame experiences, including mismatchings between the infant's interpersonal expectations and feedback from others, may actually be closely related to what is called "stranger anxiety." This possibility is suggested by differential emotions theory, which includes shame as a variable component of anxiety. The facial and body gestalts of the stranger pose a familiar (human) yet novel stimulus. Attempts to communicate with the stranger through the usual, synchrony-establishing behaviors may fail, resulting in an experience of the other as unresponsive, the self as impotent, and one's predictions as unreliable. This might partially explain why the stranger response does not occur, generally, until the stranger attempts a close interaction with the infant.

2. As the infant becomes capable of experiencing guilt, anxiety can be elicited in new interpersonal contexts. At some point in development, the parent generally begins to assume that the infant deliberately and knowingly does some wrong behaviors. As a result, expressions of disapproval appear on the face of the caregiver as the infant begins the forbidden acts. These interactions may be new and confusing experiences to the infant, since some bahaviors that were once permissible are now forbidden or even punished. The infant's motivations rather than merely its overt behaviors are being judged. This, in itself, may seem strange and may evoke an anxiety pattern in the infant (fear of the caregiver's strange behavior and guilt at the "bad" or disapproved intention).

One of the most pervasive methods of regulating (sustaining, enhancing, or attenuating) an emotion is by using another emotion. For example, in the process of socializing (regulating) fear, parents often use shame. Such socialization techniques may affect which anxiety pattern the infant predominantly experiences. The frequent message that one ought to feel shame for being afraid will, of course, result in a fear-shame anxiety pattern. Such a pattern could interfere most severely in one particular, crucial developmental task—the development of the concept of self as an adequate individual. Since frequent fear-shame experiences would result in feelings of low self-worth precisely during the most anxious, tense moments when one most wants protection, it seems likely that such an individual would have some difficulty trusting his or her own self-protective capacities. The diminished capacity for seeing alternatives (as a result of the fear component) and the lowered self-esteem and feelings of competence and strength to cope (as a result of the shame component) would make this a particularly devastating anxiety pattern in the early stages of the development of the self-image and when reliance on self (rather than caregiver) is being expanded. The effect of parental responses to infant expressions on the infant's fear and anxiety patterns has not been explored theoretically.

Tomkins (see Izard and Tomkins, 1966) differentiates left-wing socialization of fear from right-wing socialization. Left-wing (humanistic) socialization includes one or more of the following components:

1. The parent tries to keep fear experiences to a minimum.
2. Fear is regarded as noxious, and the child may be made to feel fearful of fear.
3. After fear experiences, the child is reassured; if the parent caused the fear, the child receives an apology or explanation.
4. The child's fears are tolerated, and coping skills to master fear are taught in graded steps geared to the child's capacity.
5. The parent is concerned about signs of fear in the child and treats them as signals that help is needed.

This socialization pattern is seen as likely to produce in the child a more humanistic posture, an attitude that the individual is an end in himself and not measurable by outside norms.

Right-wing fear socialization includes one or more of these elements:

1. Fear experiences are not minimized and may actually be used as teaching devices.
2. Verbally, fear is not regarded as noxious, and the child is encouraged to be unafraid of fear. However, since fear-eliciting techniques are used in socializing the child, fear becomes a frequent component

of the child's experience. As a result, and contrary to parental inten-
tions, fear may retain its noxious quality for the child.

3. There is no reassurance, apology, or explanation forthcoming when
    the caregiver causes the child to fear.
4. The child's fears are not tolerated but are the occasion for shame or
    solitude to "sweat it out" alone.
5. Techniques to counteract the experience of fear are not taught and,
    when used by the child, may even be ridiculed.
6. The parent is insensitive to signs of fear in the child and generally
    minimizes or disregards them.

These two socialization paradigms are, of course, extreme forms of
the process. In any caregiver-child interaction, elements of both types of
socialization will be present. The theory suggests that differences in emphasis,
however, will affect the development of anxiety patterns, deeply held attitudes toward emotion expression, and fundamental ideals of human behavior during stress.

Partly as a result of these parental patterns of response to infant fear
expressions, each child may develop a characteristic anxiety pattern, with
specifiable emotion components, though he or she may also experience other
patterns, depending on the interpersonal and nonpersonal context. Some
anxiety patterns, such as the linkage of fear to sadness, may be largely a
function of socialization experiences; others, such as the linkage of interest-
excitement to fear, may result from both experience and factors inherent
in interconnections between the neural substrates of these emotions. This
suggests that, particularly in infancy, when experience is limited, the interest-
excitement/fear pattern is the most common pattern of anxiety. The behavior
of infants and young children does suggest that such behavior patterns are
not uncommon. In the less frequent instance, where punitive parental attitudes toward expression of sadness foster the creation of a fear-sadness linkage,
the child may often experience anxiety since sadness is the most common
negative affect. Phenomenologically, the frequent experience of a fear-sadness
anxiety pattern (when the fear component has no objective source) would be
felt as amorphous, pervasive, or perhaps even chronic tension, less limited
by time or situational variables than discrete fear or other anxiety patterns.

When the adult experiences fear or anxiety, efforts to identify the
object and cause of the emotion involve other subsystems (primarily the
cognitive system). It may be presumed that the limited cognitive (especially
symbolic) skills of the infant and young child make certain types of "errors"
in this identification process more likely. Given that an individual child receives punitive responses from caregivers for expressions of sadness, and
therefore learns an anticipatory fear-sadness anxiety pattern, and since this
pattern may be largely at a low level of awareness (or unconscious), the

individual may well link the negative affect experience to some (actually irrelevant) contextual factor. Take, for example, the instance of a child who has been punished for expressing sadness, who wakes up from distressing dreams feeling lonely and sad. The sadness quickly recruits fear, since its open expression will bring parental disapproval. The cause of the ensuing anxiety is unclear to both the child and the parent if they are unaware of the linkage of fear and sadness in the child's experience. Consequently, something irrelevant in the situation (for example, the imminence of departure for school) could be incorrectly labeled, by both child and parent, as the "cause" of the negative affect.

When sadness is strongly linked to fear—so that, whenever the individual faces a distressing problem, he or she tends to become afraid and attempt to escape rather than cope with the source of sadness—Tomkins (1963) feels that maladjustment is likely. Lack of physical courage, panic reactions to pain, and hypochondriasis are among the hypothesized manifestations of this maladjustment.

This fear-sadness bind may also interfere in the ability to share and empathize with others who are experiencing sadness, since the individual responds to such experiences with fear-motivated avoidance. Denial of sadness, sickness, defeat, and loneliness, compulsive achievement, or withdrawal from risks—all may be the extreme strategies employed to avoid facing sadness if the individual's childhood included a strong establishment of the fear-sadness bind. In short, when the experience and expression of the (relatively common) experiences of sadness are complicated by a socialization process that makes sadness frightening, the individual may suffer a significant interpersonal and intrapersonal handicap. The sharing of problems with others and the facing of minor and more important defeats become fearful experiences to be avoided or defended against, at great cost. Some individuals may, in short, learn to fear experiencing the negative emotions. Further, it may not be the objective situation that is feared but, rather, the subjective experience of fear.

Thus, it seems likely that the predominant anxiety pattern experienced recurrently by a particular infant is affected by several variables, including parental patterns of socialization of fear, parental attitudes toward expression of sadness, and, via emotion contagion, frequency of parental expressions of fear and various anxiety patterns. The variables that shape the predominant anxiety pattern experienced by a particular infant, the effect of each anxiety pattern on the development of the self-concept, separation-individuation, development of interpersonal competence, and other crucial tasks remain areas for future study. By focusing attention on the emotions that form different anxiety patterns, differential emotions theory suggests the clinical and theoretical importance of future work to elucidate the antecedents and adaptive and maladaptive consequences of each pattern.

17

Separation Anxiety in Preschool Children

John Doris
Anne McIntyre
Michael Tamaroff

❖ ❖ ❖ ❖ ❖ ❖ ❖ ❖ ❖ ❖ ❖ ❖ ❖

Since the earliest clinical studies of Freud, the experience of anxiety has been assumed determinative of personality development and function. But analytic reconstructions and clinical observations, for all their richness, do not permit the type of manipulation and control that facilitates the integrative cross-checking of data and theory. At the same time, a direct resort to the experimental study of anxiety, though possible, involves the ethical constraints that are entailed in the study of noxious stimuli. These methodological limitations were considerably eased with the development of self-rated anxiety scales (Brown, 1938; Sarason and Mandler, 1952; Taylor, 1953), and there resulted a spate of articles in the research journals beginning in the 1950s (Levy, 1961). Unfortunately, these scales were limited in application to those age groups sufficiently advanced developmentally to cooperate in their administration. This effectively set the lower age limit for such scales at approximately that of the first-grade child (Castaneda, McCandless, and Palermo, 1956; Sarason and others, 1960). With our particular interest in separation anxiety in preschool children, we undertook, several years ago, to develop a readily usable scale that would facilitate the systematic study of separation anxiety in this age group as readily as the self-rated scales had facilitated the study of anxiety in older age groups. In this chapter we shall describe the development of such a scale, give evidence for its reliability and validity, and report on some studies that throw light on the social and cognitive concomitants of separation anxiety in preschool behavior.

Our conceptualization of separation anxiety concerns itself with the distress reaction that infants and young children experience on separation or threatened separation from the familiar caretaking adult. Although the phenomenon has been studied extensively in young infants, there is relatively less research available on the preschool or nursery school child. Since separations for such children have become more and more institutionalized in the form of day care and preschool programs, the opportunity for systematic study of the phenomenon of anxiety in this age group is readily apparent.

It is granted that the elicitation of a child's distress reaction to entrance into a day care or preschool program involves more than separation from the mother or familiar child care figure. There are new surroundings, strange adults, a large number of unfamiliar peers, and the prospect of spending an undetermined time in this novel and possibly threatening situation. Any or all of these variables could interact with separation from the mother to elicit a reaction of anxiety or distress. But we assume on theoretical and phenomenological grounds that the core component of the perceived threat in the stimulus complex is the departure of the familiar caretaking adult (Bowlby, 1973; Heinicke, 1956; Isaacs, 1933).

Parental Anxiety Rating Scale

With these considerations in mind, we undertook the development of our anxiety scale (Doris and others, 1971). We assumed difficulties in devising any sort of self-report scale of anxiety with this age group and resorted instead to developing an anxiety scale rated by the mother. Although our interest focused on separation anxiety, our selection of items was designed to sample a broad range of anxiety-arousing situations in childhood. This was desirable in that we intended to use the scale immediately prior to entrance to nursery school, and we did not wish, by focusing on separation anxiety, to set up attitudes and expectations in the mother that might unduly affect mother-child interactions upon entrance into nursery school. In addition, a broad sample of anxiety reactions would also provide us with the opportunity to assess the specificity of the separation-anxiety reaction in relationship to a more general propensity for anxiety reactions.

Table 1. Items on the Parental Anxiety Rating Scale[a]

1. Does your child show fear of dogs or other pets when he encounters them outside the home?
2. Is he afraid of the dark?
3. When you take him swimming, is he fearful or apprehensive of the water?
4. Does going to the doctor's upset him?
5. Does he ever express fear of imaginary animals, or animals with which he has not had direct contact, such as lions, tigers, dinosaurs, and so on?
6. Do loud household noises, such as the vacuum cleaner or disposal, upset him?
7. Does thunder or lightening frighten him?
8. When he goes out with you, is he upset or apprehensive unless he takes along his favorite toy or blanket with him?
9. Is he afraid of bees, wasps, or other biting or stinging insects?
10. Does he show concern around toileting, such as fear of the noise of flushing or fear of falling into the bowl?
11. Does having his head washed or hair cut upset him?
12. Is he afraid of strangers?
13. Is he afraid of harmless insects such as beetles, moths, or dragonflies?
14. Does getting dirty disturb him?
15. Is he upset when left with a babysitter for an evening?
16. Does he show fear of domestic animals, such as cows, horses, or sheep?
17. Is he afraid of snakes, toads, frogs, and so on?
18. Does he become upset at being lost, such as an accidental separation in the supermarket?
19. Do cuts and bruises upset him?
20. Is he afraid to try new foods?
21. Do loud noises from outside, such as passing fire engines or air raid sirens, frighten him?
22. Does he have difficulty mixing with a new group, such as at a party?
23. Is he upset by violence on television?
24. Is he overly concerned when he breaks a toy or household object, such as a glass?
25. How much concern or upset does he show when his father and/or mother is away overnight?

[a]PAR_6 items = 8, 12, 15, 18, 22, and 25.

As finally devised, the Parental Anxiety Rating Scale (PAR) consisted of twenty-five items, each item referring to an event or object that frequently elicits distress reactions in children (see Table 1). Parents rated their children's typical response to these situations on a five-point scale of increasing frequency or intensity of occurrence. The PAR provided two subscales. One subscale, PAR_6, consisted of six situations specifically involving actual separations or threats of separations (items 8, 12, 15, 18, 22, and 25). The remaining nineteen items, PAR_{19}, related to distress-eliciting objects or events not necessarily involving separation. Thus, the PAR_6 was designed to tap pre-nursery school proneness to separation anxiety, and the PAR_{19} to tap more general anxiety or distress proneness. The subjects for our standardization study were sixty predominantly white, middle-class children with a mean age of 27.5 months and an age range from 30 to 44 months. The children attended four classes, two in each of two different university laboratory schools. Average class size was fifteen. Both schools shared similar orientations toward meeting the individual needs and fostering the individual abilities of the children. The programs focused principally on facilitating social and emotional development and secondarily on cognitive development. The PAR was distributed to parents by mail in the week preceding the opening of school and was to be filled out and returned on the child's first day of nursery school.[1]

Using a Horst (1951) modification of the Spearman-Brown formula, we obtained a split-half reliability coefficient for the total PAR scale and for each of the subscales for all sixty children. The obtained reliability coefficients were PAR_{tot} = .82, PAR_{19} = .60, and PAR_6 = .80. The higher reliability of the PAR_6, in comparison to the PAR_{19}, might well be attributed to the higher homogeneity of the items of the PAR_6. Unlike the frequent findings from self-ratings of anxiety proneness with older children and adults, no sex-of-subject differences were found on the PAR or its subscales.

Teacher Separation Anxiety Rating Scale

In order to get an independent measure of separation anxiety, we also constructed a Teacher Separation Anxiety Rating Scale (TSAR). This scale consisted of eleven items rated on a three-point scale of increasing frequency and/or intensity of occurrence. The scale items focused on displayed emotions, tension responses, and interpersonal behavior thought to reflect anxiety (Table 2). The TSAR was rated by the teacher immediately following the end of the school day and referred to the period of time from when the child entered the nursery school until the parent or adult who brought him to school took leave and the child had become engaged in the activities of the day. The distress rating thus refers to a "behavioral unit" rather than to an arbitrary time unit and includes the period during which the parent's departure is impending as well as that during and following actual separation.

The TSAR was filled out for the children in all four groups (N = 57) for each day of the first two weeks of nursery school operation. Three

[1]For one of our four groups of parents, we were not able to distribute the scales to the parents before entrance, and so these scales were filled out after the child's first morning at nursery school. Although this could conceivably influence the parental ratings, the analysis of the data did not indicate any way in which this group differed from the other three.

Table 2. Items on the Teacher Separation Anxiety Rating Scale

1. Clings to mother
2. Cries, screams
3. Whimpers
4. Verbal protest
5. Runs after mother
6. Shadows mother
7. Periodic return to mother
8. Periodic visual contact with mother
9. Vacillates in permitting separation
10. Pulls mother into room
11. Hesitant versus eager entrance

children did not attend with sufficient regularity to attain reliable ratings.) A two-week period was chosen because preliminary study indicated that entrance distress reactions are most acute during the first two weeks of the school year.

Split-half reliabilities for the initial two-week distress ratings were obtained for two groups, each group scored by a different teacher. The Horst (1951) modification of the Spearman-Brown formula gave coefficients of .82 ($N = 16$) and .81 ($N = 13$) for these two groups. When the two groups are combined and teacher differences are ignored, the split-half reliability rises to .91. In addition to the split-half reliabilities, for Group IV both the head teacher and the assistant teacher rated each child independently for the first two weeks, and two classroom observers each made independent ratings during the same period. Interteacher reliability, based on 52 pairs of daily ratings, was found to be .65; interobserver reliability (75 pairs of daily ratings) was .64; and the reliability obtained between the head teacher's ratings and those of the principal observer, based on 52 pairs of daily ratings, was .49 (all Pearson r's). As with the PAR, no sex differences were found.

Correlations Between Parental and Teacher Ratings

Table 3 presents the correlations of the PAR scores of preschool anxiety with the TSAR scores of entrance distress summated over the first two weeks of nursery school. In addition to the total PAR scores, both subscales were separately correlated with the TSAR.

The PAR-TSAR correlations were significant and strong for three of the four groups, with an average correlation for all four groups of .41, significant at the .01 level. Although these correlations reached conventional levels of significance, inspection of Table 3 indicates that the PAR subscales bear different relationships to the TSAR. The PAR_6, with items specifically related to separation anxiety, was significantly and strongly correlated with the TSAR measure of entrance distress for all groups, but there were neither

Table 3. Correlations of TSAR Scores with PAR Scales

| | Groups | | | | |
	I (N = 14)	II (N = 16)	III (N = 13)	IV (N = 14)	Average r (N = 57)
PAR_{tot}	.54*	.46*	.03	.52*	.41**
PAR_6	.73**	.71**	.53	.76**	.70**
PAR_{19}	.34	.25	−.16	.26	.21

*$p < .05$.
**$p < .01$.

individual nor collective significant correlations between the TSAR and the measure of general anxiety proneness, the PAR_{19}. Thus, it appears that high levels of distress behavior at nursery school entrance are manifested by those children who are more prone to anxiety over events that specifically involve separation.

The differences in the correlations of the PAR_6 and PAR_{19} with the TSAR take on additional significance in view of the obtained correlation of .46 for the PAR_6 versus the PAR_{19} for all sixty subjects. The two subscales, though showing a moderately strong intercorrelation, do not show the same pattern of correlation with the TSAR measure of entrance distress.

For two of our standardizing groups, it was possible to obtain teachers' ratings on the TSAR for several additional weeks during the course of the school year; namely, the third and final weeks of the fall semester and the first two weeks of the spring semester, which followed upon a six-week intersession break. This permitted some evaluation of the overt anxiety or distress reactions of the child as the year progressed. Table 4 indicates that for these two groups the distress reactions as observed by the teachers occurred primarily in the first weeks of the semester and did not resurge after the semester break. An analysis of variance indicated a significant main

Table 4. Weekly TSAR Mean Scores

| | Weeks | | | | | |
| | Semester I | | | | Semester II | |
	1	2	3	13	1	2
Group I (N = 14)	14.0	8.4	7.5	4.9	3.6	2.4
Group II (N = 16)	10.0	2.4	3.6	2.6	1.1	1.3
Total	12.0	5.4	5.6	3.8	2.4	1.8

effect for the time, with $p < .01$ ($F = 7.37$; df 5, 150). Although the failure of the TSAR scores to resurge after the six-week intersession break might be taken as a suggestion that entrance distress is a phenomenon limited to the initial period of adjustment to school, this assumption is contradicted by the pattern of correlations between the TSAR and the PAR subscales over time (Table 5). The correlations between the TSAR and the PAR_6 did, in fact, tend to be lower after the first three-week period. However, the level of entrance distress remained significantly correlated with the PAR_6 throughout the period of observation.

Table 5. Correlations of Weekly TSAR Scores[a] with PAR Scales

	Weeks					
		Semester I			Semester II	
	1	2	3	13	1	2
	(N = 30)	(N = 30)	(N = 30)	(N[b] = 29)	(N[b] = 29)	(N[b] = 29)
PAR_6	.53**	.46*	.50**	.39*	.40*	.34*
PAR_{19}	.17	.03	.14	.22	.30	.21

[a]TSAR scores summed over one week.

[b]One child was withdrawn from the nursery school program after the first three weeks due to extreme separation anxiety; his ratings after rejoining the class at second semester are not included in these analyses.

*$p < .05$.

**$p < .01$.

Observational and Parental Interview Data on Social Adjustment

Detailed observations were made on the nursery school and home behavior of one of our four groups of children (McIntyre, Doris, and Meyer, 1975). An experienced child clinical psychologist made daily observations of the children in the nursery school and, on the basis of their entrance patterns during the fall semester, classified them as either acute distress, latent distress, or minimal distress. This classification was made without knowledge of PAR or TSAR scores. The acute-distress pattern was marked by the manifestation of numerous distress behaviors, including crying and verbal protests. The latent-distress pattern included a number of distress behaviors in the absence of crying and verbal protests. The clinician chose the label of latent distress for this group rather than moderate distress because of her belief that the covert level of anxiety was probably higher than the overt signs of distress would suggest. The minimal-distress pattern was one of relatively easy and distress-free entrance. Four children were classified as acute distress, five as latent distress, and four as minimal distress. The accuracy of these classifications was subsequently checked by comparison with the TSAR scores (summed over the first two weeks) and PAR_6 ratings. The mean TSAR scores for the groups were, respectively, 66.4, 8.4, and 1.0; those of the PAR_6 scale were similarly 12.5, 9.8, and 3.2. There was no overlap of TSAR or PAR_6 scores among the groups.

In addition to the clinical psychologist's observations, additional school observations, home visits, and parental interviews were made by various professional staff and graduate students. The combined information was discussed in seminar and dictated summaries prepared on the school and home adjustment for each child. Examination of these summaries suggested typical patterns of adjustment to nursery school for each group.

The acute-distress children were characterized by dependency on the teachers and inability to interact spontaneously with peers. At school they displayed aggression only covertly, if at all, whereas at home they displayed temporary increases in aggression toward their mothers. The latent-distress children shared most of the characteristics of the acute-distress children, particularly on the dimensions of dependence on teachers and inability to interact spontaneously with peers. In contrast, the minimal-distress children related well to peers, related positively but nondependently to teachers, expressed aggression in appropriate ways and at appropriate times, and were not likely to show any increased aggression toward the mother in association with entrance into nursery school. The patterns of adjustment of the more anxious groups, upon separations from their parents, resemble observations made by Isaacs (1933), Heinicke (1956), and others. Two abbreviated versions of our case summaries will concretize the general observations made on the adjustment of the high-separation-anxiety children.

Edward (CA: 36 months) had been enrolled in a play school the summer immediately preceding nursery school, while he and his family took their first extended trip from home since his birth. However, he had resisted going to play school with such temper tantrums that he had been withdrawn from it after only a few days. When he started nursery school, he was so tense and had such tantrums as his mother attempted to depart from the school that his mother stayed with him almost the entire time for five mornings. They tended to isolate themselves in the entrance room or washroom. Edward resisted the head teacher's attempts to get him involved in activities but responded to the supportive physical contact that she offered him. By the end of the week, he was moving about the several rooms of the nursery school more freely, responding somewhat to overtures from adults and peers, and initiating aggressive play with objects or with the nursery school guinea pig. He brought a pillow from home, which he cuddled for comfort during this period.

For the following four weeks, Edward was more enthusiastic at school, complying eagerly in activities and conforming to the group as long as the head teacher was present. However, during this same period, Edward became much less compliant at home than he had formerly been. His mother reported that he had become stubborn and rebellious toward her, had tantrums when demands were made of him, became easily angered by his 7-year-old brother, and was generally uncooperative. His noncompliance, however, appeared only in regard to her; there was no apparent change in his relationship with his father. By midsemester, when she was considering withdrawing him altogether from nursery school, this noncompliance diminished at home. But at school his enthusiasm and eagerness to comply and conform had waned. Edward initiated peer interactions less and tended to drift after the teacher in a satellite-like manner. Only with direct support from the head teacher's presence would he sustain constructive activity or peer involvement. The staff noticed that Edward often appeared angry and would manifest his anger in "sneaky" ways, either toward peers or toward animals, when he thought himself unobserved.

During the second semester, Edward remained dependent on the presence of the head teacher to sustain constructive activity and peer interaction. He rarely initiated interactions and functioned best in situations involving small groups working on structured tasks. He was still easily angered but had become somewhat less sneaky and aggressive toward the animals. He responded to unexpected events, such as field trips or the room's being darkened because of electrical failure, by clinging tensely to his mother or the head teacher.

Linda (CA: 39 months) and her family had lived in the same home except for the year previous to nursery school, which they spent in a different state. During that time, Linda had attended a cooperative nursery school along with one of her older siblings (a sister, eighteen months older). There she had been passive but had not cried. But just two weeks before Linda was to start in our nursery school, her older sister started kindergarten, crying in front of her. Simultaneously, her mother started working for the first time since Linda had been born, and a babysitter was hired to care for her at home in her mother's absence.

Linda clung to her mother and cried when she was first brought to nursery school. She defiantly resisted efforts to get her to interact with other children and either sat in her cubby (clothes locker), cuddling the blanket she had brought with her from home, or cried, kicked, and clung when the head teacher tried to encourage her to separate. For most of the first two days, she isolated herself with her mother in the cubby room or the play yard. After the first week, however, Linda began to passively comply when the teacher took her along to join in small-group activities. She was able to respond to interactions initiated by peers as long as the head teacher was available. Soon she developed a similar, though weaker, dependence on the assistant teacher. By midsemester, she could sustain interactions with peers for longer periods of time without the teacher's actual presence, but she followed the head teacher with her eyes. She had shown an early period of rebellion at home, where she was resistant to her mother, cried easily, and demanded more cuddling than usual, but this had diminished as her ability to function with the support of the head teacher had increased in the first semester.

Throughout the second semester of nursery school, Linda was able to function with peers in small groups, even initiating interactions, as long as the head teacher was present or within easy reach. But she remained hyperattentive to the teacher's whereabouts and still responded to the stresses of unfamiliar events by returning to her cubby and curling up there with her favorite blanket.

In contrast to the above, we now present two case summaries of relatively easy adjustment to nursery school.

Carol (CA: 34 months) had three siblings old enough to attend public school full day, and her mother was employed full time. Other than short trips and family visits, she had always lived in the same home; she had regularly attended Sunday School for the year preceding nursery school.

Carol entered nursery school with her mother in a relaxed but subdued manner. She scanned her surroundings intently and moved slowly, cautiously, but deliberately into activities, first with objects and then through them to peers. For the first few days, she was somewhat dependent on the teacher to bring her into peer interactions, but she was responsive to overtures from other children and after a few days started initiating peer play spontaneously. Her responses tended to be immature at this period, for she spoke unclearly and with some babytalk. However, this diminished rapidly.

By the middle of the first semester, Carol was able to sustain creative, goal-oriented play without teacher support and to interact freely and spontaneously with peers. During the second semester, there developed considerable competition between Carol and another girl over companions, toys, and dress-up materials. Each seemed to struggle for dominance over the other, and each appeared to have roughly equal successes. Carol occasionally became angry in these situations, but her anger was usually displayed in a teasing manner. Carol functioned with considerable independence during the second semester; she displayed some dependence on teachers when the lights were out unexpectedly on the winter morning and when the head teacher was absent, but she responded with enthusiasm to the anticipated events of the visit from the dog and class field trips.

Seth (CA: 40 months) had had no formal group experience prior to nursery school but had traveled extensively with his parents and baby brother and had twice stayed alone with his grandmother

for short visits. On the first day of nursery school, Seth entered quite
passively. He was appreciative of others' rights of being involved in
activities initiated by the head teacher, and he was responsive in peer
interactions. Within three days, Seth was spontaneously initiating
peer interactions, and, though he greeted the teacher joyfully and
seemed eager to be with her whenever possible, he was neither dependent on her to become involved in activities nor competitive for her
attention.

After the first week of school, Seth usually arrived late,
separated quickly and confidently from his mother, and hurried to
join activities. His peer interactions were particularly mature, for he
could take a leadership role or follow as the situation demanded.
He could permit peers to be dependent on him also. Though he never
spontaneously behaved regressively, he seemed to enjoy playing at
regressive levels when it was begun by peers. Although he sometimes
brought a baby doll from home, which he would cuddle in stressful
situations, Seth usually brought toys from home to be used for interaction with his companions. Seth particularly enjoyed clownish,
aggressive, and dramatic gross-motor play but never appeared hostile
or noncompliant. His teachers described him at the end of the year
as an exuberant, strong, leading child who could follow as well as
dominate his peers.

Separation Anxiety and Aggression

These relationships between separation anxiety and the social behavior of the children in nursery school and home suggest the need for more
extended study. The quite marked difference in patterns of aggression among
our three distress groups, coupled with the central role that aggression holds
in many theories of development and personality functioning, makes it a
likely variable for priority investigation. But it is to be noted that the patterns
of relationship between separation anxiety and aggression in these observational
and interview data suggest no straightforward relationship. The acute-distress
group (or high-separation-anxiety subjects as indicated by the rating scales),
in contrast to the minimal-distress group, tended to be aggressive toward
the mother but were less aggressive in the nursery school; when they did
aggress in that situation, the aggression (in contrast to that of the minimal-
distress group) tended to be displaced or concealed.

McIntyre and Wolfe (1973) note that the literature—conforming with
our observational and interview data—presents complex and, at times, conflicting patterns of the relationship of anxiety and aggression. For example,
both Isaacs (1933) and Sarason and associates (1960) found that anxiety in
children is related to the inhibition of aggression, whereas Heinicke (1956) and
Siegel (1956) found positive correlations between the expression of anxiety and
overt aggression in preschoolers. In their own study, McIntyre and Wolfe (1973)

sought to determine the relationship between separation anxiety as measured by the TSAR and aggressive behaviors in a frustrating situation. Children in four nursery schools were rated on the TSAR, and a group of high-separation-anxiety children, all in the upper quartile of the distribution, and ten low-separation-anxiety children, all below the median of the distribution, were selected for study.

A control condition consisted of five minutes of play at an easy, familiar task, drawing with crayons. Observations of the child's baseline level of aggressive behavior were made during this interval. Subsequently, the child was presented with a frustrating task, on the assumption that frustration frequently elicits aggressive behavior (Dollard and others, 1939). This task consisted of cutting a poster board with a plastic scissors—a difficult task that prior testing had shown to be disliked by 4-year-olds. The child was encouraged to continue at this task until five minutes had elapsed. The aggressive behaviors rated by an observer included direct and indirect physical or verbal aggression toward the experimenter, the play materials, or objects in the room. An aggressive-change measure was obtained for each subject by subtracting the aggression score in the control period from the aggression score during the frustrating task. The mean control score for the low-anxious subjects was, as the authors had predicted, higher than that of the high-anxious subjects. A Mann-Whitney U test of the difference in change scores for the two groups indicated that the difference was significant at the $p < .01$ level. McIntyre and Wolfe attempted to reconcile their results, and those of Sarason and associates (1960), with the conflicting findings of Heinicke (1956) and Siegel (1956) by assuming that the level of anxiety may determine whether it will result in the inhibition or facilitation of aggressive responses.

In a subsequent paper, McIntyre and Doris (1977) reported on the relationship between PAR_6 scores and a parental questionnaire on the child's expression of aggression toward the mother. The subjects were two samples of 3-year-olds—from intact families, racially mixed, and predominantly middle class—entering a day care center. In the first sample, a strong positive correlation (.80) between anxiety and aggression toward the mother was found among the boys ($N = 14$), while a weaker negative correlation (-.42) was obtained for the girls ($N = 12$). Means and variances were similar on both variables for both sexes. There was no evidence of response biases related to sex or to separation anxiety, and further confirmation of the objectivity of the parental ratings was provided by the high correlation between parental separation anxiety ratings and the separation distress observed in the day care center.

In the second sample of twenty-three children, a positive and significant correlation of .50 ($N = 10$) was found for the boys and an insignificant -.05 ($N = 13$) correlation for the girls. Combining the two samples gave an overall significant correlation of .59 for the boys but an insignificant negative correlation for the girls.

Striking in this study was the marked sex difference, and McIntyre and Doris attempted to relate it to differential cultural attitudes toward the expression of aggression in boys and girls and to a consideration of the functional and expressive values of aggression in relationship to attachment.

Separation Anxiety and Cognitive Performance

Tamaroff (1975), noting that personality theorists and clinicians have commonly maintained that anxiety is a significant factor in the development and manifestation of cognitive performance, undertook a determination of the relationship between separation anxiety and cognitive performance. This study has special relevance as our goals for preschool programs place increasing emphasis on the fostering of cognitive growth.

The basic hypothesis under examination was that in a test of cognitive functioning administered in an unfamiliar situation, under conditions of parent present and parent absent, the deleterious effects of the parent-absent condition will be greater in a high-separation-anxiety group than in a low-separation-anxiety group. In addition, the study attempted to determine whether high- and low-separation-anxiety children function at similar levels of proficiency on cognitive tasks under optimal conditions; that is, when the parent is present.

Nineteen high-separation-anxiety children and nineteen low-separation-anxiety children, as determined by the PAR_6, were selected from children entering, for the first time, a university laboratory school and a day care center. Each anxiety group consisted of nine males and ten females. The children's ages ranged from 39 to 57 months, with a mean of 46 months. Each child was individually administered a series of cognitive tasks by the examiner, who was unaware of the anxiety classification of the children at the time they were tested. The tasks were administered under two conditions. In the first, the child was taken from his group, accompanied by a parent, and tested in an unfamiliar room with the parent present. The parent was usually the mother. In four instances, equally divided between the anxiety groups, the father accompanied the child, either alone or with the mother. Under the second condition, the child was tested in an unfamiliar room without the parent's presence. Each subject received both conditions of administration. In this repeated observation technique, half of the subjects in each of the two anxiety groups received the parent-present condition first, and half received the parent-absent condition first. Since the design was counterbalanced for condition order, and confounding order effects were hopefully minimized. The mean time between the administration of the two conditions was twenty-two days. The administration order of the cognitive tasks was the same in each condition. In the testing room the child was seated at a low table and administered seven different cognitive tasks by the male examiner.

The parent was seated several feet from the child and invited to watch the test or to read some available magazines.

The cognitive tasks comprising the dependent variable were seven in number and presented in the same order as in the following descriptions:

1. The Seguin Form Board, as adapted for young children from the Arthur Point Scale. (Scoring was by completion time, and one trial was given.)
2. The Beery and Buktenica Developmental Test of Visual-Motor Integration, a series of age-graded line constructions which the child copied from printed designs. (Directions and scoring were according to the manual.)
3. Memory for Digits, as adapted from the Stanford-Binet and the WISC.
4. Memory for Sentences, as adapted from various forms of the Binet and Wechsler preschool scales.
5. Block Construction, as adapted from the Gesell Developmental Schedules and the Yale Scale of Child Development. Each block construction was to be reproduced from a standard model or by imitation of the examiner's demonstration.
6. The Knox Cube Test, as adapted for young children from the Arthur Point Scale. This test consisted of the child's reproduction of the serial tapping of a pattern upon a number of blocks as demonstrated by the examiner.
7. The Peabody Picture Vocabulary Test, administered and scored according to the directions of the test manual.

A separate analysis of variance was performed for each variable.[2] The p values obtained in these analyses for both main effects and interactions are reported in Table 6. Since each cognitive task gave an essentially independent test of the hypothesis, this table permits us to easily see the pattern of results.

[2] In the high-separation-anxiety group, nine children received the parent-present condition first and ten received the parent-absent condition first. For the low-separation-anxiety children, ten received the parent-present condition first and nine received the parent-absent condition first. Since no available computer program would efficiently deal with a three-factor analysis of variance with different cell frequencies, two theoretical subjects were assigned the mean scores for their respective groups on each of the dependent variables. As a check on the results, the data were reanalyzed without including the Order variable. This permitted the use of a two-factor model of analysis of variance, obviating the need for theoretical subjects. The results of the two analyses were essentially the same as regards the variables of interest.

Table 6. Anayses of Variance of Test Scores (*p* Values)

Source of Variance	Seguin Form Board	Visual-Motor Test	Memory for Digits	Memory for Sentences	Block Construction	Knox Cubes	Picture Vocabulary
				Test			
Anxiety	.16	.13	.23	.01*	.08	.06	.02*
Order	.60	1.00	.56	.18	.78	.67	.01*
Anxiety x Order	.15	.03*	.21	.50	.60	.61	.55
Parent Present or Absent	.64	.05*	.54	.005*	.17	.01*	.60
Anxiety x Parent	.15	.05*	.04*	.003*	.003*	.09	.06
Parent x Order	.12	.03*	.27	.55	.08	.71	.01*
Anxiety x Parent x Order	.51	.80	.12	.52	.005*	.58	.82

*Equals or exceeds conventional criterion for significance.

For all main effects and their interactions, there is at least one dependent variable with a significant p value. However, four of these (Order, Separation Anxiety x Order, Parent Absent or Present x Order, and Separation Anxiety x Parent Absent or Present x Order) involve the Order variable and are not of serious concern to us. As Tamaroff (1975) notes, Order was included in the analysis of variance primarily to control its possible effects. The lack of a consistent pattern and the small number of p values less than .05 in the results involving the Order variable, therefore, justify its exclusion from further consideration.

For the remaining main effects and their interactions, the p values reveal more regular patterns and are of more relevance to our interests. Separation anxiety shows a significant main effect for Memory for Sentences and the Peabody Picture Vocabulary. Block Construction and the Knox Cube Test just fail to reach significance. The parent-absent-or-present condition shows significant effects on the Visual-Motor Test, Memory for Sentences, and the Knox Cube Test. But of greater interest to us and directly relevant to the major hypothesis under test is the interaction of the separation-anxiety condition and the parent-absent-or-present condition. In this case, the Visual-Motor Test, Memory for Digits, Memory for Sentences, and Block Construction all give significant p values. In addition, the Peabody Picture Vocabulary Test barely misses significance. The overall pattern of this interaction would, therefore, justify further analysis.

In Table 7, we present the mean test scores for the anxiety groups under parent-present and parent-absent conditions for each of the seven cognitive tasks. An examination of the means for the high-separation-anxiety group indicates that, for every task, this group obtained mean scores indicative of lowered performance in the parent-absent condition. In contrast, for the low-separation-anxiety group, there is only one instance, the Knox Cubes Test, in which the means were indicative of lowered performance in the parent-absent condition. Tests of significance for the difference between correlated means were done for each anxiety group, and the respective p values are also recorded in Table 7. For the high-separation-anxiety group, the difference between the means under parent-present and parent-absent conditions were significant on five of the seven tasks: the Visual-Motor Test, Memory for Sentences, Block Construction, Knox Cubes, and the Peabody Picture Vocabulary Test. In no instance were the means of the low-separation-anxiety group significantly different for the two conditions of testing.

The combined results of the analyses of variance and the t tests therefore lend considerable support to the hypothesis that, in a test of cognitive functioning administered in an unfamiliar situation under conditions of parent present and parent absent, the deleterious effects of parent absent will be greater in a high-separation-anxiety group of preschoolers than in a low-separation-anxiety group.

Table 7. Mean Test Scores with Significance Levels for Differences Between Parent-Present and Parent-Absent Condition Within Anxiety Groups

Anxiety Group	Parent Condition	Seguin Form Board[a]		Visual-Motor Test		Memory for Digits		Memory for Sentences		Block Construction		Knox Cubes		Picture Vocabulary	
		Mean	p	Mean	p	Mean	p	Mean	p	Mean	p	Mean	p	Mean	p
High	Present	50.2		5.6		7.1		16.8		9.0		4.2		40.3	
	Absent	57.5	.15	4.8	.025	6.2	.10	11.7	.01	7.3	.01	3.0	.01	38.1	.05
Low	Present	46.3		6.1		7.4		19.9		9.8		4.8		47.5	
	Absent	44.1	n.s.	6.1	n.s.	7.8	n.s.	20.2	n.s.	10.5	n.s.	4.5	n.s.	48.4	n.s.

[a]High scores on the Seguin Form Board represent poor performance. For all other tests, high scores represent good performance.

Note: p values for the high-separation-anxiety group were ascertained by a one-tailed test of significance for the difference between correlated means (McNemar, 1969).

To determine whether high- and low-separation-anxiety children function at equal levels of proficiency on cognitive tasks when the parent is present, Tamaroff compared the mean scores for his high-separation-anxiety children with the low-separation-anxiety children under the parent-present condition for each of the seven tasks. As can be seen from the means in Table 7, in five cases—Visual-Motor, Memory for Sentences, Block Construction, Knox Cubes, and Picture Vocabulary—the mean score for the high-separation-anxiety group was lower than for the low-separation-anxiety group. However, tests of significance of mean differences for uncorrelated means were in no case significant. Therefore, there is no reason to reject the null hypothesis that, under conditions of parent present, high-separation-anxiety preschoolers perform with proficiency equal to that of low-separation-anxiety children.

Summary and Discussion

We have described the development of two scales of separation anxiety—the PAR_6 (rated by parents) and the TSAR (rated by preschool teachers)—and have presented data indicative of their reliability and significant correlation with one another. These scales differentiate children into high- and low-separation-anxiety groups, which appear to function differently in their overall social adjustment to preschool programs and in their relationships at home during the period immediately subsequent to their entrance to preschool. A particular area of social behavior in which the groups appear to differentiate themselves relates to aggressive drives and their expression or inhibition. This relationship between separation anxiety and aggression is complex. The high-separation-anxiety children apparently exhibit less direct, overt aggression in the nursery school setting and in a frustrating experimental situation than do their low-separation-anxiety peers. At the same time, parental interviews suggest that the high-separation-anxiety children may be more aggressive toward the mother subsequent to nursery school entrance than are the low-separation-anxiety children. A correlational study of separation anxiety and mother's ratings of aggression toward her by the child supports this finding for boys but not for girls. This would suggest a possible culturally determined difference in the expression of aggression for the two sexes.

There is also evidence that, in addition to differences in social behavior, the two groups differentiate themselves in the area of cognitive functioning when placed in a situation involving separation from the parent, although there is no evidence that they function differently when the parent is present.

We believe that the development of the PAR_6 and the TSAR scales and the applications that we have made of them justify the conclusion that usable rating scales can be developed for differentiating preschool children in their proneness to anxiety, thus facilitating the study of the phenomenon.

We have therefore achieved one of our basic objectives in undertaking our work. We would also note that our specific finding—that the high-separation-anxiety children identified by the scales show problematic behavior in their social and cognitive functioning in situations and circumstances eliciting separation anxiety—is analogous to the relationships that Sarason and his colleagues (1960) found between test-anxiety proneness and social and cognitive functioning of elementary school children. The appearance of these relationships in our work has relevance to the design and utilization of preschool programs, so that these programs can maximize their potential for fostering the social and cognitive growth of all children. These relationships suggest that in preschool programs we should be alert to the individual differences with which children will respond to separations from their primary caretakers. They also suggest that in high-separation-anxiety children these differences may be of such nature and intensity as to interfere with the development of the very social and cognitive skills that these programs seek to foster. This alertness should lead to a search for program, teacher, and parental adjustments to the individual needs of the children that will minimize the deleterious effects of separation anxiety on the child's development.

Since the work of Yerkes and Dodson (1908) with mice, there have been repeated demonstrations with varied species, including the human, of curvilinear relationships between learning or performance, on the one hand, and the drive state or anxiety level of the subject, on the other hand. These relationships can be further complicated by the level of difficulty of the imposed learning or performance task. Thus, a learning theory analysis might lead one to argue that, in fostering the social and cognitive learning of a child, we seek not complete elimination of anxiety but the reduction of anxiety to levels that will facilitate rather than interfere with learning.

A similar conclusion might be reached if we work within a psychoanalytic framework and conceptualize the child's attachment to his mother as a source of gratification and his separation from his mother as a source of deprivation. Then, following Kris (1948), we might argue that the education of the child—his successful resolution of conflict and development of ego strength—requires an optimal balance between gratification and deprivation. The importance, then, of the separation-anxiety response in the child and its recognition by the caring adult is that it is a sensitive index of when there is a danger of exceeding an optimal balance of gratification and deprivation and thereby risking a setback in the child's development. At the same time, if we were to organize the child's world so that anxiety is never in any degree aroused, gratification might so far outbalance deprivation that there is no impetus for growth. Within this framework, then, a continuing search for the antecedents, concomitants, and sequelae of separation anxiety—which we hope can be facilitated by the development of anxiety-rating scales for preschoolers—is a search for the individual and environmental components of optimal development in early childhood.

18

Anxiety and Stress in Later Life

Emilie F. Sobel

❊ ❊ ❊ ❊ ❊ ❊ ❊ ❊ ❊ ❊ ❊ ❊ ❊

It would be surprising if a person who found himself deprived of his liveli-hood, deteriorating physically, losing loved friends and family, and facing his own imminent death did not respond with extreme anxiety. Can any organism undergo prolonged, multidetermined stress at a time when reserve energies are waning without undergoing marked changes in personality, cognition, and adjustment? In order to document and systematically describe these changes, it is necessary to recognize that the elderly differ from younger adult neurotics. The severe external stress and deprivation of this period of life often result in long-term and significant impairment of basic ego func-tions. The regression which ensues manifests itself in narcissistic withdrawal, increased egocentricity, and in more serious regressive responses, such as profound involutional depression. There is a wide range of symptomatology: anxiety, hypochondriasis, phobic and depressive ideation, suspiciousness, and projection (Gillespie, 1963). In this population, as Zetzel (1966) points out, signal anxiety is less significant than in younger adults. She contends that anxiety in the elderly corresponds neither to Freud's primary (traumatic) anxiety nor to his secondary (signal) anxiety. It more closely resembles anxiety stimulated by fear or loss or separation. Blanck and Blanck (1974), in their descriptive developmental diagnosis, place this kind of anxiety at the earlier pregenital levels of development.

Instinctual intrapsychic danger, then, is not as much of a problem for the elderly as is anxiety related to fear of object loss from the outside world. This type of depressive anxiety contributes most to the chronic stress that precipitates and maintains regressive symptomatology in the elderly. Whanger and Busse (1976) provide a good review of some of the literature on psychiatric disorders of the elderly. They point out that many of the neurotic complaints on the part of elderly patients can be masked depressions. Sleep disturbance or interest loss are more direct expressions of this condition. Depressions may, in this age group, cause the patient to become so perplexed and withdrawn that he may appear to have an organic brain syndrome (p. 293). Another type of depression fairly common in the elderly is the agitated or excited type. Whanger and Busse point out the prevalence, particularly in older women, of hypochondriasis. Paranoid syndromes also are commonly found, as is (contrary to popular belief) alcoholism.

In addition to change in the type of anxiety level in the older person, certain breakdowns in cognitive functioning result from the aging process. Silk (1971) and Savage (1975) provide reviews of this literature. Wechsler (1958) was concerned with deterioration in the intellectual capacities of the aged and found, for example, that the subtests of the WAIS that hold up with age are Information, Comprehension, Object Assembly, and Vocabulary. Those that decline are speeded tasks, Arithmetic, and abstract reasoning tasks such as Block Design and Similarities. Schuster (1952) gave the WAIS to a well-functioning 106-year-old man and found that he had an IQ of 126 but difficulty with abstraction. Blum, Fosshage, and Jarvik (1972) have shown that such cognitive declines as can be measured by WAIS subtests are reliable predictors of mortality. This supports the idea that elderly subjects tend to be uneven in their functioning; that is, one set of abilities may decline while others may not. The measured extent of deficit or lack of deficit is a function of the specific ability assessed. During the second decade of a twenty-year follow-up on subjects with a mean age of 66, Similarities, Digits Forward, Block Design, and Digit Symbol showed significant decline (Blum, Fosshage, and Jarvik, 1972).

In a "cross-sectional" approach, Reed and Reitan (1963) show changes in test performance as associated with the normal aging process. These authors developed a battery of twenty-nine tests, including eleven of the WAIS subtests. They found that differences between age groups were minimal on stored information such as Vocabulary and maximal on tests of problem solving. Arenberg (1968) provides addition (confluent) evidence in the area of problem solving in a longitudinal study of 300 well-educated middle-class men ranging from 24 to 87. In the retest, six years later, age declines were found only for the group over 70 (Arenberg, 1968) and were significantly related to subsequent mortality. This decline in performance prior to death, which is consistently found in the literature on cognitive performance in the elderly, has been termed "terminal drop." Savage and associates (1972), studying intellectual functioning in a representative community sample as opposed to a well-educated sample, found a decline in subtest score with advancing age on both Verbal and Performance subtests. They believe that former studies did not find a significant decline because they used high-IQ subjects.

Savage (1975) points out that more widespread knowledge of the area of intellectual decline in the elderly is needed. He, too, notes that, although "g" (the concept of general intelligence as opposed to specific abilities) tends to maintain itself, specific mental abilities show differential decline. Silk (1971) suggests that too much of the work in this area is narrowly circumscribed by use of tests of general intellectual ability, which have not been standardized for use with old-age groups and are of questionable reliability and validity. Second, since these studies focus on IQ per se, they do not pinpoint deficits in specific cognitive areas. Botwinick (1970) presents a comprehensive review of this literature, which is more experimental in nature and taps areas of functioning that are not covered by general intelligence tests. Some of these areas, of interest to verbal-learning theorists, are paired associate learning, short-term and long-term memory retention, and reaction time. Decline in functioning in these areas is demonstrated in elderly groups. Other studies reviewed by Botwinick suggest that the elderly are unwilling to change concepts that are no longer adequate, have a high level of redundancy, have difficulty dealing with new concepts as problems become more complicated, and cannot take advantage of new strategies in solving problems.

In addition to the extensive literature on deficits in cognitive functioning in the elderly based on performance on standardized tests and experimental studies of learning and memory, there is a body of literature based on the idea that elderly persons "regress" in their cognitive functioning and perform much like children on problem–solving tasks. These studies, several of which are reviewed by Silk (1971), point to parallels in the cognitive functioning of the elderly and of children. For example, Rinoldi and Vanderwoude (1969), using problem-solving tasks varying in degree of concreteness-abstraction, found that 79-year-olds and 9-year-olds performed comparably. This and other similar studies suggest that cognitive functions begin to decline in reverse order to the way they developed. Additional evidence is provided by Ames, Walker, and Goodenough (1957), who conclude on the basis of Rorschach research that, as an individual grows older, increasing structuralization is reversed and Rorschach responses become more restricted and grow more like those of a child.

Another example of "regression" is provided by Denney and Lennon (1972), who found that elderly individuals instructed to classify geometric stimuli tended to make either representations of real objects or elaborate designs, just as young children often do. Middle-aged subjects, in contrast, grouped the stimuli according to dimensions such as shape or size. N. W. Denney (1974) replicated these results on 214 individuals and found that the elderly used more primitive classifications. In 1976, Denney and Wright reviewed the most current literature on cognitive changes during the adult years. They focused particularly on dimensions emerging from the Piagetian cognitive framework—dimensions such as conservation, egocentrism, animistic thinking, classification, class inclusion, and moral thinking. The results of approximately twelve studies reviewed suggest that elderly subjects perform on a more primitive level, in these dimensions, than do middle-aged subjects. Papilia and Bielby (1974) provide an overlapping review.

What precipitates and maintains the regressive phenomena in the aging individual? According to Jarvik and Blum (1971), metabolic and genetic factors, although implicated in the cognitive deterioration of the elderly, alone cannot account for these changes. They urge that psychological factors and social and environment stresses be considered in any serious attempt to understand the etiological picture. There are two trends in the literature on later life. Some authors emphasize organic factors while others concentrate on functional aspects. Clearly, an organic substrate is implicated at the extreme end of the dementia spectrum, where memory disorder and disorientation are severe and neurophysiological deterioration can be medically documented. There is, however, a very large gray area in the malfunctioning elderly, where organic brain syndrome is mild or ruled out but regressed thought and behavior are nevertheless evident.

Cath (1976) presents a balanced view of this issue. He contends that old age is that period of life where "the organic meets the functional" and that depletion of functions is multidetermined. In any case, he asserts, functional illness related to stress always has an organic or biochemical substrate in cellular or extracellular levels. Stress plays an increasingly important role over time, since vital tissues are wearing out, hormonal mechanisms are declining, and immune mechanisms are changing. He feels it would be impossible to differentiate among so-called stress, situational or environmental factors, or intrapsychic conflict in the etiology of the disorders of later life.

Thus, interpretations of the data on cognitive decline must take into consideration the physical *and* the intrapsychic. The complexity of this issue is well illustrated by the research of Britton and associates (1967). These authors, investigating eighty aged subjects living in the community, found a significant relationship between personality characteristics, psychiatric status, and intellectual decline. For example, a subgroup of the elderly with functional mental disorder performed less well than the mentally normal on certain measures of cognitive ability. Clinical scales for Hysteria, Depression, and Hypochondriasis on the MMPI correlated highly with both verbal IQ and performance IQ in a negative direction. The authors speculate that the mild functional symptoms may be precursors of organic brain syndrome; but they feel that evidence on this point is inconclusive, since other studies have not found any marked tendency for patients with functional illness to develop organic brain syndrome during follow-up periods from six months to fifteen years. This reflects the complexity of the issue of functional versus organic in an elderly population. The regressed functioning evident in the performance of these individuals may not mean that they have a competence deficit or that the poor functioning is irreversible. Perhaps the regression in performance on intellectual tasks is affected by psychological factors, in which case improvement can be expected among those who improve psychiatrically. Levin (1964), discusses this issue in relation to the depressed elderly. He asserts that even when a patient has some underlying organic brain disease or a reduced cerebral reserve, the development of a state of depression may accentuate the organic manifestations and lead to symptoms such as mental confusion. Even with the organic substrate clearly present, he feels that the mental confusion may diminish if one takes steps to counter the depression.

In dealing with the elderly, it is best to assume an interaction between psychopathology and maturational-organic factors. While the latter are presumably irreversible, this does not rule out the possibility of improvement in the cognitive sphere. Denney and Wright (1976) suggest that some cognitive processes may be more closely associated with environmental than with maturational changes. This kind of approach tends to minimize the importance of possible organic etiology and puts the issue of reversibility in a more hopeful light. The research on this aspect of the issue is contradictory. Rubin (1973), for example, compared the performance of institutionalized and noninstitutionalized elderly of similar educational backgrounds and ages. The institutionalized group performed significantly less well on the conservation tasks. Rubin postulates that the institutionalized elderly have fewer social interactions. Decrements in performance could also be accounted for, however, by the fact that the institutionalized elderly may have greater organic deficits.

Supporting the more optimistic side of the question of reversibility, N. W. Denney (1974) found that elderly persons performed a classificatory task in a childlike fashion but became capable of grouping according to a more mature classification once they observed a model grouping according to size and shape (as opposed to color and design). Denney suggests that the elderly are unlikely to use color as a dimension for grouping because of neural degeneration. According to Denney and Wright (1976), the more sophisticated modes do remain intact in the repertoires of the elderly. They found, for example, that the elderly tended to use very childlike strategies on Oliver and Hormsby's twenty-question task. Rather than asking questions that eliminate a whole class of items at a time (constraint-seeking questions), they tended to ask questions that eliminate only one item at a time. However, when exposed to an adult model who asked constraint-seeking questions, the elderly tended to adopt the constraint-seeking strategy after observing as few as one or two instances (Denney and Denney, 1974). Thus, their ability to use the more efficient problem-solving strategy does not appear to deteriorate, since it appears full blown when elicited. Unlike children, the elderly possess but do not spontaneously use the more abstract strategy. Denney and Wright suggest that the elderly, who are retired and no longer subjected to demands for the exercise of abstract, high-level modes of information processing, use those modes which are more adaptive and effective for their particular environment. Confluent evidence on this point is provided by Schultz and Hoyer (1976). They found that, in spatial egocentrism and perspective taking, feedback and practice reduce the egocentric performance of elderly individuals, whose scores on the spatial egocentrism task then improved. These authors emphasize the importance of environmental-experiential variables in the acquisition and maintenance of cognitive abilities in old age.

On the more pessimistic side, Storck, Looft, and Hooper (1972) suggest that decline in performance on Piagetian tasks may be associated with neurophysiological degeneration. Finding age-related deficits in functioning on tasks involving classification and seriation, they speculate that classification and seriation are more closely allied with measures of "fluid" as opposed to "crystallized" intelligence (Cattell, 1971), which in turn is more closely allied with the neurophysiological state of the organism. This line of theorizing suggests that the elderly are incapable of responding in a more advanced way. Papilia (1972) ascribes the decrement in conservation ability to neurological impairment *and* decreasing ability to benefit from environmental stimulation.

It is impossible to isolate the relative contribution of maturational-neurophysiological factors, on the one hand, and stress, on the other, to the cognitive decrements of later life. Nevertheless, it is interesting to speculate about the effects of stress on the level of functioning. If one follows this line of approach, then less advanced reasoning can be seen as a reinforced habitual response to stress. The more primitive modus operandi may represent an "easier" way of thinking under pressure and may have superior anxiety-reducing properties. Denney and Wright (1976) suggest that elderly adults revert to childlike response modes because their environment simply lacks conditions that would maintain high levels of cognitive performance. Perhaps primitive cognitive modes are more adaptive for the concrete here-and-now world of the elderly and young children.

Piaget (1951), in a discussion of the difference between egocentric logic and rational thought, asserts that egocentric logic, which jumps from premise to conclusion, is somehow more satisfying to the child. As he puts it, "The vision of the whole brings about a sense of belief and feeling of security far more rapidly than if each step in the argument were made explicit" (p. 162). Judgments of *value* take precedence over deduction. Thus, an earlier, less deductive, and more subjective mode of reasoning can serve an adaptive function for the elderly person undergoing severe stress.

The many stresses, both internal and external, that assault the elderly individual may precipitate regression in cognitive functioning. Fenichel (1945), following Freud, states that, in mental development, progress to the higher level never takes place completely; instead, characteristics of the earlier level persist alongside the new level. When new development meets with difficulty, it may recede to earlier stages that were more successfully experienced. If the advancing "troops" meet *too powerful* an enemy force, they may retreat to a previous position (p. 65). Losses of various kinds—death of a loved one, separation, ill health, threatened body integrity, reduced cerebral and physiological reserve, and environmental deprivation due to retirement and financially reduced circumstances—constitute the "powerful enemies" that the elderly individual encounters. In this sense, later life presents a developmental crisis which can be met by regression to earlier modes of adaptive functioning. Camaron (1967) also provides evidence that an ego function dimension is a complicating factor in the elderly. Using the relatively global concept of ego strength, as measured on the Barron Ego Strength scale, he compared young and aged samples and found that the aged groups generally had lower ego strength than the young samples.

In development, the ego gradually forms a cohesive self out of many parts (Kohut, 1977). This process, as Cath (1976) and others have pointed out, is facilitated by the early maintenance of object relations, which become the root of much of our health and sanity in later years. With advancing age, human relatedness becomes difficult or absent for what Cath calls the "ailing body-ego-object system." Then the sense of worth, identity, and cohesiveness of the self begins to fall apart. Mature ego functions are gradually replaced by more primitive forms of self-preservation and projection and introjection. Anxious dread and feelings of helplessness accelerate regression; and if important needs are not met, these ego restrictions lead to further loss of narcissistic supplies, further loss of reality testing. At times the depression and depletion give way to defensive outbursts of grandiosity as a protest against giving up narcissistic investment in the self. In any case, the severity of some of the losses of later life prompt reorganizations of the self, often on a more regressed level. Further, with the passage of object attachments based on genital sexuality, previous issues of pregenital concern come to the fore.

There is a revival of infantile concerns. Attempts to reconstruct symbiotic relationships, such as obtained at early stages of development, occur in the service of preserving the self from further narcissistic injury. Cath believes that, when restitutive attempts do not succeed and outweigh the losses and depletion, there is progressive dissolution of the structure of the ego and regression in the reverse order of that in which the ego was formed. There is decreased cathexis of the superego and especially the ego ideals. This is associated with an intensification of narcissistic cathexis of the self, certain secure ego functions, and old defensive positions. As a consequence, ego functioning operates on a regressed level that affects not only interpersonal relationships and self-esteem but cognitive functions as well.

Wedin (1977) speculates about why more primitive cognitive response may be a salient response in stressful situations. First, there is the fact that a more primitively organized response is less complex than the more abstract response. Second, it may have superior anxiety-reducing properties. Thus, such responses may have a misfired adaptive function in stressful circumstances. In states of chronic anxiety, as in later life, the egocentric approach to problem solving dominates. It may be an adaptive effort to simplify the environment and distort it in such a way that it seems less threatening. Silk (1971) discusses deterioration in senility in a context of adaptation. He feels that the decline occurs in the service of the individual's attempts to adapt to the internal and external changes that he undergoes.

During the course of a study by the author (Sobel, 1977) of an elderly, nonorganic population using thematic apperception material (the Mid Life Issues Test), this population responded differently from a younger comparison group. In the elderly group, for example, stories centered around themes of "loss" (for example, "loss of job," "friend dies of terminal cancer," "daughter or son leaving home permanently," "patient will die," "going into a nursing home").

One notable difference between the younger and older protocols was the difference in vigorous interest in the outer world. The older group relied considerably more on descriptions rather than stories. They spent a great deal of time describing the figures' states of mind, usually in negative terms: "I see an unhappy situation," "This is a lonely woman," "The future looks bleak," "This woman is sad," "She has a worried look on her face," "They all look so grim—that's all—maybe they are discussing a tragedy," "Eyes look depressed," "She looks as though she is ready to cry, there are so many memories so she keeps running." The older subjects' protocols thus illustrate Gillespie's (1963) recognition that regressive phenomena in old age entail libidinal regression to the narcissistic level. There is increasing lack of interest in external objects, whether persons or things. As illustrated by the egocentric style of the older persons' stories, everything in connection with their own person becomes of undue importance. This increase in narcissism involves a relative independence of the external world. By contrast, the younger group mentioned internal states far less. Their stories were more specific, more externally focused, and more structured, with a clear beginning, middle, and end. Older subjects spent more time describing the ambience of the story—feelings and general atmosphere—rather than the events.

The elderly person's withdrawal from the world is a form of mastery of the external stimuli. For example, Neugarten and Guttman (Neugarten and Guttman, 1958; Guttman 1969) gave the TAT to a group of 40- 70-year-old urban men and analyzed the protocols blind for age of respondent. They found an age-related movement through successive ego-mastery styles. Active mastery, instrumental and productive ways of mastering the external world, was found in the men aged 40-60. These men saw the environment as rewarding boldness and risk taking and saw themselves as possessing energies congruent with the opportunities presented in the outer world. In contrast, 60-year-old men saw the environment as dangerous and complex and the self as conforming and accommodating to outer-world demands. This change was described as a movement from active to passive mastery. After 65, the conformist mode was replaced by magical mastery, which involves projective rather than instrumental revisions of the world and the self. In this later stage, primitive defensive operations, such as projection and denial, seemed to substitute for realistic activity. Interestingly, Guttman replicated his study cross-culturally and found that the Mexican, Mayan, Druze (Israeli), and Navajo aged displayed similar approaches. The oldest men in these four societies dealt with reality projectively. Thus, age, not culture, was the crucial variable.

Treatment

Advanced age per se does not call for a differential treatment approach. Some persons function on a high level throughout life; by the same token, there are ego-deficient younger patients. The difference is that the later-life patient often faces external danger and losses that are real and continue unabated. The source of the anxiety, therefore, is not removable, and the symptomatogy is more intractable and in fact may serve an adaptive purpose. In the face of *actual* severe deprivations, the later-life patient regresses and reactivates earlier, more satisfying phases of development. These in turn call for treatment approaches which take into account the fact that regressive symptomatology serves an adaptive function in these patients. Therapy cannot aim at insights; its goals and techniques must be limited.

The anxious regressed elderly patient manifests what Fenichel (1944) describes as indications for "brief" psychotherapy. The first and foremost indication for this type of therapy is "acute difficulties of life." A second indication is an immature, childlike personality whose repressing forces are not yet internalized but are represented by anxiety about external danger. The "brief" psychotherapy approach (even though the actual treatment may extend over months or years) can be characterized as a supportive, noninterpretive mode of therapy with limited goals. Meerloo (1961), Pfeiffer (1976), Sobel (1980), Linden (1955), Goldfarb (1956), Bellak (1976), and others all suggest modifications of technique along these lines. Pfeiffer (1976), for example, advocates the following: greater activity on the part of the therapist, symbolic giving within the therapeutic relationship, specific or limited goals for therapy, empathic understanding, and differences in transference and countertransference phenomena. The patient often regards the therapist as a protective, idealized parental figure who can intervene with external dangers in a magical way. The approach provides a more active therapy—more interventions in the environment and less effort to analyze the transference. Compared to analytic therapy, those seem like second-class treatment approaches, supportive rather than revealing. They may appear to simply help the patient to function by supplying counseling, nurturance, and faith healing rather than helping the patient achieve insight (see Sobel, 1980). When the anxiety about real dangers and threats to physical, financial, and emotional integrity is given credence, supportive tactics do much to allay anxiety and thereby restore maximal functioning of the patient's ego. Cath (1976) points out that the decathexis of conscious, preconscious, and unconscious components of the self, with or without organic decrement, represents a critical time. Such "regression" demands the advent of a "reality figure who can narcissistically recathect the self-object world if resources from within are depleted or gone." The emotional investment of an interested other may compensate and postpone the yearning for an "archaic self-other fusion." This, in turn, can forestall further regression along narcissistic lines and can initiate a progressive movement toward reinvestment in the world of objects. The role of the therapist at times becomes that of being the need-satisfying object, supplier of emotional fueling, and buffer against the external world.

Death

Much of the anxiety of advanced stages of life, as has been discussed, is precipitated by the very basic fear of loss of the object. Death, essentially an unknown state, has multiple meanings and images projected onto it. One of its meanings is loss, abandonment, and violence directed at the helpless individual. Anxiety toward such an event is reality based. In therapy, anxiety about death becomes an unspoken presence, hovering in the background during phases of treatment. There is an extensive literature on death and dying and no need to duplicate those ideas here. It will suffice to mention Kübler-Ross's (1969) stages in the reaction to death and dying: (1) denial, (2) anger, (3) bargaining, (4) fear and depression, (5) acceptance. All these stages and the concomitant stress they produce are present simultaneously during the terminal phases of the life cycle. Much of the material directly related to death is disguised, however. The therapist must be attentive and be aware of his own tendency to deny much of this material. Different phases of the Kübler-Ross paradigm are activated at different points in the therapy, and the alert therapist can govern his interventions accordingly.

The therapist's active attention, for example, to the elderly patient's ruminations about his deteriorating physical integrity constitutes an acknowledgment of the patient's masked thoughts of his own progressing death. Another area frequently encountered in the material of elderly patients is obsessive, anxious concern over external events. They will become fearful of being suddenly taken off Medicaid, precipitately being evicted from their apartment, or not receiving their Social Security checks. This can be understood as a symbolic personification of death, which can come suddenly and snatch one away. Other material as well can be read as reifications of death and its action upon the undefended person. Fear of being mugged, robbed, of walking alone in the street exemplifies this concern. If the therapist gives careful attention to these obsessions, he provides an important reassuring communication with the patient that otherwise goes unspoken.

One of my supervisees (G. Perowsky) has been running a group at the senior center where she is employed. While the group was set up originally as a task-oriented group—which met to arrange visits to the sick, send get-well and condolence cards, and the like—our purpose over time was that the group would turn into a cohesive process-oriented group, with a chance for members to air anxieties and receive support around themes of death and dying. During the course of the group's development, the members began to use their weekly sessions to discuss their concerns about illness, disability, and death. It also functioned to lower the anxiety level of the members by offering support and an opportunity to express feelings. Much of the content expressed in the group reflected in various ways the Kübler-Ross categories. Anger, for example, revolved around outrage at various losses, robbery, abandonment, and feelings of being cheated, a recurring topic in the group— reflecting Kübler-Ross's idea that "the end of life . . . is always attributed to a malicious intervention from the outside by someone else" (1969, p. 2). The role of the group therapist was as empathic witness to their losses and grievances. The therapist must hear the basic anxiety over sickness and death which comes through the general outrage at minor injustices: robberies, being cheated in the dining room, and so on. It is important to avoid minimizing the seemingly petty complaints and to give them a regard commensurate with the serious object of their underlying anxiety.

Conclusion

In the course of adaptive attempts to reconstitute a coherent world view while undergoing chronic stress, many later-life people reactivate early modes of cognitive and interpersonal functioning. The elderly experience anxiety in relation to the outside world. This anxiety is qualitatively different from signal anxiety in response to threats imposed from within (Zetzel, 1966). The developmentally early level of anxiety, "fear of object loss," constitutes an important component of the stress of later life. The ensuing adaptive reorganization of ego functions along narcissistic lines, with concomitant cognitive deficits, serves the function of restituting losses and aiding "magical mastery" of the environment. At times, for example, it helps maintain the illusion that there are symbiotic magical figures that protect against the fear of death, loss, and separation. This can be seen in the kind of transference the later-life patient forms toward his therapist and in relations with his doctors, housekeepers, and children. A *too* accurate sense of reality would provide harsh disconformation of these illusions at a time when anxiety could be overwhelming. The therapist working with the regressed later-life patient does not work to remove egocentric modes of adaptation. In fact, at times he fortifies the illusion of security and comfort by intervening with the external and externalized danger (calling the Social Security office or having a talk with the housekeeper, doctor, children, or landlord). The microcosm of socialization provided by the therapy dyad also serves to improve inter-personal relationships in the environment. Still, the high premium placed on reality testing and deductive accuracy that takes place during therapy with a younger person may not be as important in this age group. Prevention of further deterioration, augmenting the inner resources, and remobilizing self-esteem through supportive techniques serve to preclude further regression along narcissistic lines.

19

Alcohol Abuse
and Anxiety

Robert J. Powers
Irwin L. Kutash

❖ ❖ ❖ ❖ ❖ ❖ ❖ ❖ ❖ ❖ ❖ ❖ ❖

Traditionally, the relief of anxiety and stress has been viewed as one of the primary motives for the use and abuse of alcohol. In addition, the repeated use of alcohol for that purpose has been viewed as an important factor in the development of habituation and addiction. Recently, several investigators have questioned the role of anxiety and stress relief in alcohol use. In experimental drinking studies, for example, researchers have discovered that alcohol frequently increases anxiety and stress levels, instead of decreasing them (McNamee, Mello, and Mendelson, 1968; Mendelson, LaDou, and Soloman, 1964; Tamerin and Mendelson, 1969). From such investigations, reviewers of the research literature have concluded that the relief of anxiety and stress does not play a salient role in the use and abuse of alcohol (Cappell, 1975; Marlatt, 1976; Williams, 1976).

It appears premature, however, to discard the hypothesis of the role of anxiety and stress relief in alcohol use and abuse. We have conducted a

series of clinical studies which support the role of anxiety and stress relief
and which are consistent with results of other clinical studies and surveys of
alcohol use. On the basis of these studies, we have concluded that, although
anxiety and stress relief is not the sole factor in the use and abuse of alcohol,
it is an especially important one.

For sake of clarity, external and internal demands on the individual
will be referred to here as *stressors,* and responses to the demands will be
referred to as *stress* or as *stress responses.* Anxiety is one type of stress response—one of numerous emotional responses, such as depression, anger,
excitement, disgust, curiosity, and elation. Anxiety is an emotional response
to threat and a feeling of apprehension that may have physiological components (for example, heart pounding, sweating), as well as cognitive elements (for example, thought that one's resources are not adequate to meet
the threat). Normal anxiety has been distinguished from neurotic anxiety;
the former is an appropriate response to objective threat, and the latter is
a disproportionate response. (May, 1950a). Both normal and neurotic anxiety
responses may exert stressor effects, but neurotic anxiety is generally the
more prolonged and debilitating.

Clinical Investigation of Stress and Alcohol Use

The relationship between stress and alcohol use is highly complex.
To investigate the relationship, we conducted a series of semistructured,
clinical interviews with thirty nonalcoholic drinkers and thirty alcoholics.
Each individual was asked to describe in detail events, thoughts, and emotions
preceding, in the course of, and following drinking occurrences. The data
were retrospective but provided important heuristic insights into the variable
nature of stress and into the complex interplay between stress and alcohol use.

First, results of the interviews demonstrated that the experience of
stress is highly individualistic. Two persons may face ostensibly similar external or internal stressors, such as job loss and guilt feelings, yet experience
very different levels and forms of stress. Individual differences in personality
needs, attitudes, and expectancies result in differences both in the perception
of the stressors and in the nature of the stress responses. For example, an
alcoholic who had been abstinent but had lost his job when his company was
bankrupted reported that he had felt extremely anxious because he had
counted on the income for support of his wife and infant son. After the job
loss, he had begun drinking again—to "settle my nerves." A second abstinent
alcoholic, who was single and had been laid off from his job, indicated that
he had felt very little stress because he had desired additional free time and
because he was able to live adequately on unemployment benefits. He stated
that he had not resumed drinking.

A study of the effects of stressors on alcohol use and abuse, therefore, must first account for individual differences in perceptions and responses to potential stressors. Several studies have attempted to assess the effects of varied stressors on patterns of alcohol use in groups of individuals (Blum and Levine, 1975; Hoffman and Noem, 1975; Morrissey and Schuckit, 1978). Their results must be considered inconclusive, however, because they failed to determine the individual meanings of each "objective" stressor for different subjects. Individual case studies appear particularly well suited for consideration of individual differences (Litman, 1974; Mitchell, 1975).

Second, the semistructured interviews revealed that stressors affecting each individual are multidetermined and often highly variable. From moment to moment, each individual may experience a large number of stressors, which vary in intensity and which often are interrelated and have combined or multiplicative interactive effects. One nonalcoholic, for example, described current stressors of financial debts, need for high achievement at work, guilt feelings about time spent away from home on route sales, concerns about getting older and losing physical vitality, and the recent death of a parent. In addition, an indeterminate number of unconscious or preconscious stressors, such as sexual and aggressive impulses and separation conflicts, may have been influential. The composite of stressors affecting an individual at any given moment may be termed a *stressor manifold*. The individual's stressor manifold is represented schematically in Figure 1.

Individuals may drink in response to certain stressors in the manifold but not to others. The subject discussed immediately above indicated that

Figure 1. An Individual's Stressor Manifold

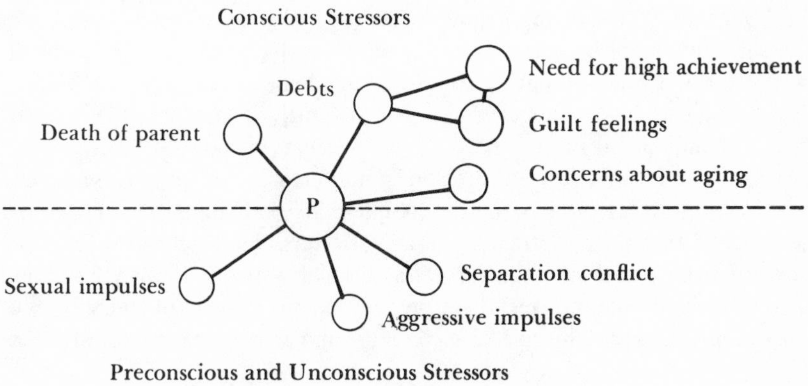

Note: P represents a person, and each circle represents a stressor. The larger the circle, the more intense the stressor.

often he had two drinks at lunch to "ease the pressures of work" but doubted that he drank to forget about debts or to relieve concerns about getting older. Other individuals may drink as a results of the combined effects of stressors. Several subjects indicated that they had many problems on their minds—a general worried feeling—when they drank. Stressors, therefore, appear often to have a composite effect on the individual. One stressor in the manifold may have relatively little influence on the incidence of drinking, but a large number of stressors in combination may have a major impact.

The stressor manifold is in continuous flux. Variations in the stressor manifold may in many cases explain variations in the intensity of the impulse to drink. As certain stressors or combinations of stressors enter consciousness or exert unconscious or preconscious influences, the individual may experience more or less intense desires to drink for relief of those stressors. It is difficult for an individual to predict changes in the stressor manifold; thus, as changes in the manifold occur, he may experience unexpected and perhaps inexplicable changes in his desire for alcohol. One abstinent alcoholic subject, for example, was walking down the street, feeling very good, and experiencing little desire for alcohol; suddenly, he thought about his separation from his wife and family several years earlier, and then he experienced a strong desire to drink to "drown the bad feelings."

Third, the semistructured interviews made clear that often stress is not simply a single response to a stressor but, rather, is a process, a series of responses that may involve different levels or stages. From subjects' descriptions of varied responses to stressors, three primary categories or stages of stress became manifest: (1) *Demand Stage,* where the individual attempts to apply existing coping behaviors and defenses to meet internal and external demands; (2) *Threat Stage,* in which the individual is unable to meet the demands with existing coping behaviors and defenses and attempts to marshal new coping behaviors or defenses; and (3) *Exhaustion Stage,* in which the individual is unable to resolve the demands and experiences feelings of helplessness or hopelessness. Alcohol may be used for the relief of stress at any or all of the three stages. Because an individual may be experiencing a wide variety of stressors simultaneously or in close sequence, the function of alcohol is highly complex. An individual may be experiencing the first stage of stress for certain stressors, the second stage for other stressors, and the third stage for yet additional stressors. He may be taking alcohol for multiple motives, therefore, related to the relief of stress. We will now be presented of the role of alcohol use and abuse at each stage of stress.

Stress Reduction Model

The data described above indicate that the relief of stress is a complex potential motive for the use of alcohol. Further support for the role of stress relief in alcohol use is found in numerous surveys and case studies. In a follow-up of 176 alcoholics discharged from a thirty-day rehabilitation program, Ludwig (1972b) found that 43 percent of the persons who relapsed to drinking gave relief of stress as the primary reason. Of those persons indicating relief of stress as the reason for relapse, 25 percent reported drinking for psychological distress ("I felt sorry for myself," "nothing to live for," "get relief from anxiety"), 13 percent mentioned family problems ("because of my wife," "couldn't see my child"), and 5 percent mentioned employment problems ("I hated my job and the pressure was building up," "bored because of not working"). Deardorff and colleagues (1975) compared 385 alcoholics and nonalcoholics on responses to a "Situations for Drinking" questionnaire. A factor analysis of item responses revealed seven major factors or reasons for drinking. Alcoholics rated reduction of stress as the most frequent reason for drinking ("I want to stop worrying about something," "I want to forget something that's bothering me," "I want to be less depressed," "I want to drown my sorrows"). Nonalcoholics rated reduction of stress third, behind "Social Liveliness" and "Personal Power." Several other surveys obtained results consistent with the surveys just described (Cahalan and Room, 1974; Horn and Wanberg, 1969; Tokar and others, 1973).

In a case study, Blane (1968) illustrates the role of stress in the onset of alcoholism. He describes the impact of an external stressor, death of a loved one, as well as the subsequent influence of some internal stressors, guilt feelings: "I saw a man in treatment who had witnessed his father's accidental death; my patient was 13 years old at the time. He portrayed himself as a carefree man-about-town who perhaps drank a bit too much. Actually, he had a serious drinking problem that had begun shortly after his father's death. Alcohol helped him to avoid facing his depressed feelings and his unconscious belief that he had caused his father's accident and, therefore, death. This later came out indirectly in his dreams and explicitly in remarks he made as he was coming out of anesthesia after an operation" (p. 40).

Mitchell (1975) conducted a series of extensive interviews with a single alcoholic subject in naturalistic settings. In the following transcript, drinking for the relief of stress is manifest as a factor in extending a period of alcohol abuse: "Well, I had to drink to do anything. I was drinking enough that I would have needed to drink to meet any requirements other than just lay in bed. It was embarrassing, feeling like I was always going to pass out, shake; I couldn't do much of anything. It's after you've been drinking, had too much, too many days, and when it besets you physically, you probably ought to know better, but you let it get beyond the line physically, like maybe you anticipate a free weekend or something and you figure, well, you'll get it straightened out in a couple days, at which time you can still do it, and then something comes up socially or businesswise unexpectedly, then you mess up your very delicate schedule where you've got two days which is what you need, and now you've got one of your shaky days, something comes up, you've got to see people, so you take some drinks to steady down and there goes your free days. . . . Once you go over that mark where you can get off it in a couple days, or get over it in a couple days, once you get past that mark then the amount of time it's going to take you to get over it keeps increasing so that when you keep drinking eventually you drive yourself to the point where you collapse and you're in the hospital" (p. 251-252).

Although the relief of stress is a commonly identified factor in alcohol use, the process whereby drinking for the relief of stress leads to excessive alcohol use and to abuse is not clear. As an attempt to clarify that process, a description will now be provided of the role of alcohol use at each of the three stages of stress.

Demand Stage. At the initial stage of stress, the individual experiences external or internal demands and attempts to respond with coping behaviors and/or psychological defenses. If the person is effectively meeting the demands, he may be experiencing relatively little anxiety, but he still may be expending much effort and experiencing considerable stress in the form of physical, mental, or emotional strain. The use of alcohol at this stage may have two primary purposes: temporary relief of strain and avoidance of strain.

Drinking for the relief of strain is a common phenomenon. It may provide a "time out" or pause from life demands merely by the change in activities, independent of any sedative or psychoactive qualities of the substance. Additionally, however, the pharmacological effects of alcohol may well contribute to cognitive and emotional changes that relieve the experience of strain. Schachter and Singer (1962), Lazarus (1966), and others have pointed out the great effect that changes in cognitive appraisal can have on emotional experiences. Alcohol may distort cognitive appraisal by altering a number of important perceptions: perceptions of demands, of capability, and of the consequences of attempts at coping (Cox, 1978). Especially at medium and high dosages, alterations in perceptions of demands may occur through limitations in attention (Barry, 1977), which may exclude from consciousness unpleasant aspects of demands related to strain. Perceptions of capacities for meeting demands may be altered through increases in fantasies, especially fantasies of power and influence (McClelland and others, 1972), which may contribute to the commonly documented feelings of confidence or "false courage." Perceptions of consequences of attempts at coping may be altered by reduction in time perspectives (Tinklenberg, 1973), which may reduce thoughts of the immediacy of the demands and thereby contribute to feelings of unconcern. Cognitive changes induced by alcohol, therefore, may clearly lead to feelings of relief from strain. Under certain circumstances, however, the cognitive distortions may result in unpleasant experiences and an increase in feelings of strain or perhaps feelings of threat. If an individual begins drinking for relief of strain but then is pressed to function effectively, as on a job, he may experience strain or threat from his impaired cognitive capacities. Just such an experience appears to occur in many laboratory studies of "experimental drinking." In a study by Mendelson, LaDou, and Soloman (1964), alcoholic subjects reported that they expected to feel calmer after drinking but instead felt more agitated.

Disinhibitory effects of alcohol also may contribute to alleviation of feelings of strain. The suppression or repression of thoughts and feelings may be a major source of strain, since considerable effort may be needed to maintain those defenses. It has been documented that the use of alcohol may bring feelings of relief, as the individual relaxes his defenses and experiences thoughts and emotions that ordinarily would be suppressed (Barry, 1977; Diethelm and Barr, 1962). Through alcohol use, individuals who are characteristically aggressive may be able to express passive aspects of their personalities, whereas individuals with passive character traits may experience increased assertiveness and even aggressiveness (Powers and Kutash, 1978). As in the case of cognitive distortions, however, the disinhibitive effects of alcohol under certain circumstances may lead to increased feelings of strain and even threat. For example, an individual's less restrained behavior while drinking may be offensive to others, which may lead to rejection and perhaps to verbal or physical abuse. An increase in strain and feelings of threat would likely result.

A second common motive for the use of alcohol at the Demand Stage of stress is the avoidance of strain. An individual may be coping adequately with demands but may be experiencing a great deal of strain. He may resort to increasingly frequent relief or "time-out" drinking episodes, which, as noted above, remove him from the stress situation and often provide him with desired euphoric or disinhibitory experiences. Drinking for temporary relief may progressively become drinking for prolonged relief, and then drinking for general avoidance of demands. A syndrome often develops wherein increased drinking creates new demands, as a spouse, for instance, begins complaining of absences from home or an employer begins complaining of impaired work performance. Anxiety may play an important, complex role in the syndrome. Anxiety frequently may act as a signal that the individual is not effectively dealing with his external demands, such as his wife's complaints, or internal demands, such as feelings of guilt. Anxiety thus may alert the individual to the need to devise new coping strategies or defenses. He may, for example, make elaborate excuses to his wife and employer and may deny or rationalize the reality of the behavior to himself. By mobilizing and maintaining such coping behaviors and defenses, the individual may reduce anxiety, but he may still experience considerable psychological strain. Drinking therefore may occur principally for the relief of strain, not for the reduction of anxiety. The increased frequency and duration of drinking episodes may lead to habituation to alcohol; then, with the appearance of withdrawal symptoms, habituation may well result in addiction.

Although alcohol is commonly used for stress relief and stress avoidance, only a minority of persons using alcohol become habituated or addicted. Many factors influence the development of excessive use and addiction. Biological factors, such as genetic strains, are associated with increased probability of alcoholism (Goodwin and others, 1977; Rodgers, 1966; Winokur and others, 1970). Cultural factors, such as ethnic customs and attitudes, may be influential, in that certain groups, such as the Chinese, have a disproportionally small number of alcoholics, while other groups, such as the Irish, have a disproportionally large number (Cahalan, Cisin, and Crossley, 1969; Chafetz and Demone, 1962; McCord, McCord, and Gudeman, 1960). Psychological factors also may have a role. Classical and operant conditioning, as well as behavioral modeling, have been associated with increased drinking (Bandura, 1969; Nathan and Lisman, 1976). Psychodynamic factors, such as overprotective and overindulgent parenting, may predispose individuals to excessive alcohol use (Knight, 1938; Wall and Allen, 1944).

It is unlikely that a single biological, cultural, or psychological factor will by itself explain why certain individuals become habituated and addicted and others do not. A multifactored approach is therefore needed in attempts to explain fully the development of alcohol abuse. Armor, Polich, and Stambul (1976), authors of the "Rand Report" on alcoholism, reach a similar conclusion. After a comprehensive review of theories of the etiology of alcoholism, they propose a multivariate approach for explaining the development of alcoholism. They present the following quotation from Plaut (1967) as a succinct summary of the multivariate perspective: "A tentative model may be developed for understanding the causes of problem drinking, even though the precise roles of the various factors have not yet been determined. An individual who (1) responds to beverage alcohol in a certain way, perhaps physiologically determined, by experiencing intense relief and relaxation, and who (2) has certain personality characteristics, such as difficulty in dealing with and overcoming depression, frustration, and anxiety, and who (3) is a member of a culture in which there is both pressure to drink and culturally induced guilt and confusion regarding what kinds of drinking behavior are appropriate, is more likely to develop trouble than will most other persons. An intermingling of certain factors may be necessary for the development of problem drinking, and the relative importance of the differential causal factors no doubt varies from one individual to another" (p. 21).

Drinking for the relief of stress is an important psychological factor in the development of alcoholism. Other psychological factors, as well as cultural and biological influences, may well be influential. It is beyond the scope of this chapter to describe in detail those other potential influences; however, several excellent reviews of those factors are available for reference (Bourne and Fox, 1973; Pattison, Sobell, and Sobell, 1977; Tarter and Sugerman, 1976).

Threat Stage. At the second stage of stress, the individual's coping mechanisms and defenses are inadequate to meet external or internal demands, and he may experience anxiety. Anxiety may have many different forms and functions, depending on the different stressors influencing the individual. A person may experience one form of anxiety in response to memories of stealing from a business partner, and he may have another form of anxiety in response to thoughts of a planned parachute jump.

The forms of anxiety experienced depend not only on different stressors influencing the individual but also on combined interactive effects of varied emotions resulting from those stressors. Just as an individual may experience multiple stressors in combination or in sequence, he may experience a variety of stress responses which have additive or multiplicative interactive effects. Emotionally, an individual may experience such affects as anxiety, excitement, and anger simultaneously or in close sequence. Izard (1977) provides an especially clear account of the composite and interactive effects of varied emotions. Anxiety, for example, may have fear-shame-guilt patterns, fear-distress-anger patterns, moderate fear-anger-interest patterns, and innumerable additional patterns.

At a given moment, the composite of emotions affecting a person may be termed an *emotional response manifold* (illustrated in Figure 2).

Figure 2. An Individual's Emotional Response Manifold

Note: See Figure 1.

The different forms of anxiety of the response manifold make the relationship between anxiety and alcohol use highly complex. Although individuals may take alcohol for some forms of anxiety, they may not take alcohol for other forms. An individual, for example, may drink to relieve feelings of anxiety from thoughts of his business dealings (fear-shame-guilt), but he may not drink to alter feelings of anxiety from thoughts of his impending parachute jump (fear-curiosity-excitement). Traditionally, researchers have failed to distinguish among forms of anxiety, tending to view all manifestations of anxiety as functionally the same. As a result, simplistic, global propositions—such as the proposition that individuals do take alcohol to relieve anxiety or that they do not take alcohol for that purpose—have often been advanced and tested. In research on anxiety and alcohol use, it is essential to distinguish clearly the particular forms of anxiety being evaluated. Conclusions should be restricted to just those anxiety forms being tested.

The effects of anxiety on drinking are highly varied. At times alcohol brings a reduction in anxiety in both nonalcoholics and alcoholics (Litman, 1974; Smith, Parker, and Noble, 1975; Vannicelli, 1972); at other times it brings no change or an increase in anxiety levels (McGuire, Stein, and Mendelson, 1966; Nathan and others, 1970; Tamerin and Mendelson, 1969; Vannicelli, 1972). In the semistructured clinical interviews described above, the highly variable effects of alcohol on anxiety were readily apparent. Alcohol's cognitive and disinhibitive effects may be effective in relieving certain forms of anxiety, but new anxiety forms may emerge. Whether drinking is effective in reducing anxiety or whether it leads to new stressors and new anxiety forms is dependent on a complex interaction of personality and environmental factors. Two case studies will be presented to illustrate the complex influences of personality and environment on the effects of alcohol use.

> *Case 1.* A nonalcoholic 26-year-old woman described the use of alcohol to relieve anxiety from inhibitions in talking with persons at social gatherings. She had attended a party where she knew only the host. As soon as she arrived, she had two drinks to make her feel "more relaxed and comfortable" in speaking with other guests. She first spoke with two female guests about mutual interests and felt at ease. Later, in speaking with a man who was attractive to her sexually, she began to feel moderately anxious. She had another drink; but then, as the conversation became more intimate, she became increasingly anxious. She began to experience an intense fear of rejection and then broke off the conversation and returned to discussions with other guests.

This case description illustrates several important considerations in the relationship between anxiety and alcohol use. Alcohol may relieve one stressor, such as inhibitions in talking with strangers, yet lead to the emergence of new stressors, such as the possibility of increased intimacy and ultimate rejection. Anxiety may be reduced at one point in time but increased at another. Personality and environmental factors play key roles in the changes in anxiety levels. An individual's personality needs, coping behaviors, and defenses can influence whether he approaches certain stressors, whether he manages them effectively, and whether they become sources of increased anxiety. An individual's changing environment is responsible for the introduction or elimination of potential stressors, such as the arrival or departure of persons of the opposite sex. The effects of alcohol on anxiety, therefore, are highly variable, depending on personality factors, the cognitive and disinhibitory effects of the alcohol, and environmental factors. Researchers have made numerous attempts to assess the effects of anxiety but typically have failed to account adequately for varying forms of anxiety and for influences of personality differences and changes in environment. In studies of drinking at experimental "parties," for instance, "objective" mood inventories, such as the Psychiatric Outpatient Mood Scale (Warren and Raynes, 1972) and the State Anxiety Scale (Holroyd, 1978), have been used. Such procedures may determine overall anxiety levels, but they overlook critical variations in forms and functions of anxiety. Anxiety levels may vary during drinking periods, and single assessments of anxiety may well overlook those variations, while multiple assessments may introduce new potential stressors, the reactive effects of the inventories themselves. Misleading conclusions as to whether alcohol increases or decreases anxiety may well result.

> *Case 2.* A 44-year-old male alcoholic who was a patient in a hospital detoxification program indicated that he had not drunk alcohol for four months prior to the three-week binge that ended in his seeking hospital admission. He had taken his first drink of the binge because he was anxious about a job interview and believed that two beers would "settle my nerves." The beers did help calm him, and he was successful in the job interview. Then he stopped for several more beers on the way home "to celebrate." His resumption of drinking created several new stressors, which increased his feelings of anxiousness. His wife and two children noticed his drinking immediately and berated him for it. He, too, felt a loss of self-worth, "felt less of a man," for his slip. By continuing to drink, he was able to "close out" his family's complaints and his negative feelings about himself. With increasing alcohol consumption, however, his performance at work suffered. He missed two days at work, and on the day before hospital admission he was fired from his job.

The second clinical case, like the first, illustrates that alcohol may be effective in relieving one stressor and one form of anxiety but may lead to other stressors and to additional anxiety. A syndrome may develop as an individual drinks to reduce or to avoid certain forms of anxiety and, in the process, creates new forms of anxiety. Continued drinking may progressively lead to habituation and, with the development of withdrawal symptoms, may lead to addiction.

Although a person may drink for many motives besides stress relief, such as power fantasies and sensation seeking, repeated use of alcohol for those other reasons may very well create new stressors. The individual may then drink for the relief of those new stressors, with the increased risk of developing a drinking syndrome that leads to habituation or to addiction.

Exhaustion Stage. At the third stage of stress, an individual's attempts to manage stressors through coping behaviors and defenses have failed, and he experiences feelings of helplessness. The emotion of helplessness, like that of anxiety, may take varied forms, depending on the nature of internal or external stressors influencing the individual and on his perception of those stressors. For example, in response to the physical decline of a loved one due to cancer, a person may experience one form of helplessness: sadness-anger-loneliness. After repeated failures to gain employment, he may feel a different form of helplessness: sadness-rejection-incompetence. An individual may drink to relieve one form of helplessness but not another. Drinking may provide relief from feelings of helplessness through cognitive distortions and disinhibition effects. Just as in the Demand and Threat Stages of stress, cognitive distortions may limit or alter an individual's perception of stressors. Disinhibition effects may "release" thoughts and emotions that counter or supersede thoughts and emotions contributing to feelings of helplessness. An individual, for instance, who feels helpless after repeated rejections on job interviews may drink to blunt cognitive awareness of his failures and also to "release" aggressive impulses, which counter his feelings of powerlessness.

Nonalcoholics as well as alcoholics use alcohol to relieve or to avoid feelings of helplessness (Blane, 1968; Sadava, Thistle, and Forsyth, 1978; Tokar and others, 1973). Whether alcohol is effective in alleviating feelings of helplessness is dependent on an interplay of pharmacological, personality, and environmental factors. If a stressor is highly potent, such as the death of a loved one, alcohol's cognitive and disinhibitory effects may only slightly alter the stressor's impact. If dosage levels are low or an individual has developed a high tolerance for alcohol's effects, the stressor's influence may again be only slightly altered. In efforts to attain levels of intoxication sufficient to overcome feelings of helplessness, and individual may resort to increased dosages or more frequent use. The increased use of alcohol may be effective in temporarily relieving feelings of helplessness. If positive changes in the stressors or in perceptions of the stressors also occur during the drinking period, such as "working through" the loss of a loved one, feelings of helplessness may more permanently be relieved. Frequently, however, little change occurs in the stressors during the drinking episode. Also, in many instances, the drinking creates new stressors, which lead to even greater feelings of helplessness. A syndrome may therefore develop as the individual increases the amount and frequency of his drinking in vain efforts to prolong the temporary effects of intoxication. The increased stressors created by the increased consumption lead to more intense and/or new feelings of helplessness, which, in turn, lead to continued drinking. Habituation to alcohol may thereby develop, and with the appearance of withdrawal symptoms, addiction may result.

In many cases, feelings of helplessness lead to or are combined with feelings of purposelessness or hopelessness. An individual may feel helpless in trying to manage stressors and therefore may also feel that there is no purpose in continued effort. Individuals experiencing both helplessness and purposelessness are particularly prone to excessive drinking and alcoholism. As Sadava, Thistle, and Forsyth (1978, p. 734) observe:

> Clinicians frequently encounter alcoholics who, after a period of abstinence, react to stress with a binge. Recalling their emotional state during stress, these alcoholics use expressions such as "I didn't give a damn about anything." Their decision to drink tends to be highly impulsive and not motivated by a "need" or "drive" to drink. The alcoholic may simply substitute "Why not?" for "Why?" That is, he may no longer see any purpose in abstinence or control. Thus, drinking may represent a loss of purpose rather than intentional escapism. . . . If repeated misuse of alcohol fails to provide relief, it also fails to provide an escape. The significant reduction in negative functions may represent a "Why not?" reaction, a loss of purposive behavior in response to stress. Thus, alcohol may be misused because the drinker feels helpless in responding to stress and helpless in controlling his drinking.

Feelings of purposelessness or hopelessness may in turn lead to the extreme response of suicidal thoughts and acts. Feelings of hopelessness, in particular, have been found to be a key determinant of suicidal intent in both nonalcoholics and alcoholics (Beck, Weissman, and Kovacs, 1976). Reviews of the literature indicate that from 7 to 21 percent of alcoholics eventually commit suicide, compared with 1 percent of the general population (Rushing, 1968). Excessive alcohol use is responsible for the heightened incidence of suicide in two primary ways. First, as noted above, syndromes may develop in which individuals drink to reduce feelings of helplessness. Suicide represents a desperate attempt at resolution of the syndrome and may reflect either a hopelessness or a self-punitiveness, an anger turned inward. Several theorists contend that alcoholism itself is a form of chronic self-destructive, suicidal behavior (Chodorkoff, 1964; Menninger, 1938; Palola, Dorpat, and Larson, 1962). Excessive alcohol use may also heighten the likelihood of suicide through the pharmacological effects of the drug. Disinhibition effects of alcohol increase the likelihood of impulsive actions, while cognitive effects impair judgments of the consequences of those actions. As Beck, Weissman, and Kovacs (1976, p. 73) point out: "Under the influence of alcohol, the typical suicide attempter tends to overcome his inhibitions and is more likely to be impulsive and his actions are likely to be more damaging than they would be if he were sober. Thus, the degree of lethality reflects not only his intent but the psychological and physiological effects of intoxication."

At each stage of stress, then, progressive increases in drinking may occur, leading to habituation and to addiction. At the Demand Stage, an individual may drink for the relief of strain but may create more intense or new sources of strain. At the Threat Stage, a person may drink for the relief of anxiety but may create more intense or new sources of anxiety. At the Exhaustion Stage, an individual may use alcohol to overcome feelings of helplessness but may engender more intense or new sources of helplessness. At each stage, habituation and addiction may develop as the individual increases amounts or frequency of use in efforts to extend temporary effects of the drug. In the last stage of stress, alcohol use may lead to the radical alternative of suicide as an ultimate attempt to gain relief from stressors.

Comment

The clinical data and theoretical perspectives presented above are contrary to the view of a number of current researchers that stress relief is not a salient factor in the use and abuse of alcohol. Typically, those researchers who discount the importance of stress relief present a limited view of stress. Often, for example, the idea of stress relief is formulated in terms of a tension reduction hypothesis (TRH). A succinct statement of the tension reduction hypothesis is put forth by Marlatt (1976, pp. 271-272): "Most research centering on the relationship between stress and drinking has involved an investigation of the validity of the so-called tension reduction hypothesis (TRH). Stated in its simplest form, the hypothesis assumes that alcohol serves to reduce tension and that the relief of tension reinforces the drinking response. An often-stated corollary of this hypothesis is that the experience of tension or stress will increase the probability of drinking."

Unfortunately, the researchers commonly use the terms *tension, stress,* and *anxiety* interchangeably. As Marlatt (1976, p. 177) notes, the terms used to define tension include "anxiety, stress, arousal, depression, lowered self-esteem, anger, and other dysphoric states." When the terms *tension, anxiety,* and *stress* are used interchangeably, the concept of stress relief being tested is often limited to anxiety reduction. Excluded from investigation are other forms or stages of stress (the Demand Stage and the Exhaustion Stage). Regrettably, therefore, researchers of the TRH commonly overlook important aspects of stress for investigation. It is recommended that future research on stress relief and alcohol take into account all three stages of stress: Demand, Threat, and Exhaustion.

In focusing on tension and anxiety, researchers of the TRH have observed that at times alcohol use will lead to an increase in anxiety, rather than to a decrease. Cappell (1975), for example, cites laboratory studies in which increased anxiety was manifested by subjects during drinking periods, despite the individuals' predrinking expectancies that alcohol use would relax them. This increased anxiety may in part be a result of the reactive effects of the laboratory settings. Williams (1976), Kalin, McClelland, and Kahn (1965), and others point out the artificiality of laboratory settings as a source of stress. Williams notes that "This type of experimental situation (laboratory or hospital setting, intravenous administration) is likely to be inhibiting and anxiety arousing. . . . Such an atmosphere is likely to inhibit any 'positive' emotional effects that may occur under more normal drinking conditions. One can only generalize to the particular situation being studied. Thus, if the interest is in why people drink, they should be allowed to drink as they normally do, in natural settings in which a choice of drinks is available for ad lib consumption" (p. 248).

In nonlaboratory settings also, alcohol use may at times be associated with increased anxiety. As noted in discussions of the three stages of stress, alcohol use may often introduce new sources of stress. Alcohol may be effective in reducing stress that leads to an initial drink but may engender numerous new stressors, such as guilt about resuming drinking. An individual may continue to drink in response to those new forms of stress, and a syndrome of stress relief drinking may develop, which eventually results in habituation and addiction. In future research, therefore, not only should the three stages of stress be taken into account but also the possible emergence of new stressors, through changes in the stressor manifold and/or the emotional response manifold.

Part IV

✳ ✳ ✳ ✳ ✳ ✳ ✳ ✳ ✳ ✳ ✳ ✳ ✳

The latest formulations in assessing, treating, and preventing stress and anxiety disorders are presented in this concluding section. Divergent major contemporary points of view are presented by experts who have utilized and researched them.

In the opening chapter, William W. K. Zung and Jesse O. Cavenar, Jr., deal with the assessment of anxiety and stress. They discuss anxiety tests, from the most subjective to the most objective, and cover in detail the Self-Rating Anxiety Scale (SAS) developed by Zung. They then review the relationship of stress to physical and emotional illnesses and describe the stress rating scales that arose out of this finding. The authors emphasize that while there is a relationship between life stress and the onset of both physical and emotional illness, the extent and mechanism of the influence remain unclear, and they urge more research leading to further refinement of assessment procedures.

Treatment of
Stress and
Anxiety Disorders

❉ ❉ ❉ ❉ ❉ ❉ ❉ ❉ ❉ ❉ ❉ ❉ ❉

In Chapter Twenty-One, Mardi J. Horowitz presents a short-term psychoanalytic approach to the treatment of stress response syndromes. The aim of such treatment is restoration of and, if possible, advance from the precrisis state of the individual. Since every person facing even the same event brings to the situation his or her individualistic history and personality —including disposition, self-image, role relationships, and strategies for coping and defending against intrapsychic conflict and interpersonal threats—working through responses to stressful events involves a consideration of individual styles in a brief psychodynamic manner that is individualized. Brief psychoanalytic therapy involves nuances related to individual style of processing information. Horowitz illustrates these nuances in his work with prototypical hysterical and obsessional cases.

Richard M. Suinn and Jerry L. Deffenbacher describe various behavioral approaches to treatment. In sharp contrast to the psychoanalytic approach, these approaches are based on the assumption that tensional response patterns can be altered by relearning and that relearning can occur through exposure to conditions for elimination of the anxiety or for acquisition of coping skills. That is, the individual does not need to confront historical origins; relearning can be derived from learning principles rather than from psychodynamic principles. The behavioral strategies for anxiety or phobias discussed here are densensitization; anxiety management training (AMT), originated by Suinn and Richardson (1971); modeling approaches to anxiety reduction; and cognitive-behavioral approaches. In conclusion, the authors stress the need for a careful diagnosis of the client's problem, the importance of examining the total gestalt that comprises the client's stresses, the importance of viewing therapy as training for real-life activities, the need for follow-up in therapy outcome evaluation, and the value of the self-control model to therapy.

In Chapter Twenty-Three, Thomas H. Budzynski and Kirk E. Peffer outline the program of biofeedback that they have successfully employed for the treatment of anxiety and stress disorders. They predicate their use of biofeedback on the assumption that the client shows evidence of maladaptive responding in one or more physiological systems. Therefore, they employ a standardized psychophysiological stress profile (PSP) as the second step after intake evaluation. They use the PSP to individualize their biofeedback training. Whether clients are taught cognitive, overt behavioral, environmental, or physiological procedures in the clinic, they must transfer or generalize to real-life situations. Consequently, the authors outline several transfer strategies, from systematic desensitization and other imagery procedures to more simple transfer procedures. For clients who require specialized training in recovery back to prestress levels, they describe recovery training procedures; for those who primarily feel loss of control in certain situations, they describe a flooding procedure. Finally, they emphasize the importance of daily practice at relaxation.

The psychopharmacological approach is discussed by Robert Hicks, Anna Okonek, and John M. Davis in Chapter Twenty-Four. They endeavor to show that pharmacological theory and treatment of anxiety are intertwined and that different types of anxiety may respond differently to different types of psychotropic agents. They present, first, a definitive classification system for the "anxiety syndrome" and, second, a description of physiological theories of etiology: the catecholamine theory, the lactate theory, the James-Lange versus Cannon-Bard theory, the beta-receptor theory, and other recognized theories. Using the classification and etiology as background, they then describe specific pharmacological regimes for specific types of anxiety, covering antipsychotic agents ("major tranquilizers"), sedative-hypnotics ("minor tranquilizers"), beta-blockers, antidepressants and lithium, and even CO_2 ("bag breathing"). They also cover drugs of abuse. They conclude this comprehensive chapter with the caution that proper medical management always includes exploration for possible causation and/or exacerbation of an anxiety state by psychological or social factors.

Miles E. Simpson deals with societal intervention and its role in states such as stress and anxiety. Simpson argues that if social institutions and social change are a primary source of anxiety and stress, then the society at large must be the level at which the ultimate reduction of stress and anxiety occurs. Simpson calls for the assessment of the input of several potential sources of stress, so that future intervention strategies can be directed at the source as well as at the symptoms. He points to recent research findings that social support—through, for example, family, friends, and therapy—is a key to reduction and even prevention of stress. The development of coping skills or styles through education is highlighted as a second and most effective preventive effort, while direct intervention through income maintenance is not viewed as a promising approach.

In the final selection, Irwin L. Kutash deals with prevention of anxiety within the context of his Equilibrium-Disequilibrium Theory. Kutash develops the point that prevention, in regard to stress and anxiety, is a misnomer and that the fostering of individually based optimal levels of stress should be the true focus of prevention of anxiety disorders. He describes the need for individuals to be aware of their intimacy, stimulation, fantasy, and sensation requirements and then to work toward adjusting these requirements to subjectively comfortable levels. Kutash also provides examples of the techniques available to help individuals understand and make these adjustments. From a global perspective, he recommends creation of a human environment that is conducive to levels of intimacy, stimulation, fantasy, and sensation that will meet the most needs, including efforts to solve such problems as overpopulation, malnutrition, pollution, and other quality-of-life factors.

20

Assessment Scales and Techniques

William W. K. Zung
Jesse O. Cavenar, Jr.

Assessment of Anxiety

The methods used to assess anxiety (that is, anxiety as a *state*, a generalized clinical disorder) can range from the most subjective to the most objective. The usual *subjective* approach is that of the clinical global impression, where values are assigned, such as from 1 to 7, based on an overall impression of the patient in an unstructured interview. Global ratings of anxiety by a clinician represent a combination of what he sees and hears and his interpretation of the patient's self-report. At another level, rating procedures could be all-inclusive and include anxiety as one of many measures in a *systematic* approach. An example of this approach is the Multiple Affect Adjective Checklist, which uses mood words that measure anxiety in addition to other moods (Zuckerman, 1960). Other rating devices use a *focused* approach and choose only one aspect of anxiety, such as fear (Walk, 1956). In the assessment of anxiety, nonspecific approaches, such as projective testing, have been used. *Semiobjective* rating scales have been developed in which specific cues for ratings of specific signs and symptoms are given as a guide to a trained interviewer. Examples of these are the Hamilton Anxiety Scale (Hamilton, 1959) and the Anxiety Status Inventory (Zung, 1971). *Objective* measurements—specific physiological measurements for the various organ systems of the body—include (1) the electroencephalogram (EEG), for the central nervous system; (2) the electrocardiogram (EKG), for the cardiovascular system; (3) measures of respiration rate and depth, for the respiratory system; (4) measures of stomach motility, and pH, for the gastrointestinal system; (5) measures of penile circumference in males and vaginal blood volume in females, for the genitourinary stystem; (6) the electromyogram (EMG), for the musculoskeletal system; (7) measures of skin potential response or palmar sweat response, for the skin.

Like other diagnostic labels used in medicine, *anxiety disorder* is a shorthand term that describes a complex set of signs and symptoms. Data from different aspects of anxiety—such as the affective-emotional, motor-behavioral, and physiological measures—do not correlate well with one another (Borkovec, Weerts, and Bernstein, 1977). Clearly, therefore, no one measure of anxiety can stand alone.

Cattell and Scheier (1961) surveyed test procedures for anxiety and reported that at least 120 specific measures had been developed as of 1961. McReynolds (1968) surveyed the available techniques for the assessment of anxiety as of 1967 and reviewed a total of 88 formal anxiety measurement procedures. DeBonis (1974) performed a systematic analysis of twenty-seven anxiety inventories and scales. A more recent review of the assessment of anxiety (Borkovec, Weerts, and Bernstein 1977) contains 191 references to rating instruments.

Anxiety rating scales are usually of two types. The self-rating scale is filled out by the patient; other scales are filled out by the examiner as he questions and listens to the patient. Some doctors do not think that the patient is capable of making valid judgments about himself. Other doctors think that only the patient can describe how he feels. Since anxiety is a disorder of feeling and not so much a disorder of thinking (such as schizophrenia), the anxious patient's comments about his feelings are usually more easily understood than an acute schizophrenic's interpretation of his delusions.

Self-rating scales have the following advantages:

1. They provide information that only the subject can provide.
2. They do not involve the use of trained personnel to administer.
3. They take a short time for the patient to complete.
4. They are easy to score.

Table 1. A Comparison of Symptoms Found in Anxiety Disorders as Reported by Various Authors.

	Kolb (1968)	Lief (1967)	Portnoy (1959)	Wheeler and others (1950)
AFFECTIVE SYMPTOMS	Apprehension, worried, inexpressible dread, painful uneasiness of mind	Apprehension, fearful, feeling of impending death, helplessness, mental disintegration	Apprehension, uneasiness, anticipation of danger, helplessness	Apprehension, Fear of death, Nervousness
SOMATIC SYMPTOMS *Musculoskeletal System*				
Tremor	Tremor	Muscle tightness, tremors, spasms, painful movements, headaches, neck and back pains	Increased tension, tremors, stiffness	Trembling, Shakiness
Tension headache	Tension headache	Weakness		Headache, Tires easily
	Weakness	Restlessness		Weakness
	Restlessness			Fatigued all the time
Cardiovascular System				
Palpitation	Palpitation, rapid heartbeat	Palpitation, throbbing pain in chest	Palpitation, rapid pulse, increased BP	Palpitation

Respiratory System Hyperventilation: dizziness, fainting, shortness of breath, feeling of choking, pressure on thorax, paresthesia	Dizziness, shortness of breath, constriction in chest, paresthesia	Rapid or irregular breathing	Dizziness Faintness Breathlessness Breath unsatisfactory Paresthesia
Gastrointestinal System Nausea and vomiting	Nausea, vomiting, diarrhea, anorexia	Nausea, vomiting, diarrhea	Vomiting and diarrhea Anorexia
Genitourinary System Increased desire to urinate	Urinary frequency, urgency	Urinary frequency	Urinary frequency
Skin Face flushed, perspiration	Flushing of face, sensation of heat	Flushing or pallor, cold, wet extremities	Flushing Sweating
Central Nervous System Mind in constant daze, absentminded	Lack of concentration, decreased memory, perceptual defects, irritability		
Difficulty in falling asleep, fearful dreams	Difficulty in falling asleep, fitful sleep, unpleasant dreams	Sleep disturbances	Insomnia Nightmares

5.   They provide objective data.
6.   They can be used as a separate measurement to document change over time.
7.   They can be used in any clinical setting, including mail returns by subjects.
8.   They are inexpensive.

Construction of The Self-Rating Anxiety Scale (SAS). In devising the Self-Rating Anxiety Scale (SAS), we selected diagnostic criteria in accordance with the most commonly found characteristics of an anxiety disorder, such as those listed in Table 1. Table 2 contains the diagnostic criteria (five affective and fifteen somatic symptoms) used to construct the Self-Rating Anxiety Scale (SAS).

For the purpose of constructing the SAS, illustrative verbatim records were made from patient interviews. The examples selected for inclusion were those that we considered most representative for the particular symptom. Table 3 is the actual form of the SAS as it is used and to be scored by the patient. It is based on the twenty diagnostic criteria listed in Table 2.

Table 2. The Operational Definition of an Anxiety Disorder.

Affective Symptoms of Anxiety
1. Anxiousness, nervousness
2. Fear
3. Panic
4. Mental disintegration
5. Apprehension

Somatic Symptoms of Anxiety	
6. Tremors	14. Paresthesia
7. Body aches and pains	15. Nausea and vomiting
8. Easy fatigability, weakness	16. Urinary frequency
	17. Sweating
9. Restlessness	18. Face flushing
10. Palpitation	19. Insomnia
11. Dizziness	20. Nightmares
12. Faintness	
13. Dyspnea	

So that the patient is less able to discern a trend in his answers, the scale was devised so that, of the twenty items used, some of the items were worded symptomatically positive and other symptomatically negative, depending on their suitability and usage. In addition, to eliminate the possibility of a patient's checking middle and extreme columns, an even number of columns was used.

In using the scale, the patient is asked to rate each of the twenty items by indicating how it applied to him within the past week: "None or a little of the time," Some of the time," "Good part of the time," or "Most or all of the time." The SAS is constructed so that the less anxious patient will have a low score on the scale, and the more anxious patient will have a higher score. In scoring the SAS, a value of 1, 2, 3, and 4 is assigned to a response, depending on whether the item was worded positively or negatively.

An index for the SAS was derived by dividing the sum of the values (raw scores) obtained on the twenty items by the maximum possible score of 80, converted to a decimal and multiplied by 100. Thus, an SAS index of 68 may be interpreted to mean that the patient has 68 percent of the anxiety measurable by the scale.

Validity and Reliability of the SAS. The validity of any rating instrument, that it measures what it is supposed to measure, can be determined by (1) expert opinions confirming that the signs and symptoms described in the scale represent a recognizable clinical condition; (2) demonstration that the results of the scale can distinguish patients with the disorder under consideration (in this case, anxiety disorders) and correlate with other scales which are conceded to be valid.

The first criterion was fulfilled when the scale was constructed on the basis of the available literature. The diagnostic criteria were not meant to be all-inclusive, and the scale does not encompass all schools of psychiatric orientation or all theories about anxiety. Rather, the list delineates the essential core symptoms. As for the second criterion, several studies performed by us have shown consistently that the SAS is able to discriminate patients with anxiety disorders from other diagnostic categories at a statistically significant level. A study was performed to demonstrate the correlation between the Hamilton Anxiety Scale (HAS) (Hamilton, 1959) and the Self-Rating Anxiety Scale. Results of this study, based on data obtained from over 500 separate HAS and SAS ratings, were analyzed, using the Pearson product-moment correlation for calculation of the coefficient r, which was .75 ($p<.01$).

The reliability of a scale, that it measures dependably the same each time and that it is free from random irrelevant sources of error, can be determined by (1) interrater reliability, which is not applicable to the self-rating version of the scale; (2) intercorrelation of items, by tests of internal consistency. Statistical analyses of the SAS results, using the alpha coefficient calculation for reliability analyses, indicate that the coefficient alpha had a value of .84, indicating highly reliable interval consistency for the profile measured.

Interpreting the SAS Results. Results from various studies have shown that there is usually some anxiety present in almost all the psychiatric disorders. Patients can have several diagnoses: low back pain *and* anxiety,

Table 3. The Self-Rating Anxiety Scale (SAS).

Name ——————————

Age —————— Sex ——————

Date ——————

	None OR A Little of the Time	Some of the Time	Good Part of the Time	Most OR All of the Time
1. I feel more nervous and anxious than usual				
2. I feel afraid for no reason at all				
3. I get upset easily or feel panicky				
4. I feel like I'm falling apart and going to pieces				
5. I feel that everything is all right and nothing bad will happen				
6. My arms and legs shake and tremble				
7. I am bothered by headaches, neck and back pains				
8. I feel weak and get tired easily				

9. I feel calm and can sit still easily				
10. I can feel my heart beating fast				
11. I am bothered by dizzy spells				
12. I have fainting spells or feel like it				
13. I can breathe in and out easily				
14. I get feelings of numbness and tingling in my fingers, toes				
15. I am bothered by stomachaches or indigestion				
16. I have to empty my bladder often				
17. My hands are usually dry and warm				
18. My face gets hot and blushes				
19. I fall asleep easily and get a good night's rest				
20. I have nightmares				

coronary heart disease *and* anxiety, depression *and* anxiety. Thus, for example, a patient with a primary diagnosis of coronary heart disease may also have an anxiety disorder and may need treatment for his anxiety in addition to treatment for his other condition. Combining results from several studies, the SAS Index can be interpreted as follows: below 45, within normal range, no anxiety present; 45-59, presence of minimal to moderate anxiety; 60-74, presence of marked to severe anxiety; 75 and over, presence of most extreme anxiety.

We have used the SAS in a number of studies. Table 4 provides a summary of our data. We are interested in developing baseline data for normal subjects (in order to answer the question "How normal is anxiety?") and for subjects with varying degrees of "risk," ranging from patients in a family practice setting, to patients with known cardiac disease, to psychiatric patients with and without diagnoses of anxiety disorders. Using the total data base available, we developed a morbidity cutoff score in order to establish the level at which individuals might be viewed as "well and not-sick" and "sick and not-well."

Several cross-national studies using the SAS have been reported, and their results are in basic agreement with those we have reported. Miao (1976) studied over 900 college students in Taiwan and reported a mean ± S.D. SAS index of 42.3 ± 8.3. Jegede (1977) reported a study performed in Nigeria, where the SAS was administered to 206 normal subjects and 142 psychiatric outpatients. The mean scores for these two groups were significantly different, and based on his study it was concluded that the SAS had sufficient reliability and construct validity to justify further use in Nigeria.

Since the publication of the initial description of the SAS (Zung, 1971), other authors have dealt with the issue of defining anxiety as a disorder. Feighner and associates in 1972 published diagnostic criteria for an anxiety neurosis. DeBonis in 1974 performed a systematic analysis of item content of twenty-seven anxiety inventories and scales. These included four rating scales specific for anxiety and filled out by the clinician, and twenty-three rating scales filled out by the subject as a self-rating scale. See Zung (1979) for a comparison of the SAS with these authors' work, as well as with the oldest and most often used interviewer-rating scale that is specific for an anxiety disorder—Hamilton (1959).

Inasmuch as we diagnose in medicine in order to treat, it is worth noting that the diagnostic criteria used by the Food and Drug Administration (1974) (in its guidelines for psychotropic drugs) when it investigates antianxiety agents are almost identical to the item contents of the SAS. The guidelines do omit sleep disturbances, insomnia, and nightmares found in anxiety states but have three items not found in the SAS: avoiding certain places and things, feeling keyed up, and dry mouth.

Application of the SAS. The SAS may not be used at all by some practitioners. But knowledge of it, and of rating scales in general, helps the practitioner to understand and interpret new findings about emotional disorders. For other practitioners, the SAS may be used at times as a simple reminder or checklist for recording impressions or observations about a patient during an interview.

The SAS also may be used in conducting studies. In drug studies, for example, the SAS has been used as part of the Standard Assessment System, a battery of rating scales included as a result of efforts among individual investigators, the pharmaceutical industry, the Psychopharmacology Research Branch of the National Institute of Mental Health, and the Biometric Laboratory of the George Washington University (Guy, 1976).

Last, the SAS could be used in the everyday practice of physicians, regardless of their specialty, to help them take the emotional pulse of their patients. Just as we take the vital signs of patients when we examine them, and obtain their blood pressure, temperature, pulse, and respiration rate, we could also take their emotional pulse by administering simple rating scales that measure their emotional status. Just as elevated blood pressure measurements would raise the index of suspicion for hypertension, such information would help each practitioner raise his or her index of suspicion for specific emotional disorders, such as anxiety.

Assessment of Stress

Stress and Illness. It has long been recognized that there is a relationship between major stressful events in a person's life and ill health. History provides multiple examples of this observation. One such situation was the study of the physical health of the population of London during the blitz of 1940-1941. Figures from sixteen London hospitals during the first two months of 1940 showed a significant increase in stomach and duodenal perforations secondary to peptic ulcer disease; this increase persisted throughout the blitz, and then the rate returned to normal following the cessation of the blitz in May 1941 (Stewart and de R. Winser, 1942; Spicer, Stewart, and de R. Winser, 1944). Other studies have demonstrated that events in the life of an expectant mother may influence the course of her pregnancy and delivery. Gorsuch and Key (1974) found significantly more complications of pregnancy and parturition in women who had experienced life changes in the six months prior to pregnancy than in women who had not experienced life changes. Dodge (1972) studied the life events in mothers of babies who developed pyloric stenosis; in contrast to the control group, these women had a history of recent family illnesses, marital difficulties, unemployment of the father, and bereavements during the last trimester of the pregnancy. Still other studies (Greene and Miller, 1958) have documented clusters of family life changes during the two years prior to the onset of leukemia in a child in the family. In young adults, Marx, Garrity, and Bowers (1975)

Table 4. Comparison of the Self-Rating Anxiety Scale (SAS) Indexes Among
Various Groups Tested, Using a Morbidity Cutoff SAS Index of 45.

Group	N	\multicolumn{2}{c	}{SAS Index}	\multicolumn{4}{c}{SAS Index}
		M	(S.D.)	44 & under N	(%)	45 & Over N	(%)
Normal Adults	196	34.4	(6.9)	178	(91)	18	(9)
Patients							
Family Practice	101	41.8	(9.7)	69	(68)	32	(32)
Cardiac Service	567	45.5	(9.8)	281	(50)	286	(50)
Psychiatry Service							
Not Anxiety Disorder	1,111	48.8	(12.7)	327	(29)	784	(71)
Anxiety Disorder	403	58.8	(11.9)	46	(11)	357	(89)
Outpatients	(351)	58.7	(11.6)				
Inpatients	(52)	59.8	(14.3)				

showed that students with the highest number of life changes reported the highest number of subsequent illnesses; students with moderate life changes developed only a moderate number of illnesses, while students with few life changes had the lowest illness rates.

Life stress and diseases of later adult life have been studied. Several reports have documented significant changes in the lives of persons during the six months prior to the development of cardiovascular disease and, at times, death. Adler, MacRitchie, and Engel (1971) have documented life changes and stress in the recent history of stroke patients. Other investigators (Theorell and Rahe, 1971; Rahe and Paasikivi, 1971; Rahe and Lind, 1971; Rahe, Bennett, and Romo, 1973; Rahe, Romo, and Bennett, 1974) have demonstrated a life-change accumulation as measured by stress rating scales developed by Holmes and Rahe (1967) in the six months prior to myocardial infarction in patients; the level reached nearly 100 percent higher than the patients' usual level of life-change events. Life-change event levels rose to between 200 and 300 percent above the usual level during the final six months of life for patients who experienced sudden death from their heart disease. DeFaire (1975) studied identical twins where only one died due to coronary artery disease; he found significantly higher life-change events over a four-year period for the twin who had died than for the twin who had survived. Still other reports, such as the study by Liberman (1961), suggest that the high death rate during the first year of persons entering nursing homes may be accounted for by the life changes incident to entering the home.

Life change and illness have been studied extensively in patients who develop psychiatric illness. Brown and Birley (1968) demonstrated significant life stresses in patients for a three-week period prior to the onset of acute schizophrenic symptomatology. They studied fifty patients, by interviews with both the patient and family, and found that personal, health, work, and other dramatic stresses were significantly greater in the patients than in 325 individuals from the general population. Jacobs and associates (Jacobs and Myers, 1976; Jacobs, Prusoff, and Paykel, 1974) studied the life-change events in patients prior to the onset of schizophrenia, compared to the life-change events prior to the onset of depression in other patients. Both the schizophrenics and the depressives were found to have undergone increased recent life-change events compared to the control groups; the depressed patients were found to have undergone a larger variety of undesirable events than did the schizophrenics. The authors concluded that the life-change events in the schizophrenics served a precipitating role in the illness, while the life-change events in the depressives had a more formative role in the depressive illness. Paykel, Prusoff, and Myers (1975) found that life-change events in hospitalized depressed patients were nearly twofold greater than the life-change events in a healthy control group, and that patients who had attempted suicide had experienced nearly four times more life-change events than the control group reported. In yet another study (Paykel, 1974a), patients at an outpatient psychiatric clinic reported a larger number of recent life-change events than controls did but fewer than those reported by hospitalized depressed patients. Those hospitalized inpatients who had attempted suicide had the most life-change events in the previous six months. Brown and associates (1973) compared 114 depressed women with a control group free of depression. The depressed women reported a fourfold increase in distressing life events over a nine-month period prior to the onset of depression, particularly during the three weeks before the depressive disorder was recognized. Thompson and Hendrie (1972) found that recent life-change events in patients who developed endogenous depression were equal to the life-change events in patients who developed reactive depression. Vinokur and Selzer (1975) studied both the desirable and undesirable life-change events in patients prior to the onset of depession. They noted that few positive life changes were found, and these showed little association with the depression. The study confirmed that undesirable life-change events were increased in patients prior to the onset of depression.

The relationship between life change and neurotic illness also has been studied. Cooper and Sylph (1973) matched thirty-four neurotic patients with thirty-four controls and reported that the neurotic patients experienced two times the life-change events that the controls reported in the three months prior to the onset of the neurosis. Tennant and Andrews (1978) also noted a significant correlation between recent life events and the onset of neurotic symptoms.

Several large epidemiological studies have been done. Myers, Lindenthal, and Pepper (1971) studied one adult in each of 938 households in New Haven, utilizing a questionnaire. The subjects were asked to report the number of life changes in the one year prior to the study. Six questions asked about depressive symptoms. The prevalence rates for individual life-change events, total events, and groups of events were highest in the respondents who were the most emotionally disturbed. Intermediate life-change rates were noted in those considered moderately impaired, and the lowest life change was reported in the healthiest respondents. This massive study was repeated two years later, utilizing 720 persons of the original sample (Myers, Lindenthal, and Pepper, 1972); the occurrence of new psychological difficulty over the two-year period was studied. When the amount of life change reported at the first interview was compared with the amount of life change reported at the second interview, persons showing increases in recent life-change levels—whether the changes were perceived as positive or negative—showed a decline in mental functioning.

Another large epidemiological study was done by Dohrenwend (1974), who studied a large, random sample of people to assess depressive symptoms and the effects of social class on the experiencing of life-change events. He found that the lower-class persons experienced more undesirable life changes than higher-class persons. A significant correlation was found between recent life changes and emotional disturbance.

These studies, by a widely divergent group of researchers throughout the world, clearly demonstrate that stress and life change are related in some manner to the onset of physical and psychiatric disease. However, all these studies are reporting on large groups of people. An in-depth, focused study of the individual patient is lacking.

Dynamically oriented psychiatrists and psychoanalysts had noted for many years that patients with similar characterological patterns tended to develop certain diseases after certain types of trauma. To evaluate these impressions, a study was undertaken at the Chicago Institute for Psychoanalysis (Alexander, French, and Pollock, 1968). Patients suffering from organic ailments—including bronchial asthma, rheumatoid arthritis, ulcerative colitis, essential hypertension, neurodermatitis, thyrotoxicosis, and peptic ulcer—were studied. The hypothesis postulated the coexistence of at least two categories of factors—a psychological and a preexisting organic factor. The research project was guided by three operational concepts. First, the psychodynamic constellation, or central intrapsychic conflict, together with the defenses against the conflict, was identified. Second, the onset situation, or the psychodynamic situation in which the patient found himself at the time the first symptoms developed, was explored. Third, it was necessary to postulate an x factor, because the same psychological pattern and even the corresponding onset situation may be present in patients who do not develop organic disease. The research design consisted of gathering data exclusive of organic-medical clues via interview, matching these psychological data with the disease formulations for the seven diseases, and arriving at a somatic diagnosis from the psychological material. The findings indicated that the psychoanalysts could identify the disease from a high of 51 percent of the time with arthritis patients to a low of 32 percent of the time for hypertension and peptic ulcer disease. However, it must be noted that these were patients who already had the psychosomatic disease in question, and, further, the x factor could not be discerned. Studies such as this have been criticized because the patients do have the disease when studied, so that their intrapsychic conflicts may be the result of regression induced by the illness. These conflicts may not necessarily be the conflicts that were present prior to the disease onset. Dynamic studies have also been criticized on the basis that the patient's verbal reaction to the life stress is studied, his thoughts, moods, and affects, instead of the life stress itself.

Stress Rating Scales. In the early 1960s, researchers developed scaling charts where typical life stresses or change events were weighed according to their assumed degree of significance for the average person (Holmes and Rahe, 1967). Various others lists of life-change items have appeared, such as that used by Dohrenwend, Krasnoff, and Askenasy (1978). Such lists of life events are designed to sample the crucial list of life adjustments rather than to cover all possible life events. As Fairbank and Hough (1979) note, nearly all lists contain five categories of events. First, there are items or events which are confounded with the psychiatric condition of the individual and for which the person may himself be responsible: events reflecting outstanding personal achievement, events reflecting inferior functioning, and events which may per se be symptoms of psychiatric illness. A fourth category of events consists of items referring to the health of the person. A fifth category consists of events outside the control of the person—for example, the death of a spouse or friend, retirement, and other items which are assumed to be equally distressing; it is this category that is most often utilized when life-change events and illness onset are studied.

All life-event scales measure only a horizontal cross section of a person's life stress and do not measure the long-standing, chronic difficulties which the person may experience. Whether the person may have significant object-relationship difficulties due to an intrapsychic conflict or personality disorder is not apparent; only the immediate result—that is, divorce or job loss—is scaled if such has occurred within a limited time. Another difficulty with the life-events scaling technique is that it does not address the group of people who have had significant life events take place and who nevertheless do not fall ill. In an attempt to clarify why some persons may fall ill, where others do not, as a result of life stresses, Rahe and Arthur (1978) have described a schema in which the person's perception of the life-change event, his psychological defenses, psychophysiological response, response management, illness behavior, and illness measurements are considered.

Most of the life-event scales that have been utilized in epidemiological studies have attempted to quantitatively deal with the most meaningful and/or significant changes in a person's life, and with most of the scales, events have been conceptualized as positive or negative in their impact on the individual. There is marked difficulty in attempting to quantitatively determine whether any single event or series of events in an individual's life may be positive or negative; many times the true significance to the individual can be determined only through careful clinical investigation. Cavenar and Werman (in press) have described persons who fall ill with a neurotic illness at the time of their greatest achievements, because of the unconscious meaning of their success. Similarly, although most people conceptualize the birth of a child as a satisfying, pleasant experience, for some persons it is not. Cavenar and Butts (1977) found that some men have great psychological turmoil on the basis of feeling sibling rivalry due to the birth of a child. Cavenar and Weddington (1978) reported on men who experienced abdominal pain during their wives' pregnancy, only to experience a cessation of the pain following the birth of the child; with the relief of the physical pain, each man experienced a psychosis. Clearly, scaling an event as positive or negative may be impossible. Thus, some investigators have attempted to scale only the degree of life change without regard to whether it may be positive or negative.

At a recent conference entitled "The Crisis in Stress Research: A Critical Reappraisal," reported by Rose and Levin (1979), many of the current problems in assessing and measuring stress were summarized. Those attending the conference generally agreed that there is a relationship between life stress and the onset of disease but that the relationship is not precise and is, at times, difficult to demonstrate and quantitate. The central problem noted was the difficulty in making adequate psychological assessments of the persons being studied. The controversy between the psychoanalytic method and the psychometric and epidemiological approaches was again discussed. Several participants noted that the psychoanalytic method seems to offer both the greatest explanatory and predictive capabilities; others suggested that it is difficult to make such observations objective and to quantitate them. It was suggested that if the relevant psychological variables—such as emotions, psychological defenses, and coping abilities—could be better understood, it might be possible to psychometrically measure and quantitate them. Further, the conference noted that research questions must be posed so that the predisposing, precipitating, and disease-sustaining factors can be studied separately. Little evidence was noted for psychological characteristics or attributes that predispose to particular illnesses; the general view was that psychological characteristics may provide a general, not a specific, vulnerability to illness. The conference again noted the problems inherent in studying psychological process after disease onset; it is impossible to determine whether the processes contributed to the illness or whether they represent a regression because of the illness. Only well-designed, prospective, longitudinal studies can answer such questions. Finally, the participants agreed that we do not yet understand the mechanism by which a nonphysical stimulus, such as a feeling state, produces a physiological event in the brain. Such understanding will come only from further studies of neural and endocrine functions.

This appears to be the state of the art of assessing and measuring stress at the present time. It seems clear that there is a relationship between life stress and the onset of both physical and emotional illness, but the extent and mechanism of the influence are unclear. There are multiple problems with both the psychodynamics and epidemiological methods of studying the stress for the reasons noted. Only through further research will the dilemma be resolved.

21

Psychoanalytic Therapy

Mardi J. Horowitz

✳ ✳ ✳ ✳ ✳ ✳ ✳ ✳ ✳ ✳ ✳ ✳ ✳

Serious life events, such as the loss of a loved one or a personal injury, can shatter a person's reality. Inner models of the world that have sustained the person must now be changed to accord with the new situation. Such revisions of mental models take time. But some persons are greatly upset during this time; others ward off the assimilative process to such a degree

Note: Research on which this chapter is based has been funded by NIMH Research Grants including a Clinical Research Center grant (MH30899). The chapter is reprinted, in part, from a paper published in the Archives of General Psychiatry (1974) and in part, on a lecture upon receipt of the Strecker Award of the Institute of the Pennsylvania Hospital (1977). The author is indebted to his colleagues at the Center for the Study of Neuroses, especially Nancy Wilner, Nancy Kaltreider, and Robert Wallerstein, who participated in initiation of the work on brief therapy; and Emanual Windholz, who collaborated on work on character variation.

that they impair their future. In such instances, brief therapy aimed at resolution of the stress response syndrome is indicated.

At a broad level of generalization, the principles of such brief therapy are clear. The aim is restoration of, and if possible advance from, the pre-crisis state of the person. Sifneos (1972), Mann (1973), Malan (1976), and earlier pioneers such as Alexander, French, Caplan, and Wolberg have described the techniques of such brief focus-oriented interventions. After a serious life event, the goal is acceptance and maximum adaptation to changed circumstances. But as we go beyond general principles and theories of stress response, the issue gets more complex. Every person brings to any serious life event, no matter how prototypical that event is, his or her own history and existential moment. Working through responses to a particular life event in the context of a brief, individual, psychodynamic psychotherapy means that the therapist will have to deal with individual styles of absorbing new information. Therapy, in general, may involve establishment of a therapeutic alliance, clarification of patterns, interpretation of conflicts, confrontation with the need to make new decisions, and learning and practicing useful changes. But the nuances of these processes will vary as individuals vary in style.

My goal in what follows is to interweave, for stress response syndromes and brief therapy for these conditions, both *general response tendencies* and the more *common variation* on these tendencies. My method in this essay will be somewhat unusual to clinical description, but it is common in musical compositions as the theme with variations. I will use the device of a fictitious but true-to-life case history. This device will allow me, for discussion purposes, to keep the life event and the core conflicts of the person constant while I deal with the dispositional variables. In that way, I can contrast the *nuances of brief therapy* of stress response syndromes with persons of hysterical, obsessional, and narcissistic styles.

These assertions, while put in a fictional construction here, are drawn from experience in developing, at the University of California's Langley Porter Neuropsychiatric Institute, a special clinic for the brief therapy of stress response syndromes. Over the last six years, we have studied over one hundred cases. Persons with varied personality styles have been seen, allowing some redundancy in observed patterns in the more hysterical, obsessional, and narcissistic personality patterns.

In a much smaller number of persons seen in psychoanalysis, I have had the opportunity to study the information-processing style used by various personality types as they encounter and work through stress events arising during the course of their years of treatment. In addition, nonpatient subjects have been studied as they elaborated their responses to vicariously experienced stress events presented on films. These varied contexts of investigation have allowed repetitive observations, guided by the body of previously established clinical psychoanalytic theories. My statements about nuances of technique for different character styles must, however, be taken as a quite preliminary effort, in need of many critical tests.

Rationale for Choices

State: Stress Response Syndromes. Stress response syndromes have been chosen because the general symptomatic tendencies are well documented, observed across various populations, and usually change rapidly during psychotherapy. Serious life events such as bereavements or accidents are usually clear and provide the therapist with a point of reference for consideration of other material.

Disposition: Hysterical and Obsessional Neurotic Styles. "Obsessional" and "hysterical" styles are important typologies in dynamic psychology. Theorization about these styles is at the same level of abstraction as theories of stress, in that both stress response syndromes and neurotic styles have been described in terms of potentially conscious ideational and emotional processes. Information-processing theory will thus provide a useful language.

Technique: Crisis-Oriented Psychodynamic Therapy. The goals of psychotherapy are infinite. Here they will be limited to conceptual and emotional working through of the stress response syndrome to a point of relative mastery, a state in which both denial and compulsive repetition are reduced or absent. I will focus on nuances of technique such as repetition, clarification, and interpretation, since these maneuvers are on an information-processing level of abstraction. I will also deal with the relationship between patient and therapist, but the focus will be on the therapeutic alliance; the complexities of transference and resistance will be touched on but not discussed in detail.

The Natural Course of Stress Response Syndromes

Multiple meanings confound the use of the word *stress*. In psychiatry, the central application is concerned with how a serious life event, or even a change in internal events (for example, a bad dream or emergent conflicted impulses), sets up a discrepancy between current actual states of the person and desired states of relative homeostasis. Serious life events and triggered internal responses combine to produce potentially disruptive quantities or qualities of information and energy. An example of a serious life event that leads to states of stress is a sudden highway accident and its consequences. Elaboration of this example will be used to provide a concrete reference.

First, however, some reminders set the stage. Freud and Breuer (1895) found that traumatic events are repressed and yet involuntarily repeated in the form of hysterical symptoms. While some "reminiscences" of their hysterical patients stemmed more from fantasy than from reality, the central observation of compulsive repetition of trauma was validated in many later clinical, field, and experimental studies (Grinker and Spiegel, 1945; Horowitz and Becker, 1972). A second common set of stress responses includes ideational denial and emotional numbing. These signs seem antithetical to intrusive repetitions and are regarded as a defensive response (Hamburg and Adams, 1967; Horowitz, 1973). Tendencies to both intrusive repetition and denial-numbing occur in populations that vary in predisposition, after stressful events that vary in intensity and quality, and may occur simultaneously in a given person or in patterns of phasic alterations.

There is a common pattern to the progression of phases of stress response. With the onset of a stress event, especially if it is sudden and unanticipated, there may be emotional reactions such as crying out or a stunned uncomprehending daze. After these first emotional reactions and physical responses, there may be a period of comparative denial and numbing. Then an oscillatory period commonly emerges, in which there are episodes of intrusive ideas or images, attacks of emotion, or compulsive behaviors alternating with continued denial, numbing, and other indications of efforts to ward off the implications of the new information. Finally, a phase of "working through" may occur, in which there are less intrusive thoughts and less uncontrolled attacks of emotion and greater recognition, conceptualization, stability of mood, and acceptance of the meanings of the event (Bowlby and Parkes, 1970; Horowitz, 1973).

Theory of Psychic Trauma

Freud's theories about trauma have two important aspects: the neurotic and the energic definitions of traumatization. In early theory, a traumatic event was defined as such because it was followed by neurotic symptoms. To avoid circularity, a theoretical explanation of traumatization was necessary. The energic explanation defined as traumatic those events that lead to excessive incursions of stimuli. In a series of energy metaphors, stimuli from the outer world were postulated to exceed a "stimulus barrier" or "protective shield." The ego tries to restore homeostasis by "discharging," "binding," or "abreacting" the energy. Energy, instinctual drives, and emotions were often conceptually blended together in this model.

While Freud repeated energy metaphors throughout his writings, he also conceptualized trauma in cognitive terms more compatible with contemporary psychodynamic models. As early as 1893, in his lecture "On the Psychical Mechanism of Hysterical Phenomena," he said that one can deal with the affect of a psychic trauma by working the trauma over associatively and producing contrasting ideas.

The concept of information overload can be substituted for excitation or energy overload (Appelgarth, 1971; Peterfreund, 1971). Information applies to ideas of inner and outer origin as well as to affects. The persons remain in a state of stress or are vulnerable to recurrent states of stress until this information is processed. It is the information that is both repressed and compulsively repeated until processing is relatively complete. Emotions, which play an important part in stress response syndromes, are seen not as drive or excitation derivatives but as responses to ideational incongruities and as motives for defense, control, and coping behavior. This view of the centrality of ideational processing is consistent with French's (1952) conceptualization of integrative fields, and the concept of emotion and ideational incongruities is concordant with cognitive formulations of emotion (Lazarus, Averill, and Opton, 1970) and cognitive-neurophysiological formulations (Pribram, 1967).

Prototypical Example

These generalizations will be given concrete reference in the form of a story. The story is intended as a prototype and will be elaborated in various ways as an exercise. That is, the story will allow a hypothetical constancy of events and problems but a variation in personality style. We shall imagine this story as if it happened to two persons—one with a hysterical neurotic style, the other with an obsessional style. Thus, similar response tendencies to the same stress event can be contrasted in terms of stylistic variations and the nuances of treatment applicable to these variations.

Harry is a 40-year-old truck dispatcher. He had worked his way up in a small trucking firm. One night he himself took a run because he was short-handed. The load was steel pipes carried in an old truck. The improper vehicle had armor between the load bed and the driver's side of the forward compartment but did not fully protect the passenger's side.

Late at night Harry passed an attractive and solitary girl hitch-hiking on a lonely stretch of highway. Making an impulsive decision to violate the company rule against passengers of any sort, he picked her up on the grounds that she was a hippie who did not know any better and might be raped.

A short time later, a car veered across the divider line and entered his lane, threatening a head-on collision. He pulled over to the shoulder of the road into an initially clear area, but crashed abruptly into a pile of gravel. The pipes shifted, penetrated the cab of the truck on the passenger's side, and impaled the girl. Harry crashed into the steering wheel and windshield and was briefly unconscious. He regained consciousness and was met with the grisly sight of his dead companion.

The highway patrol found no identification on the girl, the other car had driven on, and Harry was taken by ambulance to a hospital emergency room. No fractures were found, his lacerations were sutured, and he remained overnight for observation. His wife, who sat with him, found him anxious and dazed that night, talking episodically of the events in a fragmentary and incoherent way, so that the story was not clear.

The next day he was released. Against his doctor's recommendations for rest and his wife's wishes, he returned to work. From then on, for several days, he continued his regular work as if nothing had happened. There was an immediate session with his superiors and with legal advisers. The result was that he was reprimanded for breaking the rule about passengers but also reassured that, otherwise, the accident was not his fault and he would not be held responsible. As it happened, the no-passenger rule was frequently breached by other drivers, and this was well known throughout the group.

During this phase of relative denial and numbing, Harry thought about the accident from time to time but was surprised to find how little emotional effect it seemed to have. He was responsible and well ordered in his work, but his wife reported that he thrashed around in his sleep, ground his teeth, and seemed more tense and irritable than usual.

Four weeks after the accident, he had a nightmare in which mangled bodies appeared. He awoke in an anxiety attack. Throughout the following days, he had recurrent, intense, and intrusive images of the girl's body. These images, together with ruminations about the girl, were accompanied by anxiety attacks of growing severity. He developed a phobia about driving to and from work. His regular habits of weekend drinking increased to nightly use of growing quantities of alcohol. He had temper outbursts over minor frustrations and experienced difficulty concentrating at work and even while watching television.

Harry tried unsuccessfully to dispel his ruminations about feeling guilty for the accident. Worried over Harry's complaints of insomnia, irritability, and increased alcohol consumption, his doctor referred him for psychiatric treatment. This phase illustrates the period of compulsive repetition in waking and dreaming thought and emotion.

Harry was initially resistant, in psychiatric evaluation, to reporting the details of the accident. This resistance subsided relatively quickly, and he reported recurrent intrusive images of the girl's body. During the subsequent course of psychotherapy, Harry worked through several complexes of ideas and feelings linked associatively to the accident and his intrusive images. The emergent conflictual themes included guilt over causing the girl's death, guilt over the sexual ideas he had fantasied about her before the accident, guilt that he felt glad to be alive when she had died, and fear and anger that he had been involved in an accident and her death. To a mild extent, there was also a magical or primary process belief that the girl "caused" the accident by her hitchhiking, and associated anger with her, which then fed back into his various guilt feelings.

Before we discuss in more detail the conflicts triggered by the accident, it is helpful to consider, at a theoretical level, the ideal route of conceptualization that Harry should follow. To reach a point of adaptation to this disaster, Harry should perceive the event correctly; translate these perceptions into clear meanings; relate these meanings to his enduring attitudes; decide on appropriate actions; and revise his memory, attitude, and belief systems to fit this new development in his life. During this information processing, Harry should not ward off implications of the event or relevant associations to the event. To do so would impair his capacity to understand and adapt to new realities.

Human thought does not follow this ideal course. The accident has many meanings sharply incongruent with Harry's previous world picture. The threat to himself, the possibility that he has done harm, the horrors of death and injury, and the fear of accusation by others seriously differ from his wishes for personal integrity, his current self-images, and his view of his life role. This dichotomy between new and old concepts arouses strong painful emotions that threaten to flood his awareness. To avoid such unbearable feelings, Harry limited the processes of elaborating both "real" and "fantasy" meanings of the stressful event.

Because of complex meanings and defensive motives that impede conceptualization, the traumatic perceptions are not rapidly processed and integrated. They are stored because they are too important to forget. The storage is in an active form of memory that, hypothetically, has a tendency toward repeated representation. This tendency triggers involuntary recollections until processing is completed. On completion, the stored images are erased from active memory (Horowitz, 1976; Horowitz and Becker, 1972). (This memory is called "active" rather than "short term" because of the extended duration of intrusive repetitions of stress-related perceptions.) The repetitions, however intrusive, can be adaptive when they provoke resumption of processing. They can be maladaptive when they distract from other tasks, elicit painful emotions, evoke fear of loss of mental control, and motivate pathological defenses.

Defensive operations that oppose repetition can also be adaptive, because they allow gradual assimilation rather than overwhelming recognition. Defense maneuvers can be maladaptive if they prevent assimilation, lead to unrealistic appraisals, perpetuate the stress response symptoms, or lead to other problems, such as Harry's alcoholism.

The six problematic themes of Harry's psychotherapy can now be reconsidered as ideational-emotional structures in schematic form. These themes will provide a concrete referent during the ensuing discussion of character-style variations. In Table 1, each theme is represented as a match

Table 1. Themes Activated by the Accident.

	Current Concept	Incongruous "Enduring" Concept	Emotion
A.	Self as "aggressor"		
	1. Relief that she and not he was the victim	Social morality	Guilt
	2. Aggressive ideas about girl	Social morality	Guilt
	3. Sexual ideas about girl	Social morality	Guilt
B.	Self as "victim"		
	1. Damage to her body could have happened to him	Invulnerable self	Fear
	2. He broke rules	Responsibility to company	Fear (of accusations)
	3. She instigated the situation by hitchhiking	He is innocent of any badness; the fault is outside	Anger

between a current concept and enduring concepts. Since there is an incongruity between the new and the old, the elicited emotion is also listed.

Three themes cluster under the general idea that Harry sees himself as an aggressor and the girl as a victim. For example, he felt relief that he was alive when someone "had to die." The recollection of this idea elicited guilt because it is discrepant with social morality. He also felt as if he were the aggressor who caused a victim to die because of his wish to live—a primitive concept that someone has to die and a belief in the magical power of his thought. Similarly, his sexual ideas about the girl before the crash were recalled and were incongruent with his sense of sexual morality and marital fidelity. All three themes are associated with guilty feelings.

Three other themes center around an opposite conceptualization of himself, this time as a victim. Harry is appalled by the damage to the girl's body. It means that his body could also be damaged. This forceful idea interferes with his usual denial of personal vulnerability and is inconsistent with wishes for invulnerability. The result is fear. Harry also conceives of himself as a victim when he recalls that he broke company rules by picking up a passenger. Since the breach resulted in a disaster, and is discrepant with his sense of what the company wants, he believes that accusations would be justified and is frightened. "Harrys" with varying character styles would experience this same theme in different ways. A Harry with a paranoid style might project the accusation theme and suspect that others are now accusing him. He might use such externalizations to make himself feel enraged rather than guilty. If Harry had a hysterical style, he might have uncontrolled experiences of dread or anxiety without clear representation of the instigating ideas. Were he obsessional, Harry might ruminate about the rules, about whether they were right or wrong, whether he had or had not done his duty, about what he ought to do next, and on and on.

The last theme cited in Table 1 places Harry as a victim of the girl's aggression. His current ideas are that she made the disaster happen by appearing on the highway. This matches with his enduring concept of personal innocence in a way that evokes anger. These angry feelings are then represented as a current concept, and responses to these concepts again transform Harry's state. His felt experience of anger and his concept of the girl as aggressor do not mesh with his sense of reality. The accident was not her fault, and so, as the ideas change, his emotional experience (or potential emotional experience) changes. He feels guilty for having irrational and hostile thoughts about her. With his switch from the feelings of victim to the feelings of aggressor, there is a change in emotions from anger to guilt and, as shown in Table 1, in state from B3 to A2.

All six themes might be activated by the accident. In "Harrys" of different neurotic character styles, some themes might be more important or conflictual than others. In a hysterical Harry, sexual guilt themes (A3) might predominate. In an obsessional Harry, aggression-guilt (A2), concern for duty (B2), and "self as an innocent victim" (B3) themes might predominate. Other themes, such as fear of body vulnerability (B1) and guilt over being a survivor (A1), seem to occur universally (Furst, 1967; Lifton, 1967).

Harry had a period in which there was relative denial and numbness for all the themes. Later, at various times after the accident, some themes were repressed and others emerged; eventually some were worked through, so that they no longer aroused intense emotion or motivated defensive efforts. The first emergent themes were triggered by the nightmare of mangled bodies and the daytime recurrent unbidden images of the girl's body. The themes of bodily injury and survivor guilt (A1 and B1) were no longer completely warded off but, rather, occurred in an oscillatory fashion, with periods of both intrusion and relatively successful inhibition. In psychotherapy, these intrusive themes require first attention. The other themes, such as sexual guilt, emerged later.

General Stratagems of Treatment
for Stress Response Syndromes

At least two vectors affect stress response syndromes: the tendencies to repeated representation and the tendencies to inhibited representation to prevent disruptive emotions. The general rationale of treatment is to prevent either extreme denial, which might impede conceptual and emotional processing, or extreme intrusive-repetitiousness, which might cause panic states or secondary avoidance maneuvers. Various "schools" of therapy have evolved techniques for counteracting extremes of denial or repetitious states, and these are tabulated in Table 2.

Table 2. Classification of Treatments for Stress Response Syndromes.

| Systems | *States* | |
	Denial-Numbing Phase	*Intrusive-Repetitive Phase*

Change controlling processes	Reduce controls
	  Interpretation
	  of defenses
	  Hypnosis and
	  narcohypnosis
	  Suggestion
	  Social pressure and
	  evocative situations
	  (for example,
	  psychodrama)
	Change attitudes
	  that make con-
	  trols necessary
	Uncover inter-
	  pretations
		Supply controls externally
		  Structure time and events
		  for patient
		  Take over ego functions
		  (for example, organize
		  information)
		Reduce external demands
		and stimulus levels
		Rest
		Provide identification models,
		group membership, good
		leadership, orienting values
		Behavior modification with
		reward and punishment

Change information processing	Encourage abreaction
	Encourage:
	  Association
	  Speech
	  Use of images
	  rather than
	  just words in
	  recollection and
	  fantasy
	  Enactments
	  (role playing,
	  psychodramas,
	  art therapy)
	  Reconstructions
	  (to prime memory
	  and associations)
	  Maintenance of
	  environmental
	  reminders
		Work through and reorganize
		by clarifying and educative
		interpretive work
		Reinforce contrasting ideas
		(simple occupational therapy,
		moral persuasion)
		Remove environmental
		reminders and triggers
		Suppress or dissociate
		thinking (sedation,
		tranquilizers, mediation)

Change emotional processing	Encourage catharsis Supply objects and encourage emotional relation- ships (to counter- act numbness)	Support Evoke other emotions (benevolent environment) Suppress emotion (sedation or tranquilizers) Use desensitization procedures Encourage relaxation and provide biofeedback

Once extreme symptoms are reduced, the task is to bring stress-related information to a point of completion. This "completion" can be defined, at the theoretical level, as a reduction of the discrepancy between current concepts and enduring schemata. The crucial feature is not discharge of pent-up excitation, as suggested by the terms *abreaction* and *catharsis*, but processing of ideas. To complete the response cycle, either new information must be reappraised or previous concepts must be modified to fit an altered life. Emotional responses will occur during this process when conflicts of meanings are fully considered.

Investigation, in focal psychodynamic treatment, includes examination of conflicts present before and heightened by the immediate situation, as well as the loaded meanings given to stressful events because of prior development experiences and fantasies. Conscious representation is encouraged because it promotes the solving of problems not resolved by automatic, out-of-awareness thought or dreaming. The communicative situation encourages representation and reexamination, and techniques of repetition, clarification, and interpretation enhance the ongoing process (Bibring, 1954).

The state of stress imposed by a particular life event may impose a general regression, in which developmentally primitive adaptive patterns will be noted, latent conflicts will be activated and more apparent, and increased demand for parental objects will affect all interpersonal relationships. These general regressive signs will subside without specific therapeutic attention if the state of stress is reduced by working through the personal meanings of the particular life event.

The problem in therapy is to provide tolerable doses of awareness, because knowledge of the discrepancies between desire and reality leads to painful emotional responses. On his own, the patient has warded off such knowledge to avoid pain and uncertainty. In therapy, while the affective responses are painful, they are held within bearable limits because the therapeutic relationship increases the patient's sense of safety (Peterfreund, 1971). In addition, the therapist actively and selectively counters defensive operations by various kinds of intervention. These interventions are, most commonly, clarification and interpretation of specific memories, fantasies, and impulse-defense configurations.

The aim of these techniques is completion of ideational and emotional processing and, hence, resolution of stress state rather than extensive modification of character. However, persons of different character structure will manifest different types of defenses, resistances, and therapeutic alliances and transferences during this process. The general techniques will be used with various nuances, depending on these dispositional qualities of the patient. As illustration, hysterical and obsessional variations on these general themes will be considered.

Hysterical Style in Response to Stress

The concept of hysterical character was developed in the context of psychoanalytic studies of hysterical neuroses, even though these neuroses may occur in persons without hysterical character and persons with hysterical styles do not necessarily develop hysterical neurotic symptoms, even under stress. The discussion will briefly develop the "ideal" typology of hysterical style, with the assumption that most persons will have only some of the traits and no person will fit the stereotype perfectly.

The main symptoms of hysterical neuroses are either conversion reactions or dissociative episodes (Janet, 1907). Both symptom sets have been related to dynamically powerful but repressed ideas and emotions that would be intolerable if they gained conscious expression (Freud, 1893; Freud and Breuer, 1895). In classical analytic theory, the intolerable idea is a wish for a symbolically incestuous love object. The desire is discrepant with moral standards and so elicits guilt and fear. To avoid these emotions, the ideational and emotional cluster is warded off from awareness by repression and denial. Because the forbidden ideas and feelings press for expression, there are continuous threats, occasional symbolic or direct breakthroughs, and a propensity for traumatization by relevant external situations. While later theorists have added the importance of strivings for dependency and attention ("oral" needs), rage over the frustration of these desires, and the fusion of these strivings with erotic meanings, the correlation of hysterical symptoms with efforts at repression has been unquestioned (Easser and Lesser, 1965; Ludwig, 1972a).

Psychoanalysts view hysterical character as a configuration that either predisposes toward the development of conversion reactions, anxiety attacks, and dissociative episodes or exists as a separate entity with similar impulse-defense configurations but different behavioral manifestations. The hysterical character is viewed as typically histrionic, exhibitionistic, labile in mood, and prone to act out.

Clinical studies suggest that hysterical persons, because of their proclivity for acting out oedipal fantasies, are more than usually susceptible to stress response syndromes after seductions, especially those that are sadomasochistic; after a loss of persons or of positions that provided direct or symbolic attention or love; after a loss or disfigurement of body parts or attributes used to attract others; and after events associated with guilt about personal activity. In addition, any event that activates strong emotions, such as erotic excitement, anger, anxiety, guilt, or shame, would be more than usually stressful, even though a hysteric might precipitate such experiences by his behavior patterns.

Clinical studies also indicate that, under stress, the prototypical hysteric becomes emotional, impulsive, unstable, histrionic, and possibly disturbed in motor, perceptual, and interpretive functions.

Shapiro (1965) emphasizes the importance of impressionism and repression as part of the hysterical style of cognition. That is, the prototypical hysteric lacks a sharp focus of attention and arrives quickly at a global but superficial assumption of the meaning of perceptions, memories, fantasies, and felt emotions. There is a corresponding lack of factual detail and definition in perception, plus distractibility and incapacity for persistent or intense concentration. The historical continuity of such perceptual and ideational styles leads to a relatively nonfactual world, in which guiding schemata of self, objects, and environment have a flat, depthless quality.

Dwelling conceptually in this nonfactual world promotes the behavioral traits of hysterical romance, emphasis on fantasy meanings, and *la belle indifférence*. For example, the prototypical hysteric may react swiftly with an emotional outburst and yet remain unable to conceptualize what is happening and why such feelings occur. After the episode, he may remember his own emotional experiences unclearly and will regard them as if visited on him rather than self-instigated.

This general style of representation of perception, thought, and emotion leads to patterns observable in interpersonal relations, traits, and communicative styles. A tabular summary of what is meant by these components of hysterical style is presented below.

Information-Processing Style: Short-Order Patterns (observe in flow of thought and emotion on a topic)

- Global deployment of attention
- Unclear or incomplete representations of ideas and feelings, possibly with lack of details or clear labels in communication; nonverbal communications not translated into words or conscious meanings
- Only partial or unidirectional associational lines
- Short-circuit to apparent completion of problematic thoughts

Traits: Medium-Order Patterns (observe in interviews)

- Attention-seeking behaviors, possibly including demands for attention and/or the use of charm, vivacity, sex appeal, childlikeness
- Fluid change in mood and emotion, possibly including breakthroughs of feeling; inconsistency of apparent attitudes

Interpersonal Relations: Long-Order Patterns (observe in a patient's history)

- Repetitive, impulsive, stereotyped interpersonal relationships, often characterized by victim-aggressor, child-parent, and rescue or rape themes

- "Cardboard" fantasies and self-object attitudes
- Drifting but possibly dramatic life, with an existential sense that reality is not really real

Shapiro regards these patterns as relatively fixed, perhaps the result of constitutional predisposition and childhood experiences. Other analysts regard them as more likely to occur during conflict. The following discussion will not contradict either position, since both allow us to assume a fixed baseline of cognitive-emotional style and an intensification of such patterns during stress.

Controlling Thought and Emotion: Harry as "Hysteric." Harry will now be considered as if he responded to stress and treatment in a typically hysterical manner. One of his six conflictual themes, as described earlier, will be used to clarify the hysterical mode of controlling thought and emotion. This theme concerns Harry's relief that he is alive when someone had to die (see A1, Table 1).

Considered in microgenetic form, Harry's perceptions of the dead girl's body and his own bodily sensations of being alive are matched with his fear of finding himself dead. The discrepancy between his perceptions and his fears leads to feelings of relief. The sense of relief is then presented as a conscious experience. In the context of the girl's death, relief is incongruent with moral strictures. Harry believes that he should share the fate of others rather than have others absorb bad fate. This discrepancy between current and enduring concepts leads to guilt. Harry has low toleration for strong emotions, and the danger of experiencing guilt motivates efforts to repress the representations that generate the emotions.

While repression helps Harry escape unpleasant ideas and emotions, it impedes information processing. Were it not for controlling efforts, Harry might think again of the girl's death, his relief, and his attitudes toward survival at her expense. He might realize that he was following unrealistic principles of thought, forgive himself for feeling relief, undertake some act of penance and remorse if he could not change his attitude, or reach some other resolution of the incongruity between the current concept and his enduring schemata.

If repression is what Harry accomplishes, one can go further in microanalysis to indicate how it is accomplished in terms of cognitive operations. These operations can be abstracted as if they were in a hierarchy. The maneuver to try first in the hierarchy is inhibition of conscious representation. The initial perceptual images of the girl's body are too powerful to ward off, and, immediately after the accident, Harry might have behaved in an "uncontrolled" hysterical style. Later, when defensive capacity is relatively stronger, the active memory images can be inhibited, counteracting the tendency toward repeated representation. Similarly, the initial ideas and feelings of relief might be too powerful to avoid, but later, as components of active memory, their reproductive tendency can be inhibited.

Suppose this inhibition fails or is only partly successful. Warded-off ideas are expressed in some modality of representation. In a secondary maneuver, the extended meanings of the ideas can still be avoided by inhibition of translation from initial modes to other forms of representation. Harry could have only his visual images and avoid verbal concepts concerning death, relief, and causation.

A third maneuver is to prevent association to meanings that have been represented. This is again, hypothetically, an interruption of an automatic response tendency. Harry might conceptualize events in image and word forms but not continue in development of obvious associational connections. The purpose would be avoidance of full conscious awareness of threatening meanings.

These controlling efforts are three typically hysterical forms of inhibition: avoidance of representation, avoidance of translation of threatening information from one mode of representation to another, and avoidance of automatic associational connections. If these efforts fail to ward off threatening concepts, there are additional methods. A fourth maneuver is the reversal of role from active to passive. Harry could avoid thinking about his own active thoughts by deploying attention to other factors (fate, the girl, or the listener to his story). He could then change the attitude that he was alive because he actively wished to be alive, even if another person died, by thinking of one's passivity with regard to fate, of the girl's activity in hitchhiking, and of how she got herself into the accident.

The fifth and last "hysterical" maneuver is alteration of state of consciousness. Metaphorically, if the hysteric cannot prevent an idea from gaining consciousness, he removes consciousness from the idea by changing the organization of thought and the sense of self. Harry used alcohol for this purpose, but no outside agents are necessary to enter a hypnoid state, with loss of reflective self-awareness.

These five cognitive maneuvers can be listed as if they were a hierarchy of "rules" for the avoidance of unwanted ideas:

1. Avoid representation.
2. Avoid intermodal translation.
3. Avoid automatic associational connections (and avoid conscious problem-solving thought).
4. Change self-attitude from active to passive (and vice versa).
5. Alter state of consciousness in order to alter hierarchies of wishes and fears, blur realities and fantasies, dissociate conflicting attitudes, and alter the sense of self as instigator of thought and action.

The hysteric has further maneuvers, but these extend longer in time. Harry could manipulate situations so that some external person could be held responsible for his survival, thereby reducing the danger of a sense of guilty personal activity. As a very long-range maneuver, Harry could characterologically avoid experiencing himself as ever fully real, aware, and responsible. He could identify himself with others, real or fantasied, so that any act or thought of crime would be their responsibility and not his.

Clarity in Therapeutic Interventions: An Important Nuance with Persons Who Have Hysterical Style. If the person of hysterical style enters psychotherapy because of stress response symptoms, the therapist will try to terminate the state of stress by helping him to complete the processing of the stress-related ideas and feelings. The activity will include thinking through ideas, including latent conflicts activated by the event, experiencing emotions, and revising concepts to reduce discrepancies. The interpretation of defense may be useful to remove impediments to processing, but the main goal in the present model is to end or reduce a state of stress rather than to alter the character style. Even with such limited goals, character style must be understood and the usual therapy techniques (as in Table 2) used, with appropriate nuances.

These nuances are versions, variations, or accentuations of major techniques, such as clarification. One example is simple repetition of what the patient has said. The therapist may, by repeating a phrase, exert a noticeable effect on the hysteric, who may respond with a startle reaction, surprise, laughter, or other emotional expressions. The same words uttered by the therapist mean something different from when they are thought or spoken by the hysteric himself; they are to be taken more seriously. Additional meanings accrue, and some meanings are also stripped away. For example, a guilty statement by Harry, repeated by the therapist in a neutral or kind voice, may seem less heinous. More explicitly, to call this "repetition" is to be correct only in a phonemic sense. Actually, the patient hears meanings more clearly, hears new meanings as well, and the previously warded-off contents and meanings may seem less dangerous when repeated by the therapist.

Simple repetition is, of course, not so "simple." The therapist selects particular phrases and may recombine phrases to clarify by connection of causal sequences. At first, when Harry was vague about survivorship but said "I guess I am lucky to still be around," the therapist might just say "yes" to accentuate the thought. A fuller repetition in different words—for instance, "You feel fortunate to have survived"—may also have progressive effects; it "forces" Harry closer to the potential next thought: "And she did not, so I feel bad about feeling relief."

Left to his own processes, Harry might have verbalized the various "ingredients" in the theme, might even have painfully experienced pangs of guilt and anxiety, and yet might still not have really "listened" to his ideas. In response to this vague style, the therapist may pull together scattered phrases: "You had the thought, 'Gee I'm glad to still be around, but isn't it awful to be glad when she's dead'?" Harry might listen to his own ideas through the vehicle of the therapist and work out his own reassurance or acceptance. This seems preferable to the therapist's giving him permission by saying "You feel guilty over a thought that anyone would have in such a situation," although such a statement is, of course, sometimes necessary. As will be seen, these simple everyday maneuvers are not so effective with persons of obsessional style.

Other therapeutic maneuvers oriented toward helping the hysteric complete the processing of stressful events are equally commonplace. To avoid dwelling further on well-known aspects of psychotherapy, some maneuvers are listed in tabular form as applicable to specific facets of hysterical style (Table 3). Each maneuver listed has additional nuances. For example, with some hysterics interpretations or clarifications should be very short and simple, delivered in a matter-of-fact tone that would counter the hysteric's vagueness, emotionality, and tendency to elaborate any therapist activity into a fantasy relationship.

Table 3. Some "Defects" of the Hysterical Style and
Their Counteractants in Therapy.

Function	Style as "Defect"	Therapeutic Counter
Perception	Global or selective inattention	Ask for details
Representation	Impressionistic rather than accurate	"Abreaction" and reconstruction
Translation of images and enactions to words	Limited	Encourage talk Provide verbal labels
Associations	Limited by inhibitions Misinterpretations based on schematic stereotypes, deflected from reality to wishes and fears	Encourage production Repetition Clarification
Problem solving	Short-circuit to rapid but often erroneous conclusions Avoidance of topic when emotions are unbearable	Keep subject open Interpretations Support

Nuances of Relationship with the Hysterical Patient in a State of Stress. Hysterical persons have a low toleration for emotion, although they are touted for emotionality. Because motivations are experienced as inexorable and potentially intolerable, the ideas that evoke emotion are inhibited. If toleration for the unpleasant emotions associated with a stressful event can be increased, then cognitive processing of that event can be resumed. The therapeutic relationship protects the patient from the dangers of internal conflict and potential loss of controls, and so operates to increase tolerance for warded-off ideas and feelings. The therapist affects the patient's sense of this relationship by his or her activities or restraint. How this is typically done is also a nuance of technique.

After a stress event, the hysterical patient often manifests swings from rigid overcontrol to uncontrolled intrusions and emotional repetition. During these swings, expecially at the beginning and with a desperate patient, the therapist may oscillate between closeness and distance within the boundaries that characterize a therapeutic relationship.

The hysteric may consider it imperative to have care and attention. This imperative need has been called, at times, the "oral," "sick," or "bad" component of some hysterical styles (Easser and Lesser, 1965; Lazare, 1971; Marmor, 1953). During the period of imperative need, especially after a devastating stress event, the hysteric may need to experience warmth and human support from the therapist. Without it, the therapeutic relationship will fall apart, and the patient may regress or develop further psychopathology. During this phase, the therapist moves, in effect, closer to the patient: just close enough to provide necessary support and not so "close" as the patient appears to wish.

As the patient becomes more comfortable, he may begin to feel anxiety at the degree of intimacy in the therapeutic relationship, because of a fear of being seduced or enthralled by the therapist. The therapist then moves back to a "cooler" or more "distant" stance.

The therapist thus oscillates to keep the patient within a zone of safety by sensitive modification of his manner of relating to the patient. Safety allows the patient to move in the direction of greater conceptual clarity (Sandler, 1960; Weiss, 1971). Naturally, the therapist's manner includes his nonverbal and verbal cues. This is what the therapist allows himself to do in the context of his own real responses and qualities of being. This is not role playing. The therapist allows or inhibits his own response tendencies as elicited by the patient.

If the therapist does not oscillate in from a relatively distant position, and if the patient has urgent needs for stabilizing his self-concept through relational support, then the discrepancy between need and supply will be so painful that the patient will find it unendurable to expose problematic lines of thought. Inhibition will continue. If the therapist does not oscillate from

a relatively close position, the conceptual processing will begin, but transference issues will cloud working through the stress response syndrome.
Neither clarity nor oscillation by the therapist may be a suitable nuance of
technique with the obsessional.

Obsessive Style in Response to Stress

Contemporary theory of obsessional style evolved from analysis of
neurotic obsessions, compulsions, doubts, and irrational fears. Abraham
(1942) and Freud (1949) believed that the obsessional neuroses are secondary
to regressions to or fixations at the anal-sadistic phase of psychosexual development. In their view, the manifestations of the neuroses represent compromises between aggressive and sexual impulsive aims and defenses such as
isolation, intellectualization, reaction formation, and undoing. Underneath
a rational consciousness, ambivalent and magical thinking are prominent.
Common conflicts are formed in the interaction of aggressive impulses and
predispositions to rage, fears of assault, and harsh attitudes of morality and
duty. These conflicts lead to coexistence and fluctuation of dominance and
submission themes in interpersonal situations and fantasies.

Salzman (1968) emphasizes the obsessional's sense of being driven,
his strivings for omniscience and control, and his concerns for the magical
effects of unfriendly thoughts of both the self and others. Homosexual
thoughts may also intrude, although often without homosexual behavior.

Vagueness seems less possible for the obsessional than for the hysteric.
Since the obsessional tends more toward acute awareness of ideas, staying
with one position threatens to lead to unpleasant emotions. Seeing the self
as dominant is associated with sadism to others and leads to guilt. Seeing
the self as submissive is associated with weakness and fears of assaults; hence,
this position evokes anxiety. Alternation between opposing poles, as in alternation between sadistic dominance themes and homosexual submissive
themes, serves to undo the danger of remaining at either pole (Sampson and
others, 1972; Weiss, 1967).

To avoid stabilization at a single position and to accomplish the
defense of undoing, obsessionals often use the cognitive operation of shifting
from one aspect of a theme to an oppositional aspect and back again. The
result is continuous change. At the expense of decision and decisiveness, the
obsessional maintains a sense of control and avoids emotional threats (Barnett,
1972; Silverman, 1972).

While the obsessional moves so rapidly that emotions do not gain
full awareness, he or she cannot totally eliminate feelings. Some obsessionals
have intrusions of feelings in minor quasi-ideational form, as expressed in
attacks of rage. Even these intrusions, however, can be undone by what
Salzman calls "verbal juggling." This process includes alterations of meaning,

the use of formulas to arrive at attitudes or plans, shifts in valuation from overestimation to underestimation, and, sometimes, the attribution of magical properties to word labels.

Shapiro (1965) has described the narrowed focus of the mode of attention of the obsessional person, how it misses certain aspects of the world while it engages others in detail. Ideal flexibility of attention involves smooth shifts between sharply directed attention and more impressionistic forms of cognition. The obsessional lacks such fluidity. Shapiro also notes that the obsessional is driven in the course of his thought, emotion, and behavior by "shoulds" and "oughts" dictated by a sense of duty, by his fears of loss of control, and by his need to inhibit recognition of his "wants." In spite of his usual capacity for hard work, productivity, and "will power," the obsessional person may experience difficulty and discomfort when a decision is to be made. Instead of deciding on the basis of wishes and fears, the obsessional must maintain a sense of omnipotence and, therefore, must avoid the dangerous mistakes inherent in a trial-and-error world. The decision among possible choices is likely to rest on a rule evoked to guarantee a "right" decision or else is made on impulse, to end the anxiety. The result of these cognitive styles is an experiential distance from felt emotion. The exception is a feeling of anxious self-doubt, a mood instigated by the absence of cognitive closure.

The obsessional's cognitive style is summarized below, with common traits and patterns of behavior.

Information-Processing Style: Short-order patterns (observe in flow of thought and emotion on a topic)

- Detailed, sharp focus of attention on details
- Clear representation of ideas, meager representation of emotions
- May shift organization and implications of ideas rather than follow an associational line to conclusion, as directed by original intent or intrinsic meanings
- Avoids completion or resolution of a given problem, instead switches back and forth between attitudes

Traits: Medium-Order Patterns (observe in interviews)

- Doubt, worry, productivity and/or procrastination
- Single-minded, imperturbable, intellectualizer
- Tense, deliberate, unenthusiastic
- Rigid, ritualistic

Interpersonal Relations: Long-Order Patterns (observe in a patient's history)

- Regimented, routine, and continuous interpersonal relationships, low in "life," vividness, or pleasure: often frustrating to "be" with

- Prone to dominance-submission themes
- Duty-fulfiller, hard worker, seeks or makes strain and pressure, does what he "should" do rather than what he decides to do
- Experiences himself as remote from emotional connection with others, although feels committed to operating with others because of role or principles

Controlling Thought and Emotion: Harry as an "Obsessive." Stressful events may so compel interest that there may be little difference in the initial registration and experience of persons with hysterical or obsessional style. But, short of extreme disasters, the obsessional person may remain behaviorally calm and emotionless, in contrast to the emotional explosions of the hysteric. (This report demands such generalizations, but it should be noted that, during some events, obsessionals may become quite emotional and hysterics may remain calm. The difference remains in the quality of the person's conscious experience. The hysterical person can have a "hysterical calm" because it is based on an inhibition of some aspects of potential knowledge; no emotion occurs, because implications are not known. If and when the obsessional behaves emotionally, he may regard such behavior as a loss of control, to be "undone" by retrospective shifts of meaning, rituals, apologies, or self-recriminations.)

After a stressful event, the obsessional and the hysteric may both exhibit similar general stress response tendencies, including phases of denial and intrusion. But they may differ in their stability in any given phase. The obsessional may be able to maintain the period of emotional numbing with greater stability; the hysteric may be able to tolerate phases of episodic intrusions with more apparent stability and less narcissistic injury.

During the oscillatory phase, when the uncompleted images and ideas of the current stressful concepts tend to repeated and intrusive representation, the hysteric is likely to inhibit representation to ward off these unwelcome mental contents. The obsessional may be precise and clear in describing the intrusive images but may focus on details related to "duty," for example, and away from the simple emotion-evoking meanings of the gestalt of the image.

It is during the oscillatory phase of both intrusions and warding-off maneuvers that styles stand out in starkest form. Instead of, or in addition to, repressive maneuvers as listed earlier, the obsessional responds to threatened repetitions with cognitive maneuvers such as shifting. By a shift to "something else," the obsessional is able to jam cognitive channels and prevent emergence of warded-off contents, or to shift meanings so as to stifle emotional arousal. That is, by shifting from topic to topic, or from one meaning to another meaning of the same topic, the emotion-arousing properties of one set of implications are averted.

Treating Harry: Modeled Here as an Obsessional Personality. In discussion of a hysterical Harry, the theme of survival guilt was used as an example. An obsessional Harry might share a tendency toward emergence of the same theme but react to this threat with a style characterized by shifting rather than vagueness and inhibition.

In psychotherapy, Harry begins to talk of the unbidden images of the girl's body. He associates now to his memory of feeling relieved to be alive. The next conceptualization, following the idealized line of working through, outlined earlier, would be association of his relieved feelings with ideas of survival at her expense. This cluster would be matched against moral strictures counter to such personal gain through damage to others, and Harry would go on to conceptualize his emotional experience of guilt or shame (theme A1 in Table 1). Once clear, he could revise his schematic belief that someone had to die, accept his relief, feel remorse, even plan a penance, and reduce incongruity through one or more of these changes.

Harry does not follow this idealized route because the potential of these emotional experiences is appraised as intolerable at a not fully conscious level of information processing. A switch is made to another ideational cycle in order to avoid the first one. The second cycle is also associatively related to the images of the girl's body. A common element in both ideational cycles allows a pivotal change and reduces awareness that the subtopic has changed (G. S. Klein, 1967).

The pivot for the switch is the idea of bodily damage. In the second ideational cluster, the concept is that bodily damage could happen to him, perhaps at any future time, since it has now happened to her. Through the comparison with his wishes for invulnerability and his dread of vulnerability, fear is aroused (B1 in Table 1).

While fear is unpleasant and threatening as a potential experience, the switch allows movement away from the potential feelings of guilt (theme A1). When the second theme (B1) becomes too clear, fear might be consciously experienced. The procedure can be reversed with return to A1. Harry can oscillate between conscious and communicative meanings, between A1 and B1, without fully experiencing either set of dangerous ideas and emotions.

Harry need not limit switching operations to the two contexts for ideas about bodily damage. He can switch between any permutations of any themes. He can transform, reverse, or undo guilt with fear or anger (Jones, 1929a). He can see himself as victim, then aggressor, then victim, and so forth. These shifts dampen emotional responsivity but reduce cognitive processing of themes.

This does not imply that inhibition of representation will be absent in obsessional Harry or that shifts of theme will be absent in hysterical Harry. Obsessional Harry will attempt inhibitions and use his shifts when inhibitory efforts fail. Hysterical Harry might shift from active to passive, as noted earlier, but timing and quality of the shifts would differ. Obsessional Harry would tend to shift more rapidly, with less vagueness at either pole. The shift could occur in midphrase, between an utterance of his and a response from the therapist, or even as virtually simultaneous trains of thought.

It is because of rapid shifts that therapists who attempt clarity with obsessionals may be thwarted in their task. Suppose the therapist makes a clarifying intervention about A1, the survivor guilt theme. Obsessional Harry may have already shifted to B1, his fear of body injury, and thus hear the remarks in a noncongruent state. The clarification procedure may not work well because Harry was not unclear or vague in the first place, is not listening from the earlier position, and will undo the therapist's intervention by further shifts. An interpretation to the effect that Harry fears bodily damage as a retribution for his survivor relief and guilt would be premature, since at this point he has not fully experienced either the fear or the guilt.

Holding to Context: Important Nuances with Persons Who Have Obsessive Character Style. Holding the obsessional to a topic or to a given context within a topic is equivalent to clarifying for the hysteric. Metaphorically, the obsessional avoids conceptual time, whereas the hysteric avoids conceptual space. The goal of holding is reduction of shifting, so that the patient can progress further along a given conceptual process. The patient must also be helped to tolerate the emotions that he will experience when he cannot quickly divert ideas into and out of conscious awareness.

Holding to context is more complicated than clarification. One begins with at least two current problems, such as the dual themes of A1 and B1 in Harry. When the patient is not shifting with extreme rapidity, the therapist may simply hold the patient to either one or the other theme. The patient will not comply with this maneuver, and the therapist must not confuse "holding" with "forcing." Ferenczi (1950) in an effort to speed up analysis, experimented with various ways to make the obsessional stay on topic until intensely felt emotions occurred. For example, he insisted that his patient develop and maintain visual fantasies relevant to a specific theme. During this technical maneuver, his obsessional patients did experience emotions, they even had affective explosions, but the transference complications impeded rather than enhanced the therapy.

The therapist has to shift, even though he attempts to hold the patient to a topic. That is, the therapist shifts at a slower rate than the patient, like a dragging anchor that slows the process. This operation increases the progress of the patient in both directions. That is, with each shift, he is able to go a bit further along the conceptual route of either theme, even though he soon becomes frightened and crowds the theme out of mind with an alternative.

The therapist may use repetitions, as with the hysteric, in order to hold or slow the shift of an obsessional patient. But this same maneuver is used with a different nuance. With the hysteric, the repetition heightens the meaning of what the patient is now saying. With the obsessional, the repetition goes back to what the patient was saying before the shift away from the context occurred. With the hysteric, the repetition may consist of short phrases. With the obsessional, greater length may be necessary, in order to state the specific context that is being warded off. For example, if Harry is talking about bodily damage and shifts from a survivor guilt context to his fears of injury, then a repetition by the therapist has to link bodily damage specifically to the survivor guilt theme. With the hysteric, such wordy interventions might only diminish clarity.

At times, this more extensive repetition in the obsessional may include the technique of going back to the very beginning of an exchange, retracing the flow carefully, and indicating where extraneous or only vaguely relevant details were introduced by the patient. Reconstructions may add warded-off details. This technique has been suggested for long-term character analysis (Salzman, 1968; Weiss, 1971), during which defensive operations are interpreted, so that the patient increases conscious control and diminishes unconscious restrictions on ideas and feelings. In shorter therapy, aimed at working through a stress, this extensive repetition is still useful, because, during the review by the therapist, the patient attends to the uncomfortable aspects of the topic.

Increased time on the topic allows more opportunity for processing and hence moves the patient toward completion. Emotions aroused by the flow of ideas are more tolerable within the therapeutic relationship than for the patient alone. Also, time on the topic and with the therapist allows continued processing in a communicative state, emphasizing reality and problem solving rather than fantasy and magical belief systems. Identification with and externalization onto the relatively neutral therapist also allow temporary reduction in rigid and harsh introjects that might otherwise deflect thought.

Focusing on details is sometimes a partial deterrent to shifting in the obsessional, just as it may aid clarity with the hysteric. The nuances of focusing on details differ because the purposes differ. In general, the aim with the hysteric is to move from concrete, experiential information, such as images, toward more abstract or more extended meanings, such as word labels for activities and things. The aim with the obsessional is to move from abstract levels, where shifts are facile, to a concrete context. Details act as pegs of meaning in concrete contexts and make shifts of attitude more difficult. This maneuver utilizes the obsessional's predisposition to details but allows the therapist to select them. Again, the nuance of asking for concrete details is part of the general aim of increasing conceptualization time.

In states where shifts are so rapid as to preclude simple repetition or questioning, the therapist may use a more complex form of repetition. The therapist repeats the event—for example, Harry's intrusive image of the girl's body—and then repeats in a single package the disparate attitudes that the patient oscillates between. For example, the therapist might tell Harry that the image of the girl's body led to two themes. One was the idea of relief at being spared from death, which made him feel frightened and guilty. The other was the idea of bodily harm to himself. Were the rate of oscillation less rapid, this form of "packaged" intervention would not be as necessary, since simpler holding operations might be sufficient and the therapist could focus on a single theme.

These efforts by the therapist encroach on the habitual style of the patient. The patient may respond by minimizing or exaggerating the meaning of the intervention. The obsessional is especially vulnerable to threats to his sense of omniscience, especially after traumatic events. If the therapist holds him on a topic, the obsessional senses warded-off ideas and feelings and develops uncertainties that cause his self-esteem to fall.

To protect the patient's self-esteem, the therapist uses another technical nuance. He uses questioning to accomplish clarification and topic deepening, even when he has an interpretation in mind. The questions aim the patient toward answers that contain the important, warded-off, but now emerging ideas. The obsessional patient can then credit himself with expressing these ideas and experiencing these feelings. The therapist with the hysterical person might, in contrast, interpret at such a moment, using a firm, short delivery, since a question might be followed by vagueness.

To the obsessional, incisive interpretations often mean that the therapist knows something he does not know. A transference bind over dominance and submission arises as the patient either rebels against the interpretation with stubborn denial, accepts it meekly without thinking about it, or both.

Timing is also important with obsessionals working through stress-activated themes. After experience with a given patient, the therapist intuitively knows when a shift is about to take place. At just that moment, or a trifle before, the therapist asks his question. This interrupts the shift and increases conceptual "time and space" on the topic about to be warded off. These technical nuances are put in a crude, broad context in Table 4.

Nuances of Relationship with Obsessional Patients in a State of Stress. The oscillation described as sometimes necessary with the hysterical style is not as advisable with the obsessional style. Instead, the therapist creates a safe situation for the patient by remaining stable within his own clear boundaries (objectivity, compassion, understanding, concern for the truth, or whatever his own personal and professional traits are).

The patient learns the limits of the therapist within this frame. It gives

Table 4. Some "Defects" of Obsessional Style
and Their Counteractants in Therapy.

Function	Style as "Defect"	Therapeutic Counter
Perception	Detail and factual	Ask for overall impressions and statements about emotional experiences
Representation	Isolation of ideas from emotions	Link emotional meanings to ideational meanings
Translation of images to words	Misses emotional meaning in a rapid transition to partial word meanings	Focus attention on images and felt reactions to them
Associations	Shifts sets of meanings back and forth	Holding operations Interpretation of defense and of warded-off meanings
Problem solving	Endless rumination without reaching decisions	Interpretation of reasons for warding off clear decisions

him faith that the therapist will react neither harshly nor seductively. This trust increases the patient's breadth of oscillation. He can express more aggressive ideas if he knows that the therapist will not submit, be injured, compete for dominance, or accuse him of evil. Harry could express more of his bodily worries when he knew that the therapist would not himself feel guilty or overresponsible.

If the therapist changes with the obsessional's tests or needs, then the obsessional worries that he may be too powerful, too weak, or too "sick" for the therapist to handle. Also, the obsessional may use the situation to externalize warded-off ideas or even defensive maneuvers. The therapist shifts, not he. The obsessional does, at times, need kindly support after disastrous external events. But his propensity for shifting makes changes in the degree of support more hazardous than a consistent attitude, whether kindly-supportive, neutral-tough, or otherwise. Suppose the therapist becomes more kindly as Harry goes through a turbulent period of emotional expression of guilt over survival. Harry may experience this as an increase in the therapist's concern or worry for him. He might shift from a "little" suffering position—the position that elicited the therapist's reaction—to a "big" position from which he looks down with contempt at the "worried" therapist.

Similarly, if the therapist is not consistently tough-minded, in the ordinary sense of insisting on information and truth-telling, but shifts to this stance only in response to the patient's stubborn evasiveness, then the patient can shift from strong stubbornness to weak, vulnerable self-concepts. Within the context of this shift, the therapist comes to be experienced as hostile, demeaning, and demanding.

Unlike the hysteric, then, the obsessional's shifts in role and attitude within the therapeutic situation are likely to be out of phase with changes in demeanor of the therapist. The obsessional can chance further and more lucid swings in state when he senses the stability of the therapist.

Transference resistances will occur in spite of the therapist's effort to maintain a therapeutic relationship. The stability of the therapist will be exaggerated by the patient into an omniscience that he will continually test. When negative transference reactions occur, the therapist will act to resolve those that interfere with the goals of therapy. But some transference reactions will not be negative, even though they act as resistances. The hysteric may demand attention and halt progress to get it. The obsessional may take an oppositional stance not so much out of hostility or stubbornness, although such factors will be present, as out of a need to avoid the dangerous intimacy of agreement and cooperation. Since the therapist is not aiming at analysis of transference to effect character change, he need not interpret this process. Instead, with an obsessional patient in an oppositional stance, he may word his interventions to take advantage of the situation.

That is, interventions can be worded, when necessary, in an oppositional manner. Suppose Harry were talking about picking up the girl and the therapist knew that he was predisposed to feeling guilty but was warding it off. With a hysterical Harry, the therapist might say, "You feel bad about picking up the girl." With an obsessional and cooperative Harry, he might say, "Could you be blaming yourself for picking up the girl?" With an oppositional obsessional stance, the therapist might say, "So you don't feel at all bad about picking up the girl." This kind of Harry may disagree and talk of his guilt feelings.

Provided the context is a basically stable therapeutic relationship, one in which the patient has an image of the therapist as objective, kindly, and firmly competent, the inflection need not be the sincere, neutral, firm tone helpful with hysterics. Slight sarcasm or mild humor may help the obsessional Harry assume a tough position while trying out his own tender ideas (Salzman, 1968).

By sternness, as implied in the above comments, the therapist may have the effect of "ordering" the obsessional to contemplate warded-off ideas. This seeming unkindness is kind in that it removes responsibility from the patient and permits him to think the unthinkable. But this sternness, mild sarcasm, or slight humor has to remain a relatively consistent characteristic of the therapist.

This is not as difficult as it may sound, for these nuances involve what the therapist allows himself to do or not to do in natural response to the situation. They are not assumed or artificial roles or traits. For some therapists, kindliness, openness, gentleness, and a nonjudgmental air are preferable nuances to any toughness, sternness, sarcasm, or humor and may accomplish the same purpose. These latter remarks are meant more as illustrations than assertions because it is here that we encounter that blurred border between the "science" and "art" of psychotherapy.

In summary, even with a general goal of working through conflicted reactions to a recent serious life event, brief therapy involves nuances related to the individual style of processing information. These nuances for varied personality styles have been described in more detail elsewhere (Horowitz, 1976, 1979). Here, contrasts between the prototypical hysterical and obsessional styles have served to illustrate this point of view.

22

Behavior Therapy

Richard M. Suinn
Jerry L. Deffenbacher

❖ ❖ ❖ ❖ ❖ ❖ ❖ ❖ ❖ ❖ ❖ ❖ ❖

The model of anxiety proposed here may more appropriately be broadened to encompass *tensional states*; that is, anxiety and phobias. These states involve complex patterns of responses characterized by subjective feelings of apprehension or tension, accompanied by or associated with physiological activation or arousal (Spielberger, 1966b). These response patterns may include cognitive sets ("I am an anxious person"); autonomic responses, such as changes in heart rate, galvanic skin response (GSR), blood pressure, respiration, or gastric motility; and/or somatic-behavioral responses, such as tremors, avoidance behaviors, speech disruption, motor inhibition, or disruption of performances. The evidence is that these response patterns need not all be present simultaneously in tensional states (Lang, 1971). For example, a client may say that he feels "apprehensive" or "fearful" and yet may show only modest autonomic arousal. Similarly, a person may demonstrate heightened

392

physiological arousal and yet may approach—rather than avoid—the anxiety-provoking stimulus object (Leitenberg and others, 1971). Also, a client may exhibit avoidance behaviors or disruptions in performance but not report any subjective distress.

In the phobic tensional states, the client is able to specify the cue conditions prompting the tensional response pattern. (The more general terms *trait anxiety, free-floating anxiety,* and *anxiety neurosis* refer to those conditions where the tensional response patterns are triggered by a large number of diverse stimuli or where the stimuli are so diffuse that the client cannot identify them cognitively.) Such cues may be external or internal. External stressors may involve reality threats or excessive demands beyond the reach of the client, including certain changes in life adjustments, such as retirement or divorce (Holmes and Rahe, 1967). Seligman (1971) has proposed that some external stimuli are more likely to become phobic stimuli than others because the person is more prepared to respond. Internal stressors may involve a type of feedback-loop phenomenon. For example, a client may activate the flow of adrenaline by moving quickly and in a rushed way; this adrenaline increase may speed up the heart rate; and the client may respond to the physiological arousal by further activating behavioral systems, such as by rushing even further. Similarly, for some clients the initiation of mild anxiety responses may trigger further increments in anxiety responsiveness in an upward spiraling course. Or the first physical signs of anxiety arousal may lead to the cognition "I'm not going to be able to handle this stress," leading in turn to further autonomic arousal and performance disruptions.

In a behavioral approach to treatment, several assumptions are made: (1) Tensional response patterns are subject to alteration through relearning. (2) Such relearning can take place through exposure to conditions for elimination of the anxiety or for acquisition of coping skills, without confronting past historical origins as part of the current therapeutic process. (3) The conditions for relearning can be derived from learning principles rather than psychodynamic principles. Along with the learning principles derived from classical conditioning and extinction, operant learning, and modeling, behavioral intervention strategies also emphasize careful assessment of the client to set therapy goals and strategies, orientation of the client to programming for change through current action rather than reviewing past actions, the design of an intervention program that systematically retrains the client, and the requirement that training include the client's putting into practice *in vivo* the new adaptive skills (Deffenbacher and Suinn, 1979). Assessment and the establishment of treatment goals also follow certain requisites—specifically, concreteness and explicitness. For example, treatment goals are defined in terms of target behaviors desired at the termination of treatment—for example, sleeping for at least seven hours per night, reducing disruptive anxiety responses ("attacks") to one per month, reducing or eliminating the frequency or duration of tension headaches on a daily basis, or increasing the frequency of use of coping behaviors.

Behavioral assessment of anxiety (Hersen and Bellack, 1976; Mash and Terdal, 1976; Suinn, 1977a) examines the antecedent conditions responsible for the anxiety response. Anxiety may be precipitated when a client lacks needed behavioral skills, lacks information, has been conditioned to respond with anxiety, or is exposed to cognitive stressors. A client's skill deficit (Bandura, 1968; Staats and Staats, 1963), for example, due to his not studying for a test, can lead to his becoming anxious during final examination week. Such anxiety would be properly removed through study-skills training. An informational deficit might also contribute to anxiety arousal; for example, the anxiety one feels when uninformed about the proper etiquette for an important social gathering. Unlike the behavioral deficit category, in informational deficits the client possesses the necessary skills in his or her repertoire but simply is uninformed about which behaviors are appropriate to the situation. Conditioned anxiety derives from previous direct or vicarious experiences whereby anxiety has been elicited. A two-factor theory of fear (Eysenck and Rachman, 1965; Mowrer, 1960; Solomon, 1964) postulates that anxiety may be originally elicited by a stressor but that it persists because of avoidance behaviors. Eysenck (1976) now adds the possibility that innate predisposing factors, modeling, and incubation variables are important. Rachman (1977) has recently proposed a three-pathway theory involving conditioning, modeling, and information giving. Seligman (1971) also proposes the concept of preparedness in fear acquisition; that is, that humans may be "prepared" to have fear responses conditioned to certain stimuli and not others. The stressor prompts sympathetic nervous system reactions (anxiety), which become paired with concurrent cue conditions, as well as with fear acquisition through classical conditioning. Avoidance behaviors adopted by the client lead to anxiety reduction, thus maintaining the fear response through operant conditioning. In an animal paradigm, Solomon (1964; Solomon, Kamin, and Wynne, 1953) found that a neutral light cue presented just before unavoidable shock could elicit intense emotional responses in dogs to the light itself. Further, if the animal is given the opportunity to escape the shock, through leaving the chamber, then this animal shows a neurotic persistence of the fear/avoidance response long after the shock is no longer being delivered. Treatment approaches associated with some parts of this model may involve desensitization (whereby the anxiety cue condition is presented and paired with relaxation responses), implosive therapy (whereby the client is prevented from avoidance behaviors through anxiety induction), and anxiety management training (whereby the client is trained to initiate relaxation responses to physical or physiological signs of anxiety arousal). The conditioning may occur through vicarious experiences

(Berger, 1962); that is, where the subject observes aversive consequences or anxiety behaviors of someone else. Such data on vicarious learning have opened up vicarious extinction or modeling as another treatment method. Here, the client observes a model in the anxiety situation exhibiting non-anxious behaviors (Bandura, Grusec, and Menlove, 1967; Meichenbaum, 1971). Bandura and Barab (1973) suggest that modeling techniques may work because they provide accurate information about the feared stimulus and the process for interacting with it, as well as providing for vicarious extinction. In some cases, the anxiety response is precipitated by cognitions: anticipatory thoughts, attributions, self-evaluative statements, and other self-talk or self-statements (Girodo, 1976). Such cognitive behaviors may serve as mediating stimuli, triggering anxiety in the same way that environmental stimuli can prompt tensional reactions. When such cognitive events are critical in the chain of events leading to anxiety in a client, cognitive treatment strategies are available.

Desensitization

Desensitization, perhaps one of the most used behavioral strategies for treatment of phobias, owes its development to Salter (1949) and Wolpe (1958). Theoretically, Wolpe (1958) applies Sherrington's (1947) neurological concept of *reciprocal inhibition* to behavior therapy, stating the principle: *"If a response inhibiting anxiety can be made to occur in the presence of anxiety-evoking stimuli, it will weaken the bond between these stimuli and the anxiety"* (p. 17). In this view, a phobia is a learned reaction (fear) to an originally neutral stimulus; this reaction becomes strengthened to such a degree that any real or imagined occurrence of the stimulus precipitates it. Desensitization attempts to attach a different response to the phobic cues—specifically, a response that inhibits and hence can eliminate the fear response. In technique, desensitization aims at setting up a learning procedure which permits this new stimulus-response association (phobic stimulus-relaxation response), rather than precipitating the phobic reaction. Relaxation is selected as the inhibitory response, although other behaviors—such as assertiveness, sexual activity, eating behaviors, or even anger—may be similarly used. The relaxation is taught through a direct muscle exercise, while the pairing of the relaxation and the phobic stimuli is achieved through the use of imagery. In the imagery, the client is guided to visualize fearful situations while remaining relaxed.

Desensitizatation therapy involves three stages: relaxation training, hierarchy construction, and desensitization proper. As noted earlier, the relaxation is crucial as the response to inhibit the anxiety response; hence, the client must be well trained in this skill. The most common relaxation-training method is based on the Jacobsen (1938) deep muscle relaxation method, although relaxation also may be acquired through hypnosis (Rubin, 1972), autogenic training (Schultz and Luthe, 1959), drugs (Wolpe, 1958; Pecknold, Raeburn, and Poser, 1972), breathing exercises (Deffenbacher and Snyder, 1976), biofeedback (Wickramasekera, 1972), or meditation (Beary, Benson, and Klemchuck, 1974). In the Jacobsen approach, clients are instructed first to tense muscles, then to be aware of the relaxation as the tenseness is released. They concentrate on the contrasting sensations between the muscle tension and the subsequent muscle relaxation, moving through muscle groupings such as the hands, the biceps, the eyes, the shoulders, and the chest. Clients are instructed to practice the relaxation exercise at home prior to desensitization proper.

Hierarchy construction involves obtaining a sampling of realistic phobic events from the client's life, which evoke different levels of anxiety. The scenes are graded from low anxiety arousing to extremely high arousing. Scenes represent single phobic situations, although multiple hierarchies may be constructed. Desensitization proper combines the hierarchy scenes and the relaxation: the client is relaxed, then instructed to visualize the lowest anxiety scene and to "actually be there, involved in the situation." Since the theory of reciprocal inhibition requires that the new competing response (relaxation) be stronger than the phobic response, the therapist continues the scene presentations only as long as the client remains relaxed. As the client is able to visualize each scene without discomfort, then the next-higher scene on the hierarchy is presented. The total number of treatments required is a function of the intensity of the phobia, the number of phobias (and hence hierarchies) needing treatment, and the ability of the client to develop skill in relaxation and to experience the scenes. Wolpe (1973) reported one case with 2,000 scene presentations as one extreme, while Suinn (1970) reported success within three hours under special conditions as the other extreme.

Research over twenty years on desensitization therapy supports the conclusion that this intervention has a significant impact on anxiety responses associated with specific stimuli. Wolpe (1958) discovered that 90 percent of his personal clients were either cured or much improved. He defined successful recovery or improvement as showing fearfulness no greater than 20 percent of the original intensity prior to therapy. In a classic analogue study, Paul (1967) compared desensitization against insight psychotherapy, placebo, waiting-list, and no-contact control groups. Subjects were suffering from public-speaking anxiety. Measures included physiological, cognitive, and behavioral assessments under a stress condition. The desensitization group showed significantly greater reduction on all three measures than the untreated controls and was superior to the insight therapy and attention placebo groups. At two-year follow-up (Paul, 1967), the desensitization group still showed 85 percent improved, as compared to 50 percent for the insight and the placebo groups and 22 percent for the untreated controls. Lang and Lazovik (1963), with snake phobics, added further information that follow-up results on desensitization subjects were still favorable; in fact, the differences between treated subjects and nontreated control subjects increased at six-month follow-up. As with Paul, no evidence was found for symptom substitution. Another way of evaluating outcome is reported in a study of academic dropout rates. Two years after treatment, Paul (1968) discovered that desensitization clients showed only a 10 percent dropout, as compared to 60 percent for controls. Di Loreto (1971) compared desensitization with rational-emotive therapy, client-centered therapy, no-treatment control, and no-contact control for interpersonal anxiety. All therapies were better than controls, but desensitization was superior to rational-emotive therapy and nondirective therapy for this sample of 100 clients. Measures of improvement included self-reports, therapist ratings, and objective ratings of anxiety behavior by trained observers. Results persisted through a three-month follow-up. Desensitization therapy proved consistently effective across clients, whereas the other therapies were highly effective for some clients but not effective for others. Although studies of college students, "minor" phobias, or analogue studies have come under criticism (Cooper, Furst, and Bridges, 1969; Marks, 1975), other studies also report the use of desensitization with hospitalized phobics and anxiety patients (Dawley, Duidry, and Curtis, 1973; Cooper, Gelder, and Marks, 1965; Gelder and Marks, 1968; Gelder and others, 1967), and for symptoms such as auditory hallucinations (Slade, 1972), compulsions (McGlynn and Linder, 1971), anorexia (Ollendick, 1979; Schnurer, Rubin, and Roy, 1973), and homosexuality (Lopiccolo, 1971). For interested readers, a number of excellent reviews of desensitization research may be found in the professional literature (Kazdin and Wilcoxon, 1976; Paul, 1969; Rachman, 1967; Wilson and Davison, 1971). Given the effectiveness of desensitization as an intervention strategy, studies have now shifted toward clarifying the theoretical variables or processes, such as the basic theory itself (whether desensitization is reciprocal inhibition or habituation or extinction or cognitive learning) (Bergin and Suinn, 1975; Heckmat, 1972; Ladouceuer, 1978; Leitenberg and others, 1975; London, 1964; F. N. Watts, 1973) or the procedures needed (such as relaxation, hierarchical presentations, pairing of scenes with relaxation) (Agras and others, 1971; Aponte and Aponte, 1971; Borkovec, 1972; Goldfried, 1971; Kazdin and Wilcoxon, 1976; Marks, 1978; Murray and Jacobsen, 1978; Nawas, Welch, and Fishman, 1970; Suinn, Edie, and Spinelli, 1970; Wilkins, 1971). Additional studies have focused on innovations to improve on the delivery of desensitization; for example, through audiotapes or automated treatment (Cotler, 1970; Donner and Guerney, 1969; Lang, 1969; Sappington, Staats, and Healey, 1978; Suinn and other, 1973), self-administered desensitization (Glasgow and Rosen, 1978; Kahn and Baker, 1968; Marshall and Andrews, 1973; Marshall,

Stoian, and Andrews, 1977; Mathews and others, in press; Philips, Johnson, and Geyer, 1972; Rosen, 1976), group desensitization (Anton, 1976; Lazarus, 1966; Paul and Shannon, 1966; Suinn, 1968), and accelerated treatment (Dua, 1972; Richardson and Suinn, 1973a; Robinson and Suinn, 1969; Suinn, Edie, and Spinelli, 1970; Suinn and Hall, 1970).

Anxiety Management Training

Anxiety Management Training (AMT) was developed to solve some of the deficiencies of desensitization and other anxiety management therapies. As indicated, desensitization requires that the client be able to describe the cue conditions triggering the tensional responses; hierarchy construction and scene exposure require this preciseness. For multiple phobias, desensitization may be prolonged as the client is desensitized to each new hierarchy. Another behavior therapy, implosive therapy (Levis, 1967; Stampfl, 1967), is briefer, but it also requires some knowledge of the cue conditions prompting the anxiety response. Further, implosive therapy typically leaves the client emotionally fatigued, since it involves producing anxiety continuously during the treatment session. Finally, neither desensitization nor implosive therapy provides for generalization to fears different from those treated.

Anxiety management training (Suinn, 1975a, 1977a) was aimed primarily at general or free-floating anxiety, but it is applicable to single or multiple phobias. It is unnecessary to obtain detailed hierarchies, and each session ends with the client's experiencing controlled, low arousal rather than tension. The overall framework of AMT involves a systematic training in self-control over the tensional responses. The underlying theory is that anxiety responses can have drive or cue properties, which in turn can become associated with coping behaviors through training. In practice, AMT trains the client to recognize his specific ways of experiencing stress; for example, neck and shoulder muscle tightening, clenching of hands, throat dryness, stomach motility. The client then uses these cues to prompt tension reduction behavior; that is, the initiation of relaxation. Eventually, the client is able consciously to reduce anxiety aroused by stressors or automatically to abort the tensional state before anxiety symptoms can build.

Anxiety management training has several objectives: (1) control over the autonomic components of stress, (2) training in self-control, and (3) training to generalize such self-management skills to diverse real-life situations. Regarding the first, as the reader will recall, responses to stress may appear as autonomic arousal, cognitions, or somatic-behavioral responses. With AMT, it is assumed that acquiring control over the autonomic reactivity is a crucial step and sometimes the only needed step in stress management. One premise is that heightened uncontrolled affect arousal can disrupt behaviors, influence cognitions, and cause somatic symptoms. It is accepted that, in

some cases, the autonomic reactivity may be a response to cognitions themselves (consider, for example, a client's reaction in confronting a minority
laborer, if the client believes that all such persons are hostile, short-tempered,
and prone to physical violence). Under these conditions, AMT may still be
useful, since control over the emotionality may permit the client to reevaluate
the cognitions objectively. In cases where behavioral factors are the source
for the stress symptoms, once again AMT may be helpful in removing the
emotional obstacle to learning or adopting new behaviors (Suinn, 1972).

The self-control objective of AMT is based on the belief that the
therapy process will have greater impact where the client does not simply
resolve a problem but also learns the skill of problem solving itself (Kanfer,
1976; Mahoney and Arnkoff, 1978; Thoresen and Mahoney, 1974). AMT
aims at helping the client not only to deal with the anxiety representing
the presenting problem but also to learn self-management or self-regulation
skills. Therapy therefore becomes not merely a setting where something is
done by an expert *to* the client but a setting where the client learns new
coping skills. Toward this end, the AMT procedure gradually fades out
therapist control and fades in client self-control. This type of procedure is
also involved in the third objective, that of enabling *in vivo* applications of
stress management. AMT sessions emphasize learning to reduce anxiety
arousal reactions no matter what stressors have been the precipitating factors;
hence, AMT should lead to a generalizable skill (Deffenbacher and Shelton,
1978). Also, sessions employ steps directly aimed at *in vivo* transfer; for
example, through various homework assignments.

The actual steps in AMT include several phases: (1) assessment and
relaxation training, (2) visualization training for guided rehearsal, (3) guided
rehearsal through imagery for anxiety arousal and for anxiety reduction
through relaxation, (4) increased training in self-initiation instead of therapist initiation of anxiety reduction under stress, and (5) increased emphasis
on transfer to real-life situations. Some of these phases occur concurrently in
the training. Phase 1 involves a behavioral diagnosis and initial training in
relaxation, via the Jacobsen exercise, with homework to practice relaxing.
The session also obtains a detailed description of an actual situation in which
the client experienced -anxiety. Unlike desensitization scenes, this AMT
scene can focus on simply the setting, persons involved, and how the anxiety
was experienced, without any specific identification of what stimulus actually
was responsible for triggering the anxiety. Thus, the scene retrieves the
anxiety *experience* and its setting and not necessarily the causative stressor
itself; for this reason, AMT is appropriate for treatment of free-floating
anxiety or anxiety neurosis. In Phase 2, the therapist instructs the client to
visualize a relaxation scene, and later an anxiety scene. Through the therapist's
verbal descriptions, the client is helped to vividly reexperience these events in
this guided rehearsal. In Phase 3, these scenes are used to enable the client

to experience either controlled relaxation or heightened anxiety arousal. The therapist also guides the client in anxiety control by first switching on the anxiety scene to precipitate anxiety arousal, then turning off this scene, then switching to either the relaxation scene or relaxation exercises to reachieve low autonomic arousal or relaxation. In Phase 4, the therapist gradually fades out direct instructions aimed at helping the client to achieve either anxiety arousal or relaxation control. Instead, the client is given more responsibility —for example, in relaxation by switching off the anxiety and switching on the relaxation scene. In Phase 5, the client at various steps is helped to transfer skills from the treatment sessions to real life. For example, homework is assigned to initiate relaxation in an *in vivo* setting at home, school, or work, as soon as the client has the skill to relax within about a minute. Throughout the sessions, the client is also taught to recognize his own "stress profile"; for example, early bodily cues of the buildup of anxiety, such as clenching of the fist or shoulder tightening. Because clients are unaware of these signs, anxiety often continues to build until it reaches an irreversible level. AMT teaches the client to be aware of these "early-warning signs" both in and outside treatment sessions and to initiate relaxation control. The total number of AMT sessions depends on the ability of the client to develop the skills needed at each phase.

A number of research studies have demonstrated the efficacy of AMT. Early studies reported on the value of AMT with specific anxieties, such as public-speaking anxiety (Nicoletti, 1972), mathematics anxiety (Richardson and Suinn, 1973a; Suinn and Richardson, 1971), and test anxiety (Richardson and Suinn, 1973b). Since the special contribution of AMT is for general or free-floating anxiety, studies of this type of tensional state are particularly relevant. Edie (1972) treated clients referred with a diagnosis of general anxiety by counseling centers at two colleges. Following treatment, the clients' anxiety levels decreased to that of a control group of nonanxious students. In addition, Edie reported that some clients became able to pinpoint the precipitating stimuli of their anxieties as treatment progressed, in spite of the earlier "free-floating" nature of their anxieties. To test the validity of AMT, Shoemaker (1976) selected community mental health center clients diagnosed as anxiety neurotic. In comparison with implosive therapy, relaxation-only, placebo, and waiting list groups, AMT proved more effective on three anxiety self-report measures. Improvement in anxiety reduction was maintained after one-month follow-up. Shoemaker reports an interesting clinical observation in interviewing those AMT clients who returned to the clinic for additional treatment. These clients seemed now to be seeking help for more specific issues, such as improvement on social skills. The AMT success may have enabled the clients to reduce their extreme anxiety, which blocked efforts to develop adaptive behaviors. Once this anxiety was reduced, the clients were able either to identify other problems needing attention or to confront problems originally contributing to the anxiety. Without the threat of uncontrollable anxiety recurring, the clients could more directly deal with deficiencies.

Another way of determining the effectiveness of AMT in reducing anxieties is to measure changes in behaviors or other variables considered to be consequents of anxiety. For example, Nally (1975) theorized that delinquent behaviors are maintained because of anxiety and, further, that reduction of anxiety would lead to increases in a delinquent's ability to learn new societal rules, to display prosocial behaviors based on these rules, and to show a decrease in conduct problem behaviors and an increase in self-esteem. Using adjudicated delinquents scoring high on an anxiety measure, Nally found support for his hypotheses, using behavioral tests, self-ratings, and ratings by dormitory counselors. Using this type of logic, Suinn and his colleagues studied AMT with medical variables. The medical literature suggests that risk of heart disease is associated with the Type A behavioral patterns, such as time urgency anxiety, self-imposition of deadlines, drive toward work accomplishments, and inability to relax (Dembroski and others, 1978; Friedman and Rosenman, 1974). Suinn (1976, 1978a, 1978b) hypothesized that stress plays a crucial role in Type A behaviors, and has therefore used AMT. In a sequence of studies (Suinn, 1975b; Suinn and Bloom, 1978), AMT appeared to be useful in altering some Type A behavioral patterns. Finally, Bloom and Cantrell (in press) applied AMT to reduce the anxiety believed associated with essential hypertension. In a case report, they conclude that AMT was helpful in reducing both systolic and diastolic pressure over the six weeks of treatment and after an eight-week follow-up.

A number of studies have compared AMT with other behavioral treatment approaches. In the first publication on AMT (Suinn and Richardson, 1971), AMT proved as effective as desensitization with a specific phobia, a finding supported by later research (Richardson and Suinn, 1973a). Deffenbacher and Shelton (1978) also found that AMT and desensitization led to equivalent reductions in test anxiety. However, the level of test anxiety continued to decline six weeks after AMT treatment was ended, whereas the anxiety level increased slightly for the desensitization-treated group. Additionally, although clients were treated for the target problem of test anxiety, the AMT group showed reductions on two measures of general anxiety. This finding provides some support for the contention that AMT trains clients in self-management skills that enable them to cope with a variety of tensional states, not merely those targeted by the AMT sessions. A study by Hutchings and associates (1978) is also relevant to another premise expressed earlier in this chapter: that AMT may be valuable in resolving cognitive responses to stressors. These authors found that AMT was more effective than placebo in reducing chronic anxiety, as well as in substantially decreasing maladaptive or ruminative cognitions, under a laboratory-induced stress condition.

Modeling Approaches to Anxiety Reduction

Anxiety may also be reduced through the application of principles of observational or vicarious learning (Bandura, 1969; Rosenthal and Bandura, 1978). In the typical modeling paradigm, a client who formerly was apprehensive and avoidant is exposed to another individual (model), who behaves with calm, coping, approach behavior toward the anxiety-arousing circumstance. In turn, the model's behavior does not result in adverse consequences and may even result in positive consequences. Often the model's approach behavior is graded in small steps, and the client may be asked to imitate the model in a participant fashion—first the model and then the client engaging in the approach behavior. Through either vicarious observing alone or through the combination of vicarious experience plus guided participation, the client learns to behave less fearfully and to approach the previously anxiety-arousing situation.

Modeling procedures appear to capitalize on some combination of four basic effects of observational learning (Bandura, 1969, 1977b). The first of these is *response acquisition*. By observing a model, clients may learn new coping and/or approach behaviors, which were not previously in their repertoires. For example, snake phobics may learn how to approach and pick up a snake, where previously they did not have the knowledge or skills; or test-anxious clients might learn new strategies of moving past difficult, anxiety-arousing items on an examination. A second effect of modeling is that of *response facilitation*. In this effect, it is assumed that individuals already possess the appropriate behavior but are not employing it. The model's behavior serves to cue in this behavior. For example, some individuals are very apprehensive about job interviews and yet have the requisite verbal interactive skills with which to present themselves adequately. The opportunity to observe another individual demonstrate effective interview behavior could serve to cue in this behavior and reduce the anxiety. A third effect of vicarious learning is that of *response disinhibition*. The observation by the client that the model's approach responses do not result in adverse consequences, and in some cases result in positive consequences, can result in vicarious extinction of affective overresponsibity in the client (Bandura and Barab, 1973; Blanchard, 1970). The change in incentive information provided in the modeling sequence may also alter the cognitions and expectations about the feared situation. Either or both effects tend to disinhibit appropriate approach behavior available within response repertoires. For example, observation of others approaching and handling snakes tended to decrease the affective reactivity of snake phobics (Blanchard, 1970). A fourth effect is the *acquisition of realistic standards for self-regulation.* Some individuals experience considerable anxiety because they impose highly critical evaluations of themselves and their behavior without appropriate reference criteria. Exposure to a model who sets realistic, reasonable performance standards and then rewards himself for appropriate performance-standard matching may decrease considerably the rates of self-generated criticism and consequent anxiety. For example, M. W. Watts (1973) found that self-expectations became more realistic and task-appropriate after exposure to favorable comment from instructors. In sum, then, anxiety reduction may be achieved by exposure to a model who copes with approaching the feared object or situation, because it (1) teaches new approach and/or coping responses, (2) cues in appropriate but currently unused behavior, (3) disinhibits approach behavior as interfering anxiety is extinguished through the presentation of new information regarding the response consequences of approach, and/or (4) alters anxiety-engendering self-standards and replaces them with more realistic, less self-critical ones.

Most modeling approaches to anxiety reduction involve a principle of graduated exposure; that is, the clients observe models who engage in approach behavior, which brings them progressively into greater contact with the threatening situation. Such graduated modeling procedures have proved very effective. For example, Bandura, Grusec, and Menlove (1967) successfully treated youngsters who were highly fearful of dogs. Treatment consisted of eight brief (ten-minute) sessions over a four-day period. Fearful youngsters observed a peer who progressively came into closer and closer contact with a dog, beginning with patting the dog in an enclosed cage and ending with climbing into the pen and playing with the dog. Results showed that the modeling experience led to substantially increased approach behavior, not only to the dog involved in the modeling experience but also to another one never seen by the youngsters. Follow-up demonstrated that these gains were maintained one month later. Similar results were found when dog-phobic youngsters viewed the modeling sequences vicariously on film (Bandura and Menlove, 1968). Graduated modeling has also proved effective for socially anxious, withdrawn preschoolers (O'Connor, 1969, 1972). In these studies, withdrawn children were shown a film of peers who gradually took part in enjoyable group activities. Youngsters who observed this film increased their level of social interaction to a level equal or superior to that of nonwithdrawn children, while the untreated controls remained isolated and withdrawn. A comparison of modeling with reinforced participation (O'Connor, 1972) showed that children receiving the modeling experience increased their rate of social interaction and maintained it at follow-up, while those receiving only contingent reward reverted back to the level of untreated and still-withdrawn controls.

Participant modeling (Bandura, 1969) or *contact desensitization* (Ritter, 1969) takes graduated modeling a step further by not only exposing clients to the therapist-model but also including verbal and/or physical support while clients actively engage in approach behavior at each step. For example, snake phobics not only see the model approach and handle a snake in increasingly more direct ways; they also receive verbal and/or physical support while performing the approach behavior at each step. Participant modeling has been shown to be very effective in reducing small-animal phobias (Bandura, Blanchard, and Ritter, 1969; Blanchard, 1970), acrophobia (Ritter, 1969), aquaphobia (Sherman, 1972), and obsessive-compulsive neurotic behavior (Roper, Rachman, and Marks, 1975). In fact, some researchers argue that participant modeling may be the single most effective anxiety-reduction procedure currently available, being more effective than modeling alone, systematic desensitization, or cognitive modeling (Rosenthal and Bandura, 1978). An example of this overall comparative effectiveness can be seen in an extensive and well-designed study by Bandura, Blanchard, and Ritter (1969). At the end of treatment, 92 percent of subjects in the participant modeling condition were able to engage in the most threatening approach behavior, while only 33 percent of subjects in the modeling alone condition, 25 percent of desensitization subjects, and 0 percent of untreated controls could do so. There is, however, one serious shortcoming to participant modeling. Specifically, it may not be possible to arrange the world for participant modeling. With stationary environmental features, such as those involved in acrophobia or claustrophobia, or with stimuli that can be fixed in space and time, such as those in animal phobias, participant modeling may be possible. However, with more complex and changing anxiety-arousing conditions, such as test anxiety or various social inhibitions, it may not be possible to arrange the necessary conditions for participant modeling. With this practical caution in mind, participant modeling should be considered one of the most powerful anxiety reduction procedures available.

A number of other modeling programs, either symbolically or directly presented, have proved effective in reducing anxiety and anxiety-related problems. A few examples will be cited to demonstrate the range of such effects. For example, such programs have been effective in reducing test anxiety (D. R. Denney, 1974; Jaffe and Carlson, 1972; J. Mann, 1972; Mann and Rosenthal, 1969), spider phobias (Denney and Sullivan, 1976), fear of air travel (Denholtz and Mann, 1975), social-communication anxieties (Wright, 1976), and compulsive rituals (Rachman, Hodgson, and Marks, 1971). Additionally, videotaped modeling and demonstrations have disinhibited career information-seeking behaviors (Fisher, Reardon, and Burck, 1976); decreased anxiety, while improving school attitudes, grades, and retention of disadvantaged adults in basic education courses (Kunce, Bruch, and Thelen, 1974); reduced fear and home adjustment problems in youngsters undergoing surgery (Melamed and Siegel, 1975); and enabled individuals fearing dental offices and procedures to complete dental treatment (Shaw and Thoresen, 1974).

Another variant of modeling procedures is *covert modeling* (Cautela, Flannery, and Hanley, 1974). In covert modeling, individuals imagine the modeling sequences, rather than experiencing them directly or by stored means, such as audio or videotape, on the assumption that modeling sequences presented in imagination can have effects similar to those presented externally to the individual. For example, snake phobics imagine a graded sequence of a model gradually approaching and successfully handling a snake without untoward consequences. Covert modeling has proved effective in reducing fearfulness of and increasing approach behavior toward both rats (Cautela, Flannery, and Hanley, 1974) and snakes (Kazdin, 1973, 1974a, 1974b). Covert modeling has also been effective with socially anxious, unassertive clients (Kazdin, 1974c, 1975, 1976; Rosenthal and Reese, 1976). Comparisons of covert modeling with more overt modeling has tended to be somewhat equivocal, with some slight benefit favoring overt modeling (Cautela, Flannery, and Hanley, 1974). While some additional benefit might accrue from procedures such as participant modeling, covert modeling has the advantage of being easier and more efficient. It can be employed where the sources of anxiety are hard to arrange and control; for example, social-approach anxiety and fear of air travel.

The above review suggests that modeling is an effective anxiety reduction strategy, whether the medium of observational learning is through direct observation, imagination, or audiovisual systems. This raises questions about what factors may enhance modeling effects. As noted previously, the inclusion of therapist-model support in participant modeling greatly improved effectiveness. While the data are incomplete and should not be overgeneralized, the literature suggests some other possibilities. For example, exposure to multiple models may aid guided modeling (Bandura and Menlove, 1968), and response induction aids may facilitate participant modeling (Bandura, Jeffrey, and Wright, 1974). Variables which increase the similarity between clients and models appear to enhance effects. One effective example is to use models who have shared similar fears but who have been through treatment (Fremouw and Harmatz, 1975). Another possibility is to use coping models rather than mastery models. From the start, mastery models approach the anxiety-arousing situation directly, calmly, and competently. Coping models, in contrast, begin by showing verbally and behaviorally that they share some of the client's apprehensiveness, but they slowly gain in poise and competence over the course of the modeling sequence. Coping models are likely to be seen by clients as more similar to themselves and appear to increase modeling effects (Kazdin, 1973; Meichenbaum, 1971; Sarason, 1975a). The one exception to the coping versus mastery model appears to be situations where individuals are not already anxious and modeling is being used to prepare them for a stressor (Poser, 1976). To employ a coping model tends to suggest and vicariously condition anxiety, rather than prevent it.

Cognitive-Behavioral Approaches

Cognitive-behavioral interventions for anxiety reduction are based on the importance of cognitive mediators in the elicitation and maintenance of anxiety. According to this theoretical perspective, the stimulus situation itself does not elicit the anxiety reaction; instead, the personal constructs or meanings about that situation determine the anxiety reaction (Beck, 1976; Ellis, 1962). That is, some environmental condition prompts a set of anxiety-engendering cognitions, which in turn lead to affective arousal and behavioral disruption and/or avoidance. These idiosyncratic, yet inappropriate, nonreality-based cognitions—rather than the stimulus context per se—determine anxiety reactions. For example, Beck (1976) emphasizes the interpretation by clients of personal danger where none exists, and Ellis (1962) stresses catastrophic, absolutistic thinking as the key to the development of anxiety reactions.

Several studies have supported this cognitive-mediational conceptualization of anxiety. For example, patterns of self-verbalizations can significantly affect emotional arousal and mood (May and Johnson, 1973; Rimm and Litvak, 1969; Schacter, 1966; Velten, 1968). Individuals who overemphasize personal-social acceptance and believe that rejection is catastrophic tend to experience anxiety while imagining social situations involving rejection (Goldfried and Sobocinski, 1975). Worry (ruminative self-preoccupation and evaluation) contributes significantly to performance deterioration of highly text-anxious individuals (Deffenbacher, 1980). Additionally, worry correlated with lower performance of the highly test-anxious, while physiological arousal did not (Holroyd, 1976). Thus, at least in some situations, cognitive-interpretive patterns appear to contribute to emotional arousal and/or anxiety-related behavior.

If distorted cognitive patterns prompt anxiety, then it follows that changing these belief systems to be more rational and socially appropriate should tend to decrease affective arousal, defensive avoidance, and disrupted performance. Viewing the world in more reasonable terms may leave the individual experiencing frustration and other mildly negative emotional states but should free the person to engage in whatever problem-solving and coping behaviors are at his disposal. This is exactly the goal of cognitive-restructuring approaches; for example, for clients to develop more reasonable appraisals of themselves and the world. Therapeutic intervention is designed to (1) help clients identify dysfunctional cognitive patterns; (2) generate alternative, more reality-based cognitions; and (3) provide systematic practice in applying these alternative cognitive patterns in anxiety-arousing situations. Two such cognitive-restructuring approaches are reviewed below.

Rational-emotive therapy (Ellis, 1962) is perhaps the forerunner of most current cognitive-restructuring approaches. Ellis claims that there are twelve core irrational ideas that generate debilitating negative affect such as anxiety. One such belief is that we must be loved and approved by significant others. Endorsing such a belief could contribute heavily to social-evaluative anxiety as individuals sensitize themselves to cues of possible rejection. Rational-emotive therapy is designed to identify and root out such irrational beliefs. A first step is direct instruction and persuasion in a cognitive-mediational analysis of human emotion and behavior. Individuals then begin to monitor and record their thought patterns. These thought patterns become grist for therapy sessions. The therapist directly and forcefully confronts the illogicality and irrationality of the thoughts and provides abundant modeling of corrective alternatives. Cognitive and behavioral performance tasks are then assigned to provide individuals with practice in identifying, analyzing, and altering their thought patterns toward more realistic, nonanxiety-arousing appraisals. Controlled research focusing on outcome has shown that rational-emotive therapy is effective in reducing speech anxiety (Karst and Trexler, 1970; Meichenbaum, Gilmore, and Fedoravicius, 1971; Trexler and Karst, 1972), test anxiety (Warren, Deffenbacher, and Brading, 1976), interpersonal anxiety (Di Loreto, 1971), anxieties in older individuals (Keller, Croake, and Brooking, 1975), and stuttering (Moleski and Tosi, 1976). Additionally, *systematic rational restructuring* has proved effective in the reduction of test and speech anxieties (Goldfried, Decenteceo, and Weinberg, 1974; Goldfried, Linehan, and Smith, 1978). Systematic rational restructuring is a rational-emotive type of procedure involving greater systematization and the practice of cognitive restructuring through imaginal presentation of a hierarchy of anxiety-arousing situations.

A second major variant of cognitive-restructuring approaches is *stress inoculation* (Meichenbaum, 1972, 1977). Stress inoculation focuses less on the reduction of irrational self-statements and more on the development of task-oriented self-instruction. The emphasis, therefore is on the development of self-guiding coping instructions and skills. Stress inoculation is split into three general, overlapping phases. The first or educational phase provides clients with a cognitive understanding of anxiety and a coping rationale for treatment. While educational processes differ from program to program (Jaremko, 1979), they often include (1) a cognitive-mediational explanation of anxiety, typically in terms of both worry and emotionality—that is, cognitive distortions and heightened physiological arousal; (2) a self-management rationale for treatment, emphasizing that clients can learn ways of talking and guiding themselves through stressful situations; and (3) a description of treatment as the development of self-instructional training to control worrisome cognitions and applied relaxation skills to control heightened emotionality. The educational phase is followed by a skills-training phase, in which clients learn the skills necessary to reduce stress. In this phase, clients learn to identify dysfunctional cognitions; develop alternative, appropriate self-instructions; and develop applied relaxation skills. Next is the application phase, during which clients assemble and practice the coping skills learned in the previous phase. Clients usually practice these coping skills while confronting the anxiety-arousing situations in imagination. That is, they imagine anxiety-provoking situations and systematically apply their new repertoires of task-oriented self-instruction, including applied relaxation, to reduce any tension experienced. Application training is further broken down into four separate stages: (1) preparing for a stressor, (2) confronting a stressor, (3) confronting feelings of being overwhelmed, and (4) applying coping skills. This breakdown is thought to facilitate learning and application of coping skills to different anxiety situations. Application is transferred into real life with *in vivo* practice as clients demonstrate successful anxiety control within sessions. Variants of stress inoculation training have successfully reduced speech anxiety (Fremouw & Harmatz, 1975; Fremouw and Zitter, 1978; Glogower, Fremouw, and McCroskey, 1978), test anxiety (Deffenbacher and Hahnloser, 1979; Holroyd, 1976; Hussian and Lawrence, 1978; Meichenbaum, 1972), interpersonal anxiety (Glass, Gottman, and Shmurak, 1976), and fear of dead animals (D'Zurilla, Wilson, and Nelson, 1973).

Conclusions

Several final observations concerning intervention should be made:

1. *The importance of assessment.* Rather than emphasizing the technical value of the various treatment approaches, the therapist should first make a careful diagnosis of the client's problem. The therapy can then be made to fit the client, rather than vice versa. Thus, if cognitions seem to form a major role in determining the affective arousal or the disruption of behaviors, then a cognitive strategy or a modeling approach emphasizing thought processes would be desirable. Similarly, if affective arousal is so prominent as to prevent the client from confronting cognitions, then anxiety management training may be used first, to control the anxiety arousal, before the worry components are dealt with. This orientation reemphasizes that no one approach will cure all clients, that "stress" or "anxiety" does not comprise a single syndrome, and that clients may have differing ways of experiencing stress even when faced with similar stressors.

2. *The importance of examining the total gestalt that comprises the client's stresses.* Resolving irrational thoughts, offering models of appropriate behaviors, or applying anxiety management approaches for affect control may not be the total solution for all clients. In some cases, these treatments provide anxiety control or anxiety reduction that will permit the client to develop other needed skills for problem-solving. Thus, the socially anxious person may now be able to try out dating behaviors; the

anxiety neurotic may now be able to confront personal inadequacies; the anxious delinquent may be able to learn prosocial behaviors; and the public-speaking-anxious client may now be prepared to learn about audience management, eye contact, speech delivery, and the like. The behavioral approach assumes that anxiety can be eliminated through focus on current topics rather than past psychodynamic histories or events. At the same time, the approach also recognizes that current factors contributing to anxiety may have to be treated to prevent future reexposure to stress. In the desensitization model, the assumption is that fear responses were once conditioned to certain cues, such as heights. Through counterconditioning, these cues are no longer fear producing but neutral. In this case, no further treatment is needed. However, other clients may need further problem-solving treatment. For example, a student may reexperience failure on examinations if he does not acquire better study skills. This failure and the attending stress consequences may lead to resensitizing the client, and test anxiety might then be reacquired. Desensitization could once more eliminate the anxiety, but study-skills training would be suitable if "relapse" is to be prevented and if changes in course grades are to be expected (Mitchell and Ng, 1972).

3. *The importance of viewing therapy as training for real-life activities.* Traditional therapy approaches assumed that changes occurring in the therapy office will necessarily transfer to settings in real life. Some approaches, such as role playing and psychodrama, were introduced to permit some skill practice in the therapy hour. Coming from a tradition that emphasizes learning principles, including attention to the importance of transfer of learning, behavioral therapies are placing more and more emphasis on training for real-life events. This is achieved by designing the therapy sessions to simulate real-life circumstances (for example, through the use of imagery in desensitization scenes) or through the assigning of homework *in vivo* (as in practicing relaxation initially in nonthreatening settings in AMT). In recent reviews of the literature on biofeedback, Blanchard (Blanchard and Young, 1974; Silver and Blanchard, 1978) supports the importance of transfer training in his conclusions that homework seems to enable biofeedback results to persist after treatment is completed.

4. *The importance of follow-up in therapy outcome evaluation.* Research on the value of the treatment method should include follow-up, whether the study is a formal research project or a clinician evaluating the effects on his client. Conclusions that an approach was not effective, or only equally effective (compared to another treatment strategy), may be misleading. In some studies of anxiety management using self-control models, such as anxiety management training, it appears that improvements continue during follow-up, so that AMT might in some ways be superior to desensitization. For example, Deffenbacher (Deffenbacher and others, 1979; Deffenbacher and Shelton, 1978) discovered significant anxiety reduction

during follow-up that had not been evident immediately at termination of treatment. Furthermore, AMT skills appeared to have generalized or transferred to helping clients control anxieties other than those immediately targeted for treatment. In contrast, studies on the cessation of smoking (Hunt and Bespalec, in press) indicate that nearly any completed program will lead to cessation of smoking; however, recidivism is extremely high.

5. *The importance of a self-control model to therapy.* A current trend in behavioral therapy is the introduction of self-regulation as a therapeutic goal (Kanfer, 1976; Mahoney and Arnkoff, 1978; Thoresen and Mahoney, 1974). This trend shifts the idea of self-control to "something which a person *does* instead of something he or she *has*" (Mahoney and Arnkoff, 1978, p. 693). In this light, therapy may also shift from attempting to reduce anxiety in a client to training a client in anxiety reduction—a more difficult but possibly a more effective therapeutic task. Self-control training may require that the client learn (1) to observe and monitor both the external and the internal environment, (2) to develop new coping skills, and (3) to transfer these skills *in vivo* without reminders from a therapist. Clients may be completely unaware of cue conditions that prompt their anxieties, much less be aware of their internal signs that stress is building, until it is too late to abort the anxiety response. Even with knowledge of stimulus conditions or of coping alternatives, many clients cannot put such knowledge into practice. Knowing, as most clinicians discover, is not identical with doing. Hence, the therapeutic session must deal with training in doing and not simply with knowing or with insight. Self-regulation or self-control takes this process to the next logical step, enabling the client to know and to do, but without the dependence on a therapist. Research suggests that, even with desensitization, a self-control desensitization model enhances treatment effects (Deffenbacher and Parks, 1979; Denney and Rupert, 1977).

Behavioral Interventions: A Summary

To provide the reader with a more detailed comparison of the various interventions in this chapter, the following are samples of the way in which each therapeutic approach would deal with a client who has severe social-evaluative anxiety, such as when evaluated by an employer.

Desensitization. A hierarchy of about ten scenes would be constructed, ranging from a scene arousing very low anxiety ("I am at a party with friends I've known for years. Some of us are listening to George as he regales us with a lengthy story of his trip. The mood is friendly.") to a scene arousing high anxiety ("I am getting my first evaluation on the job. I really want to do well on this job, because it means so much. I am sitting in front of Mr. T's huge desk; he is reading my file and will soon be telling me how I did.") After relaxing, the client would be instructed to "Switch on the scene, be in that activity again. If you experience any level of tension, signal me." If the client signals, the scene is terminated, relaxation instructions are initiated, and a scene with a lower anxiety level is introduced. Success is defined as the ability of the client to visualize being in the scenes without experiencing anxiety. Completion of this process in the therapy office is considered sufficient to transfer to life events.

Anxiety Management Training. Two different scenes when anxiety was experienced are obtained, one involving high anxiety, the other involving moderate anxiety. Therapy and homework sessions train the client in the self-initiation of relaxation. Anxiety scenes are then presented, which might not be related to social-evaluative situations, provided the scene invokes anxiety. The client is told, "Switch on the scene and use it to retrieve the anxiety feeling again, noticing how you experience anxiety, what signs you notice. Permit yourself to experience a higher and higher level of anxiety. Now switch off the scene. Regain relaxation by taking a deep breath, focusing on relaxing the hands, the upper arms, and so on." As the client shows ability to switch from anxiety arousal to relaxation, the therapist gives the client more responsibility for stress management; for example, "Switch on the scene; permit the anxiety to build. Then, when you are ready, use whatever procedure helps you to regain relaxation and eliminate the anxiety." Finally, as self-control in the therapy office is observed, the client is instructed to apply the technique of relaxation to life events. Success is defined as the client's ability to actively initiate anxiety control within the sessions and *in vivo* when faced with stressors.

Modeling. A series of anxiety-arousing situations involving social-evaluative settings would be specified in concrete detail. One of these might relate to the job evaluation interview mentioned by the client as a major problem. The therapist might use videotapes demonstrating appropriate interview behavior, with the taped vignettes including a person with the mannerisms of Mr. T, the employer. The "employee" in the scene would be similar to the client—about the same age and the same sex. In the tape, the "employee" may behave somewhat apprehensively and tentatively but soon starts to demonstrate more controlled behaviors, such as looking steadily and attentively at the employer, requesting clarification, asking for advice on improvement, offering clarification. The therapist and the client view this tape together. Then the client tries out the observed skills. The therapist provides immediate positive and corrective feedback, such as "That's better. You're looking up at me rather than past me. You worded that comment in a nondefensive fashion; that shows me you've listened to my evaluation of your work. Remember, if you feel jittery, you can simply share that feeling with the supervisor. Why don't we try having you do that?" As the client makes progress in both anxiety control and adaptative responding, the therapist may then go on to other models of other anxiety situations.

Cognitive Restructuring. The therapist and client would outline a number of anxiety-arousing situations. The client lists thoughts usually associated with these situations; for example, "I won't have a perfect record. Mr. T will find out that I'm not as good as he thinks I am." The therapist then challenges the rationality of these thoughts—for example, by confronting the need to be perfect, whether other employees are that good, and whether perfection is necessary for continued employment. The client might then be instructed to imagine the situation while giving himself the following instructions: "Ok, what is my job here? Just stay cool and listen to Mr. T's feedback. Now what are the possibilities? He may say he is pleased with me and everything is going fine. That would be great! But what if he gives me negative feedback and criticizes my work? Ok, now just relax; that's it, take three deep breaths and relax (pause while doing this). That's good. Now, what is really true about negative feedback? Well, I sure would not like it, but it would not be the end of the world if I received it, and it won't mean my job. Just helpful information to think about. There is no reason why Mr. T should give me positive feedback just because I want it. If he gives me negative feedback, I am going to try to use my skills to keep the tension down, listen to what he has to say, and present myself assertively as I have learned in therapy. That's it, stay cool and on target." Similar self-dialogues for approaching and confronting social-evaluative situations are developed and practiced.

23

Biofeedback Training

Thomas H. Budzynski
Kirk E. Peffer

Although there are many definitions of anxiety, Weiss and English (1957) succinctly describe the condition as a specific, unpleasurable state of tension which indicates the presence of some danger to the organism. Like anxiety, psychological stress has many definitions but is generally considered to be a state of discomforting tension, conflict, or psychological pressure.

The stimuli causing anxiety are often difficult to delineate; however, the stimuli producing the stress response are usually known to the individual. Often the stress response increases as a result of competing motor tendencies; that is, the person is in a bind as to which of several possible courses of action should be pursued. At other times, the stress pattern may be produced when the individual is required to perform under time pressure, or in circumstances where performance failure produces real or imagined adverse consequences. Stressful episodes can precipitate anxiety or even result in an anxiety attack, in which the individual experiences a state of panic. An anxiety attack differs somewhat from generalized or pervasive anxiety, in which some level of anxiety is present almost constantly.

We can probably agree that stress and anxiety involve heightened physiological arousal. Obviously, there are times when such arousal is very adaptive. Most generally, these are situations that require fight-or-flight behavior. But if these situations do not call for or allow such vigorous muscular activity, then the arousal pattern is maladaptive. Moreover, we might say that the stress or anxiety arousal can be dysfunctional if it is inappropriate for the task at hand; that is, the arousal is either too much or too little of a preparation for the task. In this instance, the performance will not be optimal. Finally, we can consider that an inability to recover normally to a prestress level after the stressor has been removed constitutes a maladaptive response.

Summarizing: anxiety and stress become maladaptive:

1. When they are elicited too frequently.
2. When they are sustained too long.
3. When, after the stressful event, recovery to relaxed levels is too prolonged.
4. When they result in decreased performance.
5. When the response is lacking the final stage of vigorous muscular activity.
6. When they lead to mental or physical disorders.

Stress Response Factors

Examining first the response side of the stimulus-response stress equation, we note that some stimulus (stressor) comes to produce the response (stress) in the individual. As stated above, this response can become maladaptive (stress becomes distress) and, if chronic, may precipitate disease process. In most instances, this response began as a perfectly normal and adaptive reaction of the individual. The response is generally believed to be initiated by cortically generated "alarm" signals activating the hypothalamus, which in turn begins to increase the activity of the sympathetic branch of the autonomic nervous system. The hypothalamus also initiates the endocrine changes regulated by the pituitary gland. The sympathetic activation causes heart–rate and volume increases, blood pressure increases, decrease in skin temperature of hands and feet as blood is shunted away from extremities and digestive organs to the large muscles, increased emotional sweating, increased tonus in certain skeletal muscles, locked diaphragm, and tight anus.

The pituitary gland secretes ACTH (adrenocorticotrophic hormone), which in turn releases corticoids from the adrenal glands. Under acute stress conditions, stomach acidity is lowered; but with chronic, long-term stress, the level of hydrochloric acid can rise. At this point it can interact with high corticoid levels to produce ulcers, a common distress disorder. If stress is chronic, the corticoids also cause shrinkage of the thymus gland, an important contributor to the immune response, thereby lowering the ability of the body to protect itself against disease.

Although the stress response, or "fight-or-flight" response, originally evolved as a reaction to physical danger, research over the past quarter century in psychophysiology and psychosomatic medicine has generated abundant evidence that this reaction can be psychologically triggered (Greenfield and Sternbach, 1972). A number of researchers (Charvat, Dell, and Folkow, 1964; Selye, 1956; Wolff, 1968) have proposed that the stress reaction and its triggering by central nervous system (CNS) influences may be at the root of man's stress-related disorders. Psychologically mediated stress disorders probably began to occur as a result of the ability of the more recently evolved neocortical structures to symbolically portray past/future threatening events. The use of language which allows past/future verb tenses undoubtedly contributed to the ability of the individual to "distress" himself. However, this is getting into the stimulus side of the equation. Let us return to the response considerations.

Over the past twenty-five years, it has been a common observation in psychophysiological research that individuals suffering from stress disorders show hyperreactivity in a particular "preferred" system (Sternbach, 1966). That is, even though the stressors may vary, the individual with the stress disorder will tend to respond maximally with the same physiological system. Engel and Bickford (1961), for example, found that hypertensive patients produced more response specificity in their blood pressure systems than normotensive controls. These research findings imply that the healthy individual who shows marked response specificity is predisposed to the development of a stress disorder (Stoyva, 1977).

Although the specificity of a given disorder may be determined by the preferred system, research by Wenger and his colleagues (Wenger and Cullen, 1972) provides evidence that a chronic pattern of sympathetic arousal might be implicated in the predisposition to a stress disorder. During World War II, Wenger measured the autonomic patterns of thousands of young, healthy Air Force cadets. He developed an autonomic balance scoring system by which each individual was given an estimate of autonomic balance, called the A score. This index represented the composite of the values obtained on each of seven physiological variables reflecting autonomic function. Low $\bar{A}$ scores represented apparent sympathetic nervous system (SNS) dominance.

High $\bar{A}$ scores indicated apparent parasympathetic dominance. The cadet subjects showed a wide range of $\bar{A}$ scores. When Wenger applied this same procedure to patients with different types of disorders, he discovered that, with few exceptions, the patients in these groups showed $\bar{A}$ scores indicating an apparent SNS dominance.

Some fifteen to twenty years after the World War II study, Wenger sent questionnaires to the former cadets. The questionnaire was designed to allow a determination of which disorders, including mental, claimed the formerly healthy cadets. The results showed that those individuals who had low $\bar{A}$ scores (apparent SNS dominance) produced the greatest incidence of stress-related disorders. In contrast, the incidence of these problems was low in those former cadets who originally produced average or high $\bar{A}$ scores. It appears, therefore, that those individuals who show a resting autonomic pattern characterized by sympathetic functioning are more likely to develop a stress disorder in the future.

What could cause a state of chronic sympathetic arousal? Based on his extensive research, Malmo (1975) hypothesized that a deficiency of the autonomic nervous system regulatory mechanism may be characteristic of many anxiety and psychotic states. In anxious individuals, for example, Malmo noted that forearm electromyogram (EMG) levels which had increased in response to a startle stimulus took considerably longer to return to pre-stimulation levels than was the case with normals. Other researchers have uncovered similar evidence of slowed system responsivity in anxious or stressed individuals. Howe (1958) reported slower extinction of galvanic skin response (GSR) in anxious patients compared with normal controls. Stewart and associates (1959) compared anxious, schizophrenic, and manic-depressive patients on habituation to a series of auditory stimuli. The anxious people took longer to habituate than did the other two patient groups.

Further support for slowness of recovery came from the studies of Lader and Mathews (1968), who compared normals, patients with specific anxieties, and those with generalized or chronic anxiety. Habituation to white-noise stimuli took considerably longer for the chronically anxious group than for the other two groups. The more generalized, chronic group also manifested higher arousal levels when resting, as indicated by higher rates of spontaneous GSR response (Lader, 1969). These results are consistent with our own early observations when we compared subjects with generalized anxiety and those with more circumscribed phobias. The treatment program for both groups consisted of frontal EMG relaxation training (biofeedback from the frontalis muscles of the forehead) followed by systematic desensitization. We noted that the chronic-anxiety group took longer to relax after each visualized anxiety scene from the hierarchy. Furthermore, the chronic group took twice as long to learn the relaxation and required approximately twice as many desensitization sessions as did the circumscribed anxiety group (Budzynski and Stoyva, 1973, 1975; Stoyva and Budzynski, 1974).

Summarizing the research results on chronic anxiety, Malmo (1975, p. 17) concluded, "Under a variety of conditions, high-anxiety patients continue to be overactivated physiologically, when normals have returned to baseline." The physiological goal, therefore, with highly stressed or anxious individuals, might be to train them not only to produce a physiological pattern of relaxed musculature and decreased sympathetic arousal but, additionally, to be able to recover in normal time back to the prestress level (Budzynski, 1979).

An inability to recover to prestress level in a normal amount of time is a phenomenon that appears in the psychophysiological research on hypertension as well. White and Gildea (1937) compared blood pressure responding in normal controls, anxious patients, and hypertensives. During a stress procedure, the hypertensives showed the greatest pressure responses and the slowest return to baseline. Brod and colleagues (1959) compared hypertensives with normals in a situation where all were subjected to a mental arithmetic stressor. Mean blood pressure rose 21 mm in the normals and 30 mm in the hypertensives. Recovery times, however, were quite different in the two groups, with most of the normals returning to baseline in less than four minutes. Not surprisingly, the hypertensives took longer—in fact, more than sixteen minutes—to recover back to baseline. In another hypertensive study, Patel (1977), one of the first researcher/clinicians to use biofeedback with successful results with hypertension, showed that recovery of pressures after stress improved from eighteen to five minutes after training. Patel combined Yoga breathing, meditation, and two forms of biofeedback to produce the remarkable results of approximately 20 mm average decrease under baseline systolic pressures in her patients.

Thus far, the research reviewed indicates that individuals suffering from anxiety, distress, or stress disorders have a tendency to respond to a variety of stressors with a preferred system. Furthermore, once stimulated by a stressor, they do not return to prestimulation levels. Finally, healthy individuals who show a sympathetically dominated resting autonomic pattern may be unusually susceptible to stress disorders. We can now consider the stimulus side of the equation to find out what triggers the stress response.

Stimulus (Stressor) Factors

Although all psychological stress reactions are by definition triggered by cognitive interpretations, we can consider four factors that contribute to stress responding.

Cognitive. Many clients suffering from stress or anxiety problems do not realize that their subtle, fleeting thoughts or images can influence physiological functioning. Negative self-statements, often originating from incorrect premises developed early in life, can initiate the stress response. The client's interpretation of self-generated thoughts or of external events can be distorted, so that the threat potential of these stimuli is greatly exaggerated. Often a client torments himself with multiple conflicts almost simultaneously; that is, he quickly jumps from a consideration of one problem to another, ultimately finding that none gets solved by this approach. Less frequently, we find that negative visual images can precipitate a stress response.

Most difficult are those cases involving deeply held negative beliefs, values, or self-images. These maladaptive cognitions often prove relatively resistant to the conscious cognitive therapy procedures. Consequently, in these cases we have begun to employ procedures that affect primarily unconscious processes—procedures such as subliminal techniques, twilight learning (Budzynski, 1972, 1976, 1977b), and hypnosis. With the less difficult maladaptive cognitions, we have used cognitive therapy (Meichenbaum, 1977) and rational-emotive therapy (Ellis, 1962).

Overt Behavioral. Does the client possess adequate social and work skills? Is the client lacking in assertiveness? Does the client manifest potentially embarrassing behaviors of which he or she has little or no awareness? If there are such distressing behaviors, we can use role modeling, rehearsal, assertive training, videotape feedback, and other behavior modification procedures.

Environmental. The work and family environments may produce distress even in an individual with effective stress coping skills in other areas. The organizational work structure, for example, exerts its own set of unique forces on the individual. The organization uses these forces in an attempt to channel the employee's behavior toward certain goals (Huse, 1975). The employee conforms to organizational policy in return for wages and perhaps security, although the price of such conformity may be anxiety, depression, or a stress disorder. Physical escape and active manipulation of the situation are possible alternatives to aversive environmental pressures. Clients can be urged to examine such alternatives, and they can be taught how to modify environments, including the behaviors of relevant other individuals in those environments. Problems of this sort are often best treated with group training in stress management. At the Biofeedback Institute of Denver, we often teach stress coping skills in a group setting. Organizational stress problems are discussed along with a variety of coping techniques. A person's awareness and control of physiological responses is augmented by biofeedback demonstrations and training.

Family problems are handled by therapy sessions with relevant family members present. Communication skills and contract therapy are used to decrease distress in this environment.

Physiological. All the above factors influence physiology; therefore, modifying them in the direction of adaptive functioning will result in a more ideal physiological response to stress as well. We can, however, help individuals develop control over the stress response by focusing training on the physiological functioning itself.

Relaxation training of one form or another has been used in a number of programs applied to anxiety and stress-related disorders. The two most widely known techniques are progressive relaxation (Jacobsen, 1938) and autogenic training (Luthe, 1969). Both of these techniques involve the voluntary deep relaxation of the main muscle groups. Autogenic training, however, also emphasizes awareness of and control over autonomic responses associated with a decrease in sympathetic dominance. Since these approaches are intended to produce what amounts to an antistress physiological pattern, they should be well suited for the treatment of stress-linked disorders. For over half a century, progressive relaxation and autogenic training have been effective for just such problems. All biofeedback clinicians augment the biofeedback training with one or both of these relaxation procedures.

Although progressive relaxation and autogenic training are effective, the training can be lengthy, and success depends on the trainee's ability to discriminate extremely subtle proprioceptive, kinesthetic, and interoceptive sensations. Discriminations of this sort appear to be particularly difficult for those who most need the training; that is, individuals who have a chronically heightened arousal level. Because various components of their arousal patterns are frequently high, these individuals tend to become adapted to, and therefore lacking in awareness of, these sensations. Consequently, training effectiveness might be improved by the addition of a technique that would aid in the development of these fine discriminations.

Biofeedback can enhance discrimination of subtle physiological functioning because it produces an external "effect," whereas previously the effect was so subtle as to be below awareness. As Sheffield (1965) has noted, an inherent feature of Thorndike's (1911) law of effect is that the *effect* of a response determines whether it is learned. Therefore, the effect of a response must in some way be detected by the organism or recorded in its nervous system. Somehow the organism's nervous system must connect the temporal contiguity of the response and its consequences. If a physiological response has little or no sensory feedback, it is difficult to understand how the nervous system can take account of the fact that the response has occurred. This may explain why the mastery of Zen or Yoga requires years of dedicated practice before voluntary control of certain autonomic responses is acquired, and why autogenic training and progressive relaxation demand such regular practice over a relatively long period of time. The "effect," the *making of the internal external,* is the biofeedback. This electronic means of enhancing discrimination of subtle internal sensations not only provides precise, easy-to-assimilate information about the response but, in most instances, provides accurate quantification of the response as well (Budzynski, 1978).

Biofeedback Training in the Clinic

The use of biofeedback for anxiety or stress disorders is predicated on the assumption that the client shows evidence of maladaptive responding in one or more physiological systems. We have found that such dysfunction may *not* appear if the client is simply asked to relax as measurements are made. Indeed, such responding is more likely to show up in a dynamic rather than a static test situation. Consequently, since 1974, both at the Biofeedback Institute of Denver and at the biofeedback laboratory of the University of Colorado Medical Center and lately at the biofeedback clinic at Georgetown University, we have employed a standardized psychophysiological stress profile (PSP) in order to help define maladaptive responding. The PSP session, which follows the intake evaluation session, is carried out in three phases: relaxation, stress, and recovery. Measurements are made each minute of forearm extensor and frontal (frontalis) EMG, finger skin temperature, electrodermal response (EDR), and, in some cases, occipital-central EEG, heart rate, and blood pressure. The client is asked to relax in the recliner chair in a semidarkened room for roughly thirteen minutes. Next, the instructions are given for the stress part of the sequence. Essentially, the client is asked to perform a mental arithmetic task. He is told that he will be compared to grade school, high school, college, and professional populations. Following the six-minute stress period, the trainee is told once more to relax as deeply as possible. This last "recovery" period indicates how well the trainee can return to the prestress relaxed level. Relative to normative data obtained from individuals free of stress disorders, a client's response to the PSP may indicate maladaptiveness in one or more of the monitored physiological systems, and in one or more of the three phases. A headache client, for example, may show an inability to recover frontal EMG back to a prestress level; at the same time, he may look normal on skin temperature and EDR in all three phases. In contrast, the generalized-anxiety client would more likely show heightened EDR in all three phases, although the EMG levels may be normal. Labile essential hypertensives tend to differ from normals in their inability to recover peripheral skin temperature after being stressed.

The three-phase PSP enables us to tailor biofeedback training to the individual. If he is hyperreactive in the skeletal muscle system, we emphasize EMG feedback. Maladaptive peripheral skin temperature can be modified by thermal feedback. Electrodermal levels can be brought within a normal range by means of EDR feedback training. The basic structure of the biofeedback training follows a systems approach devised by the first author in 1973.

This sequence of training was designed primarily for the use of biofeedback technicians with relatively little experience with biofeedback. Transition from one type of biofeedback to another is based on criteria developed in our laboratory and clinic over the past decade. A series of flow charts (see Budzynski, Stoyva, and Peffer, 1979) details the logical progression through the training.[1]

Basically, the client first learns to relax the muscle system and then the autonomic responses. When she meets the criteria for relaxation in this near ideal (quiet, semidarkened) environment, we then begin the transfer procedures that will permit generalization to everyday life. Augmenting the biofeedback training is the very important home practice. We have found that a successful program of this sort is a six-phase cassette tape relaxation-training sequence, which will be described later. The biofeedback training is also combined with psychotherapy or other approaches if this is deemed necessary.

Individuals suffering from stress-related disorders seem to have little awareness of the hyperaroused state of their physiology. Consequently, they are ill prepared to begin to focus on the subtle internal sensations that may signal relaxation. Having adapted to a gradually increasing level of arousal, they no longer have a conscious memory of what being relaxed really feels like. In many instances, they may even "feel bad" if they find themselves inadvertently relaxing.

These individuals initially are taken through the progressive relaxation procedure (Jacobsen, 1938), which involves the tensing and then relaxing of the major muscle groups. Even though these chronically tense people may not relax to low levels, they at least perceive a contrast between moderate and high muscle tension. This exercise can be enhanced by the use of EMG feedback from the arm and frontal (forehead) areas. With biofeedback, it is much easier to be aware of the difference between the two tension levels. If there is time following the tense-relax procedure, the client practices lowering forearm extensor EMG with feedback. It is at this first stage of training where the client must learn the important distinction between passively and actively trying to relax. The active striver *tries* to make the muscles relax instead of *allowing* the muscles to relax. This client must learn to *let go* and *allow* relaxation to occur. Passive manipulation of the arm by the therapist may be necessary on several occasions in order to teach the client this distinction.

---

[1]The criteria are based on normative data gathered with biofeedback equipment manufactured by Bio-Feedback Systems, Inc., 2736 47th Street, Boulder, Colorado 80301. Details of the use of the systems flow charts are available as a cassette tape, catalog number T-18, plus flow diagrams from BMA Audio Cassette Programs, 200 Park Avenue South, New York 10003.

Once the client can produce forearm EMG levels below 2.50 micro-volts peak-to-peak with feedback, the sound or visual feedback can be faded gradually. (Biofeedback takes many forms; however, the EMG equipment used in our institute and at the medical center produces a tone that varies in pitch, or a series of clicks that vary in repetition rate, or a tricolor visual display.) When the client can maintain levels below 3 microvolts without feedback, we *add* frontal EMG feedback. (A mixer unit permits us to present multiple feedback signals simultaneously to the headphones worn by the client.) Now receiving two feedback signals, the client can be aware of the arm tension as she practices with the frontal EMG feedback. If the client does not receive two feedback signals, the arm tension tends to increase as the client focuses on the new feedback signal. The two signals can be made quite distinct: for example, the tricolor visual display for the arm EMG and the tone or clicks in the headphones tracking frontal EMG.

The frontal musculature is ordinarily much more difficult to relax to low levels than is the forearm. One of the functions of the forehead musculature is to translate thoughts and emotions into facial expressions. Some thin layers of the facial muscles are *nonstraited* and receive sympathetic innervation (Rubin, 1977). The origin of this autonomic innervation is unclear, but Miehlke (1973) has noted that "emotional control of our facial musculature is conducted by afferences from the thalamus and the globus pallidus mediated via interneurons in the reticular formation." Physicians are familiar with the apparent dual innervation of the facial musculature. An accident may deprive the patient of voluntary control or autonomic control (reflex emotional expression) or both; but the two types of control can exist independently. An individual in a biofeedback situation may easily be able to decrease voluntary afferent activity to facial muscles yet find himself frustrated in an attempt to decrease the remaining tonus due to sympathetic tone. Since 1966, when we first developed the 100-1,000 Hz bandpass EMG system, we have been aware of a peculiar plateau in learning to relax the frontal area. Often the trainee will decrease the frontal EMG over a few sessions to a level of roughly 5 microvolts (this may vary from four to six across individuals). After this, little progress is made for four to ten sessions. At this point, the learning seems to progress again, with a drop to levels of 3 microvolts or less. It is at this second decrease, after the plateau, where clients most often report feeling deeply relaxed—possibly because they are now able to decrease autonomic afferent firing to the facial musculature. Since the sympathetic branch of the autonomic system has a tendency to change as a whole rather than discretely, the decrease in sympathetic tone in the facial muscles may simply reflect a general decrease in sympathetic tone throughout the body. Because this sort of general decrease in sympathetic tone is the opposite of a stress response, we consider it important to achieve during the biofeedback training. We have therefore set the criterion of 2.5

microvolts for frontal relaxation. (It is important to note that this criterion was established with a bandpass of 100-1,000 Hz, noise subtracted.)

One final note on frontal EMG has to do with whether there is EMG activity in the frontalis muscle at rest. Basmajian (1976) has stated, "At rest all parts of the frontalis muscle in most people relax completely, but the muscle springs into vigorous EMG activity whenever the eyebrows are raised." Our own observations, however, agree with those of researchers from Osaka University Medical School (Sumitsuji and others, 1967), who found that the frontalis muscle produces continuous muscle action potentials even in the resting state. Our results with surface sensors indicate resting tonus levels in almost all individuals, although these frontal levels can drop to below 1 microvolt if the trainee falls asleep. On the one hand, in the absence of sympathetic tone, the frontal EMG may drop to low levels if the client also decreases all voluntary afferent activity; on the other hand, the client who has difficulty decreasing frontal EMG below 4 to 6 microvolts may be manifesting moderate to high levels of sympathetic tone.

Frontal EMG biofeedback training for anxiety was begun in 1967 in our biofeedback laboratory at the University of Colorado Medical Center. We first worked with anxious clients who had been unable to relax with the brief Wolpe-Jacobsen training usually employed by behavior therapists. Over the past twelve years, we have worked with a large number of chronically anxious clients (Budzynski and Stoyva, 1973, 1975). Our general conclusion was that the more pervasive or generalized the anxiety, the more biofeedback training was required to reach relaxed levels. Later, Raskin, Johnson and Rondestvedt (1973) found that a combination of frontal EMG feedback and the instruction to practice at home each day was moderately useful for severe chronic anxiety. All ten clients in this study had been troubled by severe anxiety symptoms for at least three years. Individual psychotherapy and medication had not been successful for these clients. The training resulted in dramatic lessening of all anxiety symptoms in one client, and three others showed moderate improvement. It should be remembered that these people were not trained to transfer their relaxation skills to everyday situations.

Canter, Kondo, and Knott (1975) examined the relative effectiveness of frontal EMG feedback and progressive relaxation with twenty-eight patients suffering from anxiety neurosis and having complaints of muscle tension and insomnia as well. Fourteen of these patients reported acute panic episodes, and the other fourteen were more typical chronic anxiety cases without acute panic episodes. Although both feedback and progressive relaxation reduced frontal EMG activity, the biofeedback was found to be generally superior in producing longer reductions in muscle activity and in decreasing anxiety symptoms for a greater number of patients. Townsend, House, and Addario (1976) compared frontal EMG to group psychotherapy for chronically anxious subjects. The biofeedback produced significantly greater reductions in EMG levels, mood disturbance, and trait anxiety than did the group psychotherapy.

Frontal EMG feedback has even been compared to Valium for treatment of chronic, free-floating anxiety (Lavellee and others, 1975). Forty outpatients with chronic, free-floating anxiety were used in this Montreal study. In general, the results showed that frontal EMG feedback had a more prolonged therapeutic effect than did Valium. Needless to say, biofeedback had no negative side effects.

The above excursion into some of the research concerning frontal EMG and anxiety was deemed necessary because we have tended to emphasize this form of biofeedback training (Budzynski, 1977a). We have learned, however, to rely on other forms of feedback, such as peripheral skin temperature (often called thermal feedback) and electrodermal response (EDR), which is really skin conductance. These two responses are both mediated by the sympathetic branch of the autonomic system. Therefore, if the finger skin temperature is cool and the palms are moist, it is a sign of heightened sympathetic tone. These responses can exist in the absence of high EMG levels, although it is rare for an individual to have cool, moist hands *and* a very low frontal EMG level. Cameron (1944) found that most anxious patients showed increased muscle tonus. A smaller percentage of such patients reacted most prominently with autonomic responses.

The PSP identifies, in almost all cases, the "preferred" system, whether it be EMG, EDR, or skin temperature. If, and when, a client does meet the criterion for forearm and frontal EMG and still manifests skin temperatures below 90°F, we will initiate thermal biofeedback in an attempt to teach him to self-control not only muscle tonus but peripheral skin temperature as well.

Thermal feedback is particularly useful in cases of Raynaud's Disease (Sedlacek, 1976), where excessive peripheral vasoconstriction can lead to serious consequences. This feedback technique was pioneered by Green, Green, and Walters (1970) at the Menninger Foundation. They were the first researchers to apply it to migraine headache. A serendipitous event brought to light this application. A subject in a hand-warming experiment found on several occasions that the migraine headache dissipated when the hands warmed. Further research showed that, along with EMG, thermal feedback is particularly helpful in headache conditions.

At the Biofeedback Institute, thermal training is begun after criteria levels of EMG have been demonstrated. In general, thermal control is easier if the client is relaxed muscularly. Because this response is mediated by sympathetic nerve fibers, self-control is more difficult to attain than is the case with most EMG feedback. With training, clients learn to produce finger skin temperatures in excess of 90°F. When highly vasoconstricted, the skin temperature can drop close to room ambient temperature. Decreasing sympathetic tone can cause increased peripheral blood flow to the point where skin temperature of the hands can exceed 96°F. For a "skin temperature responder," the warm/cool sensations from the hands are the best indicators of the state of arousal.

As with the transition from forearm to frontal EMG, we use simultaneous feedback as the change to thermal is made. Now the client is monitoring frontal EMG and peripheral skin temperature. She will attempt to hold a relaxed muscle tonus while warming the hands. Numerous successful strategies for temperature self-control have been reported by clinicians. No one strategy appears to work for everyone, although the autogenic exercises are widely accepted. Even this technique, however, is unsuccessful at times. One of our clients, having failed with autogenic phrases, achieved hand warmth control by means of the silent recitation of a short prayer featuring God's grace converted into a warming substance which entered her hands and feet. Some clients achieve control simply by making the feedback move in the correct direction. Children are particularly good at this. They need no more instruction than "make it go in that direction."

When the client has demonstrated that a temperature of 90°F or greater can be achieved with feedback, we fade the feedback until he can hand-warm without it. At this point, the client has learned to control both skeletal muscle tonus and peripheral vasodilation. Often this degree of control produces the sensations of very deep relaxation. A few individuals, most of them suffering from severe generalized anxiety, will still show excessive palmar sweating (EDR), even in the presence of relaxed musculature and warm hands. This response can become disassociated from skin temperature because the original sympathetic nerve pathway becomes a cholinergic fiber before the end organ. Thus, the sweat glands are activated by acetylcholine, while the smooth muscles in the arterioles of the hands and feet are activated by norepinephrine. This means that circulating epinephrine (adrenaline) in the blood stream can maintain a certain amount of peripheral vasoconstriction, although it will not affect the sweat response.

Our research with the PSP has brought us to the conclusion that a number of stress disorders may be associated with unusually low EDR values. Levels below .70 micromhos are often seen in cancer, headache, and labile hypertension patients. Our normal sample yields an average value of about 2.5 micromhos. If this observation maintains itself over time and the collection of more data, a correlate of inhibition of emotional expression may have been found.

Strangely enough, the attainment of low EMG levels and warm hands in a flat EDR responder will often *increase* the EDR level. If EDR is high, however, we will provide feedback of it until the criterion (below 2.5 micromhos) is reached. The production of an EDR level between .7 and 2.5 micromhos, along with warm hands (above 90°F) and low EMG levels, indicates to us that the client is ready to begin to transfer this ability from the near-ideal setting of the quiet, darkened room to more realistic settings.

Transfer Skills

Whether the client has been taught cognitive, overt behavioral, environmental, or physiological procedures in the clinic, she must now successfully transfer or generalize them to real-life situations. Transfer strategies range from systematic desensitization and other imagery procedures to such simple techniques as the use of small pieces of brightly colored tape pasted to wrist watches, steering wheels, telephones, refrigerators, and door knobs as a reminder to check for maladaptiveness and to correct it if found. Thus, the client must become aware of the maladaptiveness as well as skilled in the procedures to cope with it. Clients with migraine headaches or Raynaud's Disease learn to become aware of hand cooling. If detected, this response is then brought back to the normal, relaxed range. Tension headache sufferers are taught to feel slight increases in muscle tension in the neck and shoulder area as well as the forehead. Eventually, they can relax away the tension, even in difficult circumstances such as a business meeting or social gathering. An individual with irritable bowel can become aware that the abdominal distress is often preceded by a cooling of the hands and feet. If he can hand-warm when this symptom is noticed (hand cooling), he may prevent the development of the abdominal pain. Perhaps the most useful of the transfer procedures is systematic desensitization.

Systematic Desensitization. In transferring stress-coping skills, we have found it useful to rehearse these strategies in the clinic before asking clients to attempt to transfer them to real-life situations. The technique of systematic desensitization (Wolpe, 1958) is one way to do this. Over the years, this behavior therapy procedure has proved effective for anxiety disorders. At the Biofeedback Institute of Denver, we use biofeedback monitoring and some feedback of relevant physiological responses as the client goes through the desensitization. Clients are asked to visualize and describe verbally the scenes from the stress/anxiety hierarchy. If undue arousal is encountered, the scene is stopped and the client asked to relax with the aid of the biofeedback.[2] Eventually, the client can relax as he describes and visualizes all scenes from the graduated hierarchy. At this point, the automatic transfer of "less stress/anxiety" occurs outside the clinic in many cases. Some clients, however, seem to require specialized training in recovery back to prestress levels.

Recovery Training. By means of exaggeration of the visualization of typical stressful situations, the client can be made to produce some arousal.

---

[2]Details of systematic desensitization and flooding by procedures with biofeedback are available as a dual cassette, catalog number T-35, from BMA Audio Cassettes.

When this arousal is evident, the biofeedback is presented and the client attempts to recover as quickly as possible. Initially, this may require five to ten minutes. However, with continued trials, the client learns to recover in less than one minute. Next, she learns to recover without the aid of the biofeedback. The confidence gained in recovering from stressors induced in the clinic enables the client to feel more secure about her stress-coping outside the clinic.

Flooding. We have found this therapy procedure extremely useful for clients who primarily feel loss of control in certain situations. Since the technique involves the deliberate generation of high arousal by means of verbal and visual presentations of highly exaggerated scenarios of key anxiety-provoking situations, and the subsequent extinction of this arousal, the arousal response must be monitored. Biofeedback equipment is beautifully suited to do just this. Skeletal muscle and autonomic responding can be precisely measured, along with cortical responses if desired. With such monitoring, the therapist can be certain when the extinction has indeed taken place.

Daily Practice at Relaxation. We believe that it is important to take time out of a busy day to relax deeply for an extended period of fifteen to thirty minutes. This gives the body a chance to shift from the dominant sympathetic nervous system (SNS) stress pattern to a relaxed parasympathetic nervous system (PNS) dominant pattern. We accomplish this by urging that all clients go through the six-phase cassette tape home-relaxation program in parallel with their biofeedback training. The program encompasses elements of progressive relaxation, autogenic training, and systematic desensitization. Clients thereby learn a successful strategy for relaxation, which can be sharpened and refined by the biofeedback training. Our follow-up results reveal that, if symptoms recur, the clients tend to fall back on twice-a-day listening to the tapes.

Final Remarks

We have presented an outline of the program of training typically employed at our clinic for the treatment of anxiety and stress disorders. For the most part, the model is one of stress as heightened arousal in either a general or specific form, which, when chronic, becomes distress leading to anxiety or disease process. The stimuli that produce the stress response can be modified by cognitive and rational-emotive therapy as well as instruction, modeling, and rehearsal procedures. Newer techniques, such as twilight learning and subliminal processes, are being explored as therapeutic aids in the correlation of deeply held, below-conscious-awareness, maladaptive attitudinal and behavioral tendencies. The stress response itself is modified by relaxation training and biofeedback. Transfer of all skills to real life is an important phase of the program.

Group training in stress management is employed as a preventive program, often in the context of a particular organizational environment.

24

The Psycho-
pharmacological
Approach

Robert Hicks
Anna Okonek
John M. Davis

✳ ✳ ✳ ✳ ✳ ✳ ✳ ✳ ✳ ✳ ✳ ✳ ✳

To attempt a complete review of studies on the pharmacological management of stress and anxiety is itself somewhat stressful, since the literature in this field is both abundant and diverse. The reader, for example, can find among published symposia a 1976 St. Moritz presentation (Kielholz, 1977) and subsequent discussion (Siitonen and Jänne, 1977) on the "effect of beta-blockade on bowlers"(undergoing the anxiety of stressful competition in an amateur match in Finland). Kielholz (1977) also offers many broader views presented at this same symposium. One can find excellent reviews (for example, Lader, 1978) of the psychophysiological basis that we consider in rationally medicating the anxious (and/or stressed) patient. And there are concise monographs (for example, Tyrer, 1976) on the bodily feelings that produce (and/or are produced by) anxiety and stress, feelings which we in the field of psychopharmacology are often called on to treat.

428

Another problem is one of definition. If a bowler is said to have done poorly because some stress has made him too anxious to adequately exercise his skill, we tend to assume that we know what we are saying. However, as the various chapters in this volume attest, "stress" and "anxiety" mean many things to many people. So, to avoid a Tower of Babel, we will define anxiety as "apprehension, tension, or uneasiness that stems from the anticipation of danger, the source of which is largely unknown or unrecognized" (American Psychiatric Association, 1975, pp. 16-17). We will define stress as that stimulus which can *produce* anxiety, either externally (social pressures, publication deadlines) or internally (physical illness, such as hyperthyroidism). Since psychopharmacologists do not usually think of themselves as treating stress, this word will not be used further.

We will cover the psychopharmacological *treatment* of anxiety. Proper treatment is ideally based on some rationale, and we will show that pharmacological theory and treatment of anxiety are intertwined. We will also attempt to demonstrate the increasing importance of the nosology of anxiety, because of the increasing evidence that different types of anxiety may respond differently to different types of psychotropic agents. We will exclude discussions of anxiety produced by psychodynamics, conditioning, or existential crises, since these are covered elsewhere in this volume.

If anxiety is hard to define, its classification is even more difficult. Pariser and associates (1979a) point out the problems inherent in arbitrarily separating psychological and physiological factors in anxiety: "It is advantageous to adopt a holistic model for anxiety, which recognizes that causal factors are multiple, that they may operate simultaneously on several levels, and that they may be circular (that is, the patient's ineffective response to anxiety may lead to more anxiety, which leads to further ineffective response)" (p. 146). We (Hicks, McCormick, and Davis, 1979) have argued in general against the arbitrary separation of biology from psychology; that is, against the naive either/or approach which has been aptly termed "bifocal" (Chanoit and others, 1970) or "bimodal" (Docherty and others, 1977). We will thus approach anxiety from a "holistic" perspective, as Pariser and his associates suggest. We will view it in a "*uni*focal" (Hicks and McCormick, 1979) fashion, taking into account the inseparable unity of all the multidimensional factors—psychosocial and neurobiological—that comprise any psychiatric problem, especially anxiety.

Types of Anxiety

Anxiety can be broken down further than the APA definition given above. For the clinical psychopharmacologist, it can be viewed as a subjective phenomenon and also an objective one, which can be quantified by recording of rapid pulse, increased rate of respiration, and so on. It thus can be viewed medically as an entity with both (subjective) symptoms and (objective) signs, comprising a syndrome (see Feinstein, 1967).

The "anxiety syndrome" can be (and has been) classified in various ways. We will use the following:

1.   Primary anxiety
      a.   Acute and/or periodic (panic attacks) (includes "hyperventilation syndrome," "cardiac muscular exhaustion," "irritable heart," "DaCosta's Syndrome," "Soldier's Heart and Effort Syndrome," "neurocirculatory asthenia," and the APA *DSM-III* pure "panic disorder")
      b.   Chronic (includes "free-floating" anxiety, Beard's "neurasthenia," and the *DSM-III* "generalized" anxiety)
2.   Secondary Anxiety
      a.   To other psychiatric disorders (for example, schizophrenia and affective disorders such as mania and depression)
      b.   To medical conditions (for example, hyperthyroidism, but especially mitral valve prolapse syndrome (MVPS) and hyperdynamic β-adrenergic state)
3.   Agoraphobia (especially with panic disorder)
4.   Anticipatory Anxiety
5.   Obsessive-Compulsive Disorder

We recognize that this is arbitrary and that other classifications exist. We also realize that, as Feinstein (1967) has pointed out, two or more distant medical conditions, or subclasses of the same condition, may still have overlapping signs and symptoms. This can be demonstrated for panic attacks by means of a Venn diagram (see Figure 1). In addition, the diagnosis of a purely primary anxiety disorder should always be made only after the most extensive evaluation. Anxiety, as Pariser and associates (1979a) point out, is like "fever," more often a sign of some dysfunction than the pure manifestation of a pathological condition.

Primary Anxiety

Acute and/or Periodic (Panic Attacks). Probably the most common feature of all anxiety and anxiety-producing states is the anxiety (panic) attack (see Figure 1). Adams and Victor (1977, p. 991) provide a vivid description:

Fully developed, [anxiety attacks] are nearly as dramatic as a seizure. They begin with a distressing presentiment of imminent danger. Patients are assailed by a feeling of strangeness, as though

Figure 1. Relationship of Panic Attacks to Other Psychiatric
and/or Medical Conditions (by Phenomenology).

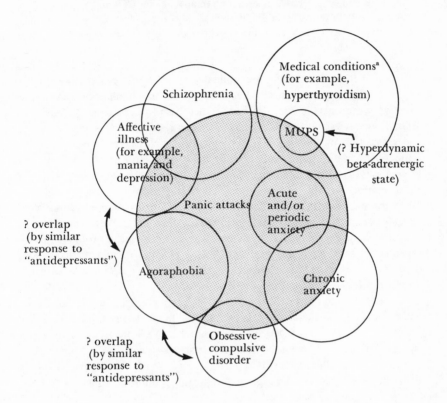

[a]Can overlap elsewhere, especially with affective illness; for example, amphetamine use
producing a mania and/or schizophrenia-like condition.

their body had changed (depersonalization) or the surroundings were
unreal (derealization). They are frightened, most often by the prospect of imminent death (angor animi), of losing their mind or self-
control, or of smothering. "I am dying," "This is the end," "Oh my
God, I'm going," "I can't breathe" are the characteristic expressions
of alarm and panic. The heart races, breathing comes in rapid gasps,
pupils are dilated, and the patient sweats and trembles. Hyperventilation induces paresthesia [tingling] of fingers, tongue, and lips and,
rarely, carpopedal [hand and foot] spasms. The palpitation and
breathing difficulties are so prominent that a cardiologist is often
called. The symptoms abate spontaneously, leaving the patient
shaken, tense, perplexed, and often embarrassed.

Such attacks may occur several times a day, or at infrequent
intervals. They may occur without easily recognizable sources of fear,

in a public place, or when patients are sitting quietly at home; or the attacks may awaken the patient from sleep. Except in minor details all the attacks are more or less alike in any one individual.

Between attacks patients may feel relatively well, or may experience the symptoms of the panic attack in lesser but persistent fashion.

If increased breathing predominates, this "attack" is sometimes called "hyperventilation syndrome." Because of the predominance of cardiovascular symptoms, it has also been called "cardiac muscular exhaustion" (Hartshorne, 1864), "irritable heart" (DaCosta, 1871) secondary to "strain and overaction of the heart" (DaCosta, 1874), "Neurocirculatory asthenia" (Oppenheimer, 1918), and "Soldier's Heart and Effort Syndrome" (Lewis, 1919). By employing "inclusion" and "exclusion" criteria, the third edition of the American Psychiatric Association's *Diagnostic and Statistical Manual of Mental Disorders (DSM-III)* will be more precise: such episodes are to be called "panic disorder" if they are discrete and occur in the absence of exertion; if there is no concomitant medical problem and no evidence for a major psychiatric disorder, such as schizophrenia, mania, and/or depression; and if there is no evidence for agoraphobia. (See Table 1 for the precise *DSM-III* classification.)

Chronic. In this category we include "generalized anxiety" of *DSM-III*, which includes occasional "attacks" similar to, though less striking than, those above, persisting for longer than six months. We also group here "freefloating" anxiety (a "pervasive fear not attached to any idea"—Linn, 1975). The condition of "neurasthenia" (Beard, 1889)—a general category, including exhaustion, depression, and other "neurotic" symptoms—might fall here.

Secondary Anxiety

To Other Psychiatric Disorders. That anxiety accompanies signals and results from major psychiatric disorders is both common knowledge and common sense. For the patient with schizophrenia—suffering from hallucinations, delusions, impaired reality perception, and sometimes fear of persecution—anxiety is a common problem, occasionally manifesting itself in actual panic attacks. Likewise, a patient with a major affective disorder is likely to be anxious. The end stages of mania often involve not euphoria but a picture very much like paranoid schizophrenia, often accompanied by irritability and all the signs and symptoms of anxiety. Depression is sometimes divided into "retarded" and "agitated" types (see, for example, Linn, 1975). That all the manifestations of anxiety, including panic attacks, are often the latter type of depression is no surprise. In fact, there is a body of literature devoted to various ways of discriminating between depression and anxiety. In addition, that certain phobic states are treated with "anti-

Table 1. APA *DSM-III* Criteria for Panic Disorder.

A. At least three panic attacks, occurring within a three-week period and occurring at times other than during marked physical exertion or a life-threatening situation, and in the absence of a physical disorder that could account for the symptoms of the anxiety. Further, these attacks do not occur only upon exposure to a circumscribed phobic stimulus.

B. The panic attacks are manifested by discrete periods of apprehension or fearfulness, with at least four of the following symptoms present during the majority of attacks:
(1) Dyspnea
(2) Palpitations
(3) Chest pain or discomfort
(4) Choking or smothering sensations
(5) Dizziness, vertigo, or unsteady feelings
(6) Feelings of unreality
(7) Paresthesia (tingling)
(8) Hot and cold flashes
(9) Sweating
(10) Faintness
(11) Trembling or shaking
(12) Fear of dying, going crazy, or doing something uncontrolled during an attack.

C. The panic attacks are not symptomatic of another mental disorder, such as Major Depressive Disorder,[a] Somatization Disorder[b] or Schizophrenia.

D. Does not meet the criteria of Agoraphobia.

[a]The "major" indicates that the disorder is a severe one—not, for example, just a temporary depression in "reaction" to some life problem. We suggest the addition of the *DSM-III* category of "Manic Disorder" to this list of exclusion criteria.

[b]"Briquet's Syndrome. The essential features are recurrent and multiple somatic complaints for which medical attention is sought but that are not apparently due to any physical disorder, beginning before early adulthood (prior to age 25), and having a chronic but fluctuating course."

depressants" suggests more than just a phenomenological similarity between depression and anxiety. Figure 1 is our attempt to demonstrate these complex relationships between schizophrenia, mania, depression (especially "agitated" type), and phobias (especially "agoraphobia").

To Medical Conditions. That such illnesses as hyperthyroidism lead to anxiety—manifest both chronically and as acute panics—is also common knowledge. It is no surprise either that metabolic derangements due to drugs—either by prescription or abuse—can produce anxiety; stimulants such as caffeine and amphetamines are well-known examples. Illnesses that produce pain and/or high mortality—such as myocardial infarction (which does both)—have well-known capabilities of producing anxiety. There has been recent interest, however, in the association of anxiety with specific types of cardiac problems, particularly mitral valve prolapse syndrome (MVPS) (Pariser and others, 1979b). The Pariser group found that patients with MVPS were more prone to extrasystoles, cardiac awareness, tachycardia, palpitations, syncope, fatigue, dyspnea, and atypical chest pain. An actual anatomical defect in the connective tissue of the mitral valve was present in six out of seventeen patients suffering from panic attacks. The incidence of MVPS in the general population, however, is uncertain; for example, in a recent study of one hundred presumably healthy young females, 17 percent had phono-cardiographic and 21 percent echocardiographic evidence of MVPS (Markiewicz and others, 1976). This all suggests, nonetheless, that the emphasis on the heart by Hartshorne, DaCosta, and Lewis may not be as fanciful as it might first appear.

Agoraphobia

In *DSM-III,* the "essential feature" of phobic disorders is "persistent avoidance behavior secondary to irrational fears of a specific object, activity, or situation." Liebowitz and Klein (in press) have provided a recent review.

Phobias can include "simple" conditioned phobias, such as avoidance of large dogs after canine attack, and "social" phobias, such as fears of speaking in public. Of most interest here is the condition of "agoraphobia," defined in the *DSM-III* (p. 226) as "a phobic disorder in which the predominant disturbance is an irrational fear of leaving the familiar setting of the home. It is *almost always* [our italics] preceded by a phase during which there are recurrent panic attacks. The individual develops an anticipatory fear of helplessness when having a panic attack and therefore is reluctant or refuses to be alone, travel or walk alone, or to be alone in unfamiliar situations, such as in crowds, closed or open spaces, crowded stores, bridges, tunnels, or churches. The fears are pervasive and dominate the individual's life, so that a large number of situations are entered into only reluctantly or are avoided. In the severe form of the disorder, the individual is "housebound.' "

Since panic attacks "almost always" occur, perhaps agoraphobia is actually synonymous with what we have called "acute and/or periodic (panic attacks)" (see Figure 1).

Anticipatory Anxiety

Even if a patient has his panic disorder treated, with whatever agent, the problem remains—at least transiently—that he will fear another attack. As Liebowitz explains (see Liebowitz and Klein, in press), anticipatory anxiety is "qualitatively different" from the panic episodes of agoraphobia with panic attacks. The role of a physician's reassurance and of deconditioning in this instance should be self-evident and will not be discussed further.

Obsessive-Compulsive Disorder

In *DSM-I*, "Obsessive-compulsive disorder" is grouped under the general heading of "Anxiety Disorders"; in contrast, in *DSM-II* (American Psychiatric Association, 1968), obsessive-compulsive disorders comprise a separate diagnostic entity. This new classification is of more than academic interest, in light of reports that obsessive-compulsive disorder—like agoraphobia—may respond to a pharmacological agent in the "antidepressant" group.

Anxiety Versus Depression

As Roth (1959) first noted, anxiety is not easily separated from other states. For example, a certain percentage of phobic patients also manifest symptoms of "depersonalization" and/or "derealization" (Roth, 1959), both of which the neurologists Adams and Victor (1977) describe as part of the "classic" anxiety attack.

There is, as reviewed by McNair and Fisher (1978), a good deal of controversy in this area, including a question of the clinical utility of such a diagnostic exercise. We do not have the space to enter into this debate, but we agree with McNair and Fisher's conclusion that there "may be five or more diagnostic groups within the two combined traditional categories [of anxiety and depression] and that several of these may be valuable indicators for choice of psychotropic agents." We have already pointed out a potential nosological dilemma presented by the fact that some "anxiety" syndromes respond to "antidepressants" (see Figure 1).

Physiological Theories of Etiology as a Basis for Treatment

The Catecholamine Theory. The fact that the catecholamines epinephrine (adrenaline) and norepinephrine (noradrenaline) could produce what Cannon (1929) called "fight" and "flight" has obvious relevance here. As Lader (1978) explains, these agents "are secreted and excreted in larger quantities during states of arousal. Strenuous sport, aircraft flights, parachute drops, vigilance situations, simulated weightlessness, exciting films, electric shocks, motor car driving, and many other stimuli are associated with raised plasma concentrations or increased urinary excretion of catecholamines. Epinephrine and norepinephrine are elevated, the former through direct stimulation of the adrenal medulla and the latter mainly through sympathetic nervous discharge. Increased muscular activity can increase norepinephrine production."

The Lactate Theory. Pitts and McClure (1967) first reported that spontaneous episodes of panic can be precipitated by the infusion of sodium lactate in patients prone to such attacks. Sodium lactate did not produce these episodes in normal controls, who experienced only mild symptomatology. These findings were replicated by other studies (Fink, Taylor, and Volavka, 1970; Bonn, Harrison, and Rees, 1971; Kelly, Mitchell-Heggs, and Sherman, 1971). In their 1967 report, Pitts and McClure postulated that "anxiety symptoms may have a common determining biochemical end mechanism involving the complexing—that is, the binding—and thus decreased availability of ionized calcium at the surface of excitable membranes by excess lactate." (Calcium exists in the blood in two forms: protein-bound and "ionized," the latter being the free and active form.) Pitts (1969, p. 75), combining the lactate theory and the catecholamine theory, hypothesized that "anxiety symptoms could occur in normal people under stress as a consequence of excess lactate production resulting from an increased flow of adrenaline, which is known to stimulate anxiety symptoms as well as to step up lactate production. The anxiety neurotic would be someone particularly subject to this mechanism because of chronic overproduction of adrenaline overactivity of the nervous system, a defect in metabolism resulting in excess lactate production, a defect in calcium metabolism, or a combination of these conditions."

These conclusions were criticized by Grosz and Farmer (1969), who reasoned that anxiety was produced *not* by the sodium lactate as such but by the metabolic alkalosis that infusion of such a basic substance would produce. Grosz and Farmer showed that infusion of lactate does indeed produce metabolic alkalosis (as measured by a rise in bicarbonate) and that the onset of anxiety symptoms occurs at a point long before serum lactate levels are sufficient to produce any significant chelation of ionized calcium (but at a point where the serum bicarbonate indicates a clear alkalosis).

Grosz and Farmer (1972) later noted that alkalization leads to a reduction in free ionized calcium. This might therefore explain the carpopedal spasms and paresthesia (both also seen in hypocalcemic tetany) that occur in the classical anxiety attack. The mechanism would thus involve the production of a respiratory alkalosis from hyperventilation, leading in turn to reduction in available free ionized calcium, causing a *relative* hypocalcemia—all producing a picture very similar to the tetany of hypocalcemia. Pitts and McClure's theory is further undermined by Pitts's own work (unpublished—personal communication, 1979) showing that intravenous EDTA (which should bind and thus decrease available calcium) produced tetany—but not panic attacks—when given to a group of panic disorder patients. However, this area requires further investigation—particularly since there is some evidence that "antidepressants" may block both lactate-induced and spontaneous attacks.

The James-Lange Versus Cannon-Bard Theory. This controversy has become of interest again because of the recent utilization, for anxiety, of the "beta-blockers," with a resulting controversy over the site—peripheral and/or central—of their purported antianxiety activity. The classical argument revolves around the site of emotion (including anxiety); that is, around whether an emotional response causes physiological changes or whether the perception of somatic manifestations induces an emotional response. In other words, do I tremble because I fear, or do I fear because I tremble? In 1884, William James presented his theory that emotion—and presumably anxiety—is the result of one's perceptions of bodily changes: "Common sense says, we lose our fortune, are sorry and weep; we meet a bear, are frightened and run; we are insulted by a rival, are angry and strike. The hypothesis here to be defended says that this order of sequence is incorrect, that the one mental state is not immediately induced by the other, that the bodily manifestations must first be interposed between, and that the more rational statement is that we feel sorry because we cry, angry because we strike, afraid because we tremble, and not that we cry, strike, or tremble, because we are sorry, angry, or fearful, as the case may be" (p. 196). Apologizing for such a crude description of the mechanism of emotion, James went on to say that emotion separated from bodily feeling is inconceivable and that, if one tries to separate an emotion from the bodily symptoms that characterize this emotion, there is nothing left with which to describe the emotion. In Copenhagen, Carl Georg Lange (1885) independently arrived at the same conclusion as James and is thus credited with the theory as well. Lange, however, emphasized that the stimulation of the vasomotor center is also responsible for inducing emotion.

Walter B. Cannon (1927) and Philip Bard (1928) proposed an alternate theory. Cannon objected to the notion that bodily changes are the determinants of emotion and denied that the subjective experience of an emotion such as fear is the result of physiological feedback from an excited sense organ in the periphery. Cannon and Bard attempted to prove that emotions can be experienced without the occurrence of bodily changes.

Possible support for the Cannon-Bard theory is provided by Young and associates (1975, p. 614), reporting on a case of "pan-dysautonomia." In this patient (whose condition was diagnosed as transient polyneuritis confined to the autonomic system), a number of serious sympathetic-adrenergic deficits—especially severe orthostatic hypotension—were present and intensively studied. However, there "were no subjective changes in his capacity to feel nervous or anxious" (ascertained by open-ended questioning only). Unfortunately there was no fuller evaluation of this patient's emotional state. If better documented, this otherwise extremely well-detailed report would be a strong argument against the James-Lange hypothesis.

The Beta-Receptor Theory. Because of antianxiety activity noted recently for the so-called beta blockers ("β-blockers"), especially propranolol, interest has focused on the β-adrenergic receptors. These receptors, largely located on the peripheral (versus central) nervous system, are one of the two types of receptors in the sympathetic portion of the autonomic nervous system. In contrast to the so-called "alpha-receptors" ("a-receptors"), they mediate physiological changes—such as increased heart rate, increased gastrointestinal motility, and facial flushing—that are classically associated with anxiety (see Table 2).

Because propranolol has both central and peripheral actions, but may exert its antianxiety effects largely through beta-blockade, a modern-day version of the James-Lange versus Cannon-Bard argument has arisen. For example, Gottschalk, Stone, and Goldine (1974) studied the effect of propranolol (60 milligrams (mg) in three divided doses over twelve hours) given to twelve "healthy, nonanxious" subjects and a matched placebo group. On a ten-minute stress interview, anxiety scores increased to equal levels in both groups. Pulse responses during the interview were significantly lower in the propranolol group. Free fatty acid (FFA) plasma-level responses were not statistically different in the two groups, although lower in the propranolol group. (Lipolysis, or breakdown of peripheral fat into FFAs, is thought to involve beta-receptors; see Table 2.) The authors (Gottschalk, Stone, and Goldine, 1974, p. 47) interpreted these findings to suggest that "basal or resting" anxiety may be reduced by peripheral beta-adrenergic blocking and that "the magnitude of acutely aroused anxiety is mediated more through the central nervous system." They concluded that the antianxiety activity of propranolol is the result of its peripheral actions, but they could not rule out some antianxiety affects produced by its central actions.

In general, studies into the central-versus-peripheral site of propranolol's antianxiety activity favor a peripheral basis for such actions. Greenblatt and Shader (1978) have recently reviewed all the literature and conclude that "direct central effects undoubtedly play some role" in the anxiolytic action of this agent. They note, however, that studies on practolol, a beta-blocker that does not cross the blood-brain barrier but does have antianxiety effects, support a peripheral antianxiety action of propranolol. Additional evidence for a role of peripheral β-adrenergic receptors in anxiety states is the responsiveness of the so-called "hyperdynamic β-adrenergic circulatory state" to propranolol.

The GABA Theory. Because of the well-known efficacy of the "benzodiazepines," considerable work—largely laboratory—has focused on the role of γ-amino butyric acid (GABA), neurotransmitter, in the antianxiety activity of these agents. Costa, Guidotti, and Mao (1976) and Haefely and associates (1976) have, in particular, proposed that the benzodiazepines exert their effects by acting on "GABA-ergic" mechanisms, which in turn presumably modulate the function of ststems in which other neurotransmitters—including catecholamines—are involved. (See Haefely, 1978, for a recent review; see also Figure 2.)

Other Theories. Included here is a work suggesting that some drugs,

Table 2. Responses of Effector Organs to Autonomic Nerve Impulses and Circulating Catecholamines (after Ganong). [a]

Effector Organs	Cholinergic Impulses Response	Receptor Type	Adrenergic Impulses Response
Eye			
Radial muscle of iris		α	Contraction (mydriasis)
Sphincter muscle of iris	Contraction (miosis)		
Ciliary muscle	Contraction for near vision	β	Relaxation for far vision
Heart			
S-A node	Decrease in heart rate: vagal arrest	β[b]	Increase in heart rate
Atria	Decrease in contractility, and (usually) increase in conduction velocity	β[b]	Increase in contractility and conduction velocity
A-V node and conduction system	Decrease in conduction velocity: A-V block	β[b]	Increase in conduction velocity
Ventricles		β[b]	Increase in contractility, conduction velocity, automaticity, and rate of idiopathic pacemakers
Blood vessels			
Coronary	Dilatation	α	Constriction
		β	Dilatation
Skin and mucosa		α	Constriction
Skeletal muscle	Dilatation	α	Constriction
		β	Dilatation
Cerebral		α	Constriction (slight)
Pulmonary		α	Constriction
Abdominal viscera		α	Constriction
		β	Dilatation

Organ		Receptor	
Renal	Dilatation	α	Constriction
Salivary glands		α	Constriction
Lung			
Bronchial muscle	Contraction	β	Relaxation
Bronchial glands	Stimulation		Inhibition (?)
Stomach			
Motility and tone	Increase	β	Decrease (usually)
Sphincters	Relaxation (usually)	α	Contraction (usually)
Secretion	Stimulation		Inhibition (?)
Intestine			
Motility and tone	Increase	$\alpha\ \beta$	Decrease
Sphincters	Relaxation (usually)	α	Contraction (usually)
Secretion	Stimulation		Inhibition (?)
Gallbladder and ducts	Contraction		Relaxation
Urinary bladder			
Detrusor	Relaxation	β	Relaxation (usually)
Trigone and sphincter	Contraction	α	Contraction
Ureter			
Motility and tone	Increase (?)	$\alpha\ \beta$	Increase (usually)
Uterus	Variable[c]		Variable[c]
Male sex organs	Erection		Ejaculation
Skin			
Pilomotor muscles		α	Contraction
Sweat glands	Generalized secretion	α	Slight, localized secretion[d]
Spleen capsule		α	Contraction
Adrenal medulla	Secretion of epinephrine and norepinephrine		

Effector organ	Cholinergic responses	Adrenergic receptor type[b]	Adrenergic responses
Liver		β	Glycogenolysis
Pancreas			
Acini	Secretion		
Islets	Insulin secretion	α	Inhibition of insulin secretion
		β	Insulin secretion
Salivary glands	Profuse, watery secretion	α	Thick, viscous secretion
Lacrimal glands	Secretion		
Nasopharyngeal glands	Secretion		
Adipose tissue		β	Lipolysis
Juxtaglomerular cells		β	Renin secretion

[a]Modified from Goodman and Gilman, *The Pharmacological Basis of Therapeutics*, 5th ed. Macmillan, 1975.

[b]The β receptors of the heart have been classified as β_1 receptors and most other β receptors as β_2 receptors.

[c]Depends on stage of menstrual cycle, amount of circulating estrogen and progesterone, and other factors. Responses of pregnant uterus different from those of nonpregnant.

[d]On palms of hands and in some other locations ("adrenergic sweating").

Figure 2. Proposed Links Between the Modification of GABAergic synaptic
Transmission and the Main Pharmacological Actions of Benzodiazepines
(After Haefely, 1978).

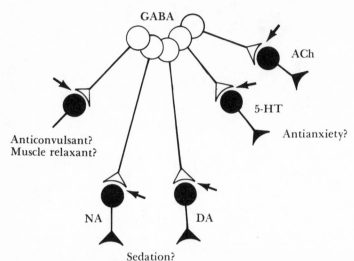

Note: Arrows indicate facilitation of GABAergic transmission by
benzodiazepines.

NA = noradrenaline (norepinephrine).
DA = dopamine.
5-HT = 5-hydroxytryptamine (serotonin).
ACh = acetylcholine.

Source: M. A. Lipton (Ed.). Psychopharmacology: A Generation of Progress. New York:
Raven Press, 1978.

such as ρ-chlorophenylalanine (PCPA), have an antianxiety effect via serotonin
depletion. Various drugs (including the benzodiazepines, chlordiazepoxide,
and diazepam) may act as phosphodiesterase inhibitors, decreasing the breakdown of brain cyclic adenosine monophosphate (CAMP). Other drugs may
affect central glycine receptors, especially the benzodiazepines, which may
exert their antianxiety, anticonvulsant, and muscle-relaxing effects by minimizing glycine. (See Sepinwall and Cook, 1978, for a further explanation
of these theories.)

Specific Treatment of Anxiety Disorders

It may seem to the reader that this section should have begun much
earlier and perhaps have constituted this entire chapter. However, it is worth
reiterating that different types of anxiety seem to respond to different types

of psychoactive agents, making classification absolutely essential. Likewise, if a medication is given without some thought about its mechanism of action and the pathophysiological condition for which it is given, such treatment is at best a "cookbook" and is certainly unlikely to produce any further progress in the field.

One group in our earlier classification of anxiety states need not concern us further: anxious disorders that are secondary to "medical conditions." In such cases, the anxiety will be eliminated when the underlying medical illness is treated. Of course, some sort of palliative treatment for anxiety may be needed concurrently if the anxiety is overwhelming enough to cause intolerable distress or to interfere with the ongoing medical regimen. In general, such palliative medication should be a benzodiazepine, since most other drugs used for anxiety involve higher risks of toxic reaction, either directly or by an adverse drug interaction. An exception may be the use of beta-blockers in certain specific medical conditions, such as "hyperdynamic β-adrenergic circulatory state," where the use of such agents may be the treatment of choice for the condition itself, or in conditions such as high blood pressure and hyperthyroidism (where beta-blockers may be more effective in treatment of such symptoms as rapid pulse).

Antipsychotic Agents ("Major Tranquilizers")

Table 3 is an outline of the classes and subclasses of medications in the antipsychotic group, with some examples given. What distinguishes the

Table 3. Classification of Antipsychotic Agents.

Phenothiazines
    Aliphatic (for example, chlorpromazine)
    Piperadines (thioridazine)
    Piperazines (trifluoperazine, fluphenazine, perphenazine)
Thioxanthines
    Aliphatic (chlorprothixene)
    Piperazine (thiothixene)
Dibenzazepines (loxapine, clozapine)
Butyrophenones (haloperidol)
Indolones (molindone)
Rauwolfia alkaloids (reserpine)

agents in this group is their antipsychotic activity. By virtue of sedation, most have antianxiety properties. However, they all possess an ability to correct or ameliorate disordered thinking of psychosis seen in schizophrenia and in extreme forms of affective illness, such as mania and depression (both of which may involve disordered mood). (Sedative and antianxiety may, however, not necessarily describe the same property; see, for example, Haefely's schema in Figure 2.)

The sedative action of these drugs generally occurs immediately and may be transient; the antipsychotic action may take days or weeks (see Davis and Cole, 1975). All agents in this group have antipsychotic activity but varying sedative properties (Davis and Cole, 1975). For example, chlorpromazine (Largactil, Thorazine) is relatively sedating whereas trifluoperazine (Stelazine) is not. For this reason, in a psychosis where agitation and anxiety are a major feature, chlorpromazine is preferred.

Because of their sedative properties, these agents are sometimes suggested for many of the other types of anxiety, including those classified in *DSM-II* as "neurotic" (for example, our "chronic primary anxiety"). A more sedative type of antipsychotic is generally chosen. Dosage is usually set low, often at subantipsychotic levels (for example, the antipsychotic properties of chlorpromazine are generally thought to require about 400 mg per day, but sedation may occur with as little as 5 to 10 mg). One rationale for such practice is that, unlike the sedative-hypnotics, there is little evidence for a physiological addiction to these agents. An argument against such a practice is that, given chronically (even in small doses), these agents may produce permanent neurological side effects (see Cole and Davis, 1975). We have seen enough examples of a permanent and crippling neurological illness produced by chronic use of antipsychotics in *non*psychotic anxiety states—especially obsessive-compulsive disorder—to suggest extremely careful monitoring with such treatment. However, if addiction or abuse is a major concern, these drugs may be preferable to the sedative-hypnotics as antianxiety agents.

Sedative-Hypnotics ("Minor Tranquilizers," "Antianxiety Agnets," "Anxiolytics")

As we have pointed out elsewhere (Cole and Davis, 1975), all "minor tranquilizers" and sedatives can be used as hypnotics ("sleeping pills") at high doses, and all hypnotics can be used for sedation at low doses; therefore, the distinction between "sedatives" and "hypnotics" is arbitrary and based more on classical usage than pharmacological properties. Similarly, the distinction between "major tranquilizers" and "minor tranquilizers" is not sharp; the minor tranquilizers are merely weaker agents. The term *antianxiety agent* has become synonymous with this group but could conceivably include any agent with antianxiety properties in the other groups. The recently popular term *anxiolytic* refers to this group and to the beta-blockers. These agents are used for all types of anxiety, except those "secondary" to a psychotic disorder (schizophrenia, mania, depression), where they are used usually only as an adjunct.

Statistics indicate that one in five Americans has been, at some time, on a psychotropic medication, of which two thirds are in this class (Cole and Davis, 1975). Interestingly, prescriptions for such agents are written largely (about 70 percent) by nonpsychiatrists. These figures may be on the decrease because of well-publicized "exposés" on the benzodiazepines, such as diazepam (Valium) and chlordiazepoxide (Librium). Within this group are several subgroups.

Barbiturates. This group, of which phenobarbital is the classic example, has been in use the longest, dating back to the beginning of this century (Harvey, 1975). Barbiturates have been used to treat all the types of anxiety, including (with relative inefficacy) that due to schizophrenia and other psychoses. Their use has been increasingly restricted for several reasons. The toxicity of these agents, which may include "paradoxical" excitement (Gibson, 1966), especially in the elderly (Stotsky, 1976), is one reason. Addiction (Wikler, 1968) and gravity of overdose (Davis, Bartlett, and Termini, 1968) are others. Their greatest liability, however, may be due to their property to induce enzymes, in the liver generally, thereby causing more rapid metabolism, especially of other pharmacological agents with which barbiturates are coadministrated. For example, a patient may be on a drug to reduce blood coagulation, a treatment requiring careful titration. If barbiturates are then added to the regimen, enzyme activity increases. The anticoagulant is thus more rapidly eliminated, resulting in the need for an increase in anticoagulant dosage to achieve the same inhibition of clotting. If barbiturates are then suddenly stopped, metabolism of the now high-dosage anticoagulant is suddenly decreased, leading to severe and sometimes fatal bleeding (see Greenblatt and Shader, 1972). As a result, the barbiturates have been condemned as archaic (Koch-Weser and Greenblatt, 1973).

Propanediols. This group is essentially represented now by meprobamate (Miltown, Equanil), which enjoyed great popularity in the 1950s (see Tinklenberg, 1977). Meprobamate has the liability of a significant addiction potential and may be lethal in low doses (Pariser and others, 1979a); clinically significant enzyme induction has not been convincingly demonstrated as yet. It appears to be less effective clinically than the benzodiazepines (Cole and Davis, 1975).

Benzodiazepines. There appears to be a general consensus (Rickels, 1968; Rickels, Downing, and Winokur, 1978; Greenblatt and Shader, 1974; Cole and Davis, 1975; Pariser and others, 1979a) that this group is clinically superior, for nonpsychotic anxiety, to the barbiturates and meprobamate. As Pariser and associates (1979a) summarize in detail, the benzodiazepines have the advantages of low incidence of side effects and toxicity; a relatively low incidence of addiction (despite recent news media criticism of their use); lack of enzyme induction; and additional positive properties, such as muscle relaxation, especially with diazepam (see Figure 2 for a schematic diagram of how the differing properties of the benzodiazepines may be carried out via different GABA-mediated pathways).

As Greenblatt and Shader (1978) have noted, there has been a remarkable proliferation of these agents, especially recently. Relative clinical superiority of one benzodiazepine over another remains to be proved (Greenblatt
and Shader, 1978). Greenblatt and Shader (1974) believe that the varying
clinical activities of the various benzodiazepines are less dependent on their
intrinsic pharmacological properties than on their "pharmacokinetics" (Dost,
1953; see also Greenblatt and Koch-Weser, 1975); that is, on how they are
absorbed, distributed, metabolized, and eliminated from the body. For
example, of the commonly used agents, diazepam (DZ) (Valium) has the
advantage (and disadvantage) of a long stay in the body (days), because
the initial ("parent") drug undergoes four metabolic changes, each producing
"active metabolites," before the final biotransformation into an inactive
metabolite, which is subsequently excreted; oxazepam (OZ) (Serax) has a
short stay in the body (several hours), because OZ is identical with the
fourth (and final) active breakdown product of DZ; chlordiazepoxide (CDX)
(Librium) has the advantage of an intermediate length of stay in the body
and slightly different metabolism from DZ and OZ; flurazepam (Dalmane)
is marketed as a hypnotic, although it could, as we explained, be used as a
sedative anxiolytic.

How long should a patient be maintained on these agents? There is
no consensus in the literature. Extremists, motivated presumably by what
Klerman (1971) has termed "pharmacologic Calvinism," deplore their use
at all. Because of their relative lack of side effects, others adopt a laissez-
faire attitude and permit their chronic use. The fact that persistent patients
have little trouble obtaining these drugs from various physicians is one
argument in support of this the laissez-faire approach (that is, if only one
physician is the source of these drugs, perhaps—through a personal relationship between doctor and patient—the use of these agents can be monitored
and minimized). We take the position that chronic *intermittent* use, especially
for "acute and/or periodic anxiety attacks," is justified, although antidepressants and beta-blockers might be tried first. For "chronic primary"
anxiety, we allow a few weeks of constant use and subsequent intermittent
use, but we insist that the patient search for the medical or psychosocial
stimulus that may underlie his anxiety. There is no general agreement on
whether patients may develop "tolerance" to these agents; that is, whether
they have to take increasing amounts to achieve the same effect. In general,
clinical experience has shown that unrestricted use leads to gradually increasing dosage over time.

Antihistamines. These drugs—for example, diphenhydramine (Bena-
dryl)—are often used as anxiolytics because of their "side effects," which
include somnolence. Dermatologists in the United States often employ the
"diphenylmethane" type of antihistamine hydroxyzine (Atarax, Vistaril)
for situations where histamine and anxiety-induced scratching are part of

a skin problem. Many nonprescription sedatives and hypnotics contain such agents. Rickels and Hesbacher (1973) studied such sedatives and found them relatively ineffective.

Beta-Blockers (β-Blockers)

This class of anxiolytic agents has aroused recent interest because of experiments such as that on propranolol (Inderal) by Gottschalk, Stone, and Goldine (1974), which revive the James-Lange versus Cannon-Bard argument and which suggest a peripheral basis for at least some types of anxiety, especially in view of the anxiolytic activity of practolol (Eraldin), which has a relative inability to cross the blood-brain barrier (Bonn, Turner, and Hicks, 1972). Practolol and oxprenolol (Trasicor) are beta-blockers available outside the United States, especially in the United Kingdom.

Interest in this group of anxiolytic agents is also raised by reports of certain anxiety syndromes which seem to be especially sensitive to beta-blockers. For example, Frohlich, Tarazi, and Dustan (1969) have suggested the existence of a "hyperdynamic β-adrenergic circulatory state." They describe this syndrome as one of increased "cardiac awareness, increased heart rate responsiveness to various stimuli, and hyperkinetic circulation"—all determined by various hemodynamic measurements—including response to the beta-agonist (and catecholamine) isoproterenol and to the beta-blocker propranolol. Nine to fourteen such patients manifested an "almost uncontrollable" "hysterical outburst" following isoproterenol infusion, an emotional reaction reported to be promptly reversed by intravenous propanolol but not placebo. Unfortunately, the emotional responses of these patients were neither quantified nor measured by standard psychometric testing, nor were the "hysterical outbursts" contrasted, even in colloquial terms, with controls. Nonetheless, this report, and that associating mitral valve prolapse syndrome (see Pariser and others, 1979b) along with the "classical" literature of Hartshorne, DaCosta, and Lewis—all suggest that anxiety states with prominent cardiovascular symptomatology might be a special group and might, therefore, be best treated first with a beta-blocker such as propranolol. This suggestion is partially supported by reports such as the following.

In 1974, Tyrer and Lader reported a study of twelve "chronically anxious" patients who were treated with propranolol, diazepam, and placebo for one week each, using a balanced cross-over design. Of the twelve subjects, six had predominantly "somatic anxiety, complaining mostly of bodily symptoms," and six had mainly "psychic anxiety, complaining primarily of psychological symptoms." Although diazepam was in general more effective than propranolol or placebo in relieving anxiety, propranolol was more effective than placebo in patients with somatic anxiety but not in those with psychic anxiety. Tyrer and Lader suggest that propranolol should be reserved for patients whose anxiety symptoms are mainly somatic.

Unfortunately, not all studies of the clinical anxiolytic efficacy of the beta-blockers are so well delineated. Such studies have been characterized by Greenblatt and Shader (1978) as "heterogeneous in design and objective, making comparative judgment a difficult and tenuous matter." Greenblatt and Shader summarize studies suggesting clinical equivalence of oxprenolol and diazepam in patients with "acute, short-term anxiety" related to situation. Becker (1976) compared oxprenolol and propranolol in patients with anxiety that we would categorize as "chronic primary." Both drugs were equally effective in treating "anxiety and tension." However, propranolol reduced palpitations to a greater degree, although producing a higher incidence of unwanted cardiovascular effects such as bradycardia and hypotension. This latter difference was thought due to either a greater "cardiac-depressant effect" of propranolol or to "intrinsic sympathomimetic" activity of oxprenolol (not shared with propranolol). We agree with Greenblatt and Shader's (1978) conclusion, however, that much "further study is needed to define the role of β-adrenergic antagonists" and that studies do not yet prove the superiority of beta-blockers over benzodiazepines in patients with chronic anxiety marked with somatic complaints.

Although no physiological dependency on beta-blockers has been shown, their potential side effects—including cardiovascular disturbances and neuropsychiatric disturbances such as depression and confusion (see Greenblatt and Koch-Weser, 1974)—are numerous and dangerous.

Antidepressants (and Lithium)

The role of antidepressants—either of MAO inhibitor (MAOI) or tricyclic antidepressant (TCA) type—in anxiety produced "secondary" to a depression should be self-evident. In the United States, the TCAs are generally employed first, because of the many adverse food and drug interactions that can occur with the MAOIs (see Baldessarini, 1977, pp. 32-33). If anxiety is a major part of the picture, a more sedating TCA is chosen; usually amitriptyline (Elavil) and/or a sedative-hypnotic is added. If a depression involves both mood *and* thought disorder, an antipsychotic is often added. Since lithium helps to treat and prevent depression and mania of a periodic type, it is given chronically for recurrent mania and/or depression, both of which manifest anxiety (see Figure 1).

One of the most exciting recent developments in psychopharmacology has been a number of reports on the efficacy of antidepressants in phobic anxiety of the "agoraphobic" type. The first breakthrough was the demonstration that the TCA imipramine (Tofranil) can block panic attacks (Klein and Fink, 1962; Klein, 1964). However, as Liebowitz points out (Liebowitz and Klein, in press), panic attacks associated with agoraphobia are made better by imipramine, while pure panic attacks (our "acute and/or periodic" type of primary anxiety) are made *worse*. Interestingly, the panic attacks of agoraphobia are often helped at dosages lower than the dosages for treating depression (depression treated with imipramine requires 150 to 300 mg per day over weeks, while panic attacks may improve immediately on as little as 5 mg per day). Antidepressants of the MAOI type also may help agoraphobic panic attacks but are recommended—because of the possible adverse reactions noted above—as drugs of second choice. As we have noted, partial or complete clearing up of panic attacks still leaves the patient fearful of another attack, suffering more from "anticipatory anxiety," for which counseling and/or a benzodiazepine is recommended.

Another startling possibility is represented by reports such as that by Ananth (1977) that obsessive-compulsive neurosis responds to the TCA clomipramine (Anafranil), a drug not available commercially in the United States. Its success involves a mechanism that cannot be explained, Ananth argues, by simple antianxiety and/or antidepressant effect. Such a drug would certainly offer hope to patients who suffer from this often crippling disorder, about which there is a wealth of psychoanalytic literature but little clear evidence of success with purely psychosocial approaches. Much work is going on, at this writing, to replicate such clinical results.

CO_2 ("Bag Breathing")

Walking through the emergency ward of any large general hospital, almost invariably one is confronted with the specter of a patient in some room breathing rapidly into a paper bag. This seemingly ludicrous situation is usually the result of a "hyperventilation syndrome" attack, which seems to produce and/or is the end product of an acute panic, involving a respiratory alkalosis. The paper bag is put over the patient's mouth and nose to ensure that he will rebreathe exhaled CO_2, which normally would produce a respiratory acidosis, but which in this instance simply restores the patient's acid-base balance to normal. Sometimes this—plus a brief physiological explanation and reassurance that the patient is not "crazy"—helps the individual with periodic attacks. However, the patient should subsequently be asked about symptoms of agoraphobia, for which an antidepressant would be the drug of choice. If this does not help the patient with attacks, then counseling and/or the occasional use of a benzodiazepine may be required as an adjunct. The physiological explanation should always be coupled with advice to breathe more slowly in an attack, or, if that fails, to self-treat with a paper bag.

Drugs of Abuse

Alcohol is an anxiolytic known for centuries. The opiates are well-known euphoriants that possess calming effects as well. They are unfortunately often abused by the anxious patient in an attempt at self-medication. For the clinician, therefore, any evaluation of an anxiety state should involve an attempt to ascertain whether these (or any) drugs are being used (or abused) by the subject. Carefully monitored, alcohol may be a useful anxiolytic, expecially for geriatric patients, for whom a party with "punch" may help meet both medical and social needs (Chien, Stotsky, and Cole, 1973).

Conclusion

Since this chapter is centered on treatment, Table 4 presents a sort of "decision-tree" guide to the psychopharmacological treatment of anxiety (reminding the reader that proper medical management *always* includes an exploration for possible causation and/or exacerbation of an anxiety state by psychological or social factors).

Table 4. Summary of Psychopharmacological Treatment for Different Types of Anxiety.

Primary Anxiety
   Acute and/or Periodic (Panic Attacks)
   if hyperventilation: CO_2 ("bag breathing")
   if somatic $>$ psychic: consider acute and chronic beta-blocker; if fails, or
   if psychic $>$ somatic: consider acute and chronic benzodiazepine

   Chronic
   if somatic $>$ psychic: consider acute and chronic beta-blocker;
   if somatic $>$ psychic: consider acute and intermittent benzodiazepine

Secondary Anxiety
   To Other Psychiatric Disorder
   schizophrenia: antipsychotic; consider more sedating type if agitated
   depression: antidepressant; consider more sedating type if agitated (and/or benzodiazepine); consider concomitant antipsychotic if psychotic; consider lithium if recurrent, to be used both acutely and chronically
   mania: lithium, chronically and probably acutely; antipsychotic if psychotic (more sedating type if agitated), used usually only acutely

   To Medical Conditions
   all: *treat medical condition first;* ? benzodiazepine as adjunct if anxious; hypertension and hyperthyroidism: ? β-blocker for medical and anxiolytic purposes; ? benzodiazepine as adjunct (usually in place of β-blockers); hyperdynamic β-adrenergic circulatory state: chronic β-blocker, preferably propranolol

Agoraphobia
   With panic disorder
   see *Acute and/or periodic (panic attacks)* above; then consider chronic antidepressant (see text), TCA before MAOI
   Without panic disorder
   see *Primary Anxiety, chronic*
   Anticipatory Anxiety: reassurance and/or benzodiazepine
   Obsessive-Compulsive Disorder: ? antidepressant (clomipramine)

25

Societal Support
and Education

Miles E. Simpson

With the intellectual climate of the early 1980s as pessimistic as at any other time in recent history, it is difficult to suggest that society can effectively intervene in such amorphous states as stress and anxiety. Still, if social institutions and social change are a primary source of anxiety and stress, then the ultimate reduction of stress and anxiety must occur on a broad social level. Therapeutic efforts, of course, are directed at the individual, but they are ultimately societal in nature, whether conducted by governmental, religious, or private agents. In general, these efforts are a patchwork and in only an indirect way get at the societal sources of stress and anxiety. At best, therapy, if successful, should reduce the transmission of negative habits and outlooks from one generation to the next. Stress and anxiety are by their very nature collective phenomena. Although they are experienced by the individual, their control requires an olympian view of society. This position came late to

451

Sigmund Freud, who in his book *Civilization and Its Discontents* realized that the malaise confronting modern society rests on its incapacity to control the aggressive and destructive impulses of man (Freud, 1930). The baser side of man, which served him so well in the past, seems ready to destroy the foundation of civilization. But, as we shall see, the foundation of society is threatened by many sources, some of which may be unknown to social scientists. Before intervention can be consistently successful, we must have a clear understanding of the societal origins of stress and anxiety.

Political Limitations of Intervention

In discussing intervention, we must keep in mind that politicians want to be identified with popular policies. Therefore, they are likely to espouse spectacular, dramatic, and ambitious proposals rather than modest ones. At the same time, despite the grand scale of a proposal, politicians want these policies and their programs to produce immediate and tangible results, which they claim for their own. Quantifiability is desired, as well, for it allows politicians to easily portray results for their own district. Intangible and long-term programs, regardless of their merits, are not looked on with favor, since the average voter cannot perceive or understand programs whose effects have not yet been felt.

Complications arise when one considers the very nature of the American political system. Its many factions and the proliferation of extremist political groups in the last quarter century compound the problem of creating a coherent long-term policy. Furthermore, the some 80,000 government units, which have overlapping jurisdiction with one another, make difficult the implementation of any policy (Binstock and Levin, 1976). Recent efforts to provide abortions as a means of reducing stresses created by unwanted births demonstrate the crisis proportions that this process has reached. Those who favor abortion point to the social costs of unwanted and poorly parented children, while those opposed to it charge that life is cheapened by abortion. Such polarized debates will not be resolved easily by political patronage, by compromise, or by scientific data. In this climate, all intervention will become closely scrutinized for its ideological implication, real and imagined; and, if such splinter-group politics continues, the formation of new and radically different modes of intervention will be impossible (Coleman, 1956).

Some are optimistic. Lakoff (1976) sees the end to interest-group politics. He believes that its demise is inevitable, given the growing technological complexity of present postindustrial society, which will lead to the reliance of government on experts and technical advisers. "In more and more cases, . . . the interaction of interest groups [will prove] an even more dubious guide to effective policymaking than it may have been when the function of government was to act simply as a broker among power blocs"

(Lakoff, 1976, p. 654). Tocqueville (1835) said much the same thing one hundred and forty years before, but interest-group politics is still the basis of too much of our political policy even today. The future, I am afraid, rests not on the demands placed on legislative bodies by the technical necessities of our cybernetic society but on the enlightenment of the interest groups themselves and their perception of the shortsightedness of their programs and demands. Technical experts will have a say in the legislative process only if the public at large understands the long-term consequence of its actions and develops a well-founded moral sense and commitment to future generations. Otherwise, as now, the experts will be consulted and generally ignored. Therefore, intervention to reduce stress and anxiety, will depend on research that lays bare the consequences of stress and anxiety and the successful widespread dissemination of such knowledge.

Intervention finds political stumbling blocks at the implementation level as well. The most severe problem is the fear of evaluative research (Ornstein, 1977). Evaluative research can determine whether a program has had an effect on its target population and, if so, how much; but such a question is political dynamite. After a politician and a political body have invested vast resources in a project, they cannot publicly declare the project a loser. Moreover, administrators have an equally heavy investment in making the project look good. Proving the program ineffective means losing one's job. Hence, evaluation or any other research is suspect and must be controlled (Rossi, 1972). Gordon and Morse (1975) point out that the control of research results may extend to research design and quality of execution. They find that evaluative research conducted by the delivery agency itself is significantly more likely to demonstrate that the program is a success than research conducted by a nonaffiliated outside agency. This finding, in part, is associated with weak and questionable research design employed by the affiliated researchers. We will focus, therefore, on studies conducted by nonaffiliated researchers.

Cause and the Crucial Place of Theory in Intervention

Social intervention, unless blind or random, implies a causal relationship between the intervention efforts and their outcomes. Powerful social theories are needed to guide these efforts. Certainly the social planner must take into consideration the resources, the press of the social problems in question, and political considerations. But the causal model must be the dominant concern of the planner, for if the extant theory is wrong or a solid theory is misinterpreted, then the program will fail. Existing scientific knowledge, however, makes it clear that single-cause models have little applicability in social intervention. The biological model that focuses attention on the proximal cause does not always work well in the social sciences. Controlling a complex chronic disease such as diabetes, as Estes and Freeman (1976) point out, can be done by a complex system of managing the sugar intake and providing insulin. Preventive measures such as vaccination can also protect against disease. Such simple responses to social problems may not be very effective. For instance, the injection of money into a household may not reduce the problems associated with poverty to the extent previously thought (we will come back to income maintenance later).

Stress and Anxiety: A Structural-Cultural Problem

As complex as the concepts stress and anxiety appear to be to practitioners and investigators, there seems to be a common core of agreement. Sells (1970) find a common theme or principle in biochemical, physiological, psychological, individual, and groups processes when the entity in question experiences "injury; illness; environmental extremes; task demands; threats to person's prestige or survival; disruptions of interpersonal relations and group activities" (p. 135). This "common principle" involves an insult to the organism which causes a breakdown and the arousal of countermeasures. Selye (1956) views this general sequence of critical events as a three-state General Adaptation Syndrome, consisting of alarm, resistance, and exhaustion. The key here is a noxious or deleterious stimulus or event, which triggers an alarm, which in turn mobilizes some defensive reaction, which finally consumes the system's resources if the situation is not released. Selye (1956) divides such reactions or coping responses into two specific actions taken against a particular stimulus and two nonspecific actions, which he defined as stress.

Stress, according to Sells (1970), occures when these conditions are met: (1) the individual cannot find an appropriate response—either the appropriate response is a physical impossibility, or the individual has not learned the appropriate response, (2) the potential gain or loss in the situation is important to the individual.

Mechanic (1970) argues that, from the sociological point of view, stress arises when the social system fails to provide adequate preparatory institutions, incentive systems, and support systems. By preparatory institutions, Mechanic (1970) meant the family, the school, and peer groups. The institutions provide training and incidental learning, set the normative limits to aspirations, and provide role relationships that give support in a crisis. A society cannot provide perfect support for its members; hence, individuals will experience some stress some of the time and a few a great deal of stress all of the time. Normal social intervention amounts to bolstering and augmenting the functions of existing institutions when they fail. Some failures are acute and short lived, for example, a natural disaster, and others are more chronic, such as inflation or unemployment. In either case, the social environment is the key and the societal response amounts to shoring up existing institutional supports.

Anxiety, in turn, poses a complex definitional problem. For, as Endler (1975b) points out, anxiety is a personality characteristic of responding to certain situations with a stress syndrome of responses. Anxiety states are then a function of the situations that evoke them and the individual personality that is prone to stress. Cattell and Scheier (1958, 1961) factor-analyzed items that reputedly measured anxiety and found two varieties, trait or chronic anxiety and state or acute anxiety. Chronic anxiety persists from situation to situation and therefore is stable over time, while state anxiety is aroused only by specific situations. Spielberger (1966a, 1972a, 1975) further specifies the relationship between the two forms of anxiety. State anxiety consists "of unpleasant, consciously perceived feelings of tension and apprehension, with associated activations in arousal of the autonomic nervous system" (Spielberger, 1975, p. 29). In contrast, trait anxiety is a generalized tendency to respond with an anxiety state when stress is induced. More important, it appears that ego-threatening situations trigger anxiety states in high trait anxiety individuals (Rappaport and Katkin, 1972; O'Neil, Spielberger, and Hansen, 1969). This qualification is crucial for understanding generalized trait anxiety. Physical threat, such as electrical shocks, can induce the state anxiety syndrome in virtually every individual, but threats to self-esteem appear to affect only certain individuals. This line of research has been confined to demonstrating the difference between state and trait anxiety. Future research should examine more carefully potential individual differences in the arousal value of different social situations. Also, we should have a clearer demographic picture of the number and social location of persons who are subject to trait anxiety. This is where sound social policy begins.

Stress and anxiety go beyond the simple situation-person analysis (see Figure 1). They constitute a structural-cultural problem within any given social system. Sociologists can contribute to the reduction of stress through providing a thorough understanding of contextual factors that produce stressful situations. Beyond the social support and economic resources available to the individual, sociologists aid the analysis by focusing attention on the individual's definition of the situation. Before beginning an analysis of stress and social structure, we should look at an extreme situation that produces an elevated level of stress—that is, a disaster. Situations can be the source of many stressful changes. Loss of relationship tops the list. Holmes and Rahe's (1967) study amplifies this point clearly. Furthermore, the rate of change has much to do with the stress of the situation. Structural changes such as industrialization, whether on a national scale or its more subtle forms within a community, produce stressful individuals—often in unpredictable ways.

Figure 1. Social and Cultural Model of Stress and Anxiety

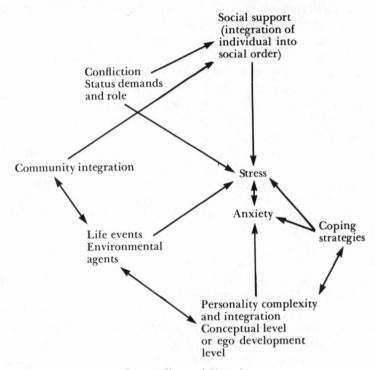

Personality and Situation

A given situation or episode may have distinctly different effects on different individuals. The research, to date, only suggests the critical factors. Durkheim (1897) saw social support and emotional involvements as critical for a person's well-being. In his classic study, Durkheim found suicide rates to be higher among individuals whose social roles give them too much freedom and not enough social support. Isolated professionals, such as doctors and lawyers in private practice, may experience "loneliness at the top syndrome." This concept has been employed to explain the differences in suicide rates among occupational categories. Individuals in top status had higher suicide rates than those holding more menial occupations. Age and marital status too have a powerful relationship with suicide. While teenage suicide may fluctuate over the years, it is relatively minor compared to the suicide rates for older persons over 50. Unmarried men from the provinces between the age of 50-60 had fourteen times the suicide rate of unmarried men under 20. But unmarried men 50-60 from Paris (Seine) had six times the suicide rate of unmarried men from rural parts of the same district (Durkheim, 1897). The general results are too complex to describe here, but it is clear that marital status, sex, age, and urban-rural residence have a complex (inter-active) effect on suicide rates. Males have generally a higher rate of success-ful suicide attemps than females, and in most studies this is accentuated for the older males. Again, a lack of emotional investment in others coupled with a sense of failure when emotional problems arise is connected to suicide. For Durkheim, social intervention, if it is to be successful and if it is truly desirable, must focus on the social structure, not the individual.

While focusing on institutions and customs, I will avoid extreme structuralism and will also take individual differences into account. Many stressful events happen to all of us. Loved ones will die. Financial setbacks will occur. Failures in life will arise unexpectedly. Sudden surprises occur at every turn. The question of stressful events (Holmes and Rahe, 1967) creates a number of problems, both methodological and theoretical, for sociologists. The phenomenological or existentially minded sociologists would warn that one cannot assume that a given event has the same meaning for all individuals. For instance, the death of a loved one is a twofold loss: first, a love object or significant other, and secondly, a major change in patterns of life. Holmes and Rahe (1967) do not sort out the two types of stress. Instead, they focus on change as the key ingredient in distress. But some individuals welcome change, and some do not. Those who like change find it pleasant when it occurs, while those who dislike change and seek the routine and familiar consider even beneficial changes stressful (Lauer, 1974). No work has been done on the impact of rapid life changes on change-receptive or change-resistive individuals. At this point, we must limit our theory to conjectures concerning the person-situation interaction. Intervention success, then, rests on a careful assessment of the individual's reaction to the situation.

Social Support

Corrective or therapeutic actions have one common denominator: they provide, in one form or another, adequate or inadequate social support. During World War II, in Saipan, for children the only source of meaningful social support was in the family (Joseph and Murray, 1951). Without the support of their family, the children were often emotionally scarred for life by the violence of war; but with family support, war experiences had little long-term effect on the Saipanese children. The loss of family ties, not the horrors of war, produced a crisis for Saipanese children. Similar patterns of stress were found in London children during the blitz. Social support is crucial for the conversion of stress to distress and anxiety. The critical nature of social support can be found in the success of moral therapy at the beginning of the nineteenth century. The rise of Christianity during the anxiety-ridden first millennium (Dodds, 1965) and armies under withering assault (Shils and Janowitz, 1948) provide examples of the pervasive need for social support and community. Dodds (1965) argues that Christianity won, despite persecution, over other religions in Rome because it provided a sense of community and place for an individual regardless of his way of life. In the communion of Christians he found social support and acceptance. Shils and Janowitz (1948) show that the German soldier was not a fighting machine or a fascist zealot; yet despite terrible risks and hardships and with no hope of victory, he fought on. The average German soldier was fighting for his friends and comrades, not Nazi ideology. When old units were broken up and reformed with fresh troops, the will to fight was lost, even for the most seasoned German soldier. Social support, or strong primary relations, is crucial for the control of anxiety. But we shall find that it is not sufficient in itself.

Several recent reviews suggest that social support has a profound effect on physical and mental health (Cobb, 1976; Kaplan, Cassel, and Gore, 1973; and Caplan, 1974). Kaplan, Cassel, and Gore (1973) emphasize the role of situations in which the individual cannot link his actions to desired consequences such as occurs in "role conflict, role ambiguity, blocked aspirations, and cultural discontinuity." They contend that social support conditions the individual's susceptibility to physiochemical disease agents such as microorganisms, toxins, and so on. Ample experimental evidence exists for the interaction between social support and stress. Liddel (1944) produced "experimental neurosis in isolated young goats but not with the mother present."

In human populations, social outsiders and loners had higher rates of tuberculosis than did socially integrated people in the same neighborhoods (Holmes, 1956). Kaplan, Cassel, and Gore (1973) cite literature linking the lack of social support to schizophrenia, multiple accidents, suicide, and other respiratory disease. Lin and associates (1979) find that, among Chinese Americans, for future illness (psychiatric symptoms) the predictive power of social support is as great as that of socioeconomic factors and stressful life events combined. Occupational prestige and marital status did not diminish the effect of social support on psychiatric symptoms. In a longitudinal study, Gore (1978) examined the effects of unemployment and social support on rural and urban populations. She found that, while unemployed, the unsupported, as opposed to the socially supported, evidenced higher levels of cholesterol, illness symptoms, and negative affective responses. Rural unemployed evidenced greater social support than urban unemployed. In sum, social support has an impact on the manifestation of symptoms of stress.

Why does social support have a salutary effect on health and wellbeing? Group pressure could enforce norms which promote health, and information from interaction could improve the individual's knowledge about disease prevention (Langlie, 1977). These explanations that avoid stress as a factor may apply to physical diseases but are hardly useful for psychiatric symptoms. Somehow social support acts as a "buffer" against the conversion of potentially stressful life events, such as unemployment, into acute stress.

Lin and associates (1979) see the buffer as information on how to reduce the consequences, either psychological or physical, of the stressful event. Pearlin and Schooler (1978) suggest other functions of social supports: modifying the conditions that produced the stress; neutralizing the meaning of experience and thereby maintaining the individual's self-esteem; and keeping emotional reactions in bounds. The mental health clinic serves as social support as well as performing its other functions. From a sociological point of view, therapy may be no more than being able to talk to a "significant other," a respected person in authority, and receiving comfort and support. Some Rogerians uphold this view.

Still, despite its promise, social support has not been thoroughly explored as a key ingredient in intervention. Kelly, Snowden, and Muñoz (1977) see the increase in social support of social structures as one of the community mental center goals. Unfortunately, the research on who responds best to what kinds of social support has not been accomplished. Only family, neighbors, and friendship groups have been demonstrated to have any major effect. Unfortunately, strangers on telephone suicide hotlines appear not to have any major effect on suicide rates. However, for first line crisis intervention, the police, if properly trained, can have a positive effect in reducing domestic disturbances (Kelly, Snowden, and Muñoz, 1977). I venture to suggest that social support works best in face-to-face situations, but we are just beginning to think through the question of immediate responses to intense crisis and of what form of intervention works best. Also, the policeman's role as an authority may be an advantage that volunteers do not possess. The utility of support from para-professionals and crisis intervention has as yet to be empirically demonstrated.

Education as Preventive Intervention

The key question for intervention is how to prevent symptoms and the damage done by stress and anxiety—not how to pick up the pieces. Events such as disasters can in part be controlled by safety and environmental measures. They cannot be eliminated, but their frequency and severity can be reduced. Economic misfortune, crime, and even marital problems may be reduced by preventive measures, which in turn should reduce some tensions. Still, we must confront the key question: Since disasters and misfortunes are inevitable, how do we allay or reduce the impact of such negative events? We have pointed to social support through family, friends, and therapy as a key ingredient. Coping skills are the second major factor. Coping skills can broadly be defined as intelligence—either Cattell's (1971) crystallized or fluid intelligence or mental flexibility—or as techniques for dealing with the symptoms of stress and for reducing ego involvement and therefore anxiety. Such coping skills can be preventive; that is, the individual's coping skills allow him to avoid crises. Also, coping skills may mitigate stress. Social learning theory provides a set of techniques for reducing the efforts of stress (Kanfer and Goldstein, 1975; Mahoney and Thoresen, 1974; Miller and Muñoz, 1976; Patterson, 1971, 1974). These efforts are successful in meeting specific problems.

But we have not explored the full power of education to prevent stress from being converted into distress. Problem-solving ability can be encouraged. Spivack and Shure have demonstrated that problem solving is positively related to adjustment (Shure and Spivack, 1972; Spivack and Shure, 1974). Unfortunately, this is a relatively isolated study and more rigorous studies are needed here.

The Stirling County Study in Nova Scotia shows that "personality assets," such as planning ability, interpersonal skills, and adaptability, are related to mental health (Beiser, 1971; Beiser, Feldman, and Egelhoff, 1972). All of these assets appear trainable. Such training efforts have been conducted. In the St. Louis County mental health programs, parents participated in a group discussion headed by a lay leader. Over a thirty-month period, the children of these parents evidenced fewer stress symptoms (Glidewell, Gilelea, and Kaufman, 1973). An educational program for low-IQ women who had a high probability of having a retarded child included cognitive and social training plus occupational and home care efforts. When the children were six years of age, massive gaps in IQ appeared between the children in the experimental group and children of similar mothers in the control groups. Still, a reduction in stress and anxiety can only be inferred from this study.

The relationship between life events, a healthy outlook, and coping and cognitive skills must be explored further. The argument advanced here has been that coping skills and education reduce stress by reducing the probability of a negative life event's occurring. We can go one step further to suggest that education could, through reducing generalized anxiety and ego involvement, reduce the stress experienced when negative life events occur. When a given negative life event occurs, psychosomatic symptoms would be less for an individual who has a flexible ego and solid coping skills than for another individual with a rigid ego and limited coping skills. Hence, coping strategies are basically a means of reducing the negative impact of setbacks and losses. Haan (1977) and many of the authors in the volume edited by Coelho, Hamburg, and Adams (1974) make similar points. But at present we have an emerging literature on adaptive functioning, with little work done on the source of coping strategies.

Income Maintenance

We have known for some time that psychological distress and anxiety are inversely related to personal income. The greater the income, with everything else held constant, the less distress and anxiety are reported (Bradburn, 1969; Department of Health, Education and Welfare, 1970; Dohrenwend and Dohrenwend, 1969; Kleiner and Parker, 1970; Phillips, 1966). Various explanations for this relationship, each with their policy implications and their mode of intervention, vie for acceptance, but we have little in the way of evidence to definitely distinguish among them. The social selection thesis (Durham, 1965) rests on downward drift; that is, the poor are mentally ill or incompetent persons who drifted into poverty. Next, an inadequate income is the cause of distress (Dohrenwend and Dohrenwend, 1969; Kohn, 1968). With limited resources, the poor are subject to more frequent and more intense crises than the rich. Simple matters such as broken appliances or minor thefts can become major crises for the poor. A third hypothesis, the life-events or life-crises approach, directs its attention to change in income. According to Dohrenwend and Dohrenwend (1974, p. 133), life events are "objective events that threaten to disrupt the individual's usual activities." Adjustments cause stress, and the continual threat of readjustments causes more stress. The accumulation of life events is associated with psychological distress (Brown and Birley, 1968; Myers, Lindenthal, and Pepper, 1971, 1972, 1974; Paykel, 1974a). Hence, even a massive and sudden increase in income would produce stress. Sudden wealth, according to Durkheim (1897), was a critical source of anomie, and he viewed it as extremely stressful.

Recent and larger-scale studies of income maintenance provided an opportunity to test the effects of income maintenance intervention. The consequences were dramatic. While the amounts of money were not large, the income of the participants changed drastically, as did their lives. In New Jersey (Middleton and Alken, 1977) recipients reported higher rates of psychosomatic symptoms than did controls, and distress symptoms had a slight positive relation to payment level. But statistical significance was not reached. But in the Rural Income Maintenance Experiment (Middleton, 1976), statistically significant effects appeared for both the recipient/nonrecipient contrast and the contrast between amounts of supplemental income. The Seattle and Denver Maintenance Program found that several sex, race, and marital status groups responded to this income maintenance program with increased distress (Thoits and Hannan, 1979). These findings are complex, varying within each site and length of treatment (three years and five years intervening). The magnitude of change, in general, appears less important than change itself. The Income Maintenance program shows that such radical intervention does not necessarily reduce stress and its consequences. Thoits and Hannan (1979) argue for a life-events hypothesis. In the same study Hannan, Tuma, and Groeneveld (1977) found a higher level of divorce in the income maintenance group. Income maintenance, then, may trigger a negative life event, divorce.

A puzzle remains. Despite the negative relationship between income and psychological distress, and income maintenance does reduce income inequality among the experimental group, it was impossible to tell from the present studies why this should be so (Middleton, 1976; Thoits and Hannan, 1979). The question then remains: Does income maintenance, after an adjustment period, reduce stress experienced by those at the bottom? Still, changes in income induce stress in the short run.

Summary

This review was short for the simple reason that literature based on sound empirical evidence is in short supply. Few intervention efforts address stress and anxiety indirectly, either as a preventive or an alleviative effort. Fewer still address the topics directly. Social support is the most developed area, with some evidence indicating that social support does reduce stress. Still, little effort has been directed at the person-situation interaction. Social support may work better with dependent individuals than independent individuals. Further, how can formal intervention efforts employ social support as a strategy? Will nonprofessional efforts be as effective as professional efforts? What role does similarity of background and outlook have on social support effects? These questions must be addressed before an adequate model of social support intervention can be created. As an intervention strategy, direct financial support did not fare well, although the studies cited involved a limited time span. The evidence, in fact, points to an increase, not a decrease, in experienced stress. Intervention into stress and anxiety, I argue, will be more effective if prevention efforts are emphasized through educational activities aimed at improving coping skills. Both the preventive and alleviative models are relevant. The critical research is yet to be done. If successful intervention strategies are to be developed, we must first build a sound body of research findings— and soon.

26

Prevention
and Equilibrium-
Disequilibrium Theory

Irwin L. Kutash

❖ ❖ ❖ ❖ ❖ ❖ ❖ ❖ ❖ ❖ ❖ ❖ ❖

Prevention in regard to stress and anxiety is actually a misnomer. No individual and no society could or would want to be stressless or without some level of objective anxiety. Hans Selye (1978) notes that "sitting in a dentist's chair is stressful, but so is exchanging a passionate kiss with a lover—after all, your pulse races, your breathing quickens, your heartbeat soars, and yet, who in the world would forgo such a pleasurable pastime simply because of the stress involved? . . . Our aim shouldn't be to completely avoid stress . . . but to learn how to recognize our typical response to stress and then try to moderate our lives in accordance with it." Anxiety theory likewise regards anxiety as serving a positive signal function (Rangell, 1955; Zetzel, 1966). Freud (1917) contrasted neurotic anxiety with objective anxiety. In his view, objective anxiety is adaptive, if the extent of the reaction is within controllable limits, since it is a response to a real danger and leads one to institute protective measures. Positive stress, or "eustress" as

463

coined by Selye, and signal anxiety, or objective anxiety as described by Freud, are, therefore, not the focus of prevention.

Furthermore, one person's stress is another person's eustress. One person's level of objective anxiety may serve as a signal; another person's level may exceed controllable limits and become paralyzing. Individual differences must not be overlooked. Selye (1978), for example, describes "racehorses, who thrive on stress and are only happy with a vigorous, fast-paced life style, and turtles, who, in order to be happy, require peace, quiet, and a generally tranquil environment." Selye concludes that "all the stress inventories are flawed because they fail to give enough weight to individual differences." Zuckerman (1978), on the basis of his experiments on sensory deprivation in humans, concluded that "some humans have an innate need for more stimulation than others" and that "knowing whether one is 'high' or 'low' can be important." He is currently developing normative data on a "Sensation-Seeking Scale," which may fill the need described by Selye.

This concept of an individually based optimal level of stress is less controversial than that of an individually based optimal level of anxiety, simply because stress can be construed to be a positive sensation, as in the passionate kiss described above, while anxiety is clearly uncomfortable. Its signal function or survival value, however, gives it its positive connotation (May, 1950a; Grinker, 1966; Costello, 1976). In fact, "The patient after therapy may well bear more anxiety than he had before, but it will be conscious anxiety and he will be able to use it constructively" (May, 1967, p. 109). Therefore, an individually based optimal anxiety level can serve as a barometer to the person of when life changes are needed.

With this prelude in mind, then, this chapter will deal with the prevention of extremes—of too much or too little stress, which can induce anxiety disorders in the individual and globally for many members of the society.

To deal with prevention in the manner described earlier, and to provide a framework for the discussion to follow, I will present an outline of my Equilibrium-Disequilibrium Theory of stress-induced anxiety. It will integrate stress and anxiety theory, incorporate the concept of optimal levels of stress and anxiety, and take into account the principle of individuality. Since even the terms *stress* and *anxiety* have almost as many meanings as there are theorists using them, and since some new concepts will be introduced, a glossary of the author's use of these terms and original nomenclature is therefore provided.

Stress. The experiencing of external environmental or internal environmental impingements or stressors.

Stressors. Environmental impingements to the individual.

1. *External Stressors.* Environmental impingements emanating from the interpersonal environment or the physical environment.

2. *Internal Stressors.* Environmental impingements emanating from the mental environment or the physiological environment.

Stress Level. The sum of all external or internal environmental impingements or stressors experienced at any given time—as measured by quantitative physical and mental examination results compared to an individual's base rate.

1. *Interpersonally Derived Stress Level.* That portion of stress level caused by stressors emanating from the interpersonal environment.

2. *Physically Derived Stress Level.* That portion of stress level caused by stressors emanating from the physical environment.

3. *Mentally Derived Stress Level.* That portion of stress level caused by stressors emanating from the mental environment.

4. *Physiologically Derived Stress Level.* That portion of stress level caused by stressors emanating from the physiological environment.

Environment. All the phenomena surrounding or affecting an individual.

1. *Interpersonal Environment.* Social or cultural phenomena that surround or affect an individual.

2. *Physical Environment.* Physical phenomena or objects that surround or affect an individual.

3. *Mental Environment.* Mental phenomena—such as conscious, preconscious, or unconscious processes or content—that affect an individual; cognition, thoughts, and feelings.

4. *Physiological Environment.* Bodily phenomena—such as the nervous system, receptors, glands, or organs—that affect an individual.

Anxiety. A generalized psychological and/or physiological experience of discomfort, resulting from a nonoptimal stress level for one's psychological and/or physiological constitution.

Tranquility. A generalized psychological and/or physiological experience of inherent comfort, resulting from an optimal stress level for one's psychological and/or physiological constitution.

Equilibrium. The state an individual is in when he is experiencing tranquility (that is, when he is at an optimal stress level for his constitution). Healthy equilibrium is found in normal individuals.

Disequilibrium. The state an individual is in when he is experiencing anxiety (that is, when he is at a less than or more than optimal stress level for his constitution). Disequilibrium is found in individuals with psychosomatic illness, neurosis, or psychosis when the disorder is ego alien.

Malequilibrium. The state an individual is in when he is experiencing tranquility through adjusting stress level in an objectively maladaptive manner (for example, by delusional thinking or substance abuse). Malequilibrium is found in individuals with disorders that are ego syntonic.

Intimacy. The application of external interpersonal energy to the individual.

Intimacy Balance. The point on the continuum from low intimacy (isolation) to high intimacy (engulfment) at which a person experiences tranquility or is in a state of equilbrium in the interpersonal environment.

Intimacy Imbalance Disorder. A disorder wherein the individual is in a state of disequilbrium in the interpersonal environment, evidenced by anxiety resulting from too much or too little intimacy for his individual intimacy needs.

Stimulation. The application of external object energy to an individual.

Stimulation Balance. The point on the continuum from low stimulation (boredom) to high stimulation (shell shock) at which a person experiences tranquility or is in a state of equilibrium in the physical environment.

Stimulation Imbalance Disorder. A disorder wherein the individual is in a state of disequilibrium in the physical environment, evidenced by anxiety resulting from too much or too little stimulation for his individual stimulation needs.

Fantasy. The experiencing by the mind of internally produced mental images.

Fantasy Balance. The point on the continuum from low fantasy production (unimaginativeness) to high fantasy production (excessive daydreaming) at which a person experiences tranquility or is in a state of equilibrium in the mental environment.

Fantasy Imbalance Disorder. A disorder wherein the individual is in a state of disequilibrium in the mental environment, evidenced by anxiety resulting from too much or too little fantasy production for his individual fantasy needs.

Sensation. The experiencing of external energy through a receptor.

Sensation Balance. The point on the continuum from low sensation (numbness) to high sensation (pain) at which a person experiences tranquility or is in a state of equilibrium in the physiological environment.

Sensation Imbalance Disorder. A disorder wherein the individual is in a state of disequilibrium in the physiological environment, evidenced by anxiety resulting from too little or too much sensation for his individual sensation needs.

Prevention. Measures to avoid too low or too high a stress level for the individual or the community and consequently the avoidance of maladaptive anxiety and its related disorders.

1.   *Primary Prevention.* Measures to avoid anxiety-related disorders.
2.   *Secondary Prevention.* Measures to limit the growth of anxiety-related disorders.
3.   *Tertiary Prevention.* Measures to reduce impairment or disability following anxiety-related disorders. (Caplan, 1964, can be credited with the conceptualization of prevention as a three-part undertaking.)

With this vocabulary in mind, the theory can be simply put forth. *Anxiety,* or a state of disequilibrium, results when one is not experiencing the optimal level of stress for one's constitution. *Prevention* refers to measures that stop anxiety from occurring. *Tranquility,* or a state of equilibrium or malequilibrium, results when one is experiencing the optimal stress level for one's constitution, either in a healthy (equilibrium) or an unhealthy (malequilibrium) balance. (See Figure 1.)

Anxiety can be adaptive if it is at a level that can serve to signal to an individual a need for change and maladaptive if it is so high as to be immobilizing or so low as to be nonmotivating. Drugs, as a treatment for anxiety, are used properly only if they bring anxiety down from a high maladaptive range to an adaptive level. If they bring an individual from an adaptive level down to a low maladaptive level, they are being misused.

Disorders that can develop within the context of each of the four environments will now be considered. These disorders can serve as examples of what can result when there is too low or too high a stress level and can serve as a more discrete focus for prevention, as will be seen later, than stress level or anxiety per se.

A most significant factor in a person's stress level emanating from the interpersonal environment is the person's intimacy balance, which involves psychological, sociological, and cultural issues. A person experiencing too little intimacy (for example, isolation) or too much intimacy (for example,

Figure 1. Diagrammatic Representation of Equilibrium-Disequilibrium Theory of Stress-Induced Anxiety.

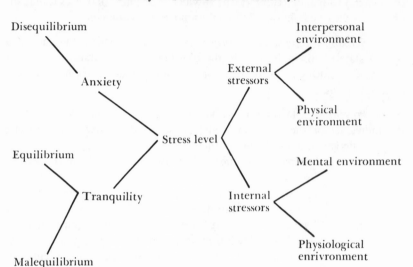

engulfment) has either a low interpersonally derived stress level or a high interpersonally derived stress level and consequently experiences anxiety as a result of the imbalance or disequilibrium it creates. Such difficulties can be termed "intimacy-level disorders." The anxiety can serve as a signal of the imbalance and function usefully or, if too great, can prove immobilizing. These anxiety-level alternatives are applicable to the other environments to be discussed as well. A person whose interpersonal intimacy balance is at a subjectively comfortable point on the continuum from low intimacy to high intimacy will experience tranquility.

A most significant factor in a person's stress level emanating from the physical environment is the person's stimulation balance, involving psychological and ecological issues. A person experiencing low stimulation (for example, boredom) or too much stimulation (for example, shell shock) has either a low physically derived stress level or a high physically derived stress level and consequently experiences anxiety as a result of the imbalance or disequilibrium it creates. Such difficulties can be termed "stimulation-level disorders." A person whose stimulation balance is at a subjectively comfortable point on the continuum from low stimulation to high stimulation will experience tranquility.

A most significant factor in a person's stress level emanating from the mental environment is the person's fantasy balance, involving psychological issues. A person experiencing too low fantasy production (unimaginativeness) or too high fantasy production (excessive daydreaming or compulsive rumination) has either a low mentally derived stress level or a high mentally derived stress level and consequently experiences anxiety as a result of the imbalance or disequilibrium it creates. Such difficulties can be termed "fantasy-level disorders." These fantasy level disorders can be related to criminal behavior (see Kutash and Schlesinger, 1977, in press; Schlesinger and Kutash, in press). A person whose fantasy balance is at a subjectively comfortable point on the continuum from low fantasy production to high fantasy production will experience tranquility.

A most significant factor in a person's stress level emanating from the physiological environment is the person's sensation balance, involving psychological and medical issues. A person experiencing too little sensation (numbness) or too much sensation (pain) has either a low physiologically derived stress level or a high physiologically derived stress level and consequently experiences anxiety as a result of the imbalance or disequilibrium it creates. A person whose sensation balance is at a subjectively comfortable point on the continuum from low sensation to high sensation will experience tranquility. The nature of the sensation as well as the absolute degree contributes to the stress level derived—as is true for intimacy, stimulation, and fantasy level as well. The best measure of level is, therefore, in terms of resultant bodily or mental wear and tear.

Of course, these environments overlap, interact, and interrelate— so that, for example, high or low intimacy or high or low stimulation level may affect fantasy or sensation level, since fantasy or sensation can result from intimacy or stimulation. They can also be independent, however, since fantasy or sensation can also be aroused by internal processes or stimuli and therefore have been considered discretely as well. In any event, a balance must exist amont the four environments a person functions in, as well as within each environment.

A person experiencing an intimacy disorder may use the anxiety as a barometer of disequilibrium and try to achieve equilibrium in the interpersonal environment through, for example, working out a dependency conflict in psychotherapy and hence achieving normality. Less adaptive solutions, creating malequilibrium, may involve altering the balance among the environments. That is, the person might compensate for too little intimacy with (1) high stimulation level (for example, going out with different people every night but experiencing them as objects), (2) high fantasy level (for example, creating imaginary or delusional involvements), (3) high sensation level (for example, developing physical complaints or psychosomatic illnesses), or (4) some combination of the above. The person can thus avoid anxiety and experience subjective tranquility but would be considered disordered by objective standards. The following case history further illustrates the maladaptive solution possibilities.

Case 1. A woman (J) who had been diagnosed as a paranoid schizophrenic came to see me for psychotherapy at a state hospital.

She said that she had been committed by relatives who did not believe that she was being pursued by the Mafia, that men hiding in the halls of her apartment were watching her, and that she had to sneak around the neighborhood passing messages to the FBI. Her history revealed an individual who, after her mother's death, had moved from a rural area to Manhattan and had gradually grown more isolated and lonely. In New York City, she had been unable to get a job or find any social involvement. Therapy over a four-year period focused on how she could become less isolated and more social; her delusional system was ignored entirely. She went to live in the more rural area near the hospital, joined some community activities, and made some friends. Gradually, her paranoid symptoms disappeared without ever being discussed after the initial sessions.

Comment. J came to understand what was missing in her life and adjusted her intimacy balance, so that she no longer needed the higher fantasy levels her delusions provided.

A person experiencing a stimulation-level disorder may use the anxiety as a barometer and try to achieve equilibrium in the physical environment by changing the ecology or relocating. Less adaptive solutions here may involve altering the balance among the environments and creating malequilibrium. That is, the individual might compensate for high or low stimulation by (1) high or low intimacy level (having no involvement in other people's lives or too much), (2) high or low fantasy level (imagining exciting circumstances or avoiding fantasy-stimulating activities such as reading fiction or watching adventure movies), (3) high or low sensation level (for example, inflicting self-pain or taking sensation-reducing drugs), or (4) some combination of the above.

Case 2. A man (M) who had been diagnosed as alcoholic came for treatment on the alcohol rehabilitation unit. He said that he had worked for over twenty years in a high-pressure executive position, never had enough time for his family life, and gradually began drinking more and more to calm his overwrought nerves. He decided, after counseling, that his job as a buyer for a department store, requiring a lot of traveling and long hours, was not worth the wear and tear. He therefore used some accumulated capital to open a small clothing store. He was able to stop drinking entirely and spend more time with his family.

Comment. M realized that he was receiving too much stimulation in his life and remedied it. He had previously lowered his intimacy level (little family life) and sensation level through alcohol abuse in a maladaptive solution.

A person experiencing a fantasy-level disorder may use the anxiety as a barometer to seek psychological treatment in order to become more or less involved in fantasy. Again, less adaptive solutions may involve altering the balance among environments and creating malequilibrium. That is, an individual might compensate for too high or too low a fantasy level by (1) avoiding external stressors or becoming overinvolved in them, (2) tuning out or heightening physiological pleasures or pains, or (3) some combination of the above.

> *Case 3.* P came for psychotherapy. He complained that he had to be constantly on the move, always out socializing or keeping busy, because he had anxiety attacks whenever he was not active. As a result, he felt that he could "never allow myself a moment to think." When he stopped running, however, he was plagued by sadistic fantasies that he could not live with and would do anything to "get away from." Psychoanalytic therapy was geared to help him discover the origins of his compulsive thinking and to work through anger originating in his childhood.
> *Comment.* P was controlling his fantasy level by being highly stimulated at all times. Once he was able to work through his need for sadistic fantasies, he was able to lower his stimulation level.

A person experiencing a sensation-level disorder may use the anxiety it generates as an impetus to seek medical treatment to cure a physiological malfunction. Less adaptive solutions would be to increase intimacy, stimulation, or fantasy levels so as to tune out pain or numbness and any anxiety accompanying it.

An imbalance in one environment may be influenced by a change in another environment to create malequilibrium as in the examples above. Such changes can also be used to create equilibrium when, for example, raising one level that is too low causes a corresponding lowering of a level that is too high. This was the result in Case 1, when increased intimacy level lowered fantasy level, and in Case 2, when decreased stimulation level contributed to increased intimacy level and sensation level.

Imbalance within or among environments, with its accompanying anxiety, is ego alien and provides anxiety as a motivation for treatment. Compensatory balance among environments when it creates malequilibrium is ego syntonic and is less amenable to treatment because of the lack of anxiety as impetus.

Finally, an important balance must be maintained between the external and internal environments as a whole. This was recognized in the Rorschach Test, which features the introversive-extratensive balance. To quote Klopfer and Davidson (1962, pp. 142-143):

> The markedly introversive person is one who has a well-developed imaginal function, either in terms of fantasy, long-range goals, or acknowledged impulses, while his responsiveness to and

involvement with the outer world are reduced. He tends to restructure the world in terms of his own values and needs. The well-adjusted introversive person is not withdrawn or retiring; he is self-sufficient. The markedly extratensive person, on the other hand, is one who is highly responsive to his environment, either in terms of overt emotional expression or affectional warmth or feeling, or a mere passive submission to forces coming upon him from without. He does not tend to restructure the world in terms of his own needs. The well-adjusted extratensive person is not passively reactive. He is creative in his relationship to objects and people external to him and strives toward goals that he has staked out in the external world.

According to equilibrium-disequilibrium theory, such well-adjusted persons have achieved a healthy equilibrium by having the optimal balance, for them, of stress levels within and between environments.

Prevention, within the context of the equilibrium-disequilibrium theory of stress-induced anxiety, is prevention of inoptimal levels of stress for one's individual comfort. On an individual level, prevention involves the person's being cognizant of his intimacy, stimulation, fantasy, and sensation needs and satisfying them. On the global level, prevention involves creating environments for people that are conducive to levels of intimacy, stimulation, fantasy, and sensation that will meet the most needs, since some levels (such as sensory deprivation, crowding, and pollution) are universally detrimental.

An individual prevention program would teach people to be aware of their levels of stress in each environment and to discover the most beneficial level for them. Data that could be useful for this purpose were obtained by the author. Each person in a "coping with stress" course was administered the Social Readjustment Rating Scale (SRRS) from Holmes and Rahe (1967), the Sensation-Seeking Scale (SSS) from Zuckerman (1978), and the Self-Rating Anxiety Scale (SAS) from Zung (1979). We found that high SRRS scale scorers with low sensation-seeking scores experienced more anxiety than high SRRS scale scorers with high sensation-seeking scores. It appears, then, that low sensation seekers can avoid anxiety by keeping life changes within their control to a minimum, while very high scorers might better tolerate life changes. Similar findings are reported by Smith, Johnson, and Sarason (1978) utilizing the life experiences survey, the SSS, and Lanyon's Discomfort Scale. In other words, individual programs to prevent anxiety become possible with more sophisticated test use. The above example is by no means a prevention program; it simply illustrates that such a program is plausible. Biofeedback; consciousness-raising groups; dynamic psychotherapies; projective tests; and objective tests and scales, including tests detecting cognitive, psychomotor, physiological, and perceptual behavior and tests that sample behavior under experimentally induced stress are other existing techniques that can be applied to prevention, as well as treatment, by creating awareness of what a person's individual intimacy, stimulation, fantasy, or sensation needs are.

Mental hygiene courses, particularly in the schools, could be used for prevention purposes as well as to educate people to the pitfalls involved with substance abuse, a factor that can exacerbate anxiety-related disorders (Powers and Kutash, 1978, and in this volume). Secondary and tertiary prevention would involve treatment immediately after trauma or particularly stressful events; for example, after the trauma of an aggressive attack. (For such intervention strategies and therapies see Kutash, 1978, and Chapter Twenty-One in this volume.) In addition to psychoanalytic psychotherapy techniques, prevention and treatment paradigms are also being developed in the behavioral model (see, for example, Poser and King, 1976, and Chapter Twenty-Two in this volume).

A global prevention program (see Levi and Andersson, 1975; Kessler and Albee, 1975) would include control of factors that create high or low stress levels in most people in their four environments. Stress-producing factors identified by Levi and Andersson (1975) include overpopulation, malnutrition, underemployment, poverty, famine, environmental polution, illiteracy, and inequality. Control of such factors—factors that affect the quality of life—would eliminate extreme environmental stressors that are bound to create inoptimal stress levels in many people.

In conclusion, if stress can be experienced in the interpersonal environment, the physical environment, the mental environment, and the physiological environment, prevention is certainly a multifaceted enterprise and needs to involve multidisciplinary input to be effective. Psychological, sociological, ecological, biological, and medical factors all figure in the equation. Ultimately, however, each person must become involved in his own individual program, as both client and practitioner on the individual level and as both agitator and effector on the global level. We all want to live in personal and universal tranquility. We must all work to achieve it.

References

Aaksten, C. W. "Psychosocial Stress and Health Disturbances." *Social Science Medicine,* 1974, *8,* 77–90.

Abel, E. L. "The Fetal Alcohol Syndrome: Behavioral Teratology," *Psychological Bulletin,* in press.

Abraham, K. "A Short Study of the Development of the Libido, Viewed in the Light of Mental Disorders." In *Selected Papers.* London: Hogarth Press, 1942.

Abrahamsen, D. *The Psychology of Crime.* New York: Columbia University Press, 1960.

Abramson, L. Y., Seligman, M. E. P., and Teasdale, J. P. "Learned Helplessness in Humans: Critique and Reformulation." *Journal of Abnormal Psychology,* 1978, *87,* 49–74.

Achenbach, T. M. "The Child Behavior Profile. I: Boys Aged 6–11." *Journal of Consulting and Clinical Psychology,* 1978, *46,* 478–488.

Ackerman, S. M., and Sachar, E. J. "The Lactate Theory of Anxiety: A Review and Reevaluation." *Psychosomatic Medicine,* 1974, *36,* 69–81.

Adam, G. *Interoception and Behavior*. Budapest: Akademiai Kiado Publishing House of the Hungarian Academy of Sciences, 1967.

Adams, R. D., and Victor, M. "The Neuroses." In *Principles of Neurology*. New York: McGraw-Hill, 1977.

Ader, R. "Experimentally Induced Gastric Lesions." *Advances in Psychosomatic Medicine*, 1971, *6*, 1–39.

Ader, R., Beels, C. C., and Tatum, R. "Social Factors Affecting Emotionality and Resistance to Disease in Animals. II: Susceptibility to Gastric Ulceration as a Function of Interruptions in Social Interactions and the Time at Which They Occur." *Journal of Comparative and Physiological Psychology*, 1960, *53*, 455–458.

Adler, R. K., MacRitchie, K., and Engel, G. L. "Psychologic Processes and Ischemic Stroke (Occlusive Cerebrovascular Disease). I: Observations on 32 Men with 35 Strokes." *Psychosomatic Medicine*, 1971, *33*, 1–29.

Agras, W. S., and others. "Relaxation in Systematic Desensitization." *Archives of General Psychiatry*, 1971, *25*, 511–514.

Agras, W. S., Sylvester, D., and Oliveau, D. C. "The Epidemiology of Common Fears and Phobias." *Comprehensive Psychiatry*, 1969, *10*, 151–156.

Ainsworth, M. D. S., Bell, S. M., and Stayton, D. J. "Individual Differences in Strange Situation Behavior of One-Year-Olds." In H. R. Schaffer (Ed.), *The Origins of Human Social Relations*. New York: Academic Press, 1971.

Ainsworth, M. D. S., Bell, S. M., and Stayton, D. J. "Infant-Mother Attachment and Social Development: Socialization as a Product of Reciprocal Responsiveness to Signals." In M. Richards (Ed.), *The Integration of a Child into a Social World*. Cambridge, England: Cambridge University Press, 1974.

Alexander, F., French, T. M., and Pollock, G. H. (Eds.). *Psychosomatic Specificity*. Vol. 1. Chicago: University of Chicago Press, 1968.

Ambrose, J. A. "The Development of the Smiling Response in Early Infancy." In B. M. Foss (Ed.), *Determinants of Infant Behavior*. Vol. 1. New York: Wiley, 1961.

Ambrose, J. A. "The Concept of a Critical Period for the Development of Social Responsiveness in Early Human Infancy." In B. M. Foss (Ed.), *Determinants of Infant Behavior*. Vol. 2. New York: Wiley, 1963.

American Psychiatric Association. *Diagnostic and Statistical Manual of Mental Disorders*. (2nd ed.) Washington, D.C.: American Psychiatric Association, 1968.

American Psychiatric Association. *A Psychiatric Glossary*. New York: American Psychiatric Association, 1975.

Ames, L., Walker, R., and Goodenough, E. "Old Age Rorschach Follow-Up." *Perceptual and Motor Skills*, 1957, *1*, 68.

Ananth, J. "Treatment of Obsessive-Compulsive Neurosis with Clomipramine (Anafranil)." *Journal of Internal Medicine Research*, 1977, *5* (15), 38–41.

Anderson, D. E., and Brady, J. V. "Pre-avoidance Blood Pressure Elevations Accompanied by Heart Rate Decreases in the Dog." *Science*, 1971, *172*, 595–597.

Anderson, D. E., and Brady, J. V. "Effects of Beta Blockade on Cardiovascular Responses to Avoidance Performances in Dogs." *Psychosomatic Medicine*, 1973, *35*, 457.

Anderson, D. E., and Tosheff, J. "Cardiac Output and Total Peripheral Resistance Changes During Pre-avoidance Periods in the Dog." *Journal of Applied Physiology*, 1973, *34*, 650–654.

Anderson, S., and Gantt, W. H. "The Effect of Person on Cardiac and Motor Responsivity to Shock in Dogs." *Conditional Reflex*, 1966, *1*, 181–189.

Andrew, R. J. "Review of Eibl-Eibesfeldt's *The Biology of Behavior*." *Science*, 1971, *171*, 53–54.

Andrews, G., and Tennant, C. "Becoming Upset and Becoming Ill: An Appraisal of the Relation Between Life Events and Physical Illness." *Medical Journal of Australia*, 1978, *1*, 324–327.

Andrews, G., and others. "Life Event Stress, Social Support, Coping Style, and Risk of Psychological Impairment." *Journal of Nervous and Mental Disease*, 1978, *166*, 307–316.

Anton, W. "An Evaluation of Outcome Variables in Systematic Desensitization." *Behaviour Research and Therapy*, 1976, *14*, 217–224.

Antonovsky, A. "Breakdown: A Needed Fourth Step in the Conceptual Armamentarium of Modern Medicine." *Social Science and Medicine*, 1972, *6*, 537–544.

Aponte, J., and Aponte, C. "Group Preprogrammed Systematic Desensitization Without the Simultaneous Presentation of Aversive Scenes with Relaxation Training." *Behaviour Research and Therapy*, 1971, *9*, 337–346.

Appelgarth, A. "Comments on Aspects of the Theory of Psychic Energy." *Journal of the American Psychoanalytic Association*, 1971, *19*, 379–416.

Aprison, M. H. "Are Some Amino Acid Neurotransmitters Involved in Psychiatric Disorders.?" In E. Usdin, D. A. Hamburg, and J. D. Barclas (Eds.), *Neuroregulators and Psychiatric Disorders*. New York: Oxford University Press, 1977.

Arenberg, D. "Concept Problem Solving in Young and Old Adults." *Journal of Gerontology*, 1968, *23*, 279–282.

Argyle, M., and Little, B. R. "Do Personality Traits Apply to Social Behavior?" *Journal for the Theory of Social Behavior*, 1972, *2*, 1–35.

Arlow, J. A. "Conflict, Regression, and Symptom Formation." *International Journal of Psycho-analysis*, 1963, *44*, 12–22.

Arlow, J. A. "Psychomania and the Primal Scene: A Psychoanalytic Comment on the Work of Yukio Mishima." *Psychoanalytic Quarterly*, 1978, *47*, 24–51.

Armor, D. L., Polich, J. M., and Stambul, H. B. *Alcoholism and Treatment*. Santa Monica, Calif.: Rand, 1976.

Arthur, R. J. "Extreme Stress in Adult Life and Its Psychic and Psychophysiological Consequences." In E. K. Gunderson and R. H. Rahe (Eds.), *Life Stress and Illness*. Springfield, Ill.: Thomas, 1974.

Asberg, M., and others. "'Serotonin Depression'—A Biochemical Subgroup Within the Affective Disorders." *Science*, 1976, *191*, 478–480.

Atweh, S. F., and Kuhar, M. J. "Autoradiographic Localization of Opiate Receptors in Rat Brain. II: The Brain Stem." *Brain Research*, 1977, *129*, 1.

Auerbach, S. M. "Trait-State Anxiety and Adjustment to Surgery." *Journal of Consulting and Clinical Psychology*, 1973, *40*, 264–271.

Averill, J. R. "Personal Control over Aversive Stimuli and Its Relationship to Stress." *Psychological Bulletin*, 1973, *80*, 286–303.

Ayers, D., and Ely, D. L. "Zona Fasciculata Ultrastructure and Plasma Corticosterone Correlates in Dominant and Subordinate Mice." *Federation Proceedings,* 1979, *38* (3), 1151.

Baade, E., and others. "Psychological Tests." In H. Ursin, E. Baade, and S. Levine (Eds.), *Psychobiology of Stress.* New York: Academic Press, 1978.

Back, K. W., and Bogdonoff, M. D. "Plasma Lipid Responses to Leadership, Conformity, and Deviation." In P. H. Leiderman and D. Shapiro (Eds.), *Psychobiological Approaches to Social Behavior.* Stanford, Calif.: Stanford University Press, 1964.

Bagley, C. "Incest Behavior and Incest Taboo." *Social Problems,* 1969, *16,* 505–519.

Baldessarini, R. J. "Mood Drugs." *Disease-a-Month,* 1977, *24* (2).

Bandura, A. "A Social Learning Interpretation of Psychological Dysfunctions." In P. London and D. Rosenhan (Eds.), *Foundations of Abnormal Psychology.* New York: Holt, Rinehart and Winston, 1968.

Bandura, A. *Principles of Behavior Modification.* New York: Holt, Rinehart and Winston, 1969.

Bandura, A. *Aggression: A Social Learning Analysis.* Englewood Cliffs, N.J.: Prentice-Hall, 1973.

Bandura, A. "Self-Efficacy: Toward a Unifying Theory of Behavioral Change." *Psychological Review,* 1977a, *84,* 191–215.

Bandura, A. *Social Learning Theory.* Englewood Cliffs, N.J.: Prentice-Hall, 1977b.

Bandura, A., and Barab, P. G. "Processes Governing Disinhibitory Effects Through Symbolic Modeling." *Journal of Abnormal Psychology,* 1973, *82,* 1–9.

Bandura, A., Blanchard, E. B., and Ritter, B. "The Relative Efficacy of Desensitization and Modeling Approaches for Inducing Behavioral, Affective, and Attitudinal Change." *Journal of Personality and Social Psychology,* 1969, *13,* 173–199.

Bandura, A., Grusec, J. E., and Menlove, F. L. "Vicarious Extinction of Avoidance Behavior." *Journal of Personality and Social Psychology,* 1967, *5,* 449–455.

Bandura, A., Jeffrey, R. W., and Wright, C. L. "Efficacy of Participant Modeling as a Function of Response Induction Aids." *Journal of Abnormal Psychology,* 1974, *83,* 56–64.

Bandura, A., and Menlove, F. L. "Factors Determining Vicarious Extinction of Avoidance Behavior Through Symbolic Modeling." *Journal of Personality and Social Psychology,* 1968, *8,* 99–108.

Bard, P. "A Diencephalic Mechanism for the Expression of Rage, with Special Reference to the Sympathetic Nervous System." *American Journal of Physiology,* 1928, *84,* 490–515.

Barnett, J. "Therapeutic Intervention in the Dysfunctional Thought Processes of the Obsessional." *American Journal of Psychotherapy,* 1972, *26,* 338–351.

Barnett, S. A. "Competition Among Wild Rats." *Nature* (London), 1955, *175,* 126–127.

Baron, M. R., and Ganz, R. L. "Effects of Locus of Control and Type of Feedback on the Task Performance of Lower-Class Black Children." *Journal of Personality and Social Psychology,* 1972, *21,* 124–130.

Baron, M. R., and others. "Interaction of Locus of Control and Type of Performance Feedback: Considerations of External Validity." *Journal of Personality and Social Psychology*, 1974, *30*, 285–292.

Barry, H., III. "Alcohol." In S. N. Pradhan and S. N. Dutta (Eds.), *Drug Abuse: Clinical and Basic Aspects*. St. Louis: Mosby, 1977.

Bartlett, E. S., and Izard, C. E. "A Dimensional and Discrete Emotions Investigation of the Subjective Experience of Emotion." In C. E. Izard (Ed.), *Patterns of Emotions: A New Analysis of Anxiety and Depression*. New York: Academic Press, 1972.

Basmajian, J. V. "Facts Versus Myths in EMG Biofeedback." *Biofeedback and Self-Regulation*, 1976, *1*, 369–371.

Bateson, G. "The Cybernetics of Self: A Theory of Alcoholism." *Psychiatry*, 1971, *34*, 1–17.

Beard, G. M. *A Practical Treatise on Nervous Exhaustion (Neurasthenia)*. New York: Treat, 1889.

Beary, J., Benson, H., and Klemchuck, H. "A Simple Psychophysiologic Technique which Elicits the Hypometabolic Changes of the Relaxation Response." *Psychosomatic Medicine*, 1974, *36*, 115–120.

Beck, A. T. *Cognitive Therapy and the Emotional Disorders*. New York: International Universities Press, 1976.

Beck, A. T., Weissman, A., and Kovacs, M. "Alcoholism, Hopelessness, and Suicidal Behavior." *Journal of Studies on Alcohol*, 1976, *37*, 66–77.

Becker, A. L. "Oxprenolol and Propranolol in Anxiety States: A Double-Blind Comparative Study." *South African Medical Journal*, 1976, *50*, 627–629.

Beckmann, H., and Goodwin, F. K. "Antidepressant Response to Tricyclics and Urinary MHPG in Unipolar Patients." *Archives of General Psychiatry*, 1975, *32*, 17–21.

Beecroft, R. S. *Classical Conditioning*. Goleta, Calif.: Psychonomic Press, 1966.

Beiser, M. "A Study of Personality Assets in a Rural Community." *Archives of General Psychiatry*, 1971, *24*, 244–254.

Beiser, M. "Personal and Social Factors Associated with the Remission of Psychiatric Symptoms." *Archives of General Psychiatry*, 1976, *33*, 941–945.

Beiser, M., Feldman, J. J., and Egelhoff, C. J. "Assets and Affects: A Study of Positive Mental Health." *Archives of General Psychiatry*, 1972, *27*, 545–549.

Bellak, L. "Crisis Intervention." In L. Bellak and T. Korascu (Eds.), *Geriatric Psychiatry*. New York: Grune and Stratton, 1976.

Bendien, J. "The Value of Questionnaires Testing the Dimensions of Neuroticism and Extraversion in Psychosomatic Research." *Journal of Psychosomatic Research*, 1963, *7*, 1–10.

Benjamin, J. D. "Some Developmental Observations Relating to the Theory of Anxiety." *Journal of the American Psychoanalytic Association*, 1961, *9*, 652–668.

Benjamin, J. D. "Further Comments on Some Developmental Aspects of Anxiety." In H. S. Gaskill (Ed.), *Counterpoint: Libidinal Object and Subject*. New York: International Universities Press, 1963.

Bennett, G. "Bristol Floods 1968, Controlled Survey of Effects on Health of Local Community Disaster." *British Medical Journal*, 1970, *3*, 454–458.

Benson, H., and others. "Behavioral Inductions of Arterial Hypertension and Its Reversal." *American Journal of Physiology,* 1969, *217,* 30–34.

Benton, D., and others. "Adrenal Activity in Isolated Mice and Mice of Different Social Status." *Physiology and Behavior,* 1978, *20,* 459–464.

Berger, S. M. "Conditioning Through Vicarious Instigation." *Psychological Review,* 1962, *69,* 450–466.

Bergin, A. E., and Strupp, H. H. *Changing Frontiers in the Science of Psychotherapy.* Chicago: Aldine, 1972.

Bergin, A. E., and Suinn, R. M. "Individual Psychotherapy and Behavior Therapy." *Annual Review of Psychology,* 1975, *26,* 509–556.

Berki, S. E., and Kobahigawa, B. "Socioeconomic and Need Determinants of Ambulatory Care Use: Path Analysis of the 1970 Health Interview Survey Data." *Medical Care,* 1976, *14,* 405–421.

Berkman, P. L. "Spouseless Motherhood, Psychological Stress, and Physical Morbidity." *Journal of Health and Social Behavior,* 1969, *10,* 323–334.

Berkman, P. L. "Life Stress and Psychological Well-Being: A Replication of Langner's Analysis in the Midtown Manhattan Study." *Journal of Health and Social Behavior,* 1971, *12,* 35–45.

Berkowitz, L. "Situational and Personal Conditions Governing Reaction to Aggressive Cues." In D. Magnusson and N. S. Endler (Eds.), *Personality at the Crossroads: Current Issues in Interactional Psychology.* Hillsdale, N.J.: Erlbaum, 1977.

Bernard, J. *The Future of Marriage.* New York: Bantam, 1972.

Bernard, J. *The Future of Motherhood.* New York: Penguin Books, 1975.

Bernstein, I. S., and Gordon, T. P. "The Function of Aggression in Primate Societies." *American Scientist,* 1974, *62,* 304–311.

Bettelheim, B. *Symbolic Wounds: Puberty Rites and the Envious Male.* New York: Free Press, 1954.

Bibring, E. "Psychoanalysis and the Dynamic Psychotherapies." *Journal of the American Psychoanalytic Association,* 1954, *2,* 745–770.

Binstock, R. H., and Levin, M. A. "The Political Dilemmas of Intervention Policies." In R. Binstock and E. Shanas (Eds.). *Handbook of Aging and the Social Sciences.* New York: Van Nostrand Reinhold, 1976.

Bird, C. *The Two Paycheck Marriage: How Women at Work Are Changing Life in America.* New York: Rawson Wade, 1979.

Bird, S. J., and Kuhar, M. J. "Ionotophoretic Application of Opiates to the Locus Coeruleus." *Brain Research,* 1977, *122,* 523.

Birley, J. L. T. "Stress and Disease." *Journal of Psychosomatic Research,* 1972, *16,* 235–240.

Bishop, D. W., and Witt, P. A. "Sources of Behavioral Variance During Leisure Time." *Journal of Personality and Social Psychology,* 1970, *16,* 352–360.

Black, A. H. "Cardiac Conditioning in Curarized Dogs: The Relationship Between Heart Rate and Skeletal Behavior." In W. F. Prokasy (Ed.), *Classical Conditioning: A Symposium.* New York: Appleton-Century-Crofts, 1965.

Black, A. H. "Operant Conditioning of Autonomic Responses." *Conditional Reflex,* 1968, *3* (2), 130.

Black, A. H., Carlson, N. J., and Solomon, R. L. "Exploratory Studies of the Conditioning of Autonomic Responses in Curarized Dogs." *Psychological Monographs,* 1962, *76* (29, Whole No. 548).

Blanchard, E. B. "The Relative Contributions of Modeling, Information Influences, and Physical Contact in the Extinction of Phobic Behavior." *Journal of Abnormal Psychology*, 1970, *76*, 55–61.

Blanchard, E. B., and Young, L. D. "Clinical Applications of Biofeedback Training: A Review of Evidence." *Archives of General Psychiatry*, 1974, *30*, 573–589.

Blanchard, R. J., and Blanchard, D. C. "Effects of Hippocampal Lesions on the Rat's Reaction to a Cat." *Journal of Comparative and Physiological Psychology*, 1972, *78*, 77–82.

Blanck, G., and Blanck, R. *Ego Psychology: Theory and Practice*. New York: Columbia University Press, 1974.

Blane, H. T. *The Personality of the Alcoholic: Guises of Dependency*. New York: Harper & Row, 1968.

Blau, A. A. "In Support of Freud's Syndrome of 'Actual' Anxiety Neurosis." *International Journal of Psycho-analysis*, 1952, *33*, 363–372.

Block, J. "Advancing the Psychology of Personality: Paradigmatic Shift or Improving the Quality of Research." In D. Magnusson and N. S. Endler (Eds.), *Personality at the Crossroads: Current Issues in Interactional Psychology*. Hillsdale, N.J.: Erlbaum, 1977.

Bloom, B. L., Asher, S. J., and White, S. W. "Marital Disruption as a Stressor: A Review and Analysis." *Psychological Bulletin*, 1978, *85*, 867–894.

Bloom, L., and Cantrell, D. "Anxiety Management Training for Essential Hypertension in Pregnancy." *Journal of Consulting and Clinical Psychology*, in press.

Blum, J., and Levine, J. "Maturity, Depression, and Life Events in Middle-Aged Alcoholics." *Addictive Behaviors*, 1975, *1*, 37–45.

Blum, T., Fosshage, J., and Jarvik, L. "Intellectual Changes and Sex Differences in Octogenarians: A Twenty-Year Longitudinal Study of Aging." *Developmental Psychology*, 1972, *1* (2), 178–187.

Bolles, R. C. "The Avoidance Learning Problem." In G. Bower (Ed.), *The Psychology of Learning and Motivation*. Vol. 6. New York: Academic Press, 1972.

Bond, P. A., Jenner, F. A., and Sampson, G. A. "Daily Variations of the Urine Content of MHPG in Two Manic-Depressive Patients." *Psychological Medicine*, 1972, *2*, 81–85.

Bonn, J. A., Harrison, J., and Rees, W. L. "Lactate-Induced Anxiety: Therapeutic Applications." *British Journal of Psychiatry*, 1971, *119*, 468–471.

Bonn, J. A., Turner, P., and Hicks, D. C. "Beta-Adrenergic-Receptor Blockade with Practolol in Treatment of Anxiety." *Lancet*, 1972, *2*, 814–817.

Bootzin, R. R., and Nicassio, P. "Behavioral Treatments for Insomnia." In M. Hersen, R. M. Eisler, and P. M. Miller (Eds.), *Progress in Behavior Modification*. Vol. 6. New York: Academic Press, 1978.

Borgatta, E. F., Fanshel, D., and Meyer, H. J. *Social Workers' Perceptions of Clients: A Study of the Caseload of a Social Agency*. New York: Russell Sage Foundation, 1960.

Borkovec, T. D. "Effects of Expectancy on the Outcome of Systematic Desensitization and Implosive Treatments for Analogue Anxiety." *Behavior Therapy*, 1972, *3*, 29–40.

Borkovec, T. D., Weerts, T. C., and Bernstein, D. A. "Assessment of Anxiety." In A Ciminero, K. Calhoun, and H. Adams (Eds.), *Handbook of Behavioral Assessment*. New York: Wiley, 1977.

Boszormenyi-Nagy, I., and Sparks, G. M. *Invisible Loyalties*. New York: Harper & Row, 1973.

Botwinick, J. "Geropsychology." In *Annual Review of Psychology*. Palo Alto, Calif.: Annual Reviews, 1970.

Bourne, P. G., and Fox, R. (Eds.). *Alcoholism: Progress in Research and Treatment*. New York: Academic Press, 1973.

Bourne, P. G., Rose, R. M., and Mason, J. W. "17-OH–CS Levels in Combat, Special Forces 'A' Team Under Threat of Attack." *Archives of General Psychiatry*, 1968, *19*, 135–145.

Bowen, R. C., and Kohout, J. "The Relationship Between Agoraphobia and Primary Affective Disorders." *Canadian Journal of Psychiatry*, 1979, *24*, 317–322.

Bowers, K. S. "Situationism in Psychology: An Analysis and a Critique." *Psychological Review*, 1973, *80*, 307–336.

Bowlby, J. *Attachment and Loss*. Vol. 1: *Attachment*. London: Hogarth Press, 1970.

Bowlby, J. *Attachment and Loss*. Vol. 2: *Separation*. New York: Basic Books, 1973.

Bowlby, J. "Human Personality Development in an Ethological Light." In G. Serban and A. Kling (Eds.), *Animal Models in Human Psychobiology*. New York: Plenum, 1976.

Bowlby, J., and Parkes, C. M. "Separation and Loss Within the Family." In E. J. Anthony and C. Kopernik (Eds.), *The International Yearbook for Child Psychiatry and Allied Disciplines*. New York: Wiley, 1970.

Bradburn, N. M. *The Structure of Psychological Well-Being*. Chicago: Aldine, 1969.

Brady, J. V. "Behavioral Stress and Physiological Change: A Comparative Approach to the Experimental Analysis of Some Psychosomatic Problems." *Transactions of the New York Academy of Sciences*, 1964, *26*, 483–496.

Brady, J. V. "Experimental Studies of Psychophysiological Responses to Stressful Situations." In *Symposium on Medical Aspects of Stress in the Military Climate*. Walter Reed Army Institute of Research. Washington, D.C.: U.S. Government Printing Office, 1965.

Brady, J. V. "Operant Methodology and the Production of Altered Physiological States." In W. K. Honig (Ed.), *Operant Behavior: Areas of Research and Application*. New York: Appleton-Century-Crofts, 1966.

Brady, J. V. "Emotion and the Sensitivity of the Psychoendocrine System." In D. Glass (Ed.), *Neurophysiology and Emotion*. New York: Rockefeller University Press, 1967.

Brady, J. V., and Harris, A. H. "The Experimental Production of Altered Physiological States." In W. K. Honig and J. E. R. Staddon (Eds.), *Handbook of Operant Behavior*. Englewood Cliffs, N.J.: Prentice-Hall, 1976.

Brady, J. V., Kelly, D., and Plumlee, L. "Autonomic and Behavioral Responses of the Rhesus Monkey to Emotional Conditioning." *Annals of the New York Academy of Sciences*, 1969, *159*, 959–975.

Brady, J. V. and others. "Avoidance Behavior and the Development of Gastroduodenal Ulcers." *Journal of the Experimental Analysis of Behavior*, 1958, *1*, 69–72.

Brain, P. F. "Endocrine and Behavioral Differences Between Dominant and Subordinate Male House Mice Housed in Pairs." *Psychonomic Science,* 1972, *28,* 260–262.

Brain, P. F., and Nowell, N. W. "The Effects of Differential Grouping on Endocrine Function of Mature Male Albino Mice." *Physiology and Behavior,* 1970, *5,* 907–910.

Bregman, E. "An Attempt to Modify the Emotional Attitude of Infants by the Conditioned Response Technique." *Journal of Genetic Psychology,* 1934, *45,* 169–198.

Brenner, C. "An Addendum to Freud's Theory of Anxiety." *International Journal of Psycho-analysis,* 1953, *34,* 18–24.

Brenner, C. "Some Problems in the Psychoanalytic Theory of Instinctual Drives." In I. M. Marcus (Ed.), *Currents in Psychoanalysis.* New York: International Universities Press, 1971.

Brenner, C. *An Elementary Textbook of Psychoanalysis* [1955]. New York: Doubleday, 1974.

Brenner, C. "Affects and Psychic Conflict." *Psychoanalytic Quarterly,* 1975, *44,* 5–28.

Brenner, M. H., *Mental Illness and the Economy.* Cambridge, Mass.: Harvard University Press, 1973.

Bretherton, I., and Ainsworth, M. "Responses of One-Year-Olds to a Stranger in a Strange Situation." In M. Lewis and L. Rosenblum (Eds.), *The Origins of Behavior.* Vol. 2: *The Origins of Fear.* New York: Wiley, 1974.

Bridges, K. M. B. "Emotional Development in Early Infancy." *Child Development,* 1932, *3,* 324–341.

Britton, D., and others. "Mental State, Cognitive Functioning, Physical Health, and Social Class in the Community Aged." *Journal of Gerontology,* 1967, *22,* 517–520.

Brod, J., and others. "Circulatory Changes Underlying Blood Pressure Elevation During Acute Emotional Stress (Mental Arithmetic) in Normotensive and Hypertensive Subjects." *Clinical Science,* 1959, *18,* 269–279.

Brody, S., and Axelrad, S. "Anxiety, Socialization, and Ego Formation in Infancy." *International Journal of Psycho-analysis,* 1966, *47,* 218–229.

Brody, S., and Axelrad, S. *Anxiety and Ego Formation in Infancy.* New York: International Universities Press, 1970.

Bronson, F. H., Stesson, M. H., and Stiff, M. E. "Serum FSH and LH in Male Mice Following Aggressive and Nonaggressive Interaction." *Physiology and Behavior,* 1973, *10,* 369–372.

Bronson, G. W. "Infants' Reactions to Unfamiliar Persons and Novel Objects." *Monographs of the Society for Research in Child Development,* 1972, *37* (3, Serial No. 148).

Brooks-Gunn, J., and Lewis, M. "Early Social Knowledge: The Development of Knowledge About Others." In H. McGurk (Ed.), *Issues in Childhood Social Development.* London: Methuen, 1978.

Brown, C. H. "Emotional Reactions Before Examination. II: Results of a Questionnaire." *Journal of Psychology,* 1938, *5,* 11–26.

Brown, G., Ni Bhrolchain, M., and Harris, T. "Social Class and Psychiatric Disturbance Among Women in an Urban Population." *Sociology,* 1975, *9,* 245–254.

Brown, G. W., and Birley, J. L. T. "Crises and Life Changes and the Onset of Schizophrenia." *Journal of Health and Social Behavior*, 1968, *9*, 203–214.

Brown, G. W., and others. "Life Events and Psychiatric Disorders. 1: Some Methodological Issues." *Psychological Medicine*, 1973, *3*, 74–87.

Brown, J., and Rawlinson, M. "The Morale of Patients Following Open-Heart Surgery." *Journal of Health and Social Behavior*, 1976, *17*, 135–145.

Bruhn, J. G., Philips, B. U., and Wolf, S. "Social Readjustment and Illness Patterns: Comparisons Between First, Second, and Third Generation Italian-Americans Living in the Same Community." *Journal of Psychosomatic Research*, 1972, *16*, 387–394.

Brunswick, D. "A Revision of the Classification of Instincts and Drives." *International Journal of Psycho-analysis*, 1954, *35*, 224–228.

Buchwald, A. M., Coyne, J. C., and Cole, C. S. "A Critical Evaluation of the Learned Helplessness Model of Depression." *Journal of Abnormal Psychology*, 1978, *87*, 180–193.

Budzynski, T. H. "Some Applications of Biofeedback Produced Twilight States." *Fields Within Fields...Within Fields*, 1972, *5*, 105–114.

Budzynski, T. H. "Biofeedback and the Twilight States of Consciousness." In G. E. Schwartz and D. Shapiro (Eds.), *Consciousness and Self-Control*. New York: Plenum, 1976.

Budzynski, T. H. "Clinical Implications of Electromyographic Training." In G. E. Schwartz and J. Beatty (Eds.), *Biofeedback: Theory and Research*. New York: Academic Press, 1977a.

Budzynski, T. H. "Tuning In on the Twilight Zone." *Psychology Today*, Aug. 1977b, pp. 40–44.

Budzynski, T. H. "Biofeedback Applications to Stress-Related Disorders." *International Review of Applied Psychology*, 1978, *27*, 73–79.

Budzynski, T. H. "Biofeedback in the Clinical Setting." Paper presented at International Course on Electrophysiological Techniques for Behavioral Analysis and Therapy, Paris, Sept. 1979.

Budzynski, T. H., and Stoyva, J. M. "Biofeedback Techniques in Behavior Therapy." In N. Birbaumer (Ed.), *The Neuropsychology of Anxiety* [*Neuropsychologie der Angst*]. Munich: Urban and Schwarzenberg, 1973.

Budzynski, T. H., and Stoyva, J. M. "EMG Biofeedback in Generalized and Specific Anxiety Disorders." In H. Legwie and L. Nusselt (Eds.), *Biofeedback Therapy: Teaching Methods in Psychosomatics, Neurology, and Rehabilitation* [*Biofeedback-Therapie: Lernmethoden in der Psychosomatics, Neurologie und Rehabilitation*]. Munich: Urban and Schwarzenberg, 1975.

Budzynski, T. H., Stoyva, J. M., and Peffer, K. E. "Biofeedback Techniques in Psychosomatic Disorders." In E. Foa and A. Goldstein (Eds.), *Handbook of Behavioral Interventions*. New York: Wiley, 1979.

Bunney, W. E., Jr., and Davis, J. M. "Norepinephrine in Depressive Reactions." *Archives of General Psychiatry*, 1965, *13*, 483–494.

Bursten, B. "Psychosocial Stress and Medical Consultation." *Psychosomatics*, 1965, *6*, 100–106.

Burton, R. V. "Generality of Honesty Reconsidered." *Psychological Review*, 1963, *70*, 481–499.

Bush, P. J., and Osterweis, J. "Pathways to Medicine Use." *Journal of Health and Social Behavior,* 1978, *19,* 179–189.

Byers, S. O., and others. "Excretion of 3-Methoxy-4-Hydroxymandelic Acid in Men with Behavior Pattern Associated with High Incidence of Coronary Artery Disease." *Federation Proceedings,* 1962, *21* (11), 99–101.

Cahalan, D., Cisin, I. M., and Crossley, H. M. *American Drinking Practices: A National Survey of Behavior and Attitudes.* New Brunswick, N.J.: Rutgers Center of Alcohol Studies, 1969.

Cahalan, D., and Room, R. *Problem Drinking Among American Men.* New Brunswick, N.J.: Rutgers Center of Alcohol Studies, 1974.

Cairns, R. B. "Attachment Behavior of Mammals." *Psychological Review,* 1966, *73,* 409–426.

Calhoun, J. B. "A 'Behavioral Sink.'" In E. L. Bliss (Ed.), *Roots of Behavior: Genetics, Instinct, and Socialization in Animal Behavior.* New York: Harper & Row, 1962.

Camaron, P. "Ego Strength and Happiness in the Aged." *Journal of Gerontology,* 1967, *22,* 199–202.

Cameron, D. E. "Observations on the Patterns of Anxiety." *American Journal of Psychiatry.* 1944, *101,* 36.

Campbell, A. "Subjective Measures of Well-Being." *American Psychologist,* 1976, *31,* 117–124.

Campos, J., and others. "Cardiac and Behavioral Responses of Human Infants to Strangers: Effects of Mother's Absence and of Experimental Sequence." *Developmental Psychology,* 1973, *9.*

Campos, J., and others. "Cardiac and Behavioral Interrelationships in the Reactions of Infants to Strangers." *Developmental Psychology,* 1975, *11,* 589–601.

Candland, D. K., and Leshner, A. I. "A Model of Agonistic Behavior: Endocrine and Autonomic Correlates." In L. DiCara (Ed.), *The Limbic and Autonomic Nervous Systems.* New York: Plenum, 1974.

Cannon, W. B. *Bodily Changes in Pain, Hunger, Fear, and Rage.* New York: Appleton-Century-Crofts, 1915.

Cannon, W. B. "The James-Lange Theory of Emotions: A Critical Examination and an Alternative Theory." *American Journal of Psychology,* 1927, *39,* 106–124.

Cannon, W. B. *Bodily Changes in Pain, Hunger, Fear, and Rage: An Account of Recent Researches into the Function of Emotional Excitement.* (2nd ed.) New York: Appleton-Century-Crofts, 1929.

Cannon, W. B. *Wisdom of the Body.* New York: Norton, 1963.

Canter, A. "Changes in Mood During Incubation of Acute Febrile Disease and the Effects of Pre-exposure Psychological Status." *Psychosomatic Medicine,* 1972, *34,* 424–430.

Canter, A., Cluff, L. E., and Imboden, J. B. "Hypersensitive Reactions to Immunization Inoculations and Antecedent Psychological Vulnerability." *Journal of Psychosomatic Research,* 1972, *16,* 99–101.

Canter, A., Kondo, C., and Knott, J. R. "Relaxation Training as a Method of Reducing Anxiety Associated with Depression." Paper presented at Biofeedback Research Society Sixth Annual Meeting, Monterey, Calif., 1975.

Caplan, G. *Principles of Preventive Psychiatry.* New York: Basic Books, 1964.

Caplan, G. *Support Systems and Community Mental Health*. New York: Human Sciences Press, 1974.

Caplan, G., and Killilea, M. *Support Systems and Mutual Help: Multidisciplinary Explorations*. New York: Grune and Stratton, 1976.

Caplan, R. D. "A Less Heretical View of Life Change and Hospitalization." *Journal of Psychosomatic Research*, 1975, *19*, 247–250.

Cappell, H. "An Evaluation of Tension Models of Alcohol Consumption." In R. J. Gibbins (Ed.), *Research Advances in Alcohol and Drug Problems II*. New York: Wiley, 1975.

Carroll, B. J. "Limbic System–Adrenal Cortex Regulation in Depression and Schizophrenia." *Psychosomatic Medicine*, 1976, *38*, 196–221.

Carver, C. S., and Glass, D. C. "Coronary-Prone Behavior Pattern and Interpersonal Aggression." *Journal of Personality and Social Psychology*, 1978, *36*, 361–366.

Casey, R. L., Thoresen, A. R., and Smith, F. J. "The Use of the SRE Questionnaire in an Institutional Health Care Setting." *Journal of Psychosomatic Research*, 1970, *14*, 149–154.

Cassel, J. "Social Science in Epidemiology: Psychosocial Processes and 'Stress' Theoretical Formulation." In E. L. Struening and M. Guttentag (Eds.), *Handbook of Evaluation Research*. Vol. 1. Beverly Hills, Calif.: Sage, 1975.

Castaneda, A., McCandless, B. R., and Palermo, D. S. "The Children's Form of the Manifest Anxiety Scale." *Child Development*, 1956, *27*, 317–326.

Cath, S. "Functional Disorders." In L. Bellak and T. Korascu (Eds.), *Geriatric Psychiatry*. New York: Grune and Stratton, 1976.

Cattell, R. B. *The Description and Measurement of Personality*. New York: World, 1946.

Cattell, R. B. *Personality: A Systematic Theoretical and Factual Study*. New York: McGraw-Hill, 1950.

Cattell, R. B. *Abilities: Their Structure, Growth, and Action*. Boston: Houghton Mifflin, 1971.

Cattell, R. B., and Scheier, I. H. "The Nature of Anxiety: A Review of 13 Multivariate Analyses Comparing 814 Variables." *Psychological Reports*, Monograph Supplement, 1958, *5*, 351–388.

Cattell, R. B., and Scheier, I. H. *The Meaning and Measurement of Neuroticism and Anxiety*. New York: Ronald Press, 1961.

Cautela, J. R. "Covert Sensitization." *Psychological Reports*, 1967, *20*, 459–468.

Cautela, J. R., Flannery, R. B., and Hanley, S. "Covert Modeling: An Experimental Test." *Behavior Therapy*, 1974, *5*, 494–502.

Cavenar, J. O., Jr., and Butts, N. T. "Fatherhood and Emotional Illness." *American Journal of Psychiatry*, 1977, *134*, 429–431.

Cavenar, J. O., Jr., and Weddington, W. W. "Abdominal Pain in Expectant Fathers." *Psychosomatics*, 1978, *19*, 761–768.

Cavenar, J. O., Jr., and Werman, D. S. "Notes on the Fear of Success." *Journal of the American Psychoanalytic Association*, in press.

Cedarbaum, J. M., and Aghajanian, G. K. "Noradrenergic Neurons of the Locus Coeruleus: Inhibition by Epinephrine and Activation by the Alpha-Antagonist Piperoxane." *Brain Research*, 1976, *112*, 413.

Cedarbaum, J. M., and Aghajanian, G. K. "Catecholamine Receptors on Locus Coeruleus Neurons: Pharmacological Characterization." *European Journal of Pharmacology,* 1977, *44,* 375.

Chafetz, M. E., and Demone, H. W., Jr. *Alcoholism and Society.* New York: Oxford University Press, 1962.

Chanoit, P. F., and others. "Epidemiology and Sociological Aspects of Neuroleptics." *Modern Problems in Pharmacopsychiatry,* 1970, *5,* 157–163.

Chapman, V., Desjardins, C., and Bronson, F. "Social Rank in Male Mice and Adrenocortical Response to Open Field Exposure." *Proceedings of the Society of Experimental Biology and Medicine,* 1969, *130,* 624–627.

Charvat, J., Dell, P., and Folkow, B. "Mental Factors and Cardiovascular Disorders." *Cardiologia,* 1964. *44,* 124.

Chien, C. P., Stotsky, B. A., and Cole, J. O. "Psychiatric Treatment for Nursing Home Patients: Drug, Alcohol, and Milieu." *American Journal of Psychiatry,* 1973, *130,* 543–548.

Chodorkoff, B. "Alcoholism and Ego Function." *Quarterly Journal of Studies on Alcohol,* 1964, *25,* 292–299.

Christenson, R. M. *Challenge and Decision.* New York: Harper & Row, 1970.

Cline, E. W., and Chosey, J. J. "A Prospective Study of Life Changes and Subsequent Health Changes." *Archives of General Psychiatry,* 1972, *27,* 51–53.

Cluff, L. E., Canter, A., and Imboden, J. B. "Asian Influenza." *Archives of Internal Medicine,* 1966, *117,* 159–163.

Cobb, S. "Social Support as a Moderator of Life Stress." *Psychosomatic Medicine,* 1976, *38,* 300–314.

Cobbin, D. M., and others. "Urinary MHPG Levels and Tricyclic Antidepressant Drug Selection." *Archives of General Psychiatry,* 1979, *36,* 1111–1118.

Coddington, R. D. "The Significance of Life Events as Etiologic Factors in the Diseases of Children. I: A Survey of Professional Workers." *Journal of Psychosomatic Research,* 1972a, *16,* 17–18.

Coddington, R. D. "The Significance of Life Events as Etiologic Factors in the Diseases of Children. II: A Study of a Normal Population." *Journal of Psychosomatic Research,* 1972b, *16,* 205–213.

Coelho, G., Hamburg, D. A., and Adams, J. E. (Eds.). *Coping and Adaptation.* New York: Basic Books, 1974.

Cohen, F., and Lazarus, R. S. "Active Coping Processes, Coping Dispositions, and Recovery from Surgery." *Psychosomatic Medicine,* 1973, *35,* 375–389.

Cole, J. O., and Davis, J. M. "Minor Tranquilizers, Sedatives, and Hypnotics." In A. M. Freedman, H. I. Kaplan, and B. J. Sadock (Eds.), *Comprehensive Textbook of Psychiatry.* (2nd ed.) Baltimore: Williams and Wilkins, 1975.

Coleman, J. C. "Life Stress and Maladaptive Behavior." *American Journal of Occupational Therapy,* 1973, *27,* 169–180.

Coleman, J. S. *Community Conflict.* New York: Free Press, 1956.

Compton, A. "A Study of the Psychoanalytic Theory of Anxiety. I: The Development of Freud's Theory of Anxiety." *Journal of the American Psychoanalytic Association,* 1972a, *20,* 3–44.

Compton, A. "A Study of the Psychoanalytic Theory of Anxiety. II: Developments in the Theory of Anxiety Since 1926." *Journal of the American Psychoanalytic Association*, 1972b, *20*, 341–394.

Compton, A. *On the Psychoanalytic Theory of Instinctual Drives*. In press.

Conel, J. L. *The Postnatal Development of the Human Cerebral Cortex*. Vol. 3. Cambridge, Mass.: Harvard University Press, 1947.

Cooley, C. H. *Human Nature and the Social Order*. New York: Scribner's, 1902.

Cooper, A., Furst, J., and Bridges, W. "A Brief Commentary on the Usefulness of Studying Fear of Snakes." *Journal of Abnormal Psychology*, 1969, *74*, 413–414.

Cooper, B., and Sylph, J. "Life Events and the Onset of Neurotic Illness: An Investigation in General Practice." *Psychological Medicine*, 1973, *3*, 421–435.

Cooper, J. E., Gelder, M. G., and Marks, I. M. "Results of Behavior Therapy in 77 Psychiatric Patients." *British Medical Journal*, 1965, *1*, 1222–1225.

Corley, K. C., Mauck, H. P., and Shiel, F. O. M. "Cardiac Responses Associated with 'Yoked Chair' Shock Avoidance in Squirrel Monkeys." *Psychophysiology*, 1975, *12*, 439–444.

Costa, E., Guidotti, A., and Mao, C. C. "A GABA Hypothesis for the Action of the Benzodiazepenes." In E. Roberts, T. N. Chase, and D. B. Tower (Eds.), *GABA in Nervous Function*. New York: Raven Press, 1976.

Costello, B. B. *Anxiety and Depression: The Adaptive Emotions*. Montreal, Quebec: McGill-Queens University Press, 1976.

Cotler, S. B. "Sex Differences and Generalization of Anxiety Reduction with Automated Desensitization and Minimal Therapist Interaction." *Behaviour Research and Therapy*, 1970, *8*, 273–285.

Cottrell, L. S., Jr. "The Adjustment of the Individual to His Age and Sex Roles." *American Sociological Review*, 1942a, *7*, 618–625.

Cottrell, L. S., Jr. "The Analysis of Situational Fields." *American Sociological Review*, 1942b, *7*, 370–382.

Cox, T. *Stress*. Baltimore: University Park Press, 1978.

Coyne, J. C. "Depression and the Response of Others." *Journal of Abnormal Psychology*, 1976a, *85*, 186–193.

Coyne, J. C. "The Place of Informed Consent in Ethical Dilemmas." *Journal of Consulting and Clinical Psychology*, 1976b, *44*, 1015–1016.

Coyne, J. C. "Toward an Interactional Description of Depression." *Psychiatry*, 1976c, *39*, 28–40.

Craig, T. J., and Van Natta, P. A. "Influence of Demographic Characteristics on Two Measures of Depressive Symptoms: The Relation of Prevalence and Persistence of Symptoms with Sex, Age, Education, and Marital Status." *Archives of General Psychiatry*, 1979, *36*, 149–154.

Cronbach, L. J. "Beyond the Two Disciplines of Scientific Psychology." *American Psychologist*, 1975, *30*, 116–127.

Cronbach, L. J., and Snow, R. E. *Aptitudes and Instructional Methods*. New York: Irvington, 1977.

Crook, J. H. "Social Organization and the Environment: Aspects of Contemporary Social Ethology." *Animal Behavior*, 1970, *18*, 197–209.

Crowcroft, P. *Mice All Over*. London: Foulis, 1966.

DaCosta, J. M. "On Irritable Heart: A Clinical Study of Functional Cardiac Disorder and Its Consequences." *American Journal of the Medical Sciences,* 1871, *61,* 17–53.

DaCosta, J. M. "On Strain and Over-Action of the Heart." *Smithsonian Miscellaneous Collections,* 1874, *15,* 1–24.

Dahlstrom, A., and Fuxe, K. "Evidence for the Existence of Monoamine-Containing Neurons in the Central Nervous System. I: Demonstration of Monoamines in the Cell Bodies of Brain Stem Neurons." *Acta Physiologica Scandinavica,* 1964, *62,* 1–55.

Darwin, C. *The Expression of Emotions in Man and Animals* [1895]. Chicago: University of Chicago Press, 1965.

Davis, D. E., and Christian, J. J. "Relations of Adrenal Weight to Social Rank of Mice." *Proceedings of the Society for Experimental Biology and Medicine,* 1957, *94,* 728–731.

Davis, D. R. *An Introduction to Psychopathology.* London: Oxford University Press, 1966.

Davis, J. M., Bartlett, E., and Termini, B. "Overdose of Psychotropic Drugs: A Review (II)." *Diseases of the Nervous System,* 1968, *29,* 241–259.

Davis, J. M., and Cole, J. O. "Antipsychotic Drugs." In A. M. Freedman, H. I. Kaplan, and B. J. Sadock (Eds.), *Comprehensive Textbook of Psychiatry.* (2nd ed.) Baltimore: Williams and Wilkins, 1975.

Dawley, H. H., Duidry, S., and Curtis, E. "Self-Administered Desensitization on a Psychiatric Ward: A Case Report." *Journal of Behavior Therapy and Experimental Psychiatry,* 1973, *4,* 201–204.

Deardorff, C. M., and others. "Situations Related to Drinking Alcohol: A Factor Analysis of Questionnaire Responses." *Quarterly Journal of Studies on Alcohol,* 1975, *36,* 1184–1195.

DeBonis, M. "Content Analysis of 27 Anxiety Inventories and Rating Scales." In P. Pichot (Ed.), *Psychological Measurements in Psychopharmacology.* Vol. 7: *Modern Problems of Pharmacopsychiatry.* Basel, Switzerland: Karger, 1974.

DeFaire, U. "Life Change Patterns Prior to Death in Ischaemic Heart Disease: A Study on Death-Discordant Twins." *Journal of Psychosomatic Research,* 1975, *19,* 273–278.

Deffenbacher, J. L. "Worry, Emotionality, and Task-Generated Interference in Test Anxiety: An Empirical Test of Attentional Theory." *Journal of Educational Psychology,* 1978, *70,* 248–254.

Deffenbacher, J. L. "Worry and Emotionality in Test Anxiety." In I. G. Sarason (Ed.), *Test Anxiety: Theory, Research, and Applications.* Hillsdale, N.J.: Erlbaum, 1980.

Deffenbacher, J. L., and Hahnloser, R. M. "Cognitive and Relaxation Coping Skills in the Reduction of Test Anxiety." Unpublished manuscript, Colorado State University, 1979.

Deffenbacher, J. L., and Parks, D. H. "A Comparison of Traditional and Self-Control Systematic Desensitization." *Journal of Counseling Psychology,* 1979, *26,* 93–97.

Deffenbacher, J. L., and Shelton, J. L. "Comparison of Anxiety Management Training and Desensitization in Reducing Test and other Anxieties." *Journal of Counseling Psychology,* 1978, *25,* 277–282.

Deffenbacher, J. L., and Snyder, A. L. "Relaxation as Self-Control in the

Treatment of Test and Other Anxieties." *Psychological Reports*, 1976, *39*, 379–385.

Deffenbacher, J. L., and Suinn, R. M. "The Chronically Anxious Patient." In D. Doleys, R. Meredith, and A. Ciminero (Eds.), *Behavioral Psychology in Medicine: Assessment and Treatment Strategies*. New York: Plenum, 1979.

Deffenbacher, J. L., and others. "A Comparison of Anxiety Management Training and Self-Control Desensitization." Unpublished manuscript, Colorado State University, 1979.

Dember, W. N. "Motivation and the Cognitive Revolution." *American Psychologist*, 1974, *29*, 161–168.

Dembroski, T., and others. *Coronary-Prone Behavior*. New York: Springer, 1978.

Denholtz, M. S., and Mann, E. T. "An Automated Audiovisual Treatment of Phobias Administered by Nonprofessionals." *Journal of Behavior Theory and Experimental Psychiatry*, 1975, *6*, 111–115.

Denney, D. R. "Active, Passive, and Vicarious Desensitization." *Journal of Counseling Psychology*, 1974, *21*, 369–375.

Denney, D. R., and Rupert, P. A. "Desensitization and Self-Control in the Treatment of Test Anxiety." *Journal of Consulting and Clinical Psychology*, 1977, *45*, 272–280.

Denney, D. R., and Sullivan, B. J. "Desensitization and Modeling Treatments of Spider Fear Using Two Types of Scenes." *Journal of Consulting and Clinical Psychology*, 1976, *44*, 573–579.

Denney, N. W. "Classification Abilities in the Elderly." *Journal of Gerontology*, 1974, *29* (3), 309–314.

Denney, N. W., and Denney, D. R. "Modeling Effects on the Questioning Strategies of the Elderly." *Developmental Psychology*, 1974, *10*, 458.

Denney, N. W., and Lennon, M. L. "Classification: A Comparison of Middle and Old Age." *Developmental Psychology*, 1972, *7*, 210–213.

Denney, N. W., and Wright, J. C. "Cognitive Changes During the Adult Years: Implications for Developmental Theory and Research." In *Advances in Child Development and Behavior*. Vol. 2. New York: Academic Press, 1976.

Department of Health, Education and Welfare. *Selected Symptoms of Psychological Distress*. Public Health Service Publication No. 1000, Series 11, No. 37. Washington, D.C.: Department of Health, Education and Welfare, 1970.

de Silva, P., Rachman, S., and Seligman, M. E. P. "Prepared Phobias and Obsessions: Therapeutic Outcome." *Behaviour Research and Therapy*, 1977, *15*, 65–77.

Dewey, J., and Bentley, A. F. *Knowing and the Known*. Boston: Beacon Press, 1949.

Dewey, R., and Humber, W. J. *The Development of Human Behavior*. New York: Macmillan, 1951.

DiCara, L. V. "Learning in the Autonomic Nervous System." *Scientific American*, 1970, *222* (1), 30–39.

DiCara, L. V., and Miller, N. E. "Instrumental Learning of Vasomotor Responses by Rats: Learning to Respond Differentially in the Two Ears." *Science*, 1968, *159*, 1485–1486.

DiCara, L. V., and Miller, N. E. "Transfer of Instrumentally Learned Heart

Rate Changes from Curarized to Noncurarized State: Implications for a Mediational Hypothesis." *Journal of Comparative and Physiological Psychology,* 1969, *62,* 159–162.

Diethelm, O., and Barr, R. M. "Psychotherapeutic Interviews and Alcohol Intoxication." *Quarterly Journal of Studies on Alcohol,* 1962, *23,* 243–251.

Di Loreto, A. O. *Comparative Psychotherapy: An Experimental Analysis.* Chicago: Aldine, 1971.

Diveky, S., and Endler, N. S. "The Interaction Model of Anxiety: State and Trait Anxiety for Banking Executives in Normal Working Environments." Unpublished manuscript, York University, Toronto, 1977.

Docherty, J. P., and others. "Psychotherapy and Pharmacotherapy: Conceptual Issues." *American Journal of Psychiatry,* 1977, *134,* 529–533.

Dodds, E. R. *Pagan and Christian in an Age of Anxiety.* New York: Norton, 1965.

Dodge, D. L., and Martin, W. T. *Social Stress and Chronic Illness.* Notre Dame, Ind.: University of Notre Dame Press, 1970.

Dodge, J. A. "Psychosomatic Aspects of Infantile Pyloria Stenosis." *Journal of Psychosomatic Research,* 1972, *16,* 1–5.

Dohrenwend, B. P. "Toward the Development of Theoretical Models, I." *Milbank Memorial Fund Quarterly,* 1967, *45* (2), 155–162.

Dohrenwend, B. P. "Problems in Defining and Sampling the Relevant Population of Stressful Life Events." In B. S. Dohrenwend and B. P. Dohrenwend (Eds.), *Stressful Life Events: Their Nature and Effects.* New York: Wiley, 1974.

Dohrenwend, B. P., and Dohrenwend, B. S. *Social Status and Psychological Disorders.* New York: Wiley, 1969.

Dohrenwend, B. P., and Dohrenwend, B. S. "Social and Cultural Influences on Psychopathology." *Annual Review of Psychology.* 1974, *25,* 417–452.

Dohrenwend, B. P., and others. "What Psychiatric Screening Scales Measure in the General Population. Part I: Jerome Frank's Concept of Demoralization." Manuscript submitted for publication, 1978a.

Dohrenwend, B. P., and others. "What Psychiatric Screening Scales Measure in the General Population. Part II: The Components of Demoralization by Contrast with Other Dimensions of Psychopathology." Manuscript submitted for publication, 1978b.

Dohrenwend, B. S. "Social Status and Stressful Life Events." *Journal of Personality and Social Psychology,* 1973, *28,* 225–235.

Dohrenwend, B. S., and Dohrenwend, B. P. (Eds.). *Stressful Life Events: Their Nature and Effects.* New York: Wiley, 1974.

Dohrenwend, B. S., and Dohrenwend, B. P. "What Is a Stressful Life Event?" In H. Selye (Ed.), *Guide to Stress Research.* New York: Van Nostrand Reinhold, in press.

Dohrenwend, B. S., Krasnoff, L., and Askenasy, A. R. "Exemplification of a Method for Scaling Life Events: The PERI Life Events Scale." *Journal of Health and Social Behavior,* 1978, *19,* 205–229

Dollard, J., and others. *Frustration and Aggression.* New Haven, Conn.: Yale University Press, 1939.

Domino, G. "Interactive Effects of Achievement of Orientation and Teaching Style on Academic Achievement." *Journal of Educational Psychology,* 1971, *62,* 427–431.

Donner, L., and Guerney, B. "Automated Group Desensitization for Test Anxiety." *Behaviour Research and Therapy*, 1969, *7*, 1–13.

Doris, J., and others. "Separation Anxiety in Nursery School Children." *Proceedings of 79th Annual Convention of the American Psychological Association*, 1971, *79*, 145–146.

Dost, F. H. *Der Blutspiegel: Kinetik der Konzentrationsablaufe der Kreislauffüsigkeit* [The Blood Indicator: The Kinetics of Concentrations in the Circulatory System]. Leipzig: Thieme, 1953.

Dua, P. S. "Group Desensitization of a Phobia with Three Massing Procedures." *Journal of Counseling Psychology*, 1972, *19*, 125–129.

Dunbar, H. F. *Emotions and Bodily Changes: A Survey of Literature on Psychosomatic Interrelationships*. New York: Columbia University Press, 1954.

Durham, H. W. *Community and Schizophrenia*. Detroit: Wayne State University Press, 1965.

Durkheim, E. *Suicide* [1897]. New York: Free Press, 1951.

Durlak, J. A. "Comparative Effectiveness of Paraprofessional and Professional Helpers." *Psychological Bulletin*, 1979, *86*, 80–92.

Dykman, R. A. "On the Nature of Classical Conditioning." In C. C. Brown (Ed.), *Methods in Psychophysiology*. Baltimore: Williams and Wilkins, 1967.

Dykman, R. A., and Gantt, W. H. "Cardiovascular Conditioning in Dogs and in Humans." In W. H. Gantt (Ed.), *Physiological Basis of Psychiatry*. Springfield, Ill.: Thomas, 1958.

D'Zurilla, T., Wilson, G. T., and Nelson, R. "A Preliminary Study of the Effectiveness of Graduated Prolonged Exposure in the Treatment of Irrational Fear." *Behavior Therapy*, 1973, *4*, 672–685.

D'Zurrilla, J. J., and Goldfried, M. R. "Problem Solving Behavior Modification." *Journal of Abnormal Psychology*, 1971, *78*, 107–129.

Easser, B. R., and Lesser, S. R. "Hysterical Personality: A Reevaluation." *Psychoanalytic Quarterly*, 1965, *34*, 390–405.

Eastwood, M. R., and Trevelyan, M. H. "Stress and Coronary Heart Disease." *Journal of Psychosomatic Research*, 1971, *15*, 289–292.

Eastwood, M. R., and Trevelyan, M. H. "Psychosomatic Disorders in the Community." *Journal of Psychosomatic Research*, 1972a, *16*, 381–386.

Eastwood, M. R., and Trevelyan, M. H. "The Relationship Between Physical and Psychiatric Disorder." *Psychology and Medicine*, 1972b, *2*, 363–372.

Eaton, W. W. "Life Events, Social Supports, and Psychiatric Symptoms: A Reanalysis of the New Haven Data." *Journal of Health and Social Behavior*, 1978, *19*, 230–234.

Ebert, M. H., Post, R. M., and Goodwin, F. K. "Effect of Physical Activity on Urinary MHPG Excretion in Depressed Patients," *Lancet*, 1972, *2*, 766.

Edie, C. "Uses of AMT in Treating Trait Anxiety," Unpublished doctoral dissertation, Colorado State University, 1972.

Edwards, D. W., and others. "National Health Insurance, Psychotherapy, and the Poor." *American Psychologist*, 1979, *34*, 411–419.

Eibl-Eibesfeldt, I. *The Biology of Behavior*. New York: Holt, Rinehart and Winston, 1970.

Eibl-Eibesfeldt, I. "The Ethology of Man." In *Ethology: The Biology of*

Behavior. (2nd ed.) (E. Klinghammer, Trans.) New York: Holt, Rinehart and Winston, 1971.

Eichelman, B. S., Jr. "Effect of Subcortical Lesions on Shock-Induced Aggression in the Rat." *Journal of Comparative and Physiological Psychology*, 1971, *7*, 331–339.

Eimerl, S., and others. *The Primates*. (Life Nature Library.) New York: Time-Life Books, 1965.

Eitinger, L. "A Follow-Up Study of Norwegian Concentration Camp Survivors' Mortality and Morbidity." *Israel Annals of Psychiatry*, 1973, *11*, 199–209.

Ekehammar, B. "Interactionism in Personality from a Historical Perspective." *Psychological Bulletin*, 1974, *81*, 1026–1048.

Ekehammar, B., and Magnusson, D. "A Method To Study Stressful Situations." *Journal of Personality and Social Psychology*, 1973, *27*, 176-179.

Ekehammar, B., Magnusson, D., and Ricklander, L. "An Interactionist Approach to the Study of Anxiety: An Analysis of an S-R Inventory Applied to an Adolescent Sample." *Scandinavian Journal of Psychology*, 1974, *15*, 4–14.

Ekehammar, B., Schalling, D., and Magnusson, D. "Dimensions of Stressful Situations: A Comparison Between a Response Analytical and a Stimulus Analytical Approach." *Multivariate Behavior Research*, 1975, *10*, 155–164.

Ekman, P. "Universal and Cultural Differences in Facial Expressions of Emotion." In J. K. Cole (Ed.), *Nebraska Symposium on Motivation*. Vol. 19. Lincoln: University of Nebraska Press, 1961.

Ellis, A. *Reason and Emotion in Psychotherapy*. New York: Lyle Stuart, 1962.

Ely, D. L., Greene, E. G., and Henry, J. P. "Minicomputer Monitored Social Behavior of Mice with Hippocampus Lesions." *Behavioral Biology*, 1976, *16*, 1–29.

Ely, D. L., Greene, E. G., and Henry, J. P. "Effects of Hippocampal Lesions on Cardiovascular, Adrenocortical, and Behavioral Response Patterns in Mice." *Physiology and Behavior*, 1977, *18*, 1075–1083.

Ely, D. L., and Henry, J. P. "Effects of Social Role upon the Blood Pressures of Individual Male CBA Mice." *Federation Proceedings*, 1971, *39*, 265.

Ely, D. L., and Henry, J. P. "Effects of Prolonged Social Deprivation on Murine Behavior Patterns, Blood Pressure, and Adrenal Weight." *Journal of Comparative and Physiological Psychology*, 1974, *87*, 733–740.

Ely, D. L., and Henry, J. P. "Neuroendocrine Response Patterns in Dominant and Subordinate Mice." *Hormones and Behavior*, 1978, *10*, 156–169.

Ely, D. L., Henry, J. P., and Ciaranello, R. D. "Long Term Behavioral and Biochemical Differentiation of Dominant and Subordinate Mice in Population Cages." *Psychosomatic Medicine*, 1974, *36*, 463.

Ely, D. L., Henry, J. P., and Jarosz, C. J. "Effects of Marihuana (Δ 9-THC) on Behavior Patterns and Social Roles in Colonies of CBA Mice." *Behavioral Biology*, 1975, *13*, 263–276.

Ely, D. L., and others. "A Monitoring Technique Providing Quantitative Rodent Behavior Analysis." *Physiology and Behavior*, 1972, *9*, 675–679.

Emde, R. N., Gaensbauer, T. J., and Harmon, R. J. *Emotional Expression in*

Infancy: A Biobehavioral Study. New York: International Universities Press, 1976.

Emde, R. N., and Robinson, J. "The First Two Months: Recent Research in Developmental Psychobiology and the Changing View of the Newborn." In J. Noshpitz and J. Call (Eds.), *Basic Handbook of Child Psychiatry.* New York: Basic Books, 1976.

Endler, N. S. "Conformity as a Function of Different Reinforcement Schedules." *Journal of Personality and Social Psychology,* 1966a, *4,* 175–180.

Endler, N. S. "Estimating Variance Components from Mean Squares for Random and Mixed-Effects Analysis of Variance Models." *Perceptual and Motor Skills,* 1966b, *22,* 559–570.

Endler, N. S. "The Person Versus the Situation—A Pseudo Issue? A Response to Alker." *Journal of Personality,* 1973, *41,* 287–303.

Endler, N. S. "The Case for Person-Situation Interactions." *Canadian Psychological Review,* 1975a, *16,* 12–21.

Endler, N. S. "A Person-Situation Interaction Model for Anxiety." In C. D. Spielberger and I. G. Sarason (Eds.), *Stress and Anxiety.* Vol. 1. Washington, D.C.: Hemisphere, 1975b.

Endler, N. S. "The Role of Person by Situation Interactions in Personality Theory." In I. C. Uzgiris and F. Weizmann (Eds.), *The Structuring of Experience.* New York: Plenum, 1977.

Endler, N. S. "The Interaction Model of Anxiety: Some Possible Implications." In D. M. Landers and R. W. Christina (Eds.), *Psychology of Motor Behavior and Sport—1977.* Champaign, Ill.: Human Kinetics, 1978.

Endler, N. S. "Persons, Situations, and Their Interactions." In A. I. Rabin (Ed.), *Further Explorations in Personality.* New York: Wiley, 1980a.

Endler, N. S. "Situational Aspects of Interactional Psychology." In D. Magnusson (Ed.), *Toward a Psychology of Situations: An Interactional Perspective.* Hillsdale, N.J.: Erlbaum, 1980b.

Endler, N. S., and Edwards, J. "Person by Treatment Interactions in Personality Research." In L. A. Pervin and M. Lewis (Eds.), *Interaction Between Internal and External Determinants of Behavior.* New York: Plenum, 1978.

Endler, N. S., Edwards, J., and McGuire, A. "The Interaction Model of Anxiety: An Empirical Test in a Theatrical Performance Situation." Unpublished manuscript, York University, Toronto, 1979.

Endler, N. S., and Hoy, E. "Conformity as Related to Reinforcement and Social Pressure." *Journal of Personality and Social Psychology,* 1967, *7,* 197–202.

Endler, N. S., and Hunt, J. McV. "Sources of Behavioral Variance as Measured by the S-R Inventory of Anxiousness." *Psychological Bulletin,* 1966, *65,* 336–346.

Endler, N. S., and Hunt, J. McV. "S-R Inventories of Hostility and Comparisons of the Proportions of Variance from Persons, Responses, and Situations for Hostility and Anxiousness." *Journal of Personality and Social Psychology,* 1968, *9,* 309–315.

Endler, N. S., and Hunt, J. McV. "Generalizability of Contributions from Sources of Variance in the S-R Inventories of Anxiousness." *Journal of Personality,* 1969, *37,* 1–24.

Endler, N. S., Hunt, J. McV., and Rosenstein, A. J. "An S-R Inventory of Anxiousness." *Psychological Monographs*, 1962, *76*, (17, Whole No. 536).

Endler, N. S., and Magnusson, D. "Multidimensional Aspects of State and Trait Anxiety: A Cross-Cultural Study of Canadian and Swedish College Students." In C. D. Spielberger and R. Diaz-Guerrero (Eds.), *Cross-Cultural Anxiety*. Washington, D.C.: Hemisphere, 1976a.

Endler, N. S., and Magnusson, D. "Personality and Person by Situation Interactions." In N. S. Endler and D. Magnusson (Eds.), *Interactional Psychology and Personality*. Washington, D.C.: Hemisphere, 1976b.

Endler, N. S., and Magnusson, D. "Toward an Interactional Psychology of Personality." *Psychological Bulletin*, 1976c, *83*, 956–974.

Endler, N. S., and Magnusson, D. "The Interaction Model of Anxiety: An Empirical Test in an Examination Situation." *Canadian Journal of Behavioural Science*, 1977, *9*, 101–107.

Endler, N. S., and Okada, M. *An S-R Inventory of General Trait Anxiousness*. Department of Psychology Reports, No. 1. Toronto: York University, 1974.

Endler, N. S., and Okada, M. "A Multidimensional Measure of Trait Anxiety: The S-R Inventory of General Trait Anxiousness." *Journal of Consulting and Clinical Psychology*, 1975, *43*, 319–329.

Endler, N. S., and Shedletsky, R. "Trait Versus State Anxiety, Authoritarianism, and Ego Threat Versus Physical Threat." *Canadian Journal of Behavioural Science*, 1973, *5*, 347–361.

Endler, N. S., and others. "The Multidimensionality of State and Trait Anxiety." *Scandinavian Journal of Psychology*, 1976, *17*, 81–93.

Endler, N. S., and others. "State and Trait Anxiety Within a Person-Situation Interaction Model: An Empirical Test in an Exam Situation." Unpublished manuscript, York University, Toronto, 1979.

Engel, B. T., and Bickford, A. F. "Response Specificity." *Archives of General Psychiatry*, 1961, *5*, 82–93.

Engel, B. T., and Gottlieb, S. H. "Differential Operant Conditioning of Heart Rate in the Restrained Monkey." *Journal of Comparative and Physiological Psychology*, 1970, *73* (2), 217–225.

Engel, G. "A Life Setting Conducive to Illness—the Giving Up–Given Up Complex." *Bulletin of the Menninger Clinic*, 1968, *32*, 355–365.

Engel, G. "Sudden and Rapid Death During Psychological Stress: Folklore or Folk Wisdom?" *Annals of Internal Medicine*, 1971, *74*, 771–782.

Engel, G. "The Need for a New Medical Model." *Science*, 1977, *196*, 129–136.

Engel, G. L., and Schmale, A. H. "Psychoanalytic Theory of Somatic Disorder: Conversion, Specificity and the Disease-Onset Situation." *Journal of the American Psychoanalytic Association*, 1967, *15*, 344.

Engel, G. L., and Schmale, A. H. "Conservation-Withdrawal: A Primary Regulatory Process for Organismic Homeostasis." *Ciba Foundation Symposium*, 1972, *8*, 57–75.

Engle, E. "Homeostasis, Behavioral Adjustment, and the Concept of Health and Disease." In R. R. Grinker (Ed.), *Mid-Century Psychiatry*. Springfield, Ill.: Thomas, 1953.

Epstein, C. F. *Woman's Place: Options and Limits in Professional Careers*. Berkeley: University of California Press, 1971.

Epstein, J. *Divorced in America: Marriage in an Age of Possibliity.* New York: Dutton, 1974.

Epstein, S. "The Stability of Behavior. I: On Predicting Most of the People Much of the Time." *Journal of Personality and Social Psychology,* 1979, *37,* 1097–1126.

Erikson, E. *Childhood and Society.* New York: Norton, 1950.

Erikson, K. T. *Everything in Its Path: Destruction of Community in the Buffalo Creek Flood.* New York: Simon and Schuster, 1976.

Estes, C. L., and Freeman, H. E. "Strategies of Design and Research for Intervention." In R. Binstock and E. Shanas (Eds.), *Handbook of Aging and the Social Sciences.* New York: Van Nostrand Reinhold, 1976.

Estes, W. K., and Skinner, B. F. "Some Quantitative Properties of Anxiety." *Journal of Experimental Psychology,* 1941, *29,* 390–400.

Evans, C. M., and MacKintosh, J. H., "Endocrine Correlates of Territorial and Subordinate Behavior in Groups of Male CFW Mice Under Semi-natural Conditions." *Journal of Endocrinology,* 1976, *71,* 91.

Extein, I., and others. "Behavior and Biochemical Effects of FK33-824, a Parenterally and Orally Active Enkephalin Analogue." In E. Usdin, W. E. Bunney, Jr., and N. S. Kline (Eds.), *Endorphins in Mental Health Research.* New York: Macmillan, 1979.

Eylon, Y. "Birth Events, Appendicitis and Appendectomy." *British Journal of Medicine and Psychology,* 1967, *40,* 317–332.

Eysenck, H. "Psychological Aspects of Anxiety." In M. H. Lader (Ed.), *Studies of Anxiety.* Kent, England: Headley Brothers, 1969.

Eysenck, H. "The Learning Theory Model of Neurosis: A New Approach." *Behaviour Research and Therapy,* 1976, *14* (4), 251–267.

Eysenck, H., and Rachman, S. *The Causes and Cures of Neurosis.* London: Routledge and Kegan Paul, 1965.

Fairbank, D. T., and Hough, R. L. "Life Event Classifications and the Event-Illness Relationship." *Journal of Human Stress,* 1979, *5,* 41–47.

Faris, R. E. *Social Disorganization.* New York: Ronald Press, 1955.

Federn, P. "The Ego as Subject and Object in Narcissism " [1929]. In *Ego Psychology and the Psychoses.* New York: Basic Books, 1952.

Feighner, J. P., and others. "Diagnostic Criteria for Use in Psychiatric Research." *Archives of General Psychiatry,* 1972, *26,* 57–63.

Feinman, S. "Infant Response to Race, Size, Proximity, and Movement of Strangers." *Infant Behavior and Development,* in press.

Feinstein, A. R. *Clinical Judgment.* Huntington, N.Y.: Krieger, 1967.

Fenichel, O. "The Concept of Trauma " [1937]. In *Collected Papers.* (2nd series.) New York: Norton, 1954.

Fenichel, O. "The Ego and the Affects " [1941]. In *Collected Papers.* (2nd series.) New York: Norton, 1954.

Fenichel, O. "Brief Psychotherapy " [1944]. In *Collected Papers.* New York: Norton, 1953.

Fenichel, O. *The Psychoanalytic Theory of Neurosis.* New York: Norton, 1945.

Fenz, W., and Epstein, S. "Gradients of Physiological Arousal in Parachutists." *Psychosomatic Medicine,* 1967, *29,* 33–51.

Ferenczi, S. *Further Contributions to the Theory and Technique of Psychoanalysis.* London: Hogarth Press, 1950.

Fiedler, F. E. "What Triggers the Person Situation Interaction in Leadership?" In D. Magnusson and N. S. Endler (Eds.), *Personality at the Crossroads: Current Issues in Interactional Psychology.* Hillsdale, N.J.: Erlbaum, 1977.

Fields, C. "Instrumental Conditioning of the Rat Cardiac Control Systems." *Proceedings of the National Academy of Sciences,* 1970, *65* (2), 293–299.

Findley, J. D., Robinson, W. W., and Gilliam, W. "A Restraint System for Chronic Study of the Baboon." *Journal of the Experimental Analysis of Behavior,* 1971, *15,* 69–71.

Findley, J. D., and others. "Continuous Cardiovascular Monitoring in the Baboon During Long-Term Behavioral Performances." *Communications in Behavioral Biology,* 1971, *6,* 49–58.

Fink, M., Taylor, M. A., and Volavka, J. "Anxiety Precipitated by Lactate." *New England Journal of Medicine,* 1970, *281,* 1129.

Fink, P. J. "Correlations Between 'Actual Neurosis' and the Work of Masters and Johnson." *Psychoanalytic Quarterly,* 1970, *39,* 38–51.

Fisher, C. "Dreams, Images and Perception." *Journal of the American Psychoanalytic Association,* 1956, *4,* 5–48.

Fisher, C. "Psychoanalytic Implications of Recent Research on Sleep and Dreaming." *Journal of the American Psychoanalytic Association,* 1965, *13,* 271–303.

Fisher, E. R., and Horvat, B. "Ultrastructural Features of Aldosterone Production." *Archives of Pathology,* 1971, *92,* 172–179.

Fisher, T. J., Reardon, R. C., and Burck, H. D. "Increasing Information-Seeking Behavior with a Model-Reinforced Videotape." *Journal of Counseling Psychology,* 1976, *23,* 234–238.

Fisher, W. F. *Theories of Anxiety.* New York: Harper & Row, 1970.

Fitzgerald, R. D. "Some Effects of Partial Reinforcement with Shock on Classically Conditioned Heart Rate in Dogs." *American Journal of Psychology,* 1966, *79,* 242–249.

Flescher, J. "A Dualistic Viewpoint on Anxiety." *Journal of the American Psychoanalytic Association,* 1955, *3,* 415–446.

Flood, M., and Endler, N. S. "The Interaction Model of Anxiety: An Empirical Test in an Athletic Competition Situation." *Journal of Research in Personality,* in press.

Folkman, S. "An Analysis of Coping in Normal Adults: A Naturalistic Investigation." Unpublished doctoral dissertation, University of California, Berkeley, 1979.

Folkman, S., Schaefer, C., and Lazarus, R. S. "Cognitive Processes as Mediators of Stress and Coping." In V. Hamilton and D. M. Warburton (Eds.), *Human Stress and Cognition: An Information-Processing Approach.* London: Wiley, in press.

Folkow, B. "Vascular Changes in Hypertension: Review and Recent Animal Studies." In C. Berglund, L. Hanson, and L. Werkö (Eds.), *Pathophysiology and Management of Arterial Hypertension.* Mölndal, Sweden: Lindgren, 1975.

Folkow, B. Häggendahl, J., and Lisander, B. "Extent of Release and Elimination of Noradrenalin at Peripheral Adrenergic Nerve Terminals." *Acta Physiologica Scandinavica,* 1967, *307,* 1–38.

Folkow, B., and Rubinstein, E. H. "Cardiovascular Effects of Acute and Chronic Stimulations of the Hypothalamic Defense Area in the Rat." *Acta Physiologica Scandinavica,* 1966, *68,* 48–57.

Folz, E. L., and Miller, F. E., Jr. "Experimental Psychosomatic Disease States in Monkeys. I: Peptic Ulcer 'Executive Monkeys.'" *Journal of Surgical Research,* 1964, *4,* 445–453.

Food and Drug Administration. "Guidelines for the Conduct of Clinical Trials: FDA Guidelines for Psychotropic Drugs." *Psychopharmacology Bulletin,* 1974, *10* (4), 70–91.

Forsyth, R. P. "Blood Pressure Responses to Long-Term Avoidance Schedules in the Restrained Rhesus Monkey." *Psychosomatic Medicine,* 1969, *31,* 300–309.

Frank, J. D. *Persuasion and Healing.* Baltimore: Johns Hopkins University Press, 1973.

Frankenhaeuser, M. "Experimental Approaches to the Study of Human Behavior as Related to Neuroendocrine Functions." In L. Levi (Ed.), *Society, Stress and Diseases.* Vol. 1. New York: Oxford University Press, 1971.

Frankenhaeuser, M. "Experimental Approaches to the Study of Catecholamines and Emotion." In L. Levi (Ed.), *Emotions: Their Parameters and Measurement.* New York: Raven Press, 1975.

Frankenhaeuser, M., and Gardell, B. "Underload and Overload in Working Life: Outline of a Multidisciplinary Approach." *Journal of Human Stress,* 1976, *2,* 35–46.

Frankenhaeuser, M., and others. "Psychophysiological Reactions to Understimulation and Overstimulation." *Acta Psychologica,* 1971, *35,* 298–308.

Frederiksen, N. "Towards a Taxonomy of Situations." *American Psychologist,* 1972, *27,* 114–123.

Freeman, L. *Catch Me Before I Kill More.* New York: Pocket Books, 1955.

Fremouw, W. J., and Harmatz, M. G. "A Helper Model for Behavioral Treatment of Speech Anxiety." *Journal of Consulting and Clinical Psychology,* 1975, *43,* 652–660.

Fremouw, W. J., and Zitter, R. E. "A Comparison of Skills Training and Cognitive Restructuring-Relaxation for the Treatment of Speech Anxiety." *Behavior Therapy,* 1978, *9,* 238–249.

French, T. *The Integration of Behavior.* Vol. 1: *Basic Postulates.* Chicago: University of Chicago Press, 1952.

Freud, A. *The Ego and the Mechanisms of Defense* [1936]. New York: International Universities Press, 1946.

Freud, A. "Adolescence." *Psychoanalytic Study of the Child,* 1958, *13,* 255.

Freud, A. "Comments on Trauma." In S. Furst (Ed.), *Psychic Trauma.* New York: Basic Books, 1967.

Freud, A. "Fears, Anxieties and Phobic Phenomena." *Psychoanalytic Study of the Child,* 1977, *32,* 85–90.

Freud, S. "On the Psychical Mechanism of Hysterical Phenomena" [1893]. In J. Strachey (Ed.), *Standard Edition of the Complete Psychological Works of Sigmund Freud.* Vol. 3. London: Hogarth Press, 1962.

Freud, S. "Project for a Scientific Psychology" [1895]. In *Standard Edition.* Vol. 1. London: Hogarth Press, 1966.

Freud, S. *Introductory Lectures on Psycho-analysis* [1917]. In *Standard Edition*. Vols. 15 and 16. London: Hogarth Press, 1963.

Freud, S. "Beyond the Pleasure Principle" [1920a]. In *Standard Edition*. Vol. 18. London: Hogarth Press, 1955.

Freud, S. *General Introduction to Psychoanalysis*. New York: Boni and Liveright, 1920b.

Freud, S. "The Ego and the Id" [1923]. In *Standard Edition*. Vol. 19. London: Hogarth Press, 1961.

Freud, S. *Inhibitions, Symptoms and Anxiety* [1926]. In *Standard Edition*. Vol. 20. London: Hogarth Press, 1959.

Freud, S. *Civilization and Its Discontents* [1930]. New York: Norton, 1961.

Freud, S. "An Outline of Psycho-analysis" [1940]. In *Standard Edition*. Vol. 23. London: Hogarth Press, 1964.

Freud, S. "Notes upon a Case of Obsessional Neurosis." In J. Strachey (Ed.), *Collected Papers of Sigmund Freud*. Vol. 3. London: Hogarth Press, 1949.

Freud, S., and Breuer, J. *Studies on Hysteria* [1895]. In *Standard Edition*. Vol. 2. London: Hogarth Press, 1957.

Friedman, M., and Bennet, P. L. "Depression and Hypertension." *Psychosomatic Medicine*, 1977, *39*, 134–141.

Friedman, M., and Rosenman, R. H. "Overt Behavior Pattern in Coronary Disease: Detection of Overt Behavior Pattern A in Patients with Coronary Disease by a New Psychophysiological Procedure." *Journal of the American Medical Association*, 1960, *173*, 1320–1325.

Friedman, M., and Rosenman, R. H. *Type A Behavior and Your Heart*. New York: Knopf, 1974.

Friedman, M., Rosenman, R. H., and St. George, S. "Adrenal Response to Excess Corticotropin in Coronary-Prone Men." *Proceedings of the Society of Experimental Biology and Medicine*, 1969, *131*, 1305–1307.

Friedman, M., and others. "Plasma Catecholamine Response of Coronary-Prone Subjects (Type A) to a Specific Challenge." *Metabolism Clinical and Experimental*, 1975, *24*, 205–210.

Friedman, S. B., and Glasgow, L. A. "Psychologic Factors and Resistance in Infectious Disease." *Pediatric Clinics of North America*, 1966, *13*, 315–335.

Frohlich, E. D., Tarazi, R. C., and Dustan, H. P. "Hyperdynamic B-Adrenergic Circulatory State." *Archives of Internal Medicine*, 1969, *132*, 1–7.

Furst, S. S. "Psychic Trauma: A Survey." In S. S. Furst (Ed.), *Psychic Trauma*. New York: Basic Books, 1967.

Gaensbauer, T., Emde, R. N., and Campos, J. J. "'Stranger' Distress: Confirmation of a Developmental Shift in a Longitudinal Sample." *Perceptual and Motor Skills*, 1976, *43*, 99–106.

Galligan, R. J., and Bahr, S. J. "Economic Well-Being and Marital Stability: Implications for Income Maintenance Programs." *Journal of Marriage and the Family*, 1978, *40*, 283–290.

Garbarino, J. "The Price of Privacy in the Social Dynamics of Child Abuse." *Child Welfare*, 1977, *56*, 565–575.

Gayral, L., and others. "Catathymic Attacks and Convulsions" [Crises et Paroxysmes Catathymiques] *Annales Médico-Psychologiques*, 1956, *114*, 25–50.

Gelder, M. G., and Marks, I. M. "Desensitization and Phobias: A Crossover Study." *British Journal of Psychiatry*, 1968, *114*, 323–328.

Gelder, M. G., and others. "Desensitization and Psychotherapy in the Treatment of Phobic States: A Controlled Inquiry." *British Journal of Psychiatry*, 1967, *113*, 53–73.

Gelles, R. J. "Child Abuse as Psychopathology: A Sociological Critique and Reformulation." *American Journal of Orthopsychiatry*, 1973, *43*, 611–621.

Gelles, R. J. "Violence and Pregnancy: A Note on the Extent of the Problem and Needed Services." *Family Coordinator*, Jan. 1975, pp. 81–86.

Gentry, W. D., Foster, S., and Harvey, T. "Denial as a Determinant of Anxiety and Perceived Health Status in the Coronary Care Unit." *Psychosomatic Medicine*, 1972, *34*, 39–44.

Gibson, I. I. "Barbiturate Delirium." *Practitioner*, 1966, *197*, 345–347.

Gil, D. "Physical Abuse of Children: Findings and Implications of a Nationwide Survey." *Pediatrics*, 1969, *44*, 857–864.

Gil, D. *Violence Against Children*. Cambridge, Mass.: Harvard University Press, 1970.

Gillespie, W. "Some Regressive Phenomena in Old Age." *British Journal of Medical Psychology*, 1963, *36*, 203–209.

Gilmor, T. M., and Minton, H. L. "Internal Versus External Attribution of Task Performance as a Function of Locus of Control, Initial Confidence, and Success-Failure Outcome." *Journal of Personality*, 1974, *42*, 159–174.

Ginsburg, G. L., Frosch, W. A., and Shapiro, T. "The New Impotence." *Archives of General Psychiatry*, 1972, *26* (3), 218.

Girodo, M. "Self-Talk: Mechanism in Anxiety and Stress Management." In I. G. Sarason and C. D. Spielberger (Eds.), *Stress and Anxiety*. Vol. 4. Washington, D. C.: Hemisphere, 1976.

Glasgow, R., and Rosen, G. "Behavioral Bibliotherapy: A Review of Self-Help Behavior Therapy Manuals." *Psychological Bulletin*, 1978, *85*, 1–23.

Glass, C., Gottman, J., and Shmurak, S. "Response-Acquisition and Cognitive Self-Statement Modification Approaches to Dating Skills Training." *Journal of Counseling Psychology*, 1976, *23*, 520–527.

Glass, D. C. "Stress, Behavior Patterns, and Coronary Disease." *American Scientist*, 1977, *65*, 177–187.

Glauber, I. P. "Federn's Annotation of Freud's Theory of Anxiety." *Journal of the American Psychoanalytic Association*, 1963, *11*, 84–96.

Glenn, N. D., and Weaver, C. N. "A Multivariate, Multisurvey Study of Marital Happiness." *Journal of Marriage and the Family*, 1978, *40*, 269–282.

Glickman, S. E., Higgins, T., and Isaacson, R. L. "Some Effects of Hippocampal Lesions on the Behavior of Mongolian Gerbils." *Physiology and Behavior*, 1970, *5*, 931–938.

Glidewell, J. D., Gilelea, M., and Kaufman, M. "The Preventive and Therapeutic Effects of Two School Mental Health Programs." *American Journal of Community Psychology*, 1973, *1*, 295–329.

Glogower, F. D., Fremouw, W. J., and McCroskey, J. C. "A Component Analysis of Cognitive Restructuring." *Cognitive Therapy and Research*, 1978, *2*, 209–223.

Glover, E. *The Roots of Crime*. New York: International Universities Press, 1960.

Gold, M. S., and Kleber, H. D. "A Rationale for Opiate Withdrawal Symptomatology." *Drug and Alcohol Dependence*, 1979, *4*, 419–424.

Gold, M. S., and Redmond, D. E., Jr. "Pharmacological Activation and Inhibition of Noradrenergic Activity After Specific Behaviors in Nonhuman Primates." *Neuroscience Abstracts*, 1977, *3* (783), 250.

Gold, M. S., Redmond, D. E., Jr., and Kleber, H. D. "Clonidine Blocks Acute Opiate-Withdrawal Symptoms." *Lancet*, 1978a, *16*, 599–602.

Gold, M. S., Redmond, D. E., Jr., and Kleber, H. D. "Clonidine in Opiate Withdrawal." *Lancet*, 1978b, *29*, 929–930.

Gold, M. S., Sweeney, D. R., and Pottash, A. L. C. "Panic Anxiety and Opiate Withdrawal: Common Neurobiological Mediation." Unpublished data, 1979.

Gold, M. S., and others. "Rapid Opiate Detoxification: Clinical Evidence of Antidepressant and Antipanic Effects of Opiates." *American Journal of Psychiatry*, 1979, *136*, 982–983.

Gold, M. S., and others. "Clonidine: A Safe, Effective, and Rapid Nonopiate Treatment for Opiate Withdrawal." *Journal of the American Medical Association*, in press.

Goldberg, I. D., Krantz, G., and Locke, B. Z. "Effect of a Short-Term Outpatient Psychiatric Therapy Benefit on the Utilization of Medical Services in a Prepaid Group Practice Medical Program." *Medical Care*, 1970, *8*, 419–428.

Goldberg, S., and Lewis, M. "Play Behavior in the Three-Year-Old Infant: Early Sex Differences." *Child Development*, 1969, *40*, 21–31.

Goldenberg, M., Snyder, C. H., and Aranow, H. "New Test for Hypertension Due to Circulating Epinephrine." *Journal of the American Medical Association*, 1947, *135*, 971.

Goldfarb, A. I. "Psychotherapy of the Aged: The Use and Value of an Adaptational Frame of Reference." *Psychoanalytic Review*, 1956, *43*, 68–81.

Goldfried, M. R. "Systematic Desensitization as Training in Self-Control." *Journal of Consulting and Clinical Psychology*, 1971, *37*, 228–235.

Goldfried, M. R., Decenteceo, E. T., and Weinberg, L. "Systematic Rational Restructuring as a Self-Control Technique." *Behavior Therapy*, 1974, *5*, 247–254.

Goldfried, M. R., Linehan, M. M., and Smith, J. L. "Reduction of Test Anxiety Through Cognitive Restructuring." *Journal of Consulting and Clinical Psychology*, 1978, *46*, 32–39.

Goldfried, M. R., and Sobocinski, D. "Effect of Irrational Beliefs on Emotional Arousal." *Journal of Consulting and Clinical Psychology*, 1975, *43*, 504–510.

Goldstein, A. "Opiate Receptors and Opioid Peptides: A Ten-Year Overview." In M. A. Lipton, A. DiMascio, and K. F. Killam (Eds.), *Psychopharmacology: A Generation of Progress*. New York: Raven Press, 1978.

Goldstein, D. S., Harris, A. H., and Brady, J. V. "Baroreflex Sensitivity During Operant Blood Pressure Conditioning." *Biofeedback and Self-Regulation*, 1977a, *2* (2), 127–138.

Goldstein, D. S., Harris, A. H., and Brady, J. V. "Sympathetic Adrenergic Blockade Effects upon Operantly Conditioned Blood Pressure Elevations in Baboons." *Biofeedback and Self-Regulation*, 1977b, *2* (1), 93–105.

Gomes-Schwartz, B., Hadley, S. W., and Strupp, H. H. "Individual Psychotherapy and Behavior Therapy." *Annual Review of Psychology*, 1978, *29*, 435–471.

Goodman, L. S., and Gilman, A. *The Pharmacological Basis of Therapeutics*. (5th ed.) New York: Macmillan, 1975.

Goodwin, D. W., and others. "Psychopathology in Adopted and Nonadopted Daughters of Alcoholics." *Archives of General Psychiatry*, 1977, *34*, 1005–1009.

Goodwin, F. K., and Post, R. M. "Studies of Amine Metabolites in Affective Illness and in Schizophrenia: A Comparative Analysis." In D. X. Freedman (Ed.), *Biology of the Major Psychoses: A Comparative Analysis*. New York: Raven Press, 1975.

Gordon, G., and Morse, E. V. "Evaluation Research." *Annual Review of Sociology*, 1975, *1*, 339–362.

Gore, S. "The Effect of Social Support in Moderating the Health Consequences of Unemployment." *Journal of Health and Social Behavior*, 1978, *19*, 157–165.

Gorsuch, R. L., and Key, M. K. "Abnormalities of Pregnancy as a Function of Anxiety and Life Stress." *Psychosomatic Medicine*, 1974, *36*, 352–372.

Goslings, W. R. O., and others. "Attack Rates of Streptococcal Pharyngitis, Rheumatic Fever, and Glomerulonephritis in the General Population. I: A Controlled Pilot Study of Streptococcal Pharyngitis in One Village." *New England Journal of Medicine*, 1963, *268*, 687–694.

Gottschalk, L. A., Stone, W. N., and Goldine, C. G. "Peripheral Versus Central Mechanisms Accounting for Antianxiety Effects of Propranolol." *Psychosomatic Medicine*, 1974, *36*, 47–55.

Graham, S., and Reeder, L. G. "Social Epidemiology of Chronic Diseases." In H. E. Freeman, S. Levine, and L. G. Reeder (Eds.), *Handbook of Medical Sociology*. (3rd ed.) Englewood Cliffs, N.J.: Prentice-Hall, 1979.

Green, E. F., Green, A. M., and Walters, E. D. "Self-Regulation of Internal States." In J. Rose (Ed.), *Progress of Cybernetics: Proceedings of the International Congress of Cybernetics, London, 1969*. London: Gordon and Breach, 1970.

Greenacre, P. "The Predisposition to Anxiety" [1941]. In *Trauma, Growth and Personality*. New York: Norton, 1952.

Greenacre, P. "The Biological Economy of Birth" [1945]. In *Trauma, Growth and Personality*. New York: Norton, 1952.

Greenberg, D. J., Hillman, D., and Grice, D. "Infant and Stranger Variables Related to Stranger Anxiety in the First Year of Life." *Developmental Psychology*, 1973, *9*, 207–212.

Greenblatt, D. J., and Koch-Weser, J. "Adverse Reactions to B-Adrenergic Blocking Drugs: A Report from the Boston Collaborative Drug Surveillance Program." *Drugs*, 1974, *7*, 118–129.

Greenblatt, D. J., and Koch-Weser, J. "Clinical Pharmacokinetics." *New England Journal of Medicine*, 1975, *293*, 702–705, 964–969.

Greenblatt, D. J., and Shader, R. I. "The Clinical Choice of Sedative-Hypnotics." *Annals of Internal Medicine*, 1972, *77*, 91–100.

Greenblatt, D. J., and Shader, R. I. *Benzodiazepines in Clinical Practice*. New York: Raven Press, 1974.

Greenblatt, D. J., and Shader, R. I. "Pharmacotherapy of Anxiety with Benzodiazepines and B-Adrenergic Blockers." In M. A. Lipton, A. Di-

Mascio, and K. F. Killam (Eds.), *Psychopharmacology: A Generation of Progress*. New York: Raven Press, 1978.

Greene, E., and Stauff, C. "Behavioral Role of Hippocampal Connections." *Experimental Neurology*, 1974, *45*, 141–160.

Greene, W. A. "Disease Response to Life Stress." *Journal of the American Medical Women's Association*, 1965, *20*, 133–140.

Greene, W. A., and Miller, G. "Psychological Factors and Reticuloendothelial Disease. IV: Observations on a Group of Children and Adolescents with Leukemia. An Interpretation of Disease Development in Terms of the Mother-Child Unit." *Psychosomatic Medicine*, 1958, *20*, 124–144.

Greenfield, N. S., and Sternbach, R. A. (Eds.). *Handbook of Psychophysiology*. New York: Holt, Rinehart and Winston, 1972.

Greenson, R. "The Working Alliance and the Transference Neurosis." *Psychoanalytic Quarterly*, 1965, *34*, 155–181.

Grings, W. W. "Inhibition in Autonomic Conditioning." In D. I. Mostofsky (Ed.), *Behavior Control and Modification of Physiological Activity*. Englewood Cliffs, N.J.: Prentice-Hall, 1976.

Grings, W. W., and Dawson, M. E. *Emotions and Bodily Responses*. New York: Academic Press, 1978.

Grinker, R. R. "The Psychosomatic Aspects of Anxiety." In C. D. Spielberger (Ed.), *Anxiety and Behavior*. New York: Academic Press, 1966.

Grinker, R. R. "The Poor Rich: The Children of the Super Rich." *American Journal of Psychiatry*, 1978, *135*, 913–916.

Grinker, R. R., and Spiegel, J. P. *Men Under Stress*. Philadelphia: Blakiston, 1945.

Grosz, H. J., and Farmer, B. B. "Pitts' and McClure's Lactate-Anxiety Study Revisited." *British Journal of Psychiatry*, 1972, *120*, 415–418.

Grosz, H. J., and Farmer, B. B. "Pitts' and McClure's Lactate-Anxiety Study Revisited." *British Journal of Psychiatry*, 1972, *120*, 415–418.

Gunderson, E. K., and Rahe, R. H. (Eds.). *Life Stress and Illness*. Springfield, Ill.: Thomas, 1974.

Gunnar-Vongnechten, M. R. "Changing a Frightening Toy into a Pleasant Toy by Allowing the Infant to Control Its Actions." *Developmental Psychology*, 1978, *14* (2), 157–162.

Guntrip, H. *Personality Structure and Human Interaction*. New York: International Universities Press, 1961.

Gutman, R. "Population Mobility in the American Middle Class." In L. J. Duhl (Ed.), *The Urban Condition*. New York: Basic Books, 1963.

Guttman, D. "The Country of Old Men: Cross-Cultural Studies in the Psychology of Later Life." Occasional Papers in Gerontology, No. 5. Ann Arbor: Institute of Gerontology, University of Michigan–Wayne State University, 1969.

Guy, W. *ECDEU Assessment Manual for Psychopharmacology*. Washington, D.C.: Department of Health, Education and Welfare, 1976.

Haan, N. *Coping and Defending: Processes of Self-Environment Organization*. New York: Academic Press, 1977.

Hackett, T. P., and Cassem, N. "Psychological Management of the Myocardial Infarction Patient." *Journal of Human Stress*, 1975, *1*, 25–38.

Haefely, W. E. "Behavioral and Neuropharmacological Aspects of Drugs Used in Anxiety and Related States." In M. A. Lipton, A. DiMascio, and K. P. Killam (Eds.), *Psychopharmacology: A Generation of Progress*. New York: Raven Press, 1978.

Haefely, W. E., and others. "Benzodiazepines and GABA." *Nature* (London), 1976, *263*, 173–174.

Halleck, S. L. *Psychiatry and the Dilemma of Crime*. Berkeley: University of California Press, 1971.

Halliday, M. S. "Exploratory Behavior." In L. Weiskrantz (Ed.), *Analysis of Behavioral Change*. New York: Harper & Row, 1968.

Hall-Smith, P., and Ryle, A. "Marital Patterns, Hostility and Personal Illness." *British Journal of Psychiatry*, 1969, *115*, 1197–1198.

Hamburg, D. A., and Adams, J. E. "A Perspective on Coping Behavior: Seeking and Utilizing Information in Major Transitions." *Archives of General Psychiatry*, 1967, *17*, 277–284.

Hamburg, D. A., Hamburg, B., and Barchas, J.D. "Anger and Depression in Perspective of Behavioral Biology." In L. Levi (Ed.), *Emotions: Their Parameters and Measurement*. New York: Raven Press, 1975.

Hamburg, D. A., Hamburg, B., and deGoza, S. "Adaptive Problems and Mechanisms in Severely Burned Patients." *Psychiatry*, 1953, *16*, 1–20.

Hamilton, M. "The Assessment of Anxiety States by Rating." *British Journal of Medical Psychology*, 1959, *32*, 50.

Hannan, M., Tuma, N. B., and Groeneveld, L. P. "Income and Marital Events: Evidence from an Income Maintenance Experiment." *American Journal of Sociology*, 1977, *82*, 1186–1211.

Hansen, J. R., and others. "Urinary Levels of Epinephrine and Norepinephrine in Parachutist Trainees." In H. Ursin, E. Baade, and S. Levine (Eds.), *Psychobiology of Stress*. New York: Academic Press, 1978.

Harris, A. H., and Brady, J. V. "Animal Learning: Visceral and Autonomic Conditioning." *Annual Review of Psychology*, 1974, *25*, 107–133.

Harris, A. H., and Brady, J. V. "Long-Term Studies of Cardiovascular Control in Primates." In G. E. Schwartz and J. Beatty (Eds.), *Biofeedback: Theory and Research*. New York: Academic Press, 1977.

Harris, A. H., Findley, J. D., and Brady, J. V. "Instrumental Conditioning of Blood Pressure Elevations in the Baboon." *Conditional Reflex*, 1971, *6* (4), 215–226.

Harris, A. H., Gilliam, W. J., and Brady, J. V. "Operant Conditioning of Large Magnitude 12-Hour Heart Rate Elevations in the Baboon." *Pavlovian Journal of Biological Science*, 1976, *11* (2), 86–92.

Harris, A. H., and others. "Instrumental Conditioning of Large Magnitude Daily 12-Hour Blood Pressure Elevations in the Baboon." *Science*, 1973, *183*, 175.

Hartmann, H. *Ego Psychology and the Problem of Adaptation*. New York: International Universities Press, 1939.

Hartmann, H. "Comments on the Psychoanalytic Theory of Instinctual Drives" [1948]. In *Essays on Ego Psychology*. New York: International Universities Press, 1964.

Hartmann, H. "Notes on the Theory of Sublimation" [1955]. In *Essays on Ego Psychology*. New York: International Universities Press, 1964.

Hartmann, H., and Kris, E. "The Genetic Approach in Psychoanalysis." *Psychoanalytic Study of the Child*, 1945, *1*, 11–30.

Hartmann, H., and Loewenstein, R. M. "Notes on the Theory of Aggression." *Psychoanalytic Study of the Child*, 1949, *3/4*, 9–32.

Hartocollis, P. "Time as a Dimension of Affects." *Journal of the American Psychoanalytic Association*, 1972, *20*, 92–108.

Hartshorne, H. "On Heart Disease in the Army." *American Journal of Medical Science*, 1864, *48*, 89–92.

Hartshorne, H, and May, M. A. "Studies in the Nature of Character." In *Studies in Deceit.* Vol. 1. New York: Macmillan, 1928.

Harvey, S. C. "Hypnotics and Sedatives: The Barbiturates." In L. S. Goodman and A. Gilman (Eds.), *The Pharmacological Basis of Therapeutics.* (5th ed.) New York: Macmillan, 1975.

Haviland, J., and Lewis, M. *Infants' Greeting Patterns to Strangers.* Research Bulletin 76-2. Princeton, N.J.: Educational Testing Service, 1976.

Hawkins, N. G., Davies, R., and Holmes, T. H. "Evidence of Psychosocial Factors in the Development of Pulmonary Tuberculosis." *American Review of Tuberculosis and Pulmonary Diseases,* 1957, *75,* 768–780.

Hebb, D. O. *The Organization of Behavior.* New York: Wiley, 1949.

Hebb, D. O. "The Mammal and His Environment." *American Journal of Psychology,* 1955, *111,* 826–831.

Heckmat, H. "The Role of Imagination in Semantic Desensitization." *Behavior Therapy,* 1972, *3,* 223–231.

Hein, P. L. "Heart Rate Conditioning in the Cat and Its Relationship to Other Physiological Responses." *Psychophysiology,* 1969, *5* (5), 455–464.

Heinicke, C. M. "Some Effects of Separating Two-Year-Old Children from Their Parents: A Comparative Study." *Human Relations,* 1956, *9,* 105–176.

Heisel, J. S., and others. "The Significance of Life Events as Contributing Factors in the Diseases of Children. III: A Study of Pediatric Patients." *Journal of Pediatrics,* 1973, *83,* 119–123.

Hennig, M., and Jardim, A. *The Managerial Woman.* New York: Simon and Schuster, 1976.

Henry, J. P., Ely, D. L., and Stephens, P. M. "Changes in Catecholamine-Controlling Enzymes in Response to Psychosocial Activation of Defense and Alarm Reactions." In *Physiology, Emotion, and Psychosomatic Illness.* Ciba Foundation Symposium 8. Amsterdam: Ciba Foundation, 1972.

Henry, J. P., Meehan, J. P., and Stephens, P. M. "The Use of Psychosocial Stimuli to Induce Prolonged Systolic Hypertension in Mice." *Psychosomatic Medicine,* 1967, *29,* 408–432.

Henry, J. P., and Stephens, P. M. "The Social Environment and Essential Hypertension in Mice: Possible Role of the Innervation of the Adrenal Cortex." *Progress in Brain Research,* 1977a, *47,* 263–276.

Henry, J. P., and Stephens, P. M. *Stress, Health, and the Social Environment.* New York: Springer, 1977b.

Henry, J. P., Stephens, P. M., and Santisteban, G. A. "A Model of Psychosocial Hypertension Showing Reversibility and Progression of Cardiovascular Complications." *Circulation Research,* 1975, *36,* 156–164.

Henry, J. P., and others. "Effect of Psychosocial Stimulation on the Enzymes Involved in the Biosynthesis and Metabolism of Noradrenaline and Adrenaline." *Psychosomatic Medicine,* 1971a, *33,* 227–237.

Henry, J. P., and others. "The Role of Psychosocial Factors in the Development of Arteriosclerosis in CBA Mice: Observations on the Heart, Kidney, and Aorta." *Atherosclerosis,* 1971b, *14,* 203–218.

Herd, J. A., and others. "Arterial Hypertension in the Squirrel Monkey During Behavioral Experiments." *American Journal of Physiology,* 1969, *217,* 24–29.

Herrnstein, R. J. "Method and Theory in the Study of Avoidance." *Psychological Review,* 1969, *76,* 49–69.

Hersen, M., and Bellack, A. *Behavioral Assessment: A Practical Handbook.* Oxford, England: Pergamon Press, 1976.

Hess, E. H. "Imprinting." *Science,* 1959, *130,* 133–141.

Hicks, R., and McCormick, M. G. F. "Clinical Negotiations in Outpatient Psychopharmacology." In A. Lazare (Ed.), *Outpatient Psychiatry.* Baltimore: Williams and Wilkins, 1979.

Hicks, R., McCormick, M. G. F., and Davis, J. M. "Psychopharmacology: The Significance (and Insignificance) of Drugs—Two Paradigms." *Psychiatric Clinics of North America,* 1979, *2,* 359–364.

Hinkle, L. E. "Ecological Observations of the Relation of Physical Illness, Mental Illness and the Social Environment." *Psychosomatic Medicine,* 1961, *23,* 289–296.

Hinkle, L. E., and Plummer, N. "Life Stress and Industrial Absenteeism: The Concentration of Illness and Absenteeism in One Segment of a Working Population." *Industrial Medicine and Surgery,* 1952, *21,* 363–375.

Hinkle, L. E., and Wolff, H. G. "Health and Social Environment: Experimental Investigations." In A. Leighton, J. A. Clausen, and R. N. Wilson (Eds.), *Exploration in Social Psychiatry.* New York: Basic Books, 1957a.

Hinkle, L. E., and Wolff, H. G. "The Nature of Man's Adaptation to His Total Environment and the Relation of This to Illness." *Archives of Internal Medicine,* 1957b, *99,* 442–460.

Hinkle, L. E., and Wolff, H. G. "Ecologic Investigations of the Relationship Between Illness, Life Experiences, and the Social Environment." *Annals of Internal Medicine,* 1958, *49,* 1373–1388.

Hinkle, L. E., and others. "The Distribution of Sickness Disability in a Homogeneous Group of 'Healthy Adult Men.'" *American Journal of Hygiene,* 1956, *64,* 220–242.

Hinkle, L. E., and others. "Studies in Ecology: Factors Relevant to the Occurrence of Bodily Illness and Disturbances in Mood, Thought, and Behavior in Three Homogeneous Population Groups." *American Journal of Psychiatry,* 1957, *114,* 212–220.

Hinkle, L. E., and others. "An Investigation of the Relation Between Life Experience, Personality Characteristics and General Susceptibility to Illness." *Psychosomatic Medicine,* 1958, *20,* 278–295.

Hinkle, L. E., and others. "An Examination of the Relation Between Symptoms, Disability and Serious Illness in Two Homogeneous Groups of Men and Women." *American Journal of Public Health,* 1960, *50,* 1327–1336.

Hodges, W. F. "Effects of Ego Threat and Threat of Pain on State Anxiety." *Journal of Personality and Social Psychology,* 1968, *8,* 364–372.

Hodges, W. F., and Felling, J. P. "Types of Stressful Situations and Their Relation to Trait Anxiety and Sex." *Journal of Consulting and Clinical Psychology,* 1970, *34,* 333–337.

Hodges, W. F., and Spielberger, C. D. "The Effects of Threat of Shock on Heart Rate for Subjects Who Differ in Manifest Anxiety and Fear of Shock." *Psychophysiology,* 1966, *2,* 287–294.

Hodges, W. F., and Spielberger, C. D. "Digit Span: An Indicant of Trait or State Anxiety." *Journal of Consulting and Clinical Psychology,* 1969, *33,* 430–434.

Hoffman, H., and Noem, A. A. "Social Background Variables, Referral Sources and Life Events of Male and Female Alcoholics." *Psychological Reports,* 1975, *37,* 1087–1092.

Hoffman, L. W. "The Professional Woman." In R. B. Kundsin (Ed.), *Women and Success*. New York: Morrow, 1974.

Holdstock, T. L. "Plasticity of Autonomic Functions in Rats with Septal Lesions." *Neuropsychologia*, 1970, *8*, 147–160.

Hollender, M. H., Brown, C. W., and Roback, H. B. "Genital Exhibitionism in Women." *American Journal of Psychiatry*, 1977, *134*, 436–438.

Holmberg, G., and Gershon, S. "Autonomic and Psychic Effects of Yohimbine Hydrochloride." *Psychopharmacologia*, 1961, *2*, 93.

Holmes, D. S., and Houston, B. K. "Effectiveness of Situation Redefinition and Affective Isolation in Coping with Stress." *Journal of Personality and Social Psychology*, 1974, *29*, 212–218.

Holmes, T. H. "Multidiscipline Study of Tuberculosis." In P. J. Sparer (Ed.), *Personality, Stress, and Tuberculosis*. New York: International Universities Press, 1956.

Holmes, T. H., and Rahe, R. H. "The Social Readjustment Rating Scale." *Journal of Psychosomatic Research*, 1967, *11*, 213–218.

Holmes, T. H., and others. "Psychosocial and Psychophysiological Studies of Tuberculosis." *Psychosomatic Medicine*, 1957, *19*, 134–143.

Holroyd, K. A. "Cognition and Desensitization in the Group Treatment of Test Anxiety." *Journal of Consulting and Clinical Psychology*, 1976, *44*, 991–1001.

Holroyd, K. A. "Effects of Social Anxiety and Social Evaluation on Beer Consumption and Social Interaction." *Quarterly Journal of Studies on Alcohol*, 1978, *39*, 737–744.

Homans, G. C. *Social Behavior: Its Elementary Forms*. New York: Harcourt Brace Jovanovich, 1961.

Hooper, D., and others. "The Health of Young Families in New Housing." *Journal of Psychosomatic Research*, 1972, *16*, 367–374.

Horn, J. L., and Wanberg, K. W. "Symptom Patterns Related to Excessive Use of Alcohol." *Quarterly Journal of Studies on Alcohol*, 1969, *30*, 35–58.

Horney, K. "The Problem of the Monogamous Ideal." *International Journal of Psycho-analysis*, 1928, *9*, 318–331.

Horowitz, M. J. "Phase Oriented Treatment of Stress Response Syndromes." *American Journal of Psychotherapy*, 1973, *27*, 506–515.

Horowitz, M. J. *Stress Response Syndrome*. New York: Aronson, 1976.

Horowitz, M. J. *States of Mind: Analysis of Change Processes in Psychotherapy*. New York: Plenum, 1979.

Horowitz, M. J., and Becker, S. S. "Cognitive Response to Stress: Experimental Studies of a Compulsion to Repeat Trauma." In R. Holt and E. Peterfreund (Eds.), *Psychoanalysis and Contemporary Science*. Vol. 1. New York: Macmillan, 1972.

Horst, P. "Estimating Total Test Reliability from Parts of Unequal Length." *Journal of Educational Psychology*, 1951, *11*, 368–371.

House, J. S., and others. "Occupational Stress and Health Among Factory Workers." *Journal of Health and Social Behavior*, 1979, *20*, 139–160.

Howe, E. S. "GSR Conditioning in Anxiety States, Normals, and Chronic Functional Schizophrenic Subjects." *Journal of Abnormal and Social Psychology*, 1958, *56*, 183–189.

Hoy, E., and Endler, N. S. "Reported Anxiousness and Two Types of Stimulus Incongruity." *Canadian Journal of Behavioural Science*, 1969, *1*, 207–214.

Huang, Y. H., and others. "In Vivo Location and Destruction of the Locus Coeruleus in the Stumptail Macaque (*Macaca Arctoides*)." *Brain Research*, 1975, *100*, 157–162.

Hucklebridge, F. H., Nowell, N. W., and Dilks, R. A. "Plasma Catecholamine Response to Fighting in the Male Albino Mouse." *Behavioral Biology*, 1973, *8*, 785–800.

Hughes, P., Senay, E., and Parker, R. "The Medical Management of a Heroin Epidemic." *Archives of General Psychiatry*, 1972, *27*, 585–591.

Hull, C. L. *Principles of Behavior: An Introduction to Behavior Therapy.* New York: Appleton-Century-Crofts, 1934.

Hunt, W. A., and Bespalec, D. A. "An Evaluation of Current Methods of Modifying Smoking Behavior." *Journal of Clinical Psychology*, in press.

Huse, E. F. *Organization Development and Change.* New York: West, 1975.

Hussian, R. A., and Lawrence, P. S. "The Reduction of Test, State, and Trait Anxiety by Test Specific and Generalized Stress Inoculation Training." *Cognitive Therapy and Research*, 1978, *2*, 25–38.

Hutchings, D. E. "Behavioral Teratology: Embryopathic and Behavioral Effects of Drugs During Pregnancy." In *Studies on the Development of Behavior and the Nervous System.* New York: Academic Press, 1978.

Hutchings, D. F., and others. "Anxiety Management and Applied Relaxation in Reducing Chronic Anxiety." Unpublished manuscript, University of Kansas, Lawrence, 1978.

Ichheiser, G. "Misinterpretations of Personality in Everyday Life and the Psychologist's Frame of Reference." *Character and Personality*, 1943, *12*, 145–160.

Ilfeld, F. W., Jr. "Current Social Stressors and Symptoms of Depression." *American Journal of Psychiatry*, 1977a, *134*, 161–166.

Ilfeld, F. W., Jr. "Low Income and Psychiatric Symptomatology." Paper presented at meeting of the American Psychiatric Association, Toronto, May 1977b.

Ilfeld, F. W., Jr. "Psychologic Status of Community Residents Along Major Demographic Dimensions." *Archives of General Psychiatry*, 1978, *35*, 716–724.

Imboden, J. B., Canter, A., and Cluff, L. E. "Convalescence from Influenza." *Archives of Internal Medicine*, 1961, *108*, 393–399.

Imboden, J. B., Canter, A., and Cluff, L. E. "Separation Experiences and Health Records in a Group of Normal Adults." *Psychosomatic Medicine*, 1963, *25*, 433–440.

Imboden, J. B., and others. "Brucellosis. III: Psychologic Aspects of Delayed Convalescence." *Archives of Internal Medicine*, 1959, *103*, 406–414.

Ingram, P. W., Evans, G., and Oppenheim, A. N. "Right Iliac Fossa Pain in Young Women." *British Medical Journal*, 1965, *2*, 149–151.

Isaacs, S. *Social Development in Young Children.* New York: Harcourt Brace Jovanovich, 1933.

Izard, C. E. *The Face of Emotion.* New York: Appleton-Century-Crofts, 1971.

Izard, C. E. *Patterns of Emotions: A New Analysis of Anxiety and Depression.* New York: Academic Press, 1972.

Izard, C. E. *Human Emotions.* New York: Plenum, 1977.

Izard, C. E. "The Emergence of Emotions and the Development of Consciousness in Infants." In J. Davidson, R. J. Davidson, and G. E.

Schwartz (Eds.), *Human Consciousness and Its Transformations: A Psychobiological Perspective.* New York: Plenum, 1978a.

Izard, C. E. "On the Development of Emotions and Emotion-Cognition Relationships in Infancy." In M. Lewis and L. A. Rosenblum (Eds.), *The Origins of Behavior.* Vol. 1: *The Development of Affect.* New York: Plenum, 1978b.

Izard, C. E. (Ed.). *Emotions in Personality and Psychopathology.* New York: Plenum, 1979.

Izard, C. E., and Buechler, S. "On the Emergence, Functions and Regulation of Some Emotion Expressions in Infancy." In R. Plutchik and H. Kellerman (Eds.), *Theories of Emotion.* Vol. 2. In press.

Izard, C. E., and Tomkins, S. S. "Affect and Behavior: Anxiety as a Negative Affect." In C. D. Spielberger (Ed.), *Anxiety and Behavior.* New York: Academic Press, 1966.

Jacobs, M. A., Spilken, A. Z., and Norman, M. M. "The Relationship of Life Change, Maladaptive Aggression and URI in Male College Students." *Psychosomatic Medicine,* 1969, *31,* 31–44.

Jacobs, M. A., and others. "Incidence of Psychosomatic Predisposing Factors in Allergic Disorder." *Psychosomatic Medicine,* 1966, *28,* 679–695.

Jacobs, M. A., and others. "Interaction of Psychological and Biological Predisposing Factors in Allergic Disorders." *Psychosomatic Medicine,* 1967, *29,* 572–585.

Jacobs, M. A., and others. "Life Stress and Respiratory Illness." *Psychosomatic Medicine,* 1970, *32,* 233–242.

Jacobs, M. A., and others. "Patterns of Maladaptation and Respiratory Illness." *Journal of Psychosomatic Research,* 1971, *15,* 63–72.

Jacobs, S. C., and Myers, J. K. "Recent Life Events and Acute Schizophrenic Psychosis: A Controlled Study." *Journal of Nervous and Mental Disease,* 1976, *162,* 75–87.

Jacobs, S. C., Prusoff, B. A., and Paykel, E. S. "Recent Life Events in Schizophrenia and Depression." *Psychological Medicine,* 1974, *4,* 444–453.

Jacobsen, E. "The Theoretical Basis of the Chemotherapy of Depression." In E. B. Davies (Ed.), *Depression: Proceedings of the Symposium Held at Cambridge, 1959.* Cambridge, England: Cambridge University Press, 1964.

Jacobsen, F. *Progressive Relaxation.* Chicago: University of Chicago Press, 1938.

Jaffe, P. G., and Carlson, P. M. "Modeling Therapy for Test Anxiety: The Role of Model Effect and Consequences." *Behaviour Research and Therapy,* 1972, *10,* 329–339.

James, W. "What Is an Emotion?" *Mind,* 1884, *9,* 188–205.

Janet, P. *The Major Symptoms of Hysteria* [1907]. New York: Hafner, 1965.

Janis, I. L. *Stress and Frustration.* New York: Harcourt Brace Jovanovich, 1969.

Jaremko, M. E. "A Component Analysis of Stress Inoculation: Review and Prospectus." *Cognitive Therapy and Research,* 1979, *3,* 35–48.

Jarvik, L., and Blum, J. "Cognitive Decline as Predictor of Mortality in Twin Pairs: A 20-Year Longitudinal Study of Aging." In E. Palmore and J. C.

Jeffers (Eds.), *Prediction of Life Span*. Lexington, Mass.: Heath, 1971.

Jefferson, J. W. "Beta-Adrenergic Receptor Blocking Drugs in Psychiatry." *Archives of General Psychiatry*, 1976, *33*, 1389–1394.

Jegede, R. O. "Psychometric Attributes of the Self-Rating Anxiety Scale." *Psychological Reports*, 1977, *40*, 303–306.

Jenkins, J. J. "Remember That Old Theory of Memory? Well, Forget It!" *American Psychologist*, 1974, *29*, 785–795.

Johnson, D. A. "Psychological Observations of Bank Robbery." *American Journal of Psychiatry*, 1978, *135*, 1377–1379.

Johnson, F. A., and Johnson, C. L. "Role Strain in High Commitment Career Women." *Journal of the American Academy of Psychoanalysis*, 1976, *4* (1), 13–37.

Jones, E. "The Early Development of Female Sexuality" [1927]. In *Papers on Psychoanalysis*. Baltimore: Williams and Wilkins, 1948.

Jones, E. "Fear, Guilt and Hate." *International Journal of Psycho-analysis*, 1929a, *10*, 383–397.

Jones, E. "The Psychopathology of Anxiety" [1929b]. In *Papers on Psychoanalysis*. Baltimore: Williams and Wilkins, 1948.

Jones, F., and others. "Diagnostic Subgroups of Affective Disorders and Their Urinary Excretion of Catecholamine Metabolites." *American Journal of Psychiatry*, 1975, *132*, 1141–1148.

Jones, M., Bridges, P. K., and Leak, D. "Correlation Between Psychic and Endocrinological Responses to Emotional Stress." *Progress in Brain Research*, 1970, *32*, 325–335.

Jones, M., and Mellersh, V. "A Comparison of Exercise Response in Anxiety States and Normal Controls." *Psychosomatic Medicine*, 1946, *8*, 180–187.

Joseph, A., and Murray, V. F. *Chamorros and Carolinians of Saipan: Personality Studies*. Cambridge, Mass.: Harvard University Press, 1951.

Justice, B., and Duncan, D. F. "Life Crisis as a Precursor to Child Abuse." *Public Health Reports*, 1976, *91*, 110–113.

Kaada, B. R. "Somatomotor, Autonomic, and Electrocardiographic Responses to Electrical Stimulation of Rhinencephalic and Other Structures in Primates, Cat and Dog." *Acta Physiologica Scandinavica*, 1951, *24*, 83.

Kaada, B. R., Feldman, R. S., and Langerfeldt, T. "Failure to Modulate Autonomic Reflex Discharge by Hippocampal Stimulation in Rabbits." *Physiology and Behavior*, 1971, *7*, 225–231.

Kaada, B. R., Jansen, J., and Anderson, P. "Stimulation of the Hippocampus and Medial Cortical Areas in Unanesthetized Cats." *Neurology*, 1953, *3*, 844–857.

Kagan, J. "Discrepancy, Temperament, and Infant Distress." In M. Lewis and L. Rosenblum (Eds.), *The Origins of Behavior*. Vol. 2: *The Origins of Fear*. New York: Wiley, 1974.

Kahn, M., and Baker, B. "Desensitization with Minimal Therapist Control." *Journal of Abnormal Psychology*, 1968, *73*, 198–200.

Kahri, A. I. "Effects of Actinomycin-D and Puromycin on the ACTH-Induced Ultrastructural Transformation of Mitochondria of Cortical Cells of Rat Adrenals in Tissue Culture." *Journal of Cell Biology*, 1970, *36*, 181–195.

Kakigi, S. "Cardiovascular Generalization and Differentiation: The Relationship Between Heart Rate and Blood Pressure." *Conditional Reflex*, 1971, *6*, 191–204.

Kalin, R., McClelland, D. C., and Kahn, M. "The Effects of Male Social Drinking on Fantasy." *Journal of Personality and Social Psychology*, 1965, *1*, 441–452.

Kanfer, F. H. "The Many Faces of Self-Control, or Behavior Modification Changes Its Focus." Paper presented at Eighth International Baniff Conference, March 1976.

Kanfer, F. H., and Goldstein, A. P. *Helping People Change*. Elmsford, N.Y.: Pergamon Press, 1975.

Kaplan, H. B. "Studies in Sociophysiology." In E. G. Jaco (Ed.), *Patients, Physicians, and Illness*. New York: Free Press, 1972.

Kaplan, H. B. *Self-Attitudes and Deviant Behavior*. Pacific Palisades, Calif.: Goodyear, 1975.

Kaplan, H. B., Cassel, J. C., and Gore, S. "Social Support and Health." Paper presented at meeting of the American Public Health Association, San Francisco, 1973.

Kaplan, H. S. *The New Sex Therapy: Active Treatment of Sexual Dysfunctions*. New York: Brunner/Mazel, 1974.

Kardiner, A., and Spiegel, H. *War Stress and Neurotic Illness*. New York: Hoeber, 1947.

Karst, T. O., and Trexler, L. D. "Initial Study Using Fixed Role and Rational-Emotive Therapy in Treating Public-Speaking Anxiety." *Journal of Consulting and Clinical Psychology*, 1970, *34*, 360–366.

Kasl, S. "Work and Mental Health." In J. O'Toole (Ed.), *Work and the Quality of Life*. Cambridge, Mass.: M.I.T. Press, 1974.

Kasl, S., and Cobb, S. "Some Psychological Factors Associated with Illness Behavior and Selected Illnesses." *Journal of Chronic Diseases*, 1964, *17*, 325–345.

Kasl, S., and Cobb, S. "Health Behavior, Illness Behavior, and Sick-Role Behavior. I: Health and Illness Behavior." *Archives of Environmental Health*, 1966a, *12*, 246–266.

Kasl, S., and Cobb, S. "Health Behavior, Illness Behavior and Sick-Role Behavior. II: Sick-Role Behavior." *Archives of Environmental Health*, 1966b, *12*, 531–541.

Kasl, S., Gore, S., and Cobb, S. "The Experience of Losing a Job: Reported Changes in Health, Symptoms, and Illness Behavior." *Psychosomatic Medicine*, 1975, *37*, 106–122.

Katkin, E. S. "The Relationship Between Manifest Anxiety and Two Indices of Autonomic Response to Stress." *Journal of Personality and Social Psychology*, 1965, *2*, 324–333.

Kawakami, M., and others. "Influence of Electrical Stimulation of Lesions in Limbic Structure upon Biosynthesis of Adrenocorticoid in the Rabbit." *Neuroendocrinology*, 1968, *3*, 337–348.

Kazdin, A. E. "Covert Modeling and the Reduction of Avoidance Behavior." *Journal of Abnormal Psychology*, 1973, *81*, 87–95.

Kazdin, A. E. "Covert Modeling, Model Similarity, and Reduction of Avoidance Behavior." *Behavior Therapy*, 1974a, *5*, 325–340.

Kazdin, A. E. "The Effect of Model Identity and Fear-Relevant Similarity on Covert Modeling." *Behavior Therapy*, 1974b, *5*, 624–635.

Kazdin, A. E. "Effects of Covert Modeling and Model Reinforcement on

Assertive Behavior." *Journal of Abnormal Psychology,* 1974c, *83,* 240–252.

Kazdin, A. E. "Covert Modeling, Imagery Assessment, and Assertive Behavior." *Journal of Consulting and Clinical Psychology,* 1975, *43* 716–724.

Kazdin, A. E. "Effects of Covert Modeling, Multiple Models, and Model Reinforcement on Assertive Behavior." *Behavior Therapy,* 1976, *7,* 211–222.

Kazdin, A. E., and Wilcoxon, L. "Systematic Desensitization and Nonspecific Treatment Effects: A Methodological Evaluation." *Psychological Bulletin,* 1976, *83,* 729–758.

Keller, J., Croake, J., and Brooking, J. "Effects of a Program in Rational Thinking on Anxieties in Older Persons." *Journal of Counseling Psychology,* 1975, *22,* 54–57.

Kelly, D., Mitchell-Heggs, N., and Sherman, D. "Anxiety and the Effects of Sodium Lactate Assessed Clinically and Physiologically." *British Journal of Psychiatry,* 1971, *119,* 129–141.

Kelly, D., and others. "Treatment of Phobic States with Antidepressants." *British Journal of Psychiatry,* 1970, *116,* 387–398.

Kelly, J. G. "Towards an Ecological Conception of Preventive Interventions." In J. W. Carter (Ed.), *Research Contributions from Psychology to Community Mental Health.* New York: Behavioral Publications, 1968.

Kelly, J. G., Snowden, L. R., and Muñoz, R. F. "Social and Community Interventions." *Annual Review of Psychology,* 1977, *28,* 323–361.

Kempe, C. H., and others. "The Battered Child Syndrome." *Journal of the American Medical Association,* 1962, *181,* 105–111.

Kemper, T. D. *A Social Interactional Theory of Emotions.* New York: Wiley, 1978.

Kendall, P. C. "Anxiety: States, Traits—Situations?" *Journal of Consulting and Clinical Psychology,* 1978, *46,* 280-287.

Kennedy, F., Hoffman, H., and Haines, W. "A Study of William Heirens." *American Journal of Psychiatry,* 1947, *104,* 113–121.

Kessler, M., and Albee, G. N. "Primary Prevention." *Annual Review of Psychology,* 1975, *26,* 357–391.

Kety, S. "Genetic and Biochemical Aspects of Schizophrenia." In A. M. Nicholi, Jr. (Ed.), *The Harvard Guide to Modern Psychiatry.* Cambridge, Mass.: Harvard University Press, 1978.

Kielholz, P. (Ed.). *Beta-Blockers and the Central Nervous System.* Proceedings of an international symposium, St. Moritz, Switzerland, January 5 and 6, 1976. Baltimore: University Park Press, 1977.

Kierkegaard, S. *The Concept of Dread.* (W. Lowrie, Trans.) Princeton, N.J.: Princeton University Press, 1944.

Kim, C., and others. "General Behavioral Activity and Its Component Patterns in Hippocampectomized Rats." *Brain Research,* 1970, *19,* 379–394.

Kimble, D., and Greene, E. "Absence of Latency Learning in Rats with Hippocampal Lesions." *Psychonomic Science,* 1968, *11,* 99–100.

Kimmel, H. "Instrumental Conditioning of Autonomically Mediated Behavior." *Psychological Bulletin,* 1967, *67* (5), 337–345.

King, L. M. "Social and Cultural Influences on Psychopathology." *Annual Review of Psychology,* 1978, *29,* 405–433.

Kiritz, S., and Moos, R. H. "Physiological Effects of Social Environments." *Psychosomatic Medicine,* 1974, *36,* 96–114.

Kizer, J. S., and Youngblood, W. W. "Neurotransmitter Systems and Central Neuroendocrine Regulation." In M. A. Lipton, A. DiMascio, and K. F. Killam (Eds.), *Psychopharmacology: A Generation of Progress*. New York: Raven Press, 1978.

Klein, D. F. "Delineation of Two Drug-Responsive Anxiety Syndromes." *Psychopharmacologia*, 1964, *5*, 397–408.

Klein, D. F. "Importance of Psychiatric Diagnosis in Prediction of Clinical Drug Effects." *Archives of General Psychiatry*, 1967, *16*, 118–126.

Klein, D. F., and Fink, M. "Psychiatric Reaction Patterns to Imipramine." *American Journal of Psychiatry*, 1962, *119*, 432–438.

Klein, D. F., Zitrin, C. M., and Woerner, M. G. "Imipramine and Phobia." *Psychopharmacology Bulletin*, 1977, *13*, 24–27.

Klein, G. S. "Peremptory Ideation: Structure and Force in Motivated Ideas." *Psychological Issues*, 1967, *5*, 80–128.

Klein, M. *The Psychoanalysis of Children*. London: Hogarth Press, 1932.

Klein, M. "On The Theory of Anxiety and Guilt" [1948]. In J. Riviere (Ed.), *Developments in Psychoanalysis*. London: Hogarth Press, 1952.

Kleiner, R. J., and Parker, S. "Social Structure and Psychological Factors in Mental Disorders: A Research Review." In H. Wechsler, L. Solomon, and B. M. Kramer (Eds.), *Social Psychology and Mental Health*. New York: Holt, Rinehart and Winston, 1970.

Klerman, G. L. "Clinical Efficacy and Actions of Antipsychotics." In A. DiMascio and R. I. Shader (Eds.), *Clinical Handbook of Psychopharmacology*. New York: Aronson, 1970.

Klerman, G. L. "A Reaffirmation of the Efficacy of Psychoactive Drugs: A Response to Turner." *Journal of Drug Issues*, 1971, *1*, 312–319.

Klerman, G. L., and Izen, J. E. "The Effects of Grief and Bereavement on Physical Health and Well-Being." In F. Reichsman (Ed.), *Epidemiologic Studies in Psychosomatic Medicine*. Basel, Switzerland: Karger, 1974.

Klinger, E. "Modes of Normal Conscious Flow." In K. S. Pope and J. L. Singer (Eds.), *The Stream of Consciousness: Scientific Investigations into the Flow of Experience*. New York: Plenum, 1978.

Klopfer, B., and Davidson, H. *The Rorschach Technique: An Introductory Manual*. New York: Harcourt Brace Jovanovich, 1962.

Knight, R. P. "The Psychoanalytic Treatment in a Sanitorium of Chronic Addiction to Alcohol." *Journal of the American Medical Association*, 1938, *111*, 1443–1448.

Kobasa, S. C. "Stressful Life Events, Personality, and Health: An Inquiry into Hardiness." *Journal of Personality and Social Psychology*, 1979, *37*, 1–11.

Koch-Weser, J., and Greenblatt, D. J. "The Archaic Barbiturate Hypnotics." *New England Journal of Medicine*, 1973, *291*, 790–791.

Kohn, M. "Social Class and Schizophrenia: A Critical Review." In D. Rosenthal and S. Kety (Eds.), *The Transmission of Schizophrenia*. Oxford, England: Pergamon Press, 1968.

Kohut, H. *The Restoration of the Self*. New York: International Universities Press, 1977.

Koikegami, H., and others. "Stimulation Experiments on the Amygdaloid Nuclear Complex and Related Structures: Effects upon the Renal Volume, Urinary Secretion, Movements of the Urinary Bladder, Blood Pressure and Respiratory Movements." *Folia Psychiatrica et Neurologica Japonica*, 1957, *11*, 157–206.

Kolb, L. *Noyes' Modern Clinical Psychiatry*. (7th ed.) Philadelphia: Saunders, 1968.

Kopin, I. J. "Measuring Turnover of Neurotransmitters in Human Brain." In M. A. Lipton, A. DiMascio, and K. F. Killam (Eds.), *Psychopharmacology: A Generation of Progress*. New York: Raven Press, 1978.

Korf, J., Aghajanian, G. K., and Roth, R. H. "Stimulation and Destruction of the Locus Coeruleus: Opposite Effects on 3-Methoxy-4-Hydroxyphenyl Glycol Sulfate Levels in the Rat Cerebral Cortex." *European Journal of Pharmacology*, 1973, *21*, 299–306.

Korf, J., Bunney, B. S., and Aghajanian, G. K. "Noradrenergic Neurons: Morphine Inhibition of Spontaneous Activity." *European Journal of Pharmacology*, 1974, *25*, 165.

Kreitman, N., Pearce, K. I., and Ryle, A. "The Relationship of Psychiatric, Psychosomatic, and Organic Illness in a General Practice." *British Journal of Psychiatry*, 1966, *112*, 569–579.

Kris, E. "On Psychoanalysis and Education." *American Journal of Orthopsychiatry*, 1948, *18* (4), 622–635.

Kris Study Group of the New York Psychoanalytic Institute. Unpublished manuscript, 1967.

Kubie, L. S. "A Physiological Approach to the Concept of Anxiety." *Psychosomatic Medicine*, 1941, *3*, 263–276.

Kübler-Ross, E. *On Death and Dying*. New York: Macmillan, 1969.

Kummer, H. *Social Organization of Hamadryas Baboons: A Field Study*. Chicago: University of Chicago Press, 1968.

Kunce, J. T., Bruch, M. A., and Thelen, M. H. "Vicarious Induction of Academic Achievement in Disadvantaged Adults." *Journal of Counseling Psychology*, 1974, *21*, 507–510.

Kundsin, R. B. (Ed.). *Women and Success: The Anatomy of Achievement*. New York: Morrow, 1974.

Kutash, I. L. "Treating the Victim of Aggression." In I. L. Kutash, S. B. Kutash, and L. B. Schlesinger (Eds.), *Violence: Perspectives on Murder and Aggression*. San Francisco: Jossey-Bass, 1978.

Kutash, I. L., Kutash, S. B., and Schlesinger, L. B. *Violence: Perspectives on Murder and Aggression*. San Francisco: Jossey-Bass, 1978.

Kutash, I. L., and Schlesinger, L. B. "Successful Psychological Defense: Probing the Defendant's Mind." *Journal of the New Jersey Bar Association*, 1977, *79*, 14–18.

Kutash, I. L., and Schlesinger, L. B. "Fantasies and Criminal Behavior." *New York University Education Quarterly*, in press.

Kvetnansky, R., Weise, V. K., and Kopin, I. J. "Elevation of Adrenal Tyrosine Hydroxylase and Phenylethanolamine-N-Methyl Transferase by Repeated Immobilization of Rats." *Endocrinology*, 1970, *87*, 744–749.

Kvetnansky, R., and others. "Enhanced Synthesis of Adrenal Dopamine B-Hydroxylase Induced by Repeated Immobilization in Rats." *Molecular Pharmacology*, 1971, *7*, 81–86.

Lacey, J., and Lacey, B. "Verification and Extension of the Principle of Autonomic Response-Sterotypy." *American Journal of Psychology*, 1958, *71*, 50–73.

Lacey, J., and Lacey, B. "The Law of Initial Value in the Longitudinal Study of Autonomic Constitution: Reproducibility of Autonomic Responses and Response Patterns over a Four-Year Interval." *New York Academy of Science Annual*, 1962, *98*, 1257–1289.

Lader, M. H. "Psychophysiology of Anxiety." In M. H. Lader (Ed.), *Studies of Anxiety*. Kent, England: Headley Brothers, 1969.

Lader, M. H. "Current Psychophysiological Theories of Anxiety." In M. A. Lipton, A. DiMascio, and K. F. Killam (Eds.), *Psychopharmacology: A Generation of Progress*. New York: Raven Press, 1978.

Lader, M. H., and Mathews, A. M. "A Physiological Model of Phobic Anxiety and Desensitization." *Behaviour Research and Therapy*, 1968, *6*, 411.

Ladouceuer, R. "Rationale of Systematic Desensitization and Covert Positive Reinforcement." *Behaviour Research and Therapy*, 1978, *16* (6), 411–420.

Laforgue, R. "On the Erotization of Anxiety." *International Journal of Psycho-analysis*, 1930, *11*, 312–321.

Lakoff, S. A. "The Future of Intervention." In R. Binstock and E. Shanas (Eds.), *Handbook of Aging and the Social Sciences*. New York: Van Nostrand Reinhold, 1976.

Lambert, M. J. "Spontaneous Remission in Adult Neurotic Disorder: A Revision and Summary." *Psychological Bulletin*, 1976, *83*, 107–119.

Lamprecht, F., and others. "Rat Fighting Behavior: Serum Dopamine B-Hydroxylase and Hypothalamic Tyrosine Hydroxylase." *Science*, 1973, *177*, 1214–1215.

Land, K. "Principles of Path Analysis." In E. F. Borgatta and G. W. Bohrnstedt (Eds.), *Sociological Methodology 1969*. San Francisco: Jossey-Bass, 1969.

Landesman-Dwyer, S., and Emanuel, I. "Smoking During Pregnancy." *Teratology*, 1979, *19*, 119–126.

Lang, P. J. "Fear Reduction and Fear Behavior: Problems in Treating a Construct." In J. M. Shlien (Ed.), *Research in Psychotherapy*. Vol. 3. Washington, D.C.: American Psychological Association, 1968.

Lang, P. J. "The Mechanics of Desensitization and the Laboratory Study of Human Fear." In C. M. Franks (Ed.), *Behavior Therapy: Appraisal and Status*. New York: McGraw-Hill, 1969.

Lang, P. J. "Stimulus Control, Response Control, and Desensitization of Fear." In D. Levis (Ed.), *Learning Approaches to Therapeutic Behavior Change*. Chicago: Aldine, 1970.

Lang, P. J. "The Application of Psychophysiological Methods to the Study of Psychotherapy and Behavior Change." In A. E. Bergin and S. L. Garfield (Eds.), *Handbook of Psychotherapy and Behavior Change*. New York: Wiley, 1971.

Lang, P. J. "Imagery in Therapy: An Information Processing Analysis of Fear." *Behavior Therapy*, 1977, *9*, 862, 886.

Lang, P. J., and Lazovik, A. D. "Experimental Desensitization of a Phobia." *Journal of Abnormal and Social Psychology*, 1963, *66*, 519–525.

Lang, P. J., Melamed, B. G., and Hart, J. H. "A Psychophysiological Analysis of Fear Modification Using an Automated Desensitization Procedure." *Journal of Abnormal Psychology*, 1970, *76*, 220–234.

Lange, C. G. *The Emotions* [1885]. Baltimore: Williams and Wilkins, 1922.

Langlie, J. K. "Social Networks, Health Beliefs, and Preventive Health Behavior." *Journal of Health and Social Behavior*, 1977, *18*, 244–260.

Langner, T. S. "A 22-Item Screening Score of Psychiatric Symptoms Indicating Impairment." *Journal of Health and Social Behavior*, 1962, *3*, 269–276.

Langner, T. S. "Life Stress, Behavior, and Intervening Variables." In *Systems Thinking and the Quality of Life*. Proceedings of 1975 Annual North American Meeting, Society for General Systems Research, January 1975.

Langner, T. S., Gersten, J. C., and Eisenberg, J. G. "The Epidemiology of Mental Disorder in Children: Implications for Community Psychiatry." In G. Serban (Ed.), *New Trends of Psychiatry in the Community*. Cambridge, Mass.: Ballinger, 1977.

Langner, T. S., and Michael, S. T. *Life Stress and Mental Health*. New York: Free Press, 1963.

Langner, T. S., and others. "Treatment of Psychological Disorders Among Urban Children." *Journal of Consulting and Clinical Psychology*, 1974, *42*, 170–179.

Langner, T. S., and others. "Factors in Children's Behavior and Mental Health over Time: The Family Research Project." In R. G. Simmons (Ed.), *Research in Community and Mental Health*. Vol. 1. Greenwich, Conn.: JAI Press, 1979.

Lapouse, R., and Monk, M. A. "Behavior Deviations in a Representative Sample of Children: Variation by Sex, Age, Race, Social Class, and Family Size." *American Journal of Orthopsychiatry*, 1964, *34*, 436–446.

Lauer, R. H. "Rate of Change and Stress: A Test of the 'Future Shock' Thesis." *Social Forces*, 1974, *52*, 510–516.

Lavellee, Y., and others. "Effects of EMG Feedback, Diazepam and Their Interaction on Chronic Anxiety." Paper presented at International College of Psychosomatic Medicine, Third Congress, Rome, 1977.

Lazare, A. "The Hysterical Character in Psychoanalytic Theory: Evolution and Confusion." *Archives of General Psychiatry*, 1971, *25*, 131–137.

Lazare, A. "Group Therapy of Phobic Disorders by Systematic Desensitization." *Journal of Abnormal and Social Psychology*, 1961, *63*, 504–510.

Lazarus, R. S. *Psychological Stress and the Coping Process*. New York: McGraw-Hill, 1966.

Lazarus, R. S. "Emotions and Adaptation: Conceptual and Empirical Relations." In W. J. Arnold (Ed.), *Nebraska Symposium on Motivation*. Lincoln: University of Nebraska Press, 1968.

Lazarus, R. S. *Patterns of Adjustment*. (3rd ed.) New York: McGraw-Hill, 1976.

Lazarus, R. S. "A Strategy for Research on Psychological and Social Factors in Hypertension." *Journal of Human Stress*, 1978a, *4*, 35–40.

Lazarus, R. S. "The Stress and Coping Paradigm." Paper presented at conference entitled "The Critical Evaluation of Behavioral Paradigms for Psychiatric Science," Gleneden Beach, Oregon, Nov. 3–6, 1978b.

Lazarus, R. S., and Averill, J. R. "Emotions and Cognition: With Special Reference to Anxiety." In C. D. Spielberger (Ed.), *Anxiety: Current Trends in Theory and Research*. Vol 2. New York: Academic Press, 1972.

Lazarus, R. S., Averill, J. R., and Opton, E. M., Jr. "Toward a Cognitive Theory of Emotion." In M. Arnold (Ed.), *Feelings and Emotions*. New York: Academic Press, 1970.

Lazarus, R. S., Deese, J., and Osler, S. F. "The Effects of Psychological Stress upon Performance." *Psychological Bulletin*, 1952, *49*, 293–317.

Lazarus, R. S., and Launier, R. "Stress-Related Transactions Between Person and Environment." In L. A. Pervin and M. Lewis (Eds.), *Perspectives in Interactional Psychology*. New York: Plenum, 1978.

Lazarus, R. S., and others. "A Laboratory Study of Psychological Stress Produced by a Motion Picture Film." *Psychological Monographs,* 1962, *76* (34, Whole No. 553).

Lazarus, R. S., and others. "Psychological Stress and Adaptation: Some Unresolved Issues." In H. Selye (Ed.), *Guide to Stress Research.* New York: Van Nostrand Reinhold, in press.

Lederer, W. *Fear of Women.* New York: Harcourt Brace Jovanovich, 1968.

Lefcourt, H. M. *Locus of Control: Current Trends in Theory and Research.* New York: Halsted Press, 1976.

Lehmann, H. E. "The Emotional Basis of Illness." *Diseases of the Nervous System,* 1967, *28,* 12–19.

Leitenberg, H. "Behavioral Approaches to Treatment of Neuroses." In H. Leitenberg (Ed.), *Handbook of Behavior Modification and Behavior Therapy.* Englewood Cliffs, N.J.: Prentice-Hall, 1976.

Leitenberg, H., and others. "Relationship Between Heart Rate and Behavioral Change During the Treatment of Phobias." *Journal of Abnormal Psychology,* 1971, *78,* 59–68.

Leitenberg, H., and others. "Feedback and Therapist Praise During Treatment of Phobia." *Journal of Counsulting and Clinical Psychology,* 1975, *43,* 396–404.

Leopold, R. L., and Dillon, H. "Psychoanatomy of a Disaster: A Long Term Study of Post-traumatic Neurosis in Survivors of a Marine Explosion." *American Journal of Psychiatry,* 1963, *119,* 913–921.

Lerner, H. "Adaptive and Pathogenic Aspects of Sex Role Stereotypes." *American Journal of Psychiatry,* 1978, *135* (1), 48–52.

Leshner, A. I., and Candland, D. K. "Endocrine Effects of Grouping and Dominance Rank in Squirrel Monkeys." *Physiology and Behavior,* 1972, *8,* 441–445.

Levi, L. *Stress and Distress in Response to Psychosocial Stimuli.* Oxford, England: Pergamon Press, 1972.

Levi, L., and Andersson, L. *Psychosocial Stress.* New York: Spectrum, 1975.

Levin, S., "Depression in the Aged: The Importance of External Factors." In R. Kastenbaum (Ed.), *New Thoughts on Old Age.* New York: Springer, 1964.

Levine, S., Goldman, L., and Coover, G. D. "Expectancy and the Pituitary-Adrenal System." In R. Porter and J. Knight (Eds.), *Physiology, Emotion and Psychosomatic Illness.* Amsterdam: Elsevier, 1972.

Levis, D. J. "Implosive Therapy: The Theory, the Subhuman Analogue, the Strategy, and the Technique. II." In S. G. Armitage (Ed.), *Behavior Modification Techniques in the Treatment of Emotional Disorders.* Battle Creek, Mich.: V. A. Publication, 1967.

Levy, L. H. "Anxiety and Behavior Scientists' Behavior." *American Psychologist,* 1961, *16* (2), 66–68.

Lewin, B. D. "Phobic Symptoms and Dream Interpretation." *Psychoanalytic Quarterly,* 1952, *21,* 295–322.

Lewinsohn, P. M., and Amenson, C. S. "Some Relations Between Pleasant and Unpleasant Mood-Related Events and Depression." *Journal of Abnormal Psychology,* 1978, *87,* 644–654.

Lewis, A. "The Ambiguous Word 'Anxiety.'" *International Journal of Psychiatry,* 1970, *9,* 62–79.

Lewis, M. "The Meaning of a Response or Why Researchers in Infant Behavior Should Be Oriental Metaphysicians." *Merrill-Palmer Quarterly of Behavior and Development,* 1967, *13* (1), 7–18.

Lewis, M., and Brooks, J. "Self, Other, and Fear: Infants' Reactions to People." In M. Lewis and L. Rosenblum (Eds.), *The Origin of Behavior.* Vol. 2: *The Origins of Fear.* New York: Wiley, 1974.

Lewis, M., and Brooks, J. "Infants' Social Perception: A Constructivist View." In L. Cohen and P. Salapatek (Eds.), *Infant Perception: From Sensation to Cognition.* Vol. 2. New York: Academic Press, 1975.

Lewis, M., Brooks, J., and Haviland, J. "Hearts and Faces: A Study in the Measurement of Emotion." In M. Lewis and L. Rosenblum (Eds.), *The Origins of Behavior.* Vol. 1: *The Development of Affect.* New York: Plenum, 1978.

Lewis, M., and Brooks-Gunn, J. "Self Knowledge and Emotional Development." In M. Lewis and L. Rosenblum (Eds.), *The Origins of Behavior.* Vol. 1: *The Development of Affect.* New York: Plenum, 1978.

Lewis, M., and Brooks-Gunn, J. *Social Cognition and the Acquisition of Self.* New York: Plenum, 1979.

Lewis, M., and Feiring, C. "Direct and Indirect Effects in Social Relations." In L. Lipsitt (Ed.), *Advances in Infancy Research.* Vol. 7. Norwood, N.J.: Ablex, 1980.

Lewis, M., and Goldberg, S. "The Acquisition and Violation of Expectancy: An Experimental Paradigm." *Journal of Experimental Child Psychology,* 1969, *7,* 70–80.

Lewis, M., and Michalson, L. "The Measurement of Emotional State." In C. Izard (Ed.), *Measurement of Emotion in Infants and Children.* New York: Cambridge University Press, in press.

Lewis, M., and Rosenblum, L. (Eds.). *The Origins of Behavior.* Vol. 4: *Friendship and Peer Relations.* New York: Wiley, 1975.

Lewis, M., and Rosenblum, L. "Issues in Affect Development." In M. Lewis and L. Rosenblum (Eds.), *The Origins of Behavior.* Vol. 1: *The Development of Affect.* New York: Plenum, 1978.

Lewis, M., and Starr, M. "Developmental Continuity." In J. Osofsky (Ed.), *Handbook of Infant Development.* New York: Wiley, 1979.

Lewis, T. *The Soldier's Heart and Effort Syndrome.* New York: Hoeber, 1919.

Liberman, M. A. "Relationship of Mortality Rates to Entrance to a Home for the Aged." *Geriatrics,* 1961, *16,* 515–519.

Liddel, H. S. "Conditioned Reflex Method and Experimental Neurosis." In J. McV. Hunt (Ed.), *Personality and the Behavior Disorders.* New York: Ronald Press, 1944.

Liebowitz, M. R., and Klein, D. F. "Assessment and Treatment of Phobic Anxiety." *Journal of Clinical Psychiatry,* in press.

Lief, H. "Anxiety Reaction." In A. M. Freedman and H. I. Kaplan (Eds.), *Comprehensive Textbook of Psychiatry.* Baltimore: Williams and Wilkins, 1967.

Liem, R., and Liem, J. "Social Class and Mental Illness Reconsidered: The Role of Economic Stress and Social Support." *Journal of Health and Social Behavior,* 1978, *19,* 139–156.

Lifton, R. V. *History and Human Survival.* New York: Vantage Books, 1967.

Lin, N., and others. "Social Support, Stressful Life Events, and Illness: A Model and Empirical Test." *Journal of Health and Social Behavior*, 1979, *20*, 108–119.

Linden, M. E. "Transference in Gerontologic Group Psychotherapy. IV: Studies in Gerontologic Human Relations." *International Journal of Group Psychotherapy*, 1955, *5*, 61–79.

Lindesmith, A. R., and Strauss, A. L. *Social Psychology*. New York: Dryden, 1949.

Linn, L. "Clinical Manifestations of Psychiatric Disorders." In A. M. Freedman, H. I. Kaplan, and B. J. Sadock (Eds.), *Comprehensive Textbook of Psychiatry*. (2nd ed.) Baltimore: Williams and Wilkins, 1975.

Lipowski, Z. J. "Psychosomatic Medicine in the Seventies: An Overview." *American Journal of Psychiatry*, 1977, *134*, 233–244.

Litman, G. K. "Stress, Affect, and Craving in Alcoholics: The Single Case as a Research Strategy." *Quarterly Journal of Studies on Alcohol*, 1974, *35*, 131–146.

Loewenstein, R. M. "Symptom Formation and Character Formation." *International Journal of Psycho-analysis*, 1964, *44*, 155–157.

London, M., Crandall, R., and Sears, G. W. "The Contribution of Job and Leisure Satisfaction to Quality of Life." *Journal of Applied Psychology*, 1977, *62*, 328–334.

London, P. *The Modes and Morals of Psychotherapy*. New York: Holt, Rinehart and Winston, 1964.

Lopiccolo, J. "Systematic Desensitization of Homosexuality." *Behavior Therapy*, 1971, *2*, 394–399.

Lorenz, K. "Der Kumpan in der Umwelt des Vogels" ["Feeding in the World of Birds"]. *Journal of Ornithology*, 1935, *83*, 137–215, 289–413.

Louch, C. D., and Higginbotham, M. "The Relation Between Social Rank and Plasma Corticosterone Levels in Mice." *General Comparative Endocrinology*, 1966, *8*, 445–454.

Luborsky, L., Docherty, J. P., and Penick, S. "Onset Conditions for Psychosomatic Symptoms: A Comparative Review of Immediate Observation with Retrospective Research." *Psychosomatic Medicine*, 1973, *35*, 187–204.

Luborsky, L., Singer, B., and Luborsky, L. "Comparative Studies of Psychotherapies: Is It True That Everyone Has Won and All Must Have Prizes?" *Archives of General Psychiatry*, 1975, *32*, 995–1008.

Ludwig, A. M. "Hysteria: A Neurobiological Theory." *Archives of General Psychiatry*, 1972a, *27*, 771–777.

Ludwig, A. M. "On and Off the Wagon: Reasons for Drinking and Abstaining by Alcoholics." *Quarterly Journal of Studies on Alcohol*, 1972b, *33*, 91–96.

Luthe, W. (Ed.). *Autogenic Therapy*. New York: Grune and Stratton, 1969.

Maas, J. W., Dekirmenjian, H., and Fawcett, J. A. "Catecholamine Metabolism and Stress." *Nature*, 1971, *230*, 330.

Maas, J. W., Fawcett, J. A., and Dekirmenjian, H. "3-Methoxy-4-Hydroxyphenyl Glycol (MHPG) Excretion in Depressive States: A Pilot Study." *Archives of General Psychiatry*, 1968, *19*, 129–134.

Maas, J. W., Fawcett, J. A., and Dekirmenjian, H. "Catecholamine Metabolism, Depressive Illness and Drug Response." *Archives of General Psychiatry*, 1972, *26*, 252–262.

Maas, J. W., and Landis, D. H. "The Metabolism of Circulating Norepin-
ephrine by Human Subjects." *Journal of Pharmacology and Experimental
Therapeutics,* 1971, *177,* 600–612.
Maas, J. W., Landis, D. H., and Dekirmenjian, H. "The Occurrence of Free
versus Conjugated MHPG in Non-human and Human Primate Brain."
Psychopharmacology Communications, 1976, *2,* 403–410.
Maas, J. W., and others. "Neurotransmitter Metabolite Production by Hu-
man Brain." In E. Usdin, I. J. Kopin, and J. Barchas (Eds.),
Catecholamines: Basic and Clinical Frontiers. Elmsford, N.Y.: Pergamon
Press, 1979.
McAdoo, W. G. "The Effects of Success, Mild Failure Feedback on A-State
for Subjects Who Differ in A-Trait." Unpublished doctoral dissertation,
Florida State University, 1969.
McClelland, D. C., and others. *The Drinking Man.* New York: Free
Press, 1972.
Maccoby, E. E. *The Development of Sex Differences.* Stanford, Calif.: Stan-
ford University Press, 1966.
McCord, W., McCord, J., and Gudeman, J. *Origins of Alcoholism.* Stanford,
Calif.: Stanford University Press, 1960.
MacDonald, J. M. *Armed Robbery: Offenders and Their Victims.* Springfield,
Ill.: Thomas, 1975.
McGlynn, F. D., and Linder, L. H. "The Clinical Application of Analogue
Desensitization: A Case Study." *Behavior Therapy,* 1971, *2,* 385–388.
McGuire, M. T., Stein, S., and Mendelson, J. H. "Comparative Psychoso-
cial Studies of Alcoholic and Nonalcoholic Subjects Undergoing
Experimentally Induced Intoxication." *Psychosomatic Medicine,* 1966,
28, 13–26.
McIntyre, A., and Doris, J. "The Role of Aggression in Attachment Rela-
tionships." Paper presented at 85th annual meeting of the American
Psychological Association, San Francisco, 1977.
McIntyre, A., Doris, J., and Meyer, M. M. "Early Childhood Separation
Anxiety and Patterns of Social Behavior." Paper presented at 83rd annual
meeting of the American Psychological Association, Chicago, Sept. 1975.
McIntyre, A., and Wolfe, B. "Separation Anxiety and the Inhibition of Ag-
gression in Preschool Children." *Journal of Abnormal Child Psychology,*
1973, *1* (4), 400–409.
McKinney, T. D., and Desjardins, C. "Intermale Stimuli and Testicular
Function in Adult and Immature House Mice." *Biology of Reproduction,*
1973, *9,* 370–378.
MacLean, P. D. "Psychosomatic Disease and the 'Visceral Brain': Recent
Developments Bearing on the Papez Theory of Emotion." *Psychosomatic
Medicine,* 1949, *11,* 338–353.
MacLean, P. D. "Sensory and Perceptive Factors in Emotional Functions of
the Triune Brain." In R. G. Grenell and S. Gabay (Eds.), *Biological
Foundations of Psychiatry.* Vol. 1. New York: Raven Press, 1976.
McNair, D. M., and Fisher, S. "Separating Anxiety from Depression." In
M. A. Lipton, A. DiMascio, and K. F. Killam (Eds.), *Psychopharmaco-
logy: A Generation of Progress.* New York: Raven Press, 1978.
McNamee, H. B., Mello, N. K., and Mendelson, J. H. "Experimental Anal-
ysis of Drinking Patterns in Alcoholics: Concurrent Psychiatric
Observations." *American Journal of Psychiatry,* 1968, *124,* 1063–1069.

McNemar, Q. *Psychological Statistics*. New York: Wiley, 1969.

McReynolds, P. "The Assessment of Anxiety: A Survey of Available Techniques." In P. McReynolds (Ed.), *Advances in Psychological Assessment*. Palo Alto, Calif.: Science and Behavior Books, 1968.

Maddison, D., and Viola, A. "The Health of Widows in the Year Following Bereavement." *Journal of Psychosomatic Research*, 1968, *12*, 297–306.

Maengwyn-Davies, G. D., and others. "Influence of Isolation and of Fighting on Adrenal Tyrosine Hydroxylase and Phenylethanolamine-N-Methyl-Transferase Activities in Three Strains of Mice." *Psychopharmacologia*, 1973, *28*, 339–350.

Magnusson, D. "An Analysis of Situational Dimensions." *Perceptual and Motor Skills*, 1971, *32*, 851–967.

Magnusson, D. *"The Person and the Situation in the Traditional Measurement Model."* Reports from the Psychological Laboratories, No. 426. Stockholm: University of Stockholm, 1974.

Magnusson, D. "The Person and the Situation in an Interactional Model of Behavior." *Scandinavian Journal of Psychology*, 1976, *17*, 253–271.

Magnusson, D. *On the Psychological Situation*. Reports from the Psychological Laboratory, No. 544. Stockholm: University of Stockholm, 1978.

Magnusson, D., and Ekehammar, B. "An Analysis of Situational Dimensions: A Replication." *Multivariate Behavioral Research*, 1973, *8*, 331–339.

Magnusson, D., and Ekehammar, B. "Perceptions of and Reactions to Stressful Situations." *Journal of Personality and Social Psychology*, 1975, *31*, 1147–1154.

Magnusson, D., and Ekehammar, B. "Similar Situations—Similar Behaviors." *Journal of Research in Personality*, 1978, *12*, 41–48.

Magnusson, D., and Endler, N. S. "Interactional Psychology: Present Status and Future Prospects." In D. Magnusson and N. S. Endler (Eds.), *Personality at the Crossroads: Current Issues in Interactional Psychology*. Hillsdale, N.J.: Erlbaum, 1977.

Magnusson, D., Gerzén, M., and Nyman, B. "The Generality of Behavioral Data. I: Generalization from Observations on One Occasion." *Multivariate Behavioral Research*, 1968, *3*, 295–320.

Magnusson, D., and Heffler, B. "The Generality of Behavioral Data. III: Generalization Potential as a Function of the Number of Observation Instances." *Multivariate Behavioral Research*, 1969, *4*, 29–42.

Magnusson, D., Heffler, B., and Nyman, B. "The Generality of Behavioral Data. II: Replication of an Experiment on Generalization from Observations on One Occasion." *Multivariate Behavioral Research*, 1968, *3*, 415–422.

Mahler, M. S., *On Human Symbiosis and the Vicissitudes of Individuation*. Vol. 1: *Infantile Psychosis*. New York: International Universities Press, 1969.

Mahler, M. S., Pine, F., and Bergman, A. *The Psychological Birth of the Human Infant*. New York: Basic Books, 1975.

Mahoney, M. J. "Cognitive Therapy and Research: A Question of Questions." *Cognitive Therapy and Research*, 1977, *1*, 5–16.

Mahoney, M. J., and Arnkoff, D. B. "Cognitive and Self-Control Therapies." In S. L. Garfield and A. E. Bergin (Eds.), *Handbook of Psychotherapy and Behavior Change: An Empirical Analysis*. (2nd ed.) New York: Wiley, 1978.

Mahoney, M. J., and Thoresen, C. E. *Self-Control: Power to the Person.* Monterey, Calif.: Brooks/Cole, 1974.

Malan, D. *The Frontier of Brief Psychotherapy.* New York: Plenum, 1976.

Malmo, R. B. *On Emotions, Needs, and Our Archaic Brain.* New York: Holt, Rinehart and Winston, 1975.

Mann, J. "Vicarious Desensitization of Test Anxiety Through Observation of Videotaped Treatment." *Journal of Counseling Psychology,* 1972, *19,* 1–7.

Mann, J. *Time Limited Psychotherapy.* Cambridge, Mass.: Harvard University Press, 1973.

Mann, J., and Rosenthal, T. L. "Vicarious and Direct Counterconditioning of Test Anxiety Through Individual and Group Desensitization." *Behaviour Research and Therapy,* 1969, *7,* 359–367.

Mann, P. "Residential Mobility as an Adaptive Experience." *Journal of Consulting and Clinical Psychology,* 1972, *39,* 37–42.

Markiewicz, W., and others. "Mitral Valve Prolapse in One Hundred Presumably Healthy Young Females." *Circulation,* 1976, *53,* 464–473.

Marks, I. *Fears and Phobias.* New York: Academic Press, 1969.

Marks, I. "Behavioral Treatments of Phobic and Obsessive-Compulsive Disorders: A Critical Appraisal." In M. Hersen, R. M. Eisler, and P. M. Miller (Eds.), *Progress in Behavior Modification.* Vol. 1. New York: Academic Press, 1975.

Marks, I. "Behavioral Psychotherapy of Adult Neurosis." In S. L. Garfield and A. E. Bergin (Eds.), *Handbook of Psychotherapy and Behavior Change: An Empirical Analysis.* (2nd ed.) New York: Wiley, 1978.

Marlatt, G. A. "Alcohol, Stress, and Cognitive Control." In I. G. Sarason and C. D. Spielberger (Eds.), *Stress and Anxiety.* Vol. 3. New York: Wiley, 1976.

Marmor, J. "Orality in the Hysterical Personality." *Journal of the American Psychoanalytic Association,* 1953, *1,* 656–675.

Marshall, W., and Andrews, W. *A Manual for the Self-Management of Public Speaking Anxiety.* Kingston, Ontario: McArthur College Press, 1973.

Marshall, W., Stoian, M., and Andrews, W. "Skills Training and Self-Administered Desensitization in the Reduction of Public Speaking Anxiety." *Behaviour Research and Therapy,* 1977, *15,* 115–117.

Martin, B. *Anxiety and Neurotic Disorders.* New York: Wiley, 1971.

Marx, K. *Selected Writings in Sociology and Social Philosophy.* New York: McGraw-Hill, 1964.

Marx, M. B., Garrity, T. F., and Bowers, F. R. "The Influence of Recent Life Experience on the Health of College Freshmen." *Journal of Psychosomatic Research,* 1975, *19,* 87–98.

Mash, E., and Terdal, L. (Eds.). *Behavior Therapy Assessment: Diagnosis, Design, and Evaluation.* New York: Springer, 1976.

Mason, J. W. "A Review of Psychoendocrine Research on the Pituitary-Adrenal Cortical System." *Psychosomatic Medicine,* 1968, *30,* 576–607.

Mason, J. W. "A Reevaluation of the Concept of 'Non-specificity' in Stress Theory." *Journal of Psychiatric Research,* 1971, *8,* 323–333.

Mason, J. W. "A Historical View of the Stress Field." *Journal of Human Stress,* March and June, 1975a, pp. 6–12, 22–36.

Mason, J. W. "Emotion as Reflected in Patterns of Endocrine Integration." In L. Levi (Ed.), *Emotions: Their Parameters and Measurements.* New York: Raven Press, 1975b.

Mason, J. W., Brady, J. V., and Sidman, M. "Plasma 17-Hydroxycorticos-
teroid Levels and Conditioned Behavior in the Rhesus Monkey."
Endocrinology, 1957, *60,* 741–752.

Mason, J. W., Brady, J. V., and Tolson, W. W. "Behavioral Adaptations
and Endocrine Activity." In R. Levine (Ed.), *Endocrines and the Central
Nervous System.* Baltimore: Williams and Wilkins, 1966.

Mason, J. W., and others. "Concurrent Plasma Epinephrine, Norepinephrine, and 17-Hydroxycorticosteroid Levels During Conditioned Emotional Disturbances in Monkeys." *Psychosomatic Medicine,* 1961a, *23,*
344–353.

Mason, J. W., and others. "Patterns of Corticosteroid and Pepsinogen
Change Related to Emotional Stress in the Monkey." *Science,* 1961b,
133, 1596–1598.

Mason, J. W., and others. "Patterns of Thyroid, Gonadal, and Adrenal Hormone Secretions Related to Psychological Stress in the Monkey."
Psychosomatic Medicine, 1961c, *23,* 446.

Mason, J. W., and others. "Selectivity of Corticosteroid and Catecholamine
Responses to Various Natural Stimuli." In G. Serban (Ed.), *Psychopathology of Human Adaptation.* New York: Plenum, 1976.

Masters, W., and Johnson, V. *Human Sexual Response.* Boston: Little,
Brown, 1966.

Masuda, M., and Holmes, T. H. "Magnitude Estimations of Social Readjustments." *Journal of Psychosomatic Research,* 1967, *11,* 219–225.

Mathews, A., and others. "A Home-Based Treatment Program for Agoraphobia." *Behavior Therapy,* in press.

Matsumoto, Y. S. "Social Stress and Coronary Heart Disease in Japan: A
Hypothesis." *Milbank Memorial Fund Quarterly,* 1970, *48,* 9–13.

May, J. R., and Johnson, H. J. "Physiological Activity to Internally Elicited
Arousal and Inhibitory Thoughts." *Journal of Abnormal Psychology,*
1973, *82,* 239–245.

May, R. *The Meaning of Anxiety.* New York: Ronald Press, 1950a.

May, R. "Centrality of the Problem of Anxiety in Our Day." In *The Meaning
of Anxiety.* New York: Ronald Press, 1950b.

May, R. *Psychology and the Human Dilemma.* New York: Van Nostrand, 1967.

May, R. *Love and Will.* New York: Norton, 1969.

Mead, G. H. *Mind, Self, and Society.* Chicago: University of Chicago
Press, 1934.

Mechanic, D. "Illness and Social Disability: Some Problems in Analysis."
Pacific Sociological Review, 1959, *2,* 37–41.

Mechanic, D. "The Concept of Illness Behavior." *Journal of Chronic Diseases,* 1962a, *15,* 189–194.

Mechanic, D. *Students Under Stress.* New York: Free Press, 1962b.

Mechanic, D. "Some Implications of Illness Behavior for Medical Sampling." *New England Journal of Medicine,* 1963, *269,* 244–247.

Mechanic, D. *Medical Sociology.* New York: Free Press, 1968.

Mechanic, D. *Social and Psychological Factors in Stress.* New York: Holt,
Rinehart and Winston, 1970.

Mechanic, D. "Discussion of Research Programs on Relations Between
Stressful Life Events and Episodes of Physical Illness." In B. S. Dohrenwend and B. P. Dohrenwend (Eds.), *Stressful Life Events: Their Nature
and Effects.* New York: Wiley, 1974.

Mechanic, D., and Newton, M. "Some Problems in Analysis of Morbidity Data." *Journal of Chronic Diseases,* 1965, *18,* 569–580.

Mechanic, D., and Volkart, E. "Illness Behavior and Medical Diagnoses." *Journal of Health and Social Behavior,* 1960, *1,* 86–94.

Mechanic, D., and Volkart, E. "Stress, Illness Behavior, and Sick-Role." *American Sociological Review,* 1961, *26,* 51–58.

Medalie, J. H., and others. "Five-Year Myocardial Infarction Incidents. II: Association of Single Variables to Age and Birthplace." *Journal of Chronic Diseases,* 1973, *26,* 329–350.

Mednick, M. T., Schuch, J. R., and Weissman, H. J. "The Psychology of Women: Selected Topics." *Annual Review of Psychology,* 1975, *25.*

Meehl, P. E. "Theoretical Risks and Tabular Asterisks: Sir Karl, Sir Ronald, and the Slow Progress of Soft Psychology." *Journal of Consulting and Clinical Psychology,* 1978, *46,* 806–834.

Meek, J. L., and Neff, N. H. "Acidic and Neutral Metabolites of Norepinephrine: Their Metabolism and Transport from Brain." *Journal of Pharmacology and Experimental Therapeutics,* 1972, *181,* 457–465.

Meerloo, J. A. "Transference and Resistance in Geriatric Psychotherapy." *Psychoanalytic Review,* 1961, *42,* 72–82.

Meichenbaum, D. "Examination of Model Characteristics in Reducing Avoidance Behavior." *Journal of Personality and Social Psychology,* 1971, *17,* 298–307.

Meichenbaum, D. "Cognitive Modification of Test Anxious College Students." *Journal of Consulting and Clinical Psychology,* 1972, *39,* 370–380.

Meichenbaum, D. *Cognitive Behavior Modification: An Integrative Approach.* New York: Plenum, 1977.

Meichenbaum, D. H., Gilmore, J. B., and Fedoravicius, A. "Group Insight Versus Group Desensitization in Treating Speech Anxiety." *Journal of Consulting and Clinical Psychology,* 1971, *36,* 410–421.

Melamed, B. G., and Siegel, L. J. "Reduction of Anxiety in Children Facing Hospitalization and Surgery by Use of Filmed Modeling." *Journal of Consulting and Clinical Psychology,* 1975, *43,* 511–521.

Mendelson, J. H., LaDou, L., and Soloman, P. "Experimentally Induced Chronic Intoxication and Withdrawal in Alcoholics. III: Psychiatric Findings." *Quarterly Journal of Studies on Alcohol* (Supplement), 1964, *2,* 40–52.

Menninger, K. *Man Against Himself.* New York: Harcourt Brace Jovanovich, 1938.

Menninger, K. *The Crime of Punishment.* New York: Viking Press, 1966.

Menninger, K., Mayman, M., and Pruyser, P. *The Vital Balance.* New York: Viking Press, 1963.

Merton, R. K. *Social Theory and Social Structure.* New York: Free Press, 1957.

Mettlin, C., and Woelfel, J. "Interpersonal Influence and Symptoms of Stress." *Journal of Health and Social Behavior,* 1974, *15,* 311–319.

Meyer, A. E., Golle, R., and Weitemeyer, W. "Duration of Illness and Elevation of Neuroticism Scores." *Journal of Psychosomatic Research,* 1968, *11,* 347–355.

Meyer, E., Unger, H. T., and Slaughter, R. "Investigation of a Psychosocial Hypothesis in Appendectomies." *Psychosomatic Medicine,* 1964, *26,* 671–681.

Meyer, R. J., and Haggerty, R. J. "Streptococcal Infections in Families: Factors Altering Individual Susceptibility." *Pediatrics,* 1962, *29,* 539–549.

Meyers-Abell, J. E. "Biofeedback Versus Habituation in the Modification of Severe Phobic Behavior: A Psychophysiological Investigation." Unpublished doctoral dissertation, Northwestern University, 1976.

Miao, E. "An Exploratory Study on College Freshmen Mental Health Status." *Acta Psychologica Taiwanica,* 1976, *18,* 129–148.

Middleton, R. "Psychological Well-Being." In *Final Report of the Rural Negative Income Tax Experiment.* Vol. 5. Madison: Institute for Research on Poverty, University of Wisconsin, 1976.

Middleton, R., and Alken, V. "Social Psychological Effects." In H. Watts and A. Rees (Eds.), *The New Jersey Income Maintenance Experiment.* Vol. 3. New York: Academic Press, 1977.

Miehlke, A. *Surgery of the Facial Nerve.* Philadelphia: Saunders, 1973.

Miller, G. A., Galanter, E., and Pribram, K. *Plans and the Structure of Behavior.* New York: Holt, Rinehart and Winston, 1960.

Miller, I. W., III, and Norman, W. H. "Learned Helplessness in Humans: A Review and Attribution-Theory Model." *Psychological Bulletin,* 1979, *86,* 93–118.

Miller, N. E. "The Influence of Past Experience upon the Transfer of Subsequent Training." Unpublished doctoral dissertation, Yale University, 1935.

Miller, N. E. "Learning of Visceral and Glandular Responses." *Science,* 1969, *163,* 434–445.

Miller, N. E. "Biofeedback and Visceral Learning." *Annual Review of Psychology,* 1978, *29,* 373–404.

Miller, N. E., and Banuazizi, A. "Instrumental Learning by Curarized Rats of a Specific Visceral Response, Intestinal or Cardiac." *Journal of Comparative and Physiological Psychology,* 1968, *65,* 1–7.

Miller, N. E., and Carmona, A. "Modification of a Visceral Response, Salivation in Thirsty Dogs, by Instrumental Training with Water Reward." *Journal of Comparative and Physiological Psychology,* 1967, *63,* 1–6.

Miller, N. E., and DiCara, L. V. "Instrumental Learning of Heart Rate Changes in Curarized Rats." *Journal of Comparative and Physiological Psychology,* 1967, *63,* 12–19.

Miller, W. R., and Muñoz, R. F. *How to Control Your Drinking.* Englewood Cliffs, N.J.: Prentice-Hall, 1976.

Miller, W. R., Rosellini, R. A., and Seligman, M. E. P. "Learned Helplessness and Depression." In J. D. Maser and M. E. P. Seligman (Eds.), *Psychopathology: Experimental Models.* San Francisco: Freeman, 1977.

Mischel, W. *Personality and Assessment.* New York: Wiley, 1968.

Mischel, W. "Continuity and Change in Personality." *American Psychologist,* 1969, *24,* 1012–1018.

Mischel, W. "Toward a Cognitive Social Learning Reconceptualization of Personality." *Psychological Review,* 1973, *80,* 252–283.

Mishima, Y. *The Temple of the Golden Pavilion.* (I. Morris, Trans.) Berkeley, Calif.: Berkeley Publishing, 1971a.

Mishima, Y. *Thirst for Love.* (A. H. Marks, Trans.) Berkeley, Calif.: Berkeley Publishing, 1971b.

Mitchell, K. R., and Ng, K. T. "Effects of Group Counseling and Behavior

Therapy on the Academic Achievement of Test-Anxious Students." *Journal of Counseling Psychology*, 1972, *19* (6), 491–497.

Mitchell, M. R. "An Existential-Phenomenological Study of the Structure of Addiction with Alcohol as Revealed Through the Significant Life-Historical Drinking Situations or Alcohol Related Situations of One Self-Confirmed Alcoholic Male." Unpublished doctoral dissertation, Duquesne University, 1975.

Moberg, G. P., and others. "Effect of Sectioning the Fornix on Diurnal Fluctuation in Plasma Corticosterone Levels in the Rat." *Neuroendocrinology*, 1971, *7*, 11–15.

Moleski, R., and Tosi, D. J. "Comparative Psychotherapy: Rational-Emotive Therapy Versus Systematic Desensitization in the Treatment of Stuttering." *Journal of Consulting and Clinical Psychology*, 1976, *44*, 309–311.

Moos, R. H. "Situational Analysis of a Therapeutic Community Milieu." *Journal of Abnormal Psychology*, 1968, *73*, 49–61.

Moos, R. H. "Sources of Variance in Responses to Questionnaires and in Behavior." *Journal of Abnormal Psychology*, 1969, *74*, 405–412.

Moos, R. H. (Ed.). *Coping with Physical Illness*. New York: Plenum, 1977.

Moot, S. A., Cebulla, R. P., and Crabtree, J. M. "Instrumental Control and Ulceration in Rats." *Journal of Comparative and Physiological Psychology*, 1970, *71* (3), 405–410.

Morgan, G. A., and Ricciuti, H. N. "Infants' Responses to Strangers During the First Year." In B. M. Foss (Ed.), *Determinants of Infant Behaviour*. Vol. 4. London: Methuen, 1969.

Morrissey, E. R., and Schuckit, M. A. "Stressful Life Events and Alcohol Problems Among Women Seen at a Detoxification Center." *Quarterly Journal of Studies on Alcohol*, 1978, *39*, 1559–1576.

Moss, C. S. *Recovery with Aphasia: The Aftermath of My Stroke*. Urbana: University of Illinois Press, 1972.

Moss, G. E. *Illness, Immunity, and Social Interaction*. New York: Wiley, 1973.

Moulton, R. "Multiple Factors in Frigidity." In J. Masserman (Ed.), *Science and Psychoanalysis*. Vol. 10. New York: Grune and Stratton, 1966.

Moulton, R. "Survey and Re-evaluation of the Concept of Penis Envy." *Contemporary Psychoanalysis*, 1970, *7*, 84–104.

Moulton, R. "Psychoanalytic Reflections on Women's Liberation." *Contemporary Psychoanalysis*, 1972, *8* (2), 197–228.

Moulton, R. "Early Papers on Women." *American Journal of Psychoanalysis*, 1975, *35*, 207–223.

Moulton, R. "The Fear of Female Power—A Cause of Sexual Dysfunction." *Journal of the American Academy of Psychoanalysis*, 1977a, *5* (4), 499–519.

Moulton, R. "Some Effects of the New Feminism." *American Journal of Psychiatry*, 1977b, *134* (1), 1–6.

Moulton, R. "Women with Double Lives." *Contemporary Psychoanalysis*, 1977c, *13* (1), 64–84.

Moulton, R. "Ambivalence About Motherhood in Career Women." *Journal of the American Academy of Psychoanalysis*, 1979a, *7* (2), 241–257.

Moulton, R. "Psychological Challenges Confronting Women in the Sciences." *Annals of the New York Academy of Sciences*, 1979b, *323*, 321–325.

Moulton, R. "Divorce in the Middle Years." *Journal of the American Academy of Psychoanalysis,* in press.

Mowrer, O. H. "On the Dual Nature of Learning: A Reinterpretation of 'Conditioning' and 'Problem-Solving.'" *Harvard Educational Review,* 1947, *17,* 102–148.

Mowrer, O. H. *Learning Theory and the Symbolic Processes.* New York: Wiley, 1960.

Mowrer, O. H., and Ullman, A. D. "Time as a Determinant in Integrative Learning." *Psychology Review,* 1945, *52,* 2, 61–90.

Muñoz, R. F., and Kelly, J. C. *The Prevention of Mental Disorders.* Homewood, Ill.: Learning Systems, 1975.

Murray, E. J., and Jacobsen, L. I. "Cognition and Learning in Traditional and Behavioral Psychotherapy." In S. L. Garfield and A. E. Bergin (Eds.), *Handbook of Psychotherapy and Behavior Change: An Empirical Analysis.* (2nd ed.) New York: Wiley, 1978.

Murray, H. A. *Explorations in Personality.* New York: Oxford University Press, 1938.

Mutter, A. Z., and Schleifer, M. J. "The Role of Psychological and Social Factors in the Onset of Somatic Illness in Children." *Psychosomatic Medicine,* 1966, *28,* 333–343.

Myers, J., Lindenthal, J., and Pepper, M. P. "Life Events and Psychiatric Impairment." *Journal of Nervous and Mental Disease,* 1971, *152,* 149–157.

Myers, J., Lindenthal, J., and Pepper, M. P. "Life Events and Mental Status: A Longitudinal Study." *Journal of Health and Social Behavior,* 1972, *13,* 398–406.

Myers, J., Lindenthal, J., and Pepper, M. P. "Social Class, Life Events, and Psychiatric Symptoms: A Longitudinal Study." In B. S. Dohrenwend and B. P. Dohrenwend (Eds.), *Stressful Life Events: Their Nature and Effects.* New York: Wiley, 1974.

Myers, J., Lindenthal, J., and Pepper, M. P. "Life Events, Social Integration and Psychiatric Symptomatology." *Journal of Health and Social Behavior,* 1975, *16,* 121–127.

Nadel, L., and O'Keefe, J. O. "The Hippocampus in Pieces and Patches: An Essay on Modes of Explanation in Physiological Psychology." In R. Bellaris and E. G. Gray (Eds.), *Essays on the Nervous System.* Oxford, England: Clarendon Press, 1974.

Nakadate, G. M., and deGroot, J. "Fornix Transection and Adrenocortical Function in Rats." *Anatomical Record,* 1963, *145,* 338.

Nally, M. "AMT: A Treatment for Delinquents." Unpublished doctoral dissertation, Colorado State University, 1975.

Nathan, P. E., and Lisman, S. A. "Behavioral and Motivational Patterns of Chronic Alcoholics." In R. E. Tarter and A. A. Sugerman (Eds.), *Alcoholism: Interdisciplinary Approaches to an Enduring Problem.* Reading, Mass.: Addison-Wesley, 1976.

Nathan, P. E., and others. "Behavioral Analysis of Alcoholism." *Archives of General Psychiatry,* 1970, *22,* 419–430.

Nauta, W. J. H. "An Experimental Study of the Fornix System in the Rat." *Journal of Comparative Neurology,* 1956, *104,* 247–272.

Nawas, M., Welch, W., and Fishman, T. "The Comparative Effectiveness of Pairing Aversive Imagery with Relaxation, Neutral Tasks, and Muscular Tension in Reducing Snake Phobia." *Behaviour Research and Therapy,* 1970, *8,* 63–68.

Needleman, H. L., and others. "Deficits in Psychologic and Classroom Performance of Children with Elevated Dentine Lead Levels." *New England Journal of Medicine,* 1979, *300,* 689–695.

Neisser, U. *Cognition and Reality.* San Francisco: Freeman, 1976.

Nelsen, E. A., Grinder, R. E., and Mutterer, M. L. "Sources of Variance in Behavioural Measures of Honesty in Temptation Situations: Methodological Analyses." *Developmental Psychology,* 1969, *1,* 265–279.

Neugarten, B. L., and Guttman, D. "Age-Sex Roles and Personality in Middle Age: A Thematic Apperception Study." *Psychological Monographs,* 1958, *72.*

Newcomb, T. M. "An Experiment Designed to Test the Validity of a Rating Technique." *Journal of Educational Psychology,* 1931, *22,* 279–289.

Newton, J. E. "Blood Pressure and Heart Rate Changes During Conditioning in Curarized Dogs." *Conditional Reflex,* 1967, *2* (2), 158.

Newton, J. E., and Gantt, W. H. "One Trial Cardiac Conditioning in Dogs." *Conditional Reflex,* 1966, *1,* 251–265.

Nicoletti, J. "Anxiety Management Training." Unpublished doctoral dissertation, Colorado State University, 1972.

Nisbet, R. E., and Wilson, T. D. "Telling More Than We Can Know: Verbal Reports on Mental Processes." *Psychological Review,* 1978, *84,* 231–259.

Nunberg, H. *Principles of Psychoanalysis.* New York: International Universities Press, 1955.

Nunberg, H., and Federn, P. (Eds.). *Minutes of the Vienna Psychoanalytic Society.* Vol. 1: *1906–1908.* New York: International Universities Press, 1962.

Obrist, P. A., and Webb, R. A. "Heart Rate During Conditioning in Dogs: Relationship to Somatic-Motor Activity." *Psychophysiology,* 1967, *4* (1), 7–34.

Obrist, P. A., and others. *Cardiovascular Psychophysiology.* Chicago: Aldine, 1974.

O'Connor, R. D. "Modification of Social Withdrawal Through Symbolic Modeling." *Journal of Applied Behavior Analysis,* 1969, *2,* 15–22.

O'Connor, R. D. "Relative Efficacy of Modeling, Shaping, and the Combined Procedures for Modification of Social Withdrawal." *Journal of Abnormal Psychology,* 1972, *79,* 327–334.

Olds, J. "Behavioral Studies of Hypothalamic Functions: Drives and Reinforcements." In R. G. Grenell and S. Gabay (Eds.), *Biological Foundations of Psychiatry.* Vol. 1. New York: Raven Press, 1976.

Ollendick, T. "Behavioral Treatment of Anorexia Nervosa: A Five Year Study." *Behavior Modification,* 1979, *3,* 124–135.

Olton, D. S., and Werz, M. A. "Hippocampal Function and Behavior: Spatial Discrimination and Response Inhibition." *Physiology and Behavior,* 1978, *20,* 597–605.

Olweus, D. "Stability of Aggressive Reaction Patterns in Males: A Review." *Psychological Bulletin,* 1979, *86,* 852–875.

O'Neil, J. F., Spielberger, C. D., and Hansen, D. N. "The Effects of State Anxiety and Task Difficulty on Computer-Assisted Learning." *Journal of Educational Psychology,* 1969, *60,* 343–350.

O'Neill, W. L. *Everyone Was Brave: Rise and Fall of Feminism in America.* New York: Quadrangle Books, 1969.

Oppenheimer, B. S. "Report on Neurocirculatory Asthenia and Its Management." *Military Surgeon,* 1918, *42,* 409–426.

Ornstein, A. C. "Politics of Accountability." *Educational Forum,* 1976, *41* (1), 61–68.

Ornstein, A. C. "Evaluation and Reform of Federal Intervention Programs." *Contemporary Education,* 1977, *48* (2), 92–97.

Ortega y Gasset, J. *Meditations on Quixote.* New York: Norton, 1961.

Oster, H. "Facial Expression and Affect Development." In M. Lewis and L. Rosenblum (Eds.), *The Genesis of Behavior.* Vol. 1: *The Development of Affect.* New York: Plenum, 1978.

Palola, E. G., Dorpat, T. L., and Larson, W. R. "Alcoholism and Suicidal Behavior." In D. J. Pittman and C. R. Snyder (Eds.), *Society, Culture, and Drinking Patterns.* New York: Wiley, 1962.

Pampiglione, G., and Falconer, M. A. "Some Observations upon Stimulation of the Hippocampus in Man." *Electroencephalography and Clinical Neurophysiology, Archives of Neurology and Psychiatry,* 1956, *8,* 718.

Papez, J. W. "A Proposed Mechanism of Emotion." *Archives of Neurology and Psychiatry,* 1937, *38,* 725–743.

Papilia, D. E. "The Status of Several Conservation Abilities Across the Life Span." *Human Development.* 1972, *15,* 229–243.

Papilia, D. E., and Bielby, D. D. "Cognitive Function in Middle and Old Age Adults." *Human Development,* 1974, *17* (6), 424–443.

Pappas, B. A., DiCara, L. V., and Miller, N. E. "Learning of Blood Pressure Responses in the Noncurarized Rat: Transfer to the Curarized State." *Physiology and Behavior,* 1970, *5* (9), 1029–1032.

Paré, W. P. "The Development of the Three-Stimulus Cardiac Discrimination Problem in Three Mammalian Species." *Psychophysiology,* 1970, *6,* 629–630.

Parens, H., McConville, B. J., and Kaplan, S. M. "The Prediction of Frequency of Illness from the Response to Separation." *Psychosomatic Medicine,* 1966, *28,* 162–176.

Pariser, S. F., and others. "Diagnosis and Management of Anxiety Symptoms and Syndromes." In J. M. Davis and D. S. Greenblatt (Eds.), *Psychopharmacology Update: New and Neglected Areas.* New York: Grune and Stratton, 1979a.

Pariser, S. F., and others. "Panic Attacks: Diagnostic Evaluation of 17 Patients." *American Journal of Psychiatry,* 1979b, *135,* 105–106.

Parkes, C. M. "Effects of Bereavement on Physical and Mental Health: A Study of the Medical Records of Widows." *British Medical Journal,* 1964, ii, 274–279.

Parkes, C. M., Benjamin, B., and Fitzgerald, R. G. "Broken Heart: A Statistical Study of Increased Mortality Among Widowers." *British Medical Journal,* 1969, *1,* 740–743.

Parkes, C. M., and Brown, R. J. "Health After Bereavement: A Controlled Study of Young Boston Widows and Widowers." *Psychosomatic Medicine,* 1972, *34,* 449–461.

Passman, R. H., and Mulhern, R. K. "Maternal Punitiveness as Affected by Situational Stress: An Experimental Analogue of Child Abuse." *Journal of Abnormal Psychology,* 1977, *86,* 565–569.

Patel, C. "Biofeedback-Aided Relaxation and Meditation in the Management of Hypertension." *Biofeedback and Self-Regulation,* 1977, *2,* 1–41.

Patterson, G. *Families: Applications of Social Learning to Family Life.* Champaign, Ill.: Research Press, 1971.

Patterson, G. "Interventions for Boys with Conduct Problems: Multiple Settings, Treatments, and Criteria." *Journal of Consulting and Clinical Psychology*, 1974, *42*, 471–481.

Pattison, E. M., Sobell, M. B., and Sobell, L. C. (Eds.). *Emerging Concepts of Alcohol Dependence*. New York: Springer, 1977.

Paul, G. L. *Insight Versus Desensitization in Psychotherapy*. Stanford, Calif.: Stanford University Press, 1966.

Paul, G. L. "Insight Versus Desensitization Two Years After Termination." *Journal of Consulting Psychology*, 1967, *31*, 333–348.

Paul, G. L. "Two Year Follow-Up of Systematic Desensitization in Therapy Groups." *Journal of Abnormal Psychology*, 1968, *73*, 119–130.

Paul, G. L. "Outcome of Systematic Desensitization. II: Controlled Investigations of Individual Treatment, Technique Variations, and Current Status." In C. M. Franks (Ed.), *Behavior Therapy: Appraisal and Status*. New York: McGraw-Hill, 1969.

Paul, G. L., and Shannon, D. "Treatment of Anxiety Through Systematic Densitization in Therapy Groups." *Journal of Abnormal Psychology*, 1966, *71*, 124–135.

Pavlov, I. P. "Über die Normalen Blutdruck-Schwankungen beim Hunde" [On Normal Blood Pressure Changes in Dogs]. *Archives Gesamte Physiologica*, 1879, *20*, 215.

Paykel, E. S. "Life Stress and Psychiatric Disorder: Applications of the Clinical Approach." In B. S. Dohrenwend and B. P. Dohrenwend (Eds.), *Stressful Life Events: Their Nature and Effects*. New York: Wiley, 1974a.

Paykel, E. S. "Recent Life Events and Clinical Depression." In E. K. Gunderson and R. H. Rahe (Eds), *Life Stress and Illness*. Springfield, Ill.: Thomas, 1974b.

Paykel, E. S., Prusoff, B. A., and Myers, J. K. "Suicide Attempts and Recent Life Events." *Archives of General Psychiatry*, 1975, *32*, 327–333.

Pearlin, L. I., and Leiberman, M. A. "Social Sources of Emotional Distress." In R. G. Simmons (Ed.), *Research in Community Mental Health*. Greenwich, Conn.: JAI Press, 1979.

Pearlin, L. I., and Schooler, C. "The Structure of Coping." *Journal of Health and Social Behavior*, 1978, *19*, 2–21.

Pecknold, J. C., Raeburn, J., and Poser, E. G. "Intravenous Diazepam for Facilitating Relaxation for Desensitization." *Journal of Behavior Therapy and Experimental Psychiatry*, 1972, *3*, 39.

Pennebaker, J. W., and others. "Lack of Control as a Determinant of Perceived Physical Symptoms." *Journal of Personality and Social Psychology*, 1977, *35*, 167–174.

Penny, D. P., Olson, J., and Averill, K. "Five Structural Studies of Rat Adrenal Cortices Following Prostaglandin Administration." *Zeitschrift für Zellforschung* [Journal of Cell Research], 1973, *146*, 297–307.

Perkins, D. N. "Evaluating Social Interventions: Conceptual Schema." *Evaluation Quarterly*, 1977, *4*, 639–650.

Perowsky, G. "Reactions and Associations to Death and Dying." Unpublished term paper, City College, New York, 1979.

Pervin, L. A. "Performance and Satisfaction as a Function of Individual-Environment Fit." *Psychological Bulletin*, 1968, *69*, 57–68.

Pervin, L. A. *Current Controversies and Issues in Personality*, New York: Wiley, 1978a.

Pervin, L. A. "Definitions, Measurements, and Classification of Stimuli, Situations, and Environments." *Human Ecology,* 1978b, *6,* 71-105.

Pervin, L. A., and Lewis, M. "Overview of the Internal-External Issue." In L. A. Pervin and M. Lewis (Eds.), *Perspectives in Interactional Psychology,* New York: Plenum, 1978.

Peterfreund, E. "Information Systems and Psychoanalysis: An Evolutionary, Biological Approach to Psychoanalytic Theory." *Psychological Issues,* 1971, *7,* 1-397.

Pfaff, D. W., Silva, M. T. A., and Weiss, J. M. "Telemetered Recording of Hormone Effects on Hippocampal Neurons." *Science,* 1971, *172,* 394-395.

Pfeiffer, E. "Psychotherapy with Elderly Patients." In L. Bellak and T. Karascu (Eds.). *Geriatric Psychiatry.* New York: Grune and Stratton, 1976.

Phares, E. J. *Locus of Control in Personality.* Morristown, N. J.: General Learning Press, 1976.

Philips, R., Johnson, G., and Geyer, A. "Self-Administered Systematic Desensitization." *Behaviour Research and Therapy.* 1972, *10,* 93-96.

Phillips, D. L. "The 'True Prevalence' of Mental Illness in New England States." *Community Mental Health Journal,* 1966, *2,* 35-40.

Piaget, J. "Principle Factors Determining Intellectual Evaluation from Childhood to Adult Life " [1930]. In D. Rapaport, *Organization and Pathology of Thought.* Austen Riggs Foundation Monograph 1. New York: Columbia University Press, 1951.

Piaget, J. *Psychology of Intelligence.* Totowa, N. J.: Littlefield, Adams, 1963.

Pitts, F. N. "The Biochemistry of Anxiety." *Scientific American,* 1969, *220,* 69-75.

Pitts, F. N., and McClure, J. N. "Lactate Metabolism in Anxiety Neurosis," *New England Journal of Medicine,* 1967, *227,* 1329-1336.

Plaut, T. F. *Alcohol Problems: A Report to the Nation by the Cooperative Commission on the Study of Alcoholism.* New York: Oxford University Press, 1967.

Popova, N. K., and Naumenko, E. V. "Dominance Relations and the Pituitary-Adrenal System in Rats." *Animal Behavior,* 1972, *20,* 108-111.

Portnoy, I. "The Anxiety States." In S. Arieti (Ed.), *American Handbook of Psychiatry.* Vol. I. New York: Basic Books, 1959.

Poser, E. G. "Strategies for Behavioral Prevention." In P. O. Davidson (Ed.), *The Behavioral Management of Anxiety, Depression, and Pain.* New York: Brunner/Mazel, 1976.

Poser, E. G., and King, M. D. "Primary Prevention of Fear: An Experimental Approach." In I. G. Sarason and C. D. Spielberger (Eds.), *Stress and Anxiety.* Vol. 2. New York: Wiley, 1976.

Post, R. M., and others. "Slow and Rapid Alterations in Motor Activity, Sleep, and Biochemistry in a Cycling Manic-Depressive Patient." *Archives of General Psychiatry,* 1977, *34,* 470-479.

Powers, R. J., and Kutash, I. L. "Substance-Induced Aggression." In I. L. Kutash, S. B. Kutash, and L. B. Schlesinger (Eds.), *Violence: Perspectives on Murder and Aggression.* San Francisco: Jossey-Bass, 1978.

Pranulis, M. "Coping with Acute Myocardial Infarction." In W. D. Gentry and R. B. Williams, Jr. (Eds.), *Psychological Aspects of Myocardial Infarction and Coronary Care.* St. Louis: Mosby, 1975.

Pribram, K. H. "Emotion: Steps Toward a Neuropsychological Theory." In

D. Glass (Ed.), *Neurophysiology and Emotion*. New York: Russell Sage Foundation, 1967.

Price, J. S. "The Ritualization of Agonistic Behavior as a Determinant of Variation Along the Neuroticism/Stability Dimension of Personality." *Proceedings of the Royal Society of Medicine,* 1969, *62,* 1107–1110.

Prokasy, W. F. (Ed.). *Classical Conditioning: A Symposium.* New York: Appleton-Century-Crofts, 1965.

Quarantelli, E. L., and Dynes, R. R. "Response to Social Crises and Disaster." *Annual Review of Sociology,* 1977, *3,* 23–49.

Rabkin, J. G., and Struening, E. L. "Life Events, Stress, and Illness." *Science,* 1976a, *194,* 1013–1020.

Rabkin, J. G., and Struening, E. L. "Social Change, Stress, and Illness: A Selective Literature Review." *Psychoanalysis and Contemporary Science,* 1976b, *5,* 573–624.

Rachman, S. "Systematic Desensitization." *Psychological Bulletin,* 1967, *67,* 93–103.

Rachman, S. "The Conditioning Theory of Fear-Acquisition: A Critical Examination." *Behaviour Research and Therapy,* 1977, *15* (5), 375–387.

Rachman, S. *Fear and Courage.* San Francisco: Freeman, 1978.

Rachman, S., and Hodgson, R. "Synchrony and Desynchrony in Fear and Avoidance." *Behaviour Research and Therapy,* 1974, *12,* 311–318.

Rachman, S., Hodgson, R., and Marks, I. "The Treatment of Chronic Obsessive-Compulsive Neurosis." *Behaviour Research and Therapy,* 1971, *9,* 237–247.

Rado, S. "Fear of Castration in Women." *Psychoanalytic Quarterly,* 1933, *2,* 425–474.

Rahe, R. H. "Life Change and Subsequent Illness Reports." In E. K. Gunderson and R. H. Rahe (Eds.), *Life Stress and Illness.* Springfield, Ill.: Thomas, 1974.

Rahe, R. H., and Arthur, R. J. "Life Change and Illness Studies: Past History and Future Directions." *Journal of Human Stress,* 1978, *4,* 3–15.

Rahe, R. H., Bennett, L., and Romo, M. "Subjects' Recent Life Changes and Coronary Heart Disease in Finland." *American Journal of Psychiatry,* 1973, *130,* 1222–1226.

Rahe, R. H., and Lind, E. "Psychosocial Factors and Sudden Cardiac Death: A Pilot Study," *Journal of Psychosomatic Research,* 1971,*15,* 19–24.

Rahe, R. H., and Paasikivi, J. "Psychosocial Factors and Myocardial Infarction. II: An Outpatient Study in Sweden." *Journal of Psychosomatic Research,* 1971, *15,* 33–39.

Rahe, R. H., Romo, M., and Bennett, L. "Recent Life Changes, Myocardial Infarction, and Abrupt Coronary Death. Studies in Helsinki." *Archives of Internal Medicine,* 1974, *133,* 221–228.

Rahe, R. H., and others. "Social Stress and Illness Onset." *Journal of Psychosomatic Research,* 1964, *8,* 35–44.

Rahe, R. H., and others. "Psychosocial Predictors of Illness Behavior and Failure in Stressful Training." *Journal of Health and Social Behavior,* 1972, *13,* 393–397.

Ramsey, D. A. "Form and Characteristics of the Cardiovascular Conditional Response in Rhesus Monkeys." *Conditional Reflex,* 1970, *5* (1), 36–51.

Ramzy, I., and Wallerstein, R. S. "Pain, Fear, and Anxiety." *Psychoanalytic Study of the Child,* 1958, *13,* 147–189.

Rangell, L. "On the Psychoanalytic Theory of Anxiety: A Statement of a

Unitary Theory." *Journal of the American Psychoanalytic Association,* 1955, *3,* 384–414.

Rangell, L. "The Scope of Intrapsychic Conflict." *Psychoanalytic Study of the Child.* 1963, *18,* 75–102.

Rangell, L. "A Further Attempt to Resolve the 'Problem of Anxiety.'" *Journal of the American Psychoanalytic Association,* 1968, *16,* 371–404.

Rapaport, D., Gill, M., and Schafer, R. *Diagnostic Psychological Testing.* (2 vols.) Chicago: Year Book, 1945.

Rappaport, H., and Katkin, E. S. "Relationships Among Manifest Anxiety, Response to Stress, and the Perception of Autonomic Activity." *Journal of Consulting and Clinical Psychology,* 1972, *38,* 219–224.

Raskin, M., Johnson, G., and Rondestvedt, J. W. "Chronic Anxiety Treated by Feedback-Induced Muscle Relaxation." *Archives of General Psychiatry,* 1973, *28,* 263–267.

Raush, H. L., Dittmann, A. T., and Taylor, T. J. "The Interpersonal Behavior of Children in Residential Treatment." *Journal of Abnormal and Social Psychology,* 1959a, *58,* 9–26.

Raush, H. L., Dittmann, A. T., and Taylor, T. J. "Person, Setting and Change in Social Interaction." *Human Relations,* 1959b, *12,* 361–378.

Raush, H. L., Farbman, I., Llewellyn, L. G. "Person, Setting and Change in Social Interaction. II: A Normal Control Study." *Human Relations,* 1960, *13,* 305–333.

Rawlings, G. B. (Ed. and Trans.). *Pascal's Pensees.* Mt. Vernon, N.Y., 1946.

Razran, G. "The Observable Unconscious and the Inferable Conscious in Current Soviet Psychophysiology: Interoceptive Conditioning, Semantic Conditioning, and the Orienting Reflex." *Psychological Review,* 1961, *68,* 81–147.

Redfield, J., and Stone, A. "Individual Viewpoints of Stressful Life Events." *Journal of Consulting and Clinical Psychology,* 1979, *47,* 147–154.

Redmond, D. E., Jr., Huang, Y., and Gold, M. S. "Anxiety: The Locus Coeruleus Connection." *Neuroscience Abstracts,* 1977, *3,* 258.

Reed, H. B., and Reitan, R. M. "Changes in Psychological Test Performance Associated with the Normal Aging Process." *Journal of Gerontology,* 1963, *18,* 271–274.

Rees, W. D., and Lutkins, S. C. "The Mortality of Bereavement." *British Medical Journal,* 1967, *4,* 13–16.

Reid, D. W., and Ware, E. E. "Multidimensionality of Internal-External Control: Implications for Past and Future Research." *Canadian Journal of Behavioural Science,* 1973, *5,* 264–270.

Reimer, J. D., and Petras, M. L. "Breeding Structure of the House Mouse, *Mus Musculus,* in a Population Cage." *Journal of Mammalogy,* 1967, *48,* 88–99.

Reiss, S. "Pavlovian Conditioning and Human Fear: An Expectancy Model." Unpublished manuscript, University of Illinois at Chicago Circle, 1979.

Rescorla, R. A., and Solomon, R. L. "Two Process Learning Theory: Relationships Between Pavlovian Conditioning and Instrumental Learning." *Psychological Review,* 1967, *74,* 151–182.

Revitch, E. "Paroxysmal Manifestations of Non-epileptic Origin: Catathymic

Attacks." *Diseases of the Nervous System,* 1964, *25,* 662–669.

Revitch, E. "Psychiatric Evaluation and Classification of Anti-social Activities." *Diseases of the Nervous System,* 1975, *36,* 419–421.

Revitch, E. "Classification of Offenders for Prognostic and Dispositional Evaluation." *Bulletin of the Academy of Law and Psychiatry,* 1977, *5,* 1–11.

Revitch, E., and Schlesinger, L. B. "Murder: Evaluation, Classification, and Prediction." In I. L. Kutash, S. B. Kutash, and L. B. Schlesinger (Eds.), *Violence: Perspectives on Murder and Aggression.* San Francisco: Jossey-Bass, 1978.

Rheingold, H. L., and Eckerman, C. O. "Fear of the Stranger: A Critical Examination." In H. W. Reese (Ed.), *Advances in Child Development and Behavior.* Vol. 8. New York: Academic Press, 1973.

Richardson, F., and Suinn, R. "A Comparison of Traditional Systematic Desensitization, Accelerated Massed Desensitization, and Anxiety Management Training in the Treatment of Mathematics Anxiety." *Behavior Therapy,* 1973a, *4,* 212–218.

Richardson, F., and Suinn, R. "Effects of Two Short-Term Desensitization Methods in the Treatment of Test Anxiety." Unpublished manuscript, 1973b.

Rickels, K. "Antineurotic Agents: Specific and Non-specific Effects." In D. H. Efron and others (Eds.), *Psychopharmacology: A Review of Progress 1957–1967.* Washington, D.C.: Department of Health, Education and Welfare, 1968.

Rickels, K., Downing, R. W., and Winokur, A. "Antianxiety: Clinical Use in Psychiatry." In L. L. Iverson, S. D. Iverson, and S. H. Snyder (Eds.), *Handbook of Psychopharmacology.* Vol. 13. New York: Plenum, 1978.

Rickels, K., and Hesbacher, P. T. "Over-the-Counter Daytime Sedatives: A Controlled Study." *Journal of the American Medical Association,* 1973, *223,* 29–33.

Riegel, K. F., and Meacham, J. A. "Dialectics, Transaction, and Piaget's Theory." In L. A. Pervin and M. Lewis (Eds.), *Perspectives in Interactional Psychology.* New York: Plenum, 1978.

Rimm, D. C., and Litvak, S. B. "Self-Verbalization and Emotional Arousal." *Journal of Abnormal Psychology,* 1969, *74,* 181–187.

Rinoldi, H. J. A., and Vanderwoude, K. W. "Aging and Problem Solving." *Archives of General Psychiatry,* 1969, *20,* 215–225.

Ritter, B. "The Use of Contact Desensitization, Demonstration-Plus-Participation, and Demonstration Alone in the Treatment of Acrophobia." *Behaviour Research and Therapy,* 1969, *7,* 157–164.

Rizley, R., and Reppucci, N. D. "Pavlovian Conditioned Inhibitory Processes in Behavior Therapy." In B. A. Maher (Ed.), *Progress in Experimental Personality Research.* Vol. 7. New York: Academic Press, 1974.

Robbins, P. R., Tanck, R. H., and Meyersburg, H. A. "A Study of Three Psychosomatic Hypotheses." *Journal of Psychosomatic Research,* 1972, *16,* 93–97.

Robinson, C., and Suinn, R. "Group Desensitization of a Phobia in Massed Sessions." *Behaviour Research and Therapy,* 1969, *7,* 319.

Rodgers, D. A. "Factors Underlying Differences in Alcohol Preferences Among Inbred Strains of Mice." *Psychosomatic Medicine,* 1966, *28,* 498–513.

Roessler, R. "Personality, Psychophysiology, and Performance." *Psychophysiology*, 1973, *10*, 315–327.

Roessler, R., and Greenfield, N. S. "Personality Determinants of Medical Clinic Consultation." *Journal of Nervous and Mental Disease*, 1958, *127*, 142–145.

Roessler, R., and Greenfield, N. S. "Incidence of Somatic Disease in Psychiatric Patients." *Psychosomatic Medicine*, 1961, *23*, 413–419.

Roghmann, K. J., and Haggerty, R. J. "Daily Stress, Illness, and the Use of Health Services in Young Families." *Pediatric Research*, 1973, *7*, 520–526.

Rolls, E. T. *The Brain and Reward*. Oxford, England: Pergamon Press, 1975.

Roper, G., Rachman, S., and Marks, I. "Passive and Participant Modeling in Exposure Treatment of Obsessive-Compulsive Neurotics." *Behaviour Research and Therapy*, 1975, *13*, 271–279.

Rose, R. M., and Levin, M. A. "The Crisis in Stress Research: A Critical Reappraisal of the Role of Stress in Hypertension, Gastrointestinal Illness, and Female Reproductive Function." *Journal of Human Stress*, 1979, *5*, 4–48.

Rosen, G. *Don't Be Afraid: A Program for Overcoming Your Fears and Phobias*. Englewood Cliffs, N.J.: Prentice-Hall, 1976.

Rosen, J. C., and Wiens, A. N. "Changes in Medical Problems and Use of Medical Services Following Psychological Intervention." *American Psychologist*, 1979, *34*, 420–431.

Rosenman, R. H., and others. "Multivariate Prediction of Coronary Heart Disease During 8.5 Year Follow-Up in the Western Collaborative Group Study." *Amerian Journal of Cardiology*, 1976, *37*, 903–910.

Rosenthal, T., and Bandura, A. "Psychological Modeling: Theory and Practice." In S. L. Garfield and A. E. Bergin (Eds.), *Handbook of Psychotherapy and Behavior Change: An Empirical Analysis*. (2nd ed.) New York: Wiley, 1978.

Rosenthal, T. L., and Reese, S. L. "The Effects of Covert and Overt Modeling on Assertive Behavior." *Behaviour Research and Therapy*, 1976, *14*, 463–469.

Ross, C. E., and Mirowsky, J. "A Comparison of Life-Event-Weighting Schemes: Change, Undesirability, and Effect-Proportional Indices." *Journal of Health and Social Behavior*, 1979, *20*, 166–177.

Rossi, A. S. "A Biosocial Perspective on Parenting." *Daedalus* (Special Issue on the Family), 1977, *106* (2), 1–31.

Rossi, P. "Boobytraps and Pitfalls in the Evaluation of Social Action Programs." In C. H. Weis (Ed.), *Evaluating Action Programs*. Boston: Allyn and Bacon, 1972.

Roth, M. "The Phobic Anxiety-Depersonalization Syndrome." *Proceedings of the Royal Society of Medicine*, 1959, *32*, 587–595.

Roth, M., and others. "Studies in the Classification of Affective Disorders. I: The Relationship Between Anxiety States and Depressive Illnesses." *British Journal of Psychiatry*, 1972, *121*, 147–161.

Rotter, J. B. *Social Learning and Clinical Psychology*. Englewood Cliffs, N.J.: Prentice-Hall, 1954.

Rotter, J. B. "Generalized Expectancies for Internal Versus External Control of Reinforcement." *Psychological Monographs*, 1966, *80* (1, Whole No. 609).

Rotter, J. B. "Some Problems and Misconceptions Related to the Construct of Internal Versus External Control of Reinforcement." *Journal of Consulting and Clinical Psychology*, 1975, *43*, 56–67.

Rubin, K. "Egoncentrism in Childhood." *Child Development*, 1973, *44*, 102–110.

Rubin, L. R. (Ed.). *Reanimation of the Paralyzed Face*. St. Louis: Mosby, 1977.

Rubin, M. "Verbally Suggested Responses as Reciprocal Inhibition of Anxiety," *Journal of Behavior Therapy and Experimental Psychiatry*, 1972, *3*, 273.

Rubin, R. T. "Biochemical and Neuroendocrine Responses to Severe Psychological Stress." In E. K. Gunderson and R. H. Rahe (Eds.), *Life Stress and Illness*. Springfield, Ill.: Thomas, 1974.

Rubin, R. T., and Rahe, R. H. "U.S. Navy Underwater Demolition Team Training: Biochemical Studies." In E. K. Gunderson and R. H. Rahe (Eds.), *Life Stress and Illness*. Springfield, Ill.: Thomas, 1974.

Rubin, R. T., and others. "The Stress of Aircraft Carrier Landings. II: 3-Methoxy-4-Hydroxyphenyl Glycol Excretion in Naval Aviators." *Psychosomatic Medicine*, 1970, *32*, 589–596.

Runyan, W. M. "The Life Course as a Theoretical Orientation: Sequences of Person-Situation Interaction." *Journal of Personality*, 1978, *46*, 569–593.

Ruotolo, A. "Dynamics of Sudden Murder." *American Journal of Psychoanalysis*, 1968, *28*, 162–178.

Ruotolo, A. "Neurotic Pride and Homicide." *American Journal of Psychoanalysis*, 1975, *35*, 1–16.

Rushing, W. A. "Individual Behavior and Suicide." In J. P. Gibbs (Ed.), *Suicide*. New York: Harper & Row, 1968.

Rushton, J. P. "Socialization and the Altruistic Behavior of Children." *Psychological Bulletin*, 1976, *83*, 898–913.

Rushton, J. P., and Endler, N. S. "Person by Situation Interactions in Academic Achievement." *Journal of Personality*, 1977, *45*, 297–309.

Russel, P. A. "Relationships Between Exploratory Behavior and Fear: A Review." *British Journal of Psychology*, 1973, *64*, 417–433.

Sachar, E. J. "Neuroendocrine Abnormalities in Depressive Illness." In E. J. Sachar (Ed.), *Topics in Psychoendocrinology*. New York: Grune and Stratton, 1976.

Sachar, E. J., and others. "Cortisol Production in Depressions." In T. A. Williams, M. M. Katz, and J. A. Shield (Eds.), *Recent Advances in the Psychobiology of the Depressive Illnesses*. (Publ. No. HSM-70-9053.) Washington, D.C.: Department of Health, Education and Welfare, 1972.

Sadava, S. W., Thistle, R., Forsyth, R. "Stress, Escapism, and Patterns of Alcohol and Drug Use." *Quarterly Journal of Studies on Alcohol*, 1978, *39*, 725–736.

Sainsbury, P. "Psychosomatic Disorders and Neurosis in Outpatients Attending a General Hospital." *Journal of Psychosomatic Research*, 1960, *4*, 261–273.

Salter, A. *Conditioned Reflex Therapy*. New York: Creative Age Press, 1949.

Salzman, L. *The Obsessive Personality*. New York: Science House, 1968.

Sampson, H., and others. "Defense Analysis and the Emergence of Warded-Off Mental Contents: An Empirical Study." *Archives of General Psychiatry*, 1972, *26*, 524–532.

Samuels, I. "Hippocampal Lesions in the Rat: Effects on Spatial and Visual Habits." *Physiology and Behavior*, 1972, *8*, 1093–1098.

Sandler, J. "The Background of Safety." *International Journal of Psychoanalysis,* 1960, *41,* 352–356.

Sandler, J. "Trauma, Strain and Development." In S. Furst (Ed.), *Psychic Trauma.* New York: Basic Books, 1967.

Sappington, A., Staats, T., and Healey, C. "An Inexpensive Flex System of Automated Desensitization." *Behavior Therapy,* 1978, *9,* 683.

Sarason, I. G. "Test Anxiety, Attention and the General Problem of Anxiety." In C. D. Spielberger and I. G. Sarason (Eds.), *Stress and Anxiety.* Vol. 1. Washington, D.C.: Hemisphere, 1975a.

Sarason, I. G. "Test Anxiety and the Self-Disclosing Coping Model." *Journal of Consulting and Clinical Psychology,* 1975b, *43,* 148–153.

Sarason, I. G., Smith, R. E., and Diener, E. "Personality Research: Components of Variance Attributable to the Person and the Situation." *Journal of Personality and Social Psychology,* 1975, *32,* 199–204.

Sarason, S. B., and Mandler, G. "Some Correlates of Test Anxiety." *Journal of Abnormal and Social Psychology,* 1952, *47,* 810–817.

Sarason, S. B., and others. *Anxiety in Elementary School Children.* New York: Wiley, 1960.

Sassenrath, E. N. "Increased Adrenal Responsiveness Related to Social Stress in Rhesus Monkeys." *Hormones and Behavior,* 1970, *1,* 238–298.

Satin, D. G. "Life Stresses and Psychosocial Problems in the Hospital Emergency Unit." *Social Psychiatry,* 1972, *7,* 119–126.

Satten, J., Menninger, K., and Mayman, M. "Murder Without Apparent Motive: A Study in Personality Disorganization." *American Journal of Psychiatry,* 1960, *117,* 48–53.

Savage, R. D. "Psychometric Techniques." In J. G. Howells (Ed.), *Modern Perspectives in the Psychiatry of Old Age.* New York: Brunner/Mazel, 1975.

Savage, R. D., and others. "A Developmental Investigation of Intellectual Functioning in the Community Aged." *Journal of Genetic Psychology,* 1972, *121* (1), 163–167.

Sawrey, J. M., and Sawrey, W. L. "Age, Weight, and Social Effects on Ulceration Rate in Rats." *Journal of Comparative and Physiological Psychology,* 1966, *61,* 464–466.

Scanzoni, J. "Sex Roles, Economic Factors, and Marital Solidarity in Black and White Marriages." *Journal of Marriage and the Family,* 1975, *37,* 130–144.

Scarr, S., and Salapatek, P. "Patterns of Fear Development During Infancy." *Merrill-Palmer Quarterly of Behavior and Development,* 1970, *16,* 53–90.

Schachter, S. "The Interaction of Cognitive and Physiological Determinants of an Anxiety State." In C. D. Spielberger (Ed.), *Anxiety and Behavior.* New York: Academic Press, 1966.

Schachter, S., and Singer, J. E. "Cognitive, Social, and Physiological Determinants of Emotional State." *Psychological Review,* 1962, *69,* 379–399.

Schaffer, H. R. "Cognitive Components of the Infant's Response to Strangeness." In M. Lewis and L. Rosenblum (Eds.), *The Origins of Behavior.* Vol. 2: *The Origins of Fear.* New York: Wiley, 1974.

Schaffer, H. R., and Emerson, P. E. "The Development of Social Attachment in Infancy." *Monographs of the Society for Research in Child Development,* 1964, *29* (3, Serial No. 94).

Schecter, D. E. "Fear of Success in Women: A Psychodynamic Reconstruction." *Journal of the American Academy of Psychoanalysis,* 1979, *7* (1), 33–45.

Schildkraut, J. J. "The Catecholamine Hypothesis of Affective Disorders: A Review of Supporting Evidence." *American Journal of Psychiatry,* 1965, *122,* 509–522.

Schildkraut, J. J. "Norepinephrine Metabolites as Biochemical Criteria for Classifying Depressive Disorders and Predicting Response to Treatment: Preliminary Findings." *American Journal of Psychiatry,* 1973, *130,* 695–698.

Schildkraut, J. J., and others. "MHPG Excretion in Depressive Disorders: Relation to Clinical Subtypes and Desynchronized Sleep." *Science,* 1973, *181,* 762–764.

Schlesinger, L. B., and Kutash, I. L. "The Criminal Fantasy Technique: A Comparison of Sex Offenders and Substance Abusers." *Journal of Clinical Psychology,* in press.

Schmale, A. "Relationship of Separation and Depression to Disease." *Psychosomatic Medicine,* 1958, *20,* 259–277.

Schmale, A. "Psychic Trauma During Bereavement." *International Psychiatric Clinics,* 1971, *8,* 147–168.

Schmale, A. "Giving Up as a Final Common Pathway to Changes in Health." *Advances in Psychosomatic Medicine,* 1972, *8,* 20–40.

Schnurer, A. T., Rubin, R. R., and Roy, A. "Systematic Desensitization of Anorexia Nervosa Seen as a Weight Problem." *Journal of Behavior Therapy and Experimental Psychiatry,* 1973, *4,* 149–153.

Schoenfeld, W. N. "Problems of Modern Behavior Therapy." *Conditional Reflex,* 1972, *7,* 33–65.

Schoenfeld, W. N., Matos, M. A., and Snapper, A. C. "Cardiac Conditioning in the White Rat with Food Presentation as Unconditional Stimulus." *Conditional Reflex,* 1967, *2* (1), 56–67.

Schultz, J. H., and Luthe, W. *Autogenic Training: A Physiologic Approach in Psychotherapy.* New York: Grune and Stratton, 1959.

Schultz, N. P., and Hoyer, W. J. "Feedback Effects on Spatial Egocentrism in Old Age." *Journal of Gerontology,* 1976, *31* (1), 72–75.

Schulz, R. "The Effects of Control and Predictability on the Physical and Psychological Well-Being of the Institutionalized Aged." *Journal of Personality and Social Psychology,* 1976, *33,* 563–573.

Schur, M. "The Ego in Anxiety." In R. M. Loewenstein (Ed.), *Drives, Affects, and Behavior.* New York: International Universities Press, 1953.

Schur, M. "Comments on the Metapsychology of Somatization." *Psychoanalytic Study of the Child,* 1955, *10,* 119–164.

Schur, M. "The Ego and the Id in Anxiety." *Psychoanalytic Study of the Child,* 1958, *13,* 190–220.

Schur, M. *The Id and the Regulatory Principles of Mental Functioning.* New York: International Universities Press, 1966.

Schuster, A. "Psychological Study of a 106-Year-Old Man." *American Journal of Psychiatry,* 1952, *109.*

Schwartz, A., Campos, J., and Baisel, E. "The Visual Cliff: Cardiac and Behavioral Correlates on the Deep and Shallow Sides at Five and Nine Months of Age." *Journal of Experimental Child Psychology,* 1973, *15,* 86–99.

Schwartz, E. K. "The Treatment of the Obsessive Patient in the Group Therapy Setting." *American Journal of Psychotherapy*, 1972, *26*, 352–361.

Schwartz, G. E. "Blood Pressure Biofeedback: Breakthrough or Bust?" Paper delivered at 86th annual convention of the American Psychological Association, Toronto, 1978.

Scotch, N. "Sociocultural Factors in the Epidemiology of Zulu Hypertension." *American Journal of Public Health*, 1963, *53*, 1205–1213.

Scott, J. P. "The Process of Primary Socialization in Canine and Human Infants." *Monographs of the Society for Research in Child Development*, 1963, *28* (1, Serial No. 85).

Sedlacek, K. "EMG and Thermal Feedback as a Treatment for Raynaud's Disease." *Biofeedback and Self-Regulation*, 1976, *1*, 318.

Sekiyama, S., and Yago, N. "A Study on the Correlation Between Function and Ultrastructure in Rat Adrenal Cortex." *Acta Pathologica Japonica*, 1972, *22*, 77–98.

Seligman, M. E. P. "Phobias and Preparedness." *Behavior Therapy*, 1971, *2*, 307–320.

Seligman, M. E. P. *Helplessness: On Depression, Development, and Death*. San Francisco: Freeman, 1975.

Sells, S. B. "On the Nature of Stress." In J. E. McGrath (Ed.), *Social and Psychological Factors in Stress*. New York: Holt, Rinehart and Winston, 1970.

Selye, H. "The General Adaptation Syndrome and the Diseases of Adaptation." *Journal of Clinical Endocrinology*, 1946, *6*, 117–230.

Selye, H. *The Physiology and Pathology of Exposure to Stress*. Montreal: Acta, Inc., 1950.

Selye, H. *The Stress of Life*. New York: McGraw-Hill, 1956.

Selye, H. *Stress Without Distress*. Philadelphia: Lippincott, 1974.

Selye, H. *The Stress of Life*. (2nd ed.) New York: McGraw-Hill, 1976a.

Selye, H. *Stress in Health and Disease*. Boston: Butterworths, 1976b.

Selye, H. *The Stress of My Life*. Toronto: McClelland and Stewart, 1977.

Selye, H. "On the Real Benefits of Eustress." *Psychology Today*, 1978, *2* (10), 60–64.

Sepinwall, J., and Cook, L. "Behavioral Pharmacology of Anxiety Drugs." In L. L. Iverson, S. D. Iverson, and S. H. Snyder (Eds.), *Handbook of Psychopharmacology*. New York: Plenum, 1978.

Serban, G. "The Significance of Ethology for Psychiatry." In G. Serban and A. Kling (Eds.), *Animal Models in Human Psychobiology*. New York: Plenum, 1976.

Shaffran, R., and Gouin-Décarie, T. "Short-Term Stability of Infants' Responses to Strangers." Paper presented at meeting of the Society for Research in Child Development, Philadelphia, March–April 1973.

Shapiro, D. *Neurotic Styles*. New York: Basic Books, 1965.

Shapiro, M. M., and Herendeen, D. L. "Food-Reinforced Inhibition of Conditional Salivation in Dogs." *Journal of Comparative and Physiological Psychology*, 1975, *88*, 628–632.

Shaw, D. W., and Thoresen, C. E. "Effects of Modeling and Desensitization in Reducing Dental Phobia." *Journal of Counseling Psychology*, 1974, *21*, 415–420.

Shearn, D. W. "Does the Heart Learn?" *Psychological Bulletin*, 1961, *58*, 452–458.

Shedletsky, R. "Trait Versus State Anxiety and Authoritarianism Rebelliousness." Unpublished doctoral dissertation, York University, Toronto, 1972.

Shedletsky, R., and Endler, N. S. "Anxiety: The State-Trait Model and the Interaction Model." *Journal of Personality*, 1974, *42*, 511–527.

Sheehan, D. V. "The Efficient Treatment of Phobic Disorders." In T. C. Manschreck (Ed.), *Psychiatric Medicine Update*. New York: Elsevier, 1979.

Sheffield, F. D. "Relation Between Classical Conditioning and Instrumental Learning." In W. F. Prokasy (Ed.), *Classical Conditioning*. New York: Appleton-Century-Crofts, 1965.

Sheldon, A., and Hooper, D. "An Inquiry into Health and Ill-Health and Adjustment in Early Marriage." *Journal of Psychosomatic Research*, 1969, *13*, 95–101.

Sherman, A. R. "Real-Life Exposure as a Primary Therapeutic Factor in Desensitization of Fear." *Journal of Abnormal Psychology*, 1972, *79*, 19–28.

Sherrington, C. S. *The Integrative Action of the Central Nervous System*. Cambridge, England: Cambridge University Press, 1947.

Shils, E. A., and Janowitz, M. "Cohesion and Disintegration in the Wehrmacht in World War II." *Public Opinion Quarterly,* ˙1948, *12*, 280–315.

Shoemaker, J. "Treatments for Anxiety Neurosis." Unpublished doctoral dissertation, Colorado State University, 1976.

Shure, M. B., and Spivack, G. "Means-Ends Thinking, Adjustment, and Social Class Among Elementary-School-Aged Children." *Journal of Consulting and Clinical Psychology*, 1972, *38*, 348–353.

Sidman, M. "Avoidance Conditioning with Brief Shock and No Exteroceptive Warning Signal." *Science*, 1953, *118*, 157–158.

Sidman, M., and others. "Quantitative Relations Between Avoidance Behavior and Pituitary-Adrenal Cortical Activity." *Journal of Experimental Analysis of Behavior*, 1962, *5*, 353–362.

Siegel, A. C. "Film Mediated Fantasy Aggression and Strength of Aggressive Drive." *Child Development*, 1956, *27*, 365–378.

Sifneos, P. *Short Term Psychotherapy and Emotional Crisis*. Cambridge, Mass.: Harvard University Press, 1972.

Siitonen, L., and Jänne, J. "The Effect of Beta-Blockers on Bowlers." In P. Kielholz (Ed.), *Beta-Blockers and the Central Nervous System*. Baltimore: University Park Press, 1977.

Silk, S. "The Breakdown of Cognitive Functions in Senile Dementia." Unpublished doctoral dissertation, Yeshiva University, 1971.

Silver, B. V., and Blanchard, E. B. "Biofeedback and Relaxation Training in the Treatment of Psychophysiological Disorders: Or Are the Machines Really Necessary?" *Journal of Behavioral Medicine*, 1978, *1* (2), 217–239.

Silverman, J. S. "Obsessional Disorders in Childhood and Adolescence." *American Journal of Psychotherapy*, 1972, *26*, 362–377.

Simmel, E. "War Neuroses." In S. Lorand (Ed.), *Psychoanalysis Today*. New York: International Universities Press, 1944.

Sipprelle, C. "Induced Anxiety." *Psychotherapy: Theory, Research, and Practice,* 1967, *4,* 36–40.

Skarin, K. "Cognitive and Contextual Determinants of Stranger Fear in Six- and Eleven-Month-Old Infants." *Child Development,* 1977, *48,* 537–544.

Skinner, B. F. *The Behavior of Organisms: An Experimental Analysis.* New York: Appleton-Century-Crofts, 1938.

Slade, P. D. "The Effects of Systematic Desensitization on Auditory Hallucinations." *Behaviour Research and Therapy,* 1972, *10,* 85–91.

Smith, M. L., and Glass, G. V. "Meta-analysis of Psychotherapy Outcome Studies." *American Psychologist,* 1977, *32,* 752–760.

Smith, R. C., Parker, E. S., and Noble, E. P. "Alcohol and Affect in Dyadic Social Interaction." *Psychosomatic Medicine,* 1975, *37,* 25–40.

Smith, R. E., Johnson, S. H., and Sarason, I. G. "Life Change, the Sensation Seeking Motive and Psychological Distress." *Journal of Consulting and Clinical Psychology,* 1978, *46* (2), 348–349.

Snapper, A. G., Pomerleau, O. F., and Schoenfeld, W. N. "Similarity of Cardiac CR Forms in the Rhesus Monkey During Several Experimental Procedures." *Conditional Reflex,* 1969, *4* (3), 212–220.

Sobel, E. "Regression in Later Life." Unpublished doctoral dissertation, Rutgers University, 1977.

Sobel, E. "Countertransference Issues with the Later Life Patient." *Contemporary Psychoanalysis,* 1980, *16* (2), 211–222.

Solomon, R. "Punishment." *American Psychologist,* 1964, *19,* 239–253.

Solomon, R. L., Kamin, L. J., and Wynne, L. C. "Traumatic Avoidance Learning: The Outcomes of Several Extinction Procedures with Dogs." *Journal of Abnormal and Social Psychology,* 1953, *48,* 291–302.

Southwick, C. H., and Bland, V. P. "Effect of Population Density on Adrenal Glands and Reproductive Organs of CFW Mice." *American Journal of Physiology,* 1959, *197,* 111–114.

Speisman, J. C., and others. "Experimental Reduction of Stress Based on Ego-Defense Theory." *Journal of Abnormal and Social Psychology,* 1964, *68,* 367–380.

Sperling, O. E. "The Interpretation of Trauma as a Command." *Psychoanalytic Quarterly,* 1950, *19,* 352–370.

Spicer, C. C., Stewart, D. N., and de R. Winser, D. M. "Perforated Peptic Ulcer During the Period of Heavy Air Raids." *Lancet,* 1944, *1,* 14.

Spielberger, C. D. "The Effects of Anxiety on Complex Learning and Academic Achievement." In C. D. Spielberger (Ed.), *Anxiety and Behavior.* New York: Academic Press, 1966a.

Spielberger, C. D. "Theory and Research on Anxiety." In C. D. Spielberger (Ed.), *Anxiety and Behavior.* New York: Academic Press, 1966b.

Spielberger, C. D. "Trait-State Anxiety and Motor Behavior." *Journal of Motor Behavior,* 1971, *3,* 265–279.

Spielberger, C. D. "Anxiety as an Emotional State." In C. D. Spielberger (Ed.), *Anxiety: Current Trends in Theory and Research.* Vol. 1. New York: Academic Press, 1972a.

Spielberger, C. D. (Ed.). *Anxiety: Current Trends in Theory and Research.* Vol. 2. New York: Academic Press, 1972b.

Spielberger, C. D. "Anxiety: State-Trait Process." In C. D. Spielberger and I. G. Sarason (Eds.), *Stress and Anxiety.* Vol. 1. New York: Halsted Press, 1975.

Spielberger, C. D. "The Nature and Measurement of Anxiety." In C. D. Spielberger and R. Diaz-Guerrero (Eds.), *Cross-Cultural Anxiety*. Washington, D.C.: Hemisphere, 1976.

Spielberger, C. D., Gorsuch, R. L., and Lushene, R. E. *Manual for the State-Trait Anxiety Inventory*. Palo Alto, Calif.: Consulting Psychologists Press, 1970.

Spilken, A. Z., and Jacobs, M. A. "Prediction of Illness Behavior from Measures of Life Crises, Manifest Distress, and Maladaptive Coping." *Psychosomatic Medicine*, 1971, *33*, 251–264.

Spitz, R. A. "Anxiety in Infancy." *International Journal of Psycho-analysis*, 1950, *31*, 138–143.

Spitz, R. A. *A Genetic Field Theory of Ego Formation*. New York: International Universities Press, 1959.

Spitz, R. A. *The First Year of Life*. New York: International Universities Press, 1965.

Spitzer, R. L., Endicott, J., and Robins, E. *Research Diagnostic Criteria*. (3rd ed.) New York: State Psychiatric Institute, Division of Biometrics Research, 1977.

Spivack, G., and Shure, M. B. *Social Adjustment of Young Children: A Cognitive Approach to Solving Real-Life Problems*. San Francisco: Jossey-Bass, 1974.

Sroufe, L. A. "Wariness of Strangers and the Study of Infant Development." *Child Development*, 1977, *48* (3), 731–746.

Sroufe, L. A., Waters, E., and Matas, L. "Contextual Determinants of Infant Affective Response." In M. Lewis and L. Rosenblum (Eds.), *The Origins of Behavior*. Vol. 2: *The Origins of Fear*: New York: Wiley, 1974.

Sroufe, L. A., and Wunsch, J. P. "The Development of Laughter in the First Year of Life." *Child Development*, 1972, *43*, 1326–1344.

Staats, A., and Staats, C. *Complex Human Behavior*. New York: Holt, Rinehart and Winston, 1963.

Stampfl, T. G. "Implosive Therapy: The Theory, the Subhuman Analogue, the Strategy, and the Technique. Part I: The Theory." In S. G. Armitage (Ed.), *Behavior Modification Techniques in the Treatment of Emotional Disorders*. Battle Creek, Mich.: V. A. Publication, 1967.

Steele, B. "The Child Abuser." In I. L. Kutash, S. B. Kutash, and L. B. Schlesinger (Eds.), *Violence: Perspectives on Murder and Aggression*. San Francisco: Jossey-Bass, 1978.

Sternbach, R. A. *Principles of Psychophysiology: An Introductory Text and Readings*. New York: Academic Press, 1966.

Stewart, D. N., and de R. Winser, D. M. "Incidence of Perforated Peptic Ulcer: Effect of Heavy Air Raids." *Lancet*, 1942, *1*, 259–261.

Stewart, G., and others. "Determinants of Sickness in Marine Recruits." *American Journal of Epidemiology*, 1969, *89*, 254–263.

Stewart, M. A., and others. "Adaptation and Conditioning of the Galvanic Skin Response in Psychiatric Patients." *Journal of Mental Science*, 1959, *105*, 1102–1111.

Stewart, W. *Psychoanalysis: The First Ten Years*. New York: Macmillan, 1967.

Stoeckle, J. D., and Davidson, G. E. "Bodily Complaints and Other Symptoms of Depressive Reaction." *Journal of the American Medical Association*, 1962, *180*, 134.

Stoeckle, J. D., and Davidson, G. E. "Communicating Aggrieved Feelings in the Patient's Initial Visit to a Medical Clinic." *Journal of Health and Social Behavior,* 1963, *4,* 199.

Stoeckle, J. D., Zola, I. K., and Davidson, G. E. "On Going to See the Doctor: The Contributions of the Patient to the Decision to Seek Medical Aid." *Journal of Chronic Diseases,* 1963, *16,* 975–989.

Stoeckle, J. D., Zola, I. K., and Davidson, G. E. "The Quantity and Significance of Psychological Distress in Medical Patients." *Journal of Chronic Diseases,* 1964, *17,* 959–970.

Stokes, P. E. "Studies on the Control of Adrenocortical Function in Depression." In T. A. Williams, M. M. Katz, and J. A. Shield (Eds.), *Recent Advances in the Psychobiology of the Depressive Illnesses.* (Publ. No. HSM-70-9053.) Washington, D.C.: Department of Health, Education and Welfare, 1972.

Stone, E. A. "Stress and Catecholamines." In A. Friedhoff (Ed.), *Catecholamines and Behavior.* Vol. 2: *Neuropsychopharmacology.* New York: Plenum, 1975.

Storck, P. A., Looft, W. R., and Hooper, F. H. "Interrelationships Among Piagetian Tasks and Traditional Measures of Cognitive Behavior in Mature and Aged Adults." *Journal of Gerontology,* 1972, *27,* 461–465.

Stotsky, B. "Use of Pharmacologic Agents for Geriatric Patients." In A. DiMascio and R. J. Shader (Eds.), *Clinical Handbook of Psychopharmacology.* New York: Aronson, 1976.

Stoyva, J. M. "A Rationale for Biofeedback Training in Stress Related Disorders." In F. Antonelli (Ed.), *Therapy in Psychosomatic Medicine.* Vol. 1. Rome: Edizioni Luigi Pozzi, 1977.

Stoyva, J. M., and Budzynski, T. H. "Cultivated Low Arousal: An Antistress Response?" In L. V. DiCara (Ed.), *Recent Advances in Limbic and Autonomic Nervous Systems Research.* New York: Plenum, 1974.

Suinn, R. M. "The Treatment of Test Anxiety by a Combination of Group and Individual Desensitization Methods." *Behaviour Research and Therapy,* 1968, *6,* 385.

Suinn, R. M. "Accelerated Massed Desensitization: Innovation in Short-Term Therapy." *Behavior Therapy,* 1970, *1,* 303.

Suinn, R. M. "Removing Emotional Obstacles to Learning and Performance." *Behavior Therapy,* 1972, *3,* 308.

Suinn, R. M. "Anxiety Management Training for General Anxiety." In R. M. Suinn and R. Weigel (Eds.), *The Innovative Psychological Therapies: Critical and Creative Incidents.* New York: Harper & Row, 1975a.

Suinn, R. M. "The Cardiac Stress Management Program for Type A Patients." *Cardiac Rehabilitation,* 1975b, *5* (4).

Suinn, R. M. "How to Break the Vicious Cycle of Stress." *Psychology Today,* 1976, *10,* 59–60.

Suinn, R. M. *Manual for Anxiety Management Training (AMT).* Fort Collins, Colo.: Rocky Mountain Behavioral Science Institute, 1977a.

Suinn, R. M. "Treatment of Phobias." In G. A. Harris (Ed.), *The Group Treatment of Human Problems.* New York: Grune and Stratton, 1977b.

Suinn, R. M. "A Behavioral Approach to Intervention." In T. Dembroski and others (Eds.), *Proceedings of the Forum on Coronary-Prone Behavior.* New York: Springer, 1978a.

Suinn, R. M. "Pattern A Behaviors and Heart Disease: Intervention Methods." In J. M. Ferguson and C. Taylor (Eds.), *Advances in Behavioral Medicine*. New York: Spectrum, 1978b.

Suinn, R. M., and Bloom, L. J. "Anxiety Management Training for Type A Persons." *Journal of Behavioral Medicine*, 1978, *1*, 25–35.

Suinn, R. M., Edie, C., and Spinelli, P. "Accelerated Massed Desensitization: Innovation in Short-Term Treatment." *Behavior Therapy*, 1970, *1*, 303–311.

Suinn, R. M., and Hall, R. "Marathon Desensitization Groups." *Behaviour Research and Therapy*, 1970, *8*, 97.

Suinn, R. M., and Richardson, F. "Anxiety Management Training: A Nonspecific Behavior Therapy Program for Anxiety Control." *Behavior Therapy*, 1971, *4*, 498–510.

Suinn, R. M., and others. "Automated Short-Term Desensitization." *Journal of College Student Personnel*, 1973, *14*, 471.

Sumitsuji, N., and others. "Electromyographic Investigation of the Facial Muscles." *Electromyography*, 1967, *12*, 77–96.

Summerskill, J., and Darling, C. D. "Group Differences in the Incidence of Upper Respiratory Complaints Among College Students." *Psychosomatic Medicine*, 1957, *19*, 315–319.

Sweeney, D. R., and Maas, J. W. "Specificity of Depressive Disease." *Annual Review of Medicine*, 1978, *29*, 219–229.

Sweeney, D. R., and Maas, J. W. "Plasma MHPG in Depressed Patients." In *Scientific Proceedings of the American Psychiatric Association*. Washington, D.C.: American Psychiatric Association, 1979a.

Sweeney, D. R., and Maas, J. W. "Stress and Noradrenergic Function in Depression." In R. A. Depue (Ed.), *The Psychobiology of the Depressive Disorders: Implications for the Effects of Stress*. New York: Academic Press, 1979b.

Sweeney, D. R., Maas, J. W., and Heninger, G. R. "State Anxiety, Physical Activity, and Urinary MHPG." *Archives of General Psychiatry*, 1978, *35*, 1418–1423.

Sweeney, D. R., Maas, J. W., and Pickar, D. "Central Noradrenergic Activity and State Variables in Affective Disorder." In E. Usdin, I. J. Kopin, and J. Barchas (Eds.), *Catecholamine: Basic and Clinical Frontiers*. Elmsford, N.Y.: Pergamon Press, 1979.

Sweeney, D. R., and others. "Plasma MHPG in Psychiatric Patients." Unpublished data, 1979.

Symonds, A. "Phobias After Marriage." *Journal of the American Psychoanalytic Association*, 1971, *31* (2), 144–152.

Szasz, T. S. "The Ego, the Body, and Pain." *Journal of the American Psychoanalytic Association*, 1955, *3*, 177–200.

Szasz, T. S. *Pain and Pleasure*. New York: Basic Books, 1957.

Szekely, L. "Biological Remarks on Fears Originating in Early Childhood." *International Journal of Psycho-analysis*, 1954, *35*, 57–67.

Takahashi, R., Nakahara, T., and Sakurai, Y. "Emotional Stress and Biochemical Responses of Manic-Depressive Patients." In *Psychoneuroendocrinology*. (Workshop conference of the International Society of Psychoneuroendocrinology.) Basel, Switzerland: Karger, 1974.

Tamaroff, M. "Separation Anxiety and Cognitive Functioning in Nursery

School Children." Unpublished doctoral dissertation, Cornell University, 1975.

Tamerin, J. S., and Mendelson, J. H. "The Psychodynamics of Chronic Inebriation: Observations of Alcoholics During the Process of Drinking in an Experimental Group Setting." *American Journal of Psychiatry,* 1969, *125,* 886–899.

Tarter, R. E., and Sugerman, A. A. (Eds.). *Alcoholism: Interdisciplinary Approaches to an Enduring Problem.* Reading, Mass.: Addison-Wesley, 1976.

Taylor, J. A. "A Personality Scale of Manifest Anxiety." *Journal of Abnormal and Social Psychology,* 1953, *48,* 285–290.

Tedeschi, J. T., Smith, R. B., III, and Brown, R. C., Jr. "A Reinterpretation of Research on Aggression." *Psychological Bulletin,* 1974, *81,* 540–563.

Teeters, N. K. *New Horizons in Criminology.* Englewood Cliffs, N.J.: Prentice-Hall, 1959.

Temerlin, M. K. "Suggestion Effects in Psychiatric Diagnosis." *Journal of Nervous and Mental Disease,* 1968, *147,* 349–353.

Tennant, C., and Andrews, G. "The Pathogenic Quality of Life Event Stress in Neurotic Impairment." *Archives of General Psychiatry,* 1978, *35,* 859–863.

Tennes, K., and Lampl, E. "Stranger and Separation Anxiety in Infancy." *Journal of Nervous and Mental Disease,* 1964, *139,* 247–254.

Theorell, T., and Rahe, R. H. "Psychosocial Factors and Myocardial Infarction. I: An Inpatient Study in Sweden." *Journal of Psychosomatic Research,* 1971, *15,* 25–31.

Thoits, P., and Hannan, M. "Income and Psychological Distress: The Impact of an Income-Maintenance Experiment." *Journal of Health and Social Behavior,* 1979, *20,* 120–138.

Thompson, C. "Cultural Pressures in the Psychology of Women." *Psychiatry,* 1942, *5* (3), 331–339.

Thompson, C. *On Women.* New York: New American Library, 1971.

Thompson, K. C., and Hendrie, H. C. "Environmental Stress in Primary Depressive Illness." *Archives of General Psychiatry,* 1972, *26,* 130–132.

Thoresen, C. E., and Mahoney, M. J. *Behavioral Self-Control.* New York: Holt, Rinehart and Winston, 1974.

Thorndike, E. L. *Animal Intelligence.* New York: Macmillan, 1911.

Thurlow, H. J. "General Susceptibility to Illness: A Selective Review." *Canadian Medical Association Journal,* 1967, *97,* 1397–1404.

Thurlow, H. J. "Illness in Relation to Life Situation and Sick Role Tendency." *Journal of Psychosomatic Research,* 1971, *15,* 73–88.

Tiger, L., and Fox, R. *The Imperial Animal.* London: Secker and Warburg, 1972.

Tighe, T. J., Graves, D. M., and Riley, C. A. "Successive Reversals of a Classically Conditioned Heart-Rate Discrimination." *Journal of Experimental Analysis of Behavior,* 1968, *11,* 199–206.

Tinklenberg, J. R. "Alcohol and Violence." In P. G. Bourne and R. Fox (Eds.), *Alcoholism: Progress in Research and Treatment.* New York: Academic Press, 1973.

Tinklenberg, J. R. "Antianxiety Medications and the Treatment of Anxiety." In J. D. Barchas and others (Eds.), *Psychopharmacology: From Theory to Practice.* New York: Oxford University Press, 1977.

Tocqueville, A. de. *Democracy in America* [1835]. Vol 1. New York: Knopf and Random House, 1945.

Tokar, J. T., and others. "Emotional States and Behavioral Patterns in Alcoholics and Nonalcoholics." *Quarterly Journal of Studies on Alcohol,* 1973, *34,* 133–143.

Tomkins, S. S. *Affect, Imagery, Consciousness.* Vol. 1: *The Positive Affects.* New York: Springer, 1962.

Tomkins, S. S. *Affect, Imagery, Consciousness.* Vol. 2: *The Negative Affects.* New York: Springer, 1963.

Townsend, R. E., House, J. F., and Addario, D. A. "A Comparison of Biofeedback-Mediated Relaxation and Group Therapy in the Treatment of Chronic Anxiety." *American Journal of Psychiatry,* 1976, *133,* 517–519.

Trexler, L. D., and Karst, T. O. "Rational-Emotive Therapy, Placebo, and No-Treatment Effects of Public-Speaking Anxiety," *Journal of Abnormal Psychology,* 1972, *79,* 60–67.

Tuddenham, R. D., Brooks, J., and Milkovich, L. "Mothers' Reports of Behavior of 10-Year-Olds: Relationship with Age, Sex, Ethnicity, and Mother's Education." *Developmental Psychology,* 1974, *10,* 959–995.

Tyrer, P. *The Role of Bodily Feelings in Anxiety.* London: Oxford University Press, 1976.

Tyrer, P., Candy, J., and Kelly, D. "A Study of the Clinical Effects of Phenelzine and Placebo in the Treatment of Phobic Anxiety." *Psychopharmacologia,* 1973, *32,* 237–254.

Tyrer, P., and Lader, M. H. "Response to Propranolol and Diazepam in Somatic and Psychic Anxiety." *British Journal of Medicine,* 1974, *2,* 14–16.

Ursin, H. "Activation, Coping, and Psychosomatics." In H. Ursin, E. Baade, and S. Levine (Eds.), *Psychobiology of Stress: A Study of Coping Man.* New York: Academic Press, 1978.

Ursin, H., Baade, E., and Levine, S. (Eds.). *Psychobiology of Stress: A Study of Coping Man.* New York: Academic Press, 1978.

Vaillant, G. E. "Natural History of Male Psychological Health. V: The Relation of Choice of Ego Mechanisms of Defense to Adult Adjustment." *Archives of General Psychiatry,* 1976, *33,* 535–545.

Vaillant, G. E. *Adaptation to Life.* Boston: Little, Brown, 1977.

Vaillant, G. E., Shapiro, L. N., and Schmitt, P. P. "Psychological Motives for Medical Hospitalization." *Journal of the American Medical Association,* 1970, *214,* 1661–1665.

Valentine, C. W. *The Psychology of Early Childhood.* (3rd ed.) London: Methuen, 1946.

Valkenburg, H. A., and others. "Attack Rate of Streptococcal Pharyngitis, Rheumatic Fever, and Glomerulonephritis in the General Population. II: The Epidemiology of Streptococcal Pharyngitis in One Village During a Two-Year Period." *New England Journal of Medicine,* 1963, *268,* 694–701.

Van Lawick-Goodall, J. *In the Shadow of Man.* Boston: Houghton Mifflin, 1971.

Van Lawick-Goodall, J. "The Behavior of Chimpanzees in Their Natural Habitat." *American Journal of Psychiatry,* 1973, *130,* 1–12.

Vannicelli, M. "Mood and Self-Perception of Alcoholics When Sober and Intoxicated." *Quarterly Journal of Studies on Alcohol,* 1972, *33,* 341–357.

Velten, E. "A Laboratory Task for Induction of Mood States." *Behaviour Research and Therapy,* 1968, *6,* 473–482.

Vernon, P. "Psychological Effects of Air Raids." *Journal of Abnormal and Social Psychology,* 1941, *36,* 457–476.

Vernon, P. E. *Personality Assessment: A Critical Survey.* New York: Wiley, 1964.

Vinokur, R., and Selzer, M. L. "Desirable Versus Undesirable Life Events: Their Relationship to Stress and Mental Distress." *Journal of Personality and Social Psychology,* 1975, *32,* 329–337.

Visotsky, H. M., and others. "Coping Behavior Under Extreme Stress." *Archives of General Psychiatry,* 1961, *5,* 423–448.

Vlachakis, N. D., and others. "Hypertension and Anxiety." *American Heart Journal,* 1974, *87,* 518–526.

Vold, G. B. *Theoretical Criminology.* New York: Oxford University Press, 1958.

Von Kugelgen, E. "Psychological Determinants of the Delay in Decision to Seek Aid in Cases of Myocardial Infarction." Unpublished doctoral dissertation, University of California, Berkeley, 1975.

Voors, A. W., and others. "Respiratory Infections in Marine Recruits, Influence of Personal Characteristics." *American Review of Respiratory Disease,* 1968, *98,* 801–809.

Voors, A. W., and others. "Prediction of Sickness in Naval Recruits by MMPI Scores." *American Review of Respiratory Disease,* 1969, *99,* 420–425.

Wachtel, P. "Psychodynamics, Behavior Therapy, and the Implacable Experimenter: An Inquiry into the Consistency of Personality." *Journal of Abnormal Psychology,* 1973, *82,* 323–334.

Waelder, R. *Basic Theory of Psychoanalysis* [1960]. New York: Schocken Books, 1964.

Waelder, R. "Inhibitions, Symptoms, and Anxiety: Forty Years Later." *Psychoanalytic Quarterly,* 1967, *36,* 1–36.

Wagner, A. R., and Rescorla, R. A. "Inhibition in Pavlovian Conditioning: Applications of a Theory." In R. A. Bokes and M. S. Halliday (Eds.), *Inhibition and Learning.* New York: Academic Press, 1972.

Wagner, A. R., Seigel, L. S., and Fein, G. G. "Extinction of Conditioned Fear as a Function of Percentage of Reinforcement." *Journal of Comparative and Physiological Psychology,* 1967, *63,* 160–164.

Walk, R. D. "Self-Ratings of Fear in a Fear-Provoking Situation." *Journal of Abnormal and Social Psychology,* 1956, *52,* 171–178.

Wall, J. H., and Allen, E. B. "Results of Hospital Treatment of Alcoholism." *American Journal of Psychiatry,* 1944, *100,* 474–479.

Wan, T. H., and Soifer, S. J. "Determinants of Physician Utilization: A Causal Analysis." *Journal of Health and Social Behavior,* 1974, *15,* 100–108.

Warheit, G. J. "Life Events, Coping, Stress, and Depressive Symptomatology." *American Journal of Psychiatry,* 1979, *136,* 502–507.

Warheit, G. J., Holzer, C. E., III, and Arey, S. A. "Race and Mental Illness: An Epidemiologic Update." *Journal of Health and Social Behavior,* 1975, *16,* 243–256.

Warren, G. H., and Raynes, A. E. "Mood Changes During Three Conditions of Alcohol Intake." *Quarterly Journal of Studies on Alcohol,* 1972, *33,* 979–989.

Warren, R., Deffenbacher, J. L., and Brading, P. "Rational-Emotive Therapy and the Reduction of Test Anxiety in Elementary School Students." *Rational Living*, 1976, *11*, 26–29.

Watson, F. M. C., Henry, J. P., and Haltmeyer, G. C. "Effects of Early Experience on Emotional and Social Reactivity in CBA Mice." *Physiology and Behavior*, 1974, *13*, 9–14.

Watson, J. B., and Rayner, R. "Conditioned Emotional Reactions." *Journal of Experimental Psychology*, 1920, *3*, 1–14.

Watts, F. N. "Desensitization as an Habituation Phenomenon. II: Studies of Interstimulus Interval Lengths." *Psychological Reports*, 1973, *33*, 715–718.

Watts, M. W. "Behavior Modeling and Self-Devaluation with Video Self-Confrontation." *Journal of Educational Psychology*, 1973, *64*, 212–215.

Watzlawick, P., Beavin, J. H., and Jackson, D. D. *Pragmatics of Human Communication*. New York: Norton, 1967.

Wayne, G. "Modified Psychoanalytic Therapy in Senescence." *Psychoanalytic Review*, 1959, *40*, 99.

Wechsler, D. *The Measurement and Appraisal of Adult Intelligence*. Baltimore: Williams and Wilkins, 1958.

Wedgewood, C. V. *The Thirty Years' War*. Harmondsworth, Middlesex, England: Penguin Books, 1957.

Wedin, R. W. "The Effects of Experimental Stress on Measures of Piagetian Intelligence in Concrete Operational Children." Unpublished doctoral dissertation, Long Island University, 1977.

Weidner, G., and Matthews, K. A. "Reported Physical Symptoms Elicited by Unpredictable Events and the Type A Coronary-Prone Behavior Pattern." *Journal of Personality and Social Psychology*, 1978, *36*, 1213–1220.

Weinraub, M., and Lewis, M. "The Determinants of Children's Responses to Separation." *Monographs of the Society for Research in Child Development*, 1977, *42* (4, Serial No. 172).

Weinraub, M., and Putney, E. "The Effects of Height on Infants' Social Responses to Unfamiliar Persons." *Child Development*, 1978, *49*, 598–603.

Weinshilboum, R. M., and others. "Elevation of Serum Dopamine-B-Hydroxylase Activity with Forced Immobilization." *Nature New Biology*, 1971, *230*, 287–288.

Weiss, E., and English, O. S. *Psychosomatic Medicine*. Philadelphia: Saunders, 1957.

Weiss, J. "The Integration of Defenses." *International Journal of Psychoanalysis*, 1967, *48*, 520–524.

Weiss, J. "The Emergence of New Themes: A Contribution to the Psychoanalytic Theory of Therapy." *International Journal of Psycho-analysis*, 1971, *52*, 459–467.

Weiss, J. M. "Psychosomatic Aspects of Symptom Patterns Among Major Surgery Patients." *Journal of Psychosomatic Research*, 1969, *13*, 109–112.

Weiss, J. M. "Somatic Effects of Predictable and Unpredictable Shock." *Psychosomatic Medicine*, 1970, *32* (4), 397–408.

Weiss, J. M. "Effects of Coping Behavior in Different Warning Signal Conditions on Stress Pathology in Rats." *Journal of Comparative and Physiological Psychology*, 1971a, *77*, 1–13.

Weiss, J. M. "Effects of Coping Behavior with and Without a Feedback Signal on Stress Pathology in Rats." *Journal of Comparative and Physiological Psychology,* 1971b, *77,* 22–30.

Weiss, J. M. "Effects of Punishing the Coping Response (Conflict) on Stress Pathology in Rats." *Journal of Comparative and Physiological Psychology,* 1971c, *77,* 14–21.

Weiss, J. M. "Psychological Factors in Stress and Disease." *Scientific American,* 1972, *226,* 104–113.

Weiss, J. M. "Ulcers." In J. D. Maser and M. E. P. Seligman (Eds.), *Psychopathology: Experimental Models.* San Francisco: Freeman, 1977.

Weissman, M., and Klerman, G. L. "Sex Differences and the Epidemiology of Depression." *Archives of General Psychiatry,* 1977, *34* (1), 98.

Weissman, M., and Paykel, E. S. *The Depressed Human: A Study of Social Relationships.* Chicago: University of Chicago Press, 1974.

Welds, K. M. "Voluntary Childlessness in Professional Women." Unpublished doctoral dissertation, Harvard University, 1976.

Wenger, M. A., and Bagchi, K. "Studies of Autonomic Functions in Practitioners of Yoga in India." *Behavior Science,* 1961, *6,* 312–323.

Wenger, M. A., and Cullen, T. D. "Studies of Autonomic Balance in Children and Adults." In N. S. Greenfield and R. A. Sternbach (Eds.), *Handbook of Psychophysiology.* New York: Holt, Rinehart and Winston, 1972.

Wershow, H. J., and Reinhart, G. "Life Change and Hospitalization: A Heretical View." *Journal of Psychosomatic Research,* 1974, *18,* 393–401.

Wertham, F. "The Catathymic Crisis: A Clinical Entity." *Archives of Neurology and Psychiatry,* 1937, *37,* 974–977.

Wertham, F. *The Show of Violence.* New York: Doubleday, 1967.

Whanger, A. D., and Busse, E. "Geriatrics." In B. B. Wolman (Ed.), *The Therapist's Handbook.* New York: Van Nostrand Reinhold, 1976.

Wheeler, E., and others. "Neurocirculatory Asthenia (Anxiety Neurosis, Effort Syndrome, Neurasthenia)." *Journal of the American Medical Association,* 1950, *142,* 878–888.

White, B. V., and Gildea, E. F. "'Cold Pressor Test' in Tension and Anxiety: A Cardio-chronographic Study." *Archives of Neurology and Psychiatry,* 1937, *38,* 964–984.

Whitehead, W. E., and others. "Anxiety and Anger in Hypertension." *Journal of Psychosomatic Research,* 1977, *21,* 383-389.

Wickramasekera, I. "Instructions and EMG Feedback in Systematic Desensitization: A Case Report." *Behavior Therapy,* 1972, *3,* 460–465.

Wikler, A. "Diagnosis and Treatment of Drug Dependence of the Barbiturate Type." *American Journal of Psychiatry,* 1968, *125,* 758–765.

Wilkins, W. "Desensitization: Social and Cognitive Factors Underlying the Effectiveness of Wolpe's Procedure." *Psychological Bulletin,* 1971, *76,* 311–317.

Williams, A. F. "The Alcoholic Personality." In B. Kissin and H. Begleiter (Eds.), *The Biology of Alcoholism.* Vol. 4: *Social Aspects of Alcoholism.* New York: Plenum, 1976.

Williams, R., Kimball, C., and Williard, H. "The Influence of Interpersonal Interaction on Diastolic Blood Pressure." *Psychosomatic Medicine,* 1972, *34,* 194–198.

Wills, T. A. "Perceptions of Clients by Professional Helpers." *Psychological Bulletin,* 1978, *85,* 968–1000.

Wills, T. A. "Comparative-Fortune Principles in Social Psychology." Unpublished manuscript, Columbia University School of Public Health, 1979.

Wilson, G. T., and Davison, G. C. "Processes of Fear Reduction in Systematic Desensitization: Animal Studies." *Psychological Bulletin*, 1971, *76*, 1–4.

Wilson, W. "Correlates of Avowed Happiness." *Psychological Bulletin*, 1967, *67*, 294–306.

Wine, J. D. "Test Anxiety and Direction of Attention." *Psychological Bulletin*, 1971, *76*, 92–104.

Winokur, G., and others. "Alcoholism. III: Diagnosis and Familial Psychiatric Illness in 259 Alcoholic Probands." *Archives of General Psychiatry*, 1970, *23*, 104–111.

Woddis, G. "Depression and Crime." *British Journal of Delinquency*, 1957, *8*, 85–94.

Wolf, S., and Wolff, H. G. *Human Gastric Function*. New York: Oxford University Press, 1943.

Wolff, H. G. *Stress and Disease*. Springfield, Ill.: Thomas, 1968.

Wolpe, J. *Psychotherapy by Reciprocal Inhibition*. Stanford, Calif.: Stanford University Press, 1958.

Wolpe, J. *The Practice of Behavior Therapy*. Elmsford, N.Y.: Pergamon Press, 1973.

Wolpe, J. "Cognition and Causation in Human Behavior and Its Therapy." *American Psychologist*, 1978, *33*, 437–446.

Woods, S. M. "Some Dynamics of Male Chauvinism." *Archives of General Psychiatry*, 1976, *33* (1), 63–65.

Wortman, C. B., and Dintzer, L. "Is an Attributional Analysis of the Learned Helplessness Phenomenon Viable?: A Critique of the Abramson-Seligman-Teasdale Reformulation." *Journal of Abnormal Psychology*, 1978, *87*, 75–90.

Wright, J. C. "A Comparison of Systematic Desensitization and Social Skill Acquisition in the Modification of a Social Fear." *Behavior Therapy*, 1976, *7*, 205–210.

Yates, A. O. *Behavior Therapy*. New York: Wiley, 1970.

Yehle, A. L. "Divergence Among Rabbit Response Systems During Three-Tone Classical Discrimination Conditioning." *Journal of Experimental Psychology*, 1968, *77* (3), 468–473.

Yerkes, R. M., and Dodson, J. D. "The Relation of Stimulus to Rapidity of Habit-Formation." *Journal of Comparative Neurology and Psychology*, 1908, *18*, 459–482.

Young, G., and Lewis, M. "Effects of Familiarity and Maternal Attention on Infant Peer Relations." *Merrill-Palmer Quarterly of Behavior and Development*, 1979, *24* (2), 105–119.

Young, M., Benjamin, B., and Wallis, C. "The Mortality of Widowers." *Lancet*, 1963, *2*, 454–456.

Young, R. R., and others. "Pure Pan-dysautonomia with Recovery: Description and Discussion of Diagnostic Criteria." *Brain*, 1975, *98*, 613–636.

Young, W. S., Bird, S. J., and Kuhar, M. J. "Iontophoresis of Methionine-Enkephalin in the Locus Coeruleus Area." *Brain Research*, 1977, *129*, 366.

Zetzel, E. R. "The Concept of Anxiety in Relation to the Development of

Psychoanalysis." *Journal of the American Psychoanalytic Association*, 1955, *3*, 369–388.

Zetzel, E. R. "Metapsychology of Aging." In M. Berezin and S. Cath (Eds.), *Geriatric Psychiatry: Grief, Loss, and Emotional Disorders in the Aging Process*. New York: International Universities Press, 1966.

Ziv, A., Kruglanski, A. W., and Shulman, S. "Children's Psychological Reactions to Wartime Stress." *Journal of Personality and Social Psychology*, 1974, *30*, 24–30.

Zola, I. K. "Culture and Symptoms—An Analysis of Patients' Presenting Complaints." *American Sociological Review*, 1966, *31*, 615–630.

Zuckerman, M. "The Development of an Affect Adjective Checklist for the Measurement of Anxiety." *Journal of Consulting and Clinical Psychology*, 1960, *24*, 457–462.

Zuckerman, M. "The Search for High Sensation." *Psychology Today*, 1978, *11* (9), 38–46, 96–99.

Zung, W. W. K. "A-Rating Instrument for Anxiety Disorders." *Psychosomatics*, 1971, *12*, 371–379.

Zung, W. W. K. "Assessment of Anxiety Disorder: Qualitative and Quantitative Approaches." In E. F. Fann and others (Eds.), *Phenomenology and Treatment of Anxiety*. New York: Spectrum, 1979.

Name Index

✤ ✤ ✤ ✤ ✤ ✤ ✤ ✤ ✤ ✤ ✤ ✤

551

Subject Index

✻ ✻ ✻ ✻ ✻ ✻ ✻ ✻ ✻ ✻ ✻ ✻ ✻

A

Adaptive/coping/defensive resources, stress related to, 67, 69-70, 75-77
Adolescents, and crime, 179-180
Adrenal weights, role of, 87, 93, 95
Adrenaline. *See* Epinephrine
Adrenal-Medullary systems: in conditioning studies, 213; in physiological theory, 82, 87, 92, 96, 104, 106, 108, 110
Adrenocortical function, role of, 88, 91, 92, 101, 102, 104, 106, 108, 109
Adrenocorticotrophic hormone (ACTH): in conditioning studies, 221; in general adaptation syndrome, 131, 133, 138; in physiological theory, 88, 91, 92, 96, 100, 107, 108; in stress response, 415
Affective Adjective Check List, 258-259
Aggression: and anxiety, 8, 9-10, 11, 18, 28; and separation anxiety, 308-310; sex differences in, 309-310
Agoraphobia, 430, 434, 448, 450
Aktual neurosis, 11-12, 29
Alcohol abuse: and addiction, 336; and anxiety, 329-343; for avoidance of strain, 335; and cognitive appraisal, 334; effects of, 338-339;

569